The Cossack Struggle
Against Communism,
1917–1945

ALSO BY BRENT MUEGGENBERG

The Czecho-Slovak Struggle for Independence, 1914–1920 (McFarland, 2014)

The Cossack Struggle Against Communism, 1917–1945

BRENT MUEGGENBERG

McFarland & Company, Inc., Publishers
Jefferson, North Carolina

ISBN (print) 978-1-4766-7948-8
ISBN (ebook) 978-1-4766-3802-7

Library of Congress and British Library
Cataloguing Data are Available

© 2019 Brent Mueggenberg. All rights reserved

No part of this book may be reproduced or transmitted in any form or by any means, electronic or mechanical, including photocopying or recording, or by any information storage and retrieval system, without permission in writing from the publisher.

Front cover: Cossack cavalrymen charging with their sabers drawn in the early months of World War I, 1914 (akg-images / WHA / World History Archive)

Printed in the United States of America

*McFarland & Company, Inc., Publishers
Box 611, Jefferson, North Carolina 28640
www.mcfarlandpub.com*

Contents

PREFACE 1

INTRODUCTION 5

1—Mobilization 21
2—Upheaval 31
3—Vacillation 50
4—Resurgence 64
5—Backwater 88
6—Rampage 113
7—Debacle 130
8—Retreat 142

9—Flight 156
10—Exile 170
11—Collaboration 190
12—Repression 206
13—Invasion 224
14—Regroup 243
15—Catastrophe 252
16—Repatriation 269

EPILOGUE 287

GLOSSARY OF TERMS, ACRONYMS AND ABBREVIATIONS 301

CHAPTER NOTES 305

BIBLIOGRAPHY 335

INDEX 341

Preface

For nearly thirty years, from 1917 to 1945, Cossacks fought and conspired against the communist regime in Russia. Their epic struggle spanned not only decades but also across immense regions of that country and beyond. It began as localized rebellions in the countryside of the Russian steppe, metamorphosized into a military campaign waged from Ukraine to Siberia, lingered abroad as a resistance movement between the world wars and was revitalized by the German invasion of the Soviet Union during the Second World War. Throughout their course, the activities of anticommunist Cossacks would impact millions of lives. Some of these affected peoples were those they lived among, such as Russians, Ukrainians, Caucasian highlanders, Central Asian nomads and Siberian aboriginals. Others lived outside of and sometimes faraway from Russia, including Chinese, Mongolians, Croatians and Italians. Yet, despite having touched so many realms, peoples and cultures, the Cossack struggle against communism never quite managed to shed its overall rustic and insular character.

Although anticommunist Cossacks possessed a collective hostility to the radical revolutionary ideology preached by Lenin and his followers, outside of that shared sentiment, their activities generally lacked any overall cohesion or clarity. Several Cossack leaders did aspire to foster greater unity among the opponents to the Soviet regime, but none managed to bridge the differeces which set them apart. Some, such as Generals Aleksey M. Kaledin and Lavr G. Kornilov, wanted to restore a strong, centralized Russian Empire. Others, like General Pyotr N. Krasnov, desired greater Cossack autonomy within the Russian state. A significant portion of Kuban Cossack politicians wanted to go even further by establishing their own Cossack nation-state completely independent of Russia. Then there were those Cossack leaders, including Grigory M. Semyonov, who simply exploited the weakness of the Russian state during the revolution to advance their self-interests. These differing motivations may be attributable in part to the diverse and, in some cases, unlikely backgrounds among the roster of Cossack leaders. A handful were former stalwarts of the old regime, such as Guards officers and landed aristocrats, while others were junior officers from lower-class families without authentic Cossack roots. The discord among them was indicative of the even greater divisions which afflicted Cossack society as a whole.

The failure of the anticommunist Cossacks to unite under a single ideology or leader was symptomatic of the wider White movement. Indeed, the Cossacks were a significant contributor to the disharmony which plagued the White campaigns. Whereas ordinary Cossacks often took up arms against the Bolsheviks to protect their lands and privileged status in their territories, the Russian officers and politicians leading the White movement did so to restore their idea of a strong, unitary Russian empire. In due course, each side willingly accepted each other's help against their common enemy without fully embracing each other's cause. This dichotomy in the anticommunist movement between the regional goals of the Cossacks and the national aims of the Russians continued beyond the Russian Civil War; it would remain a point of contention between them throughout the interwar period and into the Second World War.

The Cossacks, then, were not as sympathetic to counterrevolutionary objectives as they appeared. They certainly were not opposed to the liberal-democratic revolution which deposed tsarism, and many Cossack farmers and soldiers were willing to negotiate a peaceful coexistence with the Soviet regime. Ultimately, it was the broken promises and tyranny of Russia's ruling party that did more to drive the Cossacks into the arms of communism's enemies, whether Whites or Nazis, than any ideology or propaganda.

Chronologically, the Cossack struggle against communism can be broken down into three phases. The first phase, from 1917 to 1922, began with the revolution that eventually brought the Bolsheviks into power and ended with the defeat of the anticommunist forces in a bloody civil war. Throughout that period, the Cossacks fought the Red Army sometimes independently and other times as allies or auxiliaries of the White armies. The second phase centers on the activities of anticommunist Cossacks as members of the Russian Diaspora. Since their emigration had begun well before the civil war ended, this phase partially overlaps the first as it covers the twenty years from 1920 to 1940. Upon the German invasion of the Soviet Union in 1941, anticommunist Cossacks saw one more opportunity to achieve their goal of liberating their homelands from Soviet tyranny. In that third and final phase of their struggle, anticommunist Cossacks, as collaborators of the Nazi war machine, were to revel in the Third Reich's triumphs and, ultimately, share its fate.

Historians and writers have tended to cover the Cossacks' anticommunist activities unevenly throughout the period of 1917 to 1945. Their role in the Russian Civil War has been studied in many histories of that ruinous struggle.[1] Indeed, no account of the White movement would be complete without emphasizing the Cossacks' importance in providing recruits and a geographical base for the armies that were most dangerous to the fledgling Soviet regime. But during the interwar period, the Cossacks' visibility both inside and outside of the Soviet Union faded. In their homelands, Cossack culture was repressed while those who went abroad were often overshadowed by more prominent non-Cossack politicians, philosophers, and literary figures in the Russian Diaspora. The Cossacks regained some attention after the revival of their anticommunist movement during Second World War.[2] Most accounts of that period, however, fail to adequately portray the Cossacks' battles against the Soviets in 1942 within the context of a conflict that was by then twenty-five years in the making. Subsequently, this may give the impression that the Cossacks who fought with the Wehrmacht were opportunistic quislings rather than dedicated rebels.

This account is a synthesis of the campaigns, personalities, politics and trends which shaped the anticommunist struggle among Cossacks from the October Revolution to VE Day. It seeks to present events throughout that period as their participants saw them: the continuation of a long, desperate clash against a tyrannical foe. It is the author's hope that this perspective will not only imbue readers with a greater understanding of a period that proved epochal in the history of the Cossack people but also provide insight as to why the Cossacks' legacy continues to captivate Russians and Ukrainians to this day.

As students of Russian history well know, in the early twentieth century Russia still used the Julian (Old Style, or O.S.) calendar, which at the time was thirteen days behind the Gregorian (New Style, N.S.) calendar used in the West. Although the Bolsheviks adopted the Gregorian calendar on 14 February 1918, various White governments adhered to the

Julian calendar throughout the civil war. For the sake of simplicity, the author has elected to use Gregorian dates throughout the text whenever possible. However, two significant events in 1917, the country's liberal-democratic revolution (8–16 March N.S., 23 February–3 March O.S.) and the Bolshevik *coup d'état* (7–8 November N.S., 25–26 October O.S.) are referred to as the February and October Revolutions, respectively, since that is how they are memorialized in Russian history.

Another point of clarification is place names in the text. Many towns and cities mentioned in this book have undergone renaming according to changing demographics and political fortunes. For example, the former capital of the Kuban Cossacks, originally christened Yekaterinodar (Catherine's Gift), was renamed Krasnodar (Gift of the Reds) in 1920 and has retained that name to the present date. Other towns and cities, particularly those outside of the present borders of the Russian Federation, have been renamed according to their local indigenous names. In such instances, the text generally favors the name most familiar to readers in the English-language. Hence, the text uses Kiev instead of Kyiv, Prague instead of Praha, and so on. To help readers find their way around modern maps, the author has strived to follow outdated names of significant towns and cities with their current forms in parentheses when they first appear in the text.

Introduction

A Lazarus Taxon

For seventeen days in February 2014, much of the international community came together as it does every four years to celebrate the Winter Olympic Games. That year the event was being held in the Russian Black Sea resort of Sochi and was of course extensively covered by press from across the globe. Naturally, the reports of these correspondents centered on the performance of their countrymen and other world-class athletes on the ice rinks and ski slopes. But the Sochi Games, more so than past Olympics, also generated plenty of other headlines that had little to do with friendly competition among the global community.

Since July 2013, a heightened security threat loomed over the games after Doku Umarov, the leader of the terrorist group Imarat Kavkaz (Caucasus Emirate), urged his fellow Islamic militants to target the upcoming event. His taunts were quickly picked up by international media outlets and various governments, both of which warned that the Sochi Games, largely due to their location, presented a more inviting target than past venues.[1]

This specific threat against the games in Sochi was the culmination of years of controversy that began shortly after the International Olympic Committee (IOC) selected the seaside resort as the future site of the winter games in July 2007. The first to object to that decision were various Circassian organizations claiming to represent the people indigenous to the highlands around Sochi. The town itself had been founded by the Russians in 1838 to bring the surrounding countryside, which had been wrested from the Ottoman Empire almost a decade earlier, more firmly within the tsar's dominions. At the time, the Russians were finding it difficult to impose their rule on the region's local Circassian tribes. As a predominantly Muslim people, the latter preferred subservience to an Ottoman sultan over a Christian tsar. With their proud warrior tradition and expert use of the surrounding wilderness to evade and ambush their opponents, the Circassians continued their resistance for a generation beyond Sochi's establishment. It was not until 1864 when the last collection of defiant Circassian tribes were cornered by tsarist soldiers in a gorge forty miles from the site of the future Olympics and forced to surrender. That event marked the beginning of a new, even darker chapter in the Circassians' plight as they were subjected to forced conversions, resettlements, or even expelled from the Russian Empire altogether. Their homes, fields and pastures were then appropriated by settlers whom the authorities considered reliable, which usually meant Cossacks of Russian or Ukrainian origin.[2]

It is no wonder then that many Circassians living abroad and in Russia were inclined to regard everything about the Sochi Winter Olympics—the original purpose of the host city, its proximity to their people's defeat and the fact that the event landed on the sesquicentennial of that calamity—as an insult to their national pride and the memory of their ancestors. One Circassian group, for example, expressed its disgust by declaring that "we regard the holding of the Olympic Games in our homeland in the places of mass graves and genocide as an act of vandalism."[3] Although the IOC issued no official response, Circassians from around the world continued to protest the scheduled Sochi games over the following years. In 2010, the appearance of Circassian activists at the Vancouver Winter Olympics demanding that the next round of games be moved from Sochi perplexed journalists who had never heard of this little-known people. Further protests were staged on the streets in Istanbul and other cities right up to the fireworks which marked the opening of the games on 7 February 2014. Generally, the demonstrators demanded that the games be transferred away from Sochi or, at the very least, recognition of the events of 1864 as genocide.

Overall, their indignation garnered little press in the Western media. Nonetheless, Islamic militants readily exploited the memory of that late nineteenth-century episode of ethnic-cleansing in the western Caucasus to justify their planned attacks against the Sochi Olympics. In his July 2013 summons to terror, Umarov likened the games to "Satanic dancing on the bones of our ancestors."[4] This association was a bit of a stretch since the Circassians have little in common either ideologically or ethnically with the members of the Imarat Kavkaz, most of whom hail from the eastern Caucasus. Nonetheless, the past poor treatment of their co-religionists provided Umarov and his group a convenient *cause célèbre* to help disguise their radical and violent intentions.

Russia, as well as other countries participating in the games, took the threats presented by Imarat Kavkaz and similar groups very seriously. In December 2013, a pair of suicide bombers detonated their devices in a bus and train station in the city of Volgograd. Just days prior to the opening ceremony on 7 February 2014, U.S. officials and others expressed concerns about security at the games and the likelihood of a terrorist attack. Never before had anxieties been so high at an Olympics venue.

The Russian government, led by its presidential strongman, Vladimir Putin, was hardly of the mindset to underestimate the importance of security at Sochi. For him, the 2014 Winter Games were a personal obsession. As the first Olympics to be held in Russia since the end of the Cold War, the event was widely viewed as an opportunity to restore the country's prestige since the collapse of the Soviet Union.[5] Indeed, Moscow poured immense resources into developing Sochi from a dilapidated Soviet retreat into a world-class winter resort. Everything from the arenas to hotels to roads had to be built or upgraded to prepare for the games. The entire effort was reminiscent of a Soviet-era mega-project in terms of its fame, scale, cost and perhaps folly.[6] To prevent possible terrorists from spoiling the event, Russian authorities, during the weeks between the Volgograd bombing and the Sochi Games, conducted dragnet operations in Dagestan by rounding up anyone suspected of having ties to or sympathy towards organizations like Imarat Kavkaz.[7] They also flooded the Sochi area with troops and police, among them 800 Cossacks[8] who patrolled the streets outside of hotels and arenas in uniforms that included traditional accessories such as black sheepskin hats, striped trousers and riding boots. The Cossacks, along with other Russian security forces, ultimately succeeded in their primary mission: the Sochi Winter Olympics were unmarred by any terrorist incident. Nonetheless, more than a few eyebrows were raised on 19 February, four days before the games' closing ceremony, when at least ten Cossacks were captured on camera brutally suppressing a street performance by the female protest band Pussy Riot. Photographs taken of the encounter appeared to show the collision of two worlds: a young female member of the punk band, clad in a blue balaclava and neon

In this photograph from 14 February 2014, Pussy Riot musician Nadezhda Tolokonnikova, left, and a photographer are attacked by a whip-wielding Cossack militiaman after Tolokonnikova and her fellow bandmembers (in background) attempted to stage a protest performance on the streets of Sochi, Russia. The incident occurred on the twelfth day of the 2014 Winter Olympic Games then being held in the seaside resort (AP Photo / Morry Gash).

mini-dress, recoiling from a black-uniformed Cossack striking her with a horse whip. After the encounter, the musicians were detained by police and three of them had to be hospitalized as a result of the beating, though no charges were brought them.[9] The Cossacks' brutal treatment of them is probably best explained by Steven Lee Myers, the author of a recent biography of the Russian president. "Putin had invested so much in the Olympics," Myers wrote, "that any criticism of it—any protest that might question its benefit—was treated as blasphemous, an act of treason against the resurgent state."[10]

The Cossacks' presence at the 2014 Winter Olympic Games, and especially their beating of the Pussy Riot band members, ignited intense curiosity in the Western press. "The Cossacks Ride Again," declared a headline from *Slate*.[11] "Who are Russia's Cossack militiamen in Pussy Riot beating?" wondered *USA Today*.[12] These articles resembled a news release announcing a Lazarus taxon—the rediscovery of a species long believed to be extinct—as readers were presented with a historical background of the finding accompanied by speculation of its role in the present-day. In their search for answers, journalists struggled to shed light on both Cossacks from a century ago and their modern-day incarnates. One writer on international affairs at *Slate* touched upon the difficulty of classifying Cossacks, explaining that they are "not quite an ethnic or linguistic group" while adding that they are "more than just a military unit."[13] Other articles mentioned that Cossacks were "fierce horsemen" who had served the tsars with brutal distinction by subjugating Muslim natives in Russia's borderlands and instigating pogroms against Jews. They went on to inform their audiences how the tables turned against the Cossacks upon the Bolshevik seizure of power, after which the Cossacks themselves were subjected to mass executions, deportations and other forms of oppression. Indeed, the communists' "de-Cossackization" measures were so thorough and apparently successful that no one was quite sure what to make of the present-day Cossacks in Sochi and other parts of Russia. Were these militiamen, as they claimed, genuine ancestors of the fabled steppe horsemen who somehow preserved their heritage through decades of Soviet tyranny? Or were they, as their critics alleged, nothing more than mere pretenders, similar to so-called "urban cowboys" in North America? Moreover, were they heroes who helped shield Sochi from terrorists or were they nothing more than vile suppressors of liberty?[14]

Before baffled foreign journalists had time to fully digest the "debut" of Cossack security forces at Sochi, the world's attention turned to the Crimean Peninsula, where well-armed commandos suddenly began seizing government buildings at the end of February 2014. Although their uniforms bore no insignia, some called themselves Cossacks. Only several weeks later would Putin and other officials in Moscow admit that the men were Russians. Their operation, it turned out, had been secretly ordered by the Russian leader in retaliation for the ouster of the pro–Moscow president, Viktor Yanukovych, in Kiev (Kyiv). The unrest in the Ukrainian capital had actually begun during the previous November when demonstrators occupied Independence Square to protest Yanukovych's refusal to sign an agreement that would bring the country economically and politically closer to the European Union. Dubbed the EuroMaidan protests, the demonstration continued through the winter until 18 February 2014, when an effort by government forces to clear the square erupted into street fighting that claimed over a hundred lives in the coming days. On 22 February Yanukovych fled Kiev as government forces and his allies in the country's parliament began to turn against him, leaving his office to be taken over by a new, pro–Western successor. Five days later, the commandos, nicknamed "little green men," stormed administrative buildings in Crimea. Five weeks later, similar events took place in Ukraine's eastern cities of Donetsk, Luhansk and Kharkiv. These operations, it seems, were initiated by Putin as punishment for the country's attempt to reorient its policy towards the West.[15]

Putin was able to swiftly secure Crimea thanks to the element of surprise along with prevailing confusion in Kiev, which was in the throes of a revolution. But Russian efforts to seize the eastern districts from Kiev triggered a bitter struggle between residents who wanted to remain a part of Ukraine and irredentists seeking to join the Russian motherland. The latter may have been quickly overwhelmed by the Ukrainian military if it were not for the backing which they received from their compatriots in Russia. Among the Russian paramilitary groups which rallied to the separatists' aid were Cossack groups from the Don and Kuban regions. Amid the industrial towns and sunflower fields of eastern Ukraine, these combatants could be distinguished as Cossacks only by their black sheepskin hats and their insignias emblazoned on their sleeves and trucks. Otherwise, they bore the appearance of modern soldiers outfitted in patterned camouflage wielding automatic weapons and conspicuously lacking horses. Although the Kremlin officially denied that these Cossacks and other irregulars fighting the Ukrainians were in its service or pay, it did not provide an adequate explanation as to how so many of these well-equipped "volunteers" managed to slip across the Russian–Ukrainian border.[16]

Throughout the spring and into the early summer, the war in eastern Ukraine continued to rage with varying intensity. On 17 July 2014 the conflict acquired a new level of tragedy when a passenger jet, Malaysia Airlines Flight MH17, was shot down over the embattled Donetsk region, killing all 298 people aboard. As the world looked on in horror at the loss of so many innocent lives, both warring factions accused the other side of launching the fatal missile which struck the jetliner. In the days following the incident, however, news outlets began reporting that Flight MH17 was likely downed in a case of mistaken identity by pro–Russian rebels, possibly Cossacks, using a Russian-made SA-11 Buk surface-to-air missile. These conclusions were based on intelligence reports indicating that heavy weaponry, including rocket launchers, had been moved into separatist-controlled areas from Russia. Indeed, in the weeks leading up to the incident, two Ukrainian cargo jets and one fighter jet had been shot down by surface-to-air missiles. On the same afternoon the passenger jet was destroyed, a website used by pro–Russian elements boasted of having eliminated another enemy cargo jet.[17] Shortly after the incident, they began to realize their error. In recordings of intercepted phone conversations, later authenticated by the U.S. State Department, various separatist leaders could be heard expressing incredulity that the felled craft was a Malaysian civilian jet and not a Ukrainian military transport, as they had originally thought. Upon hearing this news, Nikolay Kozitsyn, a Don Cossack ataman in charge of local militant operations, was unapologetic. "That means they were carrying spies," declared a voice later confirmed to be Kozitsyn. "They shouldn't be fucking flying. There is a war going on."[18]

Even before the tragic demise of Flight MH17, Kozitsyn's recent activities had come under scrutiny by intelligence officials and journalists monitoring the crisis in eastern Ukraine. Several weeks earlier, the Don ataman was believed to have personally ordered an attack on Ukrainian outposts and he was implicated in the brief kidnapping on Ukrainian soil of nine observers from the Organization for Security and Cooperation in Europe. Kozitsyn also reportedly spearheaded a campaign to recruit Cossack volunteers from the Rostov-on-Don (hereafter, Rostov) area to fight in the embattled Donets Basin. In one xenophobic summons, he called on Cossacks to "defend their brethren" in Ukraine from "Poles, Romanians and Hungarians" whom he claimed were in the employ of the Kiev government.[19]

By fighting for a "Greater Russia," Kozitsyn and his accomplices appear to have been fulfilling yet another role historically assumed by Cossacks: that of proxies who facilitate Russian expansion by undermining the local authority of her neighbors. Indeed, long before Cossacks assisted tsarist police by charging demonstrators in Russia's cities, they had helped the tsars pry territories in the Caucasus, the Urals and Siberia from Turkish or Tatar control. The operations would usually begin with the Cossacks, often equipped with Russian firearms and gunpowder, destabilizing a neighbor's lightly defended frontiers through raids or the establishment of new settlements. The offended ruler—usually a sultan or khan—would often respond to this incursion by formally protesting to the tsar who, in order to avoid an all-out war, would disown the Cossacks. Sometimes the Turks or Tatars would send detachments to drive the Cossacks out, but even if they succeeded, the latter would usually return within a few years—sometimes with regular Russian troops in tow. Their persistence gradually wore down their enemies' resistance, culminating in the addition of a new territory to the tsar's dominions. Whether the present operations of the Cossacks and their Russian backers in eastern Ukraine will succeed in permanently attaching that area to the Russian Federation remains to be seen. For the present, it appears that the hostilities, like other unresolved clashes on Russia's borders in Abkhazia and South Ossetia, will become another "frozen conflict." Regardless of its outcome, one cannot help but notice the similarities between the *modus operandi* of Cossacks in those disputed lands and that of their alleged ancestors of the seventeenth century.

The motivation behind Putin's aggression, it seems, is to restore to Moscow its traditional sphere of influence by supporting irredentism among ethnic Russian populations[20] and punishing Russia's neighbors—and former subject nationalities—for adopting a too pro–Western outlook.[21] While the Cossacks, as irregulars in modern Russia's military and police forces, appear to be providing some of the muscle in this campaign, they have assumed a more visible role as mascots for the brand of Great Russian nationalism, conservatism and Orthodoxy which Putin's regime seeks to project at home and abroad. Such a narrative may be suitable for a people who are best remembered for faithfully serving the tsars, trampling revolutionary mobs and waging a bitter struggle against the supposedly internationalist Soviets, but the Cossacks were by no means preordained by their history to become symbols of Russian hyper-nationalism.

Defining the Cossacks

Author William Penn Cresson, in his book *The Cossacks: Their History and Country*, observed, "No problem of Russian history has given rise to more controversy than that of the origin of the Cossack race."[22] While that statement was hyperbolic by the time Cresson's book was published in 1919, when Russian society was in the throes of a political and social upheaval not seen since the Time of Troubles three centuries earlier, it does convey a sense of the intensity of the disputes surrounding the Cossacks' ancestry.

To medieval Slavs, a Cossack was a brigand; usually a foreigner. The term "Cossack" is derived from a Turkic word applied to horsemen who lived as renegades. It was used to describe a way of life rather than a specific ethnic group. Nonetheless, some Cossack writers[23] claim that their people are direct descendants of the early freebooters who inhabited the grassy steppe that was known as the "Wild Field" to the Slavs. On the other hand, most Russian and Western historians accept the premise that the founders of the Cossack communities which survived into the modern era were army deserters and runaway serfs who fled the repressive Polish and Muscovite states beginning in the fifteenth century. After emerging from their northern arboreal surroundings, these Slavic adventurers and fugitives quickly learned to improve their chances of survival on the open, treeless plain by banding together. They adopted the equestrian skills, weapons, costume and tactics of their Tatar and Turkic enemies. Before long, they were launching their own raids against neighboring tribes. To protect themselves and their precious loot, they constructed fortified settlements known as stanitsas, usually on a ridge or island in a river. Invariably, nearly all of these early Slavic Cossacks were men. Some of them did eventually start families with a wife or concubine—usually a woman kidnapped during a raid. This intermarriage with natives may explain why travelers often described the inhabitants of Cossack lands as having a darker complexion and slighter build than the ethnic Russians to their north.[24] Initially, those with families often gravitated back north to the more secure border settlements where they hired themselves out as frontiers guards known as "town" or service Cossacks. Those who remained in the steppe beyond the outposts, however, were free Cossacks and recognized no law but their own. By the mid-sixteenth century two distinct communities of these Slavic Cossacks had emerged: one on the Dnieper River, known as the Zaporozhian Sech, and another along the Don River.

Gradually, Russians and other peoples lost much of their previous disdain for Cossacks as marauders and began to envy them as freemen. Indeed, the southward flow of Slavs that had started as a trickle became a steady stream during the reign of Ivan the Terrible (r. 1533–1584). A series of ruinous wars waged by Muscovy, along with the eastward spread of serfdom, compelled greater numbers of Russians to seek freedom in the "Wild Field." The oppression was so great that many Cossacks with families now opted to take their chances

Cossack Hosts of South Russia.

on the steppe rather than returning to a life of servitude. Having escaped from one hierarchal and autocratic society, they were determined not allow another take root in their new homeland. To govern themselves, they drew inspiration from the crude egalitarian systems practiced by many steppe pastoralists since the days of Attila the Hun. Accordingly, all property and loot was shared equally among their army, or host, and every male could partake in the governing process. At least once per year, often in spring, the Cossacks would congregate in their capital and convene an assembly usually known as a krug (circle). It was there that decisions such as whether or not to make war against a neighboring tribe were reached by gauging the vocal feedback from the attendees. Proposals that elicited cheers from the crowd were approved, ones that were shouted down were not. A key function of the krug was the election of an ataman (chieftain) who was then tasked with the responsibility for administering the host and stanitsas when the krug was not in session. Since the early Cossacks were wary of the corrupting effects of power, the authority of the atamans was narrowly circumscribed. Only in times of war was his power absolute, and after his yearlong term expired, he was called to appear before the krug to answer for his actions. The rowdy nature of the Cossacks made the job of an ataman not only difficult but also dangerous; it was not unheard of for especially unpopular atamans to be assassinated by their own men.[25]

The free Cossacks were fiercely proud of the independent communities they carved out in the open grasslands, but even they recognized early in their history that they could not survive without allies. They did, after all, inhabit dangerous surroundings. "The steppe was both empty and filled, quiet and terrible, peaceable and full of ambushes; wild by reason of its wild plains, but wild, too, from the wild spirit of men," wrote Cresson.[26] At any moment, galloping squadrons of Crimean or Nogay Tatars could appear over the horizon and reduce a stanitsa to ashes. Cossack women and children were liable to be dragged off to Ottoman slave markets where they might be sold as an addition to the sultan's harem or as an oarsman for his galleys. Frequent raids and the Cossacks' need to maintain a vigilant defense made it impossible for them to engage in agriculture or other industries that would lead to a more advanced economy. Unable to live by plunder alone, the early Cossacks needed to import everything from grain to gunpowder. To obtain these supplies, the Cossacks turned to the states from which they had originally fled: Poland and Muscovy.[27]

While the rulers in Warsaw and Moscow were not enthused about the outflow of runaway serfs and outlaws to areas outside their reach, they still recognized that the Cossack bands could be useful as buffers on their southern borders. Until the latter sixteenth century, towns as far north as Moscow were terrorized by Tatar slave-hunting expeditions. The Tatar cavalrymen, mounted on light, hardy ponies, were simply too fast to be intercepted by the conventional armies fielded by Slavic states at the time. The Poles and Muscovites also lacked the proper mobility and logistics required to strike back at the nomads on the steppe. Their governments did try to deter the raiders by building fortified outposts on their southern borders, but these proved too few—and the steppe too wide—to have much success. A more effective countermeasure was the hiring of renegade bands of Tatars as mercenaries. Eventually, the Poles and Muscovites realized that the Cossack communities could serve a similar purpose.[28]

Despite their initially small numbers, the appearance of Cossack marauders on the steppe caused many headaches for the Slavs' traditional enemies. Slave-hunting expeditions into the northern forests became less profitable for the Tatars as Cossacks harried their columns and freed their prisoners. Not even the Ottoman garrison behind the ramparts of Azov, a fortress guarding the mouth of the Don River, could rest easy. In 1551, they experienced the first of what would become many attacks by the Don Cossacks against their strategically vital position. Two decades later, an agreement was signed between Moscow and the Don Cossacks whereby the latter, in exchange for helping guard the borderlands, would receive a regular subsidy of grain, firearms, gunpowder and other essentials the Cossacks could not produce themselves. This arrangement, which increased in importance as the Cossack communities grew, enabled them to harness the advanced technologies of sedentary societies while maintaining the lifestyle and skills of frontiersmen. This combination made them a force to be reckoned with on the steppe.[29]

It was not long before the tsars found other uses for the Cossacks. In the mid-sixteenth century, Ivan the Terrible employed them as proxies against Turkish influence in the Caucasus to help guard trade routes to Persia. Under his direction, Cossack colonization was encouraged along the Terek River. But these Grebensk Cossacks (later known as Terek Cossacks), unlike their brothers on the Dnieper or Don, were ruled directly—albeit loosely—by Moscow. Almost from their start, with few interruptions, the Terek lands were also home to garrisons of regular Russian musketeers. Indeed, due to the low influx of migrants and the high casualties they experienced in their relentless struggles with the native highlanders, the viability of the Grebensk Cossack communities depended on regular government intervention—including forced resettlement of Cossacks to there from quieter regions.[30]

As colonizers, Cossacks sometimes settled new lands on their own initiative. It is likely that Cossacks from the Don ventured eastward during the sixteenth century to found new stanitsas along the right bank of the Yaik River. This development was welcomed by the Muscovite government since the Cossacks could help contain the Kazakh and Bashkir nomads who roamed that area. Ivan the Terrible looked less favorably on the establishment of free Cossack communities along the Volga, which was a vital mercantile and communication artery for his realm. In 1577, he asserted his authority over the river by sending troops to clear it and its environs of Cossack settlers.[31] It was not until the eighteenth century when a Cossack host was formally established along the Volga. Even then, this host was to remain a tiny, widely-dispersed community that was significantly weaker than its neighbors.[32]

Ivan the Terrible's campaign against Cossacks along the Volga while supporting other Cossack communities is just one example of the complicated relations between the early Russian state and the free Cossacks. At the turn of the seventeenth century, Tsar Boris Gudonov (r. 1598–1605) tried to force the free Cossacks into submission by sending troops against them and cutting off their subsidies. As one might expect, the Cossacks were too proud to give in so easily and instead they resisted these measures by backing a pretender to the Russian throne. Their actions exacerbated the unrest during Russia's Time of Troubles (1598–1613), but eventually the Cossacks did help to bring this period of turmoil to an end by supporting the election of Mikhail Romanov (r. 1613–45) as tsar.[33] Relations between the Cossacks and the new tsar, however, were often rocky. The two especially disagreed on foreign policy as the Cossacks' insatiable appetite for plunder proved difficult to reconcile with Mikhail's desire for tranquility on his southern border when his army was engaged against the Poles or Swedes to the west. At one point, he withheld the subsidy from the recalcitrant Don Cossacks and imprisoned their envoy to Moscow. In response, the Don squadrons began rampaging through Muscovy's southern borderlands. The standoff between the tsar and Don Cossacks was brought to an end only by renewed threats from Crimean Tatar raiding parties.[34]

Such friction between the Cossacks and tsars continued throughout the seventeenth century, but as time wore on these contests clearly favored the latter. By the end of the century, the Cossacks' role had faded in importance as the Romanovs consolidated their dynastic rule and the nomads were pushed further away from the Russian heartland. On the other hand, the Don Cossacks were more dependent on Moscow than ever to feed and clothe their growing population. Less populous Cossack communities, such as those along the distant Yaik and Terek rivers, also became increasingly reliant on the tsarist government for reinforcement against hostile natives.[35] Whether they liked it or not, this dependence on Moscow boded ill for the preservation of their liberties. Obviously, the Cossacks could not pursue policies at odds with the tsarist government and still expect it to subsidize and protect their communities.

The steady erosion of the Cossacks' precarious independence was further abetted by changes within their communities. As their numbers increased, their system of direct democracy through noisy krugs became too unwieldy. Gradually, the administration of the hosts was increasingly entrusted to the atamans and their assistants, the so-called elders (*starshiny*). These men were usually long-established, often literate Cossacks who used their power to acquire wealth and lands. By the latter half of the seventeenth century, they formed an upper class that stood increasingly apart from the mass of ordinary Cossacks. In addition to the development of an elite class, Cossack societies also had to deal with a new derelict one. As fugitive serfs continued to arrive in the steppe, the host administrations became more restrictive about whom it would accept as full members of the Cossack communities. In the Don the "naked ones," as these impoverished newcomers were called, sometimes had to complete a seven-year apprenticeship before they would be granted full Cossack status. These measures, it seems, can be partially attributed to the elders' reluctance to share the tsars' subsidies and hosts' resources with the newcomers. The elites may be blamed for not only breaking the old Cossack traditions of inclusiveness and egalitarianism but also for weakening the krugs—the institution which more than any other encapsulated those values. Although the krugs still had the final say in the most contentious matters, the elders became adept at manipulating the assemblies. Such activity was encouraged by representatives of the tsars who played upon the vanity of the elders by regaling them with gifts and titles. In doing so, the tsarist government secured for itself a loyal and influential following in the Cossack communities.[36]

To their credit, the elite did try to uphold some renowned Cossack traditions—including those that were impractical. As the Cossack settlements grew, their inhabitants found it impossible to live solely off plunder, wild game and Moscow's shipments of grain. Fortunately, the rivers threading through their homelands were teeming with aquatic life; Cossack folklore claims that their ancestors had difficulty paddling their kayaks on the Don due to the abundance of fish in that river.[37] Subsequently, a booming fishing industry arose among the Don and Yaik Cossacks, and as a result salted fish became a dietary staple as well as a leading export.[38] In the upper reaches of the Don, however, the fish and game were not nearly as plentiful. It was here that the Cossacks, many of them poorer and relatively recent arrivals to the host, began to plow the steppe and sow fields of grain. This development was abhorred by elders along the lower Don; tending fields, they felt, was unsuitable for proud, freemen. In 1689, the Don elders threatened to punish any Cossack caught growing crops with death. They did not specify, however, by what other means Cossacks living in the northern Don were supposed to feed themselves. As a result, the prohibition against agriculture was ignored by the Cossack farmers and the practice continued to spread. It did not take long for the elders to embrace agriculture once they realized the potential profits they could reap if their lands were tilled. Eventually, they constructed sprawling estates that produced everything from beef and cereal grains to fruits and wines.[39]

By the onset of the eighteenth century, the Cossack lands, especially the Don Host, were beginning to bear a greater resemblance to Russia with each passing year. Belts of perennial grasses and wildflowers were being plowed under to make room for wheat fields. In some locales, a chattel dominated the countryside instead of a rickety village enclosed by stockade. This was unwelcome news to the fugitive serfs drawn south by the Cossack aura. At one time any man, as long as he could brandish a weapon, would be accepted as a full Cossack regardless of race, religion or social status, but this was no longer the case. With fewer opportunities for plunder and the most productive hunting grounds already claimed, many newcomers had to find employment as hired hands on the estates of the elite Cossacks. These laborers and their descendants, with few exceptions, would not be recognized as Cossacks and would remain peasants. The new life they sought in the Cossack lands turned out only slightly better than if they had remained serfs on Russian manors.[40] Opportunities for newcomers to become full Cossacks existed for a longer time on more distant hosts, such as the Yaik or Terek, but even these communities gradually became closed societies. Nonetheless, the fact that so many peasants were willing to abandon their homes—at the risk of severe punishment if they were caught—and make for an unknown frontier is indicative of the deplorable social and economic conditions prevalent throughout Russia at the time.

Some Cossacks launched rebellions to defend their societies from Polish or Russian encroachment. Insurgent leaders whose aims were concerned primarily with Cossack interests found little support beyond their hosts. Such was the case for Kondrati Bulavin, who in 1707–1708 led poorer Cossacks from the upper Don against the Cossack elite and troop detachments of Tsar Peter I (the Great, r. 1682-1725). A few months after Bulavin's revolt was crushed, Hetman Ivan Mazepa attempted to free the Zaporozhian Sech from Peter's tightening grip by siding with the invading army of King Charles XII of Sweden. Mazepa's gamble failed when Russian troops overran the Sech, razed it to the ground and decisively defeated the Swedes at the battle of Poltava. Both Bulavin and Mazepa fought to stave off the intrusion of the Petrine state on their homelands, but instead their actions swept away the last vestiges of their people's independence. After 1709, host atamans were no longer elected by krugs but instead were appointed by the tsar. Strongholds were constructed on Cossack lands and garrisoned by Russian troops. Before the end of the Peter's reign, the krugs, as the supreme institution of the host, were no more and Cossack delegations to the Russian capital, once honored as foreign dignitaries, were unceremoniously subordinated to military officials.[41]

In contrast, more successful Cossack rebels, such as Bohdan Khmelnytsky, Stenka Razin and Emelian Pugachev, exploited social discontent among peasants in Ukraine or Russia to make their uprisings far more widespread and potent than they would have been if they relied solely on their fellow Cossacks. Yet, of these, Khmelnytsky's revolt (1648–54) was the only one which attained any sort of lasting success by wresting the lands of the Ukrainian hetmanate away from the Polish-Lithuanian Commonwealth and making them a protectorate of Moscow.[42] Razin's rebellion (1670) attracted support from impoverished Cossacks, disgruntled peasants and even displaced nomads but as soon as it collapsed the Don elders, who were unsympathetic to his cause, had him arrested and extradited to tsarist authorities.[43] Pugachev's uprising (1773–74) was embraced by a significant number of Yaik Cossacks and ordinary peasants but failed to resonate among the Cossacks of his native

Don. After his capture and beheading, Empress Catherine II (the Great, r. 1762-96) punished the Yaik Cossacks *in toto* by renaming them the Ural Cossacks.[44]

The revolts led by Khmelnytsky, Razin and Pugachev demonstrated that the Cossack aura had a strong folk appeal to the oppressed serfs of the Ukraine and Russia. In each rebellion, peasants of non–Cossack origin readily declared themselves to be Cossacks or were galvanized by the rebel leaders' promises of Cossack status to them.[45] Nonetheless, Cossack rebels like Razin, Bulavin and Pugachev possessed a glaring weakness in the fact that none had the united support of a host behind them, much less the backing of all Cossack hosts. From the mid-seventeenth century onwards, the Cossack elders and elite in the hosts clearly identified their interests with the tsarist regime. Gradually, economic and social pressures forced even ordinary Cossacks to recoil from the populist ideology espoused by rebels and gravitate towards the established order championed by their elders. By the latter eighteenth century, at the time of Pugachev's rampage, this process was nearly complete on the Don, where the unrest fomented by its prodigal son failed to resonate in the stanitsas. Instead, the Don Cossacks were more likely to appear in the government forces as they were called upon to stamp out local uprisings in nearby districts; they even assisted in the final destruction of the Zaporozhian Sech, which had been partially rebuilt since Mazepa's ill-conceived adventure.[46]

While the Cossacks were the source of many headaches for the imperial courts in Moscow and St. Petersburg during the seventeenth and eighteenth centuries, Russia's rulers still regarded these knights of the steppe as a greater overall asset than a liability. More often than not, they could be faithfully counted upon to provide skilled cavalrymen for a military campaign or to rapidly quell revolts which flared up among tribal peoples in the Russian borderlands. The government thus went out of its way to create Cossack hosts where none previously existed as the empire expanded into Siberia and deeper into the Caucasus. Most of these new hosts were formed by transplanting a scion of Cossacks from an existing host, such as the Don or Ural (formerly Yaik) hosts, and grafting onto them non–Cossack elements that might include peasant immigrants or discharged soldiers. At times even certain non–Russian ethnicities were assigned to Cossack communities. For example, some Kalmyks, a Mongol people and followers of Buddhism who migrated into the lower Volga region during the 1630s, were incorporated into the Volga (later Astrakhan) and Orenburg Hosts, which were established in 1732 and 1755, respectively.[47] Near the end of that century, the Russian government formed a new host south of the Don on the eastern coast of the Black Sea. The nucleus of this Black Sea Host was to be former Zaporozhian Cossacks who had been chased away from the Sech only eight years earlier. Ukrainians deprived of their Cossack status several decades earlier were also brought in to fill the ranks of the new host, which encompassed a fertile plain recently depopulated by a genocidal campaign against the native Nogay Tatars.[48]

From the mid-eighteenth century onward, tsarist officials no longer regarded Cossacks as unsavory renegades but rather as cheap border guards. In their view, the Cossack communities would act as a military border, and their residents would serve in the dual role as self-sustaining farmers and ever-ready warriors. The Russian authorities were selective about choosing exactly which Cossack traditions they wanted their protégés to emulate. They desired the new Cossacks to provide their own equipment and be as adept on the horse as their designated forbearers. At the same time, they discouraged the democratic and egalitarian practices that had been a prominent feature of the early hosts. Instead, Russian officials took care to cultivate a group of elites in the new hosts in order to assure themselves a permanent base of support. This was especially true in the Black Sea Host, later to be renamed the Kuban Host, where a great land-owning class was allowed to develop.[49]

It was during the Napoleonic Wars when the Cossacks first took on the role of patriotic mascots. Their greatest test came in the summer of 1812, when Napoleon led his Grand Army of nearly 600,000 men into Russia. The Cossacks, with their smaller, shaggy ponies and motley uniforms, looked hardly a match for the French regular cavalry mounted on their larger steeds while donning glittering tunics. But what the Cossacks and their horses lacked in appearance was more than made up by their resilience to the worst winter conditions. During the Grand Army's retreat from Moscow, the horses from Western Europe, unaccustomed to the severe cold and unable to forage under snow cover, died in droves and left many French cavalrymen without a mount. Meanwhile, Cossack squadrons galloped around the retreating columns harassing their communications, taking thousands of prisoners and grabbing any loot within their reach. During the following year, they continued to trot alongside regiments of Russian infantry in the allied coalition's unrelenting drive against Napoleon. When the Russians, along with their allies, finally reached the French capital, the Cossacks were an object of curiosity among friend and foe. Among the former, the Cossacks were romanticized as noble savages whose obedience, courage and skills on the battlefield were second to none. On the other hand, many Parisians who watched the Cossacks parade into their city were repulsed by the barbaric appearance of these exotic steppe horsemen.[50]

As toasts to the Cossacks were drunk in gilded ballrooms in St. Petersburg and other European capitals, the Romanov court recognized the advantages of tying the legacy of

Front row, left to right, Duchess Anastasia, Grand Duchess Olga, Tsar Nicholas II, Tsarevich Aleksey, Grand Duchess Tatiana and Grand Duchess Maria pose with officers (back row) from a Kuban Cossack regiment during World War I, undated. This scene, along with the *cherkesskas* worn by the tsar and his heir, was one way the dynasty tied itself to the Cossack legacy (akg-images / WHA / World History Archive).

these celebrated defenders of the motherland closer to the dynasty. The past indiscretions of the Cossacks—from their outlaw origins to the rebellions of Razin and Pugachev—were deliberately glossed over by Russian historians who recast them as perpetually loyal and obedient subjects of the tsars.[51] In 1827, Tsar Nicholas I (r. 1825–55) designated the tsarevich as the ataman of all Cossack hosts, an announcement that was supposed to appear honorific but in reality bound the Cossacks more closely to the dynasty. Indeed, at the same time the regime was wrapping itself in a cloak of mythical Cossack imagery, it was seeking ways to curtail the autonomy of the hosts and to more fully integrate the borderlands into the empire. In 1832, the government defined the Cossacks as an estate with specific military obligations and a tax-exempt status.[52] Three years later, Nicholas reformed the administration and military ranking system of the Don Cossack Host to put these on the same footing as those elsewhere in Russia. It also barred the Don Cossacks and their descendants from leaving the host—unless ordered to do so by the government—and an effort was begun to standardize their military equipment. Satisfied by the results of these reforms, the government soon began applying them to other hosts.[53]

In all the hosts the Cossack elite had, with few exceptions, readily accepted a close alliance with the Romanovs. For them, the tsarist order was a source and defender of the authority, prosperity and titles which they enjoyed. Ordinary Cossacks had benefited much less by the increasing Russian intrusion in host affairs and had simply acquiesced to this fate. Still, by the nineteenth century virtually all Cossacks recognized the omnipotence of the tsar in their hosts. Each host treasured the charters from Moscow or St. Petersburg, particularly those which guaranteed the territory of the host to them and their descendants in perpetuity.[54] This claim to the steppe lands grew in importance as the Cossacks increasingly felt their way of life to be under siege—not by nomads or a foreign invader—but by Russian migrants and their descendants known disparagingly as outlanders (*inogorodnye*).

The origins of the outlander problem dated back to the early eighteenth century as admission for newcomers into Cossack society, beginning with the Don, grew more restrictive and eventually virtually impossible. As their communities became more exclusive, the Cossacks, seemingly forgetful of their own humble origins, developed a deep-seated prejudice against the peasantry as a whole. "In the eyes of the Cossack the Russian peasant is a nondescript creature, uncouth and beneath contempt," observed William Penn Cresson.[55] Nonetheless, desperate peasants continued to stream into the Don and other hosts, finding work on a Cossack estate and carving out a living despite rarely-enforced laws prohibiting non–Cossacks from settling in these lands. Occasionally, exemptions were made and the outlanders were reclassified as Cossacks, but for most they and their descendants were doomed to an inferior, semi-legal status as long as they remained in Cossack territory.[56]

The Cossacks increasingly resented the presence of the outlanders on the lands which, according to them, had been purchased with the blood of their ancestors. In the meantime, the outlanders looked upon the Cossacks as a privileged class whose prosperity was dependent upon their labor.[57] As early as 1840 relations between the two elements in the Orenburg host were so bad that Cossacks there urged the administration to either assimilate or deport the outlanders. Amid such extreme rhetoric, the situation faced by the Cossacks would grow much worse after Tsar Alexander II (r. 1855–81) emancipated the serfs in 1863. In the ensuing decades, waves of newly-freed Russian peasants departed from their crowded communes in central Russia for less-densely populated regions such as Siberia and the North Caucasus. As a result of these migrations, by 1914 many Cossacks had become a minority on their home turf. The Don Territory, for example, was the largest Cossack host, but its 1,460,000 Cossacks comprised less than 40 percent of the 4,000,000 inhabitants there. The bulk of the non–Cossack population was outlanders including not only rural agricultural laborers but also workers in mines, railways and in the industrial cities of Rostov and Taganrog.[58] The numbers were only a little better for the Cossacks in the Kuban, where they represented about 43 percent of the population, and much worse in the Terek, where they comprised a measly 20 percent of the total population. Outside of South Russia, the Cossacks often held stronger majorities in their hosts. It must be noted, however, that some of these hosts, such as those of the Astrakhan and Semirechye Cossacks, were nothing more than scattered pockets of settlements spread across one or more provinces. This arrangement allowed for large non–Cossack communities to exist within their midst without infringing upon the actual territory of their hosts. Those hosts that did form contiguous regions and held overwhelming majorities of Cossacks, such as those in the Urals or in Siberia, were situated in sparsely-populated backwaters.[59]

The Cossacks' inferior numbers posed problems for them as agitation for limited democratic reforms gained momentum in the latter nineteenth century. During that period the tsarist government, which clung stubbornly to the principle of autocracy, conceded to the establishment of local elected assemblies known as *zemstvos*. Although the jurisdiction of these organs was circumscribed to mostly apolitical matters such as public health or education, most Cossacks viewed them as a threat to their dominant position in the hosts. The *zemstvos*, they believed, might either become a dangerous rival to their traditional stanitsa assemblies or, even if they joined them, succumb to non–Cossack majorities. Subsequently, the stronger Cossack communities led a campaign of obstruction against the *zemstvos* that compelled Tsar Alexander III (r. 1881–94) to abrogate their existence in the Don and other hosts.[60] Democratic reforms did appeal to some more liberal-minded Cossacks, but even these, for the most part, had no desire to enfranchise the outlanders and natives who lived among them. Their solution was a revival of a regional *krug* that would exclusively represent Cossack interests while leaving the rest of the population, even if they were more numerous, without a political voice.[61]

The Cossack identity, then, had evolved from unlikely origins. Originally designated for marauders of Turkic-Tatar background, the term "Cossack" became associated with Slavic desperados who preferred to take their chances on the uncivilized steppe rather than integrate into the feudal societies of Poland or Muscovy. The egalitarian, warrior lifestyle of their ancestors was gradually replaced by a hierarchical, agrarian society that struggled to maintain their ancestors' equestrian and fighting abilities. Despite having once produced some of Russia's most famous rebels, after the early nineteenth century the Cossacks were increasingly viewed as devotees of the tsarist regime. Although they frequently adopted various customs of and even married among indigenous peoples, Russian conservatives from the nineteenth-century onwards embraced them as the embodiment of Russian ideals: simple folk who were ever-ready to make the ultimate sacrifice for the tsar, Orthodoxy and the motherland. The crises of the first half of the twentieth-century, however, would test these views to the utmost. The challenges wrought by modernization, war and revolution would again complicate and in some instances upend perceptions of Cossack identity in ways few could have expected.

1

Mobilization

Janissaries of the Old Order

By the dawn of the twentieth century, a little over 4.2 million Cossacks[1] resided in eleven hosts sprawled across the southern reaches of the Russian Empire. Although the lands they inhabited were broadly characterized as steppe, each host possessed its own unique characteristics. The Don Cossacks held the distinction of being members of the most senior and influential host while their southern neighbors, the Kuban Cossacks, cultivated some of the most fertile soil in the tsarist realm. In the eastern half of the isthmus between the Black and Caspian Seas, the Terek Cossacks farmed the scenic valleys below the snow-capped peaks of the Caucasus Mountains. Along the Volga and Ural rivers, communities of Astrakhan and Ural Cossacks harvested that signature Russian delicacy, caviar, and exported salted fish. In the southern range of the Ural Mountains, the Orenburg Cossacks acquired their name from the nearby fortress town which, during the previous century, had been used as a forward base for Russian expansion into Central Asia. In western Siberia, the Siberian Cossacks were mostly concentrated along a stretch of the Trans-Siberian Railway and the course of the Irtysh River. To their distant southeast, in present-day Kazakhstan, the Semirechye Cossacks had recently colonized a patchwork of oases in the semi-arid region near Lake Balkhash. In the mostly desolate Russian Far East, the Transbaikal Cossacks grazed large herds of cattle in the jagged terrain near the Manchurian frontier. Further north, the Amur Cossacks occupied the north bank of the great river after which they were named. The most easterly host was that of the Ussuri Cossacks, situated in Russia's Maritime Province and just shy of the Pacific coast. Nearly 6,000 miles separated them from their cousins in the Don Host.

Regardless of where they lived, all Cossacks shared a rural lifestyle centered on their stanitsas. Many made a living through agriculture, grazing or fishing. A few communities, especially those in the North Caucasus region, focused on the production of wines and fruits. They shunned industrial occupations such as labor in factories, mines, oil rigs or on railways. Whenever a modern industry developed on Cossack lands it was almost invariably dominated by outlanders. In nearby towns, few Cossacks were represented among the merchant class; rather, most shopkeepers were of Russian, Armenian or Tatar background. Consequently, in many of the hosts' population centers—including their capitals such as Yekaterinodar (Krasnodar), Vladikavkaz, Orenburg and Omsk—non–Cossacks outnumbered Cossacks.[2]

The seeming inability of the Cossacks to adapt to anything but a rustic way of life was actually an unavoidable outcome of the heavy military obligations imposed on them by the tsarist regime. Under the statues of 1875, which remained in effect into World War I, all able-bodied Cossack males between the ages of 21 and 33 were considered members of the active service. This twelve-year period in the Cossacks' military career was divided into three stages, or turns, with varying requirements. The heaviest obligations fell on the young Cossacks of the first turn, ages 21–24, in which they spent three years away from home usually serving in a garrison or patrol. When the Cossacks entered the second turn at about age 25, they were allowed to return home in peacetime. During this stage, they were required to leave their fields for about one month each summer to attend a training camp. For the last stage of active service, which began at about age 29, the Cossacks were supposed to be battle-ready though their horses were not required to pass military inspection. Following their period of active service, the Cossacks were moved into the reserve category for five years, which absolved them of further obligations in peacetime. After the age 38, the Cossacks were reclassified as militia, where they remained liable to be called up for another ten years.[3] Russian conscripts of non–Cossack origin, in contrast, typically saw about three years on active duty followed by fifteen years in the reserves and another five in the militia.[4]

In addition to the time the young Cossack men needed to spend away from their homes, they were further burdened by the requirement of needing to provide their own suitable horses, uniform and saddles throughout much of their military career. At the end of nineteenth-century, the skyrocketing costs of these accessories made it nearly impossible for the average Cossack family to outfit one son for active duty, much less two or more. As a sign of how bad the situation was, the tsarist government, in order to maintain the strength of its Cossack cavalry, resorted to issuing subsidies to partially cover the costs of horses for incoming recruits from several hosts.[5]

The hardships which the Cossacks endured as a result of their military obligations were not evident to neighboring Russian peasants, outlanders and natives. Instead, those groups envied the privileges which the Cossacks received from the government in exchange for their years of duty. Perhaps the most important of these was access to land: the Cossacks were entitled not only to larger allotments than peasants but also to the best ground. In mountainous regions such as the Terek, the Cossacks tilled the fertile valleys while native clans had to make do with cultivating rocky, terraced slopes. In the semi-arid climate of the Semirechye Host, the Cossacks had better access to oases and other water resources to the detriment of the Kazakh herders. Relations between the Cossacks and their neighbors were further impaired by the stanitsas' frequent need to rent land out to cover the costs of its members' military service. This practice instilled peasants and natives with the impression that the Cossacks had more land than they knew what to do with.[6] Yet the reality was that the Cossacks, or at least those in the crowded western hosts, were being required to do as much or more than previous generations but with fewer resources. This was especially true in the Don, where by 1914 the average size of each Cossack's land allotment was just over a third of what it had been in 1835.[7]

Besides their more generous land allotments, other privileges bestowed on the Cossack estate by the tsarist regime included local autonomy and the distinction of being one of the two estates in the empire exempt from most taxes. The fact that the nobility was the only other estate which enjoyed this status was a source of great pride for the Cossacks—it was a reminder that they had never been classified as serfs.[8] Still, these privileges had come to them at a high cost. By the twentieth century, the economic fortunes of most Cossacks were in such decline that there was little hope that they would become self-supporting military garrisons as the government intended. Indeed, the Cossack hosts east of the Urals never came close to such an objective and constantly required government aid in the form of funds, supplies and even recruits. But even the more closely-knit, vibrant Cossack communities of European Russia often required large grants from St. Petersburg from the late nineteenth-century onward. In 1898, a commission set up to uncover the cause of the Cossack economic crisis concluded that the terms of the Cossacks' service were unsustainable amid current conditions and recommended their reclassification as peasants. For the tsarist authorities, such a solution was unthinkable—they could not admit that the steppe warriors whom they had celebrated for the better part of a century were becoming obsolete. Their approach to the growing impoverishment of the Cossacks became one more example of how the regime, never known for embracing modernity, shunned unpleasant realities by immersing itself in its own myths.[9]

Aside from the fantasy of Cossack devotion to the Romanov dynasty, the tsarist government had one other compelling reason to keep the Cossacks around. The rapid industrialization that Russia had undergone since the reign of Tsar Alexander II brought unrest in the form of massive worker strikes and urban riots which, if left unchecked, might snowball into a revolution. Russian authorities quickly learned that mounted Cossacks could be an effective instrument to disperse unruly crowds. In case their imposing demeanor was not enough to convince a mob to disband, Cossacks on security duty were issued painful whips called *nagaika*. Although *nagaika*-wielding Cossacks were regarded as a non-lethal form of crowd control, they were not harmless. Following the failure of the 1898 Andijan uprising in Russian Turkestan, tsarist officials investigating the causes of the revolt observed that local hospitals were overflowing with patients suffering from *nagaika*-inflicted injuries. Nevertheless, the commander overseeing the punitive measures noted with satisfaction that the floggings "created a splendid impression on both the native population and on the army."[10]

For their part, the Cossacks did not relish this type of special police service. It certainly lacked the romanticism of their ancestors' feats of taming Russia's frontiers. Still, the Cossacks' steppe upbringing, political naivety and distrust of city-dwellers rendered them apathetic towards the strikers they were called upon to whip into submission. Whenever the crowds begged the horsemen to join them or to show mercy, their pleas seemed to fall on deaf ears. The authorities took note of this as well. For that reason, policemen almost invariably preferred to use Cossacks over regular soldiers against unruly crowds since the reliability of the steppe warriors seemed unquestionable.[11]

For a time, the Cossacks' service alongside the police forces cemented them to the tsarist regime, but cracks began to appear in that mortar during the revolutionary uprisings of 1905. Those insurrections began at a time when the Cossack hosts were already feeling the burden of mobilization from the ongoing Russo-Japanese War. Beginning in February 1904, all active service and some reserve Cossacks from the Siberian, Transbaikal, Amur and Ussuri hosts were called up and dispatched to the battlefields in Manchuria. After tsarist police fired into a crowd of demonstrators in St. Petersburg on 22 January 1905—the incident that became known as Bloody Sunday—the spread of the rebellion from the capital to other cities and then to the countryside compelled authorities to call up dozens of additional Cossack regiments to stamp out protests, strikes and revolts in nearly every corner of the empire. Over the next several months, even after a treaty was signed with Japan, mobilization orders continued to stream out of St. Petersburg. Before the end of the year, all Don, Kuban, Terek, Astrakhan, Orenburg and Ural Cossacks in the second turn of their active service period (age 25–28) along with some in the third turn (age 29–33) were mobilized.[12] Even so, demands for more Cossack units continued to pour into Novocherkassk, Yekaterinodar and Orenburg. The host administrations were reluctant to activate the reserves or militia since not only would this further disrupt their local economies, but also because many Cossacks frowned upon the police work they were being called to perform. Some stanitsa assemblies even echoed the widespread grievances of the masses by passing resolutions against further mobilization.[13] Meanwhile, the Cossack squadrons being shuttled from one restive district to another were growing weary from the unending spate of reprisals they were being ordered to carry out. Amid their exhaustion many turned to alcohol and as they did so their discipline, which was almost invariably well-below that of regular army units, evaporated. By 1906, the behavior of the Cossack punitive detachments was becoming unpredictable; some left a trail of smoldering villages and charred corpses in their wake, others fraternized with the insurgents they were supposed to crush.[14] The disorders also affected the Cossack homelands. To protect their stanitsas against rebellious peasants or natives, Cossacks in the Don, Kuban and Terek hosts were authorized by the War Ministry to form "self-defense units." Meanwhile, politically-active Don Cossacks, following the examples of peasants and workers in other parts of the country, began to formulate a list of demands that included the revival of the krug along with increased self-rule. But as the turmoil subsided and the tsarist government gained the upper hand, the Cossack spokesmen wisely backed off their demands.

Despite the flickering of revolutionary feeling among Cossacks in the service and at home, their overall image after the Revolution of 1905 remained the same as it was before: that they were rigid stalwarts of the tsarist regime. Tsar Nicholas II (r. 1894–1917) tried to reinforce this notion by regaling nearly all the hosts with charters stating his appreciation for their service. Distinguished units and individuals were awarded orders and medals while cash bonuses were granted to the mobilized older Cossacks. Finally, a new elite Cossack unit, the Composite Lifeguards Cossack Regiment, was formed so that troopers from each of the Cossack hosts would be represented in the tsar's convoy of bodyguards.[15]

The tsar's subjects, of course, had a much less favorable opinion of the steppe horsemen. Naturally, those who had lost property or family members to the rampages of the Cossack punitive detachments were the most resentful. This widespread animosity was irksome for the Cossack delegates to State Dumas convened during and after the crisis. Contrary to their prevailing image, the majority of Cossack deputies to the Dumas were members of liberal or centric parties generally in opposition to the government. This remained true even after tsarist authorities manipulated the electoral system to favor conservative candidates.[16] Nonetheless, the stereotype of Cossacks as janissaries of the dynasty continued to persist.[17] Later, it would be exploited by Bolshevik propagandists to the utmost during Russia's civil war.

The Cossacks in the First World War

On 1 August 1914, a Kuban Cossack teenager, Marina Yurlova, was startled from her fieldwork by the abrupt tolling of church bells emanating from her nearby stanitsa. Since it was neither Sunday nor a holy day, she later recalled that they sounded "ominous, like something calling for help."[18] Upon returning to her stanitsa, red placards—the signal for general mobilization—confirmed her misgivings. That scene was repeated over and over throughout thousands of stanitsas and Russian villages: Cossacks and peasants focused on harvesting their crops were suddenly being called to fight in a war that to them had come out of nowhere. Indeed, while the outbreak of hostilities was greeted with an outpouring of patriotic enthusiasm in the European capitals, including St. Petersburg (soon to be rechristened as Petrograd),[19] the announcement was received much more soberly in the Russian countryside. Although the relatively small Cossack intelligentsia was among those groups overcome with the patriotic fervor,[20] many if not most rural dwellers felt that the looming conflict seemed distant, its causes obscure and, on the whole, unnecessary. Nevertheless, the Cossacks and the peasants obediently laid down their scythes and set off for the depots from where they began their long journeys to the front.[21]

Since the population of registered Cossacks in each host varied considerably, the number of men they contributed to the war effort also differed greatly. The two largest hosts, the Don and Kuban, together provided well over half of the 360,000 Cossacks who served in the army during the war. On the other hand, a number of eastern hosts such as the Semirechye, Amur and Ussuri hosts could only send a few squadrons. At the outset of the war, all Cossacks were organized in mounted units, except for some infantry (*plastun*) regiments from the Kuban.[22]

Russia began the war with the highest proportion of cavalry among the belligerents, and Cossacks comprised a significant chunk of this mounted force. Each Russian cavalry division contained a regiment of Cossacks in addition to a regiment of hussars, lancers and dragoons. Despite their famed equestrian skills, it seems that the presence of boorish Cossacks was not always appreciated by other cavalrymen. As one Russian officer put it, "In each cavalry division hussars despise lancers, lancers despise dragoons, and all three despise Cossacks!"[23] Russia's enemies, on the other hand, were downright terrified by the steppe warriors, and cries of "*Der Kossak kommen!*" were known to spread panic among both soldiers and civilians in the eastern districts of the German and Austro-Hungarian Empires. In some instances their fears were kindled by sensationalized articles appearing in German newspapers of Cossack atrocities in East Prussia. In both enemy states the Imperial Russian Army was denigrated as "the Asiatic hordes," and nothing seemed to epitomize this more than the popular image of sinister Cossacks outfitted in shaggy hats and oriental costumes with curved sabers at their sides.[24]

Early in the conflict, lances were used by all Russian cavalrymen, including Cossacks, in addition to rifles and sabers. Intended as a shock weapon, the mounted lancers were deployed to break-up infantry formations as they had during the Napoleonic Wars.[25] All combatants, however, quickly learned that battlefield conditions had changed drastically in the century since the Battle of Waterloo. Back then musket-wielding infantrymen could fire at most two or three volleys before approaching cavalry might trample them down. But with the adoption of repeating rifles with improved ranges, the lethality of the foot soldier was greatly enhanced. In 1914, a trained rifleman on open ground could fire 20–30 rounds before attacking cavalry reached his position. The odds against cavalry became even more unfavorable if the infantry were supported by a machine gun, which could spew hundreds of bullets per minute at charging horsemen.[26] Despite these vulnerabilities, cavalry formations retained their effectiveness much longer in the open, less-densely defended areas of the Eastern and Caucasus Fronts than in the elaborate trenchworks of France. Unlike most other European cavalries at the beginning of the war, all Russian cavalry units were trained to fight dismounted as well as on horseback, giving them a versatility which their opponents initially lacked. Despite such training, many cavalrymen maintained a certain reluctance to fight out of the saddle. As one Russian hussar later admitted, "the spirit of the Russian cavalry still remained that of charging with drawn swords."[27] But such attacks proved increasingly futile as the war continued. Occasionally, an opportunity to utilize the full shock-effect of cavalry presented itself. In November 1915, a British correspondent attached to a Russian column in Armenia was awed by the spectacle of a Cossack squadron pursuing a retreating detachment of Turkish infantry. When the Cossacks charged, he observed, "they were like a flood let loose, long black lines streaming across the open, and raising clouds of dust."[28] By that stage of the war, however, such picturesque mounted attacks were rare. Generally, the limited role of horsemen could not justify the large amounts of inputs needed to maintain large cavalry formations at the fronts. Indeed, at times Russia's war effort could have benefited considerably if trains pulling wagons of horse fodder to the fronts were instead filled with munitions and other essentials desperately needed by the men in the trenches.[29]

With cavalry no longer decisive on the battlefield, the role of Cossacks was adjusted accordingly. Some were organized into small raiding parties and sent behind the opposing lines to wreak havoc on the enemy's communication and supplies.[30] Others were stationed behind their own frontlines to prevent Russian soldiers from shirking their duty to the crown. In the opening battle of Krasník in August 1914, Russian infantry attempting to flee the Austrian onslaught were whipped back to the firing line by Cossack squadrons blocking their path of retreat.[31] Throughout the rest of the war, Cossacks were relied upon to patrol the rear of the Russian armies and round up war-weary and homesick deserters.

The Cossacks' rear duties made them unpopular among peasant-soldiers, and before long civilians caught in the armies' path learned to resent the steppe horsemen as well. In early 1915, anti–Semitic tsarist generals, believing unfounded rumors that Jews living near the front were spying for the Central Powers, ordered the wholesale removal of Jewish populations from the war zones. The deportation, which eventually displaced tens of thousands of Jews, was carried out in the crudest manner with Cossacks cracking their painful *nagaika* on the backs of the hapless refugees as they were driven eastward.[32] For the other, non–Jewish civilians in these areas, their turn to bemoan the presence of Cossacks came that following summer as the supply-starved tsarist armies fell back across much of the Eastern Front. In order to leave nothing to the enemy, the Russians adopted a scorched-earth policy, and the Cossacks were among those units tasked with razing villages, confiscating livestock and burning crops. Not even the bewildered peasants were to be left behind, and subsequently hundreds of thousands were uprooted and forced to withdraw eastward with the Russian troops. The entire episode, and in particular the Cossacks' brutish behavior, discredited the tsarist regime among the Polish and Ukrainian peasants whose loyalties it had once sought to secure.[33]

When the Cossacks did engage the enemy, assessments of their performance ranged from glowing reports to frustrated grumblings. Cossack and some Russian historians, perhaps due to a lack of objectivity, depicted Cossack troops as the bravest and most decorated men in the tsarist army.[34] However, General Alfred Knox, a British liaison officer who observed the fighting on the Eastern Front, complained on more than one occasion that the successful forays of German cavalry were possible only because of the passiveness of their Cossack opponents. "The German cavalry advanced with fine self-sacrifice," Knox wrote of an enemy incursion near Vilna in 1915, "but its raid would never have penetrated to the depth it did if it had had to deal with Russian regular cavalry instead of with Cossacks."[35] Indeed, the Cossacks frequently failed to live up to their expectations as "noble savages" and were often afflicted by the same rumors, propaganda and disillusionment which sapped the morale of Russia's peasant-soldiers. These feelings were even manifested on the Caucasian Front, where Russian forces generally held the initiative against the Ottoman army. While serving in that theater with the 3rd Yekaterinodar Regiment, Yurlova wrote that "the army muttered to itself all during that march, till the very air seemed to be heavy with rumors."[36] The gossip she heard there was being repeated throughout the country: the tsar was said to be completely dominated by his German-born wife, who was betraying Russian military secrets to the kaiser. In the meantime, the imperial couple's spiritual guru, Grigory Rasputin, was allegedly pulling the real levers of power in Petrograd.

For Russia's soldiers, such explosive tales of treachery in the palaces seemed to be the only possible explanation for the cycles of incompetence, privations and reverses which they witnessed at the front.[37] In reality, the causes behind the empire's flailing war effort were less sensational. The Russian general staff, like their colleagues in other countries, had anticipated a conflict of brief duration. When the war extended beyond a few months, the country's industries were totally unprepared to compensate for the shortfall in materiel. By early 1915, rifles were so scarce that recruits were being trained with one rifle for every three men, and later that year unarmed replacements were sent into the trenches to snatch a firearm from those killed or wounded. At the same time, the Russians were also in desperate need of artillery shells. According to one source, in September 1914 Russian factories had a total output of 35,000 shells per month, but at the time the army was firing an average of 45,000 shells per day.[38] By 1915, the morale of Russian infantrymen crashed as they endured merciless poundings by enemy guns while their supporting artillery stood silent for want of shell. Given these circumstances, it is not surprising that the Russian lines were rolled back that year, and the fact that the tsarist armies held together as well as they did amid the crisis is a testament to the hardiness of its peasant-soldiers.

From a purely military viewpoint, Russia's fortunes improved during 1916. That June General Aleksey Brusilov, commander of the Southwest Front, launched an offensive that stunned the Central Powers and inflicted over 1,500,000 casualties on their armies before the attacks ended in October. The only drawback to the operation was that it was also costly for the Russians as they experienced grave losses, particularly in officers, that could not be easily replaced.[39] Success at the front, however, did not offset the steadily deteriorating situation in the rear. Much of the trouble could be traced to Russia's rail network, which was much less developed than the railways of Western and Central Europe. The task of supplying the armies alone strained the capacity of Russia's rolling stock, but the circumstances of the war, particularly the enemy blockade, brought additional burdens. Germany and Turkey effectively closed Russia's shipping routes through the Baltic and Black Seas, leaving only the much less accessible ports of Arkhangelsk and Vladivostok open for her overseas trade.[40] Suddenly, trains were needed to haul coal from the Donets Basin and Siberia to fuel Petrograd factories that had previously imported their coal supplies through the Baltic. In the meantime, the diversion of trade to distant ports meant that more trains were needed to shuttle munitions and other desperately needed war materiel from the White Sea and Pacific coasts to the fronts.[41] By autumn of 1916, Russian cities were suffering from acute food and fuel shortages as a result of the declining capacity of the country's overtaxed railway system. This in turn led to further unrest in Petrograd and other urban centers as hungry workers protested against shrinking bread rations.[42]

Some of the logistical difficulties which Russia experienced during the war, such as her immense distances, were unavoidable consequences of her geography. But the crisis was made immeasurably worse by the mismanagement, lapses and corruption which permeated every level of tsarist officialdom. No where were these defects more apparent than at the top, where Tsar Nicholas II ignored pleas of wiser advisors and concerned Duma representatives to appoint proven and qualified men to key ministries. Instead, by late 1916 most of the tsar's ministers were mere lackeys of the court. This state of affairs was frustrating not only for Russia's population but also for her allies who doubted their ability to defeat Germany by themselves. Although they were obliged to support the tsarist regime, it was at times difficult for their representatives in Russia to hide their frustration with the bungling monarchy. For instance, in a particularly candid report to London, an exasperated Knox complained, "If there has ever been a Government that richly deserved a revolution, it is the present one in Russia."[43]

Rehearsal for Revolution

With a prewar population estimated at 180,000,000 inhabitants, the Russian Empire held a significant manpower advantage over her adversaries, but large swaths of the tsar's subjects were ineligible for conscription.[44] Many native tribes in the Caucasus, Central Asia and Siberia, for example, were exempted from the draft. But in the summer of 1916, when the Imperial Russian Army was in dire need of recruits to replace the soaring losses from the first two years of the war, the army command prevailed upon Nicholas to mobilize Caucasian and Central Asian natives. This call-up was not intended to put the indigenous peoples in uniform but rather for them to provide labor in agriculture and other essential industries so more Russian workers could be released into the army. Nonetheless, news of the mobilization was received with trepidation among many natives; their concerns fueled in part by rumors that they would be digging trenches in no-man's land or become cannon fodder for the army.[45]

The mobilization announcement sparked the greatest uproar among the nomadic Kazakh and Kyrgyz living in the vicinity of the Semirechye Cossack Host, the site of long-simmering tensions between the natives, Cossacks and Russian colonists. In the decade prior to 1916, the Semirechye region had been the focus of intense colonization as Russian peasants were encouraged to plow the virgin steppe. Invariably, the arrival of settlers from Central Russia displaced nomads, depriving them of the best grazing lands while limiting their access to scarce water resources.[46] The subsequent call-up for native workers, following years of economic hardship caused by colonization, compelled many Kazakhs and Kyrgyz in the easternmost districts of Russian Turkestan to flee towards the Chinese frontier. Others chose to band together and resist the measure by killing the officials responsible for drawing up lists of draftees or by attacking Russian and Cossack settlements. Amid the circumstances of the ongoing war, the Cossacks and peasant settlers were especially vulnerable since many of their men were away at the front. Moreover, those remaining behind no longer possessed the firearms which had been issued by the government to defend their settlements from unruly nomads; these weapons had been collected during earlier drives to help remedy the shortage of arms at the front.[47]

In early September 1916, nearly a month after the initial uprising began in Semirechye, Cossacks and other personnel began arriving by train from Siberia and other parts of Russian Central Asia to help "pacify" the region. The insurgents, many of them armed only with spears, were hopelessly outgunned wherever they stood their ground. Throughout the remainder of the autumn, the punitive expeditions burned the natives' villages, shot suspected rebels and rounded up the nomads' livestock amid atrocities that equaled or surpassed the worst excesses of the insurgents. The native population probably suffered the most in those areas where the government authorities readily handed out rifles to any Russian colonist or Cossack willing to accept them. Amid the inflamed passions, the *ad hoc* self-defense detachments they formed made little effort to discriminate between Kazakhs and Kyrgyz that had actively participated in the rebellion and those who had complied with mobilization order.[48]

As the revolt collapsed in the autumn of 1916, as many as 300,000 Kazakhs and Kyrgyz tried to escape the wrath of the Cossack and colonial detachments by migrating to the Chinese territory of Xinjiang.[49] There they faced new hardships as Chinese authorities, in exchange for allowing the refugees cross their border, confiscated their herds of livestock and left them with nothing to eat. The hungry and defenseless refugees also came under attack by nomadic tribes indigenous to Xinjiang.[50] In the meantime, back in their homeland, the Russians and Cossacks in the Semirechye region appropriated any property or livestock the refugees had left behind. Russian authorities under the leadership of A. N. Kuropatkin, who served in the dual role as governor-general of Turkestan and as the newly-appointed ataman of the Semirechye Cossacks, drafted a plan to separate the Russian and native populations of Semirechye by creating homogeneous districts for each. Naturally, the Russian-inhabited district was to encompass the most fertile land.[51]

Cossacks, thanks to their ability to match the mobility of the nomad insurgents in the expansive, roadless steppe, were well-suited to carry out punitive operations in Semirechye and other parts of Turkestan in 1916. Among the leaders of these feared detachments was Colonel P. P. Ivanov, who acquired notoriety for the ruthless conduct of his Cossack squadrons. "Ivanov gave the order to shoot, burn, confiscate household goods and agricultural implements," recalled a survivor of the reprisals in Samarkand Province. "The units went to the *kishlaks* (native villages), burned goods, whomever they met they shot, women were raped and other bestialities [were] perpetrated."[52] While Kuropatkin did not approve of such uninhibited brutality against the native peoples,[53] he nonetheless was satisfied enough by the Cossacks' performance during the uprising to include the establishment of five new stanitsas in his blueprints for an all-Russian district in Semirechye.[54] Regardless of the economic challenges faced by Cossacks prior to 1914 and diminishing role of cavalry in the ongoing war, officials like Kuropatkin remained convinced that Cossacks would continue to fulfill a valuable role as Russia barreled deeper into the twentieth century.

At least one historian has suggested that the 1916 revolt in Central Asia might be considered an opening skirmish of Russia's civil war.[55] Although no rebellions of an equivalent magnitude broke out in other parts of the empire that year, increasing numbers if its population was becoming restive. At the outbreak of the Great War, the labor movement, caught in an upsurge of patriotic fervor, declared a truce with its opponents in industry and the government. But after two years of setbacks at the front, strict food rationing, frequent fuel shortages and soaring inflation, the patience of the working-class was exhausted. Like ominous tremors before a volcanic eruption, a series of strikes, street demonstrations and riots preceded the uprising that eventually culminated into the Russian Revolution. At one point in October, the Petrograd authorities ordered garrison troops to assist the police in clearing raucous strikers out of the city's Renault factory. But the soldiers, in a portent of the upheavals to come, fraternized with the workers and then turned their rifles on the police. Order was restored only after four Cossack regiments were dispatched to the scene to drive the mutinous troops back to their barracks.[56]

Tsarist authorities, perhaps drawing a lesson from the events of that October, reinforced the Petrograd garrison with two Don Cossack regiments from the Northern Front just weeks before Russian Revolution broke out in earnest.[57] For them, the possibility that the Cossacks themselves might be afflicted with the general malaise of demoralization was unthinkable. As a result, they probably did not give much thought to what might happen if the Cossacks, instead of charging the mobs, joined them.

2

Upheaval

The End of the Old Order

On 8 March 1917, when women frustrated by long waits in queues for meager bread rations took to Petrograd's streets in protest, the authorities responsible for preserving order in the Russian capital were not unduly concerned. Even on the following day, when over 160,000 workers from the industrial districts turned out in support of the demonstrations, the authorities still did not think the matter was serious enough to inform the tsar at Stavka. By then bread riots and massive strikes had become something of a wartime routine in Russia's cities. Besides, the authorities could take comfort in the fact that in addition to the police they could call upon a hefty garrison of 180,000 troops if the situation got out of hand. Among that number were 3,200 Cossacks from the Don, Kuban and Terek hosts who enjoyed the full confidence of tsarist officials.[1]

The authorities' absolute faith in the Cossacks blinded them to the warning signs that something was amiss in the squadrons of steppe horsemen. These signals had manifested themselves as early as the second day of the strikes when cordons of Cossacks and police were confronted by the angry crowds. According to eyewitness accounts, the Cossacks made at best only half-hearted efforts to disperse the strikers. They showed no desire to harm the demonstrators and even drove off police when the latter attempted to employ force against the crowds. Encouraged by the Cossacks' empathic smiles beneath their mustaches, the strikers invited the steppe horsemen to join them by shouting entreaties such as "Comrades, our cause is your cause!"[2] The two sides began to fraternize and soon the Cossacks, through their actions and words, adopted a neutral stance in the standoff on the streets. Nonetheless, the local authorities still ordered the Cossacks out to disperse the demonstrators on the following day.

On that day, Saturday, 10 March, the Cossacks in the capital proved no more willing to come to the rescue of policemen who were cornered and overwhelmed by the throngs of workers. To discourage the strike movement, the police attempted to round up large numbers of the most boisterous agitators, but they soon found their efforts hindered by Cossacks who turned on the police and freed the arrested individuals. The news that the Cossacks of all people had taken the side of the workers caused a sensation among the crowds, and before long they were cheering the horsemen. "By evening," observed one revolutionary, "the Cossacks had become the people's heroes."[3]

In the meantime, the unreliability of the Cossacks compelled the Petrograd authorities to acknowledge the gravity of the unrest and finally report these events to the tsar's headquarters at Mogilev (Mahilyow). Although the Cossacks comprised only a small fraction of the total troop garrison in the environs of the capital, their defection had massive symbolic importance. Both the local commanders and the strikers had anticipated the Cossacks to defend the regime to the last. The fact that they had bucked those expectations so early in the course of events did not bode well for the efforts of tsarist officers to restore order with soldiers who more readily identified with the aggrieved masses. Indeed, the fact that some of the troops had begun fraternizing with the strikers on 9 March—the same day as the Cossacks—hardly caused a stir on either side. Somewhat unexpectedly, the infantry regiments were slow to follow the Cossacks' example, but follow them they did. On 12 March, two days after the Cossacks had joined the demonstrators, the bulk of the garrison was engaged in a general mutiny and the commander of Petrograd military district acknowledged the impossibility of regaining control in the city. That evening, not one but two successors to the *ancien régime* emerged in the capital. In the Tauride Palace, a committee of members from the State Duma declared themselves a Provisional Government while almost simultaneously in the opposite wing of that building a Soviet of Workers' Deputies, soon to be joined by soldiers' deputies, was called into session. Over the next several days the revolution spread to other cities throughout the Russian Empire, culminating with the abdication of the tsar on 15 March. Three centuries of Romanov rule had arrived to an end.[4]

News of the revolution was generally welcomed throughout the army. The soldiers, having long ago lost confidence in ability of the tsarist government to prosecute the war effectively, hoped that the new order would lead them to victory or, at the very least, end the futile attacks that had proved so wasteful with their lives.[5] There were, of course, exceptions. For the most obedient Cossacks and soldiers, the tsar's abdication was akin to desertion and his absence suddenly upended their convictions of sacred duty.[6] To win the support of these confused individuals, it was essential for the new liberal regime to inspire them with fresh ideas and goals to replace the monarchical principles for which they had fought. But from the start the Provisional Government faced stiff competition in its struggle to capture the hearts and minds of the empire's peoples. The Petrograd Soviet, which quickly clenched the loyalties of the workers, peasants and even many soldiers, was its most serious challenger but it was not alone. Lenin's Bolshevik Party soon began disseminating propaganda that was far more radical than the programs of either the new government or the Soviet. The government also had to cater to the sensibilities of the empire's minorities. Throughout the borderlands, various ethnicities began promulgating their own brand of patriotism while demanding greater self-government. Many Cossacks, although they did not quite fit the definition of a distinct nationality, joined these centrifugal movements by forming organs designed to advance their own specific interests.

The Early Days of the Revolution in the Hosts

The collapse of tsarism was a readily accepted outcome in the stanitsas across Russia. Although the Cossack stanitsas, unlike Russia's northern cities, had access to reliable sources of food, their inhabitants were still impacted by rocketing inflation, railway disruptions and a dearth of manufactured goods. Most burdensome of all was the mass mobilization of their menfolk. At the war's outbreak, all Cossacks in the active service category, including those in the second and third turns, were called up.[7] In the following months, the effects of mobilization cut deeper in the stanitsas as older Cossacks from the reserves were ordered to report for duty. Although Cossack women had a tradition of taking up the plow and other duties while their men were on campaign,[8] many households still fell behind as the seemingly endless conflict drew the most productive farmhands away from the stanitsas. The result was that after three years of war cottages were falling into disrepair, fences were unmended, herds were thinned, orchards were overgrown and some fields were unsown. It should not be surprising that amid these depressing surroundings the promises of the new order—personal freedoms, popular sovereignty, national rejuvenation—were all welcome changes.

Alongside the optimism engendered by the establishment of the new liberal democratic order came uncertainty. Among the earliest decrees of the Provisional Government was a guarantee that all citizens would be considered equal regardless of class, religion or nationality. This was a cause for concern among Cossacks who under the old regime had enjoyed a favorable position in the borderlands precisely because of their status as Cossacks. Moreover, the decrees aroused their indigenous neighbors who resented the encroachment of Cossacks on their ancestral lands. Caucasian tribesmen in the Terek, Bashkir pastoralists in the Urals and Kazakh nomads of the Semirechye Hosts all hoped that the new government of the peoples would amend past injustices by returning lost lands to their possession.[9]

In ethnically-mixed hosts, the evident unrest among the natives usually drew all Russian elements—Cossacks, outlanders and colonists—into a tacit alliance against the natives. Such coalitions even formed in hosts that, like the Don, were essentially ethnically-homogenous. There Cossacks and outlanders forgot their traditional animosity long enough to form regional committees vaguely proclaiming to represent to the interests of "the people." This cooperation, however, derailed shortly after the heady enthusiasm fomented by the initial shock of the revolution wore off. Indeed, both sides soon learned that the revolutionary ideals of freedom and equality had different meanings to them. By and large, the Cossacks were unwilling to abandon their Cossack identity or the lands promised to them by ancient tsarist charters. On the other hand, the outlanders expected the revolution to be a great leveling force that would grant them full rights as well as new opportunities in the hosts. Like the various natives, the outlanders also hoped that the new government would quickly enact land reforms that would deprive their Cossack neighbors of their larger and more fertile allotments. As these opposing views became more pronounced in the weeks and months following the February Revolution, both sides began to look to other organs besides the Provisional Government to advance their agendas.

In the Don, a Cossack government was formed by the upper class, former officials and army officers nervous over what changes the new revolutionary order might bring. Rather than look forward, they peered backward and decided that freedom meant the restoration of Cossack liberties lost centuries ago. In particular, they sought to recreate krugs and elect atamans just as their ancestors did in the seventeenth century. Their activities received official sanctioning after the new War Minister, Aleksandr Guchkov, authorized all Cossacks to overhaul the civil administration in their hosts. Shortly afterwards, a Don Cossack Krug was summoned in Novocherkassk from which the outlanders were excluded. As these took shape, Guchkov, realizing that the Don Krug and others like it might compete for authority with the regional committees recognized by the Provisional Government, quickly tried to bridle the krugs by issuing a follow-up decree that they were to limit themselves to Cossack affairs.

With the weakness of the Provisional Government evident to all that spring, the Don Krug was hardly fazed by the restrictions imposed by the War Ministry. While the Cossack delegates initially recognized the Petrograd-ordained Don Executive Committee as the higher regional authority, they passed a resolution insisting that all land in the host was property of the Don Cossacks since it had been paid for by the blood of their ancestors. They did, however, make a concession to a portion of the non–Cossack population by voting in favor of providing land access to peasants whose families had resided in the Don prior to the emancipation of the serfs. Still, this decision did nothing to help the majority of outlanders whose families had migrated to the host after 1863.

Those resolutions would prove moderate in comparison to those passed by a more comprehensive krug that met from late May into mid-June 1917. That later assembly, while still willing to make lands available to "native" Don peasants, demanded all Cossacks to withdraw from non–Cossack organs, including the Don Executive Committee. From that point on, the Don Cossacks were supposed to recognize only the krug and its newly-elected ataman, General Aleksey Maksimovich Kaledin, as the only legitimate authority of the host.[10]

Aside from the Don region, throwback Cossack governments emerged in other hosts in the weeks following the February Revolution. Elected atamans replaced tsarist-appointees as the leaders of the Terek, Orenburg and Amur Cossacks while other hosts showed little inclination to concentrate power in the hands of a single individual. The Transbaikal Cossacks actually abolished the post of ataman while the Kuban Cossacks, reflecting their strong Ukrainian heritage, summoned a rada instead of a krug and neglected to elect an ataman for seven months.[11] The Ural Cossacks reveled in their newly acquired freedom by debating whether they should undo the work of Catherine the Great by reverting their host's official name back to the Yaik.[12] In addition to these regional projects, the Cossacks also tried to organize themselves on a higher level into a body that would encompass the interests of all eleven Cossack hosts. A few weeks after the revolution, an all-Cossack congress was convened in Petrograd. At this assembly and a follow-up meeting later during the summer, the delegates passed resolutions demanding that the Provisional Government grant Cossacks control of all the land in the hosts. Russia's new leaders, however, were hesitant to alienate the outlanders and ultimately refrained from taking a side on the sensitive land question in the Cossack hosts. The congress also formed its own special-interest committee in the capital, the Union of Cossack Hosts, but otherwise this bid to coalesce Cossack political activity into a single entity made little headway.[13]

The outlanders, meanwhile, watched these political developments among the Cossacks with growing apprehension. Initially, the outlanders were too weak to oppose the Cossack whims in any meaningful way. The primary cause of their impotence was their disorganization. While the Cossacks possessed stanitsa administrations and peasants elsewhere in Russia had *zemstvos*, the non–Cossack populations of the hosts had been barred from establishing their own local assemblies of self-government. This essentially abandoned the outlanders to the rule of the hosts' Cossack administrations. Under tsarism, this uneven arrangement was partially tempered by the fact that the deputy atamans, as appointees of the tsar and frequently lacking authentic Cossack pedigrees, were not strong partisans of Cossack interests. But in the aftermath of the liberal-democratic revolution, the new atamans who owed their positions to krug elections could hardly be expected to be objective mediators in disputes between the Cossacks and outlanders. The latter might have gained some reassurance that their interests would be considered if they had been permitted to establish *zemstvos*, but even the Provisional Government maintained the ban against the formation of such bodies in the hosts. This, along with War Minister Guchkov's order authorizing the formation of regional Cossack governments, was a blow to the outlanders who earnestly hoped that the new order would enable them to achieve parity with the Cossacks.

As demagogic rhetoric against them echoed throughout the stanitsas and krugs, the outlanders realized they needed their own exclusive organizations to counter such threats.[14]

In the Don Host, the first assembly of outlander representatives met in late spring and passed a resolution demanding the elimination of Cossack privileges.[15] Little else was heard from the non–Cossack population until well into the summer of 1917 when a more enduring assembly took shape in the form of a regional executive committee elected by Don soviets. These organs had been founded earlier that year by workers and coal miners in the heavily industrialized western areas of the Don territory. Initially dominated by the Social Revolutionary (SR) and Menshevik parties, the Don soviets had lent their support to the Don Executive Committee. Their moderate outlook, however, became a casualty of the political polarization that was encroaching upon the entire country. Gradually the Don soviets, like the Cossacks before them, distanced themselves from the Don Executive Committee. By autumn, as regional soviet leaders gravitated towards extremists wanting to abolish the Cossack caste, the Don territory appeared irreconcilably divided between the Cossacks on one side and the outlanders on the other. Lingering somewhere in the middle was the Don Executive Committee, a fading relic of cooperation that briefly existed between the two communities.

Actually, neither of the two sides in the emerging standoff between the Cossacks and outlanders on the Don were as unified as they would have the other believe. The poor peasants and rural laborers who constituted the majority of the outlander population in the host had different aims than the coal miners in the Donets Basin or the factory workers in Rostov and Taganrog. The former group wanted more land; the latter desired better working conditions. But they, along with a small middle-class of non–Cossack merchants and small land holders, were driven into the arms of the increasingly radical soviets by krug resolutions and stanitsa hearsays advocating the general expulsion of all outlanders from the host.[16]

Meanwhile, in Novocherkassk, Ataman Kaledin struggled to unite the Don Cossacks under his banner. Although the fifty-five-year-old general was applauded by the elites who cherished conservative concepts of the Cossack estate and its service to Russia, his earlier refusal to accommodate army committees while in command of the Russian Eighth Army made him suspect to the many ordinary Cossacks who welcomed the revolution. Indeed, Cossack delegates from the upper Don, traditionally the least prosperous area of the host, agreed to Kaledin's election only in the absence of other viable candidates.[17]

Aside from the less affluent Cossacks in the stanitsas, Kaledin was also unpopular among the Cossack rank and file. Their views had been molded by the static conditions of fighting on the Eastern Front that had broken down the traditional barriers in the army and brought them into close contact with peasant soldiers, conscripted workers and revolutionary agitators. As a result, they began to feel a greater affinity towards the "exploited classes" of peasants, laborers and soldiers than to the elite Cossack leadership. They were inclined to spurn Cossack-specific krugs in favor of more universal political organs—zemstvos, committees or soviets—where they could engage in dialogue with their non–Cossack compatriots. They also readily adopted the looser rules of discipline authorized by Order Number One, which was published by the Petrograd Soviet just days after the outbreak of the revolution. Yet, even as they acknowledged their equalization with the rest of Russian citizenry on some level, the radicalized Cossack troops still latched onto their identity by forming exclusive Cossack committees, which they viewed as an exercise of the principle of self-determination. Before long, delegates from these committees carried these ideas of Cossack republicanism with them to their homes and stanitsas.[18]

The discord between estate-minded elites and fraternally-inclined commoners was echoed to some degree in all Cossack hosts. But several hosts were saddled with additional tensions between members from heterogenous backgrounds. The Kuban Host in particular was affected by its members' diverse origins. The Kuban Host had been formally established in 1860 by combining the Black Sea Cossacks, originally from Ukraine, with the western communities of Caucasian Line, or *lineitsy*, Cossacks. This latter group, originating from transplanted Don Cossacks and Russian soldiers, guarded fortified villages on the north side of the Kuban River from fierce Circassian raiders living on the opposite bank. Although the common struggle against the Circassian tribes helped build a sense of camaraderie among these two Cossack elements, this fragile bond unraveled in the aftermath of February 1917. Previously, the less numerous, more prosperous and Russian-speaking *lineitsy* Cossacks had dominated the Kuban's administration. In the revolutionary era, however, the traditional leadership role of the *lineitsy* Cossack minority was threatened by any democratic restructuring that would transfer power to the Black Sea Cossack majority. This latter group had not forgotten their Zaporozhian roots: most still spoke Ukrainian vernacular and followed the blossoming national movement in Ukraine with great interest. Because of this strong Ukrainian influence, the elected assembly in the Kuban was christened as a rada. Since the Kuban Rada did not elect an ataman until October 1917, it was the host's only political voice during most of the Provisional Government's brief existence.[19]

Kaledin and Kornilov: Heroes of the Right

The increasing ethnic, political and social tensions observed among the populations of the Cossack hosts throughout 1917 were not limited to those regions. People all over Russia quickly became disillusioned with the new order when it failed to meet their immediate expectations. Subsequently, various nationalities, parties and other groups began asserting their own narrow interests at the expense of "Russian" unity. A significant factor behind this trend was the Provisional Government's inability to remedy the country's most pressing troubles; namely the deterioration of the railway infrastructure that contributed to an economic crisis as well as food shortages in many cities. At the root of these problems were the burdens of the war against the Central Powers, and the question of whether Russia should remain in the war—and on what terms—soon became yet another decisive issue.

Shortly after the revolution, Russia's allies demanded a pledge of the country's intention to continue the war against Germany as a condition for further shipments of munitions and other war materiel. The new foreign minister, Pavel Milyukov, quickly reassured the Allies of his office's desire to observe the existing alliances and treaties—including that which awarded Russia the Black Sea Straits upon an Allied victory. But to the other authoritative organ in the capital, the Petrograd Soviet, this policy reeked of imperialism and had no place in the new order. A few days after Milyukov's statement, the Soviet made its views on the war known by publishing an appeal that called upon the international proletariat to end the carnage by refusing "to serve as an instrument of violence and conquest in the hands of kings, landlords and bankers."[20] This declaration exposed the competing ideologies between the government nominally in charge and the Soviet which commanded the loyalty of workers and soldiers in the capital. Although the Provisional Government, in an effort to placate the Soviet, soon renounced all annexations and indemnities, the fallout from the controversy led to violent demonstrations in Petrograd, the resignations of Milyukov and

Guchkov from their posts, and the reconstitution of a new government with a greater number of socialists in the cabinet.

This first shake-up of the Provisional Government signified the growing power of the left since the abdication of the tsar. This trend was naturally disparaged by conservatives, but even many moderate patriotic Russians were alarmed by the Provisional Government's impotence against the Soviet. Milyukov and his followers in the Constitutional Democrat (Kadet) party, once the champions of liberalism, began moving to the right from the summer of 1917 onward.[21] They quickly abandoned their hopes that the Provisional Government might lead Russia to a better future and instead began to look elsewhere for a savior to rally around. They soon believed they had found the strongman they were seeking in the person of Ataman Kaledin.

Of all the atamans elected to lead a particular Cossack host in 1917, none enjoyed more national prominence than Kaledin. A graduate of the Mikhailovsky Artillery Academy and the General Staff Academy, Kaledin had won fame as a commander for his Eighth Army's successful exploits during the Brusilov Offensive. His army career ended abruptly after the tsar's abdication when he was dismissed for obstructing the democratization of the units under his command. That record, however, only further enhanced his appeal to many conservatives, Cossack and non–Cossack alike, who began to regard him as a defender of traditional Russian values endangered by the revolution.

Kaledin was able to attract a following among Russian patriots precisely because he remained committed to Russian national goals. Although he was ready to defend and even increase Cossack autonomy, he did not entertain the separatist fantasies espoused by later atamans. In his view, Russia's problems were also Cossack problems; therefore, rather than disengage from the national political struggle to focus on issues specific to the Don Host, he instead increased his visibility on the national scene even though his position in the host was far from secure.[22]

By the time Kaledin was elected ataman in June 1917, the first coalition government was already in power, yet relations between Novocherkassk and Petrograd remained proper. Indeed, the Provisional Government, as in its exchanges with the Soviet, was unwilling to risk antagonizing the Don Cossack government, even though the latter was undermining the authority of the Don Executive Committee while attracting the support of the Kadets and other disaffected elements. The Petrograd ministers, quite simply, recoiled from the thought of challenging such a well-organized and potentially powerful group as the Don Cossacks. The last thing they wanted was to provoke separatist ambitions in the Don, especially when they had their hands full trying to temper nationalism in Ukraine and other borderlands. Moreover, the Don Cossacks contributed two valuable regiments to the garrison in Petrograd, which remained a hotbed of agitation and disorder.[23] The only other alternative open to the Provisional Government to win support on the Don was an alliance with the outlanders. However, since the outlanders remained largely disorganized and politically weak well into the summer, this arrangement would have yielded few benefits for the Provisional Government at the cost of offending the Cossacks.

The Provisional Government was not only in need of Cossack troops in the capital but also at the front. Russia's charismatic new Minister of War, Aleksandr Kerensky, was committed to launching a summer offensive that had been promised to the Allies. Since the revolution, however, the martial spirit of the Russian soldiers steadily eroded as they formed themselves into committees, refused to obey orders, deserted their posts and fraternized with German agitators dispatched across no-man's land.[24] When their committees passed resolutions openly stating their unwillingness to attack, the War Minister embarked on a whirlwind speaking tour of the front to persuade the mutinous soldiers to return to the trenches.[25] Amid these disorders, the Cossacks seemed to offer Russia's commanders a ray of hope. On the eve of the offensive, the Union of Cossack Hosts in Petrograd approved a resolution stating that "an immediate and decisive aggressive forward movement of the army is the only way to attain the peace" Russia desperately needed.[26]

The combative spirit of the delegates to the Union of Cossack Hosts was not necessarily shared by rank and file Cossacks at the front. To the undiscerning eye the Cossacks maintained their cohesion and discipline much better than many infantry regiments.[27] But on the eve of the offensive an experienced cavalry officer noted that even the most orderly squadrons were showing early symptoms of the general malaise: horses were no longer well-groomed, leather saddles were left unpolished and bits were allowed to rust.[28] Indeed, the expectations which Kerensky and others placed in the Cossacks would prove misplaced. The only frontline Cossack troops to distinguish themselves during the operation were those that did so by openly objecting to serving alongside the Women's Battalion of Death.[29] Regardless, any Cossack contribution to the attack could have made little difference to the final outcome. Even in those areas of the front where the first waves of Russian shock troops had ruptured the enemy line, the demoralized reserves behind them moved forward only very cautiously—if at all.[30] Assessing the lackluster performance of the peasant-soldiers, one cavalry officer wrote, "The fervor of their revolutionary patriotism, warmed up by Kerensky's impassioned appeal, lasted so long, but no longer."[31]

While the Russian armies continued to launch follow-up attacks during the first half of July, the tense situation in Petrograd boiled over into an uprising that came dangerously close to toppling the government. The disorders began on 16 July when certain army units stationed in the capital began demonstrating against their planned redeployment to the front. They were soon joined by other garrison troops as well as workers, many of them Bolshevik followers, who were intent on transferring all power to the Soviet. Had the marchers been better organized—and had Lenin given his full backing to the rebellion—the uprising might have succeeded. Instead, the demonstrations digressed into widespread rioting that had to be crushed by Cossacks and the few loyal troops in the capital. Seven Cossacks killed in the mayhem were honored at the end of the month with an elaborate funeral service in Petrograd. The cortege, which featured several horses with vacant saddles trailing their masters' caskets, included Kerensky, Milyukov and other notable figures.[32]

In the aftermath of the crisis remembered as the "July Days," the Provisional Government cracked down on the Bolsheviks by raiding the party's headquarters and publicly discrediting their leaders as agents in German pay. Despite its triumph, the Provisional Government had not emerged unscathed. A new coalition government was formed with socialists in the majority and Kerensky holding the offices of both minister of war and premier.[33] But just as he was restoring some semblance of order in the capital, Kerensky was faced with a new crisis at the front. On 19 July the Germans began a counteroffensive against the Russian Eleventh Army on the Southwest Front. The defenders were taken by surprise and proved too disorganized to contain the enemy onslaught. Before long the Russian withdrawal turned into a rout that chased them almost completely out of Galicia.[34] The summer offensive, which the Provisional Government had hoped would raise its prestige at home and abroad, had done exactly the opposite.

The events of July 1917 rapidly dissolved the last shreds of confidence which propertied Russian classes had in the Provisional Government. As they demanded a restoration of order in the army and in the capital, they began to rally behind a new hero whose indomitable will, they hoped, could galvanize Russia in her time of need. This latest man of the hour was General Lavr Georgiyevich Kornilov, a forty-seven-year-old Siberian Cossack from a rather humble background. Kornilov, through his own merit, had gained admission into some of Russia's most prestigious military academies and had distinguished himself on missions in Turkestan and Manchuria. In 1915, while serving as a brigade commander in the Carpathians, he was wounded in battle and captured by the Austrians. He escaped from captivity the following year and, disguised as a Habsburg soldier, returned to Russia by way of neutral Romania. This exploit won him acclaim as a national hero, and his popularity was boosted further by his open revolutionary sympathies following the abdication of the tsar. In the aftermath of the February Revolution, he was appointed commander of the Petrograd Military District, but his prestige had no bearing on the unruly garrison troops. Frustrated by his inability to stem the erosion of discipline among the soldiers in the capital, he soon transferred to the front where he replaced Kaledin as commander of the Eighth Army. During the 1917 summer offensive, Kornilov's army, while launching a supporting attack on Southwest Front, penetrated up to eighteen miles behind Austrian lines. Although these gains were wiped out by the subsequent enemy counterattack, this temporary success further enhanced Kornilov's hero status and spawned a cult of personality that became fixated on the general.[35]

Initially, Kerensky jumped on the Kornilov bandwagon. Amid the emergency on the Southwest Front, he appointed the swarthy Siberian Cossack to commander-in-chief at Stavka. Kornilov sought to salvage the situation by reinstating capital punishment, which had been abolished shortly after the revolution, and cracked down on units who resisted orders by sending punitive expeditions of Cossacks against them. Yet, despite his efforts to restore some semblance of military discipline at the front, Kornilov appeared moderate enough to enjoy the confidence of the Soviet and the socialists in the Provisional Government. Indeed, whereas other generals pushed for the complete disbandment of the army committees, Kornilov merely requested limitations on their authority. But his near-universal appeal did not endure for long. As various right-wing organizations, including Kaledin's Don Cossack government, announced their support for Kornilov, the army committees grew suspicious of their commander-in-chief. Fearing that he was falling under the spell of reactionaries, the formerly moderate army committees began listening to Bolshevik agitators warning of an imminent counterrevolution.[36]

Kaledin, for his part, added to the soldiers' sense of alarm. In late August 1917 he was among the illustrious speakers at the Moscow State Conference, an event organized by Kerensky to promote national unity. To the attendees gathered inside the Bolshoi Theater in Russia's ancient capital, the Don ataman portrayed the Cossacks as champions of order and patriotic duty. They were, in his words, an example for the masses to emulate. He also evoked applause from the conservatives and Kadets seated on the right side the theater for blaming the army committees and soviets for Russia's woes. He spoke forcefully as though all Cossacks, and not just those of the Don, were ready to back his brazen statements. The socialists, trade union representatives and army delegates listening to Kaledin disapprovingly from the left side of the theater did not have to look far to discredit the ataman as a spokesman for all Cossacks. Later in the conference, a young Cossack lieutenant addressed the attendees and disavowed Kaledin as a spokesman for the Cossack rank-and-file.

Kornilov also gave a speech before the conference and although he deliberately restrained himself to appear more moderate than Kaledin, his call for reforms in the army—

along with his obvious popularity with right-wing delegates—aroused considerable concern among the left. Kerensky too began to regard Kornilov as a dangerous rival after the general was given an enthusiastic and ornate reception in Moscow by conservative groups and cadets. Before long it was clear that the Moscow State Conference, instead of bridging the gap between the right and left as Kerensky intended, instead drove them further apart.[37]

The Kornilov Affair

Kerensky's increasing distrust of Kornilov after the Moscow State Conference set the stage for a showdown between the two charismatic leaders. Even before the conference convened, Kornilov had begun positioning the Third Cavalry Corps under General Krymov well north of Mogilev from where it could, if ordered, make a swift descent on Petrograd. The commander-in-chief was convinced that the Bolsheviks were about to stage a coup in the capital, and he probably felt that Third Cavalry Corps was the perfect foil against that threat. Consisting of the First Don Cossack Division, the Ussuri Cossack Division and the Caucasian Cavalry Division, the presence of these rough-riding horsemen alone might have been expected to frighten the masses into submission. If indeed Third Cavalry Corps' proximity to Petrograd was intended as a scare tactic, it had its intended effect on Kerensky who began to regard it as the cocked weapon of a counterrevolutionary plot.

The tense situation was not helped by the fact that the two men, instead of communicating directly with each other, relayed messages through envoys who frequently possessed their own agendas.[38] Thus, any effort to mediate between the commander-in-chief at Mogilev and the prime minister in Petrograd was destined to fail as their subordinates sabotaged their communications in order to engineer a confrontation which they felt was in their sides' best interests. This scheming, when combined with nagging suspicions and faulty intelligence, was a certain recipe for disaster.

The event that initiated the Third Cavalry Corps' first ill-fated march upon the capital was the arrival at Stavka of a telegram in the early hours of 9 September announcing Kornilov's dismissal from the supreme army command. Upon being informed of the message, Kornilov refused to give up his post. He had some justification for disobeying the order: only the full cabinet was entitled to dismiss the commander-in-chief, but the telegram was signed only by Kerensky. He did not know that just hours earlier at a midnight cabinet meeting the government ministers, while listening to the premier harangue on the imminent threat from counterrevolutionaries, had resigned their posts thus making Kerensky *de facto* dictator. Amid his pondering for explanations, Kornilov concluded that Kerensky would have only issued such an order under duress, perhaps as a prisoner of the Bolsheviks. Subsequently, he ordered Krymov's Third Cavarly Corps to advance on Petrograd to suppress the long-anticipated Bolshevik insurrection which he believed to be in progress.

When Kornilov finally learned later that day that the order from Kerensky was authentic, he did not back down by recalling the Third Cavalry Corps. Instead, he appealed to his army commanders to stand with him against the Provisional Government which he claimed was now under the influence of the Bolsheviks and, by proxy, the Germans.[39] Several Russian commanders, including General Anton Denikin of the Southwest Front, responded positively by declaring their solidarity with Kornilov.[40] The rogue commander-in-chief also dispatched messages to Novocherkassk requesting Kaledin's backing, but the ataman was away from the Don capital when the crisis erupted and was unable to offer Kornilov any help. Nonetheless, erroneous reports spread throughout the country that Kaledin was indeed aiding Kornilov, causing a livid Kerensky to add the ataman's name to the list of rebels he wanted to place under arrest.

Even if Kaledin had been in Novocherkassk during Kornilov's revolt, he would have been unable to offer the commander-in-chief little beyond moral support. The Don Host was simply too far away to have a decisive outcome on a rebellion that would prove rather brief. Besides, many ordinary Cossacks—especially those in the army—were still attracted to the revolutionary ideals which Kornilov now appeared to be fighting. Like the generals at the front who sympathized with the commander-in-chief but could not depend on their troops to fight for him, any summons from Kaledin ordering the Cossack rank-and-file to take up arms on behalf of Kornilov would have probably fallen on deaf ears.[41]

Without concrete support from the army or the Don, Kornilov's chances for success hinged on the outcome of Krymov's operation. From the start the progress of Third Cavalry Corps was impeded by railway workers who delayed the troop trains and by telegraph operators who sabotaged communications between the units and their headquarters. Local garrisons along the route to the capital also dispatched propagandists to agitate among the cavalrymen, causing them to question the legitimacy of their mission.[42] Against these obstacles, Krymov's troops pushed onward until they were just a day's march from the capital. At that point, many of the lead units discovered the tracks ahead of them destroyed beyond repair by railway workers. Others, such as the First Don Cossack Division which came to a halt before Luga, found its path blocked by the local garrison consisting of 1,200 Cossack recruits—a standoff which invalidated the stereotype that Cossacks invariably sided with the counterrevolution. Meanwhile the Petrograd Soviet, which had decided to throw its full support behind Kerensky during the crisis, sent its own agitators carrying stacks of the latest newspaper editions to prove to the confused troops that the Provisional Government was not under attack by the Bolsheviks. The Soviet even cobbled together a delegation of Muslims from the North Caucasus to undermine the steadfast warriors of the Caucasian Cavalry Division. This subterfuge had its intended effect: the corps' units dissolved into a mess of debating committees. After disavowing their commanders, the soldiers' committees sent apologetic delegations to Petrograd to declare their loyalty to the Provisional Government. On 12 September Krymov acknowledged the hopelessness of his mission, reported to an irate Kerensky and afterwards committed suicide with a revolver.[43] "The campaign that began as a mutiny of the generals," remarked one revolutionary, "ended as a mutiny of enlisted men."[44]

Although Kerensky had crushed Kornilov's revolt with relative ease, in the aftermath of the crisis he found himself mired in a new conundrum. By rallying and arming Petrograd workers to form Red Guard detachments against Kornilov, he had staked the future of his government on the left. His actions during the crisis had permanently alienated the right and therefore he could no longer count on their help. During the late summer and early autumn, however, the organs of the left were succumbing to Bolshevik domination as that party won majorities in new elections to city dumas and soviets, including those in Petrograd and Moscow. With their familiar chant of "All Power to the Soviets!" the Bolsheviks made no secret of their hostility to the Provisional Government. Thus the organs which had allied with Kerensky during the Kornilov affair were soon poised to turn against him. To ward off his sense abandonment and vulnerability, the Russian dictator allegedly spent his remaining weeks in power soothing his tortured mind through delusional episodes and opioids.[45]

The Russian army, like the central government, also deteriorated steadily following the Kornilov affair. General Mikhail Alekseyev, appointed by Kerensky to Stavka after Kornilov and his alleged accomplices were imprisoned, was confronted with the impossible task of simply holding the army together. A month after the fiasco, an intelligence report on conditions in the armies on the Northern Front observed that the rank-and-file suspected their officers of harboring counterrevolutionary sympathies. As a result, orders were refused or ignored. "The soldiers," the report went on, "seem to believe that the arrest of Kornilov made void all the orders which he issued reinstating discipline."[46] As morale sank, desertion soared as homesick peasant-soldiers abandoned the front to return to their villages. Amid the shortening days of autumn, the remaining troops were suddenly struck by the fear that they might be expected to spend another long, dreary winter at the front. Subsequently, the soldiers began agitating for peace to be made before the onset of cold weather.[47] Amid these circumstances there was little Alekseyev, or any other able commander, could do to improve the situation.

The ripple effects of the Kornilov affair were also felt in the distant Don Host. Having made his anti–Soviet views public before the revolt, Kaledin was widely suspected of aiding Kornilov's adventure and subsequently was among those whose arrest was ordered by Kerensky. When that telegram reached the Don, the ataman was visiting the northern stanitsa of Ust-Medveditsa. Upon learning of the warrant for Kaledin's arrest, a local Cossack officer with strong revolutionary sympathies, Lieutenant-Colonel Filip Mironov, led a small group of soldiers in an attempt to capture the ataman and deliver him to Kerensky. Mironov's intentions, however, were leaked to Kaledin. Wasting no time, the Don ataman abruptly departed from Ust-Medveditsa and made a beeline for Novocherkassk.[48] There the question of his complicity in Kornilov's revolt was referred to the Don Krug, which ultimately cleared the ataman of any wrongdoing. Moreover, it also refused to turnover Kaledin to the Provisional Government by reviving the proud motto of its forbearers: "From the Don there is no extradition." This decision denied Kerensky the chance to settle scores with Kaledin and, more importantly, it exposed the government's weakness in the peripheries of the country.[49]

The Last Convulsions of the Provisional Government

Relations between Novocherkassk and Petrograd did not improve as the position of the Provisional Government grew direr. Increasingly, the Don Cossack government asserted its regional authority without regard to the Provisional Government. The latter became especially unpopular in food-surplus regions like the Don as it tried to solve urban food shortages by authorizing the requisitioning of grain. Meanwhile in other lands the Provisional Government's shortcomings bred considerable discontent. City-dwellers were still going hungry, the detested war was still in progress and one of the revolution's earliest promises, the convocation of a freely-elected Constituent Assembly, had not yet been fulfilled. As the Bolsheviks were making their final preparations to topple the Provisional Government, Kerensky found himself almost completely isolated. Distrusted by the right and loathed by the left, he now had no one he could turn to for help.

The Bolsheviks' intentions were known to almost everyone in the capital, yet Kerensky foolishly did almost nothing to obstruct them.[50] By the time the Bolshevik-led insurrection began on the night of 6–7 November, the vast majority of the Petrograd garrison had already declared its allegiance to the Bolshevik-controlled military revolutionary committee.[51] As

Red Guards were seizing public buildings throughout the city, a delegation from the Union of Cossack Hosts extended one final offer to rescue the beleaguered Provisional Government. Before any nearby Cossack regiments would saunter onto the streets, however, the delegation demanded a guarantee from Kerensky that he was committed to stomping out the insurgency. What they really wanted, it seems, was a declaration from the Russian leader stating that he authorized the Cossacks' actions so that their operations could not be misconstrued as "counterrevolutionary." Kerensky, with undue optimism that the Bolsheviks would be easily crushed, refused to bargain with the Cossack delegates and reminded them of their military oaths. The Cossack delegates, then, were left wondering whether he would cut a deal with the left, as he did during the Kornilov affair, and disavow any action they might take against the Bolsheviks. Subsequently the Union of Cossack Hosts, just hours after their delegation's meeting with Kerensky, announced its neutrality in the unfolding struggle between the Provisional Government and the Bolsheviks.

By dawn on 7 November, the authority of the Provisional Government was confined to the gilded interior of the Winter Palace. Protected by a motley collection of military cadets, women soldiers and two companies of Cossacks, Kerensky and his staff began to feverishly telephone local barracks and headquarters at the front for help. Upon calling the local Cossack regiments, they were told the troops would "begin to saddle their horses." Only when repeated phone calls elicited the same ambiguous response did the incensed Kerensky deduce that the majority of the Cossack garrison was, like their representatives, intent on observing neutrality. Realizing he had no significant force of reliable troops left in the capital, Kerensky slipped out of the Winter Palace later that morning in a car seized from the American Embassy bearing the U.S. flag. His motorcade headed southwest, hoping to meet the trainloads of soldiers he had ordered from the front.[52]

In the meantime, the government ministers remained barricaded in the Winter Palace as a mob gathered on the boulevards outside. As the hours ticked by, the outnumbered defenders of the palace—including the contingent of Cossacks—lost heart and walked away from their posts. By evening, perhaps only 300 of the original 3,000 troops guarding the building remained, yet the besieged ministers rejected a Bolshevik ultimatum to surrender. A few hours later the Winter Palace came under fire from the cruiser *Aurora* and guns mounted on the Peter and Paul Fortress, yet the ministers held tight. Finally, in the early morning hours of 8 November, Bolshevized sailors and soldiers pushed their way through the palace corridors, disarmed the remaining defenders and took the ministers into custody.[53]

That same night, after a ten-hour trip from Petrograd, Kerensky's motorcade arrived in Pskov, the headquarters of Russia's Northern Front. He was by then in a state of despair. During his journey from the capital, he had not observed any troop trains moving northward. It became obvious to him that his instructions were not being fully carried out—if at all—and that in the interval precious time had been lost in his campaign to crush the Bolshevik uprising. His cold reception at the army headquarters in Pskov only further dampened his spirit. A few months earlier, his appearances at the front had elicited cheers and applause from the rank and file of the Russian army. But on that frosty, dark autumn night he was gruffly warned by General Cheremisov, the commander of the Northern Front, that the soldiers who had once hailed him might now skewer him on their bayonets.[54]

Cheremisov had indeed ignored the premier's order to send troops to Petrograd. Like most senior officers in the Russian army, he distrusted Kerensky since the latter's imbroglio with Kornilov. He also had other reasons for withholding the directive to move against the capital. By then most of the soldier committees in the northern army group were under the influence of Bolshevik agitators. With good reason, he doubted whether the orders to advance on the capital would even be obeyed by the units under his nominal command. At worst they might have provoked a violent mutiny.

While Cheremisov refused to aid Kerensky, his political counterpart, Northern Front commissar Wladimir S. Woytinsky, did begin a feverish search for reliable troops to rescue the beleaguered Provisional Government. The only nearby unit he found that was ready to undertake such a mission was the Third Cavalry Corps, the same outfit which Kornilov had dispatched in his ill-fated attempt to impose his authority in the Russian capital back in September.[55]

In the weeks since the collapse of the Kornilov mutiny, the morale and discipline of the Third Cavalry Corps had revived under the leadership of its new commander, General Pyotr Nikolayevich Krasnov. A highly-decorated officer from a family rooted in military and Don Cossack traditions, Krasnov could hardly be expected to be sympathetic to the cause of the revolution. Nonetheless, Commissar Woytinsky, an ex-Bolshevik and former political prisoner under the tsars, took a favorable view of the Cossack general. He described Krasnov in flattering terms as a "a tall man of impressive appearance; [with] his gray head held high, he looked intelligent and self-confident."[56] According to his memoir, Krasnov abstained from political meddling in those critical November days and simply sought to carry out his soldierly duties. With little prodding, he accepted the assignment to lead his troops to the capital to save the Provisional Government. This operation, however, was handicapped from the start by the fact that the force he had available for this mission was not nearly as formidable as it appeared on paper. Of the three divisions in the Third Cavalry Corps, only one, the First Don Cossack Division, was on hand and even it was not at full strength; the rest of his troops were being used to guard ammunition stockpiles or quell disturbances in the rear of the army. Nonetheless, the Cossack general readied the men and horses he did have by loading them onto trains, but before they set off he was handed an order

A portrait of Gen. Pyotr N. Krasnov, undated. Krasnov led the first military expedition against the Bolshevik regime and continued his anticommunist activities until the close of the Second World War (© Sputnik / NV).

from Cheremisov not to advance on the capital. Uncertain of what to do, Krasnov motored to Pskov to make sense of the situation. There he conferred with the front commander, who informed him that the Provisional Government "no longer exists." He then met Kerensky, who saw the Cossack general as his only possible salvation for his regime. Reinvigorated with a sense of hope, the premier pleaded with Krasnov to continue with his preparations and promised him that the army would follow. The Cossack general, perhaps failing to perceive that Kerensky was no longer the darling of the Russian soldiers or people, consented to move forward with the operation. The next morning, the trains of Third Cavalry Corps began chugging northward to Petrograd.[57]

Kerensky joined Krasnov on the campaign; indeed, the premier's presence was essential to reassure suspicious railway workers and even the troops themselves that the corps was not the spearhead of another military *coup d'état*.[58] On 9 November, Krasnov's detachment, numbering less than a thousand men, reached Gatchina, which was garrisoned by a hodge-podge force of Red Guards, Kronstadt sailors and radicalized soldiers from Petrograd. Though outnumbered, the menacing presence of the Don Cossacks caused the defenders to either flee or lay down their arms without a fight. Encouraged by this easy victory, the Cossacks continued onto Tsarskoe Selo, from where the attackers could then begin direct operations against Petrograd. In the meantime, Kerensky made Gatchina his headquarters and began wiring the various army headquarters to send troops, especially infantry, to reinforce the expedition.[59]

The following morning the Don Cossacks began their assault against Tsarskoe Selo, but here the Reds showed slightly more resolve to hold their positions than at Gatchina. Commissar Woytinsky, who had initially stayed behind in Pskov to summon frontline regiments to Petrograd, joined the expedition amid its efforts to seize Tsarskoye Selo. At one point, he observed Krasnov speaking to opposing troops from a truck. When the defenders refused his demands to surrender their arms and let the expedition proceed, a crew of Don Cossacks made a show of force by firing a light field gun over their heads. The demonstration had its intended effect: the opposing troops finally turned over their rifles and cartridges. Despite this success, which enabled the Third Cavalry Corps to occupy Tsarskoye Selo that night, Krasnov began to show signs of pessimism towards the operation. "They could have shot us all like partridges," he admitted to Woytinsky. "We may bluff them this way once or twice, but no longer."[60]

As Krasnov grew increasingly concerned, relations between him and Kerensky became stormy. The latter believed that the capture of Tsarskoye Selo had been delayed by the Cossack general's lack of resolve. In the meantime, Krasnov was becoming irritated by the premier's badgering of him to march forward. In actuality, it was not the expedition's leaders but rather its soldiers who were most to blame for the disappointing progress. In a repetition of the Kornilov affair two months earlier, the advancing Cossacks were again met by skillful enemy agitators who made them doubt whether they were fighting on the right side. Woytinsky, for his part, tried to counter this subversive activity with his own addresses to the regimental committees, but he could do little to gloss over the fact that the tiny expedition was facing an uphill battle in its effort to reach Petrograd.[61]

The arrival of the substantial reinforcements which Kerensky had sent for might have reassured the Cossack soldiers and provided them with the confidence they needed to assault the capital. In any event, only three more Don Cossack companies arrived, elevating the number of troops in Krasnov's detachment to 1,200. What the Cossacks desired most was for riflemen to support their attack, but none of the infantry units called upon to defend the Provisional Government came close to reaching the city. Their absence was mostly the result of indifference as many divisions or their commanders simply chose to ignore Kerensky's pleas for reinforcements. Those that did attempt to obey his orders often did so in a half-hearted manner; subsequently they were easily stalled by opposition from the Bolshevized soldiers and railway workers they encountered along their routes.[62]

On 11 November, three days after Third Cavalry Corps began its advance, it stood just outside of Petrograd. While the Cossacks waited for the expected reinforcements and planned their next move, military cadets inside the city, in an example of the poor coordination that was to plague the White movement throughout its existence, staged an uprising against the Reds. Although the cadets' insurrection was easily quashed, it was enough to convince many local workers that the revolution was in mortal danger. Thousands of them volunteered to stand with the Red Guards and sailors already digging defensive positions on Polkovo Heights on the edge of the capital. Altogether, the Bolsheviks amassed a force somewhere in the range of 10,000–20,000 men and even women, although many workers were unarmed. Still, they had an imposing numerical superiority over the 1,200 Cossacks. The latter's situation did not improve during the day as the reinforcements did not show up and some of the Cossack troops opted to declare their neutrality.[63]

Despite his increasingly unfavorable outlook, Krasnov, goaded by Kerensky, began his attack on the following morning. When his few light artillery pieces began raking the opposing lines, many of the workers panicked and took flight, but the better-trained sailors, whose formations guarded the defenders' flanks, did not flinch. Still, the noticeable disarray in the enemy positions was enough to entice an undersized squadron of Cossacks to charge the defenders in the hope of inciting further panic and dispersing them. With sabers unsheathed, thundering hooves and shouts of "Hurrah!" the galloping horsemen certainly presented a frightening spectacle to the insurgents; the majority of whom had no experience in such types of warfare. But just when the horsemen appeared unstoppable, their charging beasts were suddenly stalled by a muddy gully that lay between the opposing forces. With the horses bogged down in the sticky muck, the enemy sailors concentrated their small-arms fire on the struggling creatures. Their Cossack masters, many of them now without a mount, were left with no choice other than to stagger back to their lines.

Although Krasnov's artillery continued to fire at the Bolshevik positions for the remainder of the day, no further serious attempts were made to dislodge the Red defenders from Pulkovo Heights. By evening, the general was informed that the guns had exhausted their supply of shells and that the Cossacks covering his flanks were fraternizing with Bolshevik sailors. Upon receiving that ominous report, Krasnov gave the order to retreat. By the time the expedition fell back to Gatchina, it was already disintegrating as Cossacks deserted or declared their neutrality. In the meantime, both sides had come under pressure by the central executive committee of the All-Russian Union of Railwaymen, or Vikzhel, to negotiate an end to the fighting on the threat that the union would freeze transportation along the railways. Writing of the negotiations with the Cossacks, Leon Trotsky, the Bolsheviks' silver-tongued firebrand, commented that "when it came to talking they were no match for us."[64] Kerensky's counterattack was doomed; the Cossack soldiers could not resist the attractive terms from a deputation of sailors that included an offer of amnesty, free passage to their Don homeland and support of a plan to replace the new Bolshevik-dominated government with a more moderate coalition formed from Russia's socialist parties. All that was asked of the Cossacks, in exchange, was for them to handover Kerensky.

When Lenin learned of the terms presented by the sailors, he and his cohorts were initially furious; not least because they had no intention of giving up one shred of the power they had seized for themselves in their recent coup. They quickly realized, however, that feigning consideration of the terms had the advantage of pacifying the Cossack units on the edge of the capital while avoiding the railway shutdown threatened by Vikzhel. For that reason, the negotiations continued and dragged on over the course of the following weeks, long after the immediate threat from the Cossacks had passed.[65]

In the meantime, Kerensky, Krasnov and several officers held military councils that lost all meaning since the soldiers nominally under their command would no longer listen to them. In the early morning hours of 14 November, Kerensky bowed to the inevitable and fled from Gatchina.[66] The Bolsheviks, deprived of their trophy in the person of the former head of the Provisional Government, had to settle for the arrest of Krasnov.

The advance of the Third Cavalry Corps against Petrograd in November 1917 was the first significant contest of the Russian Civil War, and many of its peculiar attributes would appear in the conflict's later battles. For instance, while the civil war was to affect millions of people and be fought in a range of theaters, from the frozen tundra near the Arctic Circle to the baking deserts of Central Asia, most of its battles were waged between relatively small numbers of men. In these conditions, victory often went not to the side that deployed the most men on the front but rather that which deployed the men *most willing to fight*. Soldiers on both sides, many of them survivors of the trenches in World War I, showed a considerable lack of devotion to the causes for which they were bearing arms. Most would have gladly laid down their rifles if they could return to their village and work the land in peace. For that reason, the prospect of a peaceful settlement remained tantalizing to combatants on both sides and explains why the Cossacks and sailors on the fringe of Petrograd in November 1917 quickly lost interest in hostilities when they were presented with the alternative of a negotiated agreement.

A Land Divided

Despite their easy victory at Pulkovo Heights, the Bolsheviks continued to regard the Cossacks as an existential threat to their infant regime. In the following weeks, rumors circulated throughout the country that a horde of Don Cossacks was riding into the Russian heartland in a campaign to crush the Soviet government.[67] While such hearsays had little basis in fact, they convey a sense of how closely the Cossacks were associated with counter-revolutionary tendencies. Nearly everyone anticipated the Cossacks to resist the Bolsheviks' assault on the cultural, economic, military and social traditions that had long-defined Russian society. In Petrograd, the Union of Cossack Hosts fueled these expectations with open condemnations of the ruling party. "The spectacle afforded to us by the prophets of a Socialistic cult imported from Germany and preached by an alien race is enough to disgust any lover of freedom, to whatever nation he may belong," declared a Ural Cossack member of the Union.[68] In order to ease these tensions, the Bolshevik leadership treated Krasnov with remarkable leniency after taking him into custody in November 1917. The last thing they wanted was to turn the general into a martyr for Cossackdom. After a short imprisonment, then, Krasnov was released on the condition that he would not actively oppose the Soviet regime and was allowed to return to the Don.[69]

The Cossack leadership in the borderlands was not mollified by this act of clemency. From the Don in the west to the Ussuri in the east, the host governments refused to recognize the Soviet regime as the legitimate heir to the Provisional Government. Most atamans or assemblies assumed all governing powers in their territories at least "until the Provisional Government and order in Russia are reestablished."[70] Only the Ural Cossack government avoided making such strong condemnation of the new regime. Already under pressure from restive Kalmyk, Kazakh and Bashkir natives—some of whom were undergoing their own national awakening—the last thing the Ural Cossacks needed to do was add another potential enemy to that list by aggravating the Bolsheviks.[71]

The Ural Cossack government, in fact, had acknowledged what most of the other Cossack hosts would soon learn: the Cossack governments, confronted with a myriad of social, economic and ethnic problems in their homelands, lacked the stability needed to undertake an energetic campaign against the Bolsheviks. Moreover, many of their young men and regiments were away, either at the front or stationed in a distant garrison, leaving the hosts poorly defended. Despite these weaknesses, most Cossack leaders—like a hobbling bull unable to resist charging the matador's red cape—threw themselves headlong into the fight against the new Soviet regime.

Many Cossack areas were on the verge of civil war even before the Bolshevik coup in Petrograd. In some hosts, such as the Don, the brewing conflict pitted Cossacks against the outlanders. In more ethnically-diverse hosts the impending hostilities would be three-sided or more with Cossacks, outlanders and natives all ready to turn against each other. The attempts of regional and local soviets to assert their claims of authority following the so-called October Revolution, and the determination of Cossack leaders to stop them, heralded the onset of fratricidal violence. For example, fighting broke out in Orenburg when the host ataman, Aleksandr Dutov, and his Cossacks arrested that town's soviet executive committee and leaders of the local labor movement. Although Dutov's Cossacks, with the help of Bashkir and Kazakh nationalists, succeeded in taking control of the town, they quickly found themselves under attack from Red Guards and Bolshevized soldiers who converged on the area from all directions.[72]

Predictably, a major center of resistance to the new Bolshevik regime formed in Kaledin's Don. When it learned of the Provisional Government's downfall, the Don Cossack government responded by declaring itself to be the sole authority in the host.[73] Kaledin then went a step further by inviting opponents of the Soviet government to Novocherkassk.[74] Before long, several leading politicians from the former State Duma and Provisional Government turned up in the Don Host, and they were soon followed by senior army officers. General Alekseyev arrived in Novocherkassk in mid–November and immediately began organizing an army with the objective of resisting both the Bolsheviks and the Central Powers.[75]

While Alekseyev took advantage of Kaledin's hospitality to transform the Don into the Vendée of the Russian Revolution, another anticipated hub of anti–Bolshevik activity quickly fizzled out. In the aftermath of the October Revolution, some moderate socialist leaders, angered by the exclusion of their parties from the Soviet of People's Commissars (Sovnarkom) that formed the new ruling clique in Petrograd, traveled from the capital to Mogilev in the hope that Stavka would mobilize loyal troops against the Bolshevik usurpers. There they found the acting commander-in-chief, General Nikolay Dukhonin, dithering on his next course of action. Dukhonin's position was not an enviable one: while he was receiving orders from Lenin to open peace talks with the Central Powers, Allied military representatives were reminding him of earlier Russian promises not to conclude a separate peace. Ultimately, he refused to send a delegation across enemy lines but at the same time made no preparations to battle the Bolsheviks—he was unwilling to risk soiling his hands with the blood of a civil war. As Lenin's appointee for Stavka chief, Ensign Nikolay Krylenko, and a compliment of sailors slowly made their way towards Mogilev, the socialist politicians gave up on Dukhonin and hedged their future on the freely-elected Constituent Assembly. Dukhonin's main service to the future counterrevolution was the release of several generals, including Kornilov, from imprisonment in the nearby Bykhov Monastery on 2 December 1917. The next day Krylenko and his sailors arrived in Mogilev and, upon learning that Kornilov and his cellmates had been allowed to escape, brutally beat and bayoneted Dukhonin to death.[76]

Upon their timely liberation from Bykhov Monastery, the former prisoners had agreed to regroup in Kaledin's Don. To avoid detection during the long and dangerous journey to Novocherkassk, most of them traveled alone and in disguise as civilians or simple soldiers. Only the brash Kornilov refused to hide his identity and began the cross-country trek with a band of Turkic tribesmen who in the previous months had served as his personal bodyguard. The column was quickly targeted by Bolshevized soldiers, and after several ambushes and many casualties, the dedication of the Turkic warriors began to waver. Warned of their misgivings, Kornilov swallowed his pride by abandoning his men, assumed a disguise and boarded a train.[77]

All the Bykhov generals reached the Don safely during the course of December 1917. What they found there, however, was a situation much different than they had anticipated. Against their better hopes, they discovered that relatively few Russian officers had made their way to the Don to enlist in Alekseyev's Volunteer Army. Throughout the winter, its strength would remain under 4,000 combatants.[78] An even greater disappointment, however, awaited them in the feebleness of the Don Cossack government. Denikin, who had traveled from Mogilev to Novocherkassk dressed as a simple private, wrote that they had expected the Cossacks to be a pillar of anti–Soviet stability. Instead, he was appalled to learn that that prediction "was a mystification, pure and simple, that at that time the Cossacks had no power left whatsoever."[79] Indeed, the Russian generals had gone to the Don with the hope of obtaining valuable assistance from the Cossacks, but before long the latter would turn to the generals for help.

3

Vacillation

Masters of Manipulation

After deposing the Provisional Government, the Bolshevik leaders quickly learned that staying in power would be a much more difficult task than seizing power. Indeed, the country which they aspired to rule was wrought by a catastrophic war, increasing socio-economic dislocation, disintegrating railways and refractory nationalist movements. They themselves were a political minority inexperienced in government affairs with hardly any reliable armed forces at their disposal. Opposition to their regime abounded, and not just from Cossack atamans in distant borderlands. Just hours after the Red Guards stormed the Winter Palace, the Petrograd city duma, along with some leading SRs and Mensheviks, formed "the Committee to Save the Country and the Revolution." This body condemned the Bolshevik coup and demanded the restoration of the Provisional Government.[1] Two days later, Right SRs called upon Petrograd workers to "liquidate the Bolshevik adventure" by staging a general strike.[2] Lenin and his cohorts, however, were not easily intimidated. They responded to these threats by issuing propagandistic decrees and proclamations intended to deprive their enemies of broad popular support. To the peasants they promised the land, to the workers the factories, to the soldiers peace and to the nationalities self-determination. These guarantees were effective, especially in the short term. City dwellers and peasants alike were relieved that the new regime, in contrast to its predecessors, appeared committed to ending the slaughter at the front while addressing their burning grievances closer to home.

The Cossacks were not excluded from this potent propaganda offensive. Some Cossacks, particularly the rank-and-file serving at the front, had long been predisposed towards the Bolshevik program. Trench combat had never suited the Cossack temperament. Three years of near static warfare, along with the economic hardships that accompanied it, had made Lenin's consistent antiwar message increasingly attractive to soldiers from the stanitsas. It was these radicalized Cossacks who helped the infant Bolshevik regime subvert Krasnov's expedition to Petrograd in November 1917. These men also appeared in the committees formed within various departments of the Soviet government to identify loci of support among Cossacks. With the assistance of these committees, the Bolsheviks dispatched trained agitators to Cossack regiments to win them over to the Soviet government.

The Bolshevik appeals which most effectively blunted Cossack hostility towards the new regime were those which promised that their land reforms would only break-up the plantations of the elite. This pledge to spare the petty holdings of "toiling Cossacks" assuaged the primary concern of most Cossack farmers.[3] Indeed, this propaganda was so well received among ordinary Cossacks that Sovnarkom's decision on 22 December 1917 to absolve the Cossacks of their compulsory military service and end their special privileges hardly caused a stir in the stanitsas. Essentially, this decree abolished the Cossacks as an estate and demoted them to the status of peasants. Amid the circumstances, it was natural that the majority of war-weary Cossacks did not mourn the loss of the extensive military duties which had long burdened their economy and families. It seems that few, especially among the Cossack rank-and-file, perceived the ominous implication that equalization with the peasantry in the socio-military sphere would almost certainly be followed by similar leveling in economic matters—particularly where land allotments were concerned.[4]

The Bolshevik propaganda offensive fell short of converting the mass of ordinary Cossacks into pious Marxists; nonetheless, it did succeed in estranging them from the elite. They felt that they had nothing to fear from the Bolsheviks, especially since the party appeared so accommodating to the national aspirations of Russia's minorities. Consequently, many Cossacks became indignant of their boisterous atamans, whose anti–Soviet proclamations in the aftermath of the October Revolution appeared to invite a civil war that otherwise seemed unnecessary and avoidable.

Among Don Cossacks, these benign attitudes towards Russia's new masters quickly complicated Kaledin's position. The backlash to his offer of sanctuary for the enemies of the Soviet regime was immediately felt, and at the end of November the worried ataman began urging Alekseyev to relocate his nascent anti–Bolshevik army elsewhere. In the following days, however, Kaledin's situation grew critical as various groups of non–Cossacks, including miners in the Donets Basin, workers in Rostov and even an infantry regiment stationed in Novocherkassk, challenged the authority of the Don Cossack government. Worse yet, the available Cossack troops were showing little enthusiasm for serving their ataman. Realizing that he was powerless to prevent the onset of total anarchy, Kaledin was left with no choice other than to seek help from his unwelcome guests, the White generals.

The Volunteer Army to the Rescue

When Kaledin turned to Alekseyev for help in early December, the contingent that would soon be named the Volunteer Army was hardly a respectable fighting force. The organization was barely two weeks old, and at this stage it lacked every basic necessity including money, rifles and even manpower. It probably should not have been surprising that volunteer recruits were in short supply; after all, war weariness was prevalent throughout the country and the uglier aspects of Bolshevik rule were as of yet unknown. Because of its inability to attract ordinary peasants or common soldiers to its banner, the Volunteer Army was saddled with a surplus of officers for most of its existence. For this reason, especially in its early days, many of its members had to accept posts far below their qualifications; in some instances men who had been colonels in the tsarist army would serve in the Volunteer Army as a lowly private.[5] Such selfless commitment to the anti–Bolshevik cause, along with the exceptional quality and experience of its few recruits, did have the benefit of making the Volunteer Army a far superior formation, man for man, than the enemies it would face in the early months of the civil war.

Regardless of the impressive skills and dedication of its soldiers, the Volunteer Army could not escape the fact that it consisted of only a few hundred men when Alekseyev agreed to undertake operations in the Don Host. For the White generals, the deal they struck with Kaledin was an opportunity to secure funds and arms; both of which they were desperately short. Their first task was to restore order in the Don government's capital where a non–Cossack infantry regiment had declared its hostility to the Kaledin regime. Fortunately for the Volunteers, the regiment's disgruntled soldiers had no stomach for an armed confrontation and readily surrendered their weapons. While this action defused the immediate threat to Novocherkassk, the situation throughout the rest of the Don continued to deteriorate. On 5 December, the ataman declared martial law in the host. Notably, Kaledin's announcement lacked the aggressive rhetoric that had been his earlier trademark. Instead, he tried to win over moderate workers by promising tolerance towards soviets in his realm while reassuring the population beyond the Don Host that his Cossack troops would remain within their traditional boundaries.[6]

At this time the Don Cossacks, as Kaledin very well knew, were in no condition to launch military operations outside of the host. The Don government did not even possess the strength to preserve order in its own backyard. A few days after the ataman's declaration of martial law, a Bolshevik-dominated military revolutionary committee (MRC) seized control of the industrial city of Rostov, just 30 miles downriver from Novocherkassk. Unable to summon enough Cossack troops to retake the city from the Bolshevized workers and sailors, Kaledin played the only card he had left—the Volunteer Army. With less than 500 men and minimal help from the Cossacks, the Volunteers hurled themselves headlong into the battle and defeated the much more numerous insurgents on 15 December. Entering Rostov later that day, a distressed Kaledin implored for an end to the fratricidal violence. "I come to your city not as a fortunate conqueror," he declared. "Blood was shed and we have nothing to be glad about."[7]

Although the Don ataman was now pleading for an end to the fighting between Bolsheviks and non–Bolsheviks, the Soviet government had already made up its mind that the Vendée forming in South Russia must be crushed. On 7 December Krylenko, the Soviet Commissar of War, received orders from Petrograd "to wipe off the face of the earth the counter-revolutionary rebellion of the Cossack generals."[8] Wasting no time, the next day Vladimir Antonov-Ovseyenko, a hero of the October Revolution in Petrograd, was assigned the task of mustering an armed expedition of Bolshevized workers and soldiers to march against Novocherkassk. Meanwhile, Sovnarkom declared the Don, Urals and other areas to be in a state of war, but it was careful to emphasize that its campaign was not directed against the Cossacks as a whole. "Every toiling Cossack," the proclamation read, "who will throw off the yoke of the Kaledins, Kornilovs and Dutovs will be greeted as a brother and will be given the necessary support by the Soviet Government."[9]

If the Don Host was to withstand the impending Soviet invasion, the Cossack government badly needed to get its house in order. In particular, it had to address its long-festering relations with the outlanders. William Penn Cresson, during his tour of the Cossack lands two years earlier, wrote, "An adjustment of relations between the Cossack proprietors and the non–Cossack emigrants now tilling the vast tracts of fertile territory owned in common by the 'armies' is one of the most important problems that the future has in store."[10] Kaledin recognized this too and, upon his return from Rostov, he went before the Don Krug to urge the delegates to ease tensions with the outlanders. The ataman's speech had the desired effect: the delegates approved a list of concessions to the non–Cossack population of the host, including the establishment of *zemstvos* and the limited participation of the outlanders in the government. Few non–Cossacks, however, were placated by these gestures. After months of trading demagogic taunts with their Cossack neighbors, most outlanders were by now too radicalized to trust or even listen to the Cossack leaders. Nonetheless, the krug managed to attract seven non–Cossack representatives into a new coalition government on the condition that a congress of outlanders would be convened and that the Volunteer Army would be kept on a tight leash. This announcement was too little, too late. By the time the new coalition government of the Don was declared, a regional congress of peasants had already met in Rostov and threw its support behind the Soviet regime. Moreover, with the worsening outlook of the Don government, the non–Cossack population had little incentive to switch its allegiance.

In its first proclamation, the coalition government of the Don promised to do all in its power to end the civil war and evict any "counter-revolutionary elements" from the host.[11] Despite such promises, Kaledin continued to work closely with the officers and politicians in his realm who represented those very elements. In the first days of 1918, his relationship with the White generals of the Volunteer Army was formally defined in that organization's "constitution." According to this document Kaledin, as the ataman of the Don Host, was to serve as a part of a triumvirate alongside Alekseyev and Kornilov, who were respectively placed in charge of the formation's political and military affairs. In practice, this arrangement proved difficult to implement as Alekseyev and Kornilov could agree on little other than their hostility towards Bolshevism.[12] A particularly contentious quarrel for them was the question over whether socialists should be included in the army's council of political advisors. Alekseyev was open to cooperation with moderate socialists in order to broaden the movement's base of support, but Kornilov regarded them with only slightly less contempt than he felt towards Bolsheviks. It took Kaledin to break the stalemate. Ever mindful of the suspicions which ordinary Cossacks harbored towards his government, the Don ataman sided with Alekseyev to permit the socialists a role in the advisory council. Despite their success, the decision would have no impact on the early Volunteer movement after the chastened Kornilov opted to simply ignore the council.[13]

Kaledin's counterrevolutionary activities at this time were not limited to his interactions with the White generals. His government also attempted to field anti–Bolshevik forces of its own recruited from Don Cossacks returning from the front. These efforts were not very successful since the majority of the Cossack regiments were not interested in further fighting. Besides, they believed Bolshevik propaganda that the new regime was not seeking to deprive them of their lands. The extent of their demoralization became apparent when their trains were held up by cordons of Red Guards just outside the Don territory. Rather than resist, most of the Cossacks submitted to Bolshevik demands that they turn over their weapons. Some even assured the Red delegations sent to their trains that they "intended to make short work of the generals as soon as they got back."[14] More often than not, the Cossack units simply melted away when they reached their home districts. The only reliable forces organized by the Don Cossack government were guerrilla brigades comprised mostly of officers and cadets that included many non–Cossacks among their ranks. The most successful of these detachments was led by a Cossack captain, Vasily Chernetsov, a veteran of raids behind the Central Powers' front. Drawing upon his experience in the war, Chernetsov's band now prowled throughout the Don Host stamping out opposition to Kaledin's government.

The Don Host Overwhelmed

Aside from the few volunteers willing to enlist in Kaledin's guerrilla brigades, most Cossack soldiers returning to the front merely added to the Don Cossack government's problems. In mid–January 1918 Cossack regiments deployed in the Donets district to defend the Don homeland from Antonov-Ovseyenko's approaching Red Guards convened a congress of Cossack soldiers in stanitsa Kamenskaya. There the delegates representing twenty-one Cossack regiments elected a military revolutionary committee. Under the leadership of Fyodor Podtelkov, a Left SR, the Kamenskaya MRC disavowed any allegiance to Kaledin and began negotiations for a ceasefire with Antonov-Ovseyenko. The Bolshevik commander, eager to exploit the divisions appearing among the Don Cossacks, restrained his Red forces and laid out his conditions to the delegates from the Kamenskaya MRC. His terms, especially a demand for the Cossacks to form a soviet that would include the outlanders, were not attractive to the MRC delegates who still valued their Cossack status. At this point, the Kamenskaya MRC gave no indication that it was willing to accommodate the outlanders; its primary goal was to end counterrevolutionary activities in the Don Host and thereby defuse hostilities with Soviet Russia.

The Kamenskaya MRC also presented its demands to the government in Novocherkassk. Although Kaledin had earlier threatened Podtelkov and his associates with arrest, the ataman's diminishing authority compelled him to attempt negotiations with the Cossack mutineers. Not surprisingly, the chances for an agreement were slim since the rebels wanted all power claimed by the Don Cossack government transferred onto themselves. Moreover, they also demanded the disarmament and dissolution of the Volunteer Army. The talks between Novocherkassk and the Kamenskaya MRC quickly broke down when Chernetsov's guerrillas raided Kamenskaya and forced the MRC to relocate. Accounts disagree on whether or not this strike was ordered by Kaledin; it is possible that Chernetsov acted independently. Regardless, the attack convinced Podtelkov's group that the ataman could not bargained with in good faith, and they effectively entered into an alliance with Antonov-Ovseyenko's Red Guards. Meanwhile, the Cossack rebels recovered Kamenskaya and even cut down Chernetsov and most of his detachment in the process.[15]

With the loss of Chernetsov, Kaledin was deprived of one of his most energetic warriors just as the gathering Bolshevik forces were poised to strike. The enemy faced by Kaledin's loyal units was not particularly imposing from a military perspective. Eduard Dune, an eighteen-year-old factory hand then serving with the Red Guards on the borders of the Don Host, later wrote in his memoir that he and most of his comrades had never held a rifle before the previous autumn. He added that they relied on former Hungarian war prisoners to operate the unit's more complex machine guns.[16] The inexperience of the Red forces, however, was offset by their considerable numerical superiority, especially when they were combined with the anti–Kaledin Cossacks. In the opening days of February 1918, they closed in on the Don heartland to deliver the *coup de grâce* to the Kaledin regime.

Antonov-Ovseyenko's Red Guards were divided into two main assault groups: one advancing southward against Novocherkassk and the other marching southeast towards Rostov. The latter approaches were defended by the Volunteer Army, whose strength was partially tied down by the need to maintain order among restive workers in Taganrog. On 8 February Kornilov's representative in Novocherkassk, General Aleksandr Lukomsky, informed Kaledin that the Volunteers were convinced that the fight for the Don was lost and intended to withdraw south into the Kuban Host. The beleaguered ataman, refusing an offer to retreat with Kornilov's army, succeeded in persuading the Volunteers to delay their evacuation. The prospects of the anti–Bolshevik forces, however, did not improve and two days later he issued a final public appeal for Cossack patriots to defend Novocherkassk.[17]

Kaledin's last-minute plea failed to arouse any renewed support. Subsequently, he called the government into an emergency session on 12 February. The meeting opened with the Don field ataman, General A. M. Nazarov, offering a bleak assessment of the host's military situation: the Reds were almost at the gates of Novocherkassk, which was defended by a paltry 150 Cossacks and two companies of the Volunteer Army. Following Nazarov's remarks, Kaledin declared that with the impending evacuation of the Volunteers from the Don "the struggle is now hopeless." He then recommended the government to resign and transfer its authority to the local duma. When a deputy attempted to argue against this suggestion, the ataman quickly cut him off. "Enough talk," interrupted Kaledin, "Russia has been ruined by grandiloquence."[18] He then announced his own resignation and retired to his office. After burning a few documents, he removed his uniform, drew his pistol and fired a bullet through his heart.

Kaledin's suicide briefly revived the sagging ardor of the anticommunist Don Cossacks. Representatives of the unoccupied southern Don stanitsas, traditionally the most prosperous and conservative districts, elected Nazarov as the new ataman and convened a "Little Krug." Ominously, no outlander deputies showed up for the government-sponsored non–Cossack congress that was scheduled to gather at the same time as the krug. In a last-ditch effort to save Novocherkassk, the Little Krug announced the full mobilization of the Don Cossacks. Like earlier proclamations and appeals, the order was shrugged off by the Cossack masses. Even so, Nazarov's hopes for the Don's salvation were buoyed by the arrival of the 6th Don Cossack Regiment from the front. "We could hardly believe our eyes," recalled Lukomsky of that regiment's homecoming, "all the officers were at their posts; there was full discipline, and no 'committees' of any kind."[19] With only a tiny number of men on either side willing to engage in actual combat at the front, Nazarov knew that even one reliable regiment might prove decisive in the struggle against the Red Guards. The Don leaders were so elated they venerated the unit in a Te Deum service held beneath the cupolas of Novocherkassk's cathedral. Afterwards, the 6th Don Cossack Regiment went to the front, but just two days later its men refused to partake in anymore fighting. The hopes of reviving the martial spirit of the Don Cossacks were dashed.

Just hours after the mutiny of the 6th Don Cossack Regiment, the Volunteer Army finally began its planned retreat to the Kuban. The withdrawal of Kornilov and his troops removed the last major obstacle between the Red Guards and the key centers on the Don. Rostov fell to the Bolshevik forces on 23 February and the other main task force of Red Guards driving on Novocherkassk from the north could have probably seized the Don capital that day as well. Instead, the Red commander there held off and allowed troops from the Cossack MRC under Lieutenant-Colonel V. S. Golubov take the town on 25 February. Some Don Cossacks fighting against the Bolsheviks accepted invitations to flee with the Volunteer Army. About 1,500 mounted Cossacks under the new field ataman, P. K. Popov, chose instead to head east out into the remote steppe. Others were overtaken by the advancing Reds, and a few, including Nazarov, deliberately chose to stay behind and take their chances with the Bolsheviks. The unfortunate ataman was quickly arrested by rebel Cossacks when they entered Novocherkassk and executed six days later. In the meantime, the victorious Golubov declared himself the "revolutionary ataman" of a projected Red Don.[20]

Kuban Odyssey

The Don territory was not the only area where the anti–Bolshevik movement saw defeat in the winter of 1918. Nationalists in the neighboring Ukraine, many evoking their long extinct Cossack past by labelling themselves "Free Cossacks," also fought a losing battle against invading Red Guards throughout that January. At the end of the month the Red Guards captured Kiev and initiated a reign of terror by killing hundreds of former officers from the tsarist army, regardless of whether or not they had aided the Soviets' opponents.[21] In the southern Urals, Ataman Dutov and his Orenburg Cossacks came under fire from militias dispatched by soviets in the Volga, Urals and Central Asian districts. Before long these Red detachments were reinforced by Bolshevized soldiers and sailors from Petrograd. Like Kaledin, Dutov found that many young Cossacks returning from the front did not want to fight or thought that the Bolsheviks would do them no harm. On 31 January Orenburg fell to the Red attackers, and the ataman and his followers regrouped in Verkhneuralsk. After an unsuccessful counteroffensive in February, Dutov lost that town as well and his band was pushed into the wilderness of the Kazakh steppe.[22]

By late February Cossack governments survived only in those areas that were not easily accessible or were cut off from the rest of Russia. The Ural Cossack government lasted partly due its remoteness and its decision not to openly condemn the Soviet regime. Despite their uneasy relations, the Ural Krug and local Bolsheviks coexisted until a unit of Red Guards reached the area in mid–March 1918 and claimed sole authority in the host.[23] The only other place where the Cossacks managed to hold their capital late that winter was in the Kuban Host. Shortly after the October Revolution, the Kuban Cossack government had followed Kaledin's example by refusing to recognize the authority of the Soviet regime and instead declared itself the head of an independent republic.[24] With the Don Host situated on its northern frontier, the Kuban was not immediately endangered by Red Guard detachments from Central Russia. Instead, its primary threat came from the opposite direction—the south—where troops from Russia's Caucasian Front were establishing soviets throughout the North Caucasus.

The challenges confronting the Kuban government were similar to those faced by anticommunist Cossacks in the Don and elsewhere. The host ataman, A. P. Filimonov, and Kuban Rada were slow to address the region's outlander problem, and by the time they permitted outlanders a voice in their government much of the host was already overrun by Bolshevized regiments. They also had to wrangle with the familiar problem of returning Cossack soldiers refusing to fight. Like Kaledin to his north, Filimonov's attempt to organize an army from Cossack veterans failed and instead he had to improvise with volunteer brigades. These units, despite their paltry size, won some impressive victories. On 4 February 1918 an anti-Bolshevik detachment of just 700 men under the command of a former Russian pilot, Captain Viktor Pokrovsky, stunned a Red force of 6,000 men on the outskirts of Yekaterinodar. This feat, along with another victory on its heels, resulted in Pokrovsky being promoted to commander of the Kuban Army. The Kuban government, however, lacked the strength to capitalize on Pokrovsky's victories. As a result, the Red forces, already in control of much of the host, closed in on Yekaterinodar and laid siege to the last significant anti-Bolshevik stronghold in Russia.[25]

The town's best hope for relief rested with the Volunteer Army, which crossed into the Kuban territory on 9 March with about 4,000 combatants and perhaps 1,000 civilians. Although its leaders knew the trek awaiting them would not be easy, they were driven forward by a messianic sense of duty. "We are plunging into the steppes. We can return only by God's mercy," wrote Alekseyev as his troops evacuated Rostov. "But," he added, "a torch must be lit, so that at least one speck of light will shine amid the darkness which has enveloped Russia."[26] With telegraphs effectively controlled by their enemies, the Volunteers moved forward blindly, not knowing whether Yekaterinodar would still be in friendly hands when they finally arrived there. The formation's progress was further impeded by its efforts to bypass railways whenever possible so as to avoid encounters with trainloads of hostile troops on their way home from the Caucasian Front.[27] The weather presented additional challenges. Although spring was near, the column still experienced the fury of wintry weather. "Men and horses were covered with an ice crust," wrote Denikin of a march during a blizzard, "everything seemed frozen to the very core, clothes became hard as though wooden, and hampered every movement; it was difficult to turn one's head."[28] To feed itself the army purchased grain from stanitsas along its route; the soldiers were explicitly barred from requisitioning at these settlements so as not to alienate the Kuban Cossacks who Kornilov hoped might one day rally to his banner. The villages of outlanders, on the other hand, were not given such special consideration, and this double standard naturally reinforced the pro–Bolshevik tendencies of the non–Cossack population in the Kuban.

While the Volunteer Army was plodding along a circuitous route towards Yekaterinodar, the Kuban Rada, its army and a number of stragglers, altogether about 5,000 persons, abandoned that town to the Reds on 13 March. This devastating news reached the Volunteers on the following day.[29] Upon leaving their capital, the Kuban leaders immediately began quarreling among themselves over which direction they should march. Some in the government wanted to head south into the Caucasian foothills, but Pokrovsky desired a link-up with the approaching Volunteer Army. Each side got their way: the government went south while Pokrovsky and his troops eventually made contact with Kornilov's force on 27 March.

Although both of the anti–Bolshevik armies were little better off than refugees, their commanders' first meeting in a Circassian *aoul* was not cordial. To enhance Pokrovsky's position in the impending negotiations, the Kuban government hastily promoted him to the rank of a general, but Kornilov was unimpressed. The Volunteer commander wanted nothing less than the complete submission of the Kuban Cossack Army and the disbandment of their government. These conditions, which would have effectively deprived the Kuban Cossacks of their autonomy, appeared harsh even to a non–Cossack like Pokrovsky. After parting ways, the two camps deliberated among themselves for three days until 30 March, when they met again in Kornilov's headquarters, then in stanitsa Novo-Dmitrovskaya. By then both sides were more willing to compromise. The Kuban delegation agreed to merge its army with the Volunteers, recognizing Kornilov's command. In exchange, the Kuban government and Rada were permitted to continue their functions. With the Novo-Dmitrovskaya agreement, the Volunteer Army added about 3,000 combatants to its ranks and increased its strength to a total of 6,000 men. That number would continue to rise as local Cossacks enlisted with the Whites. Unfortunately, the army was still encumbered with a massive number of civilians and non-combatants in tow—about 3,000—all of whom required food and other supplies.[30] Such a force could not continue wandering indefinitely; it needed a secure base. To accomplish this, Kornilov decided to march on the original objective of the Volunteer Army's Kuban campaign: Yekaterinodar.

The battle for Yekaterinodar commenced on 9 April when Whites fought their way across the Kuban River and to the edge of the Kuban capital. Kornilov, perhaps dismissive of the tenacity of the Red defenders, wasted no time in ordering his men to charge into Yekaterinodar despite warnings from his intelligence officers that the enemy had a hefty numerical superiority and well-prepared defenses in the form of trenches that ringed the town. Therefore, it should not have come as a surprise when the Reds held their positions and sent White casualties soaring. At a council of war attended by the senior generals and Ataman Filimonov on 12 April, Kornilov admitted that the operation was not going well. Nonetheless, he resolved to attack again on the following day since he believed the Volunteer Army must take Yekaterinodar or die trying.

The next morning, before this all-or-nothing attack commenced, Red artillerymen in Yekaterinodar scored a direct hit on a nearby farmstead that Kornilov had been using as his headquarters. The charismatic general, whose cult of personality provided substantial cohesion for the Volunteers, died shortly after the blast. Although the White leaders attempted to suppress word of his death, news of Kornilov's demise raced through the ranks, initiating an outpouring of both grief and panic. Amid these changed circumstances Kornilov's successor, Denikin, called off the scheduled attack. That night, the Volunteer Army withdrew from Yekaterinodar and immediately began a series of forced marches northward to put as much distance between it and the enemy. Still, had the Red forces been better disciplined and ably led, they might have pursued Denikin's mauled army and put a permanent end to the threat posed by the Volunteers. Instead the victors busied themselves with searching for Kornilov's gravesite in a nearby village, exhuming his corpse and then hauling it back to Yekaterinodar where they publicly desecrated it over the next two days.[31]

With seemingly nowhere else to go, the Volunteer Army's defeat before Yekaterinodar may have appeared to be a setback from which it was unlikely to recover. But as the men trudged through the muddy Kuban countryside, they began to have some reason for optimism. At one station they captured a trove of munitions in railway carriages amounting to over 400 shells and 100,000 rifle cartridges; thereby replenishing their spent ordinance. At the stanitsas along their route they learned that the Kuban Cossacks, not just the older men but also the younger veterans, were becoming disillusioned with Bolshevik rule. Cossacks from all generations more readily enlisted in the Volunteers' ranks. Then came the welcome news that the Don Cossacks were again taking up arms against the Soviet regime. After their scouts confirmed these reports, Denikin and Alekseyev immediately led their army back to the Don Host.[32]

The First Kuban Campaign, which became romanticized in White folklore as the Icy March, ended on 12 May as the Volunteer Army took up quarters in two stanitsas in the southern districts of the Don Host. For its survivors, the march had been physically grueling and often disheartening. The Volunteer Army had not only failed to achieve its main objective of securing a new base at Yekaterinodar, but it also lost its revered commander, General Kornilov. Yet, the Volunteer Army survived these setbacks; in fact, it returned to the Don stronger than when it evacuated the host. General Denikin, the army's new leader, had led the Fourth "Iron" Division during the world war and had a solid record as an able field commander. Moreover, tensions within the Volunteer leadership eased since Denikin and Alekseyev were on much friendlier terms than the latter had been with Kornilov.[33] Through the Novo-Dmitrovskaya agreement, the White generals gained control over the military resources of the Kuban Cossack government. Although the Kuban Army had been no larger than the Volunteer Army at the time of the agreement, the Kuban Cossacks, who numbered about 1,340,000, would become a potentially significant recruiting pool for the White generals.[34]

In the months following the Icy March, at least half of the Volunteer Army's strength was comprised of Kuban Cossacks; though neither Denikin nor his staff cared to openly acknowledge this fact.[35] These Kuban Cossack reinforcements, as the White generals would soon learn, did not come without any strings attached. To maintain the army's cohesion and morale, the Volunteer command had to incorporate the Cossacks' aims and sympathies in their overall campaign. At first glance, this seemed easy enough since both the Volunteers and the Kuban Cossacks had taken up arms for the same basic purpose: to rid their homeland of Bolshevik tyranny. But each group had a different concept of what constituted as "their homeland." To the officers of the Volunteer Army, it was Russia within her prewar frontiers; but to the Kuban Cossacks, it was merely the territory of the Kuban Host. This distinction was to have profound implications for the future of the White movement in South Russia as Denikin and his staff found it necessary to balance their national anti–Bolshevik objectives with the more limited regional ambitions of the Kuban Cossack rank and file.

Sovdepia Unmasked

After taking Novocherkassk in the last days of February, the Bolsheviks focused their energies on consolidating their hold on the Don territory. The most pressing issue was deciding who was actually to be in charge of the region. A number of claimants to regional power existed: Lieutenant-Colonel Golubov who appointed himself "Red ataman," the Rostov *revkom*, the Taganrog *revkom* and finally Podtelkov's Cossack MRC which soon relocated from Kamenskaya to Rostov. Soviet leaders quickly ruled out Golubov's claim; by now the title of ataman carried a powerful stigma for the non–Cossack population. Instead, Moscow granted nominal authority to a newly formed Don MRC consisting of both Cossacks and outlanders, an arrangement to which Podtelkov and his Cossacks had agreed in their pact with Antonov-Ovseyenko. Despite this arrangement, Soviet leaders doubted the reliability of locally-chosen leaders to ruthlessly squeeze the Don countryside of grain and other foodstuffs needed to alleviate the continuing food shortages in Russia's northern cities. As a result, the Don MRC would be nothing more than a fig leaf behind which outside commissars appointed by Antonov-Ovseyenko pursued the new regime's goals of nationalizing industries, extorting funds from the middle class and organizing food-requisition detachments to track down caches of grain.[36]

The Bolsheviks did not have much time to forge a stable revolutionary government on the Don before they were confronted with a new crisis in the region. The latest challenge stemmed from their attempt to make peace with the Central Powers at Brest-Litovsk. It was there that the ruling party discovered that it was much easier to agitate for peace than to actually obtain acceptable peace terms. The negotiations between the two sides at Brest-Litovsk had begun in late November 1917 and continued intermittently throughout that following winter. The Bolsheviks had hoped to convene a conference that would arrange a general "people's peace" without indemnities or annexations, but this was impractical after the Allies ignored Trotsky's invitations for them to join the proceedings. Unwilling to submit to the imperialist demands of the German Oberste Heeresleitung (OHL) which, among other things, would create a cordon of German client states in Russia's occupied borderlands, Trotsky eventually led the Soviet delegation to walk out of the conference after refusing to sign a treaty and declaring the war on the Eastern Front at an end.[37] Eight days later the Germans responded to Trotsky's "no war, no peace" proclamation with a new offensive across the breadth of the Eastern Front. The remnants of the Imperial Russian Army at the front, withered by desertion and low morale, was unable to offer any serious resistance. General Max Hoffmann, the chief of staff at Ober Ost, was delighted by the easy advance of his troops, gleefully writing in his diary that it was "the most comical war I have ever known."[38] The Bolsheviks, on the other hand, were not laughing and feared that Petrograd itself might be occupied by the kaiser's army. On 24 February, after torturous debates in the party's central committee, they announced their readiness to accept the new, harsher peace terms laid out by the Germans. Ober Ost, in response, soon halted its formations on the north end of the front, but no such orders were sent to German and Austrian troops pushing through Ukraine.

Earlier, on 9 February, the Central Powers had concluded a peace treaty with a delegation from the Ukrainian Central Rada after it had been chased from Kiev by invading Red Guards.[39] Nicknamed the "Bread Peace" (Brotfrieden), the treaty bound the Central Rada to deliver one-million tons of grain to the Central Powers in exchange for the latter's protection.[40] Therefore, even after the Soviet government agreed to accept the Brest-Litovsk Treaty in late February, the Germans continued their advance into eastern Ukraine on the pretext that they were liberating these lands on behalf of the Ukrainian government. Of course, the Germans' real motivation was to secure as much grain and other commodities as possible, and this explains why they eventually pushed beyond the old Ukrainian frontier to occupy the Donets coal fields as well as the Black Sea ports of Rostov and Taganrog.

The German march through eastern Ukraine panicked the Don MRC which, like the larger Soviet republic, lacked the forces needed to seriously oppose a disciplined, conventional army. To deter the invaders, the Don MRC declared the Don to be an independent soviet republic on 23 March.[41] The Germans, however, had no qualms against violating the territory of the new Don Soviet Republic, which they crossed into during the following month. Amid this latest threat, the Don Bolsheviks, who had earlier supported the Brest-Litovsk Treaty, now broke with the party central committee in Moscow and urged their followers to wage a "revolutionary war" against the invaders.[42] By then, the apparent inability of the Soviet regime to contain the foreign enemy was just one of many reasons why the Don population was becoming disillusioned with Lenin's dictatorship.

The Bolshevik occupation of the Don was accompanied by terror and violence for Cossack and non–Cossack alike. In the countryside, a "bread war" began as food-requisitioning detachments from urban centers descended on villages and stanitsas to confiscate grain and other foodstuffs from peasants unwilling to sell their commodities at fixed prices. Small battles inevitably broke out as angry, armed peasants resisted the expeditions.[43] In Rostov, Mensheviks and other moderate socialists were suppressed to give the local Bolsheviks unfettered control of the city's MRC.[44] Former officers residing in that town and others, even if they had not provided any assistance to the Whites, were forced to go underground to avoid arrest and possible execution. Even the local proletariat, in whose name the Bolsheviks ruled, was not safe from the excesses of the Red Guards.[45]

Since the Bolsheviks devoted most of their energies to controlling towns and cities, the Don Cossacks in the countryside were not exposed to the harshest elements of Soviet rule. Nonetheless, disillusionment quickly set in among the young Cossack soldiers who had been agreeable towards the Soviet regime. After Kaledin's defeat, they dispersed to their stanitsas and lost contact with their regiments' revolutionary committees. Before long, their revolutionary zeal was tempered by the misgivings of their fathers and particularly grandfathers, who had traditionally held a revered and authoritative position in Cossack families.[46] At home and in the frequent stanitsa assemblies, the conservative elders raised the general suspicion that their people's interests were being subordinated to those of outsiders. Those anxieties appeared to be confirmed with the arrival of armed food-requisitioning detachments in the countryside. Even those Cossacks living in stanitsas not targeted by these expeditions still heard rumors of Bolshevik atrocities and feared that their community might be next. Another concern was that the new regime might favor the outlanders. Indeed, outlanders clenched disproportionately large majorities in many local soviets and in the First Congress of Don Soviets which met in April. In the latter assembly, some outlander delegates were eager to abrogate the perceived advantages which the Cossacks held over the non–Cossack population beginning with the seizure of Cossack lands. Ordinary Don Cossacks who believed Bolshevik propaganda that only the property of the elite would be subject to appropriations were now beginning to fear that their lands might also be at risk.[47]

By April, many Don Cossacks probably felt that Soviet rule offered greater benefit to their internal enemies while leaving them vulnerable to the foreign one now on the doorstep of the Don. Subsequently, a spontaneous insurgency began in various districts. A notable defection occurred early that month when the military commander of the revolutionary Cossacks, Lieutenant-Colonel Golubov, turned against his Bolshevik allies and tried to rally anticommunist volunteers around Novocherkassk. But since few were willing to trust Golubov after his drastic change of heart, nothing became of his planned uprising and instead he had to flee when a contingent of Red Guards was sent after him.

While Golubov was on the run, the rebellion he tried to drum up broke out in earnest after Cossacks resisted a food-requisitioning detachment at a stanitsa just west of Novocherkassk on 10 April. The Cossacks won this scuffle, disarming and killing a number of Red Guards, and they followed up their victory by forming a rebel detachment of less than 400 men. Although this paltry force was unimpressive, just four days later it caught the Bolshevik garrison in Novocherkassk off-guard and captured that town against almost no resistance. The Cossack occupation of the Don capital came as a welcome relief to the persecuted officers still living there, and they used the opportunity to form a Council of Defense. This organization immediately began forming a new Don army around the extant rebel force. In the meantime, Red Guards from Rostov initiated a drive to retake Novocherkassk. On 18 April, the Cossack insurgents, aware of their need to husband their strength, made an orderly withdrawal from the Don capital and relocated their headquarters to stanitsa Zaplavskaya.

Their decision proved wise. The nascent Don Army grew rapidly in the coming days as Cossack volunteers eager to cast off the Soviet yoke converged on Zaplavskaya. Just five days after that stanitsa was transformed into the headquarters of the anti–Bolshevik rebellion, the army numbered 6,500 men.[48] Indeed, the rapid growth of the Don Army demonstrated that the Cossacks could still be a potent enemy. Their administrative system, which was left more or less intact despite the changes wrought by the revolutions, functioned expertly to accelerate their mobilization.[49] No other group in Russia could have fielded a large army as rapidly as the Don Cossacks would over the next few weeks.[50] Still, the most important factor in the mobilization of the Don Cossacks that spring was motivation. As Kaledin's experience proved, the Cossacks' advantages in training and organization were next to useless if the men were unwilling to fight. Now, just a few months later Cossacks young and old, having become thoroughly disillusioned with Bolshevism, were ready to put their warrior skills to good use to liberate their homeland from Soviet rule.

Although stanitsa Zaplavskaya became the most powerful locus of anti–Bolshevik resistance in the Don, many smaller uprisings independent of the rebellion near Novocherkassk erupted simultaneously in other areas of the host. Contrary to the depictions of later Cossack émigré historians, these revolts were not limited to the Cossack population. Indeed, many of the operations, especially in their early stages, were led by non-Cossack officers and attracted support from local peasants and even outlanders. Far from possessing a unified political ideology, some insurgencies were organized under local soviets opposed to Bolsheviks and their Left SR allies. The widespread appeal of the uprisings, particularly across sociological groups, is indicative of the difficulty encountered by the new regime in garnering support in rural locales.[51]

The Don was not the only host whose inhabitants challenged the Soviet regime that spring. In the Ural Host, the Bolsheviks, after a brief occupation, were driven out of most districts by the end of March 1918.[52] To the northeast, the Orenburg Cossacks took a bit longer to challenge the Red forces that had overrun their host late that winter. As elsewhere, it was Bolshevik atrocities—or rumors of such misdeeds—which spurred a mostly passive population into active resistance. By May, Cossack soldiers who a few months earlier had rejected their officers' authority now invited those men back to lead their detachments. As the insurgency continued to build just outside the gates of Orenburg, the rebellious stanitsas formed the Congress of United Stanitsas. For the better part of two months the congress would function as the governing body of the anticommunist Orenburg Cossacks.[53]

With lesser rebellions also taking place among Cossacks in Siberia and the North Caucasus, it appeared that the Cossack people, as a whole, were thoroughly embittered by their experience with Soviet rule. In fact, the uprisings in the hosts should be viewed as a part of a spontaneous series of revolts which broke out all over Soviet Russia in that spring. In the borderlands, non-Russian ethnicities rebelled when the Bolsheviks violated the principle of self-determination by subsidizing radical, pro-Soviet factions among the nationalities.[54] In secret conferences, patriotic socialists, horrified by the crippling terms for Russia in the Brest-Litovsk Treaty, passed resolutions against the ruling party and initiated underground activity.[55] In Central Russia, peasant disturbances and riots occurred in protest to activities of grain-requisitioning detachments. Even Red Army units, chaffing against efforts to tighten discipline in the revolutionary army, staged serious revolts.[56] Many of these uprisings, handicapped by sloppy organization and a dearth of arms, were quickly suppressed by Red Guard punitive detachments. The exceptions were those in the Cossack lands, where the insurgencies, even if they did not originate exclusively from the Cossacks themselves, co-opted Cossack institutions to overpower their enemies and sustain their momentum. The result was that these movements assumed a Cossack character.

The rebellions in the Cossack hosts were disconcerting for Soviet leaders for other reasons besides their appearance of possessing a united Cossack ideology. One was their disruption of food imports to Russia's hungry northern cities. After the German occupation of Ukraine, the uprisings in the Don and North Caucasus regions deprived the Soviet republic of some of its best remaining agricultural lands.[57] Another reason why the Cossack rebellions, particularly those in South Russia, would prove so menacing for the Soviet republic was that insurgents had access to exceptional military leaders thanks to the flight of army officers in that direction. In other areas the revolts were disjointed and led by mostly by amateurs. Although many Cossack rebellions began in a similar fashion, those in the Don gradually fell under the sway of officers, Cossack and non-Cossack, with clear strategic goals in mind. Like the majority of Cossacks, not all of these officers were initially eager to fight with or alongside the Volunteer Army. Many had simply fled to South Russia to escape persecution, but to survive the brief Soviet occupation of the region they were often compelled to go underground and form a resistance. If these officers were the brains of the anti–Bolshevik struggle in South Russia, the Don and Kuban Cossacks might be considered its muscles. Together, they proved a formidable combination. But one should be careful of making such a generalization since it would be misleading to imply that the Cossacks, for better or for worse, did not have a mind of their own.

4

Resurgence

The Welcome Invader

For all shades of anti–Bolshevik Russians, the sight of German troops marching through Ukraine, Crimea and to the Don frontier in the spring of 1918 aroused mixed emotions. Many were proud Russian patriots who could not easily set aside the antipathy which they developed towards the enemy after nearly four years of war. They were particularly resentful of Germany for its perceived roles in starting the war, unleashing the scourge of Bolshevism upon their country and, finally, inflicting one last humiliation upon the Russian people at Brest-Litovsk. Nonetheless, Baron Pyotr Wrangel, a veteran cavalryman who would shortly become a leading officer in the White armies, later admitted that he was relieved when soldiers clad in *feldgrau* arrived in his Crimean refuge and immediately restored order in the area.[1] In Kharkov, General Aleksandr Lukomsky encountered a similar sentiment a few days after the Germans entered that city. "The skin rejoices at being delivered from the Bolsheviks," a conflicted resident explained to the general, "but the soul grieves that this should be done by the hands of the foe!"[2] Meanwhile, in occupied Kiev Pavel Milyukov, the ex-foreign minister of the Provisional Government and an early collaborator with General Alekseyev, hoped that the Germans, through a negotiated agreement, might foster a stable, non–Bolshevik government throughout the whole of Russia.[3]

The Germans, it was true, had provided valuable support to Finnish and Ukrainian efforts to drive the Red menace from their territories. But in the latter case, Ukrainians quickly learned that the kaiser's troops were far more concerned about obtaining foodstuffs than respecting their self-determination. The differences between the "liberators" and the liberated were most acute in their attitude towards agrarian reforms. Earlier that year, during the Soviet invasion of Ukraine, the Central Rada made a last-ditch effort to rally the peasantry behind it by passing legislation that abolished private ownership of lands.[4] When the Rada delegates returned to their capital behind German bayonets, they persisted in their decision to implement such radical agrarian reforms, much to the dismay of the occupiers who did not want the crucial next planting delayed by uncertainty over land ownership. In order to put the issue to rest, the commander of the army of occupation, General von Eichhorn, unilaterally announced that the next harvest would belong to whoever worked the land. After the Rada protested against this and other interferences in Ukraine's domestic affairs, the Germans responded by encouraging a group of Ukrainian adventurers and landowners to overthrow the uncooperative assembly on 28 April.

The ringleaders of the coup belonged to the National Ukrainian Cossack Organization (NUCO), itself an outgrowth of the spontaneous "Free Cossack" movement that had formed during the summer of 1917 to counter anarchy in the Ukrainian countryside. The organization was the brainchild of Colonel Ivan Poltavets-Ostranitsa, a twenty-eight-year-old former cavalry officer in the tsarist army who claimed Cossack and noble ancestry. To enhance the group's prestige, Poltavets-Ostranitsa had cast his own leadership ambitions aside to elevate a former Russian Guards officer, Lieutenant-General Pavlo Skoropadsky, to NUCO's helm. To both men the Central Rada represented chaos, dysfunction and ultimately ruin. Their desire for order in Ukraine, which they believed could be obtained only through a strong leader, meshed perfectly with the Germans' immediate goals for that region.[5]

Upon seizing power in Kiev, the forty-five-year-old Skoropadsky evoked the legacy of the Zaporozhian Cossacks by adopting the title "Hetman of the Ukraine." He also outfitted himself in traditional Zaporozhian costumes and carried a dagger in his belt. Few of his subjects, however, were won over by these efforts to style himself as a modern Ukrainian folk hero. Although he was the scion of a Ukrainian aristocratic family, the Hetman's successful career in the Russian army, which included a stint as aide-de-camp to Nicholas II, rendered him unacceptable to Ukrainian nationalists. They regarded the Hetmanate as an elaborate fraud set up by Russian monarchists who were only interested in utilizing Ukraine as a base to overthrow the Bolsheviks. Nothing—not even Skoropadsky's genuine attempts to "Ukrainize" education, theater or his administration—could convince the nationalists otherwise. Meanwhile, the hetman's efforts to promote Ukrainian language and culture alienated Russians living in Ukraine, including refugees recently arrived from the north, as well as Russophone Ukrainians. These elements traditionally dominated Ukraine's urban centers and ridiculed the entire Ukrainian national movement as a farce. But the issue that caused the hetman the most trouble was his attitude toward agrarian reforms. In his inaugural proclamation, Skoropadsky committed himself to the restoration of privately-held land. Although he was willing to dismantle the great estates with compensation for their owners, this arrangement was far less attractive to poor and middle peasants than the Central Rada's policy of outright expropriation. From the outset, then, socialist agitators had little trouble depicting the Hetmanate as an instrument through which aristocrats and capitalists intended to enslave Ukraine's toiling masses. As a result, the Hetmanate, like the Rada before it, could count on the loyalty of only a minority of the population it claimed to rule. Whereas the latter had cultivated support primarily among the numerically-insignificant nationalist intelligentsia, Skoropadsky's government could depend on only a thin layer of large landowners and wealthy peasants. Of course, the regime also relied on outsiders, namely the German and Austro-Hungarian occupation forces, to keep Skoropadsky in power.[6]

The Central Powers' occupation of Ukraine also impacted the anti–Bolshevik insurgency that had broken out among the Don Cossacks that spring. The approach of German troops generated considerable panic among soviets in the western districts of the Don who feared being caught between the enemy to the west and the Cossack rebels in the stanitsas.[7] In the first days of May, the Germans occupied Taganrog and Rostov. By then the German command was aware that they had a potential ally in their midst. On 2 May, General Hoffmann, the chief-of-staff at Ober Ost, recorded in his diary that the Don Cossacks appealed to the German government for help in their fight against the Reds. "I am against mixing ourselves up in the affairs of the Don province," Hoffmann wrote, "our Eastern movement must come to an end some time."[8] Other German officers shared Hoffmann's concern against spreading their military strength too thin in the region, but they still desired a means to extract coal, grain and other commodities from the bountiful Don territory. Ultimately, they decided to support the Don Cossacks with rifles, cartridges and other manufactured goods. In exchange, the Cossacks were expected to make grain and coal resources in their host available to Germany.[9]

Purely from the standpoint of self-preservation, the decision of the Don Cossack rebels to seek friendly relations with the invaders was a practical one. They certainly were in no condition to challenge the Germans even though the OHL had transferred its best divisions from Russia to France months ago. Besides, in that area the two parties were fighting against a common enemy—the Bolsheviks—and the Don Cossack insurgents would have been foolish to pass up the opportunity to enlist such a powerful ally in their struggle.

This *realpolitik* was not appreciated by the leadership of the Volunteer Army. Alekseyev, Denikin and other White generals viewed their little force as an Allied formation at war with not only the Bolsheviks but also the Central Powers. In doing so, they believed that they were preserving Russia's honor by upholding the country's earlier promises to the Allies to not conclude a separate peace with the enemy.[10] With a mindset that valued their concept of honor above all else, the White generals refused to entertain any suggestion that they should regard the Germans with anything other than hostility. "Have no dealings whatsoever with the commanding staff of an enemy Power," Denikin instructed his army.[11] With the Volunteer Army regrouping on the southern frontier of the Don, the White generals could make such bold statements since the Germans were still some distance away. Still, it was silly to pretend that even they had not benefited indirectly from the recent German advance.

Although Ober Ost had halted its troops on the western fringes of the Don Host, the Germans, through their continued presence in the region, would remain a significant factor in the area for the next several months. The proximity of the German army of occupation in Ukraine would loom over the anti–Bolshevik movement in South Russia, effectively protecting the Whites' western flank but at the same time fueling discord between Germanophile Cossacks and the pro–Allied White generals.

The Return of the Atamans

Shortly after the Don Cossacks insurgents established their headquarters in stanitsa Zaplavskaya, Field Ataman Popov and his followers returned to the area after spending almost two months in the barren steppe to the east. By tradition, Popov, as field ataman, was entitled to take charge of the Don Army, but whether the insurgents would submit to his command was uncertain. Up to that point the politics of most Cossack rebels were still colored by revolutionary ideology. Although they hated the Bolsheviks, they still distrusted the Cossack elite that had been associated with Kaledin's regime. Still, many of the rebels held at least some reverence for Cossack traditions. That nostalgia, combined with the need to better organize their growing insurrection, compelled the rebel leaders to accept Popov as commander of the burgeoning Don Army. The recognition of Popov's powers as field ataman would prove to be a defining moment in the rebellion as traditional Cossack organization, values and goals steadily took precedence over revolutionary ideals.

The change in command in the Don Army did not slow the momentum of the Cossack rebellion. Popov organized the army into three groups: the Northern Group, Trans-Don Group and the Southern Group. The latter group was the strongest and most important of these formations. On 6 May the Southern Group, led by Colonel S. V. Denisov, went on the offensive to finally recapture Novocherkassk. Its initial attack succeeded in taking the town, but a determined Bolshevik counterattack quickly threatened to rob them of their prize. Just when it appeared that the Cossacks might have to again withdraw from their capital, help suddenly—and unexpectedly—appeared when about 1,000 White soldiers descended on the town from west. This grizzled unit, led by Colonel M. G. Drozdovsky, was formed during the previous winter by enlisting volunteers from Russians serving on the Romanian Front. When they arrived in Novocherkassk, they were at the end of an epic 800-mile journey during which they battled Red Guards in Ukraine while sometimes cooperating with their nominal enemies, the Germans and Austrians. After nearly nine weeks of continuous marching, Drozdovsky and his men were probably relieved to finally link up with friendly units, and the Cossacks were undoubtedly delighted to see them. Together, the troops of Drozdovsky and Denisov held on to Novocherkassk. In the meantime, the German capture of Rostov forced the regional Red command that had been headquartered there to relocate to Tsaritsyn (Volgograd). Around the same time Podtelkov, the former leader of the Cossack MRC and present chairman of the Don Soviet Republic, was executed in the northern Don stanitsas while trying to recruit Cossack volunteers to help crush the anticommunist revolts. His violent end in the northern Don, whose population was typically the most receptive to socialist agitation, was a stark indication of the Cossacks' widespread disillusionment with the Soviet regime.[12]

Following the liberation of Novocherkassk, the recently formed Provisional Government of the Don relocated to there from Zaplavskaya. There, on 9 May, it issued a proclamation stating that its main objective was "to free the Don from the destructive rule of the Soviet Government and the Red Guards" while adding that it "will engage in no undertaking that goes beyond the borders of the Don." The provisional government also stated its intention to replace itself with a more permanent authority. For this task, army units in the field and the liberated stanitsas were instructed to send representatives to the capital to attend a "Krug for the Salvation of the Don."[13]

The Krug for the Salvation of the Don convened for a week beginning on 11 May. The krug might have been expected to adopt moderate, even progressive, resolutions; after all, most of delegates were elected by insurgents who had taken up arms under revolutionary slogans.[14] The outcome proved quite different as the assembly chose to turn back the clock, not just figuratively but also literally, by abolishing the Gregorian calendar adopted by the Bolsheviks and returning to Julian dates.[15] This drastic shift in attitudes was precipitated by the debate over electing an ataman. One of the proposed candidates for the post was General Pyotr Krasnov, the commander of the ill-fated expedition to restore the Provisional Government shortly after the October Revolution. Since his release by Trotsky on the promise to never again take up arms against the Soviet regime, Krasnov had returned to the Don and in the following months laid low at stanitsa Konstantinovskaya. Initially, he was unimpressed by the latest series of anti–Bolshevik uprisings in the Don and refused early offers from the insurgents to lead their army. Krasnov believed that a Cossack campaign against the Soviet regime would succeed only when the men shed the toxic influences of revolutionary ideology and returned to their traditional values and ways. This was the message in his address to the krug, given on 14 May, which deeply impressed his audience. Krasnov immediately became a frontrunner in the election for ataman; but the real question was not whether they would have him, but rather if he would have them.

Before he would consider becoming the next ataman, Krasnov demanded the krug to approve a constitution that would abolish the reforms implemented since March 1917 in favor of an authority that evoked a Cossack governing system not seen since the reign of

Peter the Great. The participation of the outlanders in this new host government, a concession granted by Kaledin to the non–Cossack population, was not to be reinstated. In keeping with the old tradition where atamans demanded absolute obedience during times of crisis, the new ataman, once elected, was to be entrusted with dictatorial powers. Although these conditions were adverse to the early spirit of the rebellion, the krug was too captivated by Krasnov to resist his demands. The assembly agreed to the proposed constitution and elevated the general to the post of ataman in a landslide election. The metamorphosis of the rebellion to a genuine counterrevolution within the borders of the Don was well underway.

Krasnov was forty-eight years old when he became the Don ataman. He had been born into a proud Cossack family and, like Kaledin, he was a graduate of the General Staff Academy.[16] In addition to his successful military career, Krasnov was also an eloquent writer, and as ataman he used this talent to inspire Cossacks by reminding them of a glorious—if often embellished—past in flamboyant announcements. For example, in his first proclamation he bestowed the lofty title of "All-Great Don Host" on his new realm.[17] Besides his swaggering rhetoric, another ingredient behind Krasnov's dynamic leadership was his political shrewdness. Indeed, his record as a counterrevolutionary, émigré and later collaborationist leader left many contemporaries and historians debating his ultimate objective: did he seek to create an independent Cossack state or was he, like the White generals, committed to driving the Bolsheviks from all of Russia? Based on his activities from 1918 to 1945, it seems likely that Krasnov's most cherished goal was the restoration of a non-communist, possibly federal Russia that would grant significant autonomy to Cossacks and even other minorities. But he was always careful not alienate any group by appearing too partisan. The spectacle which this created was best described by the historian George Brinkley, who wrote: "Upon assuming office, he [Krasnov] immediately demonstrated his remarkable talent for being simultaneously pro–Russian and a border state nationalist, a monarchist and a defender of the 'conquests of the revolution,' an ally of the Volunteer Army and a collaborator with the Germans. The contradictions which he personified caused no little confusion and resentment, but no man of his day was more successful at being all things to all men."[18] Krasnov's chameleon-like political strategy, combined with his charismatic qualities, proved successful in so far that it did not undercut the widespread enthusiasm for the rebellion in the Don Host. In a struggle where soldiers on every side were prone to bouts of listlessness, this counted for a lot. By the end of May, just a couple of weeks after his inauguration as ataman, the Don Army had ballooned to 17,000 men and was still rapidly growing.[19]

Although the troops of the Don Army had plenty of fervor at this stage, their operations were hobbled by their lack of military hardware. With Taganrog and Rostov under German occupation, the All-Great Don Host had no industrial base of its own. In order to obtain the rifles and arms they needed, the Cossacks had to go through the Germans. From the start, Krasnov recognized the Germans' valuable role in ejecting the Bolsheviks from the region and openly stated his desire for a continuation of the friendly relations between Teuton and Cossack.[20] In letters to Kaiser Wilhelm II—whom he addressed as "the Illustrious Monarch of Great Germany"—he requested weapon shipments in exchange for food and advantageous economic concessions in the Don. He also petitioned Berlin to recognize the independence of the All-Great Don Host. He closed one letter to the kaiser with the statement "A friendship cemented in bloodshed on common battlefields by the warlike Germans and the Cossacks is bound to evolve into a tremendous force in the struggle against our common enemies."[21]

While the Germans were hesitant to satisfy all of Krasnov's requests, they did send him substantial quantities of rifles, artillery, machines guns, munitions and cartridges from captured Russian stockpiles along the former Eastern Front.[22] Even with this support, the Don Army faced an uphill battle. By mid-summer of 1918, Krasnov had perhaps 40,000 men under arms, but the Bolsheviks had tens of thousands more troops fighting for them throughout South Russia.[23] Moreover, the Soviet government redoubled its efforts to tempt ordinary Cossacks from the counterrevolutionary fold. "Rise, toiling Cossacks, as one man," read one communist appeal, "and declare that you remain as before in fraternal union with the workers and peasants of Russia!"[24] Although local Bolshevik forces, during their occupation of stanitsas in the Don and Urals, had shown a lack of empathy towards the Cossacks, Sovnarkom made gestures to accommodate the Cossacks' cherished sense of identity. In a decree issued at the end of May, Sovnarkom announced a blueprint for its administration of the Cossack lands. Its plan would not only preserve the Cossack hosts as administrative units but also invited the "toiling Cossacks" to influence policy by attaching delegates to the commissariats.[25]

Krasnov understood that he was confronting a numerically superior enemy that was poised to attack on every front, including the psychological one, and that to succeed the Don Cossacks needed to enlist other allies who, unlike the Germans, were fully committed to the struggle against Bolshevism. At that time, South Russia was teeming with adventurers, guerrillas and separatists who for one reason or another refused to submit to Soviet rule. In the first half of summer 1918, Krasnov embarked on an ambitious mission to bring these disparate peoples together.

The Struggle for Unity

Considering that both Krasnov and Hetman Skoropadsky were eager to accept German support in their fight against Bolshevism, one might have expected them to establish warm relations. This, however, was not the case. The two Cossack leaders sparred bitterly over the delineation of the frontier between them; both claimed the vital industrial areas of Mariupol, Taganrog, Rostov and the Donets Basin. Krasnov, as was his wont, took to his pen to appeal to the kaiser since German forces were in a position to act as the final arbiter on such matters. Most of his objectives were realized in August 1918 when the Hetmanate government, probably due to German pressure, concluded a treaty with Novocherkassk which placed Taganrog, Rostov and much of the Donets Basin on the eastern side of the Ukraine—Don frontier. Still, this territorial agreement did not settle all differences between the Don ataman and Ukrainian hetman. Krasnov, like most Russians, still desired the reunification of Ukraine with a future non–Soviet Russia. Moreover, he also suspected that the hetman had designs on his southern neighbor, the Kuban Host.[26]

While the Don ataman detested his neighbor in Ukraine, he did attempt to forge a working partnership with other regional leaders to his south and east. One of Krasnov's early pet projects was to unite his Don Cossacks and their neighbors in the North Caucasus into a regional federation. His idea was not an original one; in November 1917 representatives of the Don, Kuban and Terek Cossacks, along with other Caucasian peoples, had agreed to combine their energies into a Union of the Southeast. That plan had never materialized since the participating groups became preoccupied with local threats to their power and were unable to assist each other.[27] In July 1918, Krasnov tried to resurrect the union by bringing the representatives from the same peoples together for a new conference in

Novocherkassk, but his proposal for a Don-Caucasian Federation went nowhere. A Kalmyk chieftain, Prince Danzan Tundutov, was the only leader willing to endorse the project.[28] A big reason behind the scheme's failure was the attitude of the Kuban Cossack politicians. Many of their constituents were Ukrainophone Cossacks who admired Skoropadsky and viewed Krasnov with suspicion. Rather than seek an arrangement with the Don Cossacks, the Kuban politicians instead dispatched a delegation to Kiev to forge closer ties with the Hetmanate.

The Kuban politicians' mission to Kiev that summer dispelled the hopes they had placed in Skoropadsky after it became apparent to them that the hetman lacked broad support and was utterly dependent on the Central Powers.[29] Yet, even without this revelation, close cooperation between the Kuban Cossacks and Ukrainians, Krasnov or anyone else at that point would have been difficult without the approval of the White generals. The Novo-Dmitrovskaya agreement from earlier that spring, of course, had subordinated the Kuban Cossack troops to the Volunteer Army command. The top brass of that army, starting with General Denikin, possessed the mindset of Great Russian patriots and regarded any quasi-separatist project, whether espoused by Krasnov, Skoropadsky or any representative council, as treachery. They could hardly be expected to remain passive bystansders and allow the Kuban leaders to reorient their movement towards such ends. Denikin and his colleagues were determined to uphold the White slogan "Russia One and Indivisible"; a policy that would alienate many potential allies in their anti–Bolshevik campaign and cause them considerable trouble with the Cossacks.[30]

Originally, the senior generals of the Volunteer Army had got along well with the former Don ataman, Kaledin. The same could not be said for his successor, Krasnov, whose relations with the Volunteer commanders were rocky from the start. Their differences became apparent when they first met in the southern Don stanitsa of Manychskaya at the end of May 1918. Denikin, always looking ahead to his goal of driving Bolshevism from all of Russia, was eager to take control of the Don Army for that purpose. Unsurprisingly, Krasnov was unwilling to undercut his position by subordinating his forces to Denikin's command. At that moment, they were only able to agree to an arrangement where Krasnov would provide the Volunteer Army with funds and a share of the arms he was receiving from the Germans. In exchange, the White generals pledged to defend the southern Don from the Red forces in the Kuban and Caucasus, thereby allowing the Don Cossacks to concentrate their troops against threats to their north and east.[31]

The interactions between the Don Cossack leaders and the Volunteer Army command did not improve in the months following the Manychskaya meeting.[32] A major source of their discord was their relationship with the Germans. Although he readily accepted German weapons through Krasnov, Denikin remained openly hostile to Russia's enemy in the world war and continued to align his force with the Allies. Moreover, instead of showing appreciation for Krasnov's material support, he belittled the Don ataman for bargaining with the invaders. His pro–Allied rhetoric had not gone unnoticed by German liaison officers, and before long they were urging Krasnov to suspend weapon deliveries to the Volunteers.[33] The Don ataman resisted this demand, though he remained thoroughly irritated by Denikin's hypocrisy of condemning his dealings with the Germans while accepting the arms he obtained through them. "Yes, yes, gentlemen, the Volunteer Army is clean and undefiled," the ataman declared cynically at one point. "But I, the Don Ataman, take the dirty German bullets and shells, wash them in the quiet Don, and give them clean to the Volunteer Army. The entire shame for this matter rests with me."[34]

Although Denikin never forgave Krasnov for his Germanophile policy, other leading

White generals were more pragmatic. General Alekseyev, while regarding the Don ataman's pact with the enemy as distasteful, urged Denikin to relax his criticism of Krasnov in light of their dependency on the weapons provided by the Germans.[35] The dilemma confronting the Don leadership was also recognized by General Lukomsky, who attended a plenary session of the Don Krug at the end of August 1918 as an observer for the Volunteer Army. The German command in Rostov was also eyeing the proceedings and dispatched a telegram that was read to the gathered delegates. In no uncertain terms, it warned them that the nearby German army of occupation would continue to send rifles and munitions to the Don only if the krug retained Krasnov as ataman. Heeding this virtual ultimatum, the krug confirmed Krasnov as ataman, and even Lukomsky admitted that "the decision taken by the Krug was the only possible one at the time."[36]

Outside of diplomacy, the Don and Volunteer leaders had plenty of other disagreements. While Krasnov employed authoritarian methods to issue conservative legislation, Denikin preferred to dodge the major political and social dilemmas of the day. He felt that these questions could only be decided by a future elected national assembly—though not necessarily the Constituent Assembly. His only definite program was the restoration of a united Russia. In those few instances where Denikin did bother to enact legislation, he proved to have a more progressive outlook than Krasnov. Notably, he only abolished the laws issued since the Bolshevik coup in November 1917 whereas the Don ataman tended to invalidate all laws and reforms undertaken since the liberal-democratic revolution of March 1917.[37] Subsequently, each group attracted the dissidents of the other. Don Cossacks who had endured the hardships of the Icy March but were awed by the dynamism of the All-Great Don Host abandoned the Volunteers and joined Krasnov's forces. At the same time, liberal Cossack politicians, as well as Great Russian patriots such as Drozdovsky who had fought with the Don Army, flocked to Denikin's banner.[38]

A final item of long-lasting disagreement between the Don ataman and the Volunteer Army command was centered on strategy. At the Manychskaya meeting, both parties had their own plans for future campaigns: Krasnov wanted to launch an offensive towards the Red stronghold of Tsaritsyn while Denikin desired the liberation of the Kuban territory. Each had good reasons for embarking on campaigns that went in opposite directions. By taking Tsaritsyn, the Don Army would effectively cut off Red forces in Astrakhan and the Caucasus from communication with Moscow. On the other hand, Denikin's desire to liberate the Kuban was necessitated by the fact that at this stage the Kuban Cossacks probably comprised over half of the Volunteer Army. For them, freeing their own stanitsas from what they viewed as the rule of the outlanders was a much higher priority than quashing Bolshevism in other parts of Russia. Another consideration was Denikin's desire to establish his own base from where he could draw recruits and reduce his dependence on Krasnov. Finally, it must also be pointed out that the Red Army in the Northern Caucasus, with over 80,000 men, presented a real menace to the Don. Needless to say, it would have been risky for the Don Cossacks and Volunteers to throw all their strength against Tsaritsyn while leaving such a significant threat poised against their rear.[39]

Instead of forging a binding alliance, the consultations between the Don Cossacks and the Volunteer Army at Manychskaya and in follow-up meetings were more akin to a parting of ways. While Krasnov did provide invaluable support in the form of arms and funds to the Volunteer Army in the latter half of 1918, both he and Denikin largely concentrated on the pursuit of their own strategic goals. Fortunately for them, the enemy forces they engaged during the coming months were frequently more poorly-coordinated than their own.

The Liberation of the Don Host

At the time of Krasnov's election as ataman in May 1918, his government controlled only the southern districts of the Don Host. With the German army of occupation effectively protecting the host's western frontier, the surging Don Army directed its energies against the Red Army clinging to the northern and eastern areas of the Don. After their recent retreat from Ukraine and the spate of uprisings in their midst, however, the Red formations were unable to find secure footing on their Southern Front. Their disarray enabled the Don Army to advance during the following weeks so that Krasnov was only slightly exaggerating that summer when he boasted to the kaiser that the Don Cossacks had freed "nine-tenths" of their homeland.[40]

The incorporation of the various insurgencies in the Don under the aegis of the All-Great Don Host was not always a smooth process. The Novocherkassk government was adamant that all districts under its control must conform to an administration structured under local atamans. This was a bitter prescription for those rebels, especially those not of Cossack origin, who had been fighting for their own locally-defined revolutionary ideals. Nonetheless, the Don Army was unwilling to accept anything less than complete subordination. Stanitsas which refused to disband their soviets in favor of atamans were paid a visit by punitive detachments or, if they were near a navigable waterway, by gunboats. Similar treatment was meted out to those stanitsas which preferred to declare their neutrality in the conflict. Coercion was also employed against individuals. Upon joining the insurgency, the first act of the stanitsa leaders was to mobilize the entire male population between the ages of 17 and 50. Those Cossacks who shirked these orders were declared traitors and risked execution. An even more inglorious punishment awaited those who joined the ranks of the Red Army: they were expelled from the Cossack estate and stripped of their property. In some stanitsas, up to a quarter of all Cossack males were purged from the registries. On the other hand, hundreds of non–Cossacks, including even outlanders, who fought in the Don Army were formally granted Cossack status by the government in Novocherkassk. Not since the seventeenth century did non–Cossacks have such ample opportunities to become members of the Don Host.[41]

Krasnov's compulsory measures, regardless of their justification, were so successful in restoring most of the Don lands to his government that he soon set his sights on prizes just outside the host's traditional borders. In an appeal to the kaiser, the Don ataman requested German assistance in acquiring the cities of Tsaritsyn, Kamyshin and Voronezh on the basis that "they are strategically important for the Don."[42] This ambition clashed with the earlier promise made by the Don Provisional Government that its army would not campaign beyond the borders of the host.[43] Moreover, the inclusion of these cities into the All-Great Don Host would only further increase its non–Cossack population, to whose sensibilities Krasnov's regime appeared indifferent.

Unlike their ataman, most Don Cossacks had no desire to proceed beyond the borders of the Don. They naively believed that their struggle against the Soviet republic could be ended once the Red Army was pushed outside of the borders of their homeland. Subsequently, they concentrated on completing the liberation of the Don host by attempting to dislodge units of the Ninth Red Army from its northern districts.[44] Some of the most serious fighting on that front pitted Cossack against Cossack. The poorer Cossacks in the northern Don had a tradition of defying orders from their more prosperous brothers in the south, and in some areas that habit continued into the summer of 1918. At the start of the anticommunist rebellion, Lieutenant-Colonel Mironov, the Don Cossack revolutionary who made an unsuccessful attempt to capture Kaledin a year earlier, led a small contingent of about 160 Cossacks to fight with the Red Army in the district of Ust-Medveditsa. By mid–June, his detachment had grown to nearly 4,000 men but they were poorly equipped. While nearly all Red troops at the front suffered from supply-shortages, the local Soviet commanders were especially hesitant to send aid Mironov due to his background as a Cossack and tsarist officer. Nonetheless, in mid–July he counterattacked and inflicted heavy losses upon the Don Army units pressing against sector. Although the Don Army quickly regained its footing and forced Mironov to retreat, the operation had exhibited his talents as a field commander. In the meantime, the Novocherkassk government, fearful that a brazen leader such as Mironov might attract the fickle loyalties of the young Cossack soldiers, tried to dampen his appeal by reminding Cossacks that anyone who joined Mironov would be subject to expulsion from the estate.[45]

By late summer, the Cossacks in the Don Army found themselves combating an increasingly numerous, better organized and more expertly-led adversary than they had routed in the spring. Since the beginning of the Don insurgency in early April, Trotsky, as Commissar for War, had been busy introducing reforms to correct the glaring weaknesses of the fledgling Red Army. At first the new revolutionary army was intended to be a volunteer force of workers and peasants, but a lack of recruits soon compelled the Soviet government to resort to conscription for all male citizens between 18 and 40 years of age.[46] At the same time, the democratic system of soldier committees and elected commanders was terminated. In its place, former officers from the tsarist army, once labeled as class enemies by Bolshevik propagandists, were appointed to command Red Army units. To ensure their loyalty, Trotsky had these "military specialists" shadowed by armed commissars and threatened reprisals against their families if they defected to the Whites.[47] Before the end of the summer, these drastic measures began turning the tide against the anti–Bolshevik forces on the Soviet republic's Eastern Front. Although the reforms were slower to be adopted on the Southern Front, the mass mobilization and improved logistics of the Red forces became noticeable there as well. In late August 1918, the Tenth Red Army launched a counteroffensive west of Tsaritsyn which forced the Don Cossacks to fall back. Although Krasnov contained the attack by transferring units eastward from his northern front,[48] the experience convinced him of the need to decisively defeat the Soviet forces before they acquired any more strength.

The target which Krasnov had in mind was the Red stronghold of Tsaritsyn. That city, positioned astride the shortest overland route between the Don and Volga Rivers, was a communication hub for South Russia. Since the Don uprising, Tsaritsyn had acquired additional importance to the Bolsheviks since it guarded the river and rail routes that served as Moscow's last direct links with Red forces based in Astrakhan and the North Caucasus. Aside from this military significance, the Volga was also a vital mercantile waterway through which the Soviet republic could import oil from Baku, cotton from Central Asia and grain from the Kuban. These considerations were not lost on the Don ataman, and he calculated that the capture of Tsaritsyn might deliver a crushing blow upon his enemy.[49]

To drum up support for his Tsaritsyn offensive and other military campaigns outside the Don Host, Krasnov deployed his formidable oratory and writing skills. His efforts paid off in September when the Don Krug approved his plan to continue the army's advance to cities, railroad junctions and other objectives of strategic value which lay just beyond the host's borders.[50] In accordance with this decision, the Don Army soon began a general advance against the four Red armies arrayed against it. On the northern front, the Don Cossacks encountered stiff resistance from the Seventh and Eighth Red Armies defending the approaches to Voronezh. Further to the east, the Ninth Red Army fell back as it tried to hold the zone between Voronezh and the Volga River.[51]

The most critical sector, however, was in the vicinity of Tsaritsyn, which was garrisoned by the Tenth Red Army. Wresting the city from that army would be no easy task since those in charge of its defense, Bolshevik Party stalwarts Josef Stalin and Kliment Voroshilov, had hoarded reinforcements and supplies designated for the Soviet Southern Front.[52] Moreover, the Red troops had also ringed the city with barricades and trenches; the latter having been dug by bourgeoisie women they had pressed into hard labor.[53] But as the Don Cossacks fought their way to the edge of Tsaritsyn in late September, the local Red command was in serious disarray as Stalin and Voroshilov refused to obey the ex-tsarist general recently appointed by Trotsky as commander-in-chief of the Southern Front.[54] Writing of the situation there in a telegram to Moscow, the war commissar complained, "We have a colossal superiority in forces but total anarchy at the top."[55] Soviet leaders eventually endorsed Trotsky's reorganization, but in the meantime the Cossacks came dangerously close to seizing Tsaritsyn. The factor which prevented them from taking that prize was the unexpected arrival of the 15,000 strong Red "Steel Division." After a grueling march of 400 miles from the North Caucasus, where it was supposed to be on guard against Denikin's army, the Steel Division fell upon the Don Cossacks besieging Tsaritsyn and ended the immediate threat to the city.

The fighting between the Don Cossacks and the Red Armies on the Southern Front continued into the following winter. Although the Don Army managed to encircle Tsaritsyn again in December and for a third time in January 1919, the city, celebrated by Bolshevik propagandists as "the Red Verdun," held out.[56] Krasnov, then, was denied a great triumph on the Volga, but the efforts of his Don Cossacks there and in the northern Don had nonetheless tied down considerable Red reinforcements and supplies at the expense of Soviet armies on other fronts. In doing so, they created opportunities for other anti–Bolshevik forces to exploit, including the Volunteer Army which marched against Soviet forces in the North Caucasus that were several times more numerous than itself.

The Second Kuban Campaign

While Krasnov directed his forces toward the northern and eastern districts of the Don Host and beyond, Denikin sent his army in the opposite direction. Although the destruction of the Bolshevik regime remained his foremost goal, he decided to postpone an advance towards the Soviet heartland in order to establish a base in the Kuban which he would be able call his own. It is likely that there was another consideration behind his decision. In his memoirs, Denikin admitted that by this time the Kuban Cossacks numbered "about half" of his army. Although he claimed that he felt a moral obligation to liberate the homeland cherished by so many of his troops, he probably doubted whether the Kuban troops would willingly march in any other direction. In other words, another campaign in the Kuban was the only option available to him as long as he wished to hold his army together.[57]

During its brief sojourn in the southern Don, Denikin had reorganized the Volunteer Army into three divisions consisting of five infantry and eight cavalry regiments. The strength of his entire corps was at most 9,000 men with 21 guns; a seemingly insignificant force against the estimated 80,000 Red troops spread throughout the North Caucasus region.[58]

Although the Red Army of the North Caucasus, later renamed the Eleventh Red Army in October 1918, enjoyed a vast numerical superiority over its opponent, it was not nearly as strong as it appeared. Since it was virtually cut-off from Moscow by fighting to its north, its supplies were mostly limited to whatever it could scavenge from the munition dumps leftover from operations on the Caucasian Front. Another outcome of its relative isolation was that it had not adopted the centralizing military reforms imposed by Trotsky. Throughout most of the summer and autumn 1918, the operations of Red forces in the North Caucasus were directed by men from lower ranks who were nearly as inimical to rival Red commanders as they were their White opponents. This, along with the diversionary operations against other potential enemies, such as the German army of occupation just to the north in Rostov to the scattered bands of Kuban and Terek Cossack guerrillas in the Caucasian foothills, prevented the Red Army of the North Caucasus from bringing its immense manpower to bear down on the little Volunteer Army.[59]

The Second Kuban Campaign opened in late June 1918 when the Volunteers, advancing in several columns, attacked and defeated a Red force numbering close to 10,000 troops in the vicinity of Torgovaya. The Whites' occupation of that station immediately severed the North Caucasus Red Army's last rail link with Soviet forces to its north. From there, the Volunteers advanced to Bielaya Glina, where they crushed another sizeable force of Red troops. In that battle, they captured 5,000 prisoners, some of whom they press-ganged into their units, thus ending the "volunteer" character of their army. This approach to acquiring reinforcements, though new at the time, would soon become a common practice for the White armies in South Russia. On 15 July, the Volunteer Army seized the railway junction of Tikhoretskaya.[60] Amid this string of victories, the Whites enhanced their strength through the capture of rolling stock, commandeering of armored trains and an expanded recruiting pool. The most valuable addition to their ranks were the local Kuban Cossacks who joined the army once it reached their stanitsas. Disgruntled with their recent exposure to Soviet rule, this element infused the Volunteers with a renewed anti–Bolshevik fervor that would propel the army for the next several months.

Once Denikin's force was within striking distance of Yekaterinodar, Red commanders in other parts of the Kuban finally began to take the threat posed by the Volunteer Army seriously. At the time, the greatest menace to the Volunteer Army's position was a conglomeration of Red units on its northwestern flank. This force, numbering about 30,000 men, was led by a young Cossack subaltern, Ivan Sorokin, and was deployed as a screen against any incursion by the Germans or anti–Soviet Don Cossacks in the districts south of Rostov. To block Denikin's advance, Sorokin marched his troops to Korenovskaya, where the two sides engaged each other in nine days of grueling fighting. Throughout most of that time, the outcome hung in the balance, but ultimately the Reds were put to flight, opening the road to Yekaterinodar. The first Cossack cavalrymen galloped into that town on 15 August while Denikin, along with representatives of the Kuban government, made their formal entry on the next day.[61] The Kuban capital, which had acquired a "mystical significance" since the failure of the First Kuban Campaign, was theirs at last.[62]

The fall of Yekaterinodar was a joyous occasion for the Volunteer Army and the Kuban Cossacks, and their triumph was commemorated in a Te Deum ceremony in the town's cathedral. But even before the elation of that victory wore off, relations between the two parties chilled. Although the Kuban leader, Ataman Filimonov, assured Denikin that his people understood the importance of maintaining their unity with the Russian motherland, other prominent Kuban figures, particularly those of Ukrainian background, frowned upon the White generals as another set of outlanders. They were eager to claim supreme authority for their government in the Kuban Host and desired to be free of interference from non–Cossacks, whether Red or White. Such an outcome was rightly feared by the outlanders of the host, against whom many Cossacks wanted to exact reprisals for their supposed Bolshevik sympathies. On the other hand, Denikin intended to use the Kuban as a base from which he could build an army strong enough to capture Moscow. To do this, he needed stability and the support of both the Cossacks and the outlanders. Subsequently, he yearned to find some middle ground that would be acceptable to the two groups.[63]

Another issue which caused rifts among the White allies was their military arrangements. With the dark days of the First Kuban Campaign and the Soviet occupation nearly behind them, a faction of Kuban Cossack politicians immediately began agitating for the abrogation of the Novo-Dmitrovskaya agreement that had subordinated their soldiers to the Volunteer Army command. Their goal was to reestablish the Kuban Army and, ultimately, secure the independence of the Kuban Host. Since Kuban Cossacks comprised no less than half of the ranks of the Volunteer Army, the proposal to form them into a separate force threatened to deprive the White generals of considerable manpower. Not surprisingly, Denikin resisted this and other separatist projects with fierce determination.[64]

Although the capture of Yekaterinodar exposed fissures between Kuban Cossack politicians and Russian officers, their combined forces continued to march from one military triumph to the next. The day prior to the fall of the Kuban capital, a Volunteer column seized Timashevskaya in the northwest Kuban. Towards the end of August, the Volunteer Army captured the Black Sea port of Novorossiysk.[65] By then substantial Red forces existed only in the southeastern districts of the Kuban Host. In addition to the Volunteer troops being deployed against them, these remnants of the Red Army of the North Caucasus also had to contend with an exceptionally brazen band of Kuban Cossack insurgents who seemingly appeared out of nowhere and seized the provincial capital of Stavropol.[66]

The leader of that Kuban Cossack guerrilla detachment was Andrey Shkuro, a thirty-one-year-old colonel who had led cavalry raids behind enemy lines on the Eastern Front.[67] Now, in Russia's civil war, he was using those same hit-and-run tactics against the Red Army of the North Caucasus. Through a combination of personal charisma and the promise of loot, he had grown his band from a ten-man outfit to a force of several thousand Cossacks in the course of a few months. Nicknamed the "Wolves," Shkuro's pack quickly became notorious for numerous offenses as it rampaged through the North Caucasus region. Nonetheless, this unruly horde scored an impressive victory in July when it occupied Stavropol after persuading the Red commander there to surrender rather than endure a heavy artillery bombardment. Shkuro, in fact, had no artillery and when the Bolsheviks realized his bluff, they regrouped and laid siege to Stavropol. In the meantime, Shkuro, having learned of the Volunteer Army's recent victories, recognized Denikin's authority and appealed for his aid.[68] The Volunteer commander was initially impressed by Shkuro's accomplishments, but he changed his tune after he became familiar with the adventurer's behavior. Shkuro's willingness to employ any means—including terror—in the struggle against Bolshevism was repulsive to the White generals who still adhered to the Russian officers' code of honor.[69] Nonetheless, Denikin quickly learned that Shkuro was no ordinary subordinate whom he could reprimand or dismiss as he saw fit. The insurgent leader's exploits had earned him legendary status among the Kuban Cossacks, including members of the Rada who later recommended his promotion to the rank of general in December 1918.[70] Ultimately, the handling of rowdy Cossack heroes like Shkuro became another divisive issue between their Cossack supporters and the senior officers of the Volunteer Army who desperately wanted to enforce higher standards of discipline.

Shkuro and his followers, with the help of a relief detachment from the Volunteer Army led by General Sergey Ulagay, managed to hold Stavropol into October 1918. The surviving forces of the Red Army of the North Caucasus, now renamed the Eleventh Red Army, were regrouping in the vicinity of that town in an attempt to breakout of the Kuban and make for Tsaritsyn. During this phase of the Bolsheviks' military campaign, droves of outlanders, after hearing of indiscriminate hangings and property confiscations against the non–Cossack population in White-occupied districts, readily enlisted with the Reds. As a result, the Eleventh Red Army was more than able to replace its earlier losses in manpower as its strength swelled to nearly 125,000 men. Despite this growth, the army continued to operate in the partisan tradition and stonewalled any military specialists. On 23 October the Reds struck northward and soon drove the White defenders out of Stavropol. The fighting around Stavropol extended into days and then weeks. A cavalry division led by General Wrangel, who was a recent addition to the Volunteer Army, recaptured the town in mid–November, but the Reds were only decisively defeated when their crack formations were shattered later that month. The losses incurred in this prolonged engagement, in addition to a typhus epidemic that ravaged its ranks, dealt the Eleventh Red Army a blow from which it never recovered. Over the next two months, residual units of that force and the nearby Twelfth Red Army continued to fight on as they were pushed further east against the shore of the Caspian Sea, but these units no longer represented a grave menace to the Volunteer Army. Short of supplies, lacking a proper chain of command and still suffering from typhus, these two Red Armies crumbled under the incessant White blows. Those Red troops who did not desert and avoided capture were eventually forced to retreat through the salty flatlands along the Caspian's western shore to Astrakhan, during the course of which many froze, starved or succumbed to disease.[71]

As elsewhere, Cossacks fought on both sides in the bloody battles in the North Caucasus. Although by mid–1918 the political sympathies in most Kuban stanitsas were definitely trending toward the Whites, a few Cossacks served with the Soviet forces until the bitter end. One outstanding leader among the "Red Cossacks" in the Kuban was Ivan Kochubey, an illiterate but daring cavalry veteran of the Caucasian Front who formed a guerrilla detachment which engaged Shkuro's Wolves and other White formations. Kochubey's career as a Red partisan chief is symbolic of the fortunes of the entire Red Army of the North Caucasus. After some initial successes in early 1918, Kochubey's band found itself in desperate straits by the end of the year. Short of food, clothes and other supplies, his contingent retreated through the northeast Caucasus alongside the bulk of the Soviet forces. By the time they reached the western shore of the Caspian Sea, their band was reduced to just fourteen men and Kochubey was stricken with typhus. Too weakened by his illness to attempt the trek northward to Astrakhan, he was taken prisoner by his White pursuers.

In captivity, Kochubey was given medical treatment and began to recover his physical strength. During his convalescence, White officers attempted to flip the Red Cossack leader to their side by offering him amnesty and the rank of colonel in their forces. But his steadfast refusal to serve the Whites, even as he was sent to the gallows, vaulted him into revolutionary martyrdom.[72]

The Caucasian Quagmire

The Volunteer Army's drive against the Eleventh and Twelfth Red Armies in the winter of 1918–19 brought it into the northeastern region of the Caucasus. There Denikin's troops crossed into one of the most ethnically-diverse locales not just in Russia but also in the world. Amid the jagged peaks and fertile valleys of the Caucasus Mountains, various ethnicities and tribes, many of them descendants of armies and migrations that had passed through the area centuries ago, battled the elements and each other to survive from one generation to the next. For most, fighting was a way of life. Men always carried a dagger or sidearm. "Better without trousers than without a weapon," went a local saying.[73] The rugged terrain, coupled with the natives' tradition of resisting outside domination, made the region difficult for any power to control. Indeed, the tsarist government, despite having supported Cossack settlements in the region since the sixteenth century, only completed its subjugation of the northeast Caucasus in 1871 after an intense struggle that spanned over a half-century.[74]

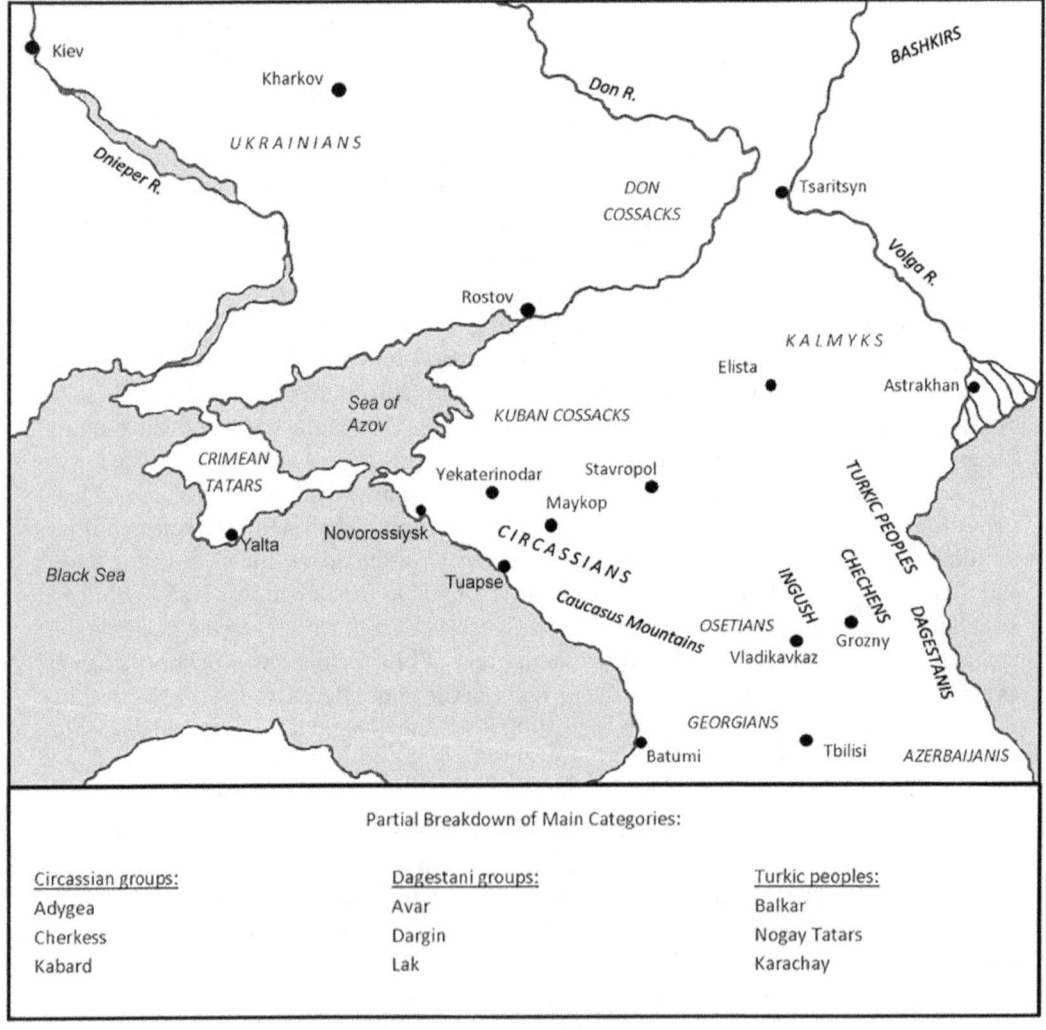

The Peoples of the North Caucasus, circa 1900.

Numerically, the Terek Cossacks who inhabited the Caucasian valleys were far more disadvantaged than their brother Cossacks in the Don or Kuban. On the eve of the world war, they possessed a population of 268,000, which meant that they comprised slightly more than 20 percent of the host's 1,200,000 inhabitants. There was also a non–Cossack Russian population of about equal size in the host, but these outlanders were not any friendlier towards Cossacks than land-hungry peasants in other parts of Russia. The rest of the host's population was a collection of natives, many of whom belonged to the so-called Mountain Peoples. This category was comprised of several ethnic groups, including Chechens, Ossetians, Kabardans, Ingush and Kumuks. Although many of these groups practiced Islam—the majority of Ossetians being the notable exception—in general they lacked cultural, linguistic or social ties. From the Russian perspective, the most problematic of these highlanders were the Chechens, with a population of just under a quarter-million, who in the previous century had heeded the calls of their imams to wage fierce, jihadist guerrilla campaigns against the Russian invaders. The latter had proven themselves equally vicious while imposing their authority over the region by systematically destroying the natives' crops and flattening their *aouls* with artillery. The end of the conflict in 1871 brought little relief to the defeated Chechens and other natives as they found themselves displaced from the productive lowlands by new Cossack settlements and estates. For the next two generations, they eked out a living by renting land from wealthy Cossack landowners or cultivating terraced fields hewn into the mountain slopes. Naturally, these people, having a tradition of blood feud, eagerly awaited an opportunity to wreak vengeance on their Cossack oppressors and reclaim the fertile valleys that had once belonged to them.[75]

After the tsarist order was swept away by revolution in March 1917, the Terek region, despite its volatile mix of ethnic rivalries, remained initially tranquil. Later that month, British correspondent Morgan Philips Price, who was passing through the area, was heartened by the sight of multiethnic committees peaceably settling outstanding questions of their local administration. "Cossacks were fraternizing with mountain Circassians," he observed, "and the enemies of centuries were now united under the banner of liberty, equality and fraternity."[76] Such cooperation, however, proved to be of short endurance, particularly at the regional level. As in other hosts, the Terek Cossacks formed a government of their own headed by an ataman elected from their ranks. Meanwhile, the outlanders established soviets though throughout most of 1917 these were dominated by socialists of the moderate variety. The various highlanders, on the other hand, proclaimed an autonomous government for themselves, the Union of Mountain Peoples, that would include the nearby region of Dagestan.

Each of these three general groups—the Cossacks, the outlanders and the highlanders—were on uneasy terms. At the heart of their discord was land: the Terek Cossacks wanted to keep the generous allotments that had been granted to them by the tsarist government while the rural outlanders wanted to increase their holdings through land appropriations. Certain native groups, particularly the Chechens, simply wanted to regain their lost ancestral lands. In the autumn of 1917, with the outlanders becoming more radical and vocal in their demands for land reforms, the Terek Cossack leaders sought an alliance with the Union of Mountain Peoples in their belief that the natives were less of an immediate threat. In early November the two groups combined their administrations into a joint Terek-Mountain government. But events in the Terek Host quickly took a tumultuous turn the following month when the Chechens and Ingush, having grown tired of waiting for a revolutionary government to return their ancestral lands, suddenly launched a guerrilla war. In the following weeks, the insurgents laid waste to stanitsas and even made nocturnal raids against Vladikavkaz. These attacks quickly turned the bulk of the Cossacks against their native allies and their leaders. In January 1918, this backlash cost the Terek ataman, M. A. Karaulov, his life after he was assassinated by Cossacks livid over his recent proposal to work out a compromise with the disgruntled highlanders. As the dysfunctional Terek-Mountain government dissolved amid the unrest, the Cossacks and outlanders who found themselves on the receiving end of the natives' raids began coordinating their defensive measures. They also sought assistance from Russian troops leaving the Caucasian Front. The soldiers, many of them radicalized, agreed to help on the condition that Soviet authority would be recognized in the Terek region.[77]

With the support of the demobilized soldiers, the Terek People's Soviet Socialist Republic was formed mainly from the Russian population, meaning Cossacks and outlanders, with minimal input from natives. It included moderate socialists in addition to Bolsheviks. This government managed to weather the upheaval unleashed by the Chechen and Ingush raiders, but it began to splinter shortly after those two groups scaled back their attacks in the spring of 1918. Amid the lull in fighting, the impatient outlanders made preparations to nationalize the land, a decision which incited the Cossacks to rebellion. As the Cossacks began to spar with the outlanders that summer, they also came under renewed attacks by the Ingush, who still hoped to seize the Cossacks' prime farmland for themselves. The Terek, by then, was torn by a multiple-sided civil war that threw the entire region into disarray.

Despite the fact that they were literally surrounded by enemies, the Terek Cossack rebels enjoyed some early successes. In July, they were joined by the Kabardans whose land holdings, which were second in size only to those held by the Cossacks, were also targeted for expropriation. On 2 August the rebels captured Vladikavkaz along with the chairman of the Terek People's Soviet Socialist Republic, whom they quickly executed. To escape a similar fate, other Bolshevik personnel, including a representative from Soviet Russia, Grigory Ordzhonikidze, sought refuge in the mountains. There they enlisted the support of the Ingush by promising to return to them the lands they had lost to the Cossacks. The Ingush, reinvigorated by the Bolshevik offer, stormed and seized Vladikavkaz just a fortnight after the Cossacks had occupied the town. The Bolsheviks, now with Ordzhonikidze at their head, returned to the Terek capital and established a new soviet regime that was intended to be much stricter than the one it had replaced.[78]

Throughout the rest of the year, bitter fighting raged in the Terek region. On one side were the Bolsheviks, supported by soldiers of the nearby Twelfth Red Army as well as Chechens, Ingush and outlanders who were motivated by their desire to seize Cossack lands. Opposing them were the Terek Cossacks, SRs and some of the more affluent natives of the region, such as the Kabardans and Ossetians. At one point, by Denikin's estimate, the anti–Bolshevik forces in the Terek boasted about 10,000 fighters.[79] In September, the White commander tried to lift their spirits by dispatching an airman to them with a message promising assistance, but the Volunteer Army was still too far away to offer direct aid. By December, the Cossack rebels were exhausted, demoralized and their units were breaking up. However, just as local victory appeared within grasp for the Twelfth Red Army, the approach of Denikin's troops placed it in an untenable position and forced its withdrawal from the Terek.[80] In the meantime, Ordzhonikidze and other Bolshevik leaders again fled into the mountains with their Chechen and Ingush allies to continue the guerrilla campaign and bide their time.[81]

Despite their support from the Terek Cossacks and some native peoples, the Whites' advance through the Terek and nearby Dagestan was a not an easy one. "In every aoul, in every cottage was an ambush against our troops," Denikin wrote of the combat in Ingush districts.[82] For the Terek Cossacks, such hostile elements always seemed near and ready to pounce at an opportue moment. Moreso than the Don and Kuban Cossacks, they recognized their dependence on Denikin's forces to maintain order in their unstable homeland. As a result, they were less imbued with separatist ideology than their brothers on the Don or Kuban, but many of them still dreamt of acquiring an army of their own.[83]

The Political Minefield

The Whites' victories in the Terek and North Caucasus brought them into contact with the Georgians, Azeris and Armenians, all of whom had been Russian subjects and proclaimed their independence after 1917. Like many ethnic groups in other parts of the former Russian Empire, the Georgians and Azeris regarded Denikin's army as a threat to their new-found freedom.[84] They were not the only peoples to view the White movement with apprehension. Many peasants feared that the White generals sympathized with the gentry on the land question. Others were concerned that the Whites would uphold the institutions which gave some groups, such as the Cossacks, disproportionate political and economic leverage over certain regions. Denikin, for his part, would have liked to put such issues on hold and defer them to a future all-Russian national government. Initially, he believed that patriotic appeals alone would be sufficient to rally the masses to his banner. But it soon became apparent to him that the peasants and plenty of others wanted to know what concept of Russia they were fighting for. Did the Whites desire an autocracy or democracy for the country? What was their agrarian policy? Which, if any, freedoms won during the revolution would be preserved? Was Russia to be governed as a unitary or federalized state?

True to his policy of non-predetermination for Russia's political future, Denikin avoided definite statements on some of these pressing issues. In regards to Russia's future form of government, he simply called for an "all-Russian legislative body" but avoided any more specifics.[85] He was even less transparent on the land question, which was the most imperative question as far as the peasantry was concerned. Behind the scenes, his political advisors made two attempts to formulate a land policy during the course of the civil war. But the White leaders, having realized that any solution which satisfied the peasants' land hunger would alienate the landlords and vice versa, ultimately refrained from announcing any legislation.[86]

Denikin did endeavor to offer more definite answers on civic rights and the separatist movements in the borderlands, but the options available to him were complicated by his dependence on the Cossacks. In a provisional constitution which he hoped would lay the foundations of a stable administration, he guaranteed equal civil rights for all citizens "irrespective of nationality, social status and religion." But for the various ethnicities and outlanders in White-occupied lands, that assurance was diminished by a declaration in the same article that "the special rights and privileges enjoyed by the Cossacks shall be held inviolable."[87] This contradictory proclamation effectively dispelled the hopes of outlanders and various natives that the White generals might promote land reforms that would equalize their holdings with those of the Cossacks. For their part, Denikin and his staff wanted to avoid the appearance of being too favorable towards the Cossacks, but they could not escape the reality that the Cossacks were a valuable source of soldiers for the army which they hoped to lead into Moscow. Indeed, throughout much of the civil war the skilled Cossack horsemen proved invaluable to the Volunteer Army as they provided superior mobility and shock effect which their more numerous opponents were unable to match. Since no other group could field a similar pool of equestrians, the Whites could not risk alienating their Cossack allies.[88]

Under these circumstances, the Kuban Cossacks were given considerable license in their treatment of non-Cossacks despite Denikin's plea to Filimonov for the Kuban government to show restraint towards the outlander population.[89] In general, the Cossacks paid little heed to the Volunteers' commander-in-chief. Following the liberation of Yekaterinodar, the Kuban government held new elections for the Rada from which the outlanders, with minor exceptions, were barred from casting ballots.[90] When the outlander problem was raised during sessions of the new Rada, Cossack delegates discussed the possibility of their expulsion. At least one fringe politician even suggested their extermination. Amazingly, the White generals, who someday hoped to establish their authority over the greater part of Russia that was overwhelmingly non-Cossack, do not appear to have made any formal objection to this venomous rhetoric or the poor treatment of the outlanders in general.[91]

As it was, the White generals had enough problems with the Kuban Cossacks without injecting themselves into the outlander controversy. Especially troublesome was the separatist agitation that intensified among Kuban political leaders in the latter half of 1918. This movement gained momentum for two reasons. One was the considerable autonomy which had been afforded to the Cossacks by the old regime. Since the tsars allowed the Cossacks to fight in their own distinct units, the Kuban separatists expected that they would be granted a similar arrangement under the White generals. The second reason why a significant element of the Kuban Cossacks wanted to loosen their ties with the Volunteer Army was that their political outlook contrasted sharply with those held by Denikin and his staff. Those Kuban Cossacks who were descended from the Black Sea Cossacks were culturally closer to Ukrainians than Russians. Denikin's plans to restore a Great Russia were anathema to those who sympathized with socialist and Ukrainian nationalist programs. For the most part, the White generals refused to recognize the Ukrainians as a distinct ethnicity. To them, Ukrainian nationalism was a machination concocted by the Germans and unpatriotic elements to undermine Russia. The White generals could look on the *lineitsy* Cossacks in the Kuban Host as a politically reliable counterweight, but this group, whose members included Ataman Filimonov, was in the minority and was careful to moderate their pro-Russian leanings.

Denikin, in a speech during the opening session of the Rada on 14 November, tried to lure the Kuban delegates away from the spell of separatism. After warning them that the Bolsheviks would never leave the Kuban Cossacks to their own devices, he declared: "It is time to cease all quarrelling, intrigue and conflict about precedency! Everything for the struggle with Bolshevism. It must be annihilated. Russia must be free—or your happiness and welfare will be but a toy in the hands of her enemies at home and abroad." He further added: "There must be no Volunteer, Don, Kuban, [or] Siberian Army. There must be one Russian Army, one front and one Command, invested with full authority, and only responsible before the Russian Nation and its future Supreme and Lawful Authority." Amid his calls for a united and indivisible Russia, Denikin's only concession to his Cossack allies was to respect their rights, privileges and way of life.[92]

The Volunteer commander's plea for overall unity was seconded by prominent Kuban military leaders, including Pokrovsky and Shkuro. They understood that the Kuban Cossacks could not prevail against the Red Army by themselves. To get this point across to the Kuban politicians, both men went before the Rada and urged the assembly to be more accommodating towards the Volunteer Army. Their efforts were only partly successful. In December 1918 the Rada approved a proposed constitution which declared the Kuban as a part of a federalized, not unitary, Russia; but it did fulfill one of the Volunteer Army's wishes by reelecting Filimonov as ataman.[93]

Despite these challenges from the Kuban Cossack separatists, Denikin was in a far stronger position at the close of 1918 than he been six months earlier. Previously, Alekseyev had been responsible for the army's civilian affairs, but after he died of cancer in early October, those duties were assumed by Denikin.[94] The latter had become, in fact if not by name, a military dictator. He also controlled an army of about 40,000 men, which was many times the strength that formation had been at the beginning of the year.[95] Finally, another momentous event occurred in the autumn of 1918. This was the collapse of the Central Powers, and for Denikin and his staff this occasion was a cause for great celebration—and hope.

The Defeat of Germany

The Central Powers' occupation of Ukraine did not proceed according to their plans. Their puppet, Hetman Skoropadsky, was less successful than even the Central Rada in preventing disturbances in the Ukrainian countryside. Within days of the coup that shoehorned Skoropadsky into power in Kiev, the peasantry in several districts revolted against his declared intention to restore private ownership of land. In the worst cases manors were put to the torch, their inhabitants lynched and violent pogroms were initiated against Jews. Although detachments of German and Austro-Hungarian soldiers were shuttled from one district to the next to suppress the uprisings, the brutal reprisals which they carried out only fueled the insurgency. The character of the rebellions varied from one province to the next; some insurgent leaders declared themselves atamans with the aim of establishing their own miniature "Cossack" republics. Others, like the soon-to-be famous warlord Nestor Makhno, fought to establish an anarchist utopia. His activities certainly contributed to the spread of lawlessness. Throughout the period from April to June 1918, Makhno and his followers reportedly launched 118 raids against estates, villages and railway stations in southeastern Ukraine.[96] The unrest even penetrated into the Ukrainian capital, where at the end of July a bomb-throwing terrorist assassinated General von Eichhorn, the commander of the German army of occupation.[97]

Amid this sea of disorder, the actual amount of grain which the central empires were able to import from Ukraine fell far short of the goal of one million tons fixed by the "Bread Peace."[98] As a result, the food crises in Germany and Austria-Hungary continued, and this, combined with the failure of their spring and summer offensives, led to revolution and defeat in the world war. Under the terms of the Armistice dictated by the Allies at Compiègne, the German armies of occupation in Eastern Europe were supposed to hold their present positions until further notice.[99] At the time, the Allies lacked a clear policy towards the chaos in the lands that had constituted the Russian Empire. For them, having German units maintain order in Eastern Europe was a more attractive alternative than abandoning that region to anarchy or Bolshevik expansion. What they did not count on, however, was that by then many German soldiers in the East were unwilling to obey their officers, much less the Allies. Soldier committees cropped up in German units, and these organs began negotiating their neutrality and trading arms with local insurgents. The German soldiers were determined to go home, and their commanders were powerless to stop them.[100] As the Germans evacuated the occupied territories, a great power vacuum began to open across Eastern Europe.

There was no shortage of various councils and parties eager to fill the void left by the Central Powers, but whether these aspirants actually had the strength to impose their will over the territories they claimed was another matter. In Ukraine, Skoropadsky made a desperate attempt to hold onto power by reorienting his government towards the victorious Allies. The hetman, like most anti–Bolshevik Russians, expected the Entente to intervene militarily in Russia, overthrow the Bolsheviks and restore their former ally to her rightful place among the Great Powers. Not wanting to stand in the way of those developments, on 14 November Skoropadsky released an edict in which he effectively denounced Ukrainian aspirations towards complete independence, stating instead that Ukraine's future would be best secured in a federated, non–Bolshevik Russia. To Ukrainian nationalists, this proclamation seemed to confirm their long-held suspicions of the hetman: the Russian wolf had at last shed his Ukrainian sheepskin. Subsequently, Skoropadsky's political opponents, organized under the Ukrainian National Union, launched an uprising with the help of defectors from the hetman's pathetically small armed forces. The rebels also formed an insurgent government in the form of a five-man directory that included veterans of the Central Rada. Throughout the rest of month and into December the rebel troops pressed towards Kiev. The main hindrance to their progress was their caution to keep a respectful distance from the evacuating German troops. On 14 December Skoropadsky finally abdicated, bringing his Cossack-styled regime to an ignominious end. Later that the same day, insurgent forces led by Symon Petliura, a member of the Directory and of the former Central Rada, entered Kiev and proclaimed a new Ukrainian People's Republic. Petliura also set out to hunt down Skoropadsky, who he denounced as a "traitor," but to no avail. The former hetman, it turned out, was among the estimated 3,000 anti–Bolshevik politicians, officers and soldiers who slipped out of Ukraine with the evacuating Germans.[101]

As the new government set up by Petliura and his associates took up quarters in Kiev, it was faced with a new opponent in the form of a Ukrainian Soviet Army, soon renamed the Ukrainian Army Group, that was being organized by Antonov-Ovseyenko. The objective of this force was to occupy Ukraine behind the withdrawing German troops and ultimately, like the previous occupying powers, extract grain and other foodstuffs from the region.[102]

The brewing struggle in Ukraine had major implications for Krasnov's All-Great Don Host. As the Germans departed from the western border of the host, the Don Army had to transfer troops to the Donets Basin in order to guard its left flank from the threat posed by the Ukrainian partisan bands, many of which were entering temporary alliances with the Red Army. This additional military burden on the Don Cossacks could not have come at a worse time. Although their army then stood at about 52,000 men,[103] this formidable size had been attained only by wringing all able-bodied Cossack males from the Don stanitsas. The only other sources of manpower available to the Don Army were the much-maligned outlanders. To provide them an incentive to fight the Red Army, Krasnov's regime promised to bestow Cossack status—and by implication Cossack lands—on non–Cossacks who took up arms against the Bolsheviks.[104] Meanwhile, the pluck of the Don Cossack troops, which had been crucial in driving the more numerous Soviet forces from the region, was beginning to waver. When the last Red troops were pushed outside the borders of the Don Host that autumn, many simple Cossack soldiers believed that their campaign was complete.

Unlike their ataman, they had no desire to advance beyond the Don and instead began to filter back to their stanitsas.[105]

To keep the Cossacks at the front, the propagandists in Novocherkassk publicized stories of Red atrocities. The Bolsheviks, they claimed, subjected their prisoners to various medieval tortures; one such method supposedly reserved specifically for Cossacks was the cutting open of their legs from the waist to the ankles in order to imitate the red stripes worn on Don Cossack uniforms.[106] These claims were not as startling as they may have appeared since both sides were known to engage in cruel practices. Subsequently, the Cossacks, long numbed to such tales, continued to desert; increasing the Don Army's numerical disadvantage against the Reds and foreshadowing the military crisis that would shortly transpire in the All-Great Don Host.

Germany's defeat not only worsened Krasnov's military position, it also upended his foreign policy. Since his election in May, the ataman had oriented his government towards Berlin in the anticipation of Germany's victory in the world war. After 11 November, however, it was clear that he had bet on the wrong horse. Like Skoropadsky, Krasnov responded to the collapse of his benefactor by making an about-face through the adoption of a pro–Allied policy. On 19 November, two emissaries from Novocherkassk arrived in Jassy (Iași) and handed a letter from their ataman to General Henri Berthelot, the chief of the French Military Mission to Romania. In a prose as colorful as his earlier messages to the kaiser, Krasnov reminded the French commander how the Allies' recent victory was made possible by the Russian army and especially its Cossack warriors. Mindful of the rivalry between Krasnov and Denikin, the two delegates also attempted to discredit the commander of the Volunteer Army in the vain hope that the Allies might replace him with someone who was more acceptable to the Don ataman. As a last resort, the delegates mentioned that if the Allies disappointed their leader by giving their full backing to Denikin, the Don government might seek a settlement with the Bolsheviks.

The Don emissaries' mixture of pleas, intrigue, and veiled threats failed to impress Berthelot and his colleagues. The French officers were already in contact with Denikin's headquarters and had made their decision to back him as the eventual supreme commander of the united anti–Bolshevik forces of South Russia. Their reason for favoring Denikin was simple: unlike Krasnov, he had remained faithful to the Allies and avoided accommodation with Germans even when it may have been advantageous for him to do so. The Allies did not trust Krasnov, and the ridiculous suggestion that he might bargain with his ideological foe did not lift their confidence in him. As a result, the French and British dispatched representatives to Yekaterinodar, but not to Novocherkassk.[107]

Krasnov's setbacks in the military and diplomatic fronts worked in Denikin's favor. Ever since the White general conferred with the Don ataman at stanitsa Manychskaya in May, he had sought to unite the anti–Bolshevik forces in South Russia under his command. Back then his movement, with an army numbering less than 10,000 men, in desperate need of arms and having no territory it could call a base of its own, appeared pitifully weak in contrast to Krasnov's All-Great Don Host. He lacked any real means to exert pressure on the egotistical Don ataman. These circumstances were completely changed in the course of a few months. By the close of 1918, the Don Army was breaking down; on the other hand, Denikin presided over a relatively stable army of 40,000, controlled the fertile Kuban region and was welcoming representatives from Britain and France at his headquarters in Yekaterinodar. The momentum within the White movement in South Russia had clearly shifted to the White generals.

Nearly all anti-Bolshevik Russians, not just those in South Russia, had high hopes that the Allies, following their victory over Germany, would begin a large-scale military intervention in Russia against the Soviet regime. They viewed the ongoing struggle in their country as a continuation of the world war since Bolshevism, in their view, had been imposed on Russia by Germany. The Allies, as far as Denikin and his ilk were concerned, were legally and morally obligated to assist them in liberating their country from communist tyranny. Absorbed as they were in upholding their own sense of honor, the White generals could not imagine that their past devotion to the Allied cause might not be reciprocated by the governments of those countries.[108]

In the weeks following Germany's defeat, the White generals had grounds for optimism in their expectations for unlimited Allied aid. On 16 November General Shcherbachev, Denikin's emissary to the French Military Mission in Jassy, reported with brimming enthusiasm that twelve divisions of French and Greek troops were en route to southern Ukraine and the Crimea.[109] A week later, a squadron of British and French warships, after sailing through the now-open Black Sea Straits, lowered their anchors in the harbor of Novorossiysk. On 3 December, a British Military Mission headed by General F. C. Poole arrived in Yekaterinodar with further pledges of Allied support.[110]

Outside assistance—whether from the Allies or the Volunteer Army—could not arrive soon enough for the Don Cossacks. As the Cossack soldiers in the northern Don deserted to their homes or, in the worst cases, defected to the Red Army, Krasnov tried to reverse his military predicament by seeking direct aid from the Allied missions and the White generals. His pleas to the latter group did not go unanswered. In December, Denikin sent a detachment of about 2,500 Volunteers to the Donets Basin in order to shore up the left flank of the Don Army and deny the enemy access to that area's immense coal resources.[111] The British and French, however, continued to remain aloof of the Don ataman. Their representatives in Russia stood unflinchingly behind Denikin and refused to extend any courtesy to Krasnov that might appear to validate his authority as the leader of a sovereign nation. In the waning days of 1918, General Poole did finally confer with Krasnov at Kushchevka train station, but only in an unofficial capacity. Amid their discussions on how to unite the Don Army and Volunteer Army under a single command, Krasnov indicated his readiness to submit to Denikin's authority although the arrangement he proposed would unify the anti-Bolshevik movement in principle but not in practice. Significantly, he wanted, as Don ataman, to retain substantial control over the Don Army after its incorporation into a unified anti-Bolshevik force. This unworkable proposal, not surprisingly, was quickly rejected by Denikin and his staff. Nonetheless, Krasnov's willingness to even consider subordinating himself to Denikin was a major departure from his earlier policy of upholding all pretensions of the Don Cossacks' independence.[112]

Although Krasnov left Kushchevka without having to give up any of his powers, the outcome of the meeting was not a victory for the ataman. Notably, he failed to secure any guarantee from Poole that the Don Cossacks would be granted a share of the forthcoming Allied supplies and assistance to South Russia. Moreover, the need for such outside help increased with each passing day. Just days after his meeting with Poole, several stanitsas in the northern Don revolted against his government and sent a delegation to negotiate with the Red Army.[113] Amid these worsening developments, the Don ataman jumped at a new offer to meet with Denikin and hash out an agreement for a united command. The conference between the two men and their closest aides took place at Torgovaya station on 8 January 1919. Despite the increasing vulnerability of the Don region, Krasnov's vigorous insistence on retaining as much autonomy as possible for his army nearly caused Denikin to walk out of the meeting on two separate occasions. Gradually, however, the two parties bridged their differences on key issues. At the end of the day, Denikin was able to announce his new position as commander-in-chief of the Armed Forces of South Russia (AFSR), in which the Don Army was included as an autonomous entity.[114]

The formation of the AFSR finally bound the Don Cossack's struggle against the Soviet regime, which they waged on a mostly regional scale, to the counterrevolution being organized by the White generals with far-reaching national goals. While such a union had been a foremost goal of the White generals, including not just Denikin but Alekseyev and Kornilov as well, it was a settlement which most Cossacks would have preferred to avoid. What ordinary Cossacks desired the most was to be left alone to tend to their farms and fields. As the failure of the Cossack governments in early 1918 showed, the majority of Cossacks were not fundamentally opposed to the Soviet regime. Rather, their antagonism towards the Bolsheviks was sparked by rumors of atrocities and fears that their land allotments would have to be shared with outlanders. In due course, they fought diligently to protect their way of life within the host but had little interest in occurrences outside their territory. The majority of Cossacks failed to grasp the reality that their privileged status was inextricably tied to the fate of the Russian motherland. This fact was apparent to most atamans, including Krasnov. Despite their best efforts, the atamans—to the detriment of the entire anti–Bolshevik struggle—never quite succeeded in ingraining this concept in their peoples.

While many Cossacks in the Don and Kuban continued to view the civil war on a regional basis, their military leaders in Yekaterinodar began to plan their campaign against the Soviet heartland. This shift in strategy was enabled by a number of factors: the unification of the AFSR, the reduction of the vestigial Red forces in the North Caucasus, the promise of Allied intervention and, finally, the emergence in Russia of other anti–Bolshevik forces, particularly in Siberia. While the counterrevolutionary governments in South Russia and Siberia were at times as much separated by politics as they were geography, they were nonetheless united by the overarching goal to depose Lenin's dictatorship. They also shared one other important similarity: Siberia, like South Russia, was home to several Cossack hosts. Generally, the Cossack communities east of the Urals were substantially smaller and weaker than their counterparts in the Don and Kuban. Nonetheless, a number of atamans, for reasons that will be explained in the next chapter, managed to wield an influence in White Siberia that was totally out of proportion to the size and actual strength of their respective hosts.

5

Backwater

The Asiatic Hosts

As the Cossack hosts in South Russia were transformed into bases for opposition against the Bolsheviks during the course of 1918, similar developments occurred in the Cossack lands of Asiatic Russia. Following in the footsteps of Kaledin, the leaders of the Siberian hosts also refused to recognize the legitimacy of Soviet rule in the aftermath of the October Revolution. Their attempts to form something resembling a Cossack state, however, were far less successful than those of the Don and Kuban Cossacks. Their failure to overcome the challenges they faced in this endeavor were mostly the result of their geographical locations and unique historical development.

To the inhabitants of medieval and early modern Russia, the lands east of the Urals were an unchartered wilderness populated by marauding horsemen whose forays were a nuisance in the best of times and terrifying in the worst of them. The most devastating invaders to ride out the east were the Mongol armies which laid waste to much of the Russian lands in the thirteenth century. Two centuries later, after the early Muscovite state had shed the Tatar yoke, the threat of raids by the nomadic and semi-nomad peoples from Asia still lingered over many of its inhabitants. A turnabout in this situation began to occur in the final decades of the sixteenth century, when a few hundred Cossack adventurers led by Yermak Timofeyevich captured the capital of the Siberian Khanate, Kashlyk, near present-day Tobolsk.[1] Their exploit touched off a torrent of Russian exploration and eastward expansion that eventually extended the tsars' dominions to the Pacific coast by the end of the seventeenth century.[2] Although most of these trailblazers and the settlers behind them were called Cossacks, few of them had any actual ties to a Cossack host. Most of them were soldiers or peasants who were forcibly resettled by the tsarist government to a stanitsa strategically placed along a Siberian river. Their population was quite small and grew only very slowly. Hence, the first host east of the Urals, the Siberian Cossack Host, was not organized until 1808.[3]

The Siberian Host, along with the Orenburg Host to its southwest, was deliberately created by the tsarist government as a cordon against the nearby Bashkir and Kazakh peoples. With the increase of Russian power during the nineteenth century, however, both hosts were factored into tsarist designs for expansion into Central Asia. The town of Orenburg became a forward base for the projected campaigns while Cossacks provided reconnaissance and cavalry support for the expeditions that eventually pushed the empire's southern frontier to Afghanistan. To help secure these new domains, a few thousand Siberian Cossacks were uprooted from Western Siberia and transplanted in Turkestan. They were to provide a "Cossack nucleus" for the thousands of Russian peasant settlers and few hun-

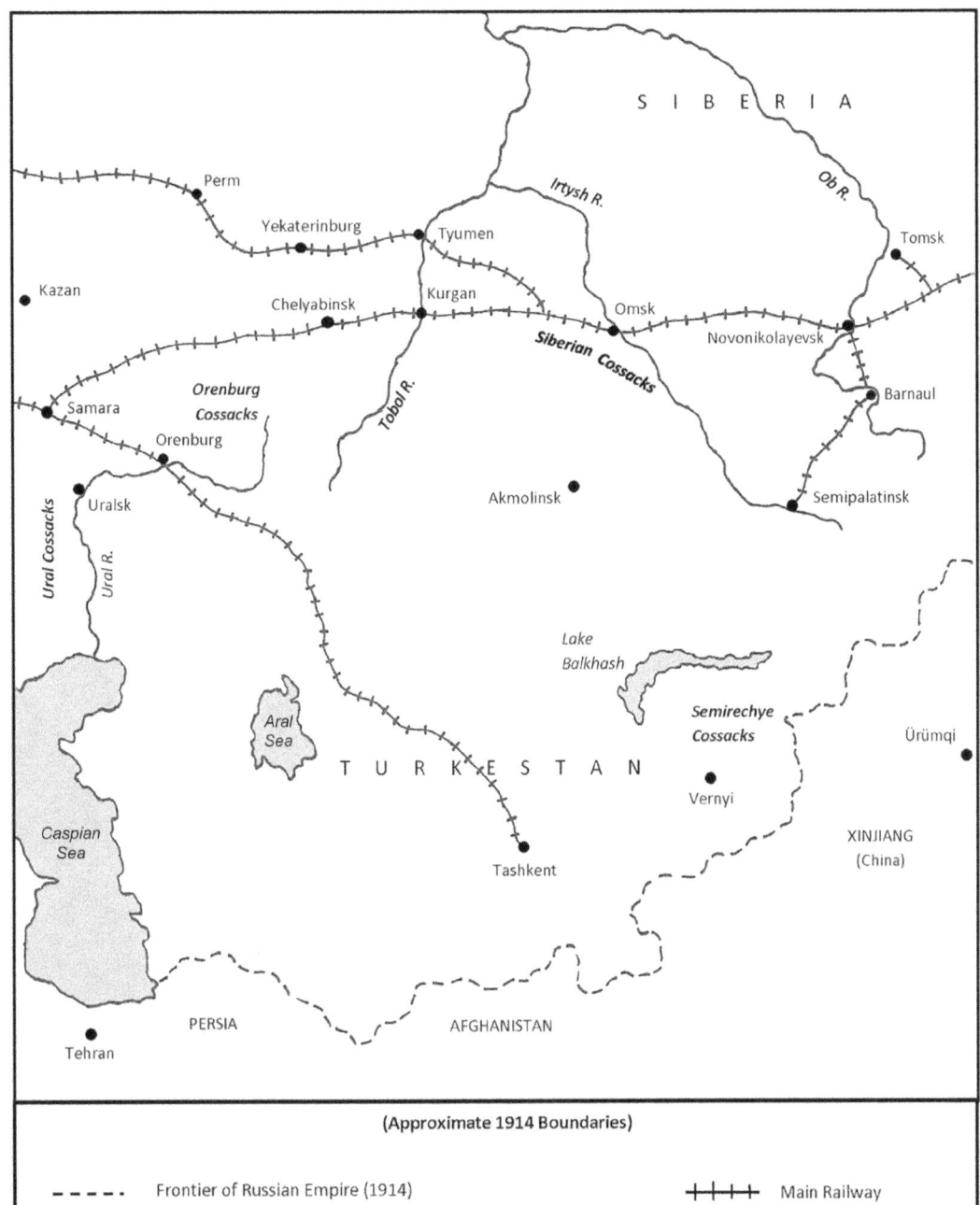

Cossack Hosts of the Urals, Western Siberia and Central Asia.

dred Chinese immigrants who were molded into the Semirechye Host in 1867. (Semirechye translates into "seven rivers." They were given this name because their territory was centered on the seven-river district southeast of Lake Balkash.)

Around the same time, the Russian government raised new Cossack hosts in its most eastern realms to create a militarized frontier against China. In 1851, the Transbaikal Host was established by registering Russian peasants, Chinese immigrants and local natives as

Cossacks. From there, the government continued to extend the Cossack line eastward by creating the Amur Cossack Host in 1858 and finally the Ussuri Cossack Host in 1889. The establishment of the latter host capped-off a four decade-long period of unprecedented growth for Cossacks as never before had so many hosts been established in such rapid succession.[4]

Obviously, the Cossack hosts in Siberia stood apart from their counterparts along the Don and Ural rivers in that they did not form spontaneously; rather, they were deliberate

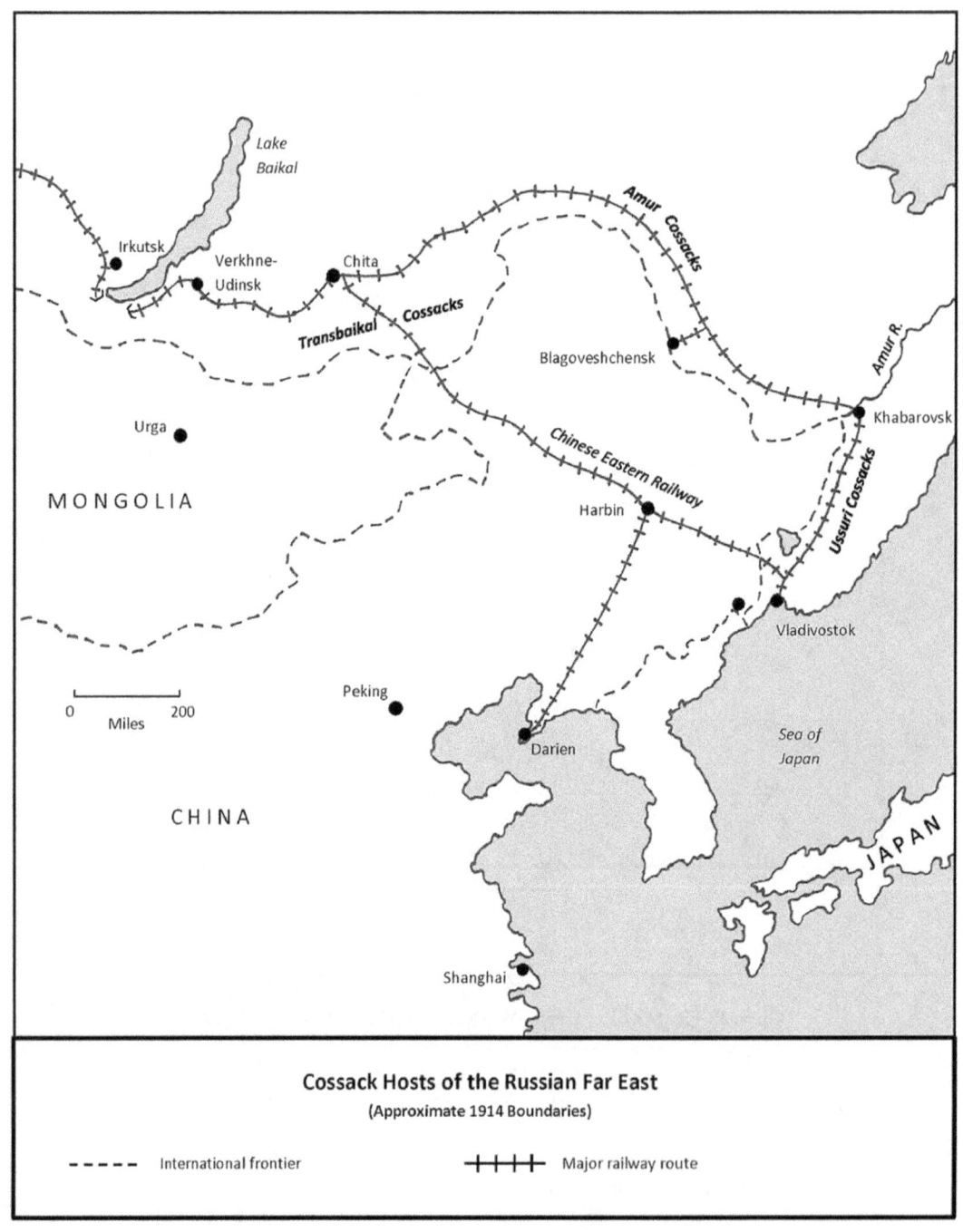

Cossack Hosts of the Russian Far East
(Approximate 1914 Boundaries)

creations of the tsarist regime. Yet the eastern hosts differed in many other ways from those to their west, including those like the Kuban and Orenburg Hosts that were also the direct offspring of government intervention. In the first place, the eastern hosts were from their outset far more ethnically diverse than the hosts in the Urals and to the west. Although it was not unusual for the Cossacks of the Don, Kuban and Urals to possess some Tatar or Turkic blood after generations of intermarriage between themselves and surrounding natives, they nonetheless remained predominantly Slavic in culture. In the eastern hosts, however, Slavs were sometimes in the minority. When forming the Transbaikal Host, for example, the government fused together Russian and Chinese settlers with local Tungus and Buryat herdsmen. We have already seen how the disparate origins of the Black Sea Cossacks and *lineitsy* Cossacks in the Kuban Host were the source of considerable friction in that region's administration. One can easily imagine how much more difficult it would have been to forge a common identity from several ethnic groups who shared neither a common religion nor alphabet.[5]

While all Cossack hosts from the Black Sea to the Sea of Japan faced their own unique socio-economic problems, these also varied considerably from European Russia to Siberia. During the latter nineteenth century, the swelling populations of the Don and Kuban Hosts made overcrowding in the countryside a dire problem as the amount of land available to ordinary Cossacks remained static. On the other hand, the Cossacks in Siberia had more land than they knew what to do with. A Ussuri Cossack, for example, had an average land allotment that was nearly six times the average parcel worked by a typical Don Cossack in 1900. This surplus of land, however, did not mean that the eastern Cossacks were better-off than their brethren on the Don. Instead, the ample land allotments given to the eastern Cossacks encouraged its inefficient use. The land was frequently rented out to Russian, Chinese or Korean immigrants who lacked any incentive to improve the soil. Relatively little of it was tilled; most of it was used for grazing. As a whole, Cossacks in Siberia, due their underdeveloped economy and late establishment, were poorer and less educated than Cossacks of the Don or Kuban.[6]

One reason the eastern Cossacks enjoyed such large land allotments was that their populations were relatively small and distributed over wide areas. The combined population of the Siberian, Semirechye, Transbaikal, Amur and Ussuri Hosts was only 526,000 Cossack men, women and children. In contrast, the Orenburg Host held 574,000 Cossacks and the much larger Don and Kuban respectively numbered 1,460,000 and 1,340,000 Cossacks.[7] One must also keep in mind that the five hosts situated east of the Urals were separated by vast distances. For example, over 3,500 miles stood between the lands of the Siberian Cossacks and those of the Ussuri Cossacks. To put that into perspective, that distance is 500 miles longer than the shortest route between Los Angeles and Boston. Moreover, not only were the Cossack hosts separated by wide areas, but the stanitsas within in the hosts were also spread thin, a fact which further inhibited their ability to develop the high-degree of fellowship enjoyed by Cossacks in the Don or Urals.

The smaller populations of the eastern hosts also meant that their potential military strength was weaker. In 1914, the mighty Don Host could mobilize 54 cavalry regiments during wartime whereas the Transbaikal and Siberian Hosts could only field 9 regiments each. The much smaller Semirechye, Amur and Ussuri Hosts counted their contributions to the army in squadrons, not regiments.[8] In fact, the combined mobilization strength of all hosts east of the Volga—which includes the Ural and Orenburg Hosts in addition to those further to the east—could not match that of the Don Cossacks.

Although the eastern hosts were artificial progenies of the tsarist regime, many of their members nonetheless valued their distinction as Cossacks which lifted them slightly above peasants in the social hierarchy of Imperial Russia. For the Cossacks in Siberia, this usually meant that they had access to better land and far larger allotments than peasants who immigrated to the region.[9] While this disparity was a source of peasant resentment, tensions between the outlanders and Cossacks in the wide spaces of Siberia were less acute than in the increasingly crowded steppe of South Russia. Still, at the turn of the twentieth century the eastern Cossacks had plenty of reason to feel insecure about the long-term prospects of their communities. Beginning in the 1880s, the tsarist government had encouraged peasants from the overpopulated villages of Central Russia to resettle in the sparsely-inhabited regions of Siberia. In its effort to attract colonists to those forbidding lands, the government offered a number of incentives—including land allotments that rivaled those given to eastern Cossacks but without the heavy military obligations imposed on the latter. The migration of peasants to Siberia was further aided by the opening of the Trans-Siberian Railway in the first years of the twentieth century: the overland journey across the breadth of the empire that had once taken months could now be completed in as little as ten days.[10] A sense of the changes that were taking place can be seen in the growth of region's centers between 1897 and 1911. During that time, the towns of Omsk, Tomsk, Novonikolaevsk (Novosibirsk), Krasnoyarsk, Irkutsk and Vladivostok all increased in size by two or more times.[11] The Cossack population, in contrast, had no chance to keep pace with this exponential population growth.[12]

Siberia in the Revolution

The belated development of the Cossacks in the Russian Far East meant that they were given only a short window to establish an identity of their own before the outbreak of the Russian Revolution in 1917. Nevertheless, many of these relatively-new Cossacks wasted no time in asserting their autonomy and defending their entitlements against the leveling forces of the revolution. In the weeks following the collapse of the tsarist regime, the eastern Cossacks formed their own governments based on the traditional model of krugs and atamans even though most had possessed neither at any time in their brief history. Although some of the atamans they elected would acquire fame—or notoriety—in the coming months, none came close to matching the prominence of Kaledin or Krasnov. Meanwhile, at the national level, delegations of eastern Cossacks from the armies and from the stanitsas joined their western peers on the Union of Cossack Hosts in an attempt to merge the political interests of all Cossacks across the empire.[13]

Like their brethren in South Russia, the political goals of the Cossacks in Siberia frequently clashed with those of the aboriginal population. Indeed, in the heady weeks following the abdication of the tsar, it did not take long for nascent national movements to surface among the Bashkirs in the Urals, the Kazakhs in Central Asia and the Buryats in Transbaikal. At a minimum, the nationally-conscious strata among these ethnic groups sought self-rule in their local affairs. Although this demand was relatively moderate, it conflicted with the claims of Cossacks whose hosts overlapped the natives' lands. But just when their interests appeared irreconcilable, the ascendancy of the Bolsheviks in Petrograd introduced a new variable which often pulled the Cossacks and natives together. Influential elders among both groups were antipathetic to Bolshevik propaganda which championed the urban proletariat and the village poor; the latter of which often included land-hungry Russian colonists in their midst. This sometimes led the Cossacks and indigenous peoples to form alliances against the common enemy. Such a pact, for example, was made between the Bashkirs, Kazakhs and Orenburg Cossacks at the end of December 1917.[14]

The cooperation worked out between the Orenburg Cossacks and local natives was rendered possible by feelings that their traditional animosities belonged mostly to a distant past. This was not the case, however, in the Semirechye Cossack Host where just a few months earlier the Russian population had brutally suppressed an uprising among the region's nomads. Apprehension between the two groups remained high into the following year as Kazakh and Kyrgyz refugees, after having eked through the freezing winter with little food in the Chinese province of Xinjiang, began filtering back to their former grazing lands in the wake of the February Revolution. They earnestly hoped that the new Russian regime would foster respect or at least tolerance towards their nomadic way of life, but they were wrong. The Cossacks and Russian colonists had no intention of returning the land and livestock they had confiscated in the aftermath of the revolt. Subsequently, they once again formed vigilante detachments which massacred the Kazakhs and Kyrgyz by the thousands.[15] Although this latest round of barbarism subsided after just a few months, savage and sometimes three-way combat between the nomads, Cossacks and Russian colonists continued to flare up in the Semirechye over the course of the revolution and civil war. As a result, the Semirechye Cossacks, concerned with defending their remote and scattered stanitsas, were much too preoccupied to lend substantial assistance to anti–Bolshevik campaigns outside of their region.

Although the fierce ethnic strife which entangled the Semirechye Cossacks was unfamiliar to most Cossacks in Siberia, the latter did have to contend with a large population of ethnic Russians that was groping towards its own political aspirations. Prior to the great wave of immigration to Siberia at the end of the nineteenth century, a regional movement had begun to germinate among the tiny Siberian intelligentsia. The primary goal of the regionalists was to obtain a degree of self-government for Siberia, but they were unable to advance their cause until after the collapse of the tsarist regime.[16] In August 1917, a Siberian Regional Conference was convened at Tomsk, and this was followed by two more conferences in the same town later that year. These conferences prepared for the convocation of an elected assembly of Siberian delegates—the Siberian Regional Duma or Sibobduma—which was scheduled to meet in January 1918. That assembly, along with the entire regional movement by then, was dominated by right-wing elements of the Socialist Revolutionary Party, which enjoyed wide support among Siberian peasants. The latter, it seems, were generally apathetic towards the regional movement; certainly its goals did not attract the same level of devotion that nationalism conjured among minorities in other parts of the empire.[17] But after the fall of the Provisional Government in November 1917, the Sibobduma, thanks to its SR affiliation, became a potentially attractive alternative to the establishment of Bolshevism in Siberia. For the feeble Cossack governments attempting to stake their authority in that same region, the Sibobduma appeared poised to become a formidable challenger.

The socio-economic climate of Siberia, it seemed, was unfavorable for the spread of Bolshevism. As the least industrialized region of the empire, Siberia's working class, which the Bolsheviks regarded as their natural base of support, was tiny and confined to mining districts, a few towns and along the railways. The overwhelming majority of the population resided in villages and worked the land, but the conditions in the Siberian countryside were far less volatile than those in European Russia, where the Bolsheviks had exploited the resentment of the village poor against the wealthier peasants, or *kulaks*, and the landed gentry. In Siberia, there was no class of great landowners for agitators to rail against. Generally, the Siberian peasants cultivated larger fields, attended to larger herds and used more modern implements than their counterparts in European Russia, and all these factors contributed to their political moderation.[18]

Although it appeared unlikely that Lenin's dictatorship of the proletariat could obtain a foothold in, much less dominate, rustic Siberia, the region actually succumbed quite easily to Bolshevik rule. In the months following the October Revolution, the Bolsheviks, sometimes in alliance with more moderate socialists, organized soviets in the towns along the Trans-Siberian Railway. Meanwhile, in the countryside, the Soviet government's abolition of Cossack privileges in December 1917 earned Russia's new masters some support from Siberian peasants who coveted the larger and better Cossack lands.[19] The only place where the Bolsheviks met serious resistance was in Irkutsk, but even that town was subdued by the new year. The Russian Far East, owing to distance, took a bit longer to bring under Soviet control, but by the end of the winter the entire railway from Chelyabinsk to Vladivostok—except the shortcut across Manchuria—had gone Red.[20]

In Siberia, as elsewhere in Russia, the Bolsheviks' triumph was made possible not by their strength but rather by the weakness of their enemies. That assessment certainly applies to Siberia's anticommunist Cossack leaders, who were confronted with the same obstacles encountered by their western cousins but with additional problems to boot. For most, the young men they needed for their defense were thousands of miles away at the front and could not be expected to return for weeks or even months. When the regiments and squadrons did finally return, the atamans were appalled to discover that the soldiers were insubordinate, war-weary and inclined to desert to their stanitsas. Older Cossacks who were supposed to keep order in major Siberian centers, such as Omsk or Krasnoyarsk, were no more reliable than the younger veterans. Generally, these Cossack garrisons offered no resistance against Bolshevik takeovers and melted away in the ensuing turmoil.[21] Subsequently, the only forces which the atamans could muster were partisan bands recruited from volunteers. These detachments were insufficient for securing the wide borders of the hosts or even taking a major town, including those which had traditionally served as the capital of their host. During February 1918, a band of Siberian Cossacks headed by a local ataman, Boris Annenkov, learned this after making two unsuccessful assaults on Omsk, which was then the seat of the West Siberian Soviet.[22]

Efforts by Cossack governments to assert their authority floundered worse of all in the hosts of the Russian Far East. As fairly recent creations of the tsarist regime, these hosts lacked the traditions and pride which cemented older Cossack communities. Since many of their ancestors had belonged to the peasantry only two or three generations earlier, large segments of their population still identified with that class and therefore were more susceptible than usual to revolutionary agitation. The turmoil within the populations of these hosts nearly destroyed their Cossack administrations long before they were confronted by enemies from the outside. For example, in August 1917, the Transbaikal Cossack Krug in Chita was sharply divided between leftist Cossacks, many of them descended from former miners, eager to dissolve the host as an obsolete relic of tsarism and more conservative members determined to cling to their Cossack identity. Somewhat unexpectedly, the latter included Cossacks of Buryat and Mongol extraction.[23] Although the Transbaikal Host weathered through this debate, the neighboring Amur Host did not. In April 1918, members of that host renounced their Cossack status. In doing so, they resigned themselves to the position of ordinary peasants and merged their political activities with the local soviets.[24] The Ussuri Cossacks further east also struggled with the question of whether or not they should abolish their host. In krugs held in March and April of 1917, the gathered delegates passed resolutions favoring disbandment only to backpedal on this decision in later krugs.[25] Other Cossack governments in Siberia gathered just enough followers to sustain a guerrilla campaign of varying intensity but failed to attract the numbers they needed to enforce their authority over a substantial area. Without a suitable capital or a foothold along a major railway or river route, they lingered as farcical affairs which were little more than nuisances to local soviet organs.

The most prominent Cossack enemy of the Soviet regime operating east of the Volga in early 1918 was Ataman Aleksandr Dutov who, we have seen, was lumped together with Kaledin and Kornilov in Bolshevik tirades against counterrevolutionary Cossack generals. Although Dutov's Orenburg Cossacks were based in the Urals, the fortunes of the civil war would soon tie their fate to that of the Siberian Whites. Initially, Dutov concentrated his operations on holding the citadel of Orenburg and its hinterland. Although he was far away from the Soviet capital, his position along the single-tracked Samara—Tashkent railway was significant since he effectively cut-off Moscow's textile factories from the cotton-producing regions of Turkestan. Even after Dutov's Cossacks were ran out of Orenburg at the end of January 1918, the Red Guards never quite succeeded in securing the railway route to Tashkent before their position in the Urals was undermined by new uprisings that following spring.[26]

Other anticommunist Cossack leaders emerged in the Russian Far East, although for the time being their forces were even weaker than those commanded by Dutov. One of these detachments had its beginnings during the summer of 1917, when a young captain of the Transbaikal Cossacks, Grigory Mikhailovich Semyonov, was dispatched to the Russian Far East to recruit a regiment of Buryats and Mongols to fight with the Russian Army. The twenty-seven-year-old Semyonov was part Buryat himself and had been twice decorated with the Cross of St. George while serving as a cavalry officer during the world war.[27] While those who met him were taken back by his bestial appearance—a British officer described him as having "an enormous head, the size of which is greatly enhanced by the flat, Mongol face, from which gleam two clear, brilliant eyes that rather belong to an animal than a man"—they were nonetheless impressed by his charm, vigor and bravery.[28] After the civil war, one of his former commanders, Baron Wrangel, who derided Semyonov's career in the White movement, still complimented him as "an exemplary soldier, especially courageous when under the eye of his superior."[29] Despite his gallant reputation in battle, however, his efforts to enlist Buryats and Mongols that summer were not very successful. In desperation, he eventually opened his ranks to anyone willing to pick up a saber. When the Provisional Government was overthrown in November, he was still trying to attract recruits in Transbaikal Province. With the Bolsheviks suddenly in power and announcing their desire to seek peace, Semyonov's project was thrown in limbo.[30]

On the night of 18–19 December 1917, Semyonov, along with his wartime comrade Baron Nikolay Roman von Ungern-Sternberg, a hard-drinking cavalry officer of Baltic German lineage, led their few hundred soldiers to seize the train stations at Manchuli and Dauria along the Chinese Eastern Railway, next to the border with Manchuria.[31] Their position was strengthened six days later when 3,500 Chinese troops restored order along the Manchurian sector of the Chinese Eastern Railway by disarming and expelling mutinous Russian militias stationed there. That action preserved the Chinese Eastern Railway Administration of General Dmitry Horvath, based in Harbin, who subsequently allowed the railway zone in Manchuria to become a haven for enemies of the Soviet regime. In the meantime, the Chinese Eastern Railway was policed by Chinese troops loyal to the Manchurian warlord General Duan Qirui. His forces, in turn, were backed by Japan and both parties were eager to halt the spread of Bolshevism in Eastern Asia.[32]

With his rear effectively secured by foreign troops hostile to Bolshevism, Semyonov decided to take the offensive. In the first days of January 1918, Semyonov led his band westward along the Chinese Eastern Railway. His army, which he christened as the Special Manchurian Detachment, was hardly imposing: it consisted of 51 Russian officers, 135 Transbaikal Cossacks, 80 Mongolians, 300 Buryats and an assortment of men from various other backgrounds; altogether about 600 men. Despite their small numbers, the Semyonovites managed to seize most of the railway between Chita and Manchuli before an enemy counterattack threw them back against the Manchurian border.[33]

Although Semyonov's first offensive ended in failure, the operation captured the attention of Japanese, British and French officials in the region who were impressed by the young captain's bold adventure. Indeed, his resolve to actually engage the Red Guards contrasted sharply with other anti–Bolshevik Russians in Harbin who were either unable or unwilling to convert their tough words into tangible deeds. Subsequently, these foreign officials began to funnel money, firearms, obsolete field guns and munitions to Semyonov's motley army. From the start, the Japanese were the most lavish in their subsidies; they even attached a small mission to Semyonov's headquarters.

These foreigners who were so enamored by the Cossack leader's determination to make war on the Bolsheviks soon learned that their protégé was impossible to control. Ignoring the recommendation of his Japanese advisors and the wishes of his British and French contacts, Semyonov decided to launch a new attack into the Transbaikal with his revitalized forces, which had grown to about 2,000 men. This second offensive, which began on the night of 20 April, got off to a promising start. A fortnight later, with the Special Manchurian Division continuing its advance, Semyonov proclaimed himself the head of an autonomous government in the Transbaikal and soon began using the Cossack title of ataman. By then his opponents, consisting of Red Guards and Bolshevized Cossacks under the leadership of a twenty-four-year-old ensign, Sergey Lazo, were holding nothing back in their efforts to stop the Semyonovites. In early May the Reds dynamited the bridge over the Onon River, rendering the Chinese Eastern Railway momentarily unpassable. They were also concentrating Soviet forces from all over Siberia in the Transbaikal. Among the reinforcements arriving in the region were Hungarian war prisoners who elected to fight for the Red Army in its "Internationalist Legion." The position of the Semyonovites was further challenged by the refusal of General Horvath's new military advisor in Harbin, Admiral Aleksandr Kolchak, to forward supplies to the Special Manchuria Detachment until its leader submitted to Horvath's authority. At the end of May, the Soviet forces finally seized the initiative in a counterattack that once again rolled the Semyonovites back towards the frontier with Manchuria. For the next several weeks, the outlook of Semyonov's renegades was dismal as they clung onto their last sliver of Russia against an enemy that probably outnumbered them two to one.[34]

If General Duan had his way, Semyonov's campaign would have been terminated by closing Manchuria as a supply route and allowing the Special Manchurian Division to retreat into Chinese territory only after it laid down its arms. With China already fractured by years of revolutionary upheaval, the last thing Duan wanted was for the mayhem in Russia to spill over his frontier. The warlord, however, was restrained from taking such drastic measures against the Semyonovites by the Japanese who were closely eyeing developments in Siberia. Powerful Japanese military and commercial circles were especially eager to exploit the breakdown of order in Russia to increase their political and economic penetration of the Asiatic mainland. With these goals in mind, earlier that spring Japan had prodded the weak Chinese central government into a series of agreements which effectively transformed northern Manchuria into a staging ground for a Japanese intervention into Eastern Siberia. Under these circumstances Duan, who like Semyonov relied on Japanese funds and weapons to maintain his army, had little choice other than to accept the Cossack rebel as an ally.[35]

Japan's growing influence in Manchuria also shielded other Cossack leaders from Chinese and Soviet troops. On Manchuria's eastern frontier, an anti–Bolshevik movement had gained a foothold among Ussuri Cossacks. Their counterrevolution began in January 1918 when the Ussuri Krug took the unusual step of electing a non–Cossack, Ivan Pavlovich Kalmykov, as their ataman. Exactly how Kalmykov, an army captain aged only in his mid-twenties, won that election has been subject to speculation. At the very least, Japanese agents appear to have actively promoted his candidacy, and they may have helped him further by assassinating his most serious challenger. Regardless, Japan's active patronage of Kalmykov was essential in another session of the Ussuri Krug, held in March, to confirm the young captain as their ataman and approve an anticommunist policy. That stance, however, failed to resonate with the Ussuri Cossack soldiers who finally returned from the front that same month. As elsewhere, the Cossack veterans ignored their officers and atamans, dispersed to their stanitsas or, in a few instances, joined a local detachment of "Red" Cossacks. Ultimately, Kalmykov could count on only a few dependable followers. Rather than make a desperate stand against stronger Red forces, they preferred to cross the border into Manchuria where, under the disapproving eye of Chinese troops, they waited for the right moment to pounce back into Russia.[36]

On Manchuria's northern frontier, another ataman, Vasily Gamov, also used Chinese territory as a base for an attack on Blagoveshchensk, which had succumbed to Soviet rule at the beginning of February 1918. A little over a month later, on the night of 6–7 March, Gamov's band of Cossack and officer insurgents launched their assault on Blagoveshchensk and took control of the town. As leader of the Amur Cossacks, Gamov expected the nearby stanitsas to rally to his banner in the aftermath of his victory. He also called upon the town's sizeable middle-class and its Japanese enclave to join his crusade. His appeals, however, failed to arouse any widespread enthusiasm. Many Amur Cossacks, as we have seen, were not necessarily hostile to Soviet rule and soon renounced their Cossack status. Other elements of the local population that were inclined to oppose Bolshevism had no desire to take up arms. Subsequently, Gamov could rely on just 800 officers, 700 Cossacks and a few dozen Japanese militamen to defend Blagoveshchensk when it was attacked on 9 March by approximately 12,000 Red Guards converging on area. Two days later, Gamov and his men, along with nearly 10,000 civilian refugees, evacuated the town by crossing the frozen Amur and sought refuge in Manchuria. The decision of so many people to abandon their home in Blagoveshchensk proved wise as the Reds celebrated their recapture of the town by shooting anyone whom they suspected of harboring counterrevolutionary sympathies.[37]

By late spring of 1918, with Semyonov, Kalmykov, Gamov and Horvath effectively hiding behind or in the proximity of Chinese bayonets, the counterrevolution in the Russian Far East appeared to have no traction on Russian soil. Even with the backing of Japan, and to a lesser extent Britain and France, the anti–Bolshevik campaigns in the Russian Far East were rather easily contained by Red forces in the region. Semyonov, Gamov and Kalmykov's appeals for ordinary Transbaikal, Amur and Ussuri Cossacks to take up arms against the Soviet regime went unheeded, and the more numerous peasants were even less responsive. By late spring, the atamans' campaigns appeared headed for certain demise until an unexpected twist of fate suddenly transformed their fortunes.

Deus ex machina: The Czecho-Slovak Legion

As the Eastern Front against the Central Powers lapsed into inactivity during the autumn of 1917, thousands of foreign troops fighting alongside the Russians began seeking a way out of the country. With Russia's nearest ports in the Baltic and Black Seas effectively blockaded by the enemy, the only options for these troops to evacuate by sea was through the northern ports of Murmansk and Arkhangelsk or the Pacific port of Vladivostok. Due to the congestion and limitations of the northern ports, several foreign units opted to cross thousands of miles of Siberian steppe and taiga by train to reach Vladivostok or the Japanese-controlled port of Darien (Dalian). One of the first such units to pass over the Trans-Siberian line was a Belgian armored car division, and it was soon followed by a brigade of South Slavs formed from Austro-Hungarian POWs. Although most of these soldiers were ordered by their officers to remain neutral in the fratricidal conflicts raging in the villages they passed through, many still traded weapons and other supplies with one side or the other. In some cases, a few deserted their countrymen and threw their lot with one side. Semyonov's Special Manchurian Division, for example, acquired over 150 Serbian deserters from the South Slav brigade.[38]

The largest formation to attempt a katabasis across Russia to the Pacific coast was the Czecho-Slovak Army Corps in Russia, better known as the Czecho-Slovak Legion. The legion began in 1914 as a battalion of Czech and Slovak volunteers eager to fight for the Allies with the goal of liberating their homelands from the Austro-Hungarian Empire. In the 1917 summer offensive, the Czecho-Slovaks, fighting as a brigade on Russia's Southwestern Front, distinguished themselves in the Battle of Zborov. Afterwards, the Provisional Government lifted its recruiting restrictions against Czecho-Slovaks war prisoners and the unit grew rapidly in subsequent months; by early 1918 the formation was a well-armed corps with a strength approaching 40,000 men.

The political leader of the Czecho-Slovaks was the president of the Czecho-Slovak National Council, Tomáš Masaryk, who was in Russia for most of the winter of 1917–18. He spent much of that time trying to plot a new course for his legionaries now that Russia appeared to be leaving the war. Ultimately, he decided that his legion, then in Ukraine, should head east for Vladivostok, where the legionaries would then embark on ships that would take them halfway across the globe to France so they could fight on the Western Front. Subsequently, the Czecho-Slovak Legion evacuated Ukraine just as the Germans were overrunning the region and entered the territory of Soviet Russia to begin their long journey for Vladivostok.[39]

In March 1918, Masaryk left Russia after having made what he thought were suitable arrangements with Soviet leaders for the legionaries' departure. However, the young secretaries from the Russian branch of the Czecho-Slovak National Council quickly found themselves having to renegotiate the terms of the legion's exodus with Soviet leaders in Moscow and in Penza, where the Czecho-Slovak trains were concentrated. At the core of their disagreement were arms: the Czecho-Slovaks wanted to retain their rifles and machine guns as they traveled along the lawless Trans-Siberian Railway while Soviet leaders, concerned that the legionaries might join counterrevolutionary bands, wanted to the corps to be completely disarmed. Eventually, the two sides reached a compromise known as the Penza Agreement where the Czecho-Slovaks would reduce their armament to 168 rifles and one machine gun per train with a limited number of cartridges, grenades and munitions. In exchange, the legionaries were to receive documentation that would grant them unobstructed passage to the east.[40]

Despite its clear provisions, the Penza Agreement failed to diffuse the tensions between the two sides. In the decentralized conditions of early Soviet Russia, commissars in Moscow and Penza lacked the ability to pressure soviets in Siberia to abide by its terms. Subsequently, these regional and local soviets frequently barred the way of the Czecho-Slovak trains, forcing the legionaries to surrender more rifles in order to continue their journey. The latter, in turn, began to doubt the trustworthiness of the Bolsheviks and wondered whether the Soviet government, in cahoots with the Central Powers, was conspiring against them. This latter suspicion was reinforced by the Bolshevik practice of arming German and Hungarian POWs to form the Internationalist battalions. By late spring, the two sides entered an impasse which left most Czecho-Slovak trains at a standstill. At the time, the corps was unevenly spread out along 5,000 miles of railway between Penza and Vladivostok.

The simmering tensions between the Bolsheviks and the Czecho-Slovak Legion finally boiled over in mid–May at the railside town of Chelyabinsk. On 14 May, a scuffle at that town's train station between eastbound legionaries and westbound Magyar POWs left a Czech soldier grievously injured and a Hungarian prisoner dead. After the local soviet decided to arrest eleven legionaries over the incident, the indignant Czecho-Slovaks, approximately 3,000 strong, marched from their trains into Chelyabinsk and forced their comrades' release without firing a shot. A few days later, a previously-scheduled Congress of the Czecho-Slovak Army Corps in Russia convened at the Chelyabinsk train station. The gathered delegates, impressed by the successful outcome of their recent demonstration of strength, decided that their outfit would surrender no more arms and instead would issue ultimatums to soviets barring their path to Vladivostok.[41] Simultaneously, War Commissar Trotsky was outraged after learning of the legionaries' march on Chelyabinsk and lost his patience with the recalcitrant legionaries. "All Soviets are hereby ordered to disarm the Czechoslovaks immediately," he wired from Moscow on the night of 25 May. "Every armed Czechoslovak found on the railway is to be shot on the spot; every troop train in which even one armed man is found shall be unloaded, and its soldiers shall be interned in a war prisoners' camp."[42]

Several hours before Trotsky ordered the local soviets to begin disarming the legionaries, fighting had already taken place between the two sides when several hundred Red Guards attempted to ambush two eastbound Czecho-Slovak trains just west of Omsk. On the following day, 400 miles to the east, legionaries under the command of Captain Radola Gajda seized control of Novonikolaevsk.[43] By the start of June, Czecho-Slovak troops and Red Guards were battling each other along the breadth of the Trans-Siberian Railway from the Volga to Lake Baikal. Although the Czecho-Slovaks experienced an occasional setback, stations and towns along the Trans-Siberian line steadily fell to them like a row of dominoes. On 1 June they took control of Chelyabinsk, and a week later Omsk fell to legionaries advancing from the west. On 20 June they seized Krasnoyarsk, and in the following month they entered Irkutsk. By then the 13,500 legionaries waiting for Allied ships in Vladivostok, who were initially hesitant to partake in the conflict, had deposed the soviet in that city and began retracing their journey back to the west. The Czecho-Slovaks, it seemed, had won victories that were completely out of proportion to their relatively small numbers. "The Czech conquest of Siberia," observed a British officer, "was like the Spanish conquest of Mexico."[44]

Just as the Spanish conquistadors were aided by local tribes, the Czecho-Slovaks received valuable assistance from Russian collaborators. After Gajda's troops overthrew the soviet in Novonikolaevsk, an underground organization of SRs formed after the Sibobduma had been disbanded by the Bolsheviks earlier that year began organizing a new government under Czecho-Slovak protection. At the same time, ex-tsarist officers emerged from hiding and organized militias to police the towns seized from the Bolsheviks. Siberian regionalists also raised armed volunteer units outfitted with green and white armbands—symbolizing the forests and snows of Siberia—to fight alongside the Czecho-Slovaks.[45] Railway workers did their part to shuttle the legionaries' trains along the railway.[46] In general, many Siberians were disaffected by their brief experience under Soviet rule and rallied behind their unlikely liberators.

The Cossacks were among those groups who flocked to the Czecho-Slovaks' banner that summer. Scattered bands of Cossack cavalry in Western Siberia and along the Yenisey River quickly joined nearby legionaries and provided them welcomed support by scouting and raiding Bolshevik positions.[47] From the Manchurian border, Ataman Kalmykov led about 250 Ussuri Cossacks into Russia to serve as an auxiliary force next to the Czecho-Slovak echelons pushing northward from Vladivostok.[48] Since Bolshevik resistance south of Lake Baikal managed to stall the Czecho-Slovaks for several weeks, Semyonov's forces, then numbering about 5,000 men, were unable to make contact with the legionaries until late summer. Nonetheless, his operations had aided the Czecho-Slovaks' progress by having diverted sizable Red echelons to the Transbaikal region, thus weakening Soviet formations in other parts of Siberia. Eventually, the legionaries broke out of the jagged terrain along Lake Baikal's southern rim and continued their unstoppable advance along the Trans-Siberian Railway. On 31 August Gajda's units, advancing from the west, finally linked up with the Special Manchurian Division at Olovianaya, thus removing the immediate danger to Semyonov's front.[49] He and other anti–Bolshevik Cossack leaders had survived the first period of Soviet rule in Siberia—though just barely.

The Czecho-Slovak uprising was also a boon for the Cossacks in the Urals. As we have seen, both the Ural and Orenburg Cossacks, after experiencing brief periods of Soviet rule in early 1918, revolted against the Bolsheviks that spring. Of the two groups, the Orenburg Cossack stanitsas were the most exposed since their homeland was bisected by the Samara–Tashkent railway. On 8 June, however, the rearguard of the Czecho-Slovak Legion, numbering approximately 8,000 troops, captured Samara from the Bolsheviks. On the heels of that victory, five Right SR delegates to the Constituent Assembly proclaimed a new government called the Committee of Members of the Constituent Assembly, known by its Russian acronym as the Komuch. The Komuch quickly began to organize a "People's Army" for its defense, but the real backbone of its military strength was provided by the Czecho-Slovaks who decided to suspend their eastward withdrawal for the time being and hold their present positions.[50]

By occupying Samara, the Komuch and its Czecho-Slovak allies effectively blocked the Red Army's most direct route to Orenburg. Initially, the Orenburg Cossack insurgency was a populist movement led by the Congress of United Stanitsas. But like the uprising occurring simultaneously in the Don, the Orenburg Cossack rebels turned to more traditional and authoritarian leadership as the fighting wore on. Eventually, they sent a delegation to recall Ataman Aleksandr Dutov back to their homeland. Dutov and his followers, who had been living a precarious existence in the arid Turgai Steppe since their reverses earlier in the year, needed little convincing and returned to Orenburg in early July. By then the Orenburg Cossacks had linked up with the territory controlled by the Komuch and Czecho-Slovaks, and as a result their future, as well as those of the Ural Cossacks further south, became intertwined with that of White Siberia.[51]

By deposing the soviets in Samara, Yekaterinburg and taking control of railways to the east of those cities, the Czecho-Slovaks had effectively swept the Bolsheviks from Siberia, the Urals and threatened a large section of the Volga. Besides its military implications, their action had one other major impact on Russia's civil war since the legionaries became the *casus belli* for Allied intervention in Siberia. If British and French leaders had their way, Allied troops would have entered Siberia months earlier to reconstitute an eastern front against Germany. Their proposals for such an operation, however, were rebuffed by U.S. President Woodrow Wilson. Although his administration opposed intervention for a multitude of reasons, its biggest concern was that such an operation might be exploited by Japan to dominate Northeast Asia.[52] The top brass in the U.S. War Department did not like the scheme either on the account that any operation in Russia would be logistical nightmare and require considerable investments of manpower that, in their opinion, could be put to better use on the Western Front.[53] But the uprising of the Czecho-Slovak Legion forced Wilson and his advisors to reconsider their unyielding opposition to intervention. The legionaries' exploits in Russia earned them considerable press and sympathy for their cause in the U.S. and in Western Europe, and as their forces in Central Siberia and in the Russian Far East struggled to open the thousands of miles of railway between them, the president faced escalating calls to help this friendly army in an unforgiving land. Wilson finally caved into this mounting pressure in early July when he decided to go into Siberia in order to "rescue" the Czecho-Slovaks. His plan, which was laid out in an *aide-mémoire* made public several weeks later, called for the U.S. and Japan to each send an expeditionary force of 7,000 troops into Siberia. After landing at Vladivostok, the Allied troops would move westward to reach the legionaries stranded in Central Siberia. The Allied expeditionary forces, as far as Wilson was concerned, had no need to proceed beyond Irkutsk, which the Czecho-Slovaks held by mid–July. Once contact was made with the Czecho-Slovak forces from Central Siberia, all foreign troops in Siberia were to withdraw in unison to Vladivostok, from where they would evacuate Russia.

The intervention envisaged by Wilson was to be primarily a humanitarian, not military, operation. He had no desire to go into Russia either to reestablish an eastern front against the Central Powers or to unseat the Bolsheviks in Moscow. But his projected limited intervention, much to his irritation, quickly spiraled out of control. Japan, which had been invited by the president to contribute 7,000 troops to the operation, quickly refused to restrict its expeditionary force to such a low number. On the other hand, Britain and France, although denied any direct role in the plan laid out by Wilson's *aide-mémoire*, were not about to let go of the objectives for which they had clamored for so long. French officers and diplomats in Russia urged the Czecho-Slovaks to help the anti–Bolshevik Russians form new fronts along the Volga and in the Urals.[54] Meanwhile, the British ordered the 25th Battalion of the Middlesex Regiment, stationed in Hong Kong, to leave for Vladivostok, where they landed on 3 August 1918.[55] It quickly became apparent that each country was intent on implementing its own plan for intervention in Siberia.

The Advent of Dictatorship

Like the Allied interventionists, the anti–Bolshevik groups that had ostensibly united behind the Czecho-Slovak Legion also were frequently at odds with each other during the summer of 1918. In nearly every place where the legionaries liberated a pocket of territory in the early days of their campaign, an anti–Bolshevik government sprung up. In addition to these local governments were the administrations of Cossack hosts as well as committees formed by Bashkir and Tatar nationalists. Since few of these organizations were willing to relinquish their pretenses of power even after the Czecho-Slovaks had cleared the entire span of the Trans-Siberian Railway, White Siberia became a political jigsaw puzzle.

Among this trove of competing authorities, two stood above the rest. One was the Komuch in Samara which, by calling for all power to the Constituent Assembly, attracted socialists and democratic elements to its banner. The other was the Siberian Provisional Government that had been proclaimed in Omsk at the end of June 1918. Initially, the Siberian Provisional Government was dominated by politicians sympathetic to democracy and regionalism, but these men soon faded into the background as the new government entrusted its affairs to experienced—in other words tsarist—bureaucrats, officers and personnel. Under their auspices, the Siberian Provisional Government abandoned its regionalist, liberal aims in favor of wider national goals, authoritarianism, a conservative land policy and traditional military discipline for its army. Gradually, it became clear that outside their opposition to Bolshevism, the Siberian Provisional Government and Komuch had little in common. For them, the civil war in Siberia became a three-way ideological struggle between the Bolsheviks and each other. Although the Samara—Omsk rivalry fell short of open conflict, they did engage each other in a customs war and other intrigue as they vied for supreme authority in the White movement east of the Volga.[56]

Among those who encouraged the conservative evolution and hardline attitudes of the Siberian Provisional Government were Siberian Cossack officers. The revolutionary turmoil of the previous year had served as a poignant reminder to the Siberian Cossacks, as well as their brethren further to the east, of just how dependent their way of life had been on the tsarist regime. Unlike Cossacks of the Don and Kuban, the Siberian Cossacks had been unable to establish anything resembling a state structure. Their communities were simply too small, dispersed and backward to dominate the far larger non–Cossack population in their midst. Subsequently, the Siberian Cossack leadership recognized that they needed a strong outside patron, as the tsar had been, to prevent themselves from being submerged in a sea of outlanders. Naturally, they believed that those conservative groups who bemoaned the passing of the *ancien régime*—political reactionaries, former bureaucrats, army officers—would be most amenable to their needs, and as a result they welcomed these elements as refugees to their host capital of Omsk. In turn, the conservatives, recalling the fabled bond between the Cossacks and the throne, were more than willing to accept the Siberian Cossacks as their allies within the anti–Bolshevik movement.

One event which had a lasting impact on Siberia's political future, though its significance was not immediately evident, was the appointment of the ataman of the Siberian Cossacks, General P. P. Ivanov-Rinov, to commander-in-chief of the Siberian Army on 5 September 1918. Just a few days after assuming his new post, Ivanov-Rinov made it clear that he refused to cater to any revolutionary sentiment by ordering the restoration of epaulets on officers' uniforms. Nor was he prepared to show any restraint towards those groups or villages who exhibited the slightest resistance to his authority. Ivanov-Rinov, who had acquired infamy for his brutality during the Kazakh rebellions in Turkestan two years earlier, gave punitive expeditions in Siberia considerable license in their efforts to stamp out partisan activity in the region. "The commanders of punitive detachments did not have to answer for their unlawful actions—on the contrary, in most cases they were rewarded," a district commissar grimly observed. "This policy of course encouraged flagrant *atamanshchina*."[57]

By late summer, while the conservative ministers and army officers, with the backing of Siberian Cossacks, were in the process of hijacking the Provisional Siberian Government, the Komuch and the Czecho-Slovaks were engaged in a bitter struggle against the Red Army. Since the Volga front was 1,000 miles away, the Omsk government was not alarmed by the growing military might of the Bolsheviks and refused to send its troops as reinforcements.[58] This utter lack of cooperation was unacceptable to the Czecho-Slovaks, who were still bearing the brunt of the fighting. In July the Czecho-Slovak National Council tried to unite the fractured White governments behind their front by inviting their delegates to a conference at Chelyabinsk. After that proved unsuccessful, they made another attempt in August in which they did not hide their frustration with the inability of their Russian allies to close ranks and devote all their energies to defeating Bolshevism. "Why is it," inquired a memorandum presented to the delegates by the National Council, "that after three months so little has been done by the Russians to form organizations of their own?"[59] Despite the Czechs' open disgust, the anti–Bolshevik Russians still failed to attain political unity. Their only agreement was to meet for a third time in the town of Ufa.

The Ufa State Conference, which began on 8 September, coincided with a military crisis on the Volga front. Two days after the conference opened, the Czecho-Slovaks and People's Army evacuated Kazan, and on the heels of that defeat came the loss of Simbirsk. While the gathered delegates bickered over politics, Czecho-Slovak observers tried to accentuate the gravity of the situation by keeping them updated on the latest setbacks at the front.[60] At least one Cossack delegate got the hint and cried, "While we are arguing the Bolsheviks will capture Ufa together with the whole conference."[61] But overall the delegates remained as polarized as ever. The Komuch representatives, supported by other socialists and Muslim spokesmen from Central Asia, wanted supreme authority to rest with the Constituent Assembly. On the other hand, an increasingly illiberal group of Kadets declared that the experiences of the past year demonstrated that democracy in Russia was doomed to failure since the masses "confuse liberty with license." Subsequently, they argued that what the country needed to weather the present crisis was a dictatorship, and their position was backed by the Omsk delegation and most Cossacks.[62] Amid the heated deliberations, the opposing sides may have never come together if it were not for the Czecho-Slovak and French observers who threatened to withdraw aid from the Whites unless a settlement was reached. On 23 September the delegations finally agreed to a compromise which entrusted supreme authority to an All-Russian Provisional Government (ARPG), composed of a directory of five, until a suitable quorum of Constituent Assembly delegates could be gathered.[63]

Even with the arrangement for the ARPG in place, the quarrels between the various factions of anti–Bolshevik Russians persisted. At first they argued over which town the ARPG should designate as its capital; eventually the socialists conceded to Omsk since it was a safe distance away from the advancing Red armies. The most troublesome negotiations concerned the appointments to the new government's Council of Ministers. Naturally, each side wanted to stack the cabinet with their own politically-reliable appointees, but as the talks dragged on for weeks the socialists found themselves in an increasingly disadvantageous position. At the front, their People's Army was being thrashed by the enemy. In early October, their leaders were forced to evacuate Samara as the Fourth Red Army closed in on that town. Amid these and other frustrations, the SR Party leaders soon repudiated the Ufa terms on the charge that the Siberian Kadets and their Cossack henchmen were making no effort to fulfill their end of the bargain.[64]

The SRs had plenty of reasons to suspect the true intentions of their political adversaries in the White movement. By then rumors were rife throughout Siberia that the ARPG would be toppled to make way for a military dictatorship. Among the most prominent advocates for a dictatorship in Siberia was Major-General Alfred Knox, head of the British Military Mission to the region. Throughout October, as the SRs locked horns with the Omsk politicians over ministerial appointments, Knox openly mused over whether the Czech General Gajda or Admiral Kolchak would make a better dictator for Siberia.[65] The brewing conspiracy was not even concealed from Major-General Vasily Boldyrev, one of the directors of the ARPG. "The idea of a dictatorship is gaining ground," Boldyrev wrote in a diary entry dated 28 October 1918. "This time the idea will most probably be connected with Kolchak."[66] Elsewhere in Siberia reactionaries flaunted their tsarist nostalgia. At a banquet attended by Russian, British and Czecho-Slovak officers at Krasnoyarsk, a tipsy Cossack officer provoked an uproar by ordering hapless Austro-Hungarian POWs in the orchestra to play the monarchist anthem "God Save the Tsar".[67]

As such incidents passed without any disciplinary action against the instigators, the Cossack renegades only grew bolder. They no longer made any effort to observe niceties when dealing with their nominal SR or democratic allies; in fact their conduct was quite the opposite. Politicians who wanted to balance the power of the Provisional Siberian Government with the Sibobduma were run out of Omsk. One SR and Cossack, Aleksandr Novoselov, refused to be easily intimidated. He was soon taken into custody by a Cossack detachment under Colonel V. I. Volkov and wound up dead. A few weeks later another Cossack band, this one headed by Major I. N. Krasilnikov, was implicated in the murder of a prominent SR whose corpse washed up on the bank of the Irtysh River. Although Omsk detectives attempted to gather evidence with the intent of bringing charges against the perpetrators of these crimes, it became apparent that their investigations were being obstructed by the government and military authorities.[68] By then most SRs and their supporters understood that they were under attack on two fronts: by the Red Army driving towards the Urals and the Cossack detachments operating in the rear. The latter and their conservative backers excused the persecution of the democratic socialists by blaming them for the disintegration of the once-proud tsarist army a year earlier.[69]

The rash of bullying and killing of socialists in Omsk had not gone unnoticed by the two socialist directors in the ARPG, A. V. Avksentev and V. M. Zinoviev. Yet, they were too proud to accept an offer of protection from the local Czecho-Slovak garrison.[70] With nothing standing in the way, two battalions of Siberian Cossacks led by Volkov and Krasilnikov took the two directors into custody shortly after midnight on 18 November 1918. Other Cossack units in Omsk disarmed a militia loyal to the ARPG, thereby preventing it from making a sortie to free the incarcerated politicians. Volkov and Krasilnikov then left the remaining directors and ministers alone to work out their next course of action among themselves, which they did at an emergency meeting held that following morning in the Omsk governor's palace amid a fierce snowstorm. The remaining directors, with the exception of General Boldyrev who was away at the front, readily acknowledged the futility of trying to continue with a coalition government. The Council of Ministers agreed and concluded that a military dictatorship was the best solution. They had little trouble reaching a consensus on who was the best man for the job: they overwhelmingly voted for Admiral Aleksandr Kolchak, whose advocates had been working behind the scenes for several weeks to promote the small-statured, eagle-eyed sailor to the helm of White Siberia. Kolchak, who was among the attendees to the meeting, accepted their decision and was proclaimed Supreme Ruler that same day.[71] The coup, as far as the Cossack renegades were concerned, had proceeded exactly as they intended.

The establishment of a military dictatorship in Omsk pleased not only Siberian Cossack leaders but also many officers, Kadets and prominent refugees in White Siberia. The coup also received support from unexpected quarters. British officers in Siberia endorsed the overturn of the ARPG by deploying soldiers from the Middlesex Battalion in Omsk's streets to defend the new government from any potential enemy—especially the local Czecho-Slovak garrison.[72] At the front, however, reactions to the events in Omsk were mixed. While Ataman Dutov, commanding the southern end of the Ural front, readily sided with the new regime, a significant number of men serving under him did not.[73] Ordinary Orenburg Cossacks, many of whom earlier in the year had taken up arms under egalitarian slogans, were estranged by the anti-democratic character of the Supreme Ruler's coup. Even more hostile to the abrupt change in leadership were the Bashkir nationalists, who had been fighting alongside the anti–Bolshevik Cossacks in the Urals for the past several months. Throughout the latter half of 1918, the chairman of the Bashkir National Council, Zek Validov, had unsuccessfully lobbied the Komuch and other anti–Bolshevik authorities for some guarantee of Bashkir self-rule. By the end of the year, his patience was wearing thin and the installation of a more conservative government in Omsk compelled him to give up his politicking altogether. In early December, Validov summoned leaders from the Bashkirs and democratically-inclined Cossacks to a secret meeting where he laid out plans to retake control of their military campaign by arresting Dutov. The scheme, however, was uncovered before the conspirators could act and the entire plot fell apart.[74] In the meantime, the Siberian Whites continued to ignore the Bashkirs' grievances at their own peril.

The Czecho-Slovaks, whose exhausted, demoralized units were beginning to disengage from the front, were also dismayed by the overthrow of the ARPG but made no serious effort to challenge the coup. In the days after his ascension to power, the Supreme Ruler did try to placate his critics by reassuring them that the Siberian Cossack officers who instigated the coup would be court-martialed.[75] Although three ringleaders—Krasilnikov, Volkov and Major Katanaev—were investigated, they were also immediately promoted by Kolchak for their "excellent military service." In a brief trial a few days later, the men were found guilty of wrongdoing but were set free without further punishment. In the meantime, their high-profile prisoners, Avksentev and Zinoviev, were escorted to a train which delivered them into exile in Harbin.[76] The entire affair, from which the SR directors were fortunate to have escaped with their lives, foreshadowed the sort of lawlessness that would be tolerated in Kolchak's Siberia.

The Cossack Kleptocracies

While the Siberian, Orenburg and Ural Cossacks gradually accepted the Kolchak regime as the paternalistic sponsor they needed preserve their estate, the Transbaikal and Ussuri Cossacks in the Russian Far East looked to Japan to fill that role. Although Japan was Russia's ally in World War I, the two countries had been longtime rivals in the Far East and had clashed in a ferocious war during the previous decade. After the outbreak of hostilities in Europe in 1914, Japanese leaders sought to strengthen their military position and economic penetration in Eastern Asia at the expense of the belligerent powers, including her allies. These ambitions were presented with a new field of opportunities during the course of the 1917 as Russia slid into revolutionary disarray. Using the tried-and-true methods they had employed in China, the Japanese sought to increase their influence in Siberia by backing one warring Russian faction against another. They had some difficulty, however, in identifying a suitable group to support. The Japanese leaders, especially those in the military, were intolerant of all socialists, and therefore they were unwilling to aid any of the early underground organizations with SR affiliations. This prejudice against socialists effectively limited their options to Cossack leaders such as Semyonov and Kalmykov, and as a result these young brigands became the focus of Japanese policy in Siberia.[77]

Although the British and French had also provided some supplies and funds to Semyonov in early 1918, they severed their aid to him after other anti–Bolshevik groups with wider appeal emerged elsewhere in Siberia. But the Japanese, who had always been Semyonov's most generous sponsor, continued to back the ataman even after the Czecho-Slovak-led campaign had swept Soviet forces out of Siberia. By then the Japanese could offer much more than just material support to their Cossack protégé. Disregarding the manpower limits set by Wilson's *aide-mémoire*, the Japanese flooded Eastern Siberia and Manchuria with soldiers; before the year was finished they had at least 70,000 troops in those regions.[78] This preponderance of strength essentially elevated the Japanese command to the role of kingmaker in the Russian Far East, and the man they wanted in power was Semyonov. As a sign of their continued devotion to the Cossack captain, the commander of the Japanese Expeditionary Force, General Otani, appointed Semyonov as the commander-in-chief of the Transbaikal region. To make his hold over that area more real, the ataman set up his capital in Chita, which was strategically located near the junction of the Trans-Siberian and the Chinese Eastern railways. Meanwhile, the Japanese permitted his faithful comrade, Baron Ungern-Sternberg, to turn the railside town of Dauria into his fiefdom. Further east, Ataman Kalmykov used the protection afforded by the Japanese to establish his base in Khabarovsk. From these centers, located thousands of miles from the pitched battles against the Red Army in the Urals, these petty White leaders began a reign of terror on the pretext that they were fighting Bolshevism.

Even before they assumed the role of tin-pot dictators, the unruly behavior of the Cossack atamans in the Russian Far East had appalled foreigners and Russians alike. In a contemporary military report on conditions in that region, a Russian general observed that Semyonov "began his career by flogging a number of Manchurian railway officials for their alleged sympathies with Bolshevism."[79] This assessment was unfair: Semyonov had engaged Soviet forces in the Russian Far East when no one else in that region would do so. But the whippings of railway workers which the report's author described did occur, and such abuse, which continued throughout Semyonov's reign, quickly eclipsed his early contributions to the anti–Bolshevik movement.

From the start of his counterrevolutionary activities, Semyonov had realized that the control of even a relatively small portion of the Trans-Siberian Railway could net him great rewards as all imports from the Allies designated for the front in the Urals had to travel along the Trans-Siberian Railway and pass through Chita. To impose his will on this vital artery, Semyonov had his hirelings build armored trains from which they could patrol the railway and interfere with its operation. From these terrestrial battleships, many emblazoned with such names as *Terrible, Destroyer* and *Merciless*, they intimidated railway workers and station masters into submission. Under their instructions, passenger cars and other rolling stock in high demand were impounded in train yards and only released to those willing to pay exorbitant prices. Passing trains were held up so the Semyonovites could pilfer their freight or rob travelers of valuables. Often trains could only resume their journeys after paying a hefty bribe. Although the brigands devoted most of their energies to prowling the railways, many unlucky villages were not spared their predations. Squadrons of Semyonovites would gallop into communities which they alleged were harboring partisans and proceed to pillage, murder, rape and carry out other horrendous acts of violence. Anyone who resisted and was not killed outright might be sent to a dungeon or, most dreaded of all, to the torture chamber in Dauria operated by the demented Ungern-Sternberg.[80] The ataman and his cronies justified these barbarities in the name of patriotism: they claimed that the property they stole was needed for their military funds while anyone whom they killed was labeled a Bolshevik.[81]

While Semyonov's detachments terrorized the railways in the Transbaikal, similar atrocities occurred on a smaller scale in the vicinity of Khabarovsk. One of the most senseless incidents in that town occurred shortly after it was occupied by the Whites and their allies on 5 September 1918. Kalmykov's Ussuri Cossacks, who were among the first to enter Khabarovsk, immediately celebrated their victory by slaughtering 16 Austro-Hungarian POWs who were armed only with clarinets and violins—the unfortunate men had belonged to an orchestra. The victims' corpses were later observed by the doughboys of the U.S. 27th Infantry Regiment when they arrived in the town behind their Cossack allies. On the heels of this incident, four employees of the Swedish Red Cross mission in Khabarovsk were killed in a robbery instigated by Kalmykov's followers.[82] As reports of such barbarities were passed up the chain of command, the commander of the American Expeditionary Force to Siberia, General William Graves, quickly formed a lasting negative opinion of the anti-communist Russians. In his memoir, Graves recalled that the main difference between Kalmykov and Semyonov was that the former "murdered with his own hands" while the latter "ordered others to kill."[83] Indeed, like Ungern-Sternberg, Kalmykov appears to have taken delight in inflicting personal tortures upon alleged Bolsheviks.[84] But despite their intense hatred of communism, neither Kalmykov nor Semyonov would send troops to battle the Reds where it counted the most: on the Ural front. In fact, the patriotic officers and enlisted men serving under them who asked to be transferred westward to fight regular Soviet forces had their requests denied and sometimes were executed.[85] Since they were eager to cower their abused subjects with an aura of invincibility, each ataman jealously guarded the manpower which they had accrued in the course of their campaigns.

As word of Semyonov and Kalmykov's behavior spread, it did not take well-meaning White officers long to figure out that the two atamans were becoming liabilities in the struggle against the Soviet regime. In late October, General Boldyrev was brooding over reports alleging that "the atamans of the Far East spread anarchy in that region at the direct instigation of the Japanese."[86] Semyonov had never shown much enthusiasm for cooperating with other anti–Bolshevik governments, but his stance turned outright hostile to Omsk after Kolchak assumed power as Supreme Ruler. He never forgave the admiral for choking his detachment's supplies while serving as General Horvath's military advisor during the previous spring. Now with their geographical positions reversed, it was Semyonov's turn to strangle Kolchak's armies. Within days of the Omsk coup, the ataman openly stated his refusal to place himself under Kolchak's authority and shunted any westbound supply trains traveling through his realm. In response, a furious Kolchak prepared to send an expedition east against Semyonov but was forced to back down after the Japanese made it clear that they were ready to defend their protégé. Semyonov's virtual blockade of Kolchak's realm continued until the summer of 1919, when the two rivals finally hammered out a deal. In that settlement, the Supreme Ruler, in exchange for the ataman's allegiance, formally recognized Semyonov as the commander of all Russian forces east of Lake Baikal. Unsurprisingly, the ataman was only partially as good as his word and continued to disrupt transportation along the railway.[87]

From the Japanese perspective, the destabilizing activities of their Cossack protégés were satisfactory since they impeded the establishment of a strong, unitary Russian authority in Eastern Siberia. Besides political benefits, their support of the Cossack warlords also yielded economic advantages for them. In the marketplaces of Eastern Siberia, Japanese products gained a competitive edge over their foreign competitors since Semyonov waived any import restrictions on their goods. The ataman also encouraged Japanese investment into the region by allowing them to purchase factories, housing and other properties at cut-rate prices.[88] In exchange for these concessions, Semyonov received a lump payment or a portion of the profits. These dealings, combined with the revenue from his Chita retail shops stocked with plundered loot,[89] transformed the ataman into a wealthy man almost overnight. He soon amassed a harem, which was housed in an elegantly-furnished railcar, and deposited his earnings in foreign bank accounts. For him and his cronies, the quest to reap greater rewards through shady business ventures and heists became a major distraction in their campaign against Bolshevism.[90]

Japanese backing was crucial for both Semyonov and Kalmykov throughout their counterrevolutionary careers. Indeed, General Graves declared that Semyonov, who eventually acquired the grandiose title of field ataman of the Transbaikal, Amur and Ussuri Cossack Hosts, "could not have existed one week in Siberia if he had not the protection of Japan."[91] Quite simply, the Cossack warlords lacked a secure, sizeable base of support among the population of their districts. Their subservience to a foreign rival compromised them in the eyes of patriotic Russians. Ordinary villagers resented the high-handedness of the Japanese troops and the brigandage which the Cossacks themselves carried out.[92] Semyonov and Kalmykov, for their part, made little effort to win over their subjects. They feared the popular will of the people and employed terror to keep their populations docile.

Terror was used against not only civilians but also on those serving in Kalmykov's little army, where poorly-clad conscripts were kept in line by beating and floggings. This practice was a contributing factor behind the mutiny in Khabarovsk of roughly 800 Ussuri Cossacks on the night of 27–28 January 1919. After abandoning their barracks and posts, many Ussuri Cossacks headed for their stanitsas, but 388 of them sought asylum at the headquarters of the U.S. 27th Regiment. The perplexed Americans took the anxious Cossacks under their protection, opening a rift between them, Kalmykov and the Japanese; the latter objecting on the grounds that they owned the deserters' rifles. For four weeks the Cossacks remained under U.S. protection where, by their own testament, they were given exemplary treatment. During that period, they drafted a manifesto addressed to the Ussuri Krug in which they defended their decision to leave Kalmykov, whom they accused of executing over 2,000 persons without trial. "Under the pretext of being Bolsheviks," the mutineers alleged, "peaceful Russians have been killed with the sole purpose of robbing them." They also asserted that they were rarely paid, underfed and regularly flogged by the ataman and his officers. Subsequently, they urged the krug to strip Kalmykov of his powers and elect a different leader. Unfortunately for the mutineers, this attempt to depose Kalmykov was doomed; the Japanese would never allow their protégé to be replaced by someone who might be sympathetic to the Americans, British or Great Russian nationalism. Eventually, an agreement was worked out between the Americans and Japanese where the Cossack mutineers were set free after turning over their arms, but the incident was nonetheless a major embarrassment for Kalmykov. In an attempt to save face, he pinned blame for the mutiny on subversion by American agitators.[93]

Semyonov's units, though they were a heterogeneous mixture of Transbaikal Cossacks, Buryats, Mongols, Serbian deserters and a handful of other foreign mercenaries, seemed to possess a bit more devotion to their commander. This may be partly attributed to the fact that the ataman, despite his grotesque appearance and savage reputation, was a captivating individual.[94] As an experienced commander and recruiter, he was also probably a bit more tactful towards his men than the more abrasive Kalmykov. In an effort to clinch the loyalties of the Buryats and Mongols who comprised a significant portion of his forces, Semyonov made a brief attempt to style himself as their national leader. In early 1919 the Cossack warlord, who one observer described as "more Mongol than Russian,"[95] sponsored a Pan-Mongolism movement. He may have hoped to become a modern Great Khan, but the entire enterprise soon withered away after the Japanese, under pressure from their allies, the Omsk government and the Chinese, withdrew their support from the project.[96]

With the failure of his Pan-Mongol movement, Semyonov's political aspirations had to settle with his dictatorship in the Transbaikal, but throughout 1919 his hold on that region grew more tenuous. While the Semyonovites directed most of their energies to piracy operations along the railways, Bolsheviks and Red Army men driven into the countryside during the summer of 1918 were left unmolested and allowed to regroup. Over the following months, they were joined by droves of abused peasants, workers and Korean and Chinese immigrants who were eager to exact revenge upon the Semyonovites and their Japanese backers. In some areas the guerrillas acquired enough strength to wipe out entire patrols. In a particularly bloody week during February 1919, the Japanese reported losing at least 330 troops to partisans just in the vicinity of Blagoveshchensk.[97] By the following summer, the insurgency in the Transbaikal and other areas of the Russian Far East was booming. In July, these partisans were reinforced by a regiment of Transbaikal Cossacks who switched their allegiance from Semyonov to the rebels; a humiliation for the warlord that was on par with the discomfiture experienced by Kalmykov the previous winter. By then, entire regions of the Transbaikal were off-limits to the Semyonovites and their allies, and their outlook did not improve. The partisans were becoming more daring, were closing in on the railways and proved themselves to be more than match for the Semyonovites in battle.[98]

Thus Semyonov and Kalmykov, both of whom withheld their forces from the main front against the Soviet republic ostensibly to keep the Red enemy from reappearing in the rear of the Siberian Whites, utterly failed to meet even that modest objective. The resulting fiasco was largely of their making. Rather than seek accommodation with the Omsk government, the Cossack warlords instead pursued their own aggrandizement by effectively hiring themselves out to the Japanese. Since the Japanese would never allow them to form a strong or stable government in Eastern Siberia, the atamans had to set their sights much lower. While nearly all Cossack governments, including those of South Russia, were guilty of emphasizing regional goals at the expense of the broader anti–Soviet campaign, the regimes of Semyonov and Kalmykov had the narrowest outlook of all. Their program was one simply based on satisfying material, sexual or violent fetishes. Their depredations antagonized the local inhabitants while their defiance of Kolchak's authority further emboldened the Whites' enemies by exposing the weakness of the Omsk government. Instead of preventing Bolshevism from taking root in Eastern Siberia, the Cossack warlords unwittingly prepared a fertile seedbed for it.

Kolchak's Front: November 1918–July 1919

When Admiral Kolchak took power in November 1918, the White armies in the Urals were in disarray. On the southern end of the front, the Orenburg Cossacks of Ataman Dutov were giving ground to the advancing Reds. The situation was not much better in the center where the remnants of the Komuch's People's Army were also in steady retreat. The only bright spot for the Siberian Whites was on the northern end of the front, to the west of Yekaterinburg, where the Czecho-Slovak Second Division and the recently-arrived Siberian Army were holding their lines. In December, these units, led by General Gajda, marched through deep snow amid bone-chilling temperatures towards the town of Perm, which they entered on Christmas Eve. "There were practically no wounded," a British colonel wrote of that battle, "for any man who sank in the snow was dead in an hour."[99] By taking that town, the Whites had dealt a crushing blow to the Third Red Army and captured 31,000 prisoners along with several armored trains, hundreds of locomotives and other valuable rolling stock.[100]

The uplifting news from Perm was badly needed by the Kolchak government. Just a few days earlier an underground cell of Bolsheviks had staged an abortive coup in the Supreme Ruler's capital. Although the uprising was too feeble to present a grave threat to the Kolchak government, it still succeeded in winning over two companies of the Siberian 8th Regiment. While the presence of a potent Bolshevik organization in Omsk was disconcerting for Kolchak's supporters, the real scandal was committed by Siberian Cossacks while they were mopping up alleged rebels. As they moved into Omsk's working neighborhoods, the Siberian Cossacks showed little discretion in distinguishing passive workers from active Bolsheviks. All were liable to be dragged out of their homes, flogged and even killed. A similar fate awaited many political prisoners who had been set free by the rebels during their brief occupation of the town's prison. Nineteen of the escapees, including some members of Constituent Assembly, turned themselves in the next morning but their voluntary surrender did not spare them from the Cossacks' worst excesses. On the following day, their corpses—some of them decapitated—were discovered on the banks of the Irtysh River. Estimates of the overall persons killed in the massacre vary, but the number of victims soared into the hundreds and may have even approached a thousand or more. In its aftermath, nothing was done by the government to bring the Cossack perpetrators to justice.

The Omsk massacre tarnished Kolchak's government at a time when it was trying to attract foreign aid and recognition from the Allies. Fortunately for it, the troubling incident was eclipsed by the exciting news of the Perm victory.[101] Still, the terrible crime was condemned by the Czecho-Slovak legionaries. Their entire corps, in the words of one Czech officer, felt that "the Ural Line was no longer worth the loss of a single Czech life."[102] That winter, the demoralized, homesick legionaries continued to withdraw from the battlelines where they were sorely missed, especially in the center of Kolchak's front. There the initiative remained with the Soviets. A week after the Whites took Perm, Ufa fell to the Fifth Red Army. Further south, the news was even worse. Morale among the Orenburg Cossacks had crashed, leading to desertion in Dutov's army.[103] In January 1919, both the Ural and Orenburg Cossacks lost their capitals to the Fourth and First Red Armies.[104]

The position of the Ural and Orenburg Cossacks was rendered difficult by their relative geographical isolation from their anti–Bolshevik allies. The Whites' loss of Samara in October 1918 was major setback for their forces in the southern Urals since their only direct railway connection with that region ran through Samara. From there on, the two Cossack groups could only maintain contact with the Siberian Whites through a combination of winding river and overland routes. That front was further weakened in February 1919 when approximately 2,000 Bashkir troops switched their allegiance after the Bolsheviks, willing to go to almost any length to divide their enemies, made a generous tactical agreement with Bashkir leaders that would grant them their own soviet republic with considerable autonomy. The Bashkirs' mass desertion left the White front with a major gap and further undercut the morale of the Ural and Orenburg Cossacks who comprised much of Kolchak's Southern Army.[105]

Even amid the unfavorable circumstances on the southern end of the Ural Front, Kolchak and his top brass were determined to go over to the offensive as early as possible. They launched their attack in the first week of March 1919 and made impressive gains, particularly in the center of their front. By the middle of the month, Kolchak's Western Army retook Ufa and just a few weeks later was approaching the east bank of the Volga River. To the south, the Orenburg and Ural Cossacks of the Southern Army also pushed westward. Their progress, however, had more to do with the Western Army's success rather than their own operations as the First Red Army before them fell back to maintain contact with the retreating Fifth Red Army to the north. Indeed, the Cossacks on that front were unable to match their successes of the previous year as a Red garrison managed to hold onto Orenburg.[106]

The Southern Army's failure to keep abreast with the Western Army eventually allowed the Soviets to form a striking force against the latter's exposed left flank.[107] On 28 April, these Red troops, commanded by Mikhail Frunze, counterattacked and put the exhausted soldiers of the Western Army to flight. In about six weeks the resurgent Red Eastern Army Group erased the gains made by the Western Army and by late June succeeded in pushing all three White armies back to their initial starting lines in the Ural foothills.

The retreat of the Siberian Whites did not end there. Throughout July, Red troops infiltrated the Urals, seizing Zlatoust, Yekaterinburg and, by the end of that month, Chelyabinsk.[108] The retreating Whites were in shambles. "From Tyumen west all disorder and panic; no one in charge," reported an American general visiting Omsk. "Officers and men leaving front [on] every train by hundreds, no apparent control, no arms, some equipment, few slightly wounded on hand, probably self-inflicted."[109] The loss of the Urals was a devastating blow for White Siberia not only because they were the best natural barrier between Omsk and the Red Army, but also because they were home to mines, foundries and other valuable industries that were nearly absent in the territories further east.

By late summer of 1919, the Kolchak regime and the Cossack hosts most directly associated with it were in dire straits. From the Urals, the remnants of the Northern and Western Armies withdrew east into Western Siberia and the lands of the Siberian Cossack Host with two Red armies in hot pursuit. Meanwhile, the Southern Army fell back southeast along the Orenburg—Tashkent railway, thus increasing the distance of undeveloped steppe between them and their allies to the north. Cut-off from White Siberia, pressed by the First and Fourth Red Armies to their west and the militias of the Turkestan Soviet Republic to their southeast, they quickly found themselves in a hopeless position.[110]

Overall, the various Cossack hosts in the Urals and further to the east proved to be a mixed blessing to the anti–Soviet campaign in that vast region. While the eastern atamans often possessed the same counterrevolutionary ardor as Kaledin or Kornilov, their hosts were much less formidable than those of the Don or Kuban Cossacks. Often, they had to resort to terror to enforce their will, and by the time the Whites rose to power in Siberia during the summer of 1918, this habit was firmly ingrained into them. At Omsk, they intimidated other anti–Bolshevik groups and engineered a political coup to install a government that was more acceptable to them. In the Russian Far East, Atamans Semyonov and Kalmykov preferred to satisfy their personal greed rather than devote their energies to wider anticommunist goals. "Generally speaking, a Cossack Ataman has no conception of any policy which would contribute towards the restoration of a great united Russia," explained the U.S. Consul General in Irkutsk, Ernst Harris, in a cable to his superiors in Washington. "His chief ambition is to remain all powerful in some Cossack districts."[111] For some reason, it was incomprehensible to them that the authority which they exercised in the hosts was inextricably tied to the fortunes of the wider anti–Bolshevik movement. Indeed, the contributions of the eastern Cossacks at the front were marginal during the most critical phases of Kolchak's operations. While most historians agree that the Cossacks of South Russia were a valuable asset to Denikin's forces, providing him with effective shock units and perhaps a majority of his troops, the same cannot be said for the eastern Cossacks. Although a Cossack brigade was attached to each corps in the Siberian Army, the Cossacks comprised only a small percentage of Kolchak's troops and before the autumn of 1919 they had done very little to distinguish themselves in a major operation.[112] That statement, however, does not mean that they did not achieve notoriety on the frontlines. When the Whites entered Ufa in March 1919, for example, the Cossacks marching with them dispatched 670 prisoners from the Red Army.[113] A few months later, Ataman Annenkov and his henchmen, already infamous for their bloody punitive expeditions in the countryside around Semipalatinsk (Semey), went to the front near Yekaterinburg and initiated a pogrom against local Jews.[114] Since such atrocities were rarely punished, their perpetrators did much to discredit the White movement in Siberia, not just among British, French and American observers, but also among the Russian peasants whose sympathies were needed on some level if the Whites hoped to win the civil war.

6

Rampage

The Collapse of the Don Army

In the first weeks of 1919, exhaustion took a toll on several groups of anticommunist Cossacks. On Kolchak's front, the Ural and Orenburg Cossacks were in steady retreat. Likewise, in South Russia the Don Cossack Army, which had recently peaked at 50,000 men, began to fall back against four Red Armies with a combined strength of 113,500 men. With most fit male Cossacks already mobilized, Krasnov's government had no other source of manpower except those it had regarded as pariahs: the outlanders. Its only hope was that the recent incorporation of the Don Army into the Armed Forces of South Russia would deliver reinforcements and Allied supplies. Even so, this relief would take weeks to reach the front; in the meantime, only a handful of Volunteer troops were available to fight alongside the Don Cossacks in the Donets Basin. Their Red opponents, in contrast, were receiving generous reinforcements after the Soviet government began to concentrate on its Southern Front that winter. Worse yet, the tenacity of the Red troops was improving. The reforms enacted by Trotsky earlier in 1918 were producing the desired results for the Bolsheviks; subsequently the Red troops were much better led, organized and supplied than they had been at the outbreak of the civil war. These achievements did much to erase some of the earlier advantages enjoyed by the Cossacks and the Volunteer Army.[1]

In addition to the fatigue experienced by the outnumbered Don Cossacks, they were being showered with Bolshevik propaganda extending verbal olive branches towards working Cossacks. These appeals once again sought to drive a wedge between the Cossacks serving at the front and those running the government in Novocherkassk. Some of the most effective leaflets were authored by the famed Red Cossack commander Lieutenant-Colonel Mironov, who was cutting a dashing figure for himself in the civil war. By the start of 1919, the unit under Mironov's command had grown to a division of well over 7,000 combatants. Among those fighting with him were hundreds of Don Cossack defectors from Krasnov's army. In his addition to his talents as a field commander, Mironov also projected the image of a lenient and benevolent leader. Even after the bloodiest of battles, Mironov released captured Cossacks back to their lines; a rare humanitarian gesture which stood out in a war where prisoners were frequently shot or drafted by their captors. Moreover, whenever his soldiers advanced Mironov attempted to enforce strict discipline to prevent looting and other acts of violence against the local population, regardless of whether they were Cossacks or outlanders. Despite the efforts of the Don government to smear his reputation, Mironov became a popular figure with Cossacks on both sides of the front. Subsequently, several breakaway stanitsas in the northern Don opted to arrange a peace settlement with the Red Cossack commander.[2]

As the disillusionment in the Don Army's ranks grew more apparent, the Soviet command of the Southern Front decided that the moment was ripe for an attack. In late January Mironov, with three Soviet divisions, launched a drive on the Ninth Red Army's sector that met no serious resistance. The offensive quickly caved in the front along the northern Don as the Red troops pushed southward toward the Donets River. In the ensuing mayhem, some bewildered Don Cossack units found their line of retreat severed, others joined the

"Cossack! Which side are you on? Are you with us or them?" asks the workers and peasants (at left) of the Cossack soldier (center) in this Soviet propaganda poster from 1920. The caricatures in the background (at right) represent the Polish nobility, foreign capitalists and the White generals (Heritage Images / Fine Art Images / akg-images).

enemy while most simply returned to their stanitsas. The deserters were so numerous, recalled one Bolshevik commissar, that advancing Reds passed whole files of them along the roads. Whenever a Red soldier jeeringly asked them whether they were done fighting, a Cossack would invariably reply, "You really can't hold out against all of Russia!"[3] Their mass decampment opened the entire upper Don to the Eighth and Ninth Red Armies, enabling them to threaten the rear of the Don Army units besieging Tsaritsyn. As Krasnov transferred units from his eastern front to shore up his retreating forces to the north, the Tenth Red Army defending Tsaritsyn began to roll back the Don Cossacks in that sector as well. The scale of the defeat stunned Krasnov who, in a frantic letter to Denikin, observed that the enemy was on the verge of wiping out the all gains so laboriously won by the Don Army over the past year.[4]

For Krasnov, the collapse of the front in the northern Don was a military setback as well as a political one. Prior to that event, he had been facing mounting criticism in the Don Krug from detractors who complained that his earlier pro–German orientation had left the host diplomatically isolated after the Allied victory in the world war. To obtain the full-backing of the Volunteer Army and especially the Allies, they felt it was necessary to jettison Krasnov and replace him with someone who enjoyed the confidence of the victorious powers. On 14 February, as the Red Army was sweeping through the upper Don, the krug returned to session and immediately demanded that the Don Army be placed under a new commander more favorable to Denikin. Krasnov took offense to the suggestion and declared he would rather resign than submit to the resolution. Most likely, the ataman expected the delegates to back down from this threat, but they did not. The krug voted against him, accepted his resignation and brought his nine-month reign of the All-Great Don Host to an ignominious end.[5]

The man elected to succeed Krasnov as ataman was General Afrikan Bogaevsky, a veteran of the Icy March in early 1918 and, more importantly, a firm supporter of Denikin. He and the new commander of the Don Army, General Vladimir Sidorin, were expected to harmonize relations with the commanders of the AFSR. The majority of Don Cossack delegates had come to appreciate that close cooperation with the White generals was essential to prevent their homeland from being completely overrun by the enemy. Indeed, the military situation which Bogaevsky inherited upon his election as ataman was anything but favorable. In just a matter of weeks, the once formidable Don Army had shriveled to only 15,000 combatants. After retreating to the right bank of the Donets River, the remaining Cossacks desperately tried to hold that line, but in some places the Red troops had crossed the ice and were poised to move against Novocherkassk. Fortunately for the Don Cossacks, a late February thaw broke up the ice sheet and forced that front to lapse into a stalemate. The stabilized situation there, along with the operations on the ends of the front, gave the Don leaders a much-needed respite. In the east, the Don Army units were making a relatively orderly withdrawal from the vicinity of Tsaritsyn. To the west, in the Donets Basin, a crack force of Volunteer troops under General May-Maevsky was waging a brilliant defensive campaign against vastly superior enemy forces. By holding the Donets Basin, the Volunteers denied the Bolsheviks access to the district's coal, barred the approaches to Taganrog and Rostov and prevented the Don Cossacks from being cut off during their retreat from the northern Don. Thanks in part to the efforts of May-Maevsky's men, the Don Army, though much reduced in size, was able to regroup south of the Donets and husband its remaining strength for future battles.[6]

While the election of Bogaevsky as ataman was welcome news at Denikin's headquar-

ters in Yekaterinodar, the crisis in the northern Don was not. At the time, the White campaign was in a transitional phase as many of their forces were being redeployed to new fronts. Under Denikin's plan, the Volunteer Army would be redeployed in the Donets Basin while the recently-formed Caucasian Army would operate on his eastern flank. His strategy, however, did not come without controversy as General Wrangel advocated for the AFSR to concentrate along the Volga with the ultimate goal of forming a junction with Kolchak's armies.[7] But Denikin would hear none of it; he still placed great hopes in the Don and

Kuban Cossack lands as a source of military recruits and would not risk abandoning them to the enemy.[8]

Although Denikin valued the Cossacks as a wellspring of manpower, he had doubts in their own ability to operate effectively against the Red armies. This assessment soon appeared to be validated by events in the eastern Don Host, where the Tenth Red Army crossed the lightly-defended Manych River and threatened the communications of the Don Army units to the north. Once again, the setback was attributed to the Cossacks' poor morale. "The susceptibility of the Don Cossacks to Bolshevist propaganda has become a recurring factor one has to reckon with," observed a British correspondent in Yekaterinodar.[9] Denikin soon restored the situation along the Manych with Wrangel's Caucasian troops, but the episode was a poignant reminder of why he was unwilling to grant other Cossacks, such as those of the Kuban or Terek, their own autonomous armies within the AFSR.[10]

The Don Cossacks were not the only ally who failed to live up to Denikin's expectations that spring. He had anticipated French and Greek expeditionary forces to secure his western flank by occupying Ukraine and Crimea, but those operations quickly came to naught after mutinies broke out among the Allied troops. By mid-spring, most of Ukraine had been seized by Soviet forces after they drove Petliura's militias into eastern Galicia.[11] The military situation of the AFSR, then, did not look particularly favorable that spring as it was pressed by enemies to the west, north and east. Yet, the position of the Red Armies on their Southern Front was not nearly as strong as it appeared, and this would soon become most apparent in the northern Don districts—the very same area where they had scored their most impressive victory earlier that year.

Déjà vu in the Upper Don

The tens of thousands of Don Cossacks who abandoned the front in the gray winter days of 1918–19 did so for slew of reasons. Among the most important of these were exhaustion and a sinking morale, both of which enhanced the appeal of Bolshevik propaganda. A particularly effective theme of the agitators was the familiar assurance that the ordinary, working-class Cossacks had nothing to fear from the Bolsheviks' program of social engineering. Other Bolshevik propaganda claimed that the Soviet government, which adhered to the principle of self-determination, would not allow the Red Army to again violate the boundaries of the Cossack hosts.[12] In the weeks following the collapse of the Don Army, however, the actions of the Red troops and the officials who followed in their wake would lay bare the falsehoods contained in these promises.

The first guarantee to be exposed as a lie was the assurance that the Red Army would not cross into the Don territory. Naturally, the Soviet commanders exploited the token resistance against them in the center of the Southern Front and occupied one stanitsa after another. Adding insult to injury was the Bolshevik practice of appointing reliable figures from within their own party to administer these "liberated" stanitsas. Since Bolsheviks native to the region were in short supply, the political workers installed in the Don were frequently non–Cossack outsiders, and many assumed their posts with the hauteur of conquerors in a newly-occupied foreign territory.[13] In general, Bolshevik attitudes towards the Cossacks hardened during the past several months. Previously, in May 1918, Sovnarkom had announced its intention to grant the Cossacks some autonomy under the Soviet regime.[14] But subsequent events, with Cossack revolts raging from Ukraine to the Ussuri, compelled many Bolsheviks to gravitate towards the extreme view that all Cossacks were inherent counterrevolutionaries who must be eradicated. This idea of "de-Cossackization" was the central theme to a 24 January 1919 circular issued by the Bolshevik Central Committee's Organizational Bureau (Orgburo). This document called for the subjugation of the Cossacks once and for all through genocidal practices of mass terror and resettlement of poor peasants from other areas of Russia to the Cossack lands. Essentially, it sought to make the outlanders the dominant element in the Cossack homelands.

Not everyone on the Red side agreed that the radical approach of de-Cossackization was the solution needed to pacify the Don territory. The Political Section of the Southern Front, for example, recognized that a campaign of widespread terror might again provoke the Cossacks into a mass revolt. For that reason, it recommended a policy of differentiating between those who led the recent anti–Bolshevik campaign in the Don and those who were merely "misled" or conscripted into Krasnov's army. While the former group was to be punished mercilessly, the latter, as long as they were not guilty of any atrocities, were to be effectively amnestied.

The more moderate policy of the Southern Front's Political Section received some support from the Don Party Bureau (Donburo) with the notable exception of its chairman, Sergey Syrtsov. A native of Rostov, the twenty-six-year-old Syrtsov had been a member of the Bolshevik Party since 1913 and had served as deputy chairman on the Don Soviet Republic formed in spring of 1918. After the Don Soviet Republic was liquidated in September 1918, he was appointed to the head of the Donburo, then operating as an underground organization in Krasnov's All-Great Don Host. As a result of his years spent in the proximity of the Cossacks; from watching the steppe horsemen charge worker demonstrations as a child in Rostov to the revolts in the stanitsas that sealed the fate of his Don Soviet Republic, Syrtsov carried with him all the anti–Cossack prejudice of a disgruntled outlander. In the Donburo, he became a proponent for the most extreme forms of de-Cossackization. Thanks to his position as chairman and the hard-line policy laid out by Orgburo, Syrtsov was able to override the objections of more moderate Donburo members as well as those of the Political Section of the Southern Front. In the early months of 1919, then, the Don Cossacks would have their first encounter with the Soviet policy of de-Cossackization.[15]

In some of the northern Don stanitsas, the advancing Red Army soldiers were greeted by Cossack women welcoming them with traditional offerings of bread and salt. The inhabitants' enthusiasm for the new regime, however, evaporated quickly. The political workers and armed detachments that arrived on the heels of the combat troops immediately set about requisitioning grain and livestock, first to meet the needs of the army and then to alleviate the food crisis in Russia's industrial cities. Worst of all were the revolutionary tribunals set up to investigate and punish alleged counterrevolutionaries. Under these organs, mass shootings of Cossack men, particularly those of military age, were carried out for their suspected service in the Don Army without any regard as to whether or not they had enlisted voluntarily. Cossacks who demanded payment for their requisitioned property were shot. Those who were denounced as counterrevolutionaries, even if the evidence against them was flimsy, were shot. In just a few weeks, the revolutionary tribunals' tally of victims soared into the thousands.[16]

The widespread terror forced the Cossacks to either kill or be killed. Predictably, they chose the former option. When they left the front, many Cossack soldiers, in keeping with their military traditions, had carried their rifles back to their stanitsas. The Southern Red Army Group was aware of this and ordered the Cossacks to turn over their arms to occupation authorities or face the threat of execution, but few men complied.[17] On 10 March 1919, disgruntled Cossacks from several stanitsas in the upper Don retrieved their hidden rifles and turned them against the Reds in their midst. Like the Don rebellion a year earlier, the latest uprising was initially more anti–Bolshevik than it was pro–White. For example, one popular rebel slogan was "Long live the soviets and down with the communists!"[18] Within days, the rebel forces in the upper Don had grown to more than 15,000 fighters that included boys, old men and women. Red detachments in the rear, overwhelmed by the scale of the revolt, were unable to contain the unrest.[19]

The upper Don rebellion broke out at an especially inopportune time for the Red Armies on the Southern Front. By pure coincidence, the uprising flared up just as Kolchak's offensive got underway on Soviet Russia's Eastern Front. For the next several weeks, the bulk of the Red Army's reinforcements were directed against the Siberian Whites. Moreover, the number of effective combatants in the Red Southern Army Group was diminished by a typhus epidemic that began towards the end of February and persisted well into the spring.[20] Despite these strains on their manpower, the Bolsheviks still managed to scratch together a counter-insurgency force, the Don Expeditionary Corps, to suppress the rebellion. The subsequent fighting between the rebels and the counter-insurgency detachments proved especially ferocious. The Red troops destroyed anything that might be of use to the insurgents by putting entire villages to the torch and gunning down livestock. Neither side bothered to take prisoners.[21] Yet, despite these severe reprisals, the upper Don rebellion continued to gain momentum. By late April the rebels had 30,000 persons under arms, although they were poorly equipped and desperately short of ammunition. To add to their woes, the Soviet counter-insurgency forces in the Don eventually grew to number over 45,000 men, including Cheka squads and 5,000 cavalrymen armed with 341 machine guns and 62 field guns.[22] Amid their predicament, the Cossack insurgents gradually made common cause with the AFSR. Communication between them and the Whites further south was effected through pilots who flew their planes over the Red lines and landed them in rebel-held areas. "They welcomed our airmen with peals of bells and smothered them in flowers," noted Denikin.[23]

For the Whites, the upper Don rebellion was a godsend that, for the time being, prevented a renewal of the enemy's drive towards Novocherkassk. Indeed, by severing the supply and communication channels of the Ninth Red Army, the uprising and the subsequent failure of the Red counter-insurgency units to restore order in the upper Don sapped the initiative from the forces that had spearheaded the earlier Soviet offensive. In the meantime, the pressure against the Don Army's northern front was greatly eased, allowing Sidorin to rest and reorganize his Cossack units following their disastrous winter retreat. Amid these favorable developments, it was no wonder that the Whites readily embraced the Cossack rebels who just a couple months earlier had effectively opened up the front to the Red Army.

For the Bolsheviks, the outbreak of a violent, popular uprising among poor Cossacks who had been predisposed against the White movement prompted their side to contemplate what went wrong. Some, such as Syrtsov and other anti–Cossack extremists, attributed the rebellion to the failure of party officials to firmly apply the policy of de-Cossackization. The Cossacks, they believed, were a thoroughly monolithic counterrevolutionary element. One commissar, in a report on Soviet reverses in the Don during the spring of 1919, reinforced this notion by declaring, "there were no groups among the Cossacks with whom we could have come to an agreement."[24] Regardless of how valid this assessment was, the overwhelming suppression of the Cossacks favored by Syrtsov and his ilk could have worked only if the

Red troops maintained a formidable presence in the conquered stanitsas. Such an occupation, however, was beyond the capabilities of the Red Army at the time. Some party officials at the front tried to alert their comrades of this reality by warning that their recent victory in the northern Don was more attributable to the Cossacks' low morale than to the Reds' military strength.[25] Syrtsov and his allies, however, were undeterred by such cautions. Even after the revolt was well underway, they continued to move forward with their plans to transform the Don by resettling the region with impoverished peasants, dividing its traditional lands between two new provincial administrations and outlawing the striped trousers that were a distinguishing feature on Cossack uniforms.[26]

For their part, Cossacks serving the Soviet cause echoed those moderates in the party who desired an enlightened approach towards subduing the Cossack lands. Mironov, in a letter addressed to Lenin, blamed the upper Don uprising on the insensitive behavior of political workers who knew "nothing of the Cossacks' psychology or their special traits."[27] In a similar vein, Valentin Trifonov, a Don Cossack and commissar on the Southern Front, urged the Bolsheviks to win the Cossacks' confidence by placing adequate supplies of lubricant oil, cloth and tobacco at their disposal—a tall order when such items were scarce in the rest of Soviet Russia.[28] Overall, Mironov and Trifonov, along with their colleagues on the Cossack Section of the All-Russian Central Executive Committee of Soviets, condemned the extermination campaign directed against the Cossacks in occupied districts of the Don and Urals in spring of 1919. Their solution was to pacify the Cossacks by granting a general amnesty for working Cossacks and removing those political workers from the regions who had compromised themselves by their involvement in de-Cossackization measures.[29]

The debate among commissars, commanders and other Bolshevik leaders as to what was the best policy to apply towards the Cossacks continued into late summer 1919. But by then the question was largely of academic interest since the Red armies had once again been pushed out of the Cossack territories. The de-Cossackization policies instituted earlier that year had thoroughly discredited Bolshevik propaganda in the stanitsas, and many Cossacks in the Don and Urals fought the Reds that summer with a renewed fervor that matched their spirited campaigns a year earlier.

The AFSR Ascendant

In early May 1919 the Red Southern Army Group, already hindered by Cossack rebellions and a typhus epidemic, experienced yet another setback after a major revolt erupted among Ukrainian partisan bands serving with the Thirteenth Red Army. The disarray in the Soviet ranks brought immediate relief to General May-Maevsky and his Volunteer troops defending the Donets Basin, and after the arrival of a few British tanks on his front, his army launched a northerly drive that badly mauled units of the Thirteenth and Eighth Red Armies. May-Maevsky continued his offensive into the following month, capturing Kharkov (Kharkiv) on 25 June. Five days later, General Shkuro, then in command of Kuban Cossack cavalrymen on the Volunteers' left flank, captured Yekaterinoslav (Dnipro) after putting Makhno's anarchist partisans to flight.[30]

Those operations were part of a wider offensive by the AFSR which rolled back the Red lines from the Crimea to the Volga River. In the center of the front the revitalized Don Army struck northward and joined hands with the rebels in the upper Don districts on 7 June.[31] By the end of the month, the rejuvenated Don Cossack Army was about 40,000 strong and once again was able to celebrate the liberation of its homeland from Soviet occupation.[32] Further to the east, the Caucasian Army drove to the outskirts of Tsaritsyn. That army's commander, Wrangel, was perhaps the most qualified commander to lead the otherwise difficult Kuban Cossacks who comprised the majority of its troops. Although he was the product of the Baltic German nobility, he had commanded a regiment of Transbaikal Cossacks during the world war and from that experience he learned to gain the confidence of Cossack soldiers by demonstrating bold leadership while showing deference towards their customs.[33] Hence, as commander of the Caucasian Army, he outfitted his lean frame in costumes favored by the Kuban Cossacks and other Caucasian peoples: a sheepskin cap (*kubanka*) and cloak (*cherkesska*) complete with decorative cartridge holders stitched on the chest. Under his intelligent command, the Kuban Cossacks, Terek Cossacks and mix of other Caucasian soldiers performed admirably. Unlike other White commanders, Wrangel also tried to enforce a strict code of discipline that bucked the stereotype that many of the ethnicities serving under him were "savages." Still, the fearsome reputation of the exotic Caucasian warriors heightened the anxieties of the Red defenders holding onto Tsaritsyn in June 1919.

Wrangel's exceptional leadership skills and the *élan* of his troops were by themselves not enough to overrun Tsaritsyn's formidable defenses. For a fortnight after reaching the city, the undersupplied Caucasian Army appeared fated to endure the same frustrations before Tsaritsyn as Krasnov's Cossacks during the previous year. That changed after White trains bearing provisions and heavy weapons reached the besieging army along the repaired railway from Yekaterinodar. Among the hardware which Wrangel received were a handful of British Mark V tanks. These armored leviathans were not the only contribution the Allies made on that front. In the skies, Sopwith Camel biplanes of Royal Air Force Squadron 47, piloted by British volunteers, chased down Bolshevik aviators and strafed enemy supply convoys on the rivers and railways.[34] This Allied support, along with the artillery forwarded to that front by Denikin, demoralized the Reds and softened their defenses, enabling the Caucasian Army to break into Tsaritsyn on 30 June after a three-day battle.

Wrangel's capture of the "Red Verdun" capped off a string of impressive feats for the AFSR. Just days after the city fell to the Caucasian Army, Denikin himself traveled to Tsaritsyn to celebrate the Whites' latest prize with a parade and Te Deum in the city's cathedral.[35] Brimming with unfettered optimism, it was there that the commander-in-chief of the AFSR announced his Moscow Directive, which called on the Caucasian, Don and Volunteer armies to converge on the Soviet capital. It was an ambitious plan: at the time the objective of Moscow was about 350–400 miles from the spearheads of the Volunteer and Don Armies and it was nearly twice that distance for the Caucasian Army.[36] It also became a source of contention between Denikin and Wrangel, who later criticized it as a "death sentence" for the AFSR. "All the principles of strategy were ignored," he later complained, "there was no concentration of the bulk of the troops in this direction and no maneuvering. It merely prescribed a different route to Moscow for each of the armies."[37] While Wrangel's charges were valid, there was also merit in Denikin's desire to achieve a decisive victory as quickly as possible. He understood that continued success on the battlefield was necessary to maintain both Allied support and Cossack enthusiasm for his overall campaign. Moreover, he feared that the Bolsheviks would grow stronger with each passing week since they controlled far greater human and industrial resources than he could ever attain in the borderlands. Time, in other words, was not on Denikin's side.[38]

As the fighting along the Southern Front raged into the latter half of the summer, the

Bolsheviks were indeed focusing their energies on the rising threat posed by the AFSR. They reinforced that front with troops transferred from the Urals and mounted a major counteroffensive in mid-August. The initial phase of that operation managed to drive a deep wedge between the Volunteer and Don armies, but after ten days the Red task force had to retreat to avoid encirclement. Along the Volga, the Soviet attack stopped Wrangel's northward advance and permanently dashed any White hopes of threatening the rear of the Red Eastern Army Group as well as the dream of joining hands with the Siberian Whites. Earlier, at the end of July, the Whites had come the closest they ever would to that objective when a scouting party from the Caucasian Army reached some Ural Cossack guerrillas. This tenuous connection, however, had no lasting significance for the fortunes of the White movement.[39]

In the end, the Soviet counterattack in August 1919 failed to rob the AFSR of the military initiative. One reason for the operation's miscarriage was a spectacular raid behind the Red armies' front by the Fourth Don Cavalry Corps under General Konstantin Mamontov. Like Shkuro, Mamontov was one of those leaders who endeared himself to his Cossack soldiers as a result of his energetic command, bold maneuvers and utter disregard for strict discipline. His most impressive exploit began on 10 August 1919 when his massed corps of 9,000 cavalry burst through the Red front along the northern boundary of the Don Host and then seized the provincial capital of Tambov eight days later. After thoroughly pillaging that town, Mamontov's corps galloped west to Kozlov, the headquarters of the Red Southern Army Group. Wherever they went, the Don Cossacks looted, dynamited bridges, tore up railroad tracks and burned supply dumps in the rear of the Soviet forces. They spread further mayhem by encouraging peasants along their route to ambush food-requisitioning detachments, arrest local soviets and attack state farms. Those peasants who welcomed Mamontov's rough-riding Cossacks to their villages, however, were quickly disillusioned as the raiders helped themselves to horses, carts and anything else not nailed down before withdrawing. Eventually the Cossacks' carts and wagons, piled high with stolen goods, formed a column that stretched over thirty miles in length. This baggage slowed their progress considerably, raising concern among the corps that the Red detachments frantically pursuing them might finally catch up and deprive them of their plunder. As a result, Mamontov turned southward after spending a month behind the Red front. On their way back to White lines, the Don Cossacks briefly captured Voronezh, where they crossed the Don, and continued to ride south until they and their loot reached the safety of White-controlled territory on 19 September.[40]

Mamontov's raid was a stunning enterprise: he had operated behind the enemy's lines for nearly forty days, covered nearly 500 miles and spread untold chaos in the rear of the Red armies. Yet, despite these accomplishments, the Fourth Don Cossack Corps would never again present a significant threat to the Soviet forces. As soon as Mamontov returned to White-occupied territory, his jubilant Cossacks left the front to escort their wagons brimming with booty back to their stanitsas in the Don. In the coming weeks, during which the decisive battles of the civil war would be fought, his once formidable corps had practically melted away. By then it was down to only 2,000 men and was unable to make any significant contribution in the campaign.[41] Even the raid itself was less of a triumph than it appeared. Had Mamontov's corps been more focused on military objectives and not plunder, the operation could have been far more devastating for the Eighth and Ninth Red Armies.[42] Moreover, the Cossacks' tendency to loot and engage in other poor behavior had the drawback of creating an unfavorable image of the Whites among the peasants who were victimized during the raid. In the words of a British officer serving with the Don Army that summer, the raid "seemed to exemplify all the good and bad qualities of the Cossacks."[43]

Although Mamontov's raid accomplished less than it should have, the disruption it caused in the rear of the Red Southern Army Group was substantial enough to facilitate another round of White victories. On 20 September a crack corps of the Volunteer Army, supported by armored trains, captured Kursk. Ten days later, General Shkuro's Kuban Cossacks retook Voronezh and, unlike Mamontov, held on to the city.[44] Simultaneously, the troops on the AFSR's left flank were plunging deep into Ukraine even though Denikin's Moscow Directive had made no provisions for operations west of the Dnieper River. Their officers, it turned out, simply could not resist the temptation to advance against the weaker and fragmented Ukrainian partisan bands opposing them. Before August was out they had added Kiev and Odessa to their territory and continued to drive the Ukrainian insurgents to the north and west.

The impressive gains made by Whites in Ukraine and further north were offset by the stalemate which characterized the eastern half of Denikin's front. On the AFSR's most easterly flank, the Whites were unable to break into Astrakhan while Wrangel's Caucasian Army was content to simply hold Tsaritsyn. In the center of the front the Cossacks of the Don Army, having completed the liberation of their stanitsas months ago, were once again afflicted with the homing spirit that made them lose interest in pushing any further north. Despite these disappointments, the western half of the front, specifically the advance of the Volunteer Army, continued to feed the optimism of the White generals. On 13 October Denikin's headquarters received the welcome news that the Volunteer troops entered Oryol and were now within 250 miles of Moscow.[45] The Bolsheviks, they were certain, would be driven out of the Kremlin before winter set in.

Denikin's Front: A House of Cards

Even as Denikin's risky gamble of an all-out offensive towards Moscow appeared to come within a tantalizing reach of a jackpot, his forces were considerably less formidable than they appeared. After having achieved numerical superiority against its Red opponents in late spring and summer of 1919, the AFSR found itself heavily outnumbered again that autumn as the Bolsheviks concentrated their military resources on the Southern Front. The precise number of combatants who faced each other on the Southern Front at that time is difficult to gauge due the widespread disorder and desertions which affected both sides, but one historian has estimated the AFSR's strength at 100,000 and that of the Southern Red Army Group at 148,000.[46] For the hardened White troops, their numerical inferiority was not as discouraging as might have been to other soldiers; after all, they had prevailed against much worse odds in the past eighteen months. Still, there were of indications that any setback might precipitate disaster. To man their expansive front, the Whites press-ganged Red prisoners into service and denuded their rear of troops. Without anyone to enforce order behind the front, near-lawlessness prevailed throughout much of Denikin's Russia. Corruption abounded, particularly among AFSR military and civilian administrators who demanded bribes and siphoned off valuable supplies designated for troops at the front. When, in turn, the soldiers on the frontlines lacked supplies, they resorted to forceful requisitioning and, in doing so, discredited the Whites in the eyes of the aggrieved peasants.[47]

In addition to the widespread disorder in its realm, the AFSR's position in 1919 was further complicated by its leaders' unyielding attitude towards restive nationalities in the borderlands. The White generals continued to condemn any proposal for the reorganization of Russia, regardless of whether it suggested mere autonomy for the minorities or their full independence, as a Bolshevik or German scheme. This led those peoples who had effectively established their independence during the revolution to remain distrustful of any emissaries from Denikin's headquarters. Subsequently, neither the Georgian nor Polish governments, though hostile towards the Bolsheviks, would assist the AFSR as long as its commander-in-chief refused to offer any binding guarantees to respect their sovereignty or borders. Moreover, the White generals were so dismissive of the Ukrainian national movement that that any possibility of seeking a rapprochement with Petliura's anti–Bolshevik bands was unthinkable.

The area where the Whites' hostility toward national movements proved especially damaging was in the ethnically-diverse Terek region and Dagestan. In May 1919, the AFSR completed its occupation of the lowland towns in Dagestan with the capture of the Caspian port of Petrovsk. By then Denikin had already injured the local pride of the various native groups by refusing to grant them local self-rule while ordering their menfolk to report for duty with the Caucasian Army. These callous measures greatly eased the task of Bolshevik operatives who remained in the mountains, intent on fomenting anti–White resistance among the natives. In June, the Ingush staged an unsuccessful revolt, and in the following month unrest broke among the Dargos and Avars in Dagestan. Hardly had the Whites finished restoring order there when a new uprising erupted in nearby Chechnya in August. This insurrection, led by Muslim emirs and tribal nationalists organized into the North Caucasus Defense Council, continued to gain momentum as summer transitioned into autumn. In September, with White troops having been driven out of large swaths of Dagestan and Chechnya, the rebel leaders declared their independence under an emirate. Local Bolsheviks, who would have been antagonistic towards such a theocracy in any other setting, lent their temporary support to the emirate in its struggle against the Whites. By October, with Denikin diverting an ever-increasing number of reinforcements from his main front to the northeastern Caucasus, the insurgency was becoming a major drain on White manpower at a crucial moment. It also battered the morale of the Terek Cossacks who grew reluctant to depart for battlefields several hundred miles away while their own stanitsas and families were in peril.[48]

Hardly less problematic for the White cause were the separatist tendencies which gained traction among the Cossacks. Throughout much of 1919, the Don Cossacks appeared to be fully on board with the anti–Bolshevik campaign being pursued by Denikin. Ataman Bogaevsky, unlike his predecessor, regarded the White leader with the highest esteem and tended to side with him amid his disagreements with the recalcitrant Kuban Cossack politicians. Those who knew him described the Don ataman as an easy-going personality; which may explain his deferential attitude towards Sidorin, the commander of the Don Army. Sidorin was a man of imposing physical features; he possessed a large frame topped off with a shaved-head, scarred face and gruff voice. He was also an experienced pilot and a former staff officer. According to Major H. N. H. Williamson, a British officer attached to Sidorin's headquarters, the Don Army commander conducted his operations with minimal oversight.[49] This lackadaisical arrangement functioned smoothly when the Don Army's immediate objectives matched those of the rest of the AFSR. For example, under Sidorin's command, the Don Cossacks drove the Red troops out of their homeland in early summer and successfully repulsed the Soviet counterattack in August. But Sidorin and his troops proved less reliable when carrying out Denikin's orders to march on Moscow. One of their first objectives in that directive, Voronezh, was ultimately taken not by them but rather by Kuban Cossacks. Denikin, when writing of the Don Army's halfhearted advance some years later, alleged that Sidorin and his staff were "entirely subordinate to Cossack mentality," meaning that they were reluctant to pursue the wider national goals of the anti–Bolshevik campaign.[50] Stuck in their regional view of the civil war, it seems most Don Cossacks could not be persuaded into truly adopting the struggle to eradicate Bolshevism from the entirety of Russia as their own.

Although the performance of the Don Cossacks dropped considerably as soon as their squadrons ventured outside of their host, they at least did not agitate openly against the AFSR. Radical separatism among the Don Cossacks, it seems, was tempered by the retention of the Don Army as an autonomous fighting force even after they subordinated themselves to Denikin's command. The Kuban Cossacks, on the other hand, possessed no such outlet for their pent-up regional patriotism. For them, the fact that the Don Cossacks were allowed to fight in an autonomous army while they were denied the same privilege was an unequal arrangement in need of correction. Denikin certainly had numerous reasons to oppose a separate Kuban army; the last thing he needed was more Cossack units over which his officers lacked a firm control or were prone to passivity. Yet, the AFSR command's stonewalling of Kuban Cossack aspirations merely compelled the latter to seek more extreme solutions that drove the two sides further apart. This trend would have lasting and tragic repercussions for the anti–Bolshevik movement in South Russia.

In early summer of 1919, Denikin relocated his headquarters from Yekaterinodar to Taganrog to escape the unrelenting political distractions in the Kuban capital.[51] Even after this move, the unrest among the Kuban Cossack politicians continued to cause headaches for the AFSR command. Earlier in the year, Kuban separatists had tried to plead their case before the peacemakers in Paris. In fact, the Kuban politicians were so divided among themselves that they ultimately sent two delegations to the Paris Peace Conference; one delegation advocated a mild form of autonomy for their homeland while the other wanted the Kuban to become part of a federated Russia. Their inability to come together on this matter was not conducive towards gaining the confidence of the Allied statesmen.[52]

Despite their failure to elicit any sympathy for their cause in Paris, the separatists in the Kuban Rada continued to look for ways to strengthen their hand against the White generals. One project that piqued their interest was a conference between representatives of the Don, Terek and Kuban Cossack hosts. This assembly, which convened in Novocherkassk in late June 1919, was intended to increase cooperation between the three major Cossack hosts of South Russia. The Kuban delegation, however, sought to make it a referendum on AFSR leadership, whom they accused of anti-democratic tendencies. Their charges, however, fell on mostly unsympathetic ears. After their setback at the front during the previous winter, the Don politicians had come to appreciate their dependence on the White generals. Likewise, the Terek representatives knew that they needed the AFSR to prevent their stanitsas from being overrun by hostile natives and outlanders. Amid the chagrin felt by the Kuban delegates as their efforts to stoke opposition to the AFSR were rebuffed by their Cossack brethren, their chairman and an outspoken separatist, N. S. Ryabovol, was gunned down during their stay in Novocherkassk. The details surrounding this crime are murky and Ryabovol's killer was never caught. It is possible that he was the casualty of an assassin acting alone, but his fellow Kuban Cossacks preferred to believe that he was a victim of a hit issued from Denikin's headquarters. In any case, Ryabovol's untimely death provided the

Kuban delegation a convenient excuse to quit the conference that was not going their way. Subsequently, they hastily packed up and returned to Yekaterinodar to mourn their fallen comrade.[53]

Not all Kuban leaders were pleased with their colleagues' increasing intransigence towards their allies. Among these were Ataman Filimonov and other *lineitsy* Cossacks who dreaded a complete break with the AFSR and other Cossacks. As a result of their prodding, the Kuban delegation eventually headed back to Novocherkassk to resume the negotiations towards a united Cossack political program. The arrangement which the Don and Terek Cossack representatives had in mind was centered on a general framework that would uphold certain aspects of Cossack autonomy while recognizing the authority of Kolchak and Denikin. This relatively moderate program encountered stiff resistance first from the Kuban delegation, which wanted it to be less accommodating towards the White leadership, and then from Denikin's administrative body known as the Special Council, which thought demands for limited autonomy to be too extreme. Ultimately, the wrangling between the Cossack representatives and the Special Council dragged on for months, lasting until the very existence of the AFSR was in doubt.[54]

As their frustrations mounted during the summer, the separatists in the Kuban Rada resorted to ever bolder action in order to make it harder for Denikin to ignore their demands. Their agitation was even felt at the front, particularly in Wrangel's Caucasian Army where the Kuban Cossacks comprised the majority of troops. That army was forced to remain on the defensive around Tsaritsyn for much of the latter half of 1919 due to lack of reinforcements from the Kuban. Wrangel suspected that this frustrating state of affairs was the result of intrigue more substantial than the usual inefficiency and corruption which characterized the AFSR's logistics. To remedy the issue, he and General Romanovsky, the AFSR's top quartermaster, met with Kuban leaders Filimonov and Field Ataman Vyacheslav G. Naumenko. Although both Filimonov and Naumenko held favorable attitudes toward the AFSR, they admitted their inability to rein in the raucous separatists in the Kuban Rada.[55] That faction grew even more assertive and extreme as the Volunteer Army's victories seemed to portend a decisive victory for the Whites. They believed that it was imperative for them to achieve their objectives before the Bolsheviks were crushed and Denikin was free to turn his attention on the Kuban. To that end, they had Naumenko ousted from the post of field ataman after he failed to arrange for a separate Kuban army. Their next target was Filimonov, whom they hoped to replace with an outspoken federalist inimical to the AFSR command. These developments in Yekaterinodar were eyed dubiously by both Denikin and Wrangel. Although they would have preferred to continue to focus on the battles then raging against the Red Army, the White generals were not about to stand idly by while their Kuban base slipped from their control. They also had at their disposal a deputy in command of a contingent of crack soldiers eager to bring the Rada to heel—or worse. That individual was General Pokrovsky, the non-Cossack who had led the Kuban troops prior to their merger with the Volunteer Army. But Pokrovsky had such a notorious reputation for exceptional brutality that the upright Denikin was reluctant to unleash such an unsavory character on his political adversaries in Yekaterinodar.

The factor that changed Denikin's mind was the uncovering of a secret treaty signed between representatives from the Kuban, Chechens and Ingush in Paris a few months earlier, in July 1919. The treaty was primarily a symbolic affair that had no practical meaning in the North Caucasus, where the Kuban Cossacks continued to fight with the AFSR against the Bolsheviks and, by extension, their Chechen and Ingush allies.[56] Nonetheless, the revelation of the treaty compelled Denikin to authorize severe measures against the Rada, which he felt "was virtually in the hands of pro-Bolshevist extremists."[57] On 7 November he ordered Wrangel, who had gone to Yekaterinodar with Pokrovsky, to court-martial several Kuban leaders on charges of treason.[58] Despite attempts by Filimonov to mediate a peaceful resolution between Denikin and the Rada, Wrangel had Pokrovsky's detachment surround the Rada's chambers and present it with an ultimatum to turnover thirty-three wanted deputies. Amid the standoff, Filimonov continued to act as a go-between and eventually persuaded Pokrovsky to accept a lower bag of eleven prisoners instead of the original thirty-three. Eventually, that group of suspects, minus one who fled, gave themselves up. Among those apprehended was A. I. Kalabukhov, a member of both the Rada and the Kuban delegation to Paris that had signed the treaty. On the following morning, he was court-martialed, found guilty and hanged in the center of Yekaterinodar; afterwards his corpse was left to dangle with a placard declaring him a traitor to Russia. The remaining prisoners were expelled from the Kuban.

After this poignant show of force, Wrangel entered the Rada's chambers and gave an impassioned speech where he blamed the recent intrigues in the Kuban for the Caucasian Army's dismal supply situation. In the intimidating presence of Wrangel and Pokrovsky's troops the Rada, though now overwhelmingly dominated by the Black Sea Cossacks, meekly accepted the constitutional reforms demanded by Wrangel and affirmed its support of the AFSR.[59]

Through the actions of Wrangel and Pokrovsky, Denikin effectively executed a *coup d'état* against the Black Sea Cossacks who comprised the majority of Kuban Cossacks and were foremost advocates of separatist goals. His victory in Kuban politics, however, would prove fleeting. As the military outlook turned against the AFSR late that autumn, the Black Sea Cossack representatives regained their audacity and returned to their old ways.[60] Ataman Filimonov was cashiered on account of his ineffectual leadership during the crisis and was eventually replaced by a non-Cossack, General Bukretov. It seems that Bukretov was elected to post of ataman mainly for his well-known antipathy towards the White generals.[61]

Around the same time Denikin clamped down on the meddlesome Kuban politicians in Yekaterinodar, he also had to contend with the familiar problem of faltering morale among his Cossack soldiers, especially those from the Kuban. While he later blamed their loss of spirit on the irresponsible politicians in the Rada,[62] it is doubtful as to whether ordinary Kuban Cossack troops had much insight into the political maneuvering then underway in their regional capital. Most likely, the declining performance of the Kuban Cossacks he and others observed was caused by increasing exhaustion and homesickness.[63] With their districts no longer threatened by the enemy, the Cossack rank and file had grown indifferent to the conflict. The AFSR's goal of liberating Russia from Soviet tyranny aroused little enthusiasm among them. They would have been content to return to their farms and let the rest of Russia's population fight the civil war to its conclusion as long as they could be left alone.

To overcome this apathy, Cossack officers coaxed their men forward with the prospect of plunder. Mamontov's great raid was but one example of this approach. In Ukraine, squadrons of Kuban and Terek Cossacks fanned out across the countryside on a similar quest. Since their detachments were much smaller than the corps led by Mamontov, they had to ransack with more discretion to avoid the fury of the restive Ukrainian peasantry. Subsequently, their predations were directed against the most vulnerable group in Ukraine's towns and villages: the Jews.[64] In prerevolutionary Russia, the Jewish people had always led a precarious existence. Under the tsarist regime, they were barred from owning land, confined to the Pale of Settlement and lived under the constant threat of pogroms. Although the Provisional Government ended the legal discrimination against Jews, the anti–Semitic traditions of the general population were much harder to expunge. Among Whites, there was a widespread perception that Bolshevism and the Red Terror were products of a "Jewish conspiracy." Ukrainian peasants held onto their prejudice that Jews were an exploitative class second only to the landlords. Such misconceptions were dangerous in an era of lawlessness and inflamed passions, and it is hardly surprising that the frequency of pogroms increased during the revolutionary period.[65]

When Denikin and other high-ranking officers in the AFSR learned that their troops were responsible for pogroms, they condemned such activities and demanded that they not be repeated.[66] These directives were seemingly ignored by the Kuban and Terek Cossack brigades in Ukraine, over which the AFSR commander lacked much control. One of the most appalling incidents occurred in September 1919 at Fastov (Fastiv), a town about 45 miles southwest of Kiev with a population of 15,000 people, when a Terek Cossack brigade went on a three-day rampage. One survivor of the massacre later recounted how the Cossacks began their outrages:

> A group of Cossacks would break into a Jewish house and cry: "Money." If they had already been preceded by some other Cossacks, who had taken all the money in the house, then this group of Cossacks would call for the head of the family, put a noose around his neck, and half strangle him. If any of the family now began to cry or ask that the torture cease, the Cossacks beat him or her nearly to death. Naturally the family would give everything it possessed, even to the last kopeck. If, however, there was no money, the Cossacks loosened the noose and the unhappy wretch fell half-dead to the ground. They brought him back to consciousness with the butt ends of their rifles and a bucket of cold water. The tortures then recommenced, and if the poor man could not give any money after the process had been repeated five or six times in vain, the Cossacks would take everything in the house of use to them, smash everything else, make the whole house uninhabitable by smashing doors, windows, stoves, and so forth, and then leave the family to the tender mercies of the next lot of Cossacks, who would come along, generally very soon, and repeat the terrible tortures.[67]

In the aftermath of the Fastov pogrom, entire neighborhoods were left in ruins, an indeterminable number of women and young girls had been raped and some 1,300–1,500 persons lay dead. Other Cossack–led pogroms, though usually less destructive, occurred throughout Ukraine that autumn, including in Kiev where 300 Jews were killed in a spate of violence during 17–20 October 1919.[68]

As in past wars, the property which the Cossacks acquired during these pogroms and raids was funneled to Don, Kuban or Terek stanitsas. This influx of furnishings, implements and other stolen goods, backed by the rich agricultural resources of the North Caucasus region, made existence in the stanitsas among the most tolerable anywhere in revolutionary Russia. Due to its distance from the frontlines and hostile natives, the Kuban countryside was perhaps the most idyllic. But even there everyday life was far from perfect; the Cossack farmers, like peasants elsewhere in Russia, were in dire need of manufactured goods to maintain their equipment and work their fields. The shipments of loot, though helpful, could not compensate for the widespread dearth of implements and spare parts. The mobilization of the male population, along with the requisition of horses and carts, also contributed to the region's overall decreasing output. Nonetheless, the availability of foodstuffs in White-held territory was far better than in Soviet Russia. Indeed, the White occupation of a town or village was usually followed by a substantial decrease in the price of bread.

Unfortunately for the Whites, the peasants' greater access to bread could not compensate for the indignities they suffered at the hands of Cossacks. While other AFSR troops also partook in pogroms and pillaging, the sight of Cossacks, the so-called bloodhounds of the tsarist regime, engaging in such misdeeds evoked memories of atrocities committed by Cossack punitive expeditions during the reaction of 1905–06. That counterrevolution heralded the return of corrupt tsarist officials and vindictive landowners to their districts. For the peasants at least, the Cossacks' conduct during 1919 appeared to validate Bolshevik propaganda alleging that the Whites were bent on restoring the injustices of the *ancien régime*, and for most there was no question of wanting to go back.

For the Whites, the quickest path to victory in the civil war was a popular peasant uprising in their favor. That this did not happen when the AFSR reached Central Russia in autumn 1919 can be attributed to a multitude of factors: Denikin's lack of a clear agrarian policy, his refusal to commit to a specific form of future government and his shortcomings in propaganda; to name a few. One could add to that list his reliance on Cossacks, as the peasantry was more likely to regard them as fiends than folk heroes. The AFSR commander, however, was unwilling to change his attitudes towards the Cossacks since he highly valued them as a source of skilled and reliable recruits for his armies. Hence, the AFSR's dependence on the Cossacks would only become more apparent as its campaign was suddenly confronted with the prospect of total defeat.

7

Debacle

Retreat to the Don

In the months after their coup in Petrograd, the Bolshevik leaders demonstrated that no party doctrine was too sacred if its violation might save the revolution. To avoid the wrath of Germany, they gave up their attempts to negotiate a peace without annexations or indemnities and instead signed an imperialist peace at Brest-Litovsk. To pacify the restless peasantry, they refrained from embarking on their ideal solution to the land question—collectivization—and instead proclaimed that "the right to use the land belongs to those who cultivate it."[1] To defend their nascent regime, they eventually formed an army of conscripts led by professional officers—even though they had opposed both concepts prior to November 1917. There was, however, one item on which they were slow to reverse their position: their disdain for cavalry. To them, cavalry seemed obsolete on the industrial age battlefield; moreover, they associated that arm with the aristocracy, Cossacks and other elements viewed as counterrevolutionary.[2]

Gradually, the Whites' successes with mounted units compelled the Red military planners to appreciate the value of cavalry, especially in the wide-open spaces of South Russia. As the Ninth Red Army was being driven out of the Don Host in June 1919, one of its commanders concluded that "in a war of field maneuvers cavalry is essential, even more so in an area where there are no railways and vast roadless expanses have to be crossed."[3] Around the same time Trotsky, in a secret message to Lenin, emphasized the importance of cavalry and the timely deliveries of forage needed to maintain the horses. "We have just got to realize that this makes the difference between victory and defeat," the war commissar warned.[4] Despite these early revelations, the Bolsheviks continued to procrastinate in their efforts to assemble a cavalry force that could rival their opponents' more numerous and more experienced horsemen. The event which finally spurred them into action was the disarray on their front caused by Mamontov's raid. That operation taught the Red commanders that a massed cavalry group could still thrash opponents with devastating consequences. In September 1919, as the Fourth Don Cavalry Corps was concluding its operation behind the Soviet front, Trotsky called for the rapid development of Red cavalry units under the slogan "Proletarians, to horse!"[5] Subsequently, the Red Army frantically began organizing Cossacks and other experienced horsemen serving in its ranks into cavalry units. For quite a few commissars behind the front, this new policy required them to make an about-face since they had resisted all attempts to form Cossacks serving with the Red Army into a cavalry corps.[6]

The man chosen to lead the new Red Cavalry Corps was Semyon Budyonny, a Don outlander and veteran cavalryman. Budyonny, whose most distinguishing physical feature was a flowing moustache that resembled a horse's tail,[7] had served with the tsarist cavalry since 1903, where he rose to the rank of sergeant-major. During the revolution, he cast his lot with the Bolsheviks; leading a Red cavalry detachment, then a brigade, division and eventually a corps.[8] In October 1919, shortly after Shkuro's Kuban Cossack cavalry captured Voronezh, Budyonny concentrated his cavalry corps against that sector. In response to this threat, Shkuro led his horsemen in a surprise spoiling attack against the Red Cavalry Corps on the cold, misty night of 19 October. Budyonny's men, however, fought back and, with their visibility reduced by the weather, the two sides engaged each other at close quarters with sabers. Traditionally, the Cossacks, especially those of the Kuban, excelled at this sort of combat, but on that night it was they who were routed from the battlefield. In a panic, Shkuro's cavalry galloped back to Voronezh but were too shaken by their recent defeat to make a stand there. Four days later Budyonny's horsemen entered Voronezh, from where the Red squadrons began pouring across the Don to drive a wedge between the Volunteer and Don Armies.[9]

Shkuro's setback before Voronezh was not the only troubled sector on the AFSR's vast, fragile front. A Soviet counterattack west of Oryol forced the Whites to evacuate that town on 20 October. For the better part of the following month, the crack Volunteer regiments and the Don Cossack cavalry supporting them put up a stiff fight as they fell back on Kursk.[10] Meanwhile, a new threat had emerged in the AFSR's rear. At the end of September, Makhno and perhaps 15,000 of his followers, having been driven into western Ukraine by White detachments, suddenly gave battle and crashed through their opponents' lines. After achieving their breakthrough, they found the Whites' rear unpoliced and immediately headed due east towards their home districts. Traveling in four-wheel carts studded with rifles and machine guns, Makhno's insurgents moved swiftly and virtually unopposed through the Ukrainian countryside tearing up railroads, executing White officials and throwing open jail cells along the way. As their columns of carts snaked through villages, the Ukrainian peasantry cheered the partisans and even joined them. On the same day the Whites withdrew from Oryol, Makhno's bands occupied Yekaterinoslav and went on to menace the AFSR's headquarters at Taganrog. To address this unexpected threat, Denikin withdrew Terek and Don Cossack cavalry from the front, including a brigade from Shkuro who, as we have seen, already had his hands full with Budyonny. At the cost of weakening the AFSR's frontlines, the transferred Cossacks dispersed the insurgent army but failed to completely eliminate the danger from Makhno as he and his core of followers survived to fight another day.[11]

As troubling as the situations were on the Volunteer Army's front and in southeastern Ukraine, it was Budyonny's corps which continued to present the most serious risk to the AFSR's entire campaign. After defeating Shkuro around Voronezh, the Red Cavalry Corps dashed towards the railway junction of Kastornoye in an effort to cut the shortest route of communication between the Volunteer Army to the west and the Don Army to the east. To defend Kastornoye, General Mamontov tried to amass a Don Cossack cavalry group large enough to stand up to Budyonny's corps. His task was not easy: the units he wanted were being directed to other threatened sectors of the front or to restore order in the rear. His Fourth Don Cossack Corps also remained under strength after thousands of riders had opted to escort their baggage trains of loot to their stanitsas. Therefore, Mamontov's Cossacks were outnumbered as the bulk of the Red Cavalry Corps closed in on Kastornoye. The ensuing engagement proved to be both prolonged and fierce, lasting for weeks, but when it was over Mamontov's Cossacks were put to flight and Budyonny took possession of the junction on 15 November.

Two days after losing Kastornoye, the Volunteer Army was forced to give up Kursk. These defeats left the Volunteers with no choice other than to retreat, but they had no secure position on which they could fall back. Makhno's recent foray and the activities of underground Bolshevik cells helped convince the wavering peasants and townsfolk that the Whites were doomed, turning the masses actively against them. The Volunteers soon found themselves practically cut off from supplies from Taganrog as partisans and Red cavalry dismantled the railways in their rear. To feed themselves, the fleeing Whites pillaged the countryside, further lowering their popularity among the peasantry. As winter set in another enemy, typhus, appeared on the scene and began reaping a horrific toll among the exhausted men. The situation was not helped by the increasingly erratic behavior of the Volunteer Army's commander, General May-Maevsky, who neglected his duties to immerse himself in drinking binges and orgies.[12]

Amid the worsening crisis, Denikin did not give up hope. To end Budyonny's rampage, he made a new attempt to amass a cavalry group consisting of the Fourth Don, Second Kuban and Third Kuban Cossack Corps east of Kharkov.[13] He also dismissed May-Maevsky from command of the Volunteer Army and replaced him with Wrangel, whose talents as a cavalry general and proven effectiveness at commanding Cossacks, it was hoped, would ensure the success of the projected shock cavalry force. But when Wrangel arrived at Kharkov on 8 December, he found the task before him more daunting than he had imagined. He was dismayed by the riotous behavior of the troops he was supposed to lead and complained to Denikin that their uninhibited requisitioning habits had turned them into "a collection of tradesmen and profiteers." He found corps whittled down to brigades and regiments reduced to battalions. Most disconcerting of all was the condition of the cavalry on which Denikin was pinning his hopes. "The horses," Wrangel informed him, "have not been shod for a long while and have nearly all gone lame whilst many of them are ill from exhaustion."[14]

While Denikin may have been overly optimistic about his chances of stabilizing the front, Wrangel's presence in the Kharkov sector did not help the situation. He quarreled with the officers whom he deemed responsible for allowing the soldiers' discipline to get so out of hand. He fired Mamontov from his field command of the projected cavalry corps and replaced him with a Kuban Cossack general, Sergey Ulagay. This appointment offended the Don Cossacks who idolized Mamontov and regarded Kuban Cossacks as inferior. Since their pride would not allow them to serve under a Kuban Cossack general, they refused to fight. The outrage of the ordinary Don Cossacks was echoed by their leaders, Ataman Bogaevsky and General Sidorin, who pressured the AFSR headquarters and ultimately Wrangel into reinstating Mamontov. All of this bickering among the leadership did not improve the confidence of the Cossack soldiers, whose morale was already shaken by their recent setbacks and political disputes. Meanwhile, the new cavalry group failed to reach the formidable size envisioned by Denikin as the planned reinforcements were stalled amid the logjam of southbound trains on the railways leading from Kharkov. In its first encounter with Budyonny's horsemen, now renamed the First Cavalry Army, its contingent of Don Cossacks were routed, fomenting a panic which spread to the Kuban Cossacks and effectively caused the entire formation to break up. Afterwards, a furious Denikin fired Mamontov for second time and the remnants of what had been Fourth Don Corps, seemingly oblivious to the impending disaster, showed solidarity with their disgraced hero by leaving the front.[15]

The abject failure of the cavalry group to manage the crisis left the Volunteer and Don armies with no option but to continue their flight, effectively giving up most of Ukraine without a fight. Wrangel wanted to pull back as many units as possible into Crimea in order to hold that peninsula while the remaining AFSR units further east organized a limited defense of the North Caucasus. Once again, Denikin turned down the baron's suggestion in order to save his base in the Cossack lands. "I have not the moral right to abandon the Cossacks to their fate," Denikin declared, according to Wrangel. "We must retreat together."[16]

Denikin, it seems, was more loyal to the Cossacks than they were to him. Undoubtedly, the AFSR commander clenched at the hope that the resistance of the Don Cossacks would stiffen as the enemy approached their stanitsas, which had happened so often in the past. He failed, however, to appreciate the extent to which the recent bout of defeats had crushed the Cossacks' spirits. Besides the dejected state of the Cossack rank-and-file, he also had to contend with worsening relations with the commander of the Don Army, Sidorin. The latter had already failed Denikin at key moments in the campaign: he did not carry out the Moscow Directives with any enthusiasm and he had neglected an order from Denikin to strengthen his left wing in order to maintain contact with the Volunteer Army, which might have prevented Budyonny's devastating breakthrough at Voronezh.[17] Now, as Denikin sought to hold the Red armies on a line in the Don region, disconcerting rumors began swirling around that Sidorin was conspiring against him, either with dissident officers in the AFSR or through a separate peace with the Bolsheviks.[18]

Denikin's concerns that subordinate commanders were plotting against him were not unjustified. There was indeed a movement afoot within the AFSR, coalescing around Wrangel, to oust him as the supreme commander-in-chief. As his headquarters received credible reports of the baron's alleged machinations, Denikin became convinced that both Wrangel and Sidorin were unreliable and soon demanded that all communication between them take place through him.[19] This unwieldy state of affairs could not last and before the year's end Bogaevsky, at Denikin's urging, assumed titular command of the Cossack armies in the hope of bringing Sidorin to heel.[20] Meanwhile, Wrangel was relieved from the command of the Volunteer Army and sent to the Kuban in a last ditch effort to organize new cavalry units.

Upon Wrangel's departure, the Volunteer Army was renamed the Volunteer Corps, placed under the command of General Aleksandr Kutepov and adjoined to the Don Army.[21] This reorganization was just one indication of the deteriorating state of the AFSR. A few days earlier, Denikin hastily relocated his headquarters from Taganrog to the railway junction at Tikhoretskaya. The Whites were making last-minute preparations to defend Rostov and the Don Cossack leaders held out similar hope for Novocherkassk. However, the swiftness of the Red advance, along with the unreliable communications between the armies and rear, created a state of heightened anxiety in the Don capital. Residents and refugees began looking for any means to leave the town. Some crowded the railroad station only to find few trains still running. Those with a draft animal departed on sleighs or sledges, many outfitted with bells which a British major found "strangely gay in view of the gloomy news."[22] For most, the only way out of the town was to set out on foot across the frozen Don River and then continue through the snow-covered steppe in biting cold. The temperatures were so frigid that retreating Cossacks on horseback wrapped cloth around their stirrup irons as extra protection from frostbite. Adding to their misery was typhus, the spread of which was accelerated by the utter breakdown in medical services and sanitation.

Eventually, the leaders of the Don Army also gave up their optimistic forecast of holding the Red Army at bay. As the Cossack soldiers fell back on their capital, the chaos there only increased. The troops turned to drink and looting with some units trying to escort carriages full of booty along the railways while haggard refugees unable to find accommodation on a train looked on in disgust. Officers and officials hoping to stem the flow of troops towards the rear resorted to draconian measures, such as publicly hanging deserters and looters from trees, but these demonstrations had little effect. At Don Army headquarters, staff officers hurriedly burned sheaves of documents and archives that could not be evacuated in time.[23]

On 5 January 1920 the Reds reached Taganrog and the Sea of Azov, isolating the White units in southwest Ukraine and Crimea from the main body of the AFSR to the east. Three days later, on 8 January, Red Army cavalry galloped into Rostov and claimed to have seized over 10,000 prisoners along with nine regimental commanders, 32 guns and 200 machine guns.[24] That day also saw the fall of Novocherkassk to the enemy. Further to the east, the Caucasian Army began to pull back from the line it had held since the summer, surrendering Tsaritsyn on 3 January.[25] The new year had not brought a change in fortunes for the AFSR.

The retreat of the Volunteer troops and Don Army units which had begun the previous October ended on the south bank of the Don River. On the AFSR's east flank, the Caucasian Army was forced to retire across the Manych River by the Ninth and Tenth Red Armies. The defense of these river lines was aided by the operation of icebreakers on the Don and a mid-winter thaw, thereby increasing the difficulty of any crossing by Red troops.[26] The pursuers themselves had plenty of problems to address as they were affected by the same freezing weather, epidemics and inoperable railroads which had hindered their opponents. The rapid advance of the Red armies and of Budyonny's First Cavalry Army in particular meant that the troops often outran their supplies, causing them to resort to indiscriminate plunder. This behavior concerned Soviet commissars in the wake of the army's advance who knew all too well that in the past such deeds led to popular rebellions and military defeat. A message from one commissar to the Bolshevik Party Central Committee that winter warned, "The peasants are asking 'What is the difference—first we were robbed by the Whites and now we are being robbed by the Reds!'"[27] Indeed, the Red units were displaying many of the same signs of weariness and disorganization experienced by the Whites. Denikin's cause, then, was not yet hopeless as the remnant of his armies tried to bar the Soviet advance into the North Caucasus.

The Politics of Defeat

The crushing defeat suffered by the AFSR in late 1919 was not just a military failure; it also reflected the grave shortcomings of the Whites' civil administration. Had they done a better job of establishing order in the rear and winning the confidence of the masses, particularly the peasantry, the AFSR might have withstood the Soviet counterattack or made an orderly withdrawal. Instead, the Whites found themselves losing control everywhere; from Dagestan to the Dnieper and from the countryside to the cities.

The Cossack governments contributed to the unrest in the rear. At the time of the Whites' military reverses, representatives of the Don, Kuban and Terek Cossacks were still negotiating the limits of their autonomy with Denikin's Special Council. As the AFSR's military outlook took a turn for the worse, the Cossack representatives became less willing to compromise with the generals demanding a unitary policy. Ultimately, the talks ended without reaching any agreement after the Special Council was forced to evacuate its offices in Rostov in late December 1919. In the meantime, the separatist movement in the Kuban underwent a resurgence after a new round of elections gave the Black Sea Cossacks an unassailable majority to the Rada. As the Rada elected one of Denikin's detractors, General Bukretov, to the post of ataman and recommenced its agitation for a separate Kuban army, there was little anyone within the AFSR could do to mend the situation. Officials and representatives of the Don and Terek governments were among the thousands of refugees who flooded Yekaterinodar that winter as their homelands were being overrun by the Red Army or anti–White insurgents. Denikin's Special Council also fled to Yekaterinodar after leaving Rostov but, unlike the Don or Terek governments, it was refused quarters by the Kuban officials. As a new year dawned, Denikin, as a sop to the Cossacks, replaced the Special Council with a smaller cabinet of ministers to be presided Ataman Bogaevsky.[28]

Bogaevsky's appointment to president of the cabinet did little to revive the Cossacks' flagging support for the anti–Bolshevik cause. The Don Cossacks did regain some of their composure once they had evacuated the right bank of the Don, but that had more to do with their desire to defend their remaining stanitsas than with any enthusiasm for the new government. On the other hand, the Kuban Cossacks had lost their overall will to fight. Desertion was so rife in their units that Denikin estimated that only 5,000–8,000 remained with the AFSR when the front stabilized at the Don and Manych Rivers.[29] Back in the Kuban steppe, Wrangel found the majority of Cossacks apathetic to his summons for them to enlist or rejoin their units. Having produced no appreciable results, he soon gave up that mission and departed for Novorossiysk.[30] The Kuban Cossacks, by and large, had let go of any hope in a White victory.

Meanwhile, the Cossack leaders and politicians became more confused and divided as they sought a way out of the crisis that was encroaching upon their homelands. Amid their search for a solution, they summoned the three main South Russian hosts to send fifty representatives each to a Supreme Krug. That assembly, which met in Yekaterinodar on 18 January 1920, was the product of desperate times: it had no precedent in Cossack history and two thirds of the delegates could be relegated to the status of refugees. Nonetheless, the pride of the gathered representatives was hardly diminished. Many Kuban politicians, of course, were ready to cut their ties with Denikin. They deluded themselves into believing that they could defend their homeland by themselves or that the Bolsheviks would respect their right for self-determination by not infringing upon their territory. These attitudes were not shared by the moderate Terek Cossacks, who knew they needed outside help to secure their lands from the native highlanders. Many Don Cossacks were also loyal to Denikin, although there was a considerable segment among them which blamed him for the recent military catastrophe and had lost confidence in him. Unexpectedly, this group, which included socialists on the left and pro–Krasnov conservatives on the right, came together with the Kuban delegation to facilitate the election of I. P. Timoshenko, a Social Democrat from the Kuban, as president of the krug. Under Timoshenko's leadership, the Supreme Krug deliberated fantastical projects such as uniting the three hosts into an independent Cossack state with its own army.[31]

On 29 January Denikin went before the Supreme Krug and tried to reverse this prevailing separatist mood by informing the gathered delegates that the military outlook was not as bad it appeared. The enemy, he declared, had overextended himself during his recent advance and as a result "only one last great effort on our part is required to finish him off."[32]

He also announced his willingness to make radical changes in his government by proposing the creation of a representative assembly with legislative functions. This was a significant departure from the principle of military dictatorship which he and the Special Council had long defended in their earlier negotiations with Cossack politicians. Yet, perhaps the greatest shock for Denikin's audience was his proclamation that the land was to be given to the peasants and working Cossacks.

Denikin's speech momentarily calmed those moderate Cossack representatives who were questioning their faith in him. On the other hand, his most resolute opponents were skeptical of his sudden change of heart, which they felt had come too late. Nonetheless, in the first days of February Denikin made good on his promises to the Supreme Krug by dissolving the cabinet of ministers chaired by Bogaevsky which, like the Special Council before it, had been a purely consultative body. In cooperation with the Supreme Krug, he formed a new South Russian Government that would answer to a future elected assembly. Notably, the new government had a Don Cossack, N. M. Melnikov, as its prime minister while Nikolay Tchaikovsky, a seasoned revolutionary, was named Minister of Propaganda. Until the elections were held and the projected assembly could meet, its legislative functions were taken up by a provisional commission of which half of its members would be elected by the krug and the other half appointed by Denikin.

Under the arrangements of the South Russian Government, the Cossacks at last gained an authoritative political voice in the White movement. Almost simultaneously, Denikin made one other important concession to Cossack pride by establishing a separate Kuban Army. Once again, this move was an act of desperation; he hoped that it might attract the Kuban Cossacks back to front and rejuvenate their fighting spirit. Ultimately, he was to be disappointed. The Kuban Cossack deserters ignored the call to arms issued by both the Rada and the South Russian Government, preferring instead to hide in their stanitsas. Not even extreme measures such as the dispatch of Don Cossack punitive detachments into the Kuban countryside returned any appreciable number of men into the army. On the political side, the Kuban politicians continued to cause Denikin difficulties. The separatist Black Sea Cossacks among them remained aloof of the South Russian Government and refused to recognize its authority. The only real success of the new government was that it prevented moderate Cossacks, including *lineitsy* Cossacks from the Kuban, from straying to the opposition.[33]

The predicament confronted by Denikin in early 1920 compelled him not to only modify his views towards Cossack political aspirations but also towards those of the border nationalities; especially the Georgians and Azeris. On 14 January he finally recognized the independence of Georgia and Azerbaijan and made friendly relations with both governments a priority.[34] But despite the recasting of his government into an institution more amiable towards the Cossacks and some nationalities, his efforts came too late to have any appreciable effect on the AFSR's campaign. There was little he could do at that stage to overcome the misgivings which his person and his movement conjured up in the minds of most peoples of the former empire. Bolshevik propaganda had been very effective in portraying the White movement as a reactionary one bent on restoring the ills of tsarism. Ultimately, the greatest obstacle to Denikin's efforts to reinvigorate his campaign at this stage came from his own troops and the Cossack soldiers in particular. They were thoroughly demoralized and had little inclination to continue the fight. In contrast, the spirits of the Red Army men opposing them were exuberant. For them, another victory held the prospect of ending the civil war, but for the Whites another victory could only prolong it. It was this mentality which sealed the fate of the AFSR.

The Cossack Avalanche

The upbeat assessment of the military situation which Denikin provided to the Supreme Krug at the end of January 1920 was not completely unwarranted. At the time, the opposing armies facing each other across the Don and Manych Rivers had similar strengths: the Whites, the majority of them Cossacks, numbered about 40,000–50,000 while the Reds had perhaps 50,000–60,000 troops.[35] The Whites even managed to thwart a Soviet attempt to establish a bridgehead on the left bank of the Don, thereby preventing the need for further retreat.

Still, the AFSR's prospects were not good. The military reverses which it had suffered during the past months had shaken its support not only among the Cossacks and other peoples under its control but also the Allies, who had provided it with everything from field guns and rifles to uniforms and medical supplies. Therefore, Denikin and his staff were thunderstruck when in November 1919 British Prime Minister David Lloyd George, whose country had been the most generous in aid, announced to the House of Commons that Britain would be disengaging from further involvement in the Russian Civil War.[36] The Whites further found themselves being marginalized when on 19 January 1920 the Allied Supreme War Council decided to lift its blockade of Soviet Russia. Essentially, the Allies had deemed the intervention in Russia a failure and were finally coming to grips with the survival of the Bolshevik regime.[37]

In an attempt to take the initiative and reignite foreign enthusiasm in the White cause, the Don Army and the Volunteer Corps launched a series of attacks which culminated with the recapture of Rostov on 20 February. At the AFSR headquarters in Yekaterinodar, this triumph raised hopes that the Soviet forces really had overextended themselves to the point of exhaustion. Actually, the success was partly enabled by the transfer of Budyonny's cavalry army to the more fluid eastern flank of the North Caucasus front, where the Kuban Cossacks continued to give ground to the Ninth and Tenth Red Armies. There, in mid–February, the First Red Cavalry Army began a powerful drive to the southwest along the Tsaritsyn–Yekaterinodar railroad. To block their advance, which threatened the Don Army's rear, Sidorin sent 10,000–12,000 of his best horsemen under General Pavlov. But before this expedition made contact with the enemy, it was overtaken on the open steppe by a snowstorm that induced hypothermia in thousands of Cossacks and their horses. By the time Pavlov's frostbitten cavalry corps reached its destination at Belaya Glina, its effective strength was reduced by as much as half. There, on 25 February, it fought a disastrous engagement against Budyonny's cavalry and infantry from the Tenth Red Army. Two days earlier, the Whites had again evacuated Rostov, and this loss, combined with the defeat at Belaya Glina set into motion an uncontainable retreat on all fronts of the AFSR.[38]

The inability of the Whites to organize any serious resistance after February 1920 stemmed from their loss of cohesion as a fighting force. The Don Cossacks no longer felt that the Kuban Cossack units were dependable while the Russian officers in the Volunteer Corps held a similar attitude towards all Cossacks. The various components grew mistrustful of each other and since they lacked the necessary strength to hold the front themselves, the only option left to them was to retreat.[39] Panic ensued as officers and soldiers left their posts to evacuate their families living as refugees in railcars or towns just behind the front.[40] Certainly no one wanted to abandon their loved ones to Bolshevik atrocities and tortures that were colorfully depicted in the White propaganda posters plastered on the walls of trains stations.[41]

Realizing that the North Caucasus was lost, Denikin turned his attention to saving as much of his army as possible by evacuating it to the Crimean Peninsula, which was being held by General Slaschev's detachment. Due to his earlier optimism, he had not made any serious preparations for such an operation. In order to buy some desperately needed time, he issued directives to stall the Red armies at the Kuban River and hold the Taman Peninsula, but by then discipline had broken down in his units to such an extent that his instructions were largely ignored. Everyone—the Volunteer Corps, the Don Cossacks and the Kuban Cossacks still in uniform—could think of nothing else except for reaching Novorossiysk as soon as possible. Subsequently, Denikin, who made his latest headquarters in a carriage in Novorossiysk's harbor, was soon faced with the prospect of tens of thousands of soldiers, Cossacks and civilians converging on that port, knowing full well that there were not enough enough ships to evacuate the military personnel, much less everyone else fleeing alongside them.[42]

The White retreat through the Kuban quickly snowballed from a military disaster into a humanitarian one. Although escaping the Red onslaught was the main concern of the soldiers and refugees, they also had to contend with the equally lethal hazards of freezing weather and typhus. As refugees crowded into trains headed for Novorossiysk, they unwittingly created an ideal environment for the transmission of typhus-bearing lice. After the passengers became conscious of this threat, they ejected from the carriage anyone with a fever or showing symptoms of illness, leaving them to perish in the cold next to the railways. The death rate was so high that Major Williamson, withdrawing with the British Military Mission, was appalled by the frozen corpses that were "stacked like piles of timber for engines" next to the tracks.[43]

Besides the cold and disease, another enemy cropped up along the Whites' paths of retreat. In the final days of January, a well-organized group of partisans chased the White garrison out of Sochi and began operating in other areas along the rugged Black Sea coast. The insurgents, who called themselves Greens, possessed strong socialist influences, were uncompromisingly hostile to the Whites and desired some level of accommodation with the Bolsheviks. Their forces were quickly augmented by local peasants and Cossacks who either deserted from the Whites or joined the insurgents in order to dodge Denikin's latest draft. As the AFSR disintegrated late that winter, the Green bands were emboldened by their enemy's vulnerability and soon began wreaking havoc on the outskirts of Novorossiysk. Each night searchlight beams from British warships anchored in town's harbor scanned the mountains overlooking the port in an effort to keep the insurgents at bay.[44]

Although the Greens caused the fleeing Whites considerable distress, their detachments were still no match for the organized remnants of the AFSR. In March, Kuban Cossack cavalry under General Shkuro checked a pro–Bolshevik insurgent army that was attempting reach Novorossiysk. Other Kuban Cossack units encountered the guerrillas as they and their communities retreated south towards Georgia. To spare their men from further fighting, some Kuban politicians tried to negotiate terms with the guerrilla leaders for their unmolested passage through partisan-controlled areas. When these talks failed to produce a ceasefire, the Kuban horsemen battled the insurgents and forced them to abandon Tuapse and later Sochi.[45]

While Georgia was an attractive haven for those Cossacks that no longer wanted anything to do with the AFSR, the vast bulk of fleeing soldiers and refugees headed for Novorossiysk. Congestion mounted on the roads and railways leading to the port as carts and trains followed one another so closely that they appeared to be coupled to each other.

Overall, this flood of peoples was a kaleidoscope of the classes and cultures who opposed the Soviet regime. The distinctly Russian element was represented by officers and soldiers of the Volunteer Corps as well as displaced aristocrats, former industrialists, ex-tsarist officials and educated professionals—teachers, bankers, doctors, lawyers—who were all considered pariahs by the dictatorship of the proletariat. Non-Russian peoples who had thrown their lot with the Whites added an exotic touch to the tragic sight; particularly the Kalmyk families who were fleeing in carts pulled by camels. Yet it was the Cossacks, especially those from the Don, whose numbers overwhelmed all others in this wreckage of humanity. Like the Kalmyks, entire Cossack communities attempted to reach Novorossiysk to escape the Red onslaught. The approach of this "Cossack avalanche," as Denikin called it, was disconcerting for those who knew there were not enough vessels in the port to evacuate everyone to the Crimea.[46] The panic and chaos which prevailed along the roads rendered the Whites unable to organize a sturdy defense around the port that might have won them a few more days to carry out their evacuation.[47]

The final days of the Whites' presence in Novorossiysk were marked by utter confusion, tragedy, waste and fighting among themselves. The weather contributed to the misery as a heavy gale swept across the town from the mountains; its winds howled continuously while adding an icy chill to the air. British and French warships were on hand for the evacuation and occasionally fired their ten-inch guns at the approaches to the town in an effort to keep the pursuing Bolsheviks at a distance. Vessels belonging to the White-controlled Russian Black Sea Fleet also took part in the evacuation but neither they nor the foreign ships could carry everyone away to the Crimea. In order to fit as many people on the boats as possible, no artillery, armored vehicles, stocks of munitions or horses were to be loaded on them. Since nothing was to be left to the enemy, orders were given to destroy anything of military value. Field guns were rolled off the piers and crates of ammunition were dumped into the choppy seawater.[48] Along the shoreline, British airmen caught up in the unfolding catastrophe destroyed their planes by crushing the partially disassembled machines under the tracks of a Mark V tank. Once this task was completed, the tank itself was locked in gear and sent trundling into the harbor.[49] Nearby petrol storage tanks were set ablaze, triggering thunderous explosions and filling the sky with billows of black smoke.[50] Horses were brought down to the water's edge and then shot, their bodies left tumbling in the surf. Many Cossacks who arrived in the town were unable to dispatch their mounts; not due to sentimental reasons but rather because they had thrown away their heavy firearms during the long retreat. As their owners embarked on ships, hundreds of abandoned horses waded along the shoreline as carcasses and other debris floated around them.[51] Other Cossacks unable to reach a vessel from a pier swam their horses out to a waiting ship, grabbed onto a net or ladder and then climbed on board, leaving their bewildered mounts behind to drown in the dark waters.[52]

The Cossacks who reached a ship were the lucky ones; many were fated to be left behind. Denikin and Sidorin had anticipated, perhaps wistfully, that only a fraction of the Don Army would want to continue the struggle in the Crimea. But as the Don Cossacks converged on the port, many with their families in tow, they made it clear that they expected to go to the Crimea. Their decision did not alter Denikin's original plan, which was to give priority to the embarkation of the Volunteer Corps over the Cossacks. To reserve their places on a waiting vessel, Volunteer officers posted armed guards at the docks next to their ships and drove the Cossacks away by shouldering their rifles. In the meantime, Sidorin was infuriated by Denikin's seemingly expendable attitude towards the Cossacks and, during one of his visits to AFSR commander's carriage, accused his superior of treachery and betrayal.[53]

On 26 March Denikin and his staff abandoned their railcar headquarters and boarded a destroyer, from where they watched Novorossiysk's final hours of agony. Cracks of gunfire could be heard as officers, having realized that time had run out, shot themselves on the quays. Others made a desperate attempt to swim out into the harbor, hoping that a sympathetic ship might pick them up, and drowned. Late that evening, the victorious Red troops entered Novorossiysk, taking 22,000 prisoners—many of them Don Cossacks—and a trove of munitions, horses and other materiel that the Whites had neglected to destroy.[54]

Gathering the Pieces

The Whites landed in the Crimea in the same condition as shipwreck survivors when they reach a shore: exhausted, destitute and yet relieved at having escaped their ordeal. The figures for how many men from the AFSR were evacuated from Novorossiysk to Crimea are imprecise, but most sources agree that 19,000–25,000 Volunteer troops made the journey along with 10,000–12,000 Cossacks.[55] The fact that more troops from the Volunteer Corps reached the Crimea than from the much larger Don Army is compelling evidence of the preferential treatment given to the Russian officers and soldiers during the evacuation. To their credit, the Volunteers still carried their arms and retained their overall discipline; the Cossacks, on the other hand, lacked rifles and were without mounts. Still, these Cossacks could at least take comfort in having made it to the Crimean refuge; many of their brothers were not so fortunate.

The vast majority of Cossacks to reach the Crimea in the immediate aftermath of the evacuation from Novorossiysk were those from the Don. The bulk of the Kuban Army remained in the Caucasus after having been cut off from the retreat while fighting the Green insurgents in the mountains south of Novorossiysk. Many Kuban political leaders with the army actually preferred to seek sanctuary in Georgia rather than rejoin the Whites in Crimea. Its southward progress was hampered by the difficult mountain terrain as well the horde of refugees accompanying it. Altogether, this mass of humanity probably numbered about 40,000 persons, and it was soon augmented by some 20,000 Don Cossacks that had fled along the coast from Novorossiysk. Everyone, including the horses, lacked food; moreover, they bitterly resented Denikin and the White generals whom they felt had abandoned them to an uncertain fate.[56]

Denikin, in fact, did try to arrange for the Transcaucasian states to provide an escape route for his armies as the front crumbled. His envoys' pleas were ill-received; the last thing the Georgian and Azerbaijani governments wanted to do was to draw the ire of the victorious Red Army.[57] Still, throughout April the remnants of Denikin's shattered army, left with nowhere else to go, continued to march south towards Georgia.

While the stranded Cossacks retreated along the Black Sea coast, significant changes occurred in the rest of the army following its arrival in the Crimea. Just days after landing at Theodosia, Denikin dismissed the South Russian Government for failing to revive the Cossacks' willingness to fight.[58] Three days later, AFSR commander-in-chief resigned his post and authorized a military council to elect his replacement. That military council, which met in Sebastopol in 3–4 April, selected the man with whom he was no longer on speaking terms: Baron Pyotr Wrangel.[59] The baron, who had been staying in Constantinople following his recent discharge from the AFSR, quickly rejoined the army in the Crimea as its leader.

Immediately upon Wrangel's arrival in Sebastopol, one of his former commanders, General Ulagay, pleaded for an operation to rescue the Cossacks still retreating in the western Caucasus. On paper, the predicament of the Cossack units in that region did not look serious. Although they were exhausted and short of supplies, they outnumbered the equally tattered Red cavalry pursuing them. But the Cossack units, as Ulagay put it, "completely lost their nerve" and had no stomach for further combat. Throughout the month, the question of what to do with the Cossack units in the western Caucasus ignited a heated debate within the anti–Bolshevik camp. Ulagay, whose assessment was corroborated by other reports concerning the beleaguered units, maintained that the Cossacks would not fight and should be evacuated to the Crimea. However, many Kuban politicians, including Ataman Bukretov, were averse to transporting the remainder of their army to the peninsula where Wrangel was imposing a strict, unified command over the armed forces. More than anything else, they wanted to preserve the autonomous army they obtained from Denikin just few months earlier. At a conference convened by Wrangel to settle the matter, Bukretov rejected any proposal to evacuate the Cossacks from the mainland and insisted that their units would regain their former valor if they were led by more determined officers. Although Wrangel was skeptical, he nonetheless gave Bukretov to chance to back up this claim by appointing the ataman to overall command of the Cossacks in the western Caucasus.

In mid–April, shortly after Bukretov rejoined the Cossack units, the Red cavalry renewed their drive towards the coast. Despite the Kuban ataman's confident assurances, the Cossacks folded and fled in face of the enemy. In desperation, he and some members of the Rada attempted to initiate negotiations with the Bolsheviks. When this news reached Wrangel, he immediately ordered the Russian fleet to evacuate those Cossacks unwilling to surrender. Most Don Cossacks, along with a brigade of Terek Cossacks, readily boarded the vessels, but the Kuban Cossacks were hesitant to accept the Whites' hospitality. Some distrusted the White generals, a sentiment that was encouraged by Bukretov who publicly scorned the Crimea as a trap. Ultimately, a significant number of Kuban Cossacks recognized the hopelessness of their position and embarked for the Crimea, where they arrived on 4 May.

After the failure of his attempt to reach a settlement with the Bolsheviks, Bukretov resigned as ataman and, along with other members of the Kuban government and Rada, sought asylum in Georgia. As for the Cossack rank-and-file who stayed behind, many simply laid down their arms and surrendered to Soviet forces. A smaller number of Cossacks did vanish into the mountains to continue their anti–Bolshevik resistance as guerrillas, while others also crossed the border into Georgia where they were disarmed. With Allied connivance, many soldiers who were interned in Georgia were allowed to rejoin the White army in the Crimea.[60]

As the Bolsheviks completed their conquest of the North Caucasus in May 1920, the last organized resistance to their rule in South Russia was confined to the Crimea. That peninsula, however, was not the only area of the former Russian Empire where Cossacks continued to fight alongside Whites. In the Russian Far East, the civil war, intervention and terror continued, only slightly abated. Developments in this theater, however, like those in South Russia, did not offer anticommunist Cossacks much hope.

8

Retreat

The Counterstrike

After the Red Army crossed the Urals in the summer of 1919, the various groups who formed the White movement in Siberia were facing increasingly insurmountable odds. Although they remained in nominal control of most of Siberia, much of that vast area was an empty wilderness with few railroads and a sparse population. Their enemy, on the other hand, was backed by the much greater industrial and human resources of Central Russia, leaving the Whites with no options other than to retreat.

This general retreat sealed the fate of the Ural and Orenburg Cossacks who constituted the core of Kolchak's Southern Army. By the end of the year, the First and Fourth Red Armies had overrun the better part of both Cossack hosts, forcing thousands of refugees to migrate for distant frontiers. The flight of the Ural Cossacks began in the first days of January 1920 as soldiers and their families, numbering 15,000 persons total, fled from Guryev (Atyrau) and journeyed southward along the eastern littoral of the Caspian Sea. A key town in that area, Krasnovodsk (Türkmenbaşy), was captured by pro-Soviet forces on 10 February, preventing the hungry and weary Cossacks from obtaining any relief there. Having no other option, they plodded onward through the desert wilderness towards the Persian frontier. They left behind numerous dead along their route; by late spring, only 215 survivors had crossed into Persia after a 800-mile trek.[1] Further north, Orenburg Cossack units embarked on an even greater odyssey. Under the leadership of Ataman Dutov, tens of thousands of Cossack men, women and children fled from the First Red Army as it pushed southeast from Orenburg. When in September 1919 they found their way blocked by militias from the Turkestan Soviet Republic, many of these refugees gave themselves up. However, Dutov and several thousand of his most dedicated followers continued their exodus by abandoning the railway and heading due east into the desert wastes of Central Asia. For a time, they hoped to defend Semipalatinsk and, when that became impossible, hold out in the Semirechye Cossack Host, which continued to be the scene of bitter fighting between local Cossacks, Kazakh tribesmen and Russian colonists.

Dutov's Cossacks were too hungry and dispirited to provide useful assistance to the Semirechye Cossack guerrillas, who had recently elected Annenkov as their ataman. In the spring of 1920, as Soviet forces were encroaching upon the region, both groups of Cossacks retreated east towards Xingjian. As their ragged columns approached the Chinese frontier, the Cossack atamans sent envoys ahead to Xingjian's warlord, Yang Zengxin, to seek his permission to enter his territory with their arms. Unsurprisingly, Yang was lukewarm to the idea of allowing bands of unruly, armed desperados to enter his realm and complicate relations with his Soviet neighbor. The cunning warlord resolved the matter by inviting the

Cossack leaders to his headquarters at Ürümqi to negotiate an agreement. Ataman Annenkov, accompanied by three adjutants, accepted Yang's offer and went ahead to Ürümqi. Once they arrived, the four men were immediately detained. In the following months of his confinement, Annenkov's captors force-fed him opium to nurture an addiction and undermine his leadership capabilities. In the meantime, his troops, along with those loyal to Dutov and their civilian stragglers, were compelled to surrender their weapons as they crossed the Chinese frontier. Altogether, at least 30,000 persons, mostly Cossacks, were interned in northern Xingjian.[2]

From Omsk, Kolchak had no time to mourn the loss of the Ural and Orenburg Cossack contingents. The crises on his front had left his remaining regiments understrength and demoralized. The Allies, disheartened by the Supreme Ruler's recent string of defeats, began to divert their aid to South Russia where at that time Denikin seemed a better bet. To salvage the situation, Kolchak cleaned house at his army headquarters and appointed a quartermaster from the tsarist army, General Mikhail Diterikhs, as his new commander-in-chief. Diterikhs, amid his deliberations on how to restore the combat worthiness of the army, unimaginatively turned to two pillars of the *ancien régime*: church and Cossacks. The former institution was used to draw manpower into Kolchak's depleted corps by evoking a "holy war," but the promises from the priests and mullahs that their flocks could punch their ticket to eternal salvation by killing Red infidels failed to stir the Siberian believers into action.[3]

Greater expectations were placed in the recruitment of a Cossack cavalry corps. In contrast to South Russia where the cavalry arm frequently decided battles, on Kolchak's front cavalry hitherto operated mainly as an auxiliary force organized in relatively small detachments. But as the White foot soldiers fell back from the forested slopes of the Urals and into the grass-plumed steppes of Western Siberia, Diterikhs perceived that the deployment of a massed cavalry force in the open terrain—combined with the element of surprise—might throw the enemy off balance. The only problem with Diterikhs' scheme was that Siberia, compared to South Russia, lacked a large pool of expert horsemen to execute the feat he had in mind.

Naturally, Diterikhs looked to the Cossacks of Siberia to provide the mounted force, but when he began preparing his counterstroke in August 1919, Kolchak's recruiters had relatively few Cossacks available to them. By then they had lost contact with most of the Ural and Orenburg Cossacks while on the other end of Siberia the Transbaikal and Ussuri Cossacks were too bound by the Japanese to even be considered for the project. This left them only with the Siberian Cossacks, numbering a mere 114,000 individuals, who lived in widely-scattered settlements across the Western Siberian plain.[4] Up to the summer of 1919, ordinary Cossacks of the Siberian Host had by and large remained aloof of the civil war even though their officers, as demonstrated by the coup which brought Kolchak to power, played an outsized political role in the counterrevolution east of the Urals. Like many other rank-and-file Cossacks, including those on the Don and Kuban, they were by no means inherently sympathetic to the goals of the White movement. But unlike the Cossacks of South Russia, most Siberian Cossacks, due to the remoteness of their settlements, had not directly experienced Soviet terror or misrule. The Bolsheviks had ruled Siberia for only a brief, six-month period in early 1918. Subsequently, they were still largely an unknown entity to many Cossacks and peasants in that region. Although many heard stories of the depredations of grain-requisitioning detachments or of violent de-Cossackization policies, most Siberian Cossacks probably dismissed such accounts as fiction or exaggerations of whimsical anti–Bolshevik propagandists. Even foreign observers perceived that the Siberian Cossacks "are not disposed to fight vigorously for the Kolchak government."[5]

Diterikh's plan called for the recruitment of 20,000 cavalrymen to fill his mounted corps. The White and Siberian Cossack leaders knew that the only realistic means for them to obtain such manpower from the apathetic ordinary Cossacks was through conscription. This measure was announced in early August 1919 during a session of the Siberian Cossack Krug in Omsk by calling for the mobilization of all Cossack males 17–55 years of age. In the meantime, the White leaders, including Kolchak, went out of their way to regale their Cossack saviors with banquets, honors and elaborate ceremonies. Most of all, they heaped praise upon the Siberian ataman, Major-General P. P. Ivanov-Rinov, who was to personally lead the decisive charge. The entire spectacle reeked of desperation. "Kolchak is compelled to rely more and more on Cossack support in the present crisis because he has no other support left," reported an American diplomat from Omsk.[6]

The objective of Diterikh's counteroffensive was to eliminate the threat to Omsk by attacking the Third and Fifth Red Armies and restoring a stable defensive line at the Tobol River. To ensure long-term success of the operation, Ivanov-Rinov's corps was supposed to gallop around the right flank of the Fifth Red Army and into its rear at Kurgan, thereby blocking its path of retreat and forcing its destruction. It was, to say the least, an ambitious plan for Kolchak's gutted forces, now reorganized into three small armies, but its goals, as subsequent events were to show, were not out of reach.

Diterikhs' counterattack, which began on 1 September 1919, gave its architect some initial reasons for optimism as the Red soldiers were taken by complete surprise and forced to make a hasty withdrawal. After a week into the operation, Ivanov-Rinov's Cossack Cavalry Corps began its critical maneuver. The actual strength of the corps was estimated to be at most 7,500 men—less than half of the projected goal of 20,000 sabers. Nonetheless, the corps succeeded in penetrating the rear of the Fifth Red Army, causing considerable panic and throwing it into further disarray. By the middle of the month, the victory which Diterikhs had envisaged was within reach. Both Red armies were continuing their westward flight and only a measly enemy regiment stood between Ivanov-Rinov's corps and their objective at Kurgan. At that point, the Cossack commander inexplicably halted his men, ignoring several orders from Diterikhs to ride onto Kurgan and blow up the bridges and railways the Fifth Red Army needed to cross the Tobol. When the corps remained more or less stationary despite these instructions, a furious Diterikhs sacked Ivanov-Rinov on 19 September and announced his replacement with a more compliant commander. Illogically, the Siberian Cossack leaders in Omsk cried foul at this dismissal of their elected ataman and prodded Kolchak into reinstating Ivanov-Rinov to lead the corps only five days later. By then, however, the Whites had missed the window of opportunity to trap the Fifth Red Army. Both Red armies had retired safely to the west bank of the Tobol, where they momentarily paused to lick their wounds and replenish their regiments for a renewed push towards the Supreme Ruler's capital.

The Downfall of Kolchak

Omsk, the prize which the Red Eastern Army Group had set their sights on late that autumn, was already a chasm of hardship and misery for the hundreds of thousands of refugees who had flocked to that town. To refugees from Central Russia, it seemed strange, backward and uninviting: the landscape was treeless, streets were unpaved and Kazakh yurts still dotted its hinterlands.[7] Many visitors and refugees described Omsk as "a sad and depressing place"[8] that was "cut off from all civilization."[9] The turmoil wrought by the civil war did not improve these perceptions. Refugees fleeing persecution and famine in Soviet Russia swelled the town's population, previously at 200,000, to more than a half-million during the course of 1918–1919. Unable to find housing, many of the refugees lived in parked railcars or in dugouts in the nearby steppe.[10] With such an influx of newcomers living in improvised shelters, conditions in Omsk became unsanitary and soon epidemics, particularly of cholera and typhus, swept through the population. "The typhoid patients were so numerous," recalled a Cossack refugee in Omsk, "that it was impossible to isolate them completely, and it sometimes happened that dead men lay among the living for hours before they were discovered."[11] In addition to disease, the population also suffered from hunger and other privations since the needs of the army were given priority on the Trans-Siberian Railway.[12]

Although Omsk may have seemed like an unworthy seat for a dictator claiming to rule the lands that had constituted the vast Russian Empire, Kolchak was decidedly reluctant to leave his capital. On the other hand, Diterikhs recognized that the September counterattack as a strategic failure and urged its evacuation.[13] The commander-in-chief's misgivings were soon proved to be valid. In mid–October, the two reinforced Red armies attacked across the Tobol and broke out of their bridgeheads after just a few days. In response, Diterikhs begged his master to relocate the government to Irkutsk but Kolchak, like an honorable captain refusing to abandon his ship, would not hear of it. Instead, he accepted Diterikhs's resignation and appointed in his place General Konstantin Sakharov, whose main qualification was his assurances that the capital could still be defended. Sakharov lost his nerve just a week into his new post; his belated admission that Omsk could not be held left the Kolchak government, its armies and throngs of civilian refugees with no time to organize an orderly withdrawal. Chaos and panic broke out as thousands of desperate refugees crowded into the station and railyards pleading for admission onto an eastbound train. Others grabbed whatever they could carry and set out on the Great Siberian *trakt*, the ancient road which paralleled much of the Trans-Siberian Railway. Joining them were the ragged soldiers of Kolchak's armies and many Siberian Cossacks, some of whom had not lost their appetite for terror amid the looming disaster. Just hours before Omsk was abandoned to the enemy, several Cossack detachments reportedly converged on the town's penitentiary and carried out a wholesale slaughter of political prisoners.[14]

Kolchak, having bowed to inevitable, finally departed from his capital on the night of 13–14 November in a convoy of five trains that included the Russian gold reserve captured earlier at Kazan. The following morning, the spearheads of the Fifth Red Army entered the town against no resistance, netting some 40,000 prisoners and massive quantities of war materiel that had been abandoned by the Whites.[15] Indeed, the latter had left Omsk in such disarray that the Soviet command ordered just five divisions from the Fifth Red Army to continue the pursuit east of the town. Meanwhile, the Third Red Army, which soon reached Omsk via the railway from Yekaterinburg, was transformed into a "labor army."[16] The Bolsheviks, now confident in their victory, were looking beyond the immediate military campaigns.

The Soviet assessment that Kolchak's forces would be unable to regroup deeper in Siberia proved correct. Of all the exhaustive retreats which occurred in the Russian Civil War—and there were many—none was more unforgiving than the Whites' eastward flight along the Trans-Siberian Railway during the winter of 1919–20. The sheer distances involved, combined with the subzero temperatures, long hours of darkness, blizzards, typhus epidemics, stalled trains, vengeful partisans and hungry wolf packs sapped the last bit of energy from the remnants of Kolchak's army. Most of the soldiers retreated on foot along the *trakt*, mingling with plodding columns of desperate civilians. Some of the most fortunate refugees, along with many Cossacks, headed east via sleigh or horseback. Still, the trek was easy for no one. Even those who had managed to secure a spot on an eastbound train made frustratingly slow progress. The Trans-Siberian Railway, already in a state of disrepair from the heavy burdens of war and previous fighting along it, was overwhelmed by the sheer number of trains heading east. Everything from the coal needed to fuel the locomotives to spare parts for repairs on rolling stock were in short supply. As in South Russia, typhus-bearing lice readily dispersed throughout the packed railcars.[17]

The greatest hindrance for the Russian trains fleeing Omsk was the presence of foreign contingents which had spent the better part of 1919 grudgingly adhering to Allied orders to defend the 1,100 mile stretch of railway between Novonikolaevsk and Irkutsk from partisans. These formations included Polish, Romanian and South Slav units of varying size, but the largest by far these were the three divisions of the Czechoslovak Legion. Relations between the Russians and their Czech and Slovak "liberators" remained stormy since the latter had left the front in late 1918. Many Siberians, from the leaders in Omsk to villagers in the countryside, resented the Czechoslovaks for their interference in Russian affairs, their supposed exploitation of Russian labor in local industries and their refusal to return to the front.[18] Meanwhile, the legionaries regarded the Supreme Ruler's regime as a hopelessly reactionary, corrupt and criminal enterprise.[19] The homesick Czechoslovaks wanted nothing other than to return home, but the Allies, to whom they were beholden, ignored their repeated requests to leave Siberia. As Kolchak's collapse became inevitable in late October 1919, the legionaries finally took matters into their own hands by seizing control of depots, telegraph networks and locomotives in their sector. As they facilitated the eastward progress of their own trains, most Russian echelons behind them were immobilized for days or weeks. In the meantime, Red Army spearheads, streaking along the snow-covered *trakt* by sleighs, began overtaking dozens of idle trains daily. By 23 December, they had captured at least 120 trains from Omsk.[20] Outraged by these losses, various White leaders and officers protested in vain the Czechoslovaks' actions to the Legion's commanders, Generals Janin and Syrový.

The Czechoslovaks further aggravated the Whites by negotiating local truces with the partisans operating along the Trans-Siberian Railway. The insurgency in Siberia, often led by demobilized veterans and former Red Guards, had been building momentum since the autumn of 1918. Like guerrillas in other parts of Russia, many were not disciples of Lenin and possessed at best only a hazy understanding of the issues at stake in the civil war. Given the popularity of the Socialist-Revolutionary Party in Siberia, it is possible that some partisans were motivated by the growing hostility of that party's leaders towards the White movement.[21] But undoubtedly, the best recruiting tools which the Siberian partisans had at their disposal were the Whites' counterinsurgency measures. Throughout most of 1919, Cossack punitive expeditions stoked the peasants' outrage by razing problematic villages, annihilating their entire adult male population, confiscating their property or seizing hostages. Only in late autumn did Diterikhs try to rein in these detachments by forbidding them from burning villages, but by then the peasants were lost to the White cause.[22] The guerrillas held nothing back in the Whites' moment of agony, and with vengeful delight they threw themselves on the weary columns of civilians and soldiers retreating through their districts. In many areas Czechoslovak officers, hoping to avoid further combat while in Russia, negotiated settlements with the insurgents whereby the legionaries agreed not to interfere in the rebels' operations as long as they respected a neutral zone along the Trans-Siberian Railway.[23]

Under such arrangements, the partisans began to establish their authority in the towns and countryside adjacent to the railway in Czechoslovak-controlled sectors, greatly complicating the position of the White refugees and soldiers who still hoped to pass through these areas. As White garrisons melted away, underground SR organizations took advantage of the power vacuum to proclaim authority in the name of the Political Center. Such was the case in Krasnoyarsk, where in late December a new government under the Political Center was declared while Kolchak's train sat idle at the local rail station.[24] The regime change there was unwelcome to not only the helpless Supreme Ruler, but also to his remaining loyal troops who were still east of the town and had hoped to find relief there. These men, organized under the able leadership of General Vladimir Kappel, had been on the run for nearly six weeks during which time they traversed almost 900 miles of the wintry Siberian countryside. Hungry and weary, many of them had tossed aside their rifles during the retreat, leaving Kappel unable to even make an attempt to retake Krasnoyarsk. Instead, he and his most resolute followers bypassed the town by taking a treacherous detour through the surrounding taiga, but many soldiers, refugees and Cossacks who had previously accompanied them were unable to go any further. The hardships which they experienced had even claimed the lives of two Cossack officers responsible for instigating Kolchak's coup: General Volkov committed suicide during the retreat while his former accomplice, Krasilnikov, succumbed to typhus.[25]

Although the Political Center in Krasnoyarsk had little to fear from the demoralized Whites, its survival was still in doubt as the Fifth Red Army approached the town. After just a fortnight in power, it was overthrown by a Bolshevik *revkom* on the night of 3–4 January 1920. Four days later, the vanguard of the Red Army reached the town, cutting off many White trains as well as those of a Polish division.[26] With silent resignation, many White soldiers and Cossacks simply laid down their rifles, swords and revolvers, and soon huge piles of their discarded arms formed at collection points outside of the town. So many officers surrendered at Krasnoyarsk that a British officer visiting there a few days later observed that the epaulets torn from their uniforms littered the streets like "fallen leaves in autumn."[27] The town was also full of abandoned horses, most of them having belonged to the Cossacks or having been stolen from villages during the retreat. Since neither their former owners nor the newly-arrived Bolsheviks could provide fodder for these creatures, many were doomed to starvation in the following days and weeks.[28]

As it turned out, the White soldiers who continued the retreat beyond Krasnoyarsk were not Siberian Cossacks or the hard-line reactionary officers in whom the Kolchak regime had invested so much faith. The majority of these men and their two leading officers, Generals Kappel and Voitsekhovsky, were veterans of the Komuch's People's Army from the Volga and Urals. Although they were among the earliest opponents of Bolshevism east of the Volga, they were never held in high regard by the Supreme Ruler because of their past association with democratic socialists.[29] Indeed, Kolchak remained entrenched in his anti-socialist prejudices even as his power rapidly receded during his long train ride across Siberia that winter. In Irkutsk, the town designated as his new capital, his ministers undertook negotiations with local socialists to bring the latter into a new coalition government. The White ministers realized that their administration needed to broaden their support in order to survive, but their master, kept abreast of the talks by wire dispatches to his train, was unwilling to compromise with the socialists. Instead, he once again looked to Cossacks to save what was left of his regime.

The Supreme Ruler dreaded the thought that Irkutsk, like other towns along the Trans-Siberian line, might be lost to rebel SRs or Bolsheviks before he or the remnants of his army arrived in time. Desperate to prevent such a catastrophe, he began to sound out his old nemesis in Chita, Ataman Semyonov, for help in securing Irkutsk for the White cause. By then the Cossack warlord had thoroughly lost his earlier zeal for fighting Bolsheviks. Instead, he preferred to live in the company of his harem, gorge himself at banquets and instructed his men to pilfer valuable freight being hauled through his territory. He was willing to reinforce the Irkutsk garrison, but only for a price: a promotion to a new rank of commander-in-chief of all forces in the Russian Far East. Kolchak at first refused the suggestion, but he soon wavered after hearing reports of increasing rebel activity in the outskirts of Irkutsk. On 23 December 1919 the tormented dictator finally caved and granted the ataman the title he was so desperately wanted.

The Supreme Ruler's appointment of a brigand such as Semyonov to save what was left of his authority was to be his final undoing. In Irkutsk, SR representatives, wanting nothing to do with the rogue ataman, broke off negotiations with Kolchak's ministers.[30] Allied officials in Siberia, upon hearing that news, began to question the admiral's sanity.[31] Moreover, Semyonov quickly failed to fulfill his end of the bargain. He did send an expedition to reinforce the White garrison in Irkutsk, but it proved inadequate to hold back the insurgents. As they withdrew, the band of Semyonovites further inflamed local anti–White sentiment by committing several outrages that included bank robbery, hostage-taking and then the savage murders of their 31 prisoners.[32]

Once the Semyonovites were gone from Irkutsk, an SR-led Political Center proclaimed its authority in the town and effectively brought the Kolchak regime to an ignominious end. On 4 January 1920, the Supreme Ruler, whose trains were marooned at the railside town of Nizhneudinsk, finally acknowledged the absurdity of his title by transferring it to Denikin in South Russia. Two days later he accepted an Allied offer of a Czechoslovak escort for himself, his dwindling entourage and the railcars containing the gold reserves. The Czechoslovaks, however, found themselves under increasing pressure by local partisans to turn over the fallen White leader, especially as news of the Semyonovite atrocities in Irkutsk spread. Although Kolchak never had much control over the Semyonovites, he was held responsible for their offenses due to his recent decision to promote Semyonov. The legionaries, for their part, were never fond of the admiral and were even more suspicious of him as rumors circulated that he had recently conspired with Semyonov to dynamite the critical tunnels south of Lake Baikal in order to prevent their further evacuation.[33]

As the Fifth Red Army finally caught up to the Czechoslovak rearguard at Kansk, the legionaries grew anxious to cut a deal that would grant them safe passage through the rest of Siberia. To placate local partisans and the restless residents of Irkutsk, they handed Kolchak over to the Political Center on 15 January. A week later, after the Political Center liquidated itself in favor of a Bolshevik revolutionary committee, the admiral found himself a prisoner of his sworn enemy. Meanwhile, the legionaries negotiated an agreement with the Fifth Red Army's military revolutionary council whereby the Czechoslovaks were to be allowed to withdraw unmolested to the Pacific coast in exchange for their strict neutrality in the civil war. The Czechoslovaks also agreed to leave the gold reserve in Irkutsk and make no attempt to rescue Kolchak. In fact, on 7 February, just hours before this treaty was finalized,

Kolchak had been executed by a Cheka firing squad to prevent his possible rescue by a nearby White army under General Voitsekhovsky.[34]

Atamanschina in the Russian Far East

Although the Red Army was still a thousand or more miles away from the Russian Far East during the latter half of 1919, the repercussions of the Soviet triumph over Kolchak's armies were still felt in the distant stomping grounds of the Cossack warlords. News of the Whites' collapse in Western Siberia spread throughout the region and emboldened the partisans while bruising the morale of the Cossacks and peasants forced to serve under Semyonov and Kalmykov. It was becoming apparent that the atamans' campaigns to intimidate the region's population into submission were failing. Their wicked treatment of the peasants, railway workers and alleged political opponents merely encouraged the masses to join or at least support local resistance movements. Conscripts mobilized by the Cossack warlords shared the grievances of the general population, and as a result many officers rightly feared that these men would defect to the insurgents' ranks at their first opportunity. Even with the direct assistance of Japanese battalions, the Cossack leaders were unable to prevent partisan armies from taking over large swaths of forest and countryside in the Russian Far East.[35] Nonetheless, despite their increasingly troubled outlook, the Cossack warlords made little or no effort to widen their appeal among the Russian population. Even more irrational was their decision to challenge friendly units such as the Czechoslovaks and Americans.

During the autumn of 1919, the obvious decline of the Kolchak regime threatened order in Vladivostok, where an active SR underground was known to be plotting a putsch against the port's iron-fisted governor general, Sergey Rozanov. Before he was appointed to that post by Kolchak, Rozanov had earned notoriety for his ruthless suppression of a local insurgency while serving as a commandant in Krasnoyarsk.[36] His penchant for brutal methods meshed well with the inclinations of Ataman Kalmykov in Khabarovsk, and subsequently the two men began to work together to safeguard their hold on the Maritime Province.

As Rozanov caught wind that something was afoot, Kalmykov dispatched trainloads of his Ussuri Cossacks to Vladivostok reinforce his ally. If the governor-general had his way, the Cossacks would have been used to raid suspected SR offices, arrest the conspirators and smash their printing presses. But the democratically-minded SRs enjoyed considerable sympathy among various Allied contingents in the city, particularly the Americans and Czechoslovaks. Thus Rozanov, rather than risk offending the foreign interventionists, held back for the time being. Meanwhile, the presence of Kalmykov's rowdy Cossacks in the city caused a hike in the local crime rate. Accustomed to the loose discipline and predatory behavior permitted by their ataman, the Ussuri Cossacks engaged in widespread drunkenness, thievery and abuse. Occasionally they dabbled in more violent offenses, such as the abduction and murder of a Ussuri Cossack colonel who was also one of Kalmykov's most prominent critics. The Cossacks also harassed foreign troops, particularly Czechoslovaks and Americans. Such encounters occasionally resulted in serious incidents, including the death of a legionary and the flogging of a doughboy. Before long, the Allied representatives in the city had had enough of this gangster violence and demanded Rozanov to pull Kalmykov's men out of the port. If he refused, they threatened to restore order with their own forces. Their ultimatum, however, was shortly retracted when Kolchak protested their demarche as a violation of Russia's sovereignty.[37] For those Allied officials who never ventured much further west of Vladivostok, the Cossacks' barbarous conduct, along with Supreme Ruler's defense of them, appeared to confirm all the bloody accusations that were leveled against the Whites in other parts of Siberia.

Throughout the remainder of the autumn, Rozanov, with Kalmykov's Cossacks on standby, waited for the SRs to launch a revolt aimed at toppling White rule in Vladivostok. The planned uprising was to be led by the Czech General Radola Gajda, who had been recruited to the SR cause after he broke with Kolchak a few months earlier. The developing conspiracy was not a carefully guarded secret. Russians, Americans, Czechoslovaks and Cossacks in Vladivostok were all aware that Gajda and his fellow SRs were plotting something; the only doubt was when they would strike. That question was answered on 17 November, just three days after the fall of Omsk, when SR operatives began distributing leaflets on Vladivostok's streets proclaiming the establishment of a "Provisional Government in Siberia." Gajda, who was designated the commander-in-chief of a new "People's Army," hoisted the green and white flag of autonomous Siberia above his carriage in the city's train yard. The uprising showed some promise of popular appeal as local dock workers, in order to demonstrate their sympathy for the revolt, went on strike. Two companies from Rozanov's garrison also defected to the insurgents. That, however, was the pinnacle of the rebellion's success. Critically, the few thousand of Gajda's fellow legionaries in the city, whose intervention might have tipped the contest in the insurgents' favor, declared their neutrality in the affair. While they held back, Rozanov, the Japanese and Kalmykov's Cossacks ferociously crushed the rebellion. They quickly cornered Gajda's "army" in the railway yard near the harbor, occupied nearby rooftops and began spraying the rebels' carriages with machine gun fire at will. Nightfall brought no relief for the besieged insurgents as searchlights from Japanese warships just offshore exposed targets for White artillery. The following morning, barely twenty-four hours after their revolt got underway, Gajda and his men emerged from the smoldering ruins of the railway yard with their hands above their heads. The Czech general, who had been lightly wounded during the fighting, was savagely beaten by his Cossack captors before being turned over to local Czechoslovak authorities and given three days to leave Siberia. Other SR leaders implicated in the uprising sought asylum at the American headquarters in the city. Far less fortunate were the 1,500 rebels taken prisoner by Rozanov's forces, many of which were subsequently machine-gunned or bayoneted within hours of their capture.[38]

Although Gajda's putsch was suppressed with relative ease, the Whites' position in the Russian Far East was far from secure during the following months. In desperation, Semyonov and his underlings began to lash out at anyone suspected of harboring socialist sympathies, including Czechoslovak and American soldiers. By the first days of 1920, relations between Semyonov and the legionaries were strained. Tensions between them had been building during the previous weeks: at one point the Cossack warlord had threatened to attack the Czechoslovaks if they did not do more to assist the White soldiers and refugees fleeing along the Trans-Siberian Railway. Rumors that Semyonov, at Kolchak's bidding, was preparing to blow the railway tunnels south of Lake Baikal added to the legionaries' anxiety. Yet, relations between them did not boil over until 8 January, when Semyonov demanded the Czechoslovaks to turn over 300 railcars. The next day, when Semyonovites in the Baikal railway sector tried to enforce their master's ultimatum, the legionaries fought back with an intensity that stunned the Cossacks, leaving 15 of them dead, a similar number wounded and 600 held as prisoners. The Czechoslovaks also captured several of their opponents' trains, including some armored ones, and continued their operations in the coming days until the remaining Semyonovites were swept from the Baikal sector.[39]

At the same time as those clashes were taking place, Semyonovites further to the northeast picked a fight with doughboys of the U.S. 27th Infantry Regiment, who had been deployed as sentries over the railway between Mysovaya and Verkhneudinsk (Ulan-Ude). The Americans had just received orders to begin their evacuation when the Semyonovites struck. Fortunately for them, they were not taken by complete surprise since the Cossacks' increasingly erratic behavior had put them on high alert. After several brief skirmishes, the Americans, like their fellow legionaries, easily prevailed over the Semyonovites. Since by then both they and the Czechoslovaks were looking to travel through Semyonov's domain in order to reach Vladivostok, it momentarily appeared that the Allied contingents might continue their operations eastward and run the Cossack warlord out of Chita. At that moment, in mid–January, the Japanese, who hitherto had remained aloof from the fray, stepped in to shield their protégé from further defeats. Their declaration of support on behalf of Semyonov compelled the two interventionists to not only suspend their operations against the Transbaikal ataman but also to release the Semyonovites they had captured in their earlier skirmishes. For good reason, both the Americans and Czechoslovaks hated Semyonov, but they were unwilling to jeopardize their evacuation by antagonizing his Japanese sponsors.[40]

Although the seasoned Czechoslovak and American soldiers proved to be more than a match for Semyonov's thugs along the Trans-Siberian Railway, his underlings could still inflict plenty of agony in the Siberian countryside. That winter, a Semyonovite punitive expedition against areas of intense partisan activity in the Selenga River valley rounded up some 800 alleged political opponents and guerrillas. According to one chronicler, when the Semyonovites were ready to begin putting the captives to death, they decided to make their work more entertaining by employing different methods of killing. On 17 January the first batch was dispatched by firing squads, on the next day they used swords, on the third day they employed asphyxiation and the fourth and final day they burnt the victims alive.[41] Meanwhile, along the railway, the Semyonovites continued to beat railway workers and carry off any passing freight which they deemed useful. Yet, for all their swagger, the Semyonovites were mostly a paper tiger. During those first weeks of 1920, Semyonov could claim to have 20,000 men under him but of that number less than half were fully-armed while maybe a fifth could be considered reliable.[42] These were ominous numbers for a force that would soon be up against the Red juggernaut.

For the time being, the escalating partisan movement was a more immediate threat to the Cossack warlords. On 26 January a mutiny staged by the White garrison in Nikolsk (Ussuriysk), which included some Ussuri Cossacks, enabled local partisans to seize control of that crucial railway junction. Nearby foreign troops, including some Japanese units, did not lift a finger against the rebels and instead declared their neutrality. This development sealed Rozanov's fate as it cut him off from Semyonov as well as Kalmykov. Five days later, as the insurgents marched into Vladivostok unchallenged, the governor-general abdicated and went into hiding at the local Japanese headquarters. With Rozanov ousted, the partisans established the "Provisional Zemstvo Government of the Maritime Province" which, to appear acceptable to the Allied expeditionary forces in the region, was a Bolshevik-dominated government in an SR disguise.[43]

Just over a fortnight later it was Kalmykov's turn to make his getaway. On 16 February a partisan army advancing from the south swamped Khabarovsk. The Ussuri ataman, along with 800 of his closest followers and a cache of ill-gotten gold, had fled the town just ahead of the guerrillas. While he was on the run, an assembly of Ussuri Cossacks at Grodekovo stripped Kalmykov of his powers and declared their intention to place him before a revolutionary tribunal. Wanted by peasant and Cossack alike, he decided to cross the border into Manchuria, where he was arrested by Chinese troops on 5 March. Over the next several months, Chinese authorities debated whether they should extradite their infamous prisoner to face revolutionary justice in Khabarovsk. Eventually, during the following September, his guards resolved the matter for them by shooting him; ostensibly for trying to escape. Most likely, his captors were eager to eliminate Kalmykov so they could take permanent possession of his gold.[44]

Semyonov's Flight

The fall of Kalmykov in February 1920 did not bode well for Semyonov. Other developments region also appeared to signal that his days in power were numbered. On 1 March the last train of the ataman's erstwhile Czechoslovak allies departed from Irkutsk, and a week later the Fifth Red Army held a triumphal parade in that town.[45] But even though the Bolsheviks were flush with victory, their leaders were hesitant to continue regular military operations further east since they wanted to avoid a direct clash with the Japanese army. Instead, they maneuvered to gradually regain those lands in a war by proxies. In the political arena, they organized two sections of the Far Eastern Bureau (Dalburo) of the Russian Communist Party in Verkhneudinsk and Vladivostok. On the military side, they dispatched advisers and agitators to coordinate the activities of the various partisan groups in the region, all of which had their sights on Semyonov.[46] Before long the only sizable and reliable force standing between the Transbaikal ataman and the guerrillas were the soldiers of Japanese 5th Division in Chita.

With the Americans, Czechoslovaks and other foreign contingents pulling out of Siberia late that winter, Semyonov had to consider that his Japanese patrons might follow suit. In Japan, the Siberian intervention was not popular in the government, the press or public opinion; and Allied diplomats were adding their voices to the chorus of those calling for her to evacuate Russian territory.[47] While Semyonov was determined to hold onto his shrinking fiefdom as long as possible, he was also a practical man who was prepared to flee his capital at the first sign that all was lost. Throughout his reign, the ataman deposited profits from his bribes, boutiques and looting sprees in foreign bank accounts. As a safety precaution, he kept an airplane on standby at Chita to airlift him from the town in the event the railways were overrun by partisans. He was determined to avoid the fate of Kalmykov or Kolchak.

In mid-February, prospective reinforcements reached Semyonov's realm as the surviving remnants of Kolchak's armies began trudging onto the eastern shore of frozen Lake Baikal. Numbering about 30,000, these troops' crossing of that icy expanse was the final leg in a treacherous and epic retreat that had begun almost five months earlier at the Tobol River. Although they were under the leadership of General Voitsekhovsky, they called themselves Kappelites in honor of the inspirational General Kappel, who had died of severe frostbite a few weeks earlier. Semyonov showed pity towards the tattered White soldiers by welcoming them to the Transbaikal region with food, medical supplies and trains to carry them to Chita, but this outpouring of goodwill was not reciprocated by the Kappelites. They blamed him, not without justification, for undermining Kolchak's rear and selling out to the Japanese. Rather than join Semyonov, they looked to continue their resistance to Bolshevism under a more centrist regime. Voitsekhovsky had hoped that the Provisional Zemstvo Government in Vladivostok might fit this ticket; he did know that it was dominated by Bolsheviks concealed behind a SR façade.[48]

Without the Kappelites, Semyonov's position looked vulnerable as winter transitioned into spring. Neither his men nor the Kappelites, reported a British newspaper correspondent from Harbin, "display the slightest inclination to fight."[49] Earlier, Tokyo had announced its intention to withdraw its forces from Siberia in unison with the Americans and Czechoslovaks, seemingly leaving the Transbaikal ataman to fend for himself. But on 4 April, just a few days after the last American troops departed from Vladivostok, the Japanese launched a surprise offensive which reasserted their control over the Ussuri and Chinese Eastern sections of the Trans-Siberian Railway. That operation, which stemmed from the unwillingness of Japanese miltiary leaders to leave Siberia empty-handed, gave Semyonov a new lease on life.

With their fears allayed by the presence of their Japanese protectors, Cossack bandits continued their incessant crime spree along the railways of the Russian Far East. Even after two years of sadistic excesses, they still found new ways to top their previous monstrosities. For example, a band of Cossacks led by V. I. Bochkarev, a disciple of Kalmykov, acquired notoriety for executing three prominent Siberian Bolsheviks by heaving them into the fiery furnace of a locomotive. Among Bochkarev's victims was Sergey Lazo, the young ensign who had led the Red campaign against Semyonov in 1918 and most recently served on the *zemstvo* government's military council.[50]

Yet, beyond those areas occupied by the Japanese, the threat to Semyonov remained very much alive. On 6 April the Dalburo in Verkhneudinsk declared the establishment of a liberal-appearing Far Eastern Republic (FER) in the hope that it would serve as a buffer against further Japanese aggression. Although it was a puppet of Moscow, the FER was not without teeth. With the help of Red Army specialists, the FER set up a People's Revolutionary Army (PRA) and began coordinating partisan operations throughout the region. These contingents proved to be more than a match for the remaining Semyonovites defending the approaches to Chita. Just days after the FER's inaugural proclamation, its militias launched two major drives against the Semyonovites; one attack even brought them within miles of the ataman's base.[51]

Despite such narrow misses, Semyonov managed to cling to Chita throughout the following summer. Even so, his prospects continued to worsen. On 15 July the Japanese command agreed to a treaty with the FER that established a neutral zone between their forces and would allow them to effectively disengage from the civil war.[52] With their departure on the horizon, Japanese military leaders encouraged the Cossack warlord to secure as much power as possible before they pulled out. Japanese officers still hoped to preserve their influence in the Russian Far East by maneuvering Semyonov and other friendly elements into key positions of authority in the region's post-occupation government. To reach such an arrangement, Semyonov tried to open negotiations with the FER, but its leaders refused to have any official dealings with him. After being rejected by the government in Verkhneudinsk, Semyonov sent a delegation to Vladivostok, where in August groups representing a broad range of Russian political opinion, from conservatives to communists, met to discuss proposals for a future government in the Russian Far East. At that conference, Semyonov's delegation advocated their leader as the logical commander of the armed forces of the projected state since that role had been awarded to him by Kolchak. Unsurprisingly, the other delegates were unimpressed with that argument. Indeed, although they agreed on little else, the representatives were virtually unanimous in their opposition to entrusting any power to a man of such ill repute.[53]

Ironically, while the delegation from Chita was urging the Vladivostok conference to recognize Semyonov as the commander of all Russian troops in the region, the ataman's existing forces continued to atrophy. In August 1,500 men of the so-called Asian Cavalry Division, under the command of the ataman's deputy, Baron Ungern-Sternberg, decamped for Mongolia. Ungern-Sternberg's abandonment of the Chinese Eastern Railway ended his reign of terror in Dauria where, during a span of nearly two years, he and his underlings tortured and killed thousands of political opponents, war prisoners, Jewish refugees and Chinese laborers; all in the name of eradicating Bolshevism.[54] "In Dauria," explained one Cossack officer, "death is looked upon as a dear friend, who, if he will but come, relieves one of unbearable horror and torture."[55] By the final weeks of the summer of 1920, even the mad baron had realized that no amount of cruel flagrance could stop the infiltration of Bolshevism into the Russian Far East. Having given up on the region's Russian population, he still maintained faith in the ability of other neighboring ethnic groups, particularly the Buryats and Mongolians, to resist communist temptations by embracing militant Buddhism.[56] All they needed, he thought, was a strong, determined leader—such as himself—to organize them against the Red menace. Therefore, the baron's flight into Mongolia was the first step in this eccentric plan to continue the Russian Civil War in the east among non-Russian peoples. As it turned out, some Mongolian nationalists welcomed Ungern-Sternberg's arrival in their country; not because they wanted to make war upon their Bolshevik neighbors but rather because they hoped the White Russians spilling across their frontier might help liberate their homeland from Chinese exploitation.[57]

Baron Ungern-Sternberg, despite his many delusions, was correct in his assessment that Semyonov's days in Chita were dwindling. As the chill of autumn descended upon the surrounding region, the Transbaikal ataman continued to look for a Russian government that would sanction his authority. That quest led him to suddenly recognize Wrangel, then struggling to hold on to the Crimea, as "the successor of the legitimate Russian Power" as though their belated union could avert their impending fate.[58] In the meantime, the Japanese troops packed their personnel and property into eastbound trains that carried the last of them out of Transbaikal Province on 15 October. Their departure was eagerly anticipated by the PRA and its partisan allies. Just a few days later, they opened a general offensive that forced the Semyonovites and some lingering Kappelites to make a fighting withdrawal into Manchuria. When the PRA troops entered Chita on 22 October, Semyonov was nowhere to be found. Sometime in the previous days he had abandoned his capital, probably in an aircraft he had on hand for such an emergency. Before the month was out, Chita was proclaimed the new capital of a Far Eastern Republic that would finally unite all of the Russian Far East.[59]

The declaration of an enlarged Far Eastern Republic stretching from Verkhneudinsk to Vladivostok proved to be a bit premature. Although the Japanese had pulled out of Transbaikal Province, their troops stayed put along the railways in Manchuria and the Maritime Province. They were unwilling to permit the PRA or any communist organs to operate openly in the areas under their control. They also coerced the *zemstvo* government in Vladivostok, which they allowed to function in an emasculated state, to open the borders of the Maritime Province to the Kappelite and Semyonovite bands that had recently escaped from the Transbaikal region. The presence of these residual White forces, some of which were still armed, was bound to add volatility to the already unstable Russian Far East. Indeed, tensions between these troops and their reluctant hosts spiked after 27 November when Semyonov rejoined his men at Grodekovo, just a few miles inside the Maritime Province. There he immediately began plotting a putsch in Vladivostok, but his plans went nowhere as the Kappelites still refused to collaborate with him. Meanwhile, the presence of the hated Cossack warlord in the province caused such an uproar in the Popular Assembly, the nominal governing body of the region, that the ataman decided to slip back into Manchuria after spending only a few days on Russian soil. For the next several months he resided in Darien, located on the Japanese-controlled Liaotung Peninsula, where he continued to dabble in schemes aimed at regaining his former glory in the Russian Far East.[60]

9

Flight

The Crimean Bastion

For the Cossack soldiers that landed in the Crimea alongside the AFSR in late March 1920, that peninsula represented the beginning of their exile. Although they stood on soil that had belonged to Russia since the latter eighteenth century, the Crimea was not the Don, the Kuban or the Terek. They pined for a return to their stanitsas so they could plant their fields and tend to their herds. Many no longer cared to fight, but at the same time they were unwilling to take their chances with the Bolsheviks. They were confused, anxious and above all mistrustful, especially towards the AFSR command. From their perspective, the White generals, either due to neglect or malice, had abandoned thousands of their brothers to an unforgiving enemy during the disastrous evacuation of Novorossiysk. Overall, the Cossack units that landed in the Crimea were so thoroughly rattled that they were of little combat value during their first weeks there.

That peninsula offered little to improve their outlook. It had almost no industrial base that could churn out the rifles and cartridges they needed to replace those they had ditched during their recent retreats. Despite its wealth of pastures, it also had too few horses to provide mounts for most of the Cossacks. Even that most basic of necessities—food—was too limited in supply to sustain the local inhabitants and the tens of thousands newly-arrived soldiers.[1] But what the Crimea did have to offer the Cossacks and the rest of the White army was the security of being nearly invulnerable to an overland attack. It was surrounded on all sides by seas and its only natural link to the mainland, the five- to ten-mile-wide Isthmus of Perekop, was crisscrossed by an ancient stone wall and thickets of barbed wire overlooked by machine gun nests. From that strongpoint, General Slashchev's Crimean Corps, numbering only 5,000 men, was able to fend off an enemy force nearly twice its size. For its part, the Red Army made no determined effort to break into the Crimea and finish off its opponents that spring. One reason was the demand on Soviet forces elsewhere: the most combat-worthy units were needed to counter a Polish attack in Ukraine while others were held back to preserve order in the newly-occupied areas of the North Caucasus. Another consideration was the assessment by the Red command that the remnants of the AFSR would simply disintegrate on their own. Having written the Whites off as a substantial threat, only a token force, the Thirteenth Red Army, was left in Northern Taurida to menace Wrangel's troops.[2]

Indeed, if the Whites had been under a less able commander, it is likely that they never would have recovered from their harrowing defeat in the North Caucasus. But Baron Pyotr Wrangel was no ordinary officer. His combination of aristocratic bearing and an energetic style of command predisposed him to expect exceptional performance and behavior from the troops under him. Indeed, as leader of the Caucasian Army, he had distinguished himself among AFSR commanders by unceasingly punishing those who engaged in looting or corruption.[3] Convinced that discipline was essential for an army to retain its effectiveness and earn civilian trust, he immediately set about enforcing a higher standard of conduct among the soldiers in the Crimea by organizing a commission to punish looting and other violations. This stricter regimen was a major adjustment for the Cossacks, and many of the commission's early cases involved Cossacks accused of stealing horses from the local population.[4] Although the baron did not abolish requisitioning in the areas occupied by his army, he at least restrained that practice so it did not become a widespread euphemism for pillaging.

For Wrangel, rejuvenating the combat-worthiness of Cossack units under him was a project that required a blend of tact and firmness. To encourage Cossack and peasant alike to disassociate his forces with the AFSR and its past indiscretions, he renamed his forces the "Russian Army." Yet, he was unwilling to allow the Cossacks or their leaders to exploit any perceived injustice in order to challenge his authority. He made this clear in his quarrel with the commander of the Don Corps, General Sidorin, who remained bitter over the abandonment of tens of thousands of Don Cossack soldiers and their families at Novorossiysk. In his first weeks in the Crimea, Sidorin rankled the White leadership by demanding the anti–Bolshevik movement to adopt more liberal, democratic and federalist policies. He even threatened to desert the baron and lead his remaining Don Cossack troops in a unilateral—and almost certainly suicidal—campaign to take back their homeland. By 19 April, Wrangel had enough of Sidorin's antics and ordered his arrest. The Don commander, along with his chief-of-staff, subsequently turned himself in, was court-martialed, found guilty of treason and sentenced to hard labor. Wrangel, no doubt eager to put the entire affair behind him and repair his relations with the Cossacks, commuted their sentence to dishonorable discharges from the army.[5]

Wrangel's brazen handling of Sidorin was a portent of the treatment he was to accord to the Cossacks. He was even more unwilling than Denikin to offer many concessions towards Cossack pretentions, and he made use of every opportunity to restrict their freedom of action. In one of his earliest decrees, he abolished the autonomous armies of the Don and Kuban Cossacks and placed them directly under his command. At the same time, the Cossack governments were extended internal autonomy in their homelands, but this guarantee had no practical value while the hosts were under Soviet occupation. All civil and military authority in the Crimea, then, was concentrated in the hands of the commander-in-chief, who had assumed the title of regent.[6] A few months later, in August 1920, the baron went even a step further when he was contemplating an amphibious invasion of the Kuban. To prevent Cossack leaders from recovering some of their smugness as soon as they returned to their native soil, Wrangel summoned the atamans of the Astrakhan, Don, Terek and Kuban hosts to his headquarters in Sebastopol. There he compelled them to sign a convention that placed even more restrictions on the local authority of the Cossack governments once they were back in their homelands.[7]

In better times, the Cossack leaders would have protested Wrangel's high-handed approach by walking out or by attempting to drag out such negotiations. But after the spring of 1920, the Cossack leaders were painfully aware that they lacked any bargaining chips of their own. All were residing in the Crimea as refugees; they could no longer argue, as they had in the previous year, that the White generals were their guests. The rowdy Don Cossacks had been cowed by Sidorin's dismissal and his replacement by the more compliant

General Fyodor Abramov. Other Cossack groups were in an even less favorable position to challenge Wrangel than those from the Don. The Astrakhan and Terek Cossacks, whose leaders had traditionally been the most amenable towards the White generals, were present in Crimea in too few numbers to cause the army much difficulty even if they wanted to. The Kuban Cossacks, many of whom were evacuated from the North Caucasus only in early May, continued to be among the least dependable soldiers in the White army. Still, Wrangel was able to rein in the recalcitrant Kuban Cossacks to a considerable degree by exploiting their political disarray. The Kuban politicians had long been divided between pro–Russian and left-leaning separatist factions, but after the Red Army's conquest of the North Caucasus in early 1920, the two opposing groups became geographically separated as well. Those most favorable to the Russian officers followed the Whites to the Crimea. On the other hand, many separatists, after failing to arrange a truce with the enemy, sought asylum in Georgia and recongregated its capital, Tiflis (Tbilisi). The politics of the Kuban Cossacks sank into further confusion after their ataman, Bukretov, resigned and the two sides were unable to agree on a candidate to fill that post.[8]

Although the political freedom of the Cossacks was substantially curtailed under Wrangel, they remained a significant component of his army. That force was reorganized into four corps: the First Corps, comprised of the former Volunteer Army under Kutepov; the Second Corps, consisting of the Crimean troops and two cavalry brigades of Astrakhan and Terek Cossacks led by Slashchev; the Don Corps, composed of Don Cossacks under General Abramov; and the Mixed Corps, consisting mainly of Kuban Cossacks belatedly evacuated from the North Caucasus. Obviously, three of these four corps relied heavily on Cossack manpower. Most of the cavalry, Cossacks included, were dismounted due to lack of horses. Any horses the army did have at this point had been requisitioned from the Crimean population and were used to pull supply carts or artillery pieces. By early June 1920 the army would claim to have approximately 40,000 combatants, but this number was still woefully small when compared to the size of the entire Red Army, which had started the year with upwards of 5,000,000 men in its ranks.[9]

Wrangel was aware that he was the clear underdog in his contest against the Soviets. Shortly after assuming command of the army, he declared, "It is not by a triumphal march from the Crimea to Moscow that Russia can be freed, but by the creation, on no matter how small a fragment of Russian soil, of such a Government with such conditions of life that the Russian people now groaning under the Red yoke will inevitably submit to its attractions."[10] Wrangel's ultimate objective, then, was not to conquer but rather to inspire a regime change favorable to the Whites. To that end, the baron adopted measures which his predecessors in the White movement had been reluctant or too timid to undertake. Unlike Denikin or Kolchak, both of whom preferred to postpone decisions on major questions such as agrarian reform, state structure and border rectifications to a future Russian national assembly, Wrangel realized that the Whites needed to take a definitive and more progressive stance in order to appeal to a wider base. To win over the peasants, he enacted a land law allowing them to retain most of the land they seized during the revolution in return for compensation that would be paid as installments over a 25-year period.[11] To attract the support of the nationalities and other regional groups, the baron veered from the earlier White mantra of "Russia, One and Indivisible" by making overtures to the Poles, Petliura's Ukrainians, the Georgians and even Makhno's anarchists.[12] In retrospect, the baron's more flexible approach to key issues in the civil war was admirable but probably made little difference in his overall campaign. The land law would have been difficult to sell to the peasantry since it fell short of their dream of acquiring land without any strings attached—a prospect which was seemingly being offered by the Bolsheviks.[13] As for the various groups courted by Wrangel's emissaries, some, such as the Poles, entertained the possibility of an alliance as long as it suited them while others, like Makhno, rejected any cooperation outright.

Despite the emphasis which Wrangel placed on establishing an enlightened and stable administration for the Crimea, a renewal of military operations against the Bolsheviks remained foremost in his thoughts. Battlefield victories, he believed, were the only way for his army to arouse support from within and outside Russia. The capture of a food-producing region was especially important if the Whites were to ward off starvation. With this objective in mind, the baron launched a carefully-planned attack northward on 7 June 1920. The offensive consisted of two main drives: one against the Thirteenth Red Army at Perekop isthmus and the other in the enemy's rear by landing troops from the Second Corps on the northern coast of the Sea of Azov. In just four days, the Whites succeeded in occupying most of Northern Taurida up to the left bank of the Dnieper River and, for the moment at least, ending their food insecurity woes.

The Whites hardly had time to celebrate their break-out of the Crimea before a Soviet cavalry corps attacked along the front held by the unsteady Don Corps at the end of June. Initially, the Don Cossacks, who were fighting as *plastun*, fell back against the Red onslaught, but a bold counterstroke by the First and Second Corps ended the Don Corps' retreat and encircled the Red cavalrymen. Unable to return to their lines, most of the enemy troops were either killed or captured. This victory, on the heels of the triumph a few weeks earlier, did much to rejuvenate morale among the Whites. In addition to taking thousands of prisoners, the Whites had seized dozens of guns along with several armored trains. Most importantly from the Cossacks' perspective, about 3,000 horses had been captured from enemy. These animals, along with horses requisitioned from the population in Northern Taurida, provided mounts for many grateful Cossacks. Wrangel too was relieved by the acquisition of so many equine since he was unimpressed with the Cossacks' performance as infantry.[14]

After securing Northern Taurida, Wrangel was confronted with the difficult decision of where to strike next. The option of continuing his offensive northward deeper into Ukraine was not a very attractive one, especially since the seemingly pro-anarchist peasantry there was unlikely to provide the steadfast recruits needed for his army. Indeed, White losses had been so heavy in the recent battles that Wrangel gutted the civil and military administrations in his rear to provide replacements at the front. This need for additional manpower compelled Wrangel to select the Cossack lands to his east as his next objective. His conclusion was somewhat ironic given the fact that he had frequently criticized his predecessor's Cossack-centric strategy. Indeed, in the spring of 1919 it was Wrangel who wanted Denikin throw every ounce of strength against Tsaritsyn and the Volga region to link up with Kolchak's armies—even if that meant abandoning the largest Cossack hosts to their fate. Later that year, he had again opposed Denikin's decision to withdraw into the Cossack territories rather than pull the bulk of the AFSR directly into the Crimea. Now Wrangel, at last wielding the authority once held by Denikin, began echoing his predecessor by admitting that the Cossack lands were "the only possible source of recruitment still open to us."[15]

Besides its potential as a wellspring of manpower, the Kuban was an attractive target since the Bolshevik occupation there remained tenuous. The Ninth Red Army, numbering 24,000 men, had its hands full as it tried to impose Soviet authority across that restive region. Its task was made more difficult by the renewed operations of food-requisitioning detachments. As these outfits descended on stanitsas and villages, local resistance mounted as they spared neither Cossack nor outlander from their ravages. In the Caucasian foothills of the southern Kuban, residual White contingents began to augment their ranks with discontent Cossacks and natives ready to once again take up arms against the Bolsheviks. The largest of these formations, organized by General Fostikov, called itself the "Army for the Regeneration of Russia" and numbered between 15,000 and 30,000 Cossacks by early summer of 1920. Fostikov, who maintained a tenuous line of communication with the Crimea by way of Georgia, intended to coordinate his operations with those of the White invasion force.[16]

The relatively good fortunes of the Whites that summer fed their optimism for launching a daring campaign in the Kuban. The frequent fighting along the front in Northern Taurida won them more trophies in the form of thousands of prisoners, dozens of artillery pieces, machine guns and even a handful of armored trains. Beyond its military triumphs,

the Wrangel regime also secured a much-needed diplomatic victory when, in late July, the French government granted it *de facto* recognition. In reality, this decision was not as generous towards the Whites as it appeared. Paris, concerned that its Polish ally might buckle under the weight of a massive Red Army counterattack, hoped Wrangel's operations would draw Soviet reinforcements away from the decisive battles raging in East-Central Europe. Still, the Whites were heartened by the recognition from Paris since it raised the possibility of them obtaining foreign aid.[17]

On 3 August, Wrangel's main operation got underway as Cossack detachments from the Crimea made amphibious landings on the Kuban coast. The main force, consisting of 8,000 Cossacks under the command of General Ulagay, crossed the Sea of Azov and stormed ashore at the coastal town of Primorsko-Akhtarskaya. A smaller contingent of 1,500 troops made landfall west of Novorossiysk with the objective of making common cause with Green partisans. These landings initially met little resistance since the Ninth Red Army defending the area was concentrated in the zone between the Taman Peninsula and Novorossiysk. Morale among the invaders was high: they were excited to be returning to their beloved homeland where they expected to be welcomed as liberators. In fact, they were so optimistic that some Cossack soldiers brought their families with them. A few former Kuban officials, eager to reclaim their offices in Yekaterinodar, also trailed Ulagay's army. Altogether, the expeditionary force was encumbered by an estimated 4,000 noncombatants.

The first few days of the campaign seemed to validate the Cossacks' optimism. Having caught the Ninth Red Army off-guard, Ulagay led his expeditionary force about 50 miles inland to seize the railway junction of Timoshevskaya. Only 40 miles to the south of there stood Yekaterinodar, where panicked Soviet officials, frightened by the imminent return of the "White Guards," crowded into departing trains. Still further south was General Fostikov's insurgent army, with whom establishing contact was a key objective of the entire campaign. But after taking Timoshevskaya, Ulagay halted his advance amid anxieties that he might lose contact with the coast. His column wasted a valuable three days as it remained stationary and tried to mobilize Cossacks from the liberated stanitsas. Meanwhile, a third landing consisting of 2,900 troops was made in the Taman Peninsula as the Red defenders there moved against Ulagay. This expeditionary force, however, did not advance very far inland before it was blocked by stiff resistance. In the southern Kuban, near Novorossiysk, the Whites were driven back into the sea after the Green insurgents would have nothing to do them. On 22 August, the Reds deployed against Ulagay's column seized the initiative by retaking Timoshevskaya. Just over a fortnight later, his expeditionary force was back in the Crimea. The failure of the operation doomed Fostikov's insurgency in the Caucasian foothills. Due to poor communications, he had learned of Wrangel's invasion only when it was in its waning stages. With their ammunition supplies dwindling and now devoid of any hope of aid from the outside, Fostikov and his most loyal followers crossed into Georgia in early October. From there, nearly 2,000 of them managed to join the White army in the Crimea.

The failure of the Kuban invasion was a devastating blow to the Cossacks in the Crimea. The defeat dispelled their dreams of an imminent return to their homeland. Perhaps most disappointing of all was that the operation failed to stimulate a general uprising in the Kuban stanitsas. During the operation, the main expeditionary force did manage to recruit a few thousand Cossacks from the stanitsas along its route. Indeed, Ulagay returned to the Crimea with more men and horses than he had left with, a fact that was lauded by White propagandists. But overall the Kuban Cossacks, though unhappy with Bolshevik rule, had lost their ardor for rebellion. They were tired of war, pessimistic towards the Whites' chances of victory and ready to resign themselves to the new order.[18]

In the aftermath of the abortive Kuban offensive, Wrangel refocused his energies on the front in Northern Taurida. In September, he consolidated his forces there into two armies: First Army, consisting of the First Army Corps and Don Cossack Corps, on the left flank facing the Dnieper, and Second Army, comprised of the Second Army Corps and the Mixed Corps, covering the right flank. Early the following month, the Whites attempted to drive across the Dnieper River in an ambitious effort to make contact with the Poles, whose army had made a miraculous recovery during the previous month and was rolling back the Red Army. On their front, however, the Whites only managed to seize Nikopol on the west bank of the Dnieper, which they were soon forced to give up after heavy losses. On the heels of this failure came more bad news: on 18 October an armistice between Poland and Soviet Russia went into effect. As military trains bearing units from Poland began reinforcing the reformed Red Southern Army Group, Wrangel's army could do little else other than brace itself for the inevitable attack. Before the end of the month, the Soviets had deployed 133,000 troops against a mere 37,000 Whites.[19]

Although the eventual outcome of this unequal contest could hardly remain in doubt, many Whites and their supporters pretended that victory was still within their grasp. On 27 October the Don Cossacks convened a krug at Eupatoria that was attended by Wrangel and the French diplomat Count de Martel, who had arrived in the Crimea barely ten days earlier. At a banquet following the assembly, the Frenchman provided the Cossack leadership with words of encouragement. "Another effort," he assured them, "and you will reach your goal; you will achieve peace for the Don and your villages."[20] Events would soon prove otherwise.

The following day, the Red Southern Army Group began its general offensive amid unseasonably cold weather that was particularly harsh for the poorly-clad White defenders, later prompting Wrangel to complain that "nature herself seemed to be against us."[21] He had hoped to hold his opponents at bay long enough to collect the grain harvest from Northern Taurida, but this became impossible as his army was thrown back by the sheer weight of the attack. Especially menacing for the White defenders was the Soviet bridgehead at Kakhovka, on the east bank of the Dnieper, from which Budyonny's First Cavalry Army hoped to seize Perekop and block the Whites' withdrawal into the Crimea. Also active along the Dnieper front was the Second Cavalry Army commanded by the famed Red Cossack commander Filip Mironov. The horsemen serving under Mironov, including many Red Cossacks, fought with considerable zeal—some 200 members of the unit were later awarded the Order of the Red Banner for their performance in this campaign. Nonetheless, the Red cavalry were unable to secure the isthmus and prevent the Whites from pulling back into their Crimean fortress. Still, Wrangel's army was badly mauled by the Red onslaught, having lost approximately 20,000 men, several armored trains, dozens of guns and vast quantities of irreplaceable munitions, rolling stock and grain in the fields of Northern Taurida.[22]

Once its troops reached the wire belts and trenches at the Perekop isthmus, the Red command immediately initiated operations to break into the Crimea—they were not about to repeat their previous mistake of underestimating the Whites' ability to regroup. On 7 November, the third anniversary of the Bolshevik coup, they began hurling men against the Perekop defenses without regard to casualties. From his headquarters in Sebastopol, Wrangel tried to calm the jitters of soldiers and civilians in the peninsula by declaring the fortifications on the isthmus to be impregnable. The baron, to his credit, did not let himself be deluded by his own public assurances. Behind the scenes, he and his staff had been planning for an orderly evacuation by stockpiling fuel and readying ships at ports across the Crimean coastline.

Wrangel's preparations were wise since defeat arrived sooner than he or anyone else probably expected. Although the costly frontal assaults against the Perekop fortifications failed to make headway, the freezing weather afforded the Reds a rare opportunity to outflank two of the defensive lines by crossing ice which formed on the salty marshes just east of the isthmus. A unit of Red shock troops did just that on the first night of the attack, forcing the Whites to fall back on the third and final defensive line on the isthmus. Meanwhile, even further east, Kuban Cossacks under General Fostikov, only recently arrived from the North Caucasus, were driven from the Chonger Peninsula, which was connected to the Crimea's northern coast by two bridges. Two days later, on 11 November, a Red division broke out of that tiny peninsula and into the open country of the northern Crimea.[23] By then Wrangel was prepared to accept the inevitability of defeat and ordered his units to begin forced marches to pre-assigned ports. On 14 November they evacuated Sebastopol. Over the following days the ports of Yalta, Feodossia and Kerch were also evacuated. At the latter port, which was the designated embarkation point for Kuban and Terek units, the Cossacks shot their mounts at the shoreline just as they had done earlier at Novorossiysk. Otherwise, that previous evacuation bore little resemblance with the one the Whites carried out under Wrangel. Embarkation on the ships was completed in an orderly manner; there was none of the madness as seen at Novorossiysk. When it was all over, approximately 100,000 officers and soldiers, along with nearly 50,000 civilians, had embarked on 126 vessels for Constantinople.[24] Not every White officer and soldier made it to a boat, however, and perhaps as many as 12,000 were arrested and ultimately put to death by a revolutionary committee led by the deposed Hungarian Communist leader, Béla Kun, during the coming weeks and months.[25]

The Last Russia

In many chronicles of the Russian Civil War, the fall of Wrangel's Crimea in late 1920 is frequently presented as the conclusion of the military struggle between the Red and White armies. In fact, organized White units lingered on for another two years in the Russian Far East thanks to the continuation of the Japanese intervention. The scant attention which this phase of the struggle has received is due mainly to the fact that White victory—as defined by Great Russian patriots like Denikin or Kolchak—was no longer attainable in this theater. Not only were the Siberian Whites too weak to resist the Red juggernaut after the collapse of Kolchak's armies, but the lands into which they fell back were too undeveloped to exist as an independent entity. The best outcome that they could have realistically hoped for was that they might be allowed to establish a regional government under Japanese tutelage—a far cry from the goal of a restored, unitary Russian state. Thus, from 1920 onward the civil war in the Russian Far East was really a contest between Soviet Russia and Japan for control of that region. Neither of the main opponents desired to fight each other directly. Instead, both preferred to achieve their aims through proxies. For this, the Bolsheviks used the armed forces of the Far Eastern Republic and local partisans while the Japanese exploited residual White and Cossack detachments.

The notion of establishing an anti–Bolshevik puppet government in Eastern Siberia was not unwelcome to the Japanese interventionists. The problem they faced was locating a Russian leader capable of setting up such a regime without becoming a constant drain on Japanese resources. Their preferred candidate, Semyonov, failed to meet this condition. He had outlasted the Japanese occupation of Transbaikal Province by only a few days. Nonetheless, Japanese officers continued to aid the beleaguered Semyonovites by pressuring both the Chinese and the *zemstvo* government in Vladivostok to allow the fleeing Whites to enter their districts. The *zemstvo* government, which was covertly communist, was especially unwelcoming of the Semyonovite and Kappelite bands but it could do little as long as Japanese troops patrolled the towns and railways of the Maritime Province. It was that strip of Russian territory, wedged between Manchuria and the Pacific Ocean, that for the next two years would continue to be rocked by aftershocks from the civil war.

The brewing turmoil there was hastened by the decision of the *zemstvo* leaders in Vladivostok, taken in mid–December 1920, to resign and declare the Far Eastern Republic their successor. This proclamation alarmed the 25,000–30,000 Semyonovites and Kappelites who had no desire to see this final haven succumb to communism. Throughout that winter and into the following spring, the remnant Whites conspired to replace the local authority of the FER, which was more nominal than real, with an anti–Bolshevik or at least a non-socialist alternative. The Cossacks were not ignored by these schemers. The Semyonovites, with many Transbaikal Cossacks among them, were concentrated around Grodekovo while the stanitsas of Ussuri Cossacks lay in the countryside to the north. Both groups were viewed as a natural base of anti–Bolshevik support.

Semyonov, then settling into a comfortable exile in a Darien villa, was consulted in these secret deliberations due to his continued popularity among Cossacks, his name recognition and his connections with the Japanese. In particular, he was courted by one key conspirator, Nikolay Merkulov, who promised to restore him to commander-in-chief of the armed forces in the Russian Far East in exchange for financial assistance. Simultaneously, the Cossack warlord was in contact with conservative groups in Harbin whose designs conflicted with those of Merkulov. For their part, the Japanese command was aware of these plots and even encouraged them, especially those which appeared favorably disposed towards their exiled protégé. They were unwilling, however, to undertake large-scale military operations to install a non-socialist regime. Ideally, they wanted such a government to take power with little bloodshed and with minimal disruption to the ongoings of the Maritime Province.

Even at this late stage, the anti–Bolshevik conspirators were afflicted with the divisions which had long hindered their movement, and one of the most polarizing issues was Semyonov himself. For most of the region's population, Semyonov's reputation was irreparably tarnished by memories of the terror, corruption and senseless violence which he promulgated during his two-year reign in Chita. Many of the plotters were aware of Semyonov's unpopularity, and subsequently, they began to look to the Kappelites as a far more acceptable backbone to their operation. These men, it will be remembered, generally had a moderate political outlook, despised Semyonov and were apathetic toward Cossack goals in general. Their leaders even preferred a *modus vivendi* with the FER over submission to the Transbaikal ataman. But when their talks with the Vladivostok authorities proved fruitless, the Kappelites had little choice other than to seek an arrangement with conservative non-socialists. Together they formed an alliance that was as much opposed to the FER as it was Semyonov.[26]

The Kappelites began their uprising against the FER on 23 May 1921 by disarming militias in the towns of Nikolsk and Razdolnoye. The Japanese, while attempting to maintain the appearance of neutrality, assisted them by hindering the northward progress of security forces from Vladivostok. By noon on 26 May, the Whites were pushing into Vladivostok itself, where they engaged the defenders in a seesaw battle that lasted into the following day. Just when it appeared that the Vladivostok militia might be gaining the initiative, Japanese troops intervened on behalf of the Whites and decided the contest in their favor. In the meantime, a group of non-socialists headed by Spiridon Merkulov, brother to the aforementioned Nikolay, claimed authority in the Maritime Province as the Provisional Priamur Government.

The new government aspired to unite the population of the Russian Far East against communism, but first it had to resolve the differences among the Whites who supported the putsch. Nikolay Merkulov, who became minister of war in the new government, had secured the cooperation of the Semyonovites by guaranteeing their exiled leader the post of commander-in-chief. Such an arrangement, however, was unacceptable to the Kappelites and many others who regarded Semyonov as a thug. In the coup's aftermath, then, Merkulov broke his promise and instead appointed a Kappelite officer, General Verzhbitsky, as commander of the armed forces.

Semyonov, unwilling to acquiesce to this beguilement, chartered a boat for Vladivostok to assert his claims as commander-in-chief as well as his recently-acquired title of Field Ataman of the Cossacks. His arrival in Vladivostok on 3 June was not accompanied by the cordial reception he might have anticipated. Instead, his presence generated a barrage of protests from Kappelite officers, foreign consuls and the city duma. His machinations received a further setback a week later when a krug of Cossack representatives at Grodekovo, fearing that the controversy surrounding Semyonov might lead to a violent internecine struggle among the Whites, urged him to leave the Maritime Province. Meanwhile, the torrent of outcries and denunciations against Semyonov forced the Japanese to reassess their backing of him. Although they continued to desire an official role for their protégé in the Maritime Province, they could not ignore the fact that his presence there was counterproductive to the regional stability that was becoming an increasingly pertinent goal.[27]

Unperturbed by the widespread hostility towards him, Semyonov's stay in the Maritime Province spanned just over three months. He spent most of that time among his supporters in Grodekovo searching for a way he could assist the operations of his former deputy, Baron Ungern-Sternberg, in Outer Mongolia. Like China, that country had become a haven for thousands of Russians fleeing the revolution. Among the refugees were veterans of broken White armies as well as Buryats and Transbaikal Cossacks from settlements south of Lake Baikal. When the baron and his 1,500-strong Asian Cavalry Division entered northern Mongolia in the autumn of 1920, the displaced Russians already there found themselves in the crosshairs of the Chinese forces which occupied the country. Fearful that the refugees might act as a ready-made fifth column for the baron, the Chinese began to persecute Russians in the Mongolian capital of Urga and other strongholds. These measures compelled the Russians to band together and retaliate against the Chinese, unleashing a cycle of horrendous violence. A Russian officer who joined these marauders in Mongolia later recalled the cruel logic which prevailed in his unit. "Killing was a great pleasure to them," he wrote of his comrades, "not only because it postponed their own deaths, but also because it increased their strength, providing new ammunition, food and clothing."[28] Caught between two fires, many of these ruffians eventually sided with the baron's forces as their only hope for survival.

Although an estimated 2,500 Cossacks and 1,500 Buryats eventually served under Ungern-Sternberg, by far the largest proportion of his army was comprised of 5,000 Mongolians eager to cast off the Chinese yoke. In late October 1920, on the advice of his Buddhist soothsayers, the baron made two attempts to capture Urga. Despite the favorable predictions made by the fortune-tellers, his ragtag army was easily repulsed by the town's 12,000 Chinese defenders.[29] Unwilling to accept defeat, he attacked Urga again in the first days of February 1921 and this time succeeded in taking the town. Any illusions which upright Mongolian patriots had of their Russian liberators were quickly dispelled when the baron granted his men three days to pillage and rape in celebration of their victory.[30] In light of such atrocities, the Mongolian Communists who, with the backing of the PRA, began pushing into northern Mongolia from the FER, could hardly appear less malicious. Meanwhile, Ungern-Sternberg, rather than consolidate his hold over the country, began planning on offensive operation to liberate the Buryats' homeland in Transbaikal Province from the FER.[31]

Back in Grodekovo, Semyonov earnestly desired to support this attack, which was launched in early summer of 1921, but his efforts were frustrated by the uncooperative attitudes of the Japanese, the Manchurian warlord Zhang Zuolin and local Cossacks towards this project. As a result, Ungern-Sternberg's forces were on their own. Their invasion of the FER quickly turned into a disaster: the attack was easily contained by the PRA and the local Buryats offered no significant support to the invaders, causing the baron to vent his frustration by terrorizing their villages.[32] That defeat was soon followed by the loss of his capital, Urga, and a spate of mutinies in his army. The Transbaikal Cossacks serving with him were among those who joined these insurrections by shooting their commander and then hunting down the baron's henchmen. "All executioners and stool pigeons were brought in and chopped with swords by infuriated Cossacks," recalled a witness.[33] Eventually, most of the Cossacks sought refuge in Manchuria. After surrendering their arms to Chinese border guards, they were graciously allowed to join Semyonov at Grodekovo. Isolated groups of Cossacks took a more treacherous route southward through the Gobi Desert to reach the safety of Chinese territory. In the meantime, Ungern-Sternberg was taken captive by Mongolian mutineers and turned over to the Red Army. He was then transported Novonikolaevsk, given a show trial and executed on 15 September.[34] With him died Mongolia's dream to achieve imminent independence—it became a Soviet satellite—and Semyonov's hope to regain some of his former influence in the Far East.

By mid-summer the controversial ataman was struggling just to preserve his clout among Cossacks in Grodekovo. Many Cossacks resented the tensions caused by his continued presence in the Maritime Province. This Cossack opposition to Semyonov soon prevailed at another krug in Grodekovo, depriving him of the title of field ataman. The final blow to his ambitions for power in the Russian Far East came on 13 September when many of his followers formally recognized the authority of the Merkulov government. A few days later, Semyonov again left the Maritime Province for a second, much longer exile in foreign lands.[35]

As Semyonov's supporters deserted him during in the summer of 1921, the Cossacks' political clout faded in a corresponding manner. Simply put, the Cossacks of the Far East lacked an alternative figure with the charisma, boldness, charm and foreign contacts which had made Semyonov so influential. Nonetheless, they maintained a significant presence in the armed forces of the Merkulov government, and as with the Kolchak regime, their frequently uncouth demeanor discredited the anti–Bolshevik cause among the general population. Even inhabitants in areas untouched by the earlier *atamanshchina* learned to despise the Cossacks. In late October 1921, a 200-man expedition led by the notorious Cossack officer V. I. Bochkarev landed at Petropavlovsk and proclaimed himself military governor of Kamchatka Peninsula. Initially, he met no resistance from the local population which thus far had experienced little of the turmoil wrought by the ongoing civil war. But they too soon came to resent their White "liberator" after he began aping his former master, Ataman Kalmykov, by terrorizing fishing villages. Still, the Cossack adventurer managed to hold out in the region for over a year, though very few Whites opted to join his venture. Northeast Asia, with its remote wilderness and harsh climate, was the last place they wanted to go. Therefore, it took only the landing of a small party of GPU commandos in Petropavlovsk to bring Bochkarev's rule to an end in December 1922. A few months later, a GPU patrol cornered him in a Kamchatkan village and had him executed.[36]

Bochkarev's attempt to secure Kamchatka stemmed from the Whites' growing doubts about their long-term prospects in the Maritime Province. Their anxieties were stoked by the efforts of the Japanese, whose soldiers were the primary enablers of the White regime in Vladivostok, to seek a diplomatic solution to their intervention through negotiations with FER and Soviet plenipotentiaries at Darien. Moreover, partisan warfare continued to rage throughout the countryside of the Maritime Province, wearing down the strength of the Kappelite units attempting to keep order. Knowing that the Kappelites could not fight both the partisans and the FER's People's Revolutionary Army (PRA), which for the moment kept its distance from the Japanese, the Whites had hoped to transform northeastern Asia into an anticommunist redoubt, just as Chinese nationalists would do in Taiwan in 1949.

The Merkulov government reached the height of its power in the last months of 1921, when the Kappelites ventured north of the Japanese-occupied zone of the Maritime Province to capture Khabarovsk from the PRA. But the Whites, running low on men and ammunition, were thrown back south behind the Japanese outposts early in the following year. Amid that reverse, the various groups within the anti–Bolshevik coalition again turned on each other, eventually leading to the downfall of the Merkulov brothers in July 1922 and their replacement with a *zemskii sobor*, an archaic assembly comprised mostly of conservative elements that included Cossack officers. It did little to win the confidence of the general population; particularly after it passed a pro-monarchist resolution. Since no immediate Romanov restoration was possible, it named the new commander-in-chief of the anti–Bolshevik forces in the region, General Mikhail Diterikhs, regent until a member of the dynasty could be coaxed back to preside over this distant corner of Russia.

On the heels of Diterikhs' appointment to commander-in-chief, the Whites were stunned by Tokyo's bombshell announcement that it would be evacuating its troops from all of the Russian mainland in a few months. In desperation, Diterikhs made a last-ditch effort to secure the southern Maritime Province by launching a vigorous counter-insurgency operation, but after this failed he acknowledged the hopelessness of his position. On 15 October, as the Whites were being driven southward by the combined strength of the PRA and the partisans, Diterikhs ordered his units to evacuate the Maritime Province either by boat or by crossing the Manchurian border.

Over the next ten days, approximately 9,000–15,000 desperate refugees, soldiers and Cossacks crowded onto rusty freighters and any dilapidated vessel they found available in Vladivostok's harbor. Alongside them, homebound Japanese soldiers conducted their own orderly evacuation.[37] Further evacuations occurred at smaller nearby ports, including Posyet, where 1,500 Cossacks under a Semyonovite officer, General Glebov, ransacked the town before embarking with their families on trawlers bound for Korea.[38] Their conduct ensured that Poyset's inhabitants, regardless of their attitude towards communism, would not mourn the departure of the Whites. Back in Vladivostok, the last Japanese troops boarded their transports on 25 October, and just hours later the PRA marched triumphantly into the city. A few weeks later, the FER, having outlived its usefulness now that the Japanese were gone, was absorbed into the Russian Soviet Federal Socialist Republic.[39]

As the Bolsheviks were busy consolidating their victory in the Russian Far East, the bulk of Diterikhs' army, which had retreated to the south of Vladivostok, was getting a taste of the difficulties which awaited them as a stateless people. Diterikhs earnestly hoped to keep his army intact as it sought refuge on foreign soil. His goal was for this force, consisting of about 9,000 persons, including 1,800 Cossacks and 2,000 women and children, to cross into Manchuria and eventually join the Russian enclave in Harbin.[40] But as the Whites congregated near the Russian-Chinese border, Diterikhs' plan hit several snags. One was the desire of the Manchurian warlord, Marshal Zhang, to avoid entanglement in Russia's civil war despite his favorable disposition towards the anti–Bolshevik movement. Another was that the Chinese were less than eager to receive more destitute Russian refugees. Also working against Diterikhs were the machinations of the Soviet government, whose agents were tempting the Chinese central government to turn its back on the Whites by dangling control of the Chinese Eastern Railway as a reward.

News of the pillaging in Posyet carried out by General Glebov's Cossacks gave the Chinese yet another reason to be wary of the Whites. Diterikhs, despite assurances to Zhang that the units directly under him behaved in an exemplary manner, was eventually forced to accept the Whites' disarmament as a minimal condition for their entry.[41] To the very end, the Whites' association with unruly Cossacks remained a millstone around their necks.

In the first days of November 1922, then, the Whites laid down their weapons and crossed the frontier at Hunchun. They were not allowed to proceed to Harbin, as they had hoped, and instead they remained interned at Hunchun throughout the winter. Although the entire force was reduced to the status of refugees once they surrendered their arms, Diterikhs overhauled its military organization so that it might one day resume the fight against Bolshevism. Under his reforms, the Cossack contingent was divided into two regiments; one consisting of Siberian and Transbaikal Cossacks and the other of Ural and Orenburg Cossacks, some of whom had been transported by British vessels to the Russian Far East a year earlier.[42] Despite his efforts to keep the army together, the poor living conditions experienced by the refugees, coupled with the rigors of the Manchurian winter, strained their endurance to the limit. Tempted by communist offers of amnesty, a number of men and even some officers deserted the camp to return into Soviet territory.[43]

The expulsion of the Whites from the Maritime Province at the end of 1922 was one of the final acts in the civil war that had begun 6,000 miles away on the outskirts of Petrograd five years earlier. It had been an apocalyptic experience for all peoples of the former Russian Empire as well as for foreigners unfortunate enough to be swept into the maelstrom, such as the Mongolians or the war prisoners from Central Europe. Estimates for the number killed in the prolonged struggle vary considerably due to the often fluid-nature of the fighting, the unreliable record-keeping of both sides and the habit of armies to melt away or reform with stunning rapidity. Among soldiers serving in the armies on both sides of conflict, anywhere from 800,000 to 1,287,000 died with at least half of those losses caused by disease epidemics such as typhus. All sources agree that the death toll was far higher among non-combatants. Some were the victims of chaotic bouts of violence—the Red Terror, pogroms, ethnic conflicts, rampages of local warlords—while others were claimed by disease, famine and exposure; particularly during the mass retreats through the North Caucasus and across Central Asia and Siberia. Their numbers comprise the overwhelming majority of the seven to twelve million deaths directly and indirectly attributed to the fighting which raged across the tsars' former domains during 1917–22. These horrific figures do not include Russia's losses in the First World War, which was estimated at 1,700,000 men, nor do they account for those who fled abroad during the revolutionary turmoil—a number that was probably well over a million.[44]

It is difficult to separate losses among Cossacks from those of the non–Cossack population, not least because substantial numbers from the latter category called themselves "Cossacks" or were granted Cossack status for their service to "the Cossack cause." Nonetheless, one historian has arrived at the estimate that as many as 1,300,000 Cossack men, women and children—a whopping 30 percent of the Cossacks' total prewar population of 4,200,000—perished in the civil war.[45] Notwithstanding the accuracy of that number, there can be no doubt that the conflagration affected the Cossacks disproportionately to rest of Russia. The populous Cossack homelands of South Russia—especially the Don—had been the scene of some of the most prolonged and savage fighting between the Bolsheviks and their enemies during the entire course of the civil war. The two main contestants, rather than ignore the Cossacks in their proximity, paid special attention to them. The Soviet government for a time tried to woo the Cossacks with limited autonomy and, when that failed, then demonized them. The Whites, dependent upon an uninterrupted supply of food, horses and recruits from the stanitsas, applied the carrot and stick approach. Generally, when a side felt weak, it would be more accommodating toward Cossack aspirations and sensitivities. On the other hand, whenever it was more confident in its strength, it took a sterner approach towards them. Subsequently, each side's alternations in their policies towards the Cossacks corresponded to their fluctuating fortunes in the civil war. The insecurities of their existence weighed heavily on all Cossack groups; by the time the fighting subsided in the early 1920s their communities, economy and culture had suffered on a scale unknown to other peoples. Unfortunately, the end of the civil war would not bring them much relief. Regardless of whether they opted to remain in the familiar surroundings of their stanitsas or seek refuge abroad in strange new lands, their misery was far from over.

10

Exile

An Army in Limbo

Constantinople, the former seat of the great empires of the Byzantines and Ottomans, had long possessed a special attraction to Russia and its peoples. It was, first and foremost, the cradle of Orthodox Christianity; the site of the magnificent Hagia Sophia which, according to legend, inspired Vladimir the Great (r. 980–1015) to adopt that confession as the official religion of his realm. To Great Russian nationalists, the city's position along the narrow straits between the Black and Mediterranean Seas rendered it an object of strategic importance: control of the city would assure Russia unfettered access to the Mediterranean. It was these considerations which made its annexation a primary objective of the tsarist government during World War I. For most Cossacks, Constantinople's religious and strategic significance was immaterial; yet, for them the city still evoked pride for the epic raids which their seafaring forbearers had launched against it during the early seventeenth century.

In light of these sentiments, the fact that Constantinople became the first stopover for the tens of thousands of Russians and Cossacks who fled from the Crimea in November 1920 seems to have been a cruel irony: their arrival in that prized city marked not their triumph but rather their utter defeat. They had come there as refugees, not conquerors. Still, in the following weeks, the Russian presence there—from officers in tsarist uniforms milling about the boulevards to the national tricolor waving from the masts of over a hundred ships in the Bosporus—reawakened the delusions of grandeur. "One might have thought that the ancient Russian dream had come true," recalled General Lukomsky, "and that Tsargrad had become a Russian city."[1]

The dream was just that: a fantasy. Constantinople was the beginning of years, even decades, of new tribulations for the soldiers and civilian followers of Wrangel's army. Numbering approximately 149,000, they were the largest single wave of émigrés to flee Russia during the revolutionary period, but they were hardly alone. Estimates of the number of individuals who went abroad to escape Soviet oppression from 1917 into the early 1920s vary considerably: from just below 1,000,000 to almost 2,000,000.[2] They had left their homeland from every direction: by crossing into Finland or Poland in the west or by fleeing into Persia or China in the south and east; by boarding vessels at White Sea ports in the north or at Black Sea ports in the south. Some had left with the Germans in 1918, many more fled alongside the Allied interventionists and White armies in 1920. Several thousand, as we have seen, would depart with the Japanese expeditionary forces in the final months of 1922. Spread among these émigrés were anywhere from 80,000 to 100,000 Cossacks. Over 40,000 of that number had evacuated the Crimea with Wrangel in November of 1920.[3] The travails which had compelled these men, occasionally with their families in tow, to leave their country did not end once they boarded ships bound for foreign lands. Indeed, many boats in the fleet of 126 vessels which carried Wrangel and his army from the Crimea were barely seaworthy due to a lack of repairs and maintenance. One destroyer even went down amid a gale during the journey to Constantinople.[4] Once again, it seemed that nature was no less relenting than the communists.

Nearly all of the émigrés who fled Russia during this period expected their exile to be brief. Many were said to have kept packed suitcases on hand so they could return home the instant the Bolshevik regime fell. Others were reluctant to learn any language besides Russian or seek more permanent living arrangements while abroad.[5] Even Wrangel was inclined to believe that the communist experiment could not last much longer. Subsequently he was determined to keep his army intact so it could depart for Russia when the right moment presented itself. For him and many of his subordinates, the army was more than just a military organization, it was "the sole remaining depository of the idea of national regeneration."[6] Their mission, as they now saw it, was to protect and nurture this institution so that it might one day return to their homeland and restore Russian culture, religion and heritage to its rightful place.[7]

Holding the army together upon its arrival in the Bosporus was no easy task. The soldiers had just suffered a shattering defeat, survived a treacherous journey through stormy seas and now had no idea what lay ahead of them. Most lacked money, and what few rubles or valuables they did have were soon lost to Turkish vendors who took advantage of their plight by charging outrageous prices for food and drink.[8] To meet the army's most basic needs, a few days earlier Wrangel had concluded an agreement with the French whereby the latter would feed and shelter the army on the condition that the Russian vessels would be turned over to them as security.[9] But this arrangement did not bring much relief to the soldiers, who had to subsist on meager food rations, or their commander-in-chief, who was dismayed to learn that his closest foreign ally wished to see his army demobilized.

Despite these challenges, Wrangel reorganized the remnants of his army to make it more manageable and, most importantly, preserve some degree of its *esprit de corps*. In doing so, he grouped the largest contingents of the army into three corps: the First Army Corps, consisting of 29,000 non–Cossack officers and soldiers under General Kutepov; the Don Cossack Corps, numbering 23,000 men commanded by General Abramov; and the Kuban Cossack Corps, formed from 12,000 combatants led by General Fostikov. Each corps was then assigned to former war prisoner camps in the vicinity of Constantinople while Wrangel haggled with the French over the future of the army. The First Corps was sent to battle-scarred Gallipoli, the Don Cossacks were transported to a collection of camps northwest of Constantinople and the Kuban Cossacks were landed on the Aegean island of Lemnos. Most of the civilians who evacuated with the army, including some 6,500 Don Cossacks, entered separate camps operated by Russian and foreign charitable organizations.[10]

Unsurprisingly, the conditions which the Russians and Cossacks endured in the decrepit camps that winter were anything but pleasant. Many slept in tents supplied by the American Red Cross while living on minimal food rations provided by the French. The camp surroundings did improve at Gallipoli, where General Kutepov's draconian regimen of strict discipline coupled with hard work compelled the men to construct better facilities. However, the same could not be said for the camps where the Cossacks resided. The Cossack rank-and-file was unaccustomed to the stern discipline of regular soldiers, and in exile their officers made no effort to reverse that habit. Subsequently, some Cossacks formed gangs which preyed on the local population while others simply wandered off. They also ignored orders to use latrines, contributing to an outbreak of cholera in a Don Cossack camp near Chatalga. The Cossacks' unruliness made them unpopular with their French guardians. In early January 1921, the French commander in Constantinople, General Charpy, announced that the Don Cossacks were to be relocated to the island of Lemnos, which already held the Kuban Cossack Corps. This news outraged both Wrangel, who was not made privy to the order, and the Don Cossacks since many had heard rumors that the camps on Lemnos were worse than those at Chatalga. Subsequently, on one night two companies of Don Cossacks attempted to break out of the Chatalga camp to avoid being transferred to that barren island. When their French guards attempted to halt their escape, the two sides engaged each other in a shootout before the renegade Cossacks slipped away, leaving two Frenchmen wounded.

Although the Don Cossack Corps soon agreed to transfer to Lemnos, the firefight at Chatalga did irreparable harm to the already strained relations between the French and Wrangel's army. The former became more adamant that the Russians must disarm, a point which the baron resisted since it would spell the end of his army as a military force. The French began to take energetic measures to reduce the men in the Russians' ranks, attempting everything from recruiting them into the French Foreign Legion to encouraging them to emigrate to Brazil. Surprisingly, they were most successful at convincing the desperate refugees and soldiers to return to the land from which they had fled only a few months earlier.

The French government had decided upon voluntary repatriation of the Russians before any formal arrangements, including a guarantee of full amnesty, had been made with Soviet government.[11] Nonetheless, the Kremlin had appeared open to the possibility of permitting the defeated Whites to reside peacefully within its borders. On 12 November 1920, just as the Whites announced their intention to evacuate the Crimea, the Red Army command transmitted a message to Wrangel's headquarters guaranteeing the safety of anyone who laid down their arms, including the officers. Wrangel, who viewed capitulation as dishonorable and doubted the Bolsheviks' trustworthiness, suppressed news of the offer.[12] However, beginning in January 1921, French commandants went over Wrangel's head by posting notices in the camps which promised the Russians that they had nothing to fear by returning to their country. Moreover, the French government pressured the camp dwellers into repatriation by threatening to sever their food supplies in just a matter of weeks. To counter these efforts, Wrangel and his closest associates warned the men against trusting French assurances that they would not be harmed upon their arrival in Soviet Russia. They also protested these actions to the French High Commissioner in Constantinople, but their objections, it seems, were largely ignored.

The French campaign promoting the voluntary repatriation of the refugees and soldiers back to Russia resonated much better among Cossacks than with the soldiers in Kutepov's corps. The most plausible explanation for this was differences in morale between the Cossack corps and that of Kutepov's. Whereas the latter pulled together amid the hardship of the camps, many Cossacks lost their sense of military duty under the uninspired leadership of their officers. Additionally, French General Broussaud, the commandant of the Lemnos camp where most Cossacks were staying, zealously supported his government's decision to disband the White army. To compel the Cossacks to leave the army, he was content to keep camp conditions at Lemnos as miserable as possible and doubled down on threats to halt the distribution of food rations.[13]

Homesick, demoralized and fed up with the deprivations of the camps, thousands of

Cossacks jumped at the opportunity to return to Russia. Quite simply, they preferred to endure misery at home than abroad. On 16 February the first vessel carrying 3,285 refugees, most of them Cossacks, departed from the Bosporus for Novorossiysk. Over the following two months, an additional 6,135 émigrés boarded vessels for Russia.[14] Although the Soviet government briefly halted the repatriations later that year, the operation soon proceeded apace and continued throughout the 1920s as the Bolsheviks recognized the propaganda value of repatriations at home and abroad. Indeed, the fact that so many of their bitter enemies opted to return to the worker's utopia in Russia rather than live in the capitalist West appeared to vindicate the communists against their critics. If nothing else, the repatriations could be seen by Moscow as a means to enfeeble their counterrevolutionary opponents residing abroad.[15]

Given the inflamed passions and brutality unleashed by the civil war, one cannot help but wonder what became of the tens of thousands of Cossack émigrés who eventually chose to return to their homeland now under Bolshevik control. The regime, for its part, tried to portray itself as welcoming of its former enemies. For example, shortly after the first batch of Cossack émigrés arrived on its shores, a wireless message from Moscow announced that the returnees were granted full amnesty and would "find the friendliest reception in their homeland where they now return as fellow workers."[16] Officially, the government did not grant a blanket amnesty to ordinary Cossacks and soldiers who served the Whites until an announcement issued later that year on 7 November 1921, the fourth anniversary of the October Revolution.[17] Just over three years later, after additional waves of repatriated émigrés had arrived in Soviet Russia, the OGPU reported that nearly 30,000 Cossack returnees resided in the North Caucasus region.[18] Representatives from the League of Nations who were allowed to visit several North Caucasus villages reported that the repatriated Cossacks appeared no worse off than the rest of the population.[19] It may be surmised that the ordinary Cossacks, more often than not, were permitted to return to their stanitsas; their transgressions against the regime seemingly forgiven but—as later events would show—not forgotten. Former officers who returned to Soviet Russia, as well as anyone implicated in White atrocities, were likely interned in camps, sentenced to hard labor or shot.[20]

For the Russian refugees and soldiers who remained in the vicinity of the Bosporus, the onset of spring in April 1921 brought welcome changes, and not just in the weather. Their relations with their French guardians improved when General Pellé was appointed French High Commissioner in Constantinople. Under Pellé, the French took a more considerate approach to resolving the question over the future of Wrangel's army. General Broussaud, the unsympathetic commandant of the Lemnos camp, was removed from that post while threats of starvation were no longer made against the Russians.[21]

Despite these changes, the French remained adamant that the Russians could not remain dependent on foreign relief indefinitely. Wrangel, though he earnestly desired to keep the army organized as a concentrated, active force, gradually bowed to reality that the soldiers must somehow earn their keep. Since the surroundings at Gallipoli and Lemnos offered virtually no employment opportunities, the baron knew that the men would have to relocate elsewhere. Moreover, it quickly became apparent to him that no single country was likely to accept the army as a body; in other words, it would have to be broken up among several states. Over the next several months, Wrangel's representatives negotiated with various governments to accept units from their army. Their goal in these talks was to make arrangements where, ideally, regiments would work together and even live together in barracks or other communal housing, thus maintaining a skeleton military organization and the mentality of soldiers.²² This design was supposed prevent the men from indulging in civilian life while enabling them to quickly reform the army once the situation in Russia warranted its return.

Beginning in spring 1921, the White units began to be parceled out to countries in the Balkans and Central Europe. The Kingdom of Serbs, Croats and Slovenes was among the most inviting destinations for the Russians. The country was in need of laborers to rebuild roads, railways and other infrastructure ravaged by the fighting during the Balkan Wars and the Great War. Traditional ethnic and religious affinities, especially among Orthodox Serbs, factored into the desire of the Yugoslav leaders to help the Russians in their time of need. Ultimately, 25,000 soldiers from the camps near Constantinople were resettled in the Kingdom of Serbs, Croats and Slovenes. The majority were assigned to manual labor jobs though some 5,000 cavalrymen, many of them Kuban Cossacks, were hired to patrol the borders of the new state. Other Slavic states also welcomed men from Wrangel's army. Bulgaria, which had fought on the side of the Central Powers, accepted 19,000 Russian soldiers.²³ Czechoslovakia took in slightly more than 2,000 Cossacks to work in agriculture.²⁴ Wrangel also hoped his troops might find a warm reception in certain non–Slav countries, particularly Hungary, which after a spell of revolutionary turmoil was now under the helm of an anticommunist government led by Admiral Miklós Horthy. Although the Hungarian government was not adverse to the idea, the Allies nixed the project on the grounds that it would "excite commotion and facilitate anti–Bolshevist intrigues which are contrary to the true interests of Hungary and of all the civilized world."²⁵ Nonetheless, Wrangel's attempt to redistribute his army in a way that preserved some semblance of military organization was generally successful. Just a year after the Whites arrived in the Bosporus, only 2,000 soldiers remained in Gallipoli. In 1923, this last group was finally allowed to leave the Dardanelles for Hungary.²⁶

Despite Wrangel's tireless efforts to hold the army together, time was destined to take its toll on these arrangements. As the prospect for an imminent return to Russia faded in the early 1920s, the soldiers naturally began looking for new job opportunities and better living conditions. As a result, beginning in 1923 hundreds and later thousands of men, including Cossacks, left the Balkans for the more developed countries of Western Europe, particularly France. Wrangel, to his credit, made no attempt to hold the men back and even encouraged them to better their lot. He did, however, seek to preserve their military mentality and organization. Whenever possible, the men and officers were encouraged to move and resettle as entire units.²⁷ Still, Wrangel could not counter the toll which time and distance exacted on the soldiers' *esprit de corps*. He therefore sought a means to maintain his authority over these disparate elements and prevent them from falling under the sway of the numerous émigré organizations or claimants which might lead them astray.

The Contest of Ideas

In the Crimea, the Cossacks were incorporated into the White movement to a degree that had eluded Denikin as well as other anti–Bolshevik leaders, including Kolchak. The overall unity achieved by Wrangel was attributable, in part, to the weakness of his geographical position after March 1920: the area left to him was confined and relatively easy to control. There were no remote or inaccessible regions from where a rogue ataman could carve out a fiefdom and challenge his rule. Hence, the Cossack leaders who stayed for the duration of his campaign were completely subordinate to his regency. Those who caused him difficulty, such as Sidorin, were not tolerated. At the time, Cossacks with a record of aloofness towards the White generals often acquiesced to Wrangel's domination since his forces offered the only prospect of snatching victory from the jaws of defeat. The evacuation of the Crimea, however, permanently dispelled even that forlorn hope. It also undercut Wrangel's prestige. His hold over the Whites further unraveled in exile when he quickly disbanded his remnant government. Almost overnight, his standing had diminished to that of other pretentious though powerless émigré leaders and politicians. In the coming months and years various exile groups and spokesmen would vie with one another to position themselves as Wrangel's successor to supremacy over a consolidated anti–Bolshevik movement.

Although the desire to unite the Russian Diaspora was widespread, the highly-charged political atmosphere among the émigré community made this objective elusive. Even like-minded émigrés found it impossible to work together towards a common goal. Monarchist elements, for example, were left in disarray by the slayings of the tsar and other members of the imperial family during the revolution, and by autumn of 1922 they were bitterly divided over the question of who was the legitimate heir to the Russian throne. One group, the Supreme Monarchist Council, was dominated by a pro–French outlook and advocated the former commander of the Imperial Russian Army, Grand Duke Nikolay Nikolayevich, a first cousin once removed to the last tsar, as the rightful heir. Rivaling them were monarchist elements organized around the association known as Reconstruction: Economic-Political Organization of the East (Aufbau: Wirtschafts-politische Vereinigung für den Osten; hereafter Aufbau). This group, which possessed strong anti–Semitic and Germanophile leanings, supported the claim of Grand Duke Kirill Vladimirovich, a first cousin to Nicholas II.[28]

The disarray in the monarchist camp reverberated among those émigrés who were ready to accept the revolution in some form. Émigrés of liberal, Socialist-Revolutionary and Menshevik persuasion all quarreled over what was the best course to rescue Russia from communism without stepping into a counterrevolutionary trap. In early 1921, thirty-two representatives to the extinct Constituent Assembly met in Paris to formulate a new program that would appeal to and hopefully unite the entire Russian Diaspora. The attendees at the Paris conference, which included such former political heavyweights as Aleksandr Kerensky and Pavel Milyukov, agreed that armed intervention against Soviet Russia must cease. "Further bloodshed now appeared not only useless but criminal," wrote Milyukov, who had been one of General Alekseyev's early collaborators in the White movement.[29] He and others clung to the hope that Bolshevism, if left to its own devices, would collapse on its own and clear the way for the establishment of a democratic, federative Russia. Instead, it was their own parties which fractured into quarreling factions while Lenin's regime, at least from external appearances, remained solidly intact.[30]

Wrangel, too, attempted to forge a political union of the Russian Diaspora. His plan, unveiled in the spring of 1921, was to create an umbrella organization to be known as the Russian Council. However, his intention to appoint himself supreme leader of that organization garnered no support from liberal groups, such as the Paris-based Russian National Council, or even the monarchists. After months of mostly fruitless negotiations with émigré politicians, Wrangel acknowledged the failure of his project and dissolved the Russian Council before the close of 1922.[31]

In the meantime, the ongoing failures of the White cause and dilemmas in which the émigrés found themselves fomented an identity crisis among some of their intellectuals and spokespersons. Their efforts to make sense of their situation led to such movements as the Changing Landmarks (*Smena Vekh*), which was founded in 1921 by émigrés impressed by the Red Army's recent success in reuniting most of the lands of the former Russian Empire. The Bolsheviks' abandonment of war communism that same year convinced this group that the ruling party was moderating its policies, returning to the cycle of Russian history and no longer deserved their enmity. "We are ready to go to Canossa," conceded one Changing Landmarks supporter. "We have erred."[32] Many eventually applauded efforts to repatriate émigrés to their homeland. Meanwhile, other émigré intellectuals reexamined Russia's people, their history and culture in its entirety. Their approach spawned Eurasianism, which held that Western influences were incompatible with the traits that Russian peoples had inherited from the East and the steppe. The Eurasianists regarded Bolshevism as simply the latest perversion of Western ideas in their country. The solution, according to them, was to steer Russia off the path towards Westernization, which it had more or less followed since Peter the Great, and embrace her Asiatic past alongside her European roots.[33]

Aside from the émigrés' political and philosophical disagreements, the Diaspora was further divided by ethnic and cultural differences. Some of these non–Russian émigrés had served under the White generals while others, such as Petliura's Ukrainians, had fought against them. Often, these ethnic offshoots of the Diaspora had their own subdivisions. Throughout much of the interwar period, Skoropadsky, the former hetman of the Ukraine, tried to present himself as a legitimate Ukrainian leader to skeptical officials in the German Foreign Office. He went as far as to improve his fluency in the Ukrainian language and, in 1933, announced that his son was to succeed him as hetman of Ukraine despite his abdication of that title fifteen years earlier. His claims were opposed by various Ukrainian nationalists, republicans and even his former collaborator, Colonel Ivan Poltavets-Ostranitsa. The latter, as head of the mostly imaginary National Ukrainian Cossack Organization (NUCO), promoted himself to the Germans as the rightful head of Ukraine.[34]

Like the Ukrainians and other nationalities, the Cossacks too were fractured by political and historical disagreements. Though most were veterans of the White armies, not all were eager to continue that association. As in the civil war, they remained broadly divided into two camps. The more conservative faction subscribed to a Cossack form of Russian patriotism; arguing that Cossack goals could only be realized in a close partnership with Russia. Cossacks, they argued, represented not a separate ethnicity but rather the highest form of Russian culture. Opposing them were those who viewed themselves strictly as Cossack patriots. They resented Russian influence and regarded the tsars as enslavers of the Cossack people since the reign of Peter the Great.[35] To strengthen their claims that Cossacks were a distinct nationality, they indulged in revisionist theories that their earliest-known ancestors were ancient Christian warriors who established a state in the North Caucasus region as early as 948 A.D.[36] The claim that the Cossacks originated from fugitive Slavs in the sixteenth century, they argued, was a myth created by Moscow "in order to knock the historical weapon from the hands of the Cossacks in their struggle for survival of their own national freedom and life."[37] From their viewpoint, the majority of Cossacks who fought against the Bolsheviks during the civil war were not counterrevolutionaries but rather freedom fighters defending their homeland and natural rights against the latest version of Russian imperialism. They portrayed their cause as an enlightened struggle for self-determination and glossed over the reality that, more often than not, the ultimate fulfillment of their aims would have meant the oppression of millions of natives and outlanders living in the Cossack territories. Overall, this romanticized interpretation of the Cossacks' past and role in the civil war dovetailed nicely with the less-developed logic of former separatist politicians, many of whom embraced this revamped Cossack patriotism.[38] In exile, with their activities no longer constrained by White security forces, they began formulating their own political program to challenge the unitary Russian idea promulgated by most White generals.

It did not take the Cossack patriots long to strike out on their own. In December 1920, just weeks after the Russian refugee fleet arrived in the Bosporus, a group of separatist Cossack politicians formed the "Union for the Resurrection of Cossackdom." Their program deflected responsibility for the Cossacks' defeat in the civil war away from themselves and towards the White generals. According to them, the White leaders' refusal to recognize Cossack claims of independence sapped the morale of the freedom-loving Cossack people. They stated that democratic republics were their ideal form of government and dreamt of creating an independent "Cossackia" encompassing the Don, Kuban, Terek, Astrakhan, Ural and Orenburg hosts. Like the meeting of the former Constituent Assembly members in Paris, the Union for the Resurrection of Cossackdom did not believe that its political goals should be attained by continuing the armed struggle and intervention against Bolshevism. Instead, they placed their faith in internal forces to eventually effect a favorable change in Moscow.[39] A few months later another group with Cossack-centric political views, the All-Cossack Agrarian Union, was founded in Constantinople. Like the Union for the Resurrection of Cossackdom, it too sought to wean the Cossacks from the White generals.[40]

The newfound momentum of the Cossack separatists was a major concern for the Cossack atamans of the Don (Bogaevsky), Kuban (Naumenko) and Terek (Vdovenko). Throughout much of the civil war, these men had regarded Russia's fight as the Cossacks' fight and had developed close ties with the White generals. But on 14 January 1921, fearing that the new Cossack political organizations might eclipse their leadership, the atamans stepped out from Wrangel's shadow by establishing the United Council of the Don, Terek and Kuban. Although this action contravened the treaty which most of them had signed the previous August, Wrangel, who was busy attempting to resist French efforts to disband his army, was in no position to rein in the Cossack leaders. Under the founding guidelines of the United Council of the Don, Terek and Kuban, the three atamans agreed to consult and cooperate with one another in all political and economic matters. Significantly, they immediately began courting the moderate elements among the left and separatist Cossacks by stating their support for a democratic and federal Russia.[41]

The Cossack atamans' espousal of more progressive principles quickly soured their relations with Wrangel. Later that year, when the baron invited them to join his Russian Council, the United Council of the Don, Terek and Kuban declined on the grounds of its authoritarian character. This refusal infuriated the baron, who responded by severing contact with the atamans.[42]

Despite their break with Wrangel, the Cossack atamans were no more successful in uniting the Cossack emigration as a whole than the baron had been in his attempt to unify the Russian Diaspora. Eventually, several factions within the Diaspora did manage to come together to promote a shared regional, ethnic, religious, occupational or social interest. Among these groups were the Cossacks. In August 1924 their representatives convened a congress in Paris which established the Union of Cossacks. Initially headed by Don Ataman Bogaevsky, the Union of Cossacks was tasked with the responsibility of advocating and defending the interests of Cossack émigrés in Europe and Asia regardless of their host of origin. To do so, it divided Cossack émigré communities across the globe into over 140 branches; the larger being referred to as stanitsas while smaller ones were dubbed *khutors*. On a practical level, the Cossack Union and its subsidiaries sought to provide aid and guidance to enable Cossack refugees to improve their cultural, social and most of all economic well-being. In this line of work, it would be instrumental in assisting with the migration of Cossack workers from the impoverished Balkans to find better-paying jobs in France. Like other émigré groups, the Cossack Union printed a newssheet to educate its members, encourage contact among them and, most importantly, advance its causes. Among the most depressing items to be found in this and other émigré publications were ads pleading for information on loved ones who had gone missing during the turbulence of the civil war. Notably, one activity which the Cossack Union shunned was politics. By avoiding the divisiveness of politics, which in any case were of little practical value while they remained abroad, the members of the Cossack Union were able to transcend the parties and factions that existed among them.[43]

That following autumn, Wrangel copied this formula when he established the Russian General Military Union (Russky Obshche-Voynsky Soyuz, ROVS) from his headquarters in the Yugoslavian town of Sremski Karlovci. Like the Cossack Union, the ROVS largely dodged political questions by adapting basic tenants for its program: unrelenting hostility towards Bolshevism and the belief that the Russian people should be free to choose their own form of government. Its ultimate goal was to resurrect Russia's military legacy and help restore order in the country as soon as the Bolsheviks fell from power. For most of the interwar period, the ROVS was the leading organization in the Russian Diaspora. At its peak, its members included not only the officers and soldiers who served under Wrangel but also White veterans of the Baltic, North Russian and Siberian theaters of the Russian Civil War. From Finland to France and even as far away as Manchuria, the ROVS sought to keep White veterans psychologically engaged in the struggle against Bolshevism by organizing lectures, conferences and other social events in émigré communities.[44]

The ROVS was remarkably successful in fostering a degree of fellowship among the scattered White veterans. It also preserved the influence of Wrangel and senior officers over a considerable body of the troops throughout the 1920s and beyond. For many of the ranks, the army had become their only family, and the ROVS reinforced that bond. This extraordinary camaraderie was even felt by Cossack veterans, many of whom showed more loyalty to their commanders than to their atamans. Indeed, one of the leading figures in ROVS was the Don Cossack General Abramov, who headed that organization's branch in Bulgaria.[45]

Under the ROVS, the scattered veterans of the White armies maintained their identity and sense of duty as soldiers. A few dedicated individuals even participated in covert operations against the Soviet Union. Yet the White armies never again physically reunited after leaving Russia. The closest they came to a full-fledged gathering was during the burial ceremony for General Wrangel. In April 1928, the baron had died in Belgium after a brief bout with tuberculosis. Over a year later, in early October 1929, his remains were transported to Belgrade. White regiments from all over Europe sent honor guards to the Yugoslavian capital to pay their respects to their deceased commander. Among them were Cossacks donning their traditional attire. In addition to the regimental representatives, delegations from Russian émigré organizations also attended the ceremony.[46] For many, it was a nostalgic and much-too-brief respite from the doldrums and rigors of life as an émigré.

The Reality of Exile

For most ordinary Cossack émigrés, political activities were a hobby for which they had neither the funds nor time. While the founders of the Union for the Resurrection of Cossackdom were sketching the frontiers of their projected state of "Cossackia" on maps of southeastern Russia, the majority of Cossack émigrés were struggling to readjust to life in foreign lands.[47] They quickly learned that the skills which had made them masters of the Eurasian steppe had little practical use in most of Europe. The one exception was those Kuban Cossacks who were among the 5,000 Russian cavalrymen hired by the Yugoslavs to patrol the borders of new South Slav state. Unfortunately, many of them did not remain employed in that role for long. In November 1922, the Belgrade government released about 3,300 Russians from the border service, forcing them to join their comrades engaged in construction and other manual labor where they worked long hours for low pay.[48] Even those Cossacks who went to work as agriculturalists found it difficult to adapt to the new conditions—the intensive agricultural techniques of Central and Western Europe were drastically different than the more primitive style of farming they had known on the steppe.

The majority of émigrés, whether they were Cossacks or Russians, found their host countries unwelcoming. "We were not received very well in France," recalled an émigré who as a young girl fled from the Crimea and wound up in Paris.[49] While her experience was not unusual for displaced persons or refugees in general, it was still a major letdown for Russian émigrés—particularly war veterans—who perceived their callous treatment as another slight by their wartime allies. In the following years, Russian veterans suspected that the sacrifices made by their countrymen in the Great War were not just unappreciated but actually forgotten by the rest of the world.[50] Casual incidents seemed to validate their concerns. In his memoir, Prince Lobanov-Rostovsky recalled the astonishment of an American lady when she learned that he saw action against the Germans during the world war. "I did not know Russia had been in the War!" she exclaimed. Unwittingly heaping insult upon injury, she added, "I guess you Russians didn't do very much, did you?"[51]

Most Cossacks and Russian émigrés were determined to remain faithful to their nationality, culture or even regiment by refusing to assimilate into their host country. Aside from the early conviction that their stay abroad would be temporary, their resistance to assimilation was further reinforced by the judgement of émigré writers that the postwar European societies were degenerate and in terminal decline.[52] They refused to identify themselves as anything but Cossacks or Russians; an insular mindset that was bound to impede their social and economic mobility in exile. Their legal existence became even more uncertain in 1921 after Moscow announced that all émigrés refusing to obtain a Soviet passport would be deprived of their Russian citizenship.[53] Fortunately, a partial remedy to their statelessness was developed by the League of Nations' Commission for Refugee Affairs, headed by Norwegian explorer Fridtjof Nansen, through the issuance of identification certificates known as "Nansen Passports." These documents, which remained valid throughout the interwar period and beyond, suited most Russian émigrés since it enabled them to remain abroad without having to renounce their Russian identity. Among the soldiers, the tendency to remain aloof from the surrounding population was encouraged by Wrangel and the ROVS since it complimented their efforts to hold the military formations together as much as possible. The reluctance of the émigrés to assimilate was also reflected among civilians, who formed vibrant Russian enclaves in Paris, Prague, Berlin and other European cities. Meanwhile, rural-minded Cossacks tried to recreate stanitsas in farming regions of Europe and even as far away as South America.[54]

The durability of these émigré communities, large or small, was quite varied. Indeed, a number of factors worked against their success. First, the jingoism unleashed by World War I lingered in many European countries into the postwar period. The nation-states of East-Central Europe, having freed themselves or their compatriots from Habsburg, Hohenzollern or Romanov rule, were among the most susceptible to such hyper-nationalism. The arrival of destitute Russian refugees, especially among those peoples who had suffered under the tsarist yoke, was the last thing many countries desired. Yet, even those countries where public opinion was predominantly pro–Russian had reasons to want the refugees to be settled somewhere else. With their industries transitioning to peacetime production, thousands of demobilized soldiers entering the workforce and their treasuries struggling to pay out pensions, bonds and loans from the war, they were unlikely to welcome refugees in need of subsidies and jobs to get on their feet. An exceptional situation did exist in northeastern France during the early 1920s where construction workers were in high demand to rebuild that war-torn region. But while the government in Paris readily granted work permits to unskilled Russians seeking employment as laborers, it was far less generous towards well-educated émigrés who might have competed with French white-collar workers.[55]

The shifting political and economic trends of the interwar period prevented many émigrés from remaining in one spot for very long, making it difficult for communities, organizations and units to maintain contact with their roaming members. As we have seen, during the 1920s a number of the White veterans who initially settled in the Balkans later migrated to Western Europe in search of better paying jobs. Some would be forced to seek new opportunities once again when the markets collapsed at the end of that decade. Elsewhere, émigrés attracted to postwar Germany by its low cost of living later left that country to escape the effects of skyrocketing inflation or, if they weathered that crisis, the political repression of National Socialism. For many émigrés the interwar period was a time of wandering. Regardless of where they went, they found it difficult to escape the reality of their situation. "Wherever we lived during those years," recalled one émigré, "the land under our feet was not our land, the language spoken around us was not our language, and, no matter how hospitable and friendly the people were with whom we worked, we were foreigners among them."[56]

The viability of Russian émigré communities was further undermined by their lopsided gender ratio, especially among Cossacks. As one might expect among an emigration comprised mostly of soldiers, the vast majority were young men—three-quarters were estimated to be in their twenties or thirties. Women comprised only 4 percent of the Cossack emigration while another 3 percent were children aged below sixteen years.[57] This meant, of course, that few Cossack men had fled abroad with their families. Some tried to stay in touch with their wives and children in their homeland by writing to them, but rarely did these tenuous links last. Often, their families in Soviet Russia simply quit replying to their letters since mail from abroad invited unwanted scrutiny from the OGPU.[58] Even if the Cossack émigrés were willing to move on, their prospects for starting families were low. Many did not interact outside their enclaves or regiments, particularly those who resided in barracks. Since they were struggling to make ends meet few lacked the resources to raise a family. Nonetheless, some Cossacks did marry non–Cossack women, but it was difficult to for them to pass on their Cossack heritage to the next generation as long as they remained in a foreign land. Most émigré pupils, rather than attend Russian schools which were opened abroad, completed their education in more accessible and better-funded non–Russian schools in their host countries. This trend further accelerated the assimilation process among émigré youth.[59]

Despite the many hardships they faced, some Cossack émigrés devised creative ways to preserve and even showcase their culture and famed equestrian skills outside of their homeland. During the interwar period, several Cossack choirs were formed to serenade European audiences. The most famous of these was the Don Cossack Choir whose concert tours crisscrossed the globe.[60] Other Cossack musicians found employment in balalaika orchestras which performed nightly in cabarets.[61] Cossack skills were also exhibited in circus acts where the fabled warriors performed folk dances or a series of acrobatic stunts on horseback known as the *dzhigitovka*. Having originated with Caucasian natives, the *dzhigitovka* was adopted by Kuban and Terek Cossacks as a means to display their expert equestrian abilities.[62] The daring horsemanship of these acts was unlike anything most Western audiences had ever seen. Among the most well-known Cossack circus performers was General Shkuro, although his career in the ring appears to have been brief. Shkuro seems to have preferred that other favorite Cossack past-time of imbibing hard drink: during the interwar period he was a loyal patron of taverns in Munich and Belgrade.[63]

Another famous Cossack leader, Krasnov, also turned to cultural pursuits in emigration by writing several novels. His eloquent prose which had become his trademark during his stint as Don ataman served him well in this endeavor as many of his books were commercial successes and translated into multiple languages. His best-known work is *From Double Eagle to the Red Flag*, first published in Berlin in 1921, which revolves around the experiences of a fictional aristocratic tsarist officer from the Revolution of 1905 to the civil war. He actually began that novel shortly after his release from Bolshevik custody in late 1917 and put it on hold while he served as ataman for nine months from 1918 to 1919. After his resignation

A Cossack entertainer demonstrates his proficiency with swords during a performance in New York City on 24 May 1926. For Cossack émigrés, employment as circus performers was one of the rare opportunities where they could earn a living from the military and equestrian skills they learned on the steppes (akg-images / Universal Images Group / Underwood Archives).

from that post, he returned to writing and finished the book in exile. Although *From Double Eagle to Red Flag* is not regarded with the same level of literary acclaim as works by other Russian émigrés, Krasnov does display an impressive grasp of the motivations and mentalities which guided participants on both sides of the revolutionary struggle.[64] His other books included works of historical fiction centered on heroes of the Russia's past, such as Yermak Timofeyevich, the conqueror of Siberia, and the Cossacks who helped thwart Napoleon's invasion of Russia.

Such prestigious careers were the exception, not the norm, among Russian and especially Cossack émigrés. Many, as we have seen, went to work in construction or mines. During the 1920s, thousands of Cossack émigrés migrated from the Balkans to Paris, which became the undisputed capital of the Russian Diaspora. There they found employment in the city's automobile factories while others drove taxis. These Cossack proletarians, along with non–Cossack émigrés, took over entire neighborhoods in the French capital as local drugstores, pubs, bakeries and restaurants catered to Russian customers with a combination of Cyrillic window signs and ethnic dishes. Such enclaves made the existence in a foreign land more palatable to the homesick émigrés; particularly those that were determined to resist assimilation into French culture.

In some instances the émigrés refashioned their surroundings to remind them not only of a different land but also of a different time. This was particularly the case among Cossack veterans who continued to live and work with their regiments. When possible, their living quarters were transformed into barracks with separate dormitories and mess halls for officers and men. The walls inside them were adorned with regimental standards, relics and even portraits of the martyred tsar.[65] Such was the environment into which weary Cossack factory hands and construction workers retreated after a long workday.

Naturally many Cossacks, as a rural-bred people, preferred the solitude of the countryside over the bustle of a city. After a few years in Paris, some Cossack workers purchased small lots on the outskirts of the city where they could construct a shanty and cultivate a garden.[66] Perhaps the most fortunate Cossacks were those who managed to escape the city altogether by settling in a farming community that resembled their native stanitsas. As in their homeland, these new settlements became a central component in their inhabitants' social and economic lives. In addition to their traditional administrative functions, some émigré stanitsas organized relief efforts for their less-fortunate members, especially those suffering from medical conditions or chronic unemployment.[67]

Of the new European stanitsas, those which best replicated the traditional model were found in Yugoslavia. Several factors contributed to this development. First was their proximity to the senior leadership of the Cossacks and the White movement: during the early 1920s the country was home to the atamans of the Don, Kuban and Terek, Wrangel and his staff, three cadet corps and one cavalry training school. The town of Sremski Karlovci, in addition to being the seat of Wrangel's headquarters until 1926, was also one of the main centers of the Russian Orthodox Church Abroad, which refused to recognize the authority of the Moscow Patriarch. Another element which cannot be overlooked was the Yugoslav government itself, which was a monarchy, pro–Slavic and provided generous subsidies for the émigré communities in the early 1920s.[68] The Belgrade government also had no patience for communist agitation and, unlike France and Czechoslovakia, banned the Communist Party and its organizations from its territory beginning in late 1920. As a result of these combined influences, the émigré community in Yugoslavia as whole had a strong militarist and conservative outlook.[69] This, of course, boded well for nostalgic Cossacks who desired to recreate the life they had known prior to 1917.

The Czechoslovak Republic, by contrast, was a more preferable destination for émigrés with democratic views. Indeed, the close relationship which developed between the Czechoslovak legionaries and the Russian Socialist Revolutionaries during the civil war continued into the 1920s. For its part, the Prague government adopted a program known as the Russian Action that was intended to bolster Russian academia and innovation for the benefit of a future post–Soviet Russia. Under its progressive leadership, Czechoslovakia became a haven for opponents to the conservative White generals. Among those who were welcomed into the new state were 2,500–3,000 Cossacks. The vast majority of them, if not all, belonged to the All-Cossack Agrarian Union which had repudiated Wrangel's command. Great disappointment, however awaited them. Unlike in Yugoslavia, the Cossacks sent to Czechoslovakia were not provided the means to establish close-knit farming communities. Instead, most found themselves toiling on large estates where working conditions left much to be desired.[70]

A third region where Cossacks were resettled into a rural environment was in southern France. Some took up residence in villages along the Côte d'Azur, which had been a fashionable getaway for spendthrift Russian royalty and aristocrats in the decades prior to the world war. Of course, the doors of the plush hotels, diners and casinos frequented by the elite remained shut to the penniless Cossacks who settled in the nearby countryside. Unfazed, most of them eked out a living as sharecroppers raising poultry and cultivating produce for the local markets. After 1925, Cossacks were also relocated to under-populated rural areas of southeastern France with help from the Cossack Union and French Ministry of Agriculture. To improve their chances of success, aspiring Cossack farmers were encouraged to work as hired hands for one or two years so they could acquaint themselves with local farming practices before renting land of their own. After they had familiarized themselves with local conditions, the Cossacks would then cultivate their own fields as sharecroppers. Although these Cossacks were unable to establish as strong communities as their brethren in Yugoslavia, they at least enjoyed greater independence than those who toiled on Moravian estates.[71]

Among the most eccentric schemes was that to establish stanitsas in South America. Efforts to resettle Russian refugees to there began in 1921 after Brazilian and French agents invited soldiers from Wrangel's army to embark for that continent. Approximately 1,000 soldiers—mostly Cossacks—were seduced by the notion of taming a wild, unforgiving frontier as their ancestors had once done. Few of these adventurers, however, got that chance since the project was abruptly discontinued before the vessel carrying them left the Mediterranean. Five years later, a new campaign was launched to resettle Russian refugees in sparsely populated areas of Paraguay, Bolivia and Peru. Once again, the proposal appealed mainly to Cossacks, several hundred of whom scraped together enough francs to purchase a ticket for the transoceanic voyage. Unfortunately, they quickly found the new lands designated for them far less idyllic than they imagined: trees needed to be cleared, swamps had to be drained and shelters had to be constructed. Added to this was the constant harassment they experienced from local fauna: venomous snakes, vampire bats and swarms of mosquitoes. These challenges proved to be too much for most, causing the would-be pioneers to abandon the planned stanitsas and relocate to a settled area or—if they could come up with enough money—buy a ticket back to Europe.[72]

Although the majority of the Cossack émigrés who sought shelter in Europe hailed from the two largest, proudest, and most venerated hosts—the Don and the Kuban, the stanitsas which they founded still fell short of duplicating the Cossacks' traditional way of life in exile. Remarkably, the stanitsas which came closest to achieving that goal were not located in Europe but rather were much farther east, in Manchuria, which became primary destination for Russians and Cossacks fleeing Soviet Russia in that direction.

Lost Russia

As we have seen, the revolution in Russia sent ripples across northeastern Asia which further destabilized that already volatile region. Especially problematic were the tens of thousands of refugees from Asiatic Russia who sought refuge across borders. Like their brethren who escaped Russia by heading west, those who fled eastward came from an array of backgrounds. Besides Russians and Cossacks, Kazakhs, Buryats, Koreans and even Chinese who previously immigrated to Russia all sought sanctuary abroad. Most ultimately settled in China, which was suspended in its own limbo of warlordism.

Russian émigrés had begun seeping into China following the Bolsheviks' first conquest of Siberia in the winter of 1917–18. A Russian officer who traveled the Trans-Siberian Railway to reach the safety of Manchuria during that period later recalled the relief his fellow passengers expressed the moment their train crossed the border. "Without ceremony," he wrote, "they congratulated one another upon their good fortune in effecting their escape."[73] The exodus of refugees reached epic proportions two years later after the Red Army shattered Kolchak's forces and steamrolled across much of Asiatic Russia. Some, like the aforementioned Cossacks of Dutov and Annenkov, sought refuge in the Chinese province of Xinjiang. There, in a region where towns were often nothing more than a primitive cluster of mud huts, they were reduced to begging or eating rats in order to survive.[74]

By far, the majority of Russians and Cossacks fleeing eastward in 1920 headed for Manchuria. This stream of émigrés into that region continued in spurts until the autumn of 1922, when General Diterikhs led the last organized group of Whites across the Chinese frontier near Hunchun. During the latter part of that decade, the number of Russians living in Manchuria was estimated between 150,000 and 200,000 persons.[75] Their plight was rendered a bit easier than that of their countrymen who fled to Xinjiang thanks to the aid provided by the Russian colony at Harbin. That city, which had been founded by the Russians only a quarter century earlier in the extraterritorial zone around the Chinese Eastern Railway, became the heart of the Russian emigration in the East. Even before the 1917 revolution, Harbin had been more Russian than Chinese, and events thereafter only strengthened the Russians' influence. Throughout the 1920s, tens of thousands of Russian refugees continued to migrate to that city which, despite the rickshaws and occasional temple, reminded them of the pre-revolutionary way of life. Russian schools were in regular session, Russian theaters continued to put on shows and the Orthodox churches remained open and unviolated. Traditions that had disappeared in the Soviet Republic, such as the ringing of church bells throughout Easter Sunday, lived on in Harbin.[76] As one émigré observed, that city "was more like an old colonial settlement that stayed on after the Empire had fallen."[77]

While Harbin was the cultural and political nexus of the Russian émigré community in Manchuria, some refugees settled in the Manchurian countryside to farm or herd livestock. Prominent among these rural settlers were Cossacks. As was their habit, the Cossack émigrés preferred to put as much distance as possible between themselves and authorities.

Hence, they tended to form communities in nearly inaccessible, sparsely-inhabited regions far from any administrative center. The largest of these was the area that became known as Trekrechye (Three Rivers) along the east bank of the Argun River, a tributary of the Amur that also the designated the Sino-Soviet frontier. There, nearly 10,000 Transbaikal Cossacks engaged in their former pursuits of cattle-grazing and dairy farming. Their efforts to pursue peaceful endeavors, however, were occasionally interrupted by the partisans and bandits who terrorized the near-lawless Manchurian countryside throughout the 1920s. Some of the marauders were the flotsam from the Whites' defeat in the civil war: displaced peasants, renegade Cossacks and desperate veterans of Kolchak's army. While most of these units sought to continue the anticommunist struggle by slipping across the border to raid villages in Soviet territory, others found it more profitable to exact tribute from defenseless Chinese peasants and Russian émigrés in Manchuria. Similar rackets were run by gangs of *hunghutze* who remained active in the region. A final danger to the Cossack settlements originated from their close proximity to Soviet territory. This threat could assume many forms; from bold raids by Red Army commandos against suspected pockets of White partisans to disguised OGPU hitmen seeking to assassinate partisan leaders. The Trekrechye Cossacks, then, kept their rifles on hand and knew how to use them. Like their soldier-farmer ancestors, they could never quite let their guard down.[78]

Although the Cossack settlers frequently mingled with Buryats and other neighboring tribes, they did not mix with or assimilate into the Chinese population of Manchuria. This reluctance to assimilate into the surrounding Chinese culture was pronounced among the entire Russian émigré community in the Far East and distinguished them from émigré youth in Europe. To an American scholar who visited Manchuria in the late 1920s, the Russian émigrés he encountered during his travels appeared self-absorbed and unappreciative of their Chinese hosts: "The Russian exile community in Manchuria is not even a victorious community; it is a community of defeat. Yet, in spite of loss of prestige, and political impotence, it remains stubbornly ignorant of China and uninterested in China. To intermarry with Chinese or live like Chinese, in spite of the fact that Russians are conspicuously less influenced by 'race-feeling' than are most Westerners, is a mark of failure."[79] Despite their reluctance to assimilate, some Russian émigrés in Manchuria did eventually take Chinese citizenship; especially after a 1924 agreement between Peking and Moscow for joint administration of the Chinese Eastern Railway restricted employment to either Soviet or Chinese citizens. Still, a number of émigrés instead applied for Soviet citizenship and became so-called radishes: persons who appeared Red on the outside but were White on the inside.[80]

While the weak central Chinese government observed proper relations with the Soviet Union, Manchuria's warlord, Marshal Zhang Zoulin, was more antagonistic towards his communist neighbor. Subsequently, he imposed few restrictions on émigré activities even though, as a whole, they seemed to show him little gratitude. Under his lax rule, White partisan bands were able to terrorize Soviet border communities from bases inside Manchuria. Zhang dispatched expeditions against these marauders only when such action was necessary to diffuse tensions with Moscow. In the meantime, a few émigré organizations, eager to make the most of the opportunities afforded by the warlord, attempted to coordinate the guerrillas to make their operations even more devastating. One such group, the Brotherhood of Russian Truth, sought to continue the struggle against Bolshevism by planning assassinations, terrorist attacks and sabotage operations in the Soviet Union. Although it was headquartered in Berlin, the organization was most active in the more unrestrained environment of Manchuria. Still, neither the Brotherhood of Russian Truth nor any other organization succeeded in uniting the various anti-Soviet bands there. The White guerrillas fiercely clung to their autonomy and rightly suspected that many émigré organizations were infiltrated by Soviet operatives.[81]

Not all Russians and Cossacks who wanted to continue the battle against communism turned to conspiracy and hooliganism. Some, particularly many veterans, found jobs as mercenaries in the private armies and security outfits of various Chinese warlords. Indeed, the number of émigrés who joined Marshal Zhang's forces is estimated at anywhere from 4,000 up to 12,000.[82] Although a few of these soldiers may have been idealists hoping that one day they would be ordered to march against Soviet Union, most were probably motivated by the more immediate need to earn a living.

While China's political instability provided employment opportunities for some Russian émigrés, the lawlessness and corruption which proliferated under many warlords made life for most refugees difficult, dangerous and unpredictable. This point is best illustrated by the plight of the predominantly Cossack refugees who settled in the remote villages and oasis towns of Xinjiang. Their troubles began in the summer of 1928 when a new warlord, Jin Shuren, seized power in Ürümqi following the assassination of his predecessor. Even by the poor standards of local warlords, Jin's regime demonstrated exceptional harshness, incompetence and corruption. In 1930, his misrule triggered unrest among the Uyghurs, an indigenous Muslim Turkic group, which soon escalated into a massive uprising. As violence swept across the countryside, the Cossack émigrés in Xinjiang found it impossible to remain neutral and formed themselves into a regiment which fought on the side of the ruling Chinese minority. The assistance which Jin received from these mercenaries proved invaluable at times, particularly in early 1933 when the brave deeds of a few hundred Cossack defenders decisively thwarted a rebel assault on Ürümqi. Eventually, though, the Cossack garrison in Ürümqi turned on Jin and helped to overthrow the inept despot in April 1933. This coup brought Sheng Shicai to assume power in the strife-ridden province. The Cossacks would shortly regret their aid to Sheng since his answer for suppressing the ongoing insurrection was to invite the Red Army into his realm. The Kremlin was all too glad to intervene since it was concerned that the rebellion in Xinjiang might spread to the Muslim population in Soviet Central Asia. In the closing days of 1933, Red troops, wearing uniforms and riding in armored cars devoid of any insignia, crossed the frontier into Xinjiang. The technological superiority of their weapons—particularly their warplanes—stunned the Uyghur insurgents and quickly scattered them. Although the Soviet units withdrew from Xinjiang once order was restored, NKVD squads stayed behind to direct a purge of Cossack "White Guardists" and other elements that were supposedly dangerous to Sheng's authority.[83] The tragic fate of the Cossacks in Xinjiang was a stark case in point of the unintended consequences any unrest might have for Russian émigrés in China.

The poverty and turmoil that was familiar to many ordinary Cossack émigrés in the Far East meant that they, like their brethren in European exile, had little time to spare for politics. Nevertheless, they did form their own groups to advance political agendas, preserve their links or retain some vestige of their military organization in anticipation of their triumphal return to a post-Soviet Russia. The initial efforts were led by their atamans who met in Harbin in January 1923 and established the Union of Cossacks in the Far East. This organization included representatives of all Cossack regions east of the Volga: the Ural, Orenburg, Siberian, Semirechye, Transbaikal, Amur and Ussuri hosts. In addition to acting as a single voice for these seven hosts, the Union of Cossacks in the Far East also tried to coordinate its activity with the Union of Cossacks formed later in Paris.[84] A parallel situation arose among veteran organizations in the Far East. Initially, the veteran groups were spearheaded by General Diterikhs who, like Wrangel, took a keen personal interest in the welfare of his former soldiers. In 1928, he set up a branch of ROVS in Manchuria, thus nominally subordinating its members to that organization's headquarters in Paris.[85] Although such an arrangement worked on paper, it remained difficult for either organization to implement it in practice due to geographical challenges and, in the 1930s, increasingly widespread political instability and repression.

In the Shadow of the Motherland

Throughout the interwar period, Russian émigrés remained intensely interested in events in their homeland. Most scoured news articles for signs that the Bolshevik regime was tottering. Reports of popular uprisings or revolts at Kronstadt naval base, in Tambov Province and Western Siberia during the early 1920s buoyed their anticipation. In addition to what they read in the press, the émigrés tried to get a better understanding of conditions in their homeland by maintaining contact with anticommunist sympathizers inside the Soviet Union.[86] Indeed, Wrangel instructed his representatives in various countries to get in touch with senior Red Army officers whenever the latter traveled outside the Soviet Union. He was certain that Red Army leaders, many who had served in the tsarist army in some capacity, would be amenable to the goals he set for his army in exile.

Meanwhile, the émigrés themselves had not escaped the notice of Soviet authorities. The ruling party was hardly inclined to underestimate the threat posed by the Diaspora; after all, many of its leading figures had been exiles during the tsarist period. A key objective of Soviet agents abroad was to recruit informers among the émigrés to monitor and sabotage the activities of the so-called "White Guardists." In this game of espionage and counter-espionage, the Soviets had the clear upper hand. Their operations were, after all, backed by a state apparatus which gave them access to a near-infinite amount of resources. In contrast, the émigrés, including the ROVS, were frequently cash-strapped. This, in turn, provided Soviet operatives countless opportunities to exploit the desperate economic situation of the émigrés by offering bribes in the form of money or other rewards. Furthermore, the knowledge that enemy agents were constantly attempting to infiltrate the émigrés' ranks sowed distrust, paranoia and ultimately disunity between them. When inevitable disagreements broke out in their camp, it was not unusual for the opposing factions to fling accusations of communist treachery at each other.[87]

One of the first major setbacks to the émigrés that was attributed to Soviet operatives occurred in Bulgaria, where nearly 19,000 soldiers, including many Don Cossacks, were resettled in 1921. The Whites had been granted generous terms of asylum in that country: they were not required to fully disarm and they were provided housing in barracks that otherwise would have sat empty following the reduction of the Bulgarian army after the First World War. However, the arrival of White regiments did not sit well with the Bulgarian Communist Party. Before long, the Bulgarian Communists began printing propaganda, possibly at the instigation of Moscow, alleging that the Whites were preparing a coup against the democratic government in Sofia in order to provoke a war with Soviet Russia. These charges stirred the Bulgarian government into action in March 1922 by demanding the disarmament of the Russian units. Two months later, during a search for illicit weapons, Bulgarian authorities claimed to have stumbled upon documents which supposedly proved that certain White officers were involved in a plot to overthrow the government. Although the damning papers were most likely forgeries planted by GPU agents, they gave the Bulgarian government the pretext it needed to take action against the Russians in the hope of quieting its opponents on the left. General Kutepov, the iron-willed commander of the First Corps, was among those officers who were implicated, arrested and expelled from the country as a result of the bogus evidence. In the following months, more White officers were given the same treatment as Bulgarian searches of émigré quarters turned up additional incriminating—and ultimately false—documents.[88]

Amid their crackdown on the White émigrés, the Bulgarian leaders began looking favorably upon the idea of repatriation as a means to rid themselves of the burdensome émigrés. As we have seen, repatriations of White soldiers, mostly Cossacks, began only a few months after the evacuation of the Crimea and continued intermittently thereafter. Nansen, the League of Nations' High Commissioner for Refugee Affairs, also looked favorably upon the idea of repatriation as the simplest solution to the Russian refugee crisis. In July 1922 Nansen's commission reached an agreement with the Soviet Foreign Commissariat whereby the latter confirmed their earlier offer of amnesty for returning White soldiers. This development was cheered by homesick émigrés who in May had formed the Union for the Return to the Motherland, known by its Russian acronym as Sovnarod. The Sofia government lent Sovnarod its direct support, as did GPU agents in a more surreptitious manner. That backing, plus the government's crackdown on the émigrés combined with the dismal economic realities in the country, induced many Don Cossacks to choose to go back to Russia. Subsequently, Sovnarod attracted its greatest following in Bulgaria, from where nearly 8,000 émigrés—most of them Cossacks—embarked on vessels which carried them across the Black Sea from Varna to Soviet Russia.[89]

The Cossacks in Bulgaria were hardly alone in succumbing to the urge to return home. Many Cossack émigrés in Czechoslovakia, disillusioned with their working conditions, readily volunteered for repatriation.[90] In their efforts to lure dejected émigrés back to Russia, the Soviets once again exploited the refugees' poor economic standing. Bolshevik propagandists, as well as fellow-travelers in the West, spread rosy reports of life under communism. In the Russian Far East, such propaganda was broadcast to émigrés across the border via radio transmissions.[91] This devious campaign had its intended effect, particularly on Cossacks, who continued to stream back to Russia throughout the 1920s. By the early 1930s, only 40,000 Cossacks remained abroad—about half of the original number which fled Soviet Russia. Repatriation was the greatest factor behind that reduction of the Cossack émigré community.[92]

In addition to summoning the Cossack rank-and-file back to the motherland, Soviet *agent provocateurs* also set their sights on certain high-profile targets. These operatives were especially effective in China. One agent persuaded the ataman of the Siberian Cossacks, Ivanov-Rinov, to voluntarily return to the Soviet Union in the autumn of 1925. Not surprisingly, upon his homecoming he was arrested by the OGPU and executed during the following year.[93] A similar fate befell Ataman Annenkov who was either abducted by enemy agents in Xinjiang or enticed to enter Soviet territory. Regardless of exactly how he fell into Soviet hands, he was eventually brought to Semipalatinsk and put to death in 1927. Some key figures in the emigration were killed outright, such as Lieutenant General Dutov, ataman of the Orenburg Cossacks, who was slain in Xinjiang by Bolshevik assassins in February 1921.[94] Later that same year, in November, another Soviet assassin squad in Manchuria made an unsuccessful attempt against the life of Transbaikal Ataman Semyonov.[95]

Prominent White émigrés in China were not the only ones who were in the crosshairs of the OGPU. In Europe, that agency also dealt the ROVS several major blows during the 1930s. That decade saw the abduction of two heads of ROVS, first General Kutepov and then his successor, General E. K. Miller, from the streets of Paris by OGPU agents. The investigation into Miller's disappearance in September 1937 produced the damaging revelation that the organization's head of counterintelligence operations, Major-General Nikolay Skoblin, had been working for the Soviets. This treachery left the ROVS in disarray and widely discredited. The next in line to succeed Miller, the Don Cossack General Abramov, was reluctant to accept the post and did so only on a provisional basis. One reason for his hesitation was that he knew the government of his host country, Bulgaria, had no desire to complicate its relations with Moscow by allowing an anticommunist organization to operate from its territory; particularly one that was compromised by Soviet spies. In March 1938 he gratefully handed over the reins of ROVS to Lieutenant-General A. P. Arkhangelsky in Belgium. But the difficulties for the Don general and ROVS were not over since later that year the general's son, Nikolay Abramov, was arrested by Bulgarian police on charges that he too was secretly working for the Soviets and ordered to leave the country. Regardless of whether there was any truth to the allegations, the incident seemed to confirm the worst émigré suspicions that one of their leading organizations was teeming with Soviet operatives.[96]

Of course, ROVS was hardly the only émigré organization to be riddled with Soviet spies. A 1934 scandal uncovered the presence of OGPU agents in the Brotherhood of Russian Truth, leading to the dissolution of that organization.[97] Such revelations crushed many émigrés' last hopes in the White cause. After more than a decade in exile, they had endured numerous trials—resettlement, poverty, economic hardship—and yet their prayers for the demise of communism in Russia went unanswered. During that time, the White movement failed to produce a leader with the ability to unite the fractious émigrés, instead their organizations succumbed to Soviet provocations and meddling. Among right-wing émigrés, both Cossack and non–Cossack, there was a sense that a fresh, more dynamic movement was needed to replace the decrepit, obsolete Whites. This desire for a revitalized anti–Bolshevik operation would lead them into a number of anticommunist adventures—some of which were bizarre, others disreputable and some that were both.

11

Collaboration

A Stillborn Crusade

A popular tenet among anti–Bolshevik émigrés was that their cause represented the homegrown and organic elements of Russian society and culture. Communism, many of them asserted, was completely alien to the Russian character. They attributed the Bolsheviks' ultimate victory in the revolution and civil war to a vast, shadowy international conspiracy operated by Jews, Freemasons, socialists or a combination thereof. According to their narrative, though the communists might dominate Russia; Russia, at her core, was not and never would be communist.

Paradoxically, those same émigrés appeared oblivious to their side's extensive associations with foreign entities. The armies of Denikin and Kolchak had been far more dependent on external benefactors than their Red opponent. Beyond them, a number of Cossack leaders had accepted support from countries that were traditional rivals or even a formal enemy of the Russian state. Semyonov and Kalmykov, for example, had cooperated extensively with the Japanese while Skoropadsky and Krasnov cultivated German support. Often, those atamans who survived the collapse of the White movement and went abroad often gravitated towards those countries that had backed them: Semyonov settled in Japanese-controlled Darien, Skoropadsky retired to Berlin and Krasnov too spent much time in Germany. Although none had much authority over their ostensible followers and even less over Cossack émigrés *en toto*, they gleefully entertained the unauthorized schemes of Japanese or German army officers who shared their anticommunist ideology. To them, no plan was too troubling or far-flung to keep the flame of the anti–Bolshevik movement alive.

The Russian Diaspora, as a whole, had mixed feelings towards the premise that the émigrés should continue or renew their armed struggle against the Soviet regime. Democratic and left-leaning politicians, including the members of the Constituent Assembly who convened in Paris in January 1921, generally agreed that they should refocus their efforts to aid oppositional forces within Russia.[1] Their more conservative counterparts, however, were less willing to throw in the towel. For them, resistance to Bolshevism by any and all means was a patriotic obligation. Hence the effort of army commanders such as Wrangel and later Diterikhs to keep their troops in a psychological state of war even as they were disarmed in exile. They and other officers were convinced that if the communist regime did not collapse on its own, it would soon be destroyed by outside forces. Surely, they thought, the international community would come to its senses and make war on Soviet Russia in the interests of decency, humanity and world peace. After all, the Communist International made no secret of its desire to overturn the existing order throughout the globe by promoting violent social revolution. Conflict between these ideologies appeared unavoidable. When war did break out, the White generals wanted their men to be ready.

Throughout the interwar period, the most uncompromising elements among the émigré community anxiously eyed global affairs in anticipation of the inevitable crusade against the communist menace. Their observations provided them with some grounds for optimism. In the early 1920s, relations between the Western democracies and the Soviet government were frequently strained. Amid the postwar atmosphere of disillusionment, economic stagnation and heightened social tension, governments throughout Europe were haunted by fears of communist subversion. Until 1924, many countries refused to enter into normal diplomatic relations with the Soviet Union. In a few states, leaders made anticommunism a major plank of their platform. Such was the case in Hungary, where the Horthy regime's desire to eradicate communism was second only to its goal of Hungarian revisionism.[2] The upsurge in fascist movements, particularly after Benito Mussolini clenched power in Italy in autumn 1922, also seemed to portend a major confrontation with Moscow.

This anticipation of conservative émigrés made them particularly gullible to outlandish whispers of war. In early 1923, one group, the Supreme Monarchist Council, was electrified by rumors that the French and their allies in East Central Europe were preparing to invade Soviet Russia. Since the Supreme Monarchist Council was dominated by a Francophile orientation, its members felt that the impending Franco-Soviet conflict raised the chances that they or their preferred candidate for the throne, Grand Duke Nikolay Nikolayevich, would be ushered into power in Moscow. But not all conservative émigrés rejoiced at such prospects. Pro-German Russian exiles, especially those associated with the organization known as Aufbau, were horrified by the idea of a French-led campaign and, according to one account, viewed a Soviet victory as a more preferable alternative in such an event.[3]

The men who staffed Aufbau, like their rivals in the Supreme Monarchist Council, held predominantly monarchist political views. Their similarities, however, mostly ended there. The founders of Aufbau, unlike those of the Supreme Monarchist Council, mourned the fall of the Hohenzollerns in addition to that of the Romanovs. This, along with Aufbau's outspoken desire for close cooperation between Russia and Germany, enabled it to broaden its appeal to disaffected German monarchists in addition to those from Russia. Aufbau's leaders reconciled the recent bloodletting between the two countries by attributing the world war to the machinations of Jews and Marxists. It was this disdain for "Judeo-Bolshevism" which formed the basis for what one historian has called the "mutual flirtation" between rightwing Russian émigrés and Germans disillusioned with the Weimar Republic.[4] They saw in each other not only validation for their distorted views but also potential sources of funding. In its quest for the latter, Aufbau seems to have come up short. Although its German friends included General Erich Ludendorff, the ex-generalissimo of the kaiser's army, and Adolf Hitler, then a little-known orator for the fledgling German National Socialist Workers' (hereafter Nazi) Party, neither man was in an economic position to dole out hefty allowances. The Nazis, on the other hand, appeared to have fared better in their dealings with the émigrés since Aufbau's preferred candidate for the Russian throne, Grand Duke Kirill, and his German-born wife, Viktoria, were among those captivated by the Austrian corporal's fiery oratory. During the early 1920s, the royal couple is believed to have provided financial aid to both Aufbau and the Nazis.

Another factor which differentiated Aufbau from other monarchist émigré groups was its vision for post–Soviet Russia. While many conservative émigrés, beginning with the White generals, sought to restore Russia to her imperial splendor, Aufbau at times appeared open to the prospect of a federalized or even dismembered Russia. This unconventional outlook may be attributed to the presence of Russian minorities among many of Aufbau's leading members: its president and founder, Max von Scheubner-Richter, was a Baltic German as were several of his top associates, including Arno Schickedanz and Alfred Rosenberg. All three men also became early members of the Nazi Party. The organization's vice-president, the unscrupulous General Vasily Biskupsky, was a product of the Ukrainian aristocracy and had served as a divisional commander in Skoropadsky's inchoate armed forces during 1918. Another Skoropadsky follower, Ivan Poltavets-Ostranitsa, joined Aufbau in 1921 as the head of its Ukrainian department.[5]

By 1923, when rumors of an imminent Franco-Soviet war were circulating in the émigré community, Aufbau and Nazi leaders had been collaborating on some level for nearly two years. During that period, Aufbau had devised a general plan aimed at fomenting a popular anticommunist rebellion in the Soviet Union. The uprising, if successful, was supposed to pave the way for Grand Duke Kirill to assume power. At least two Cossack leaders were among those privy to this plot. One was Poltavets-Ostranitsa who, as chief of the National Ukrainian Cossack Organization, appears to have made the scheme more amenable to Ukrainian national interests. The other was Krasnov, the ex-Don ataman.[6] In exile, Krasnov busied himself not only with writing but also with a number of anti–Bolshevik activities. In that sphere, he helped co-found the anti–Soviet terrorist organization known as the Brotherhood of Russian Truth.[7] He was also active in the field of monarchist politics where, true to his *modus operandi*, he refused to pick a side in the contentious rivalry between the Supreme Monarchist Council and Aufbau. Although he later served as an advisor on Cossack affairs in the staff of Grand Duke Nikolay Nikolayevich, he was careful to avoid endorsing either of the main pretenders to the Russian throne. This dexterity enabled him to cultivate amiable relations with Aufbau and enter its roster of participants in its grand conspiracy.[8] Although the precise role which Aufbau intended for Krasnov is unclear, it may be surmised that the organization hoped that the former ataman, possibly through propaganda, would rally Cossacks inside the Soviet Union to a general anticommunist uprising.[9]

Ultimately, the internal anti–Soviet revolt planned by Aufbau, like the rumored French attack on the Soviet Union, proved to be more imaginary than real. It is doubtful whether it, or any émigré organization for that matter, had any substantial following behind the sealed borders of the Soviet Union. Though failing to make any headway in its struggle against communism, Aufbau did proceed with another set of conspiratorial plans on its anti–Weimar front. On the evening of 8 November 1923, Scheubner-Richter, Schickedanz and Rosenberg joined Hitler and his brownshirts in a *putsch* in Munich. Their uprising, however, collapsed after a fusillade from Bavarian police wounded about a dozen demonstrators and killed another sixteen, including Scheubner-Richter. With his death, Aufbau lost its most important link with the Nazis and disintegrated into two competing camps: a Russian faction led by Biskupsky and a Ukrainian one headed by Poltavets-Ostranitsa.[10] Ultimately, Aufbau's legacy in the Russian Diaspora was that its members were to bear the distinction of being the first, but certainly not the last, Russian émigrés to collaborate on some level with Hitler and his followers.

The far-flung and ultimately futile schemes of émigré conspirators in 1923 revealed the extent to which the more extreme elements were willing to go in an effort to regain their lost lives. Their desperation is understandable since by then most of the hapless émigrés had been abroad for three or more years. They yearned to again see the homeland and loved ones they left behind but, contrary to expectations, the Soviet regime proved remarkably durable. Indeed, many émigrés sensed that with each passing day Bolshevism became more entrenched while the Russia they knew and loved faded further from memory. With time interminably ticking way, nothing, not even collaboration with their country's one-time enemy or its unappreciative former ally, was off-limits in their quest. The failures of the early 1920s did not end émigré intrigues against Soviet Russia, rather it drove many to look for fresh ways to bridge the rifts among the emigration while attracting foreign support for their anticommunist adventures.

The Rise of Russian Fascism

It is widely accepted that some variant of monarchism, ranging from a restricted constitutional form or an all-powerful autocracy, had the broadest appeal among Russian émigrés and their organizations. Many White generals and officers, though they refrained from publicly advocating a restoration during the civil war, held monarchist sympathies. Wrangel, for example, considered the disappearance of the monarchy to be the greatest disaster to befall Russia and its army.[11] In exile, the baron regarded Grand Duke Nikolay Nikolayevich as the rightful successor to the Russian throne even though he refused to adopt an explicitly pro-monarchist program for ROVS.[12] The latter organization, though nominally committed to a policy of non-predetermination for Russia's future form of government, did at times lean towards advocating a monarchist restoration. Such predilections, however, was not enough for ROVS to secure the unqualified support of the most extreme monarchists in the Russian Diaspora.[13] Indeed, the ultra-conservative element believed that ROVS was mistaken in its decision not to explicitly endorse monarchy as the ideal form of government for a post–Soviet Russia. These reactionaries convinced themselves that Russia's suffering masses, once they cast off the shackles of Bolshevism, would gratefully welcome a Romanov restoration. As a member of the Supreme Monarchist Council put it, "When we get back to Russia, spoiled as we have been by living so long in the West, we are going to be surprised to find the people much more conservative than we are."[14]

As years passed without the emigration appearing to make any progress towards achieving some form of overall unity, much less its ultimate goal of a triumphal return to Russia, its younger members began to question the political wisdom of their elders and, in doing so, looked for new inspiration. Monarchism, it seemed to them, was a relic of the past with no relevance in modern times. They naturally held socialism in low esteem and thought that democracy fostered only gridlock and instability.[15] Gradually, they came to regard authoritarianism as the system which gave them the best chance of producing a national rebirth. Looking to Italy as an example, the young, conservative émigrés were impressed by Mussolini's apparent success in reinvigorating Italian patriotism, unifying a fractured society and staving off the threat of communist subversion. Likewise, the Italian *Duce* personified their ideal leader by exuding charisma, fortitude and authority. As a result, the Russian Diaspora produced several individuals who styled their public image after Mussolini amid their efforts to portray themselves as a Russian *vozhd* (leader).[16]

The task of uniting the entire Russian emigration, or even a like-minded segment of émigrés, behind a single *vozhd* would prove far more difficult than the proponents of authoritarianism imagined. A major obstacle for them was the wide geographic distribution of Russian émigrés. Whereas Mussolini and his blackshirts only needed to concentrate their activities in a modest area extending from Padua to Palermo, a Russian political organization aspiring to unite all right-wing émigrés needed to canvas disparate communities stretching from Paris to Peking. Since the would-be Russian *vozhds* lacked name recognition outside of their immediate communities, it was imperative for them to reach audiences directly. Yet most—with one notable exception—could afford neither the travel expenses nor the postage needed to disseminate their messages to distant lands. Nonetheless, a few individuals or groups did manage to attract a significant following or fame—even if only for a brief time. The earliest of these was the Union of Young Russia (*Soyuz Molodoi Rossii*), founded in Munich by Aleksandr Kazem-Bek in 1923, which called for Russia to be ruled by a seemingly antipodal combination of a Romanov tsar responsible to freely-elected Soviets. Although the Young Russians were attracted to the theatrics of Mussolini, they never quite openly embraced fascism.[17] Other leaders and émigré groups on the far right, however, lacked such scruples. Anastase Vonsiatsky, founder of the Connecticut-based All-Russian Fascist Organization, modeled his wardrobe and that of his few followers after the uniforms of Nazi stormtroopers.[18] In Germany, the members of another émigré organization, the Russian National Liberation Movement (*Russkoe Osvoboditelnoe Natsionalnoe Dvizhenie*, ROND), also donned swastika armbands and greeted each other with Nazi salutes.[19] Yet, none of these leaders or organizations were able to stay in the limelight for very long. The enthusiasm of the Young Russians ebbed in the latter 1920s. Vonsiatsky remained marginally relevant only because his marriage to a wealthy American heiress provided him the hefty allowances he needed to continue his political dabbling. ROND, ironically, had its activities curbed by those it sought to emulate. In October 1933, barely ten months after Hitler had assumed the chancellorship in Germany, Nazi authorities disbanded ROND in its current form and reconstituted it into a more pliable organization.

The demise of ROND at the hands of the Nazis foreshadowed the complicated relationship which ultra-conservative émigrés were to have with Hitler's regime. Initially, many were impressed by the German dictator. They applauded him for seemingly restoring Germany's greatness in less than a generation after a devastating war and revolution. Certainly, these accomplishments inspired them to continue working towards their own goal of achieving a similar transformation in their beloved homeland. Gradually, the Young Russians became outspoken critics of Hitler as they recognized his open-prejudice against Slavs, but other fascist-leaning émigrés were either blind to his xenophobia or they refused to take his racist rants seriously. This willful naïveté persisted among them even after the Nazis dissolved ROND, which appears to have occurred for no other reason than the Führer's aversion to watching Slavs, whom he regarded as sub-humans (*untermenschen*), ape national socialists.[20]

The most successful group among rightwing Russian émigrés in Europe found secure footing by striking a careful balance between support and opposition to the continent's ascendant fascist governments. This organization was the National Labor Alliance (*Natsionalnoe Trudovoy Soyuz*, hereafter NTS) which, like the Young Russians and the All-Russian Fascist Organization, had its own strongman in the person of its founder, Viktor Baydalakov. A Cossack and veteran of Wrangel's army, Baydalakov worked as a stevedore in Constantinople after the evacuation of the Crimea. Later, he went to Yugoslavia and labored there on a road-construction crew before enrolling in the University of Belgrade. There he earned a degree in chemical engineering, but after his graduation in 1929 he appears to have directed most of his energies into politics. During the following year, the National Labor Alliance of the New Generation, as Baydalakov's newly minted-organization was originally called, held its first congress in the Yugoslavian capital. It was attended by representatives from émigré communities in Yugoslavia, France, Bulgaria, Czechoslovakia and the Netherlands.[21] Like the Young Russians, the NTS attracted disaffected youth among White émigrés searching for a viable alternative to communism in Russia. Eventually, they became proponents of their own brand of dictatorship as the ideal form of government for Russia by advancing the slogan "Neither communism nor fascism, but national labor Solidarism."[22]

In its early years, the NTS, coordinating its activities with ROVS, attempted to infiltrate its members into Soviet Russia to carry out espionage and acts of terrorism. Although nothing more was heard of these would-be saboteurs as soon as they crossed the frontier, the NTS, like many émigré groups, boasted that they had an extensive network embedded within the Soviet Union. Despite its evident failures to engineer a stunt in the homeland, the group continued to garner strength as the result of its work abroad. By the late 1930s, it was transforming itself into a professional political organization where inductees were required to complete training before they could be accepted as full members.[23] The curriculum included instruction on propaganda, infiltration and intimidation tactics, such as public brawling and shouting down orators, which earned them considerable notoriety among the elder political class in the émigré community.[24]

Although the group's leader, Baydalakov, was a Cossack, the NTS subscribed to a Great Russian nationalist outlook and spurned any proposal to divide Russia along ethnic frontiers. The NTS's support for an indivisible Russia was compatible with the views of the White generals who headed the ROVS, and as a result the two groups formed a partnership during much of the 1930s. Yet at the same time the NTS, despite its Russo-centrism and supposedly anti-fascist stance, did not disassociate with groups whose views were anti–Russian and certainly fascist. Indeed, its infiltration schemes made such contacts imperative. Subsequently, NTS members readily hired themselves out as experts, translators and propagandists in the intelligence departments of the German military, Propaganda Ministry and the Foreign Office. They did so despite the fact that the Führer showed no desire whatsoever to entertain émigré dreams of restoring a great, nationalist Russia. Although they were frequently looked down upon by their German employers, NTS personnel nonetheless managed to secure positions from which they could wield considerable influence in the event that any Soviet opposition movement arose within the borders of the Third Reich.[25]

Even though many conservative Cossack émigrés subscribed to organizations that, like the NTS, were oriented towards Great Russian nationalism, a faction of Cossack separatists still managed to claw out a niche on the far right of the political spectrum. As we have seen, a Cossack émigré separatist movement, under the Union for the Resurrection of Cossackdom, had taken shape within weeks after Wrangel's army went into exile. Since their main argument was based on the principle of self-determination that the Cossacks, which they alleged were a distinct nationality, had a right to their own sovereign state, many originally held leftist views.[26] The ascension of Hitler, however, challenged this prevailing tendency. Like certain Ukrainian and Caucasian émigré leaders who were delighted by the Nazis' anticommunist and anti–Russian rhetoric, some Cossack separatists also saw Germany's new Russophobe masters as a desirable ally to their cause. Subsequently, in the mid–1930s, a Cossack National Center was formed in Prague. The organization's doyen, Vasily G. Glazkov, was a young Don Cossack who fled Russia as a child, acquired a military education in Yugoslavia and completed his university degree in Prague.[27] His book, entitled *History of the Cossacks*, published after the Second World War, is revealing of his romantic brand of Cossack nationalism. "The Cossacks have been well known from olden times as a freedom-loving people," he proclaimed. "When despotism and tyranny raged, at a time when there was slavery even in the enlightened West, the Cossack Lands were islands of true human liberty, equality and genuine fraternity."[28] Such progressive ideals, he argued, had always put them at odds with their Russian neighbors, and these differences became evident in 1917. "In the Revolution the Cossacks saw, in contrast to the Great Russians, an opportunity not for robbery, plunder and anarchy but for the people to obtain the right to direct their own fate and to organize their life as they saw fit."[29] By emphasizing the contrasts in the Cossacks' character and history from the Russians, he sought to legitimatize his argument for a separate Cossack state.

Unlike other right-wing leaders among the Russian Diaspora, Glazkov did not seek to emulate the Führer. Ultimately, his aim was to enlist German help in the establishment of a Cossack state—Cossackia—that would encompass the territories of the Don, Kuban, Terek, Astrakhan, Ural and Orenburg Hosts as well the Kalmyk steppe.[30] Overall, his program does not seem to have resonated well with most Cossack émigrés since the Cossack National Center appears to have attracted only a few dozen followers prior to the Second World War.[31] Nonetheless, Glazkov acquired some importance since his Russophobic and frequently anti–Semitic demagogy was compatible with Hitler's goals in Eastern Europe. After the Third Reich annexed the Czech homelands in March 1939, the Cossack National Center became the only legal organization of Cossack émigrés in the newly-established Protectorate of Bohemia and Moravia.[32]

The upsurge of right-wing political movements among Russian émigrés during the interwar period was not limited to those living in Europe. Indeed, the most successful openly-fascist Russian émigré organization was the Russian Fascist Party, whose followers were concentrated primarily in the Far East. Originating from a right-wing student organization established in Harbin during the late 1920s, this group eventually fell under the sway of Konstantin V. Rodzaevsky, who fled from the Soviet Union as an eighteen-year-old in 1925. While borrowing heavily from Italian Fascism, Rodzaevsky also enthusiastically embraced many aspects of German Nazism, including use of the swastika as its emblem and a virulent anti–Semitic ideology.[33] Yet, the Russian Fascist Party owed its achievements neither to its antics or demagoguery but rather to Japanese army officers who, unlike Hitler, recognized the rightwing émigrés as a potentially useful weapon against their Soviet neighbor.

Salvation from the East

At a glance, Manchuria appeared to be an inviting destination for Russian émigrés. Harbin, with its collection of Russian schools and Orthodox churches, offered all the amenities of any Russian provincial city before the revolution. In the remote countryside along the Argun River, Cossacks lived in stanitsas that were hardly different from those they left behind on the opposite river bank. But beneath this veneer of nostalgic charm lurked an underworld of organized crime, banditry and corruption which encumbered the struggling refugee communities. Villages were terrorized by *hunghutze* gangs which robbed travelers and operated protection rackets. Sectors along the extensive Soviet-Manchurian frontier were contested by White partisans and Soviet commandos. In Harbin itself, Chinese, Japanese and Russian kingpins oversaw vast criminal enterprises which engaged in heists, prostitution, kidnapping and drug trafficking. Destitute Russians, having crossed into Manchuria with little more than the clothes on their back, provided these cartels with an endless source of pawns, thugs and victims. The upshot of this nefarious atmosphere was that it did raise new employment opportunities for émigrés, especially those with military backgrounds, to serve as bodyguards to former aristocrats, wealthy businessmen or local officials who might be targeted by kidnappers seeking hefty ransoms.[34]

In addition to the localized disorders, Manchuria was caught in a tug-of-war between the three regional powers—China, Japan and Soviet Russia—for economic, military and political supremacy in Northeast Asia. Amid this struggle, the Russian émigrés were at times accursed, courted and manipulated by the various contestants. While Russian refugees in Manchuria fared relatively well under the regime of Marshal Zhang Zoulin, many felt that neither he nor other Chinese leaders were properly asserting themselves against their Soviet neighbor. Their pessimism, however, was briefly put on hold in July 1929 when Marshal Zhang Zoulin's son and successor, Zhang Xueliang, attempted to acquire complete control over the Chinese Eastern Railway in violation of the 1924 agreement between Pe-

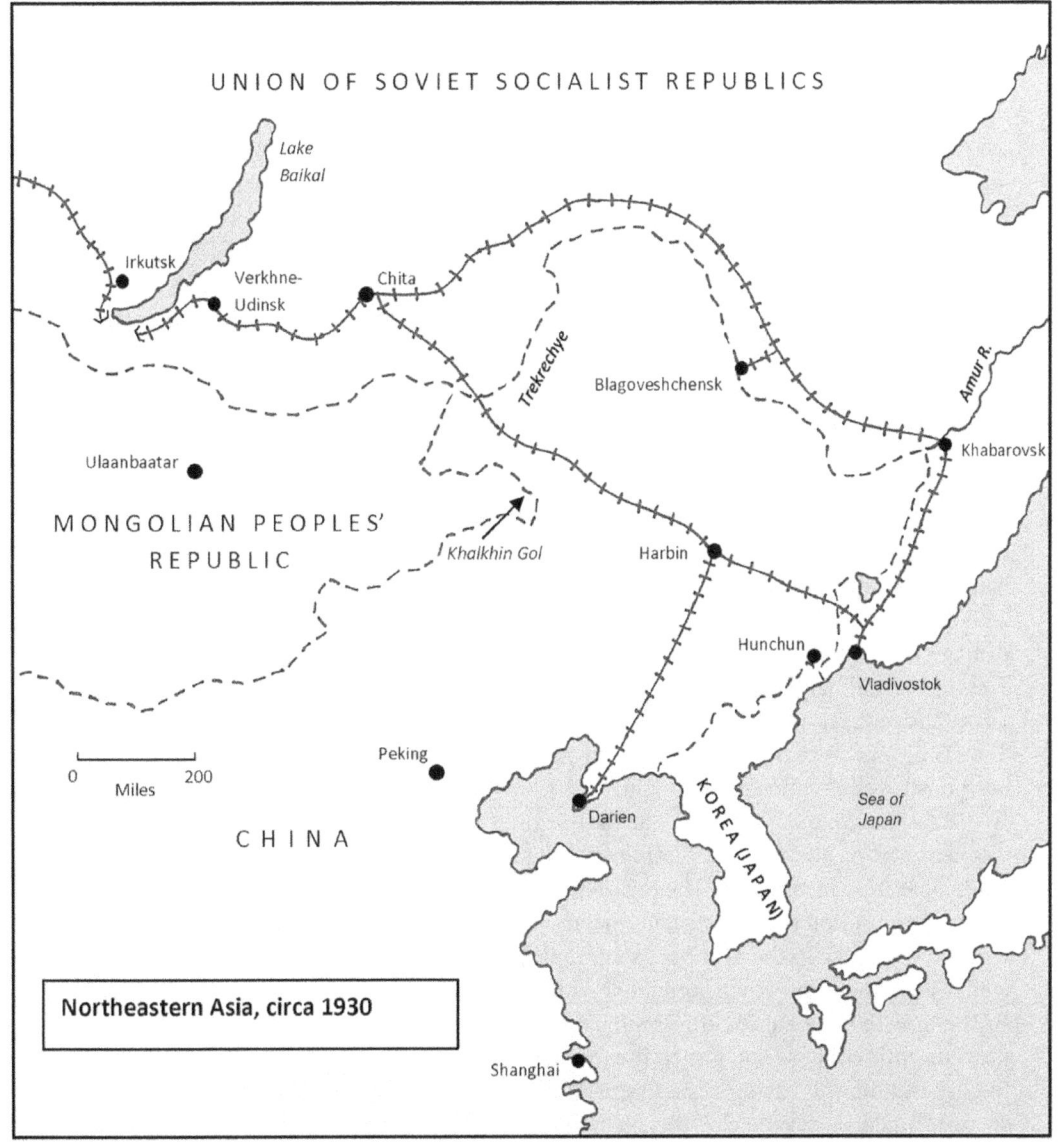

king and Moscow. His challenge was most acutely felt near the western end of the railway, near Semyonov's old stomping grounds of Manchuli, and along the Argun River, where Chinese-sponsored raiding parties terrorized the Soviet side of the frontier by rustling livestock and razing villages. These marauders were accompanied by émigré Russian and Cossack auxiliaries eager to cut down Soviet commissars.[35] Skirmishes along the border flared and ebbed into the following autumn, and for a time the Chinese and their White collaborators probably thought that their opponents had no fight left in them. Events soon proved otherwise. On 17 November, ten divisions of the Soviet Special Far Eastern Army, including nearly 1,600 cavalry, tore through Chinese positions north of the Chinese Eastern Railway in a maneuver intended to take the defenders at Manchuli in their rear. When the Red forces reached Manchuli three days later, they found themselves no longer up against a disciplined enemy but rather a riotous mob. Zhang's troops, driven to hysteria by the intensity of the Soviet offensive, had thrown away their arms, replaced their uniforms with civilian clothing and begun plundering the town. With his forces unable to mount further resistance, the warlord hastily sued for peace.[36]

Despite their role in instigating hostilities and the totality of their subsequent defeat, the Chinese fared relatively well in the conflict's aftermath. The Soviets demanded no border rectifications or concessions from their opponent; only a return to the 1924 status quo of joint administration over the Chinese Eastern Railway. This leniency was partly by design: Bolshevik propagandists, ever eager to stoke revolutionary embers in its eastern neighbor, emphasized that its military operations were directed against greedy warlords and their White Guardist stooges, not at China's multitude of oppressed workers and peasants. Chinese property was respected and Chinese deserters were welcomed to Soviet lines by Comintern agitators.[37] No similar courtesies, however, were extended to the Russian émigrés who were caught up in the maelstrom. Those residing near the border, especially the Trekrechye Cossacks, suffered the most. When the Soviet onslaught began in late November, thousands of Cossacks hurriedly packed their families and a few belongings onto carts and headed east in the freezing weather. Those that stayed behind or were overtaken by the advancing Reds risked being deported to the Soviet Union, where they might be executed or shipped to a labor camp. Even those refugees who evaded the Red Army encountered plenty of hardship. Many were robbed and assaulted by demoralized Chinese troops retreating along with them. Indeed, the ill-disciplined Chinese units were reported to have inflicted as much damage in the countryside as the Red Army. Before the month-long Soviet occupation of Trekrechye and neighboring areas was over, émigré casualties were tallied at more than 200 killed and several hundred wounded while over 800 disappeared into the Soviet Union.[38] The livelihoods which the Cossacks and peasants had constructed over the last decade had been destroyed practically overnight.

Russian émigrés outside of the battle zones were affected as well. The conflict, which was centered on the main arterial line of the Chinese Eastern Railway, disrupted the railroad's operation for months. The regional instability further scared off investors and foreign companies, leading to bankruptcies, payroll cuts and the closure of firms, all of which contributed to a spike in the number of unemployed émigrés living in Harbin. The crash of the global stock markets, which coincided with the standoff, made recovery next to impossible. By the time the railway could resume normal operations, Manchurian farmers learned that the economic collapse had gutted the market value of soybeans, the region's leading export. In desperation, increasing numbers of unemployed or underemployed émigrés turned to crime to make ends meet.[39] Others sought revenge against the Chinese population, whom they accused of desertion and betrayal during the Sino-Soviet conflict. Vigilante detachments formed from Cossacks and other rural folk who lost everything in the recent fighting began ambushing Chinese villages and slaughtering their inhabitants. The violence in the countryside soon became self-perpetuating when Chinese troops were moved in to put a stop to the bloodshed.[40]

Russian émigrés were not the only ones left unnerved by the Soviet triumph. It also raised the alarm among the Japanese, who feared that Moscow was pulling away in the ongoing tug-of-war over Manchuria. Therefore, barely two years after the conclusion of the Sino-Soviet conflict, Japan's Kwantung Army, which controlled southern Manchuria, picked a fight with Zhang's troops. In the following months the Kwantung Army, under the pretext of liberating Manchuria from Chinese misrule, began overrunning the region. These events buoyed the spirits of Russian émigrés in Manchuria since they believed the Japanese would become a protector that could hold more than their own in a showdown with the Red Army. A few months later, on 18 February 1932, Chinese collaborators declared Manchuria's succession from the Republic of China. On the heels of this announcement, a new state, Manchukuo, was proclaimed in its place. Although ostensibly administered by "Manchukuoans," Japanese advisers attached to Manchukuo's government, army and police institutions were installed behind the scenes to pull the real strings of power. It did not take long for the fiction of Manchukuo's sovereignty to become apparent to all in Manchuria.[41]

When the first Kwantung Army units entered Harbin on 5 February 1932, they were given a raucous welcome by thousands of Russian émigrés in the city's streets. The downtrodden émigrés looked forlornly to their new overlords to usher stability into the region while halting the spread of communism. Their hopes were quickly dispelled. Almost from the start, the conduct of the Japanese evoked memories of the notoriety which they had earned during the Siberian intervention nearly fifteen years earlier. With unbecoming arrogance, they demanded complete submission from the Chinese majority and Russian minority in Manchukuo. They censured the press, hired networks of informants and dissolved various émigré organizations. Worst of all, the Japanese security organs proved no less prone to corruption than those under the Chinese warlords. Japanese police stings against the Chinese and Russian mafias were designed not to stop their illicit activities but rather to acquire a chunk of their profits. Certain Japanese military and police officers, using Chinese or Russian thugs as intermediaries, amassed personal fortunes in the narcotics trade. To boost sales, some even mounted advertising campaigns to encourage opium use among the Chinese and Russian populations.

In between their profiteering rackets, Japanese officials attempted to simplify their administration of Manchukuo's White Russian population by setting up the Bureau of Russian Émigré Affairs. Although the bureau was ostensibly apolitical, the Japanese ensured that the most important posts in the organization were held by Konstantin Rodzaevsky and members of his Russian Fascist Party. Although in 1932 his party numbered no more than a few thousand members and was short of funds, the noisy boasts of Rodzaevsky had grabbed the attention of Japanese agents even before their forces reached Harbin. By the time the Kwantung Army occupied that city, the Russian Fascists were accepting subsidies and taking orders from Japanese agents. As a reward for their collaboration, the *vozhd* and his colleagues not only acquired a level of power which they could not attain by themselves but were also spared the strict Japanese interference which forced many émigré organizations in Manchuria to fold.

Aside from the authority entrusted to them by the Japanese, another motivation behind the Russian Fascists' collaboration was the expectation that they would be reserved a central role in a supposed anti–Soviet army that was to be recruited from Manchukou's Russian population. This prospect elevated the standing of the Russian Fascists among those in the Diaspora who believed that hostilities between the Soviet Union and Japan were imminent. The NTS made friendly overtures to them and Vonsiatsky, the Connecticut *vozhd*, went a step further by embarking on a pilgrimage to the Far East to coordinate the activities of Russian fascists in the U.S. and Manchuria. Although both were enthused by the prospect of Russian territory being "liberated" by Japanese bayonets, poignant discrepancies in doctrine and their gaping geographical separation inhibited any genuine cooperation.[42]

Ultimately, the Japanese occupation of Manchuria proved disappointing even for collaborators like Rodzaevsky. Although the Japanese did keep their promise to recruit White Russians into a military formation, the number of émigrés placed under arms never came near the powerful army that the *vozhd* envisioned. Moreover, for the time being these men were dispatched to fight *hunghutze* and Chinese warlords, not the Red Army.[43] Equally displeasing for the Russian Fascists was the push by influential Japanese officers to tout Ataman Grigory Semyonov as the commander-in-chief of the projected White Russian army.

Although the Transbaikal ataman was perhaps the best known White Russian leader living in the Far East, his counterrevolutionary career was unremarkable since his failed attempt in 1921 to provide assistance to the operations of Ungern-Sternberg in Outer Mongolia. After leaving Vladivostok that year, he made brief tours of cities in Korea, Japan and China. In early 1922 Semyonov and his current wife decided to head for France by sailing across the Pacific, taking a train across North America and then setting out into the Atlantic. But while traveling through the United States, newspaper correspondents began reporting the presence of the former "Ogre of Chita" in America. By the time he approached the end of his transcontinental journey in New York City, the publicity surrounding him had ignited a firestorm of indignation. American veterans of the Siberian intervention and their supporting groups, reminding the press of Semyonovite attacks on U.S. troops, laid out their case against the Cossack warlord in formal protests and newspaper editorials. Meanwhile, several U.S. companies that had their exports plundered by Semyonovites filed lawsuits against the ataman. In Washington, D.C., a U.S. Senate committee even explored whether new legislation was needed to bar unsavory foreigners, like Semyonov, from entering the country. The legal imbroglio prevented him from continuing his journey towards France and ultimately forced him into hiding. In early June 1922, after three months of uncertainty, Semyonov escaped his legal woes by crossing into Canada and making a beeline westward to board a liner that would carry him across the Pacific, eventually returning to Darien.[44]

Semyonov's bitter experience in the U.S. seems to have discouraged him from further peregrinations. He spent the remainder of his exile in the comfort and security of his Darien villa interrupted by only an occasional excursion to Japan or Harbin. His influence in the emigration was tempered by his distance from Harbin, although he did employ trusted subordinates to represent his interests among the various émigré organizations there, including the Union of the Cossacks in the Far East. He also cooperated closely with Japanese intelligence agencies by providing them with émigré contacts and raw recruits for covert missions into the Soviet Union. These services succeeded in maintaining Semyonov's popularity among certain Japanese army officers, who sought to repay their loyal protégé with the top post in the planned White Russian army. For his part, the ataman never doubted that he was the right man to lead that army. Indeed, he was quick to remind his critics and potential rivals that his title of commander-in-chief of all Russian forces in the Far East had been accorded to him by none other than the Supreme Ruler himself, Admiral Kolchak.

Semyonov remained a controversial figure among Russian émigrés. Transbaikal Cossacks generally continued to admire him as a bold, heroic leader. Still, his stature was not enough to prevent them from staging a brief but intense revolt in Trekrechye against his intrusive Japanese sponsors during August 1935.[45] Other Cossack groups had more mixed views towards him while non–Cossacks frequently despised him as a degenerate or even a traitor. Indeed, the prospect of cooperating with the ataman became a divisive issue between Vonsiatsky and Rodzaevsky which contributed to their parting of ways. The former, a veteran of the Volunteer Army, wanted nothing to do with such a notorious brigand and publicly declared that he should be shot. On the other hand, Rodzaevsky could not afford to aggravate Semyonov since doing so may have jeopardized his party's connections with the Japanese. Subsequently, the Harbin *vozhd* denounced the Connecticut *vozhd* to appease the ataman and, more importantly, his Japanese patrons.[46]

Although Rodzaevsky wanted to avoid antagonizing Semyonov, the relations between the two men and their respective followers, Fascists and Cossacks, were rocky. In the latter 1930s, the Russian Fascist Union, as Rodzaevsky's group was then called, provoked a backlash from Cossack émigrés after it launched a propaganda campaign aimed at youths in Manchurian stanitsas. To quell the unrest, Semyonov led a delegation representing the Union of Cossacks of the Far East to meet with Rodzaevsky and his Fascist henchmen in Harbin. As Japanese officers supervised their lackeys from the sidelines, the conference proceeded cordially. By the time they adjourned, the two groups resolved to work more closely towards their common anticommunist goals. Despite their agreement, lingering differences between the Fascists and Cossacks in Manchuria impeded their future cooperation. This discord was encapsulated in their leaders who, behind their veneer of fellowship, loathed each other. Rodzaevsky detested Semyonov as a failed White leader and had no sympathy for Cossack ethos. Meanwhile, Semyonov considered the *vozhd* as an upstart brainwashed by an ideology that was alien to Russia. Ultimately, it was not any anticommunist solidarity but rather their mutual dependency on the Japanese which compelled them to superficially tolerate each other.[47]

By the eve of the Second World War, both Rodzaevsky and Semyonov were confident that they were about to reap the fruits of their collaboration. Although the Japanese still had not delivered on their earlier promises to organize a sizable army of White Russians in Manchukuo, they had begun enlisting émigrés into the Asano Brigade, named after its Japanese attaché, Colonel Asano Takashi. Émigré leaders expected the brigade to become the nucleus of their long-awaited army.[48] Equally exciting for them were the frequent clashes along Manchukuo's 3,000-mile border with the Soviet Union. The émigré leaders reasoned that it was only a matter of time before one of these incidents escalated into a full-scale conflict that would compel the Japanese to make more extensive use of Manchukuo's White Russian émigrés. In the meantime, both Rodzaevsky and Semyonov, like two attentive canines, eagerly complied with the commands uttered by their Japanese masters. Neither the *vozhd* nor the ataman hesitated to sacrifice the lives of some of their most ardent disciples by placing them at the disposal of Japanese intelligence officers. After a hasty training, the Japanese dispatched the young agents on assignments to carry out reconnaissance and sabotage inside the Soviet Union. The survival rate of these operatives was not good, especially after 1938 when the NKVD took drastic steps to tighten security along its border with Manchukuo.[49] Those who did beat the odds by managing to return fell under the shadow of Japanese counterintelligence officers who suspected that they had been flipped by the NKVD.[50]

In mid–May 1939, an attempt by Japanese forces to wrest a disputed strip of land along the Khalkh River (Khalkhin Gol) from the Mongolian People's Republic sparked an intense border conflict in western Manchukuo. At last, the émigré collaborators believed that their long-awaited war was imminent. After the initial fighting proved indecisive, the Soviet Union began dispatching troops and military aid to its Mongolian satellite while Japan reinforced its ranks with artillery, tanks, warplanes and infantry, including Chinese and White Russian auxiliaries. In July, the Japanese renewed their drive. Despite their additional reinforcements, their progress was difficult in the treeless desert terrain. Their infantry, though skilled and brave, were vulnerable to machine guns and artillery on the open battlefield. Adding to their woes was the inferiority of their hardware: their tanks were slower, their artillery had less range and their fighter planes packed only half the firepower of their Soviet counterparts. By the end of the month, the battered Japanese units suspended their attacks and went on the defensive.

While the Japanese were digging in, the Soviet First Army Group facing them, under the command of General Georgy Zhukov, was gathering its strength to launch a major counteroffensive. By late summer the Soviets had amassed 57,000 soldiers, 542 artillery, 498 tanks and 515 warplanes against their opponents' 38,000 men, 318 guns, 130 tanks and 225 aircraft. In the early morning hours of 20 August, the Soviet forces began a massive bombardment along the 45 mile front while their tank brigades ripped into the Japanese flanks. Within days, the Red onslaught encircled thousands of Japanese soldiers who were eventually killed or taken prisoner. Any White Russians captured alongside the Japanese were shot as traitors, even if they had been born in Manchuria. When news of the military disaster reached Tokyo, the Japanese government, which had not authorized the provocations leading to the battle of Khalkhin Gol, readily agreed to a ceasefire while suppressing any public reports of the defeat.[51] Like the Chinese a decade earlier, the Japanese had drastically underappreciated Soviet military capabilities in the Far East.

The hopes of restless émigré collaborators, which had been soaring to new heights during the previous spring, were thoroughly crushed by the time the Soviets and Japanese brokered a ceasefire on 16 September. The unrecorded number of their countrymen who fell while fighting alongside the Japanese in western Manchukuo was only a small cause of their despair. It was difficult for them to accept the fact that their intelligence networks were discredited for failing to warn the Japanese of the Soviet buildup that summer. At the same time, the influence of their closest patrons in the Japanese army was imperiled by the defeat and humiliation at Khalkhin Gol. The clear superiority which the Red Army demonstrated on that remote battlefield was a powerful rebuke to the recommendations of anticommunist officers that Japan should strike at more important targets in the Soviet Far East. Tokyo, it appeared, would have to redirect its expansionist policies elsewhere. Finally, and most unexpected of all, were the headlines of 23 August 1939 announcing that Japan's partner in the Anti-Comintern Pact, Nazi Germany, had concluded a nonaggression pact with the Soviet Union. Russian émigrés all over the world reacted to this news with indignation and disbelief. It was especially disheartening for the Russian Fascists in Manchukuo, who for the last several years had adorned their uniforms with swastikas in the hope that one day Nazi Germany, along with Japan, might champion their cause. With their faith seemingly misplaced, émigrés began distancing themselves from the Russian Fascist Union, initiating what would prove to be a slow and interminable decline for that organization.[52]

For all Russian émigrés, the events of that summer were irrefutable evidence of their fading significance in international affairs. It was a trend that had been building for some time. In 1935, France and Czechoslovakia, which had harbored and subsidized émigré activities so that they might one day reestablish a friendly national government in Moscow, concluded alliances with the Soviet Union as a counterweight against German rearmament.[53] Now, four years later, Hitler and his cronies brushed aside the adulations they received from sycophant émigrés on their own soil to cut a deal with communist leaders. Meanwhile, the Japanese backed away from further confrontation with the Soviets after their debacle at Khalkhin Gol. Yet, even as the Japanese lost interest in anti–Soviet schemes, they continued to use Russian émigrés whenever it suited their needs. In March 1940, for example, they deployed 3,000 White Russian recruits to central China to fight in a conflict that could hardly be construed with the struggle to liberate their homeland from communism.[54] Clearly, the Japanese regarded Russian émigrés within its domains not as allies but as assets, and expendable ones at that.

Conflicted Loyalties

In the years prior to the Nazi—Soviet nonaggression pact, war between the two ideological foes appeared increasingly likely. Such a scenario, and the Russian Diaspora's appropriate response to it, weighed heavily on the minds of various émigré leaders and groups. The Young Russians, despite their attraction to fascism, came to regard Hitler as a greater evil than Stalin. This view was shared by most left-wing émigrés who abhorred Nazi persecution of political opponents and Jews. Among the most outspoken émigré critics of Nazism was the former Kadet leader Pavel Milyukov. His position was all the more surprising since in 1918 he had urged fellow Whites to adopt a pro–German orientation. But Milyukov was astute enough to realize that Nazi Germany, as far as Russia was concerned, was a much more sinister creature than Hohenzollern Germany.[55] His view that Hitler must be resisted at all costs was echoed by General Denikin in lectures and articles where the former White commander stated that a Nazi conquest of the Soviet Union would only lead to "even greater enslavement" for their homeland.[56] Thus, advocates of a "defensist" stance—meaning that the emigration should support the Soviets in a war of defense against any rapacious invader—encompassed a diverse assortment of émigrés.

In contrast, those émigrés who were open to some form of collaboration with Hitler in the event of a Nazi—Soviet war almost invariably held right-wing political views. Some, like the aforementioned Russian National Labor Movement (ROND), readily embraced fascist ideology while others, such as the NTS and ultra-monarchists, sympathized with the Nazis' anti-democratic and anti–Marxist program.[57] Among Russian minorities, there were a number of groups and committees, like the Cossack National Center, eager to insert their people's acquisition of statehood into Hitler's blueprints for the dismantling of the Soviet Union.

While émigré politicians, journalists and other public figures spilled considerable ink over the question of which side the Russian Diaspora should support if hostilities broke out between Berlin and Moscow, the majority of ordinary émigrés, including Cossacks, gave little thought to the matter. As with politics, they were too preoccupied with their daily grind—whether that meant long shifts in a factory assembly line, hours spent behind the wheel of a taxi cab, or back-breaking work in a field—to concern themselves with international affairs. But what they may have regarded as a hypothetical exercise soon became very real dilemma; although not in the precise form which émigré leaders had anticipated.

Rather than having to choose whether to support the oppressor of their homeland or Nazi ambitions, the émigrés instead were faced with the question of whether to back their host country against Hitler's Germany.

The Nazi—Soviet nonaggression pact signed in late August of 1939 was a devastating blow for those émigrés who had bet on Hitler as their best chance against Stalin. Baydalakov, writing in the NTS's official organ, lamented, "Hopes of foreign support have failed to materialize; now as before the foreigners think only of themselves."[58] On 1 September, while the NTS leader and his followers were wrestling with their feelings of abandonment, German panzers surged forward into Poland and provoked France and Great Britain into declaring war two days later. The Second World War was underway in Europe, but events were not unfolding as the émigrés had long imagined it.

In France, authorities tended to be suspicious of émigré loyalties now that Moscow was essentially complicit in Nazi aggression. Some émigrés were even detained as enemy aliens in the early weeks of the war. Despite such treatment, many émigrés sought to prove their fealty to their host country by rallying behind the French war effort. By the time the Wehrmacht subdued the country in June 1940, approximately 10,000 Russian émigrés were serving in the French army.[59]

Another victim of Hitler's aggression, Yugoslavia, also received an outpouring of support from its Russian émigré community when it was invaded during the following year, in April 1941. But the short window separating the overthrow of the pro-German government in Belgrade on 27 March, which made hostilities inevitable, and the surrender of the Yugoslav army just three weeks later limited émigré participation in that conflict mainly to those already enlisted in the country's military. Like their brethren in France, most émigrés serving in the Yugoslav army were confined to POW camps though some were later released.[60]

The great struggle in Eastern Europe which so many émigrés had anticipated did not get underway until 22 June 1941, when over 3,650,000 Axis troops attacked eastward along a front stretching from the Black Sea to the Arctic Ocean.[61] News of this campaign had the immediate effect of partially redeeming the Nazis in the eyes of collaborators and former admirers who had felt let down by the Nazi—Soviet pact nearly two years earlier; including followers of the NTS. Although it officially opposed Nazism, the NTS continued to serve and cooperate with the Germans in the belief that there was no other realistic alternative to overthrowing Stalin.[62] In contrast, ROVS followed the example set by Denikin a generation earlier by refusing to have any dealings with the German invaders of their homeland. As a result of their differences on this issue, the long partnership between the NTS and ROVS was terminated and the two groups went their separate ways.[63] At this stage, Cossack émigrés by and large appeared to share ROVS's sentiments. Overcome by a sense of Russian patriotism, many Cossack émigré organizations adopted a defensist position towards the war raging in Eastern Europe.[64]

Cossack émigrés who found themselves in German-occupied lands were initially attracted to the resistance groups taking shape in them. They were soon disillusioned, however, by the prevalence of communist influences in the underground factions. This was especially true for those in occupied-Yugoslavia. Throughout the interwar period, the Belgrade government's ban on the Communist Party had made its members experts in clandestine activity. During the war, this experience gave the communists an edge over rival resistance groups also attempting to harry the enemy and win the loyalties of South Slavs.[65] Alarmed by the appearance of the Red menace in their adopted homeland, significant numbers of Cossack and Russian émigrés eventually collaborated with the Germans; a decision which they justified with the logic that "the enemy of my enemy is my ally."[66] By September 1941, the Germans were able to recruit a sufficient number of volunteers from Russian émigrés in Serbia to form three armed regiments to protect factories, mines and other enterprises valuable to the Nazi war effort. A major incentive for joining this unit, eventually known as the Russian Protective Corps, was the promise that its members would be granted land in Russia after the war.[67] Later in the conflict, Cossack émigrés who had been residing in Yugoslavia, many of them graduates of the Russian cadet schools that had been established there, would enlist as officers in the German-sponsored Cossack cavalry division.[68]

While some Cossack and Russian émigrés eventually collaborated with Nazi Germany to defend their host countries or Europe in general against the spread of communism, others had no qualms against supporting a war of naked aggression against the Soviet Union. They did so in the belief that such a conflict would be welcomed by the majority of their compatriots in the homeland. Certainly, they predicted, Soviet citizens would never make great sacrifices to defend the oppressive and godless institutions which governed them. They fervently believed that the moment Stalin put arms in the hands of peasant recruits, the people would turn on him and the party. Although such an uprising failed to materialize during the Red Army's operations in eastern Poland, the Baltic States and Finland during 1939, the émigré collaborators remained convinced that a determined push from the outside would be enough to stir the downtrodden population to resistance.[69] The massive German attack in the summer of 1941 certainly qualified as that "push" but the Soviet population, contrary to émigré expectations, did not use the crisis to rid themselves of the Bolshevik yoke. Gradually, the émigrés—though they were loath to admit it—realized that they lacked a genuine understanding of the mentality of their compatriots who had endured a generation under communist rule. This fact even became apparent to ordinary Germans who had been heartened by newspaper articles, written by émigré "experts," predicting the imminent collapse of the Soviet Union at the outset of the invasion. "Not only is the White Russian ignorant of the Russia today, but he even tends to paint a wholly imaginary picture of it, born of his own wishful thinking," complained a Waffen-SS corporal.[70] Thus, before we continue with our survey of the anticommunist movement among Cossacks during the Second World War, we must step back and examine the ordeal of those who remained behind in the steppe following the collapse of the White movement in the early 1920s. It is at that point that the experiences of the two groups—the Cossacks who went abroad and those who stayed in the homeland—diverged on two very different courses. Ultimately, their dissimilar experiences would have significant repercussions when they regained contact amid the hellish backdrop of the conflict that raged across Eastern Europe from 1941 to 1945.

12

Repression

Red Spring

The arrival of spring in 1920 was bittersweet for the Cossacks who did not flee with the retreating White armies. The prospect of peace and onset of warmer weather brought them relief from the ravages of war and the winter season; but as the snowcover receded it exposed the remains of refugees, soldiers and horses that had perished in the previous months. Reminders of the recent turmoil appeared everywhere; in the rivers, corpses dumped in them by Red and White execution squads churned amid the thawing ice.[1] The landscape bore the scars of damaged property and infrastructure: depot walls pockmarked with bullet holes, villages reduced to charred remnants and flimsy wooden bridges standing in the place of dynamited steel structures. In some areas, the stanitsas and villages had been stripped of carts, draft animals and food by the fleeing Whites. The Red units which followed in their wake were hardly less forgiving. Regardless of whether they were retiring or advancing, soldiers from both sides, concerned with only their own progress, pillaged from the countryside with no thought to the needs of the local population.[2]

When the victorious Red troops swept through the Cossack lands of South Russia late that winter, they found some stanitsas nearly deserted after entire communities, fearing the reimplementation of the genocidal operations practiced by Soviet security organs a year earlier, had left with the White armies. In other stanitsas only women, children and the elderly were left behind. For all stanitsas, their most significant losses were in young men who had been drafted into military service and were either killed in battle or retreated with their regiments into exile. Some Cossack soldiers did desert to the Red Army in a last-ditch effort to earn redemption from the victorious Bolsheviks. According to Eduard Dune, a commissar with the Ninth Red Army in the Kuban region, many of these Cossacks eagerly embraced communist doctrine after leaving the AFSR. "The 'whiter' their soul, the redder they now wanted to become," he observed.[3] He was far from the only one in the Red Army who was fascinated by the conversion of so many Cossack warriors. Indeed, Soviet correspondent Isaak Babel was bewildered by the preponderance of former anticommunist Cossacks now fighting under Budyonny. "This isn't a Marxist revolution, it's a Cossack rebellion," wrote Babel of the First Cavalry Army's advance against the Poles in Galicia.[4] For those Red Cossacks serving under Budyonny or Mironov, many battles still awaited them that year against Poland and Wrangel's army. This continued fighting, combined with previous losses from war, epidemics and emigration, would leave many stanitsas with a steep gender imbalance after the civil war.[5] With the loss of so many adult male laborers, their recovery was made immeasurably more difficult.

With most Cossack communities experiencing shortages of just about everything from labor to food to horses, the casual observer would have been justified to dismiss the hosts as a serious threat to Soviet regime. Moscow, however, was taking no chances. In late February 1920, just as the White forces in South Russia entered their last convulsions, the "First All-Russian Conference of Toiling Cossacks" convened in the Soviet capital. The decisions made at this conference were to set the tone for the Cossacks' future under the victorious regime. Speaking to the assembly, Bolshevik leaders like Mikhail Kalinin made it clear that their party no longer felt bound by their past promises or proposals for Cossack autonomy in the Soviet state. Instead, the Cossacks were to be regarded as "an indivisible part of the Russian people."[6] Taking the cue from party leaders, the Cossack delegates subsequently passed resolutions disavowing the formation of any separate Cossack administration or soviet republic. During the following month, the Soviet government confirmed these decisions in a decree which largely reiterated the earlier statute from December 1917 that had abolished the Cossacks as an estate. The Cossack people were slated to become indistinguishable subjects of Soviet Russia.[7]

One consequence of these decisions was the loss of the Cossacks' territorial autonomy, which enabled Russia's new masters to redraw the administrative frontiers of the borderlands. They embarked on this task with two goals in mind. The first was to deprive the Cossacks of the focal point for their local patriotism. Bolshevik leaders wanted the Cossacks to abandon their fealty to the Don, the Ural and other regions and instead view themselves as members of a greater Soviet polity. The second objective of the reorganization of the borderlands was to defuse the ferment among various ethnic groups in these territories. During the civil war, Lenin and his cronies had learned to tame the separatist ambitions of nationalities by promising them some form of autonomy—even though such concessions bucked their Marxist instincts towards centralization. Eventually, Soviet leaders settled on a formula that gave their state the appearance of a federation of autonomous regions and republics governed by the highly-centralized Communist Party, meaning that they would remain under the *de facto* control of Moscow. New autonomous regions and republics, then, were formed in the borderlands bearing the names of the peoples that the Cossacks had once suppressed. For example, several autonomous Circassian regions were carved out the territory that had belonged to the Kuban Host. The Terek was eventually broken up into autonomous regions for the Chechens—Ingush, North Ossetians and Kabardans. The Ural and Orenburg lands were split among the autonomous Bashkir and Kazakh soviet republics. The Semirechye stanitsas were absorbed into the Turkestan Autonomous Socialist Soviet Republic. Those former Cossack lands without a substantial ethnic minority, such as the heartlands of the Don and Kuban Hosts, were simply divided up among existing provinces or arranged into new ones.[8]

Officially, the Cossacks' displacement on administrative maps was not be equated with their physical extermination or removal. The Communist leadership, not wanting a repetition of the ferocious insurgencies which had been ignited by de-Cossackization policies a year earlier, authorized their local party organs to persecute only the implacable class-enemies among Cossacks. By restricting their reprisals to prosperous or *"kulak"* Cossacks, they wished to avoid provoking resistance from the middle and poorer elements in the stanitsas.[9] It was essentially the same approach which the party was using throughout rural Russia to obtain a foothold in the villages. By mollifying the greater part of the rural population, the Soviet leaders sought to end the ongoing conflict between the party and peasants which had raged in background of the war between the Reds and Whites. Most of all, they wanted the rural economy to recover its productivity to help alleviate Russia's ongoing food crisis. This was a high priority for the Don and Kuban regions, which had been among the country's leading agricultural regions prior to 1914.

Moscow's rather conciliatory approach towards ordinary Cossacks was not popular among certain regional and local Communist officials in the borderlands. As a result of the Cossacks' outsized role in the White movement, the stereotype that Cossacks were monolithic counterrevolutionaries persisted among a number of party activists and functionaries. Such prejudices, along with the wide interpretations as to what exactly constituted a *kulak*, meant that many Cossacks were inevitably victimized by Soviet security organs and administrators.[10] The reprisals usually began when Cheka squads, following on the heels of the Red Army vanguard, arrived in an occupied stanitsa to hunt down any Cossack "White Guardists" hiding in the community or the nearby countryside. To safeguard their personnel, the Cheka frequently took local women hostage to deter their husbands or sons from taking up arms or joining partisan detachments. In some former hotbeds of resistance, punitive troikas were established to pass death sentences upon Cossacks suspected of service in the White armies. Any widows and young children whom the executed Cossacks left behind were often quarantined in hastily-assembled camps where the inmates languished from hunger, exposure and sexual assaults.[11]

The Cossacks which suffered the most in the early years of Bolshevik rule were those of the Terek. In the mountainous terrain of that former host, as well as in neighboring Dagestan, the Soviets struggled for years to quash the rebellions and inter-ethnic conflict which raged among the various Mountain Peoples. One solution, promulgated by Stalin, then Commissar of Nationalities, was to reassemble the territory's crazy patchwork of ethnicities into more homogenous segments. The biggest losers of this plan for segregation and resettlement were the region's Cossacks, especially those residing in what had been the eastern valleys of the Terek. Many of them were dispossessed of their land, livestock and homes so these could be handed over to the Chechens and Ingush as repayment for their support during the civil war. In some areas, entire Cossack stanitsas were deported so that the only remaining ethnic Russians were those living in nearby cities or working in oilfields.[12]

The extent to which Cossacks were persecuted in 1920 and subsequent years has been a subject of debate among historians. While some have accepted the contention of Cossack émigrés that the mass terror unleashed against the stanitsas in early 1919 was continued more surreptitiously in subsequent years,[13] others have declared such allegations to be overblown. According to the latter, after 1919 the regime only punished Cossacks for what they did and not because of who they were. In other words, Soviet security organs targeted them for suspected involvement with the White or rebel movements, not for being Cossacks.[14] Likewise, the wholesale eviction of Terek Cossacks from their homelands had less to do with their identity than with their perceived association with Russian imperialism.[15] Still, such assertions do not rule out the possibility that many Communists, particularly those on the lower rungs of the party hierarchy, regarded a Cossack and an "enemy of the people" as one of the same.

Local Cheka chiefs and party workers, some of whom presided over the terror-campaigns against Cossacks a year earlier, were only one source of the tyranny in the former hosts. Food-requisitioning detachments also reappeared as they combed the countryside for hidden stores of grain. Officially these contingents were supposed to confiscate only surplus food items, but they rarely heeded this restriction since if they had done so they never would have come close to meeting the appropriation quotas set by the Food Supply Commissariat in Moscow. Subsequently, they seized any and all grain regardless of whether the owners were Cossacks or peasants, wealthy or poor, or even if the grain was required for future sowing.[16] But now that the civil war practically over, it dawned on the rural population that these confiscations were not an exigency measure in the life and death struggle against the Whites but rather a permanent system favored by the Soviet government in its drive to socialize the national economy.[17] With their grain reserves depleted, and taking heed of the omens which foreshadowed an abnormally dry growing season, the Cossack and peasant farmers had reached the limit of their endurance.[18] It was under these circumstances that the very uprisings which Lenin hoped to avoid burst forth throughout the North Caucasus in the spring of 1920. Even the Chechens, who had cooperated with the Bolsheviks during most of the civil war, found Soviet rule intolerable enough to raise the banner of rebellion that May.[19] In the former lands of the Don and Kuban Hosts, disgruntled Cossacks joined neighboring communities of peasants and outlanders to ambush food-requisitioning detachments or Cheka squads. Unlike in the past, the insurgency did not assume an explicitly Cossack dimension and continued to transcend sociological boundaries throughout its duration.[20] Moreover, the unrest was by no means confined to Cossack territories. In the Urals, peasants who had sniped at Kolchak's soldiers a few months earlier now turned their rifles against Bolsheviks.[21] Later, in August 1920, a new wave of intense peasant uprisings broke out just north of the Don region in Tambov Province.[22]

Although the insurgents in the former Cossack hosts fought with a fanaticism born of desperation, their efforts never acquired the significance of the anti–Bolshevik rebellions staged in previous years. The simplest explanation for this was the uprisings generally lacked any coordination. The White generals and officers who in the past provided a central command for anti–Soviet campaigns in South Russia had been expelled from most of the region.[23] Although Wrangel's army was still in the nearby Crimea for most of 1920, he was, as we have seen, unable to spare adequate numbers of men from his northern front to make contact with the main insurgent groups holding out in the Caucasian foothills.[24] In most cases, the extant anti–Bolshevik armies would not have been well-received in the tumultuous countryside of the Don, Kuban or anywhere else in Russia since the partisans, despite being anticommunist, were far from turning pro–White.

The resistance in the Don and Kuban, despite its operational deficiencies, persisted into early 1921 as the food-requisitioning detachments continued their efforts to squeeze the last kernels of grain from peasant and Cossack communities. Despite reports that peasants continued to play a prominent, if not the leading, role in the unrest,[25] a cloud of suspicion still lingered over the Cossacks, at least as far as local party organs were concerned. Even Cossacks who had heroically served the Bolsheviks were not trusted. In February 1921, Filip Mironov, the former commander of the Soviet Second Cavalry Army, was arrested in the northern Don on the charge that he was plotting a rebellion there. After being taken into custody, the famous Red Cossack leader was sent to Moscow and imprisoned at the Cheka's headquarters in the Lubyanka Building. A few weeks later, he was shot dead by a guard. Although the treason charges brought against Mironov were bogus, he was not given a posthumous rehabilitation until nearly four decades later, in 1960.[26]

For all its brutality, the resistance in the Cossack homelands was mild in comparison to the insurgencies raging elsewhere in Russia. In Western Siberia, a SR-led revolt that began in January 1921 spanned across several provinces, interrupted traffic on the Trans-Siberian Railway and attracted the support of anywhere from 55,000 to 100,000 peasant-insurgents.[27] Meanwhile, guerrilla bands in Tambov Province comprised of peasants and Red Army deserters continued to evade and frustrate the Soviet forces sent to crush them.[28] Even the sailors stationed at Kronstadt naval base, who had rallied to the Bolsheviks' defense during some of party's most desperate moments, turned against Russia's new masters in March 1921.[29] The uprising in Kronstadt, so near to the cradle of revolution in Petrograd, was a major embarrassment for Lenin and his cohorts, not least because it coincided with the sessions of the Tenth Congress of the Russian Communist Party in Moscow.

Confronted with nationwide unrest, the delegates at that party congress could not avoid the reality that their efforts to socialize the national economy were causing the country to spiral out of control. Lenin's answer to salvage the situation was to make a tactical retreat on the economic front while pushing ahead on the political one. The result was the New Economic Policy (NEP), approved by the Tenth Party Congress on 15 March, which effectively ended the hated system known as war communism. The NEP was essentially a moderation of the Bolsheviks' economic policy by allowing for the partial restoration of capitalism in the form of small, privately-owned enterprises. In the countryside, it ended the drive to force the peasants into collective farms as well as the practice of arbitrary grain requisitioning. Instead, the peasants were to turnover a fixed amount of grain, produce or other foodstuffs to the government as a tax. Furthermore, to encourage the peasants to optimize agricultural production, they were allowed to sell any post-tax surplus on the free market.

The party's appeasement of the disaffected population through the NEP had its intended effect. As news of the reform spread throughout the Soviet countryside, the war-weary peasants and Cossacks, by and large, accepted its terms and turned their backs on the insurgencies. Deprived of support from the villages, the most resolute partisans were left to face the wrath of the Red Army and Cheka detachments alone. A similar ignominious fate befell remnant rival political parties, particularly the SRs, as the communists consolidated their total political domination over the country. In the meantime, the placated peasants and Cossack farmers returned to cultivating their allotments, which in some instances were larger than those prior to the revolution thanks to attrition and the appropriation of lands formerly belonging to the upper classes and *kulaks*. Fields that were left fallow in recent years were again turned over by plows. No longer harassed by roving food-requisitioning detachments and permitted to market their surplus commodities, the peasants and Cossacks finally had an incentive to grow more than their families could eat.[30]

Still, the production deficits wrought by years of civil war and economic dislocation could not be restored overnight. This was especially true in the devastated homeland of the Don Cossacks. In 1920, the number of acres under cultivation in that region was less than half of the area sowed in 1916.[31] Some of this reduction in agriculture was due to war communism: farmers were unwilling to grow more grain only to watch it be seized from them without any compensation. In other cases, fields were left idle since their new holders, the poor peasants and outlanders who benefited the most from land redistribution, lacked the animals and implements needed to till the soil.[32] In the areas that were particularly hard-hit by promiscuous requisitioning, the farming operations of all peasants and Cossacks suffered from shortages of draft animals, machinery and even seed grain. The harvest outlook for that year was made even worse by the onset of a drought which led to crop failures in two northern Don districts and reduced yields in others. The grain quotas set by the Food Supply Commissariat, however, remained unchanged.

Despite the abolition of arbitrary grain-requisitioning under the NEP in spring of 1921, the food supply situation in the Cossack homelands in the southeastern part of European Russia continued to deteriorate over the following months. In the Don, the number of acres sowed that year actually fell from 1920 due to the depleted stocks of seed grain.³³ The dry spell from the previous year did not abate and impacted a wider area. Neither winter nor spring brought precipitation to replenish the inadequate soil moisture, and by summer the river levels, including that of the mighty Volga, were sinking to their lowest in memory.³⁴ These conditions produced a grain harvest that was almost half of the country's average grain output in the years prior to World War I.³⁵ While devastating droughts and crop failures were not unknown to Russia, the dismal yields in 1921 were made immeasurably worse by years of incessant plundering and declining harvests under war communism which left no adequate grain reserves anywhere in the country.³⁶ By that summer, a famine was underway in some of its most fertile regions, from the left-bank of the Dnieper eastward to Orenburg and as far north as Perm. The crisis was most acute in the lower Volga and southern Urals, an area that included the cities of Astrakhan, Tsaritsyn, Kazan, Ufa and Orenburg. Starving peasants, unable to find anything to eat in the villages, began to converge on these centers to seek meals from Soviet-sponsored public kitchens.³⁷ Many found no relief and succumbed to malnutrition or diseases which they were unable to resist amid their weakened state. They fell in such numbers that the authorities struggled to keep up with removal of the victims' emaciated bodies from the streets and sidewalks. "A human corpse on the streets of Kazan became a familiar appearance and it no longer frightened any one," claimed a Volga Tatar who fled abroad later that year. "We stepped over them without minding it."³⁸

Conditions were no better for those who stayed behind in the villages. Famished peasants resorted to boiling grasses, wild roots and tree bark into stews. Others tried to bake bread from acorns, weeds and clay. Livestock, including horses, were slaughtered due to a lack of fodder and for human consumption, but this practice had the serious drawback of leaving many families without draft animals for the next season's fieldwork. Any strangers who came seeking food were driven away—the last thing the peasants wanted was another mouth to feed. In some locales there were rumors of cannibalism. Meanwhile, parents unable to provide for their children abandoned them in cities or at train stations in the desperate hope that they would have better luck as beggars.³⁹

The initial response of the Soviet government to the unfolding humanitarian crisis was to officially deny that any catastrophe was taking place within its borders. Only in late June did *Pravda*, the Communist Party's official newspaper, admit that twenty-five million Soviet citizens faced the prospect of starvation. Another month passed before the regime appealed for outside aid, and even then it was done only through intermediaries. Finally, on 20 August, the Soviet Assistant Commissar of Foreign Affairs, Maksim Litvinov, signed the Riga Agreement to allow the American Relief Administration (ARA), led by Herbert Hoover, to import and distribute food within famine-stricken areas of Soviet Russia. A year later, at the peak of the ARA's relief operations, the organization was feeding well over ten million Soviet citizens a day. Not to be overlooked was another two million persons whose daily nutritional needs were being covered by other charitable organizations. The relief effort was carried out with the goal of not only assisting the population with its present needs but also enabling them to provide for themselves as soon as conditions improved. Hence the ARA, instead of focusing its feeding programs in the provincial cities, as the Soviet government had done, extended its food distribution into rural areas so the peasants could return to their villages and sow a new crop. While the ARA's massive undertaking spared countless of Soviet citizens from further malnourishment and death, as many as five million persons still lost their lives in the famine of 1921–22.⁴⁰ Even though the situation remained critical into 1923, the Soviet regime began exporting grain gathered during the previous autumn to obtain desperately needed foreign currency. Amid these circumstances, the ARA was compelled to suspend its feeding programs—no one was willing to contribute money towards Russian famine relief when the country's government was shipping its own grain abroad.[41]

The improving situation after late 1922 was made possible through more favorable weather and the government's efforts to restock the depleted horse herds in southeastern Russia with equine imported from Siberia and Central Asia.[42] The new policies enacted by the regime also played a part: the NEP began to revive the moribund economy and encouraged farmers to maximize their agricultural production. The recovery continued in the following years as peasants improved their crop rotation systems, sowed better seed and acquired more draft animals. The persecution of *kulaks*, who were generally the most efficient peasants, was scaled back and amnesties were granted to peasants and Cossacks who served in the White armies or rebel detachments. According to Soviet historians, the country's average annual grain production finally caught up to and then surpassed prewar levels in the mid-1920s.[43] This recovery, however, was not felt in all regions—the grain harvests in Ukraine and the North Caucasus still lagged behind their prewar output.[44] Still, after surviving the horrors of revolution, civil war and famine, the general improvement in conditions gave Cossack and peasant alike sufficient reason for optimism.

Collectivization: The Final Reckoning

From the mid-1920s until the final years of the decade, the Cossack homelands enjoyed a period of relative serenity, stability and prosperity under the relaxed conditions of the NEP. As brigandage all but disappeared, farmers could venture into their fields unarmed. They only had to worry about an occasional hailstorm, and not hordes of cavalry, devastating their crops. Herders could raise livestock without fear that their beasts would be taken from them by a food-requisitioning detachment. Social antagonisms subsided as Bolshevik propaganda tempered its reproaches against Cossack and *kulak* "class enemies." The countryside, it seemed, was settling into its normal way of life.

The revolutionary upheaval, to be sure, had left its mark in the stanitsas. First of all, the economic recovery was slow: it took time for herds to be replenished, railways to be repaired and trade to revive after years of devastation and chaos. Cossacks and peasants, ever distrustful of the urbane Bolsheviks, also needed time to be convinced that the ruling party would uphold the promises of the NEP by allowing them to reap the fruits of their labor.[45] In the cultural sphere, Cossack folk dress once worn with pride became a less familiar sight in the stanitsas. Although donning such wear was not outlawed by the Soviet government, it appears to have been discouraged or mostly abandoned—perhaps because it invited unwanted scrutiny from local party organs. The performance of Cossack folk songs, dances and the *dzhigitovka* was accorded similar treatment.[46] The near-absence of these cultural expressions was noticeable to visitors aware of the steppe's Cossack past. "Something had erased every visible mark of the once picturesque, valiant, ruthless military caste," recalled correspondent Maurice Hindus of his 1926 tour of the Kuban. "Nearly five centuries of history and battle, conquest and triumph, had, to all outward appearances, gone up in smoke. Only the ancient names of villages remained."[47]

For Cossack and peasant alike, the most palpable change brought by the revolution was in land use. In the Cossack regions, lands once guaranteed to the hosts in perpetuity by the tsars were—along with the rest of the land in Russia—nationalized by the Bolsheviks and put at the disposal of those who worked it. Most of the land, including the fields once privately held by individual Cossacks and peasants, was incorporated into new or reorganized communes. The communes, in turn, divided it into equitable allotments among their members. Throughout the early 1920s, the People's Commissariat of Agriculture struggled to promote the orderly repartition of land among Cossack stanitsas, peasant villages, and native *aouls*. The repartitions were concerned not only with the amount of land held by each commune, but also its suitability for cropping or grazing.[48] Since Cossack communities traditionally controlled the largest parcels and most fertile soils in the regions, it may be surmised that they were the biggest losers in the land reorganizations. It has been already been mentioned how entire stanitsas of Terek Cossacks were uprooted after the civil war to make way for Chechen and Ingush clans previously restricted to the barren mountain slopes.[49] From the Kuban to Siberia, land was transferred from Cossack control to that of less privileged peasants or natives in a similar, albeit less dramatic, manner. Despite the loss of these lands, the rural Cossack economy as a whole was not grievously injured. Indeed, the acquisition of land once controlled by the Cossack elite, along with the reduced competition through either the deaths or flights of hundreds of thousands of Cossack males during the civil war, helped to offset the stanitsas' losses in property. Most of all, the Cossacks were unburdened from the military obligations which had required their young men to spend long periods away from the fields. These factors, combined with the limited capitalism allowed by the NEP, enabled many Cossack economies to flourish at a local level.

The reorganization of land into communes hardly different from those which had existed prior to 1917 was wanted by neither the peasantry nor the Communist Party. The majority of the former would have liked to consolidate their fields into individual holdings which were legal under the Land Code of 1922. The enclosed holdings had many advantages over communes: the consolidation of fields reduced the time the peasants spent walking between their scattered strips, it obliterated the common problems of narrow strips and it gave the peasant farmers the freedom to make their own management decisions regarding tillage, crop rotation and grazing. Subsequently, the enclosed smallholders tended to consist of the more enterprising and better-off Cossacks and peasants. Virtually all farmers, including those categorized as poor, aspired to break away from the communes and consolidate their shares of the land.[50] Only their limited means, and the high taxes imposed by the regime for forming enclosed holdings, prevented most from doing so.[51] According to Soviet historians, at the beginning of 1927 less than 5 percent of land in the Russian Soviet Federative Socialist Republic fell into the category of enclosed holdings. In the former Cossack strongholds of the North Caucasus Territory, that number was even lower. In both that region and the country at large, communes controlled approximately 95 percent of the arable lands.[52]

The consolidation of land into enclosed homesteads was anathema to the party since it encouraged individualism, decentralization and the development of a prosperous stratum of peasants. In effect, it appeared to strengthen the mindset and class enemies that were inherently hostile to communism. At the same time, the party tended to view the communes as an inefficient anachronism. Their solution to the agrarian problem was to transition to a system of centralization and, eventually, mechanization. Their idea of centralization sought to transpose the consolidation of workers in factories onto peasants and farms. Everything from fields and farms to livestock and tools were to be combined into a larger, theoretically more-efficient unit: the collective farm. The peasants were to be transformed into a rural proletariat. Their bosses, the collective farm managers, would be politically-reliable functionaries who would foster their charges' sense of duty towards the state. Ideally, collectivization would not only dominate the peasants' economy but also their political, social and even cultural activities.

The other primary goal for collectivization, the desire for increased mechanization in agriculture, was sensible enough though difficult to achieve given the limitations of Russia's industrial output and its foreign trade at the time.[53] Indeed, as much as zealous party activists would have liked to impose widespread collectivization after the civil war, the more sober officials in the People's Commissariat of Agriculture recognized that the regime lacked the strength, money and goods to embark on such a drastic reform. Instead, organizations overseeing land reorganization were advised to focus their limited resources on discouraging the establishment of enclosed peasant holdings.[54] Collective farms, then, remained an uncommon fixture in the Soviet countryside; as late as 1928, less than one out of every fifty peasant households belonged to a collective farm.[55] Still, throughout the 1920s party leaders remained devoted to the need to collectivize agriculture, even to the point that they quickly quashed any internal debate on that topic.[56]

The economic recovery and preponderance of the commune in the mid-1920s came to an abrupt end in the twilight of the decade as the party ramped up its efforts to complete the transition to socialist agriculture and effectively annul the armistice with the peasantry that was the NEP. The move towards mass collectivization began in early 1928 after the Soviet Union experienced a shortfall in marketable grain despite several successive good harvests.[57] For the party, there was only one explanation for this anomaly: the devious internal enemy, the *kulak*, had organized a "grain strike" against the regime. Soviet leaders refused to consider the possibility that the shortage could have apolitical origins, such as the artificially-low grain prices which encouraged the peasants to withhold their grain or divert it to more lucrative endeavors, such as the fattening of livestock or the distillation of moonshine.[58] Therefore, instead of addressing its manipulation of the markets, Politburo enacted "extraordinary measures" to forcibly take the peasants' grain. This action achieved immediate success as procurement agents quickly seized more than enough grain to compensate for the grain deficit. However, the long-term repercussions of the measure were nothing short of disastrous. The temporary suspension of the grain market and confiscations had a demoralizing effect on the peasants as they could no longer be certain whether they would receive any payment for their surplus produce. As a result, their overall productivity declined as they planted less or downsized their herds, activities which again resulted in tightened grain supplies before the year was out.[59] In the meantime, a new law was instated throughout the Soviet Union demanding that further land reorganization was to explicitly favor the poor peasants and the formation of collective farms, the latter of which were to be granted the most desirable lands.[60]

When the spring of 1929 brought a renewal of the grain crisis, the party again authorized the arbitrary procurement of foodstuffs. The new round of confiscations was accompanied by an escalating campaign of "dekulakization."[61] In fact, "dekulakization" was a guise to conceal the regime's real intention: to wipe out the peasantry in its traditional form and eradicate those cultures which appeared too rustic and incompatible with the modern Soviet state, a category which included Ukrainian, nomadic and vestigial Cossack societies. Subsequently, local officials and party activists did not restrict their campaign of intimidation and terror to homesteading or wealthy peasants who were typically branded as *kulaks*. Instead, they attempted to coerce entire communities—regardless of their members' socioeconomic status—into establishing and joining collective farms. The North Caucasus Territory Committee, which oversaw many of the lands that had encompassed the Don,

Kuban and Terek hosts, aspired to lead the way by transforming the former homelands of the Cossack counterrevolutionaries into utopias of collective farms that would serve as models for the rest of the country.[62] As a result of its frenzied efforts, by October 1929 the North Caucasus Territory Committee was able to claim that nearly one in five peasant households in its region had been collectivized at a time when the figure for the rest of the Soviet Union stood at less than one in ten. Six months later, almost four-fifths of all rural households in the North Caucasus Territory belonged to a collective farm, still well ahead of the national figure which stood at slightly under three-fifths.[63]

As one might expect, the reorganization of so much land and property within the brief span during the winter of 1929–30 led to considerable disorganization, confusion and wastage. As a result, Moscow backed off its drive toward wholesale collectivization during the spring of 1930, causing droves of rural households to quit the collectives before fieldwork was underway. This slackening, however, proved only temporary.[64] In the meantime, both Cossacks and peasants adopted various forms of resistance against the measures. Some illegally sold their caches of grain or buried it in nearby woods. Others butchered most of their livestock in order to sell or store the meat. Their reasons for engaging in such activities varied from wanting to avoid the confiscation of their assets to evading persecution as *kulaks*.[65] Regardless of the precise motives, the slaughter of livestock was so widespread that between 1929 and 1933 the number of horses in the Soviet Union plummeted by 51 percent, beef cattle by 43 percent, sheep and goats by 65 percent and swine by 42 percent.[66] The staggering losses of horses and cattle were especially debilitating since the country did not have nearly enough tractors to replace draft animals in the fields.[67] The shortage of draft animals and tractors became one the many impediments of collectivization. Peasant antipathy, unrealistic expectations and the ignorance of collective farm managers whose only qualification for that post was their party membership all added to the malaise. Rather than accept the "second serfdom" of the collectives,[68] some Cossacks and peasants, particularly those in the fertile lands of Ukraine and the North Caucasus, tried to boycott the system by ostracizing or even terrorizing any locals who cooperated with local party organs.[69] These staunch holdouts, however, risked being shunned themselves if the greater part of the community caved into the pressure to enlist in the collectives.[70]

In at least a few instances, Cossacks and peasants resorted to more than just passive resistance against the drive towards mass collectivization. Riots broke out in villages as their angry inhabitants attempted to block grain requisitioning activities or release arrested *kulaks*. Some disorders snowballed into localized rebellions, such as in the southeastern Don where an insurrection in February 1930 blazed across the countryside for a week before it was finally extinguished by Red Army brigades. Other "mass demonstrations," as Communist officials termed them, flared up throughout the North Caucasus Territory and nearby autonomous republics. Several were fully suppressed only after cavalry, armored cars and even warplanes were sent against them. The party attributed these incidents to underground *kulak* and former White Guard organizations, but in reality much of the resistance, especially in the early stages, appears to have been fomented by peasant women. Although Soviet authorities tended to treat women demonstrators more lightly than their male counterparts, all participants in these disorders risked punishments ranging from summary execution to deportation.[71] Those given the latter sentence were not necessarily luckier as they faced years of misery as exiles or prisoners in the OGPU hard labor camps that developed into the Main Administration of Corrective Labor Camps and Labor Settlements; better known by its Russian acronym as Gulag. Regardless of whether they were sent to concentration camps or "special settlements," the inmates and exiles were utilized as an expendable workforce to help the Soviet Union reach its ambitious goals for industrialization and modernization. Some prisoners wound up in the far north where they were used to unlock the oil and mineral wealth trapped in the arctic tundra. Others were sent to logging camps in the Siberian taiga. Prisoner labor was also used to construct the regime's famous mega-projects, including the Baltic—White Sea Canal, the Magnitogorsk steel works and a hydroelectric dam across the Dnieper River. The Gulag was not only ruthless but also mismanaged; the first prisoners or exiles to arrive in an area often lacked adequate shelter or food. Exiles were frequently expected to cultivate infertile land.[72] Confinement to the worst of these camps was equivalent to a sentence of slow death.

Those Cossacks and peasants who were not run out of their homes during the mass collectivization campaign endured plenty of tribulations of their own. This was especially true after unfavorable growing conditions, combined with rural economic dislocation wrought by collectivization, led to a poor harvest in Ukraine and South Russia in 1932. When local officials, including some Communists, appealed to Moscow to reduce the grain quotas to be collected from these regions, they were accused of being too soft.[73] Indeed, a key premise of collectivization, and one which rural producers found especially objectionable, was that the state's grain requirements were to be met before those of the peasants. The center had no compunctions against employing a combination of violent terror and forced extractions to fill the grain levies even when this left practically nothing for those who actually produced the grain. "The bear takes the top of the crop and only the roots are left," went a peasant saying at the time.[74]

The result of such a policy was another terrible famine—this time entirely man-made—which lasted well into 1933. Starving peasants, as they had done a decade earlier, again converged in nearby cities to beg for food. Each morning, municipal workers cleared the streets of victims who died during the previous night. A Kiev resident who observed this ghoulish ritual later recalled: "Everyone gradually built up an immunity to such sights. The instinct of self-preservation didn't permit us to react to things in the usual human way. People turned to avoid meeting the eyes of dying women and walked, unseeing, past people going through the terrible agonies of a hungry death."[75] Unlike the previous famine, the existence of widespread starvation in 1932–33 was officially denied by the Soviet government, which prevented any foreign relief from reaching the affected areas.[76] The disaster, which was to claim the lives of millions of Soviet citizens, was effectively used by the government to bend a reluctant population into accepting its will.

The drive towards mass collectivization spared no one under Moscow's rule. In Soviet Central Asia, a misguided attempt by the regime to transform the arid grazing lands of the Kazakhs into grain-producing collectives ended in crop failure, massive livestock losses, hunger and in some instances rebellion. In the eastern part of that realm, thousands of natives again tried to flee to Xinjiang. Traditionally nomadic or semi-nomadic peoples in other regions also suffered badly from attempts to leash them to collectives or resettle large swaths of their populations. In the Russian Far East, tens of thousands of Buryats migrated across the border into Manchuria. A similar flight occurred among Cossacks in the region in the winter of 1932 as whole stanitsas desperate to escape the disruption and food shortages wrought by collectivization crossed the frozen Argun, Amur and Ussuri rivers into Manchukuo. There they joined established émigrés in Trekrechye or founded new communities in northern Manchuria.[77]

As in the early 1920s, the Cossacks were more likely to experience severe treatment amid the new terror due to the lingering anti–Cossack prejudices of local officials and party activists. On occasions the latter treated even poor Cossacks as *kulak* pariahs by barring them from village soviets or collective farms. More frequently, Cossacks suspected of having served with the Whites during the civil war were arrested, shot or exiled to labor camps. Despite the regime's past offers of amnesty towards the White rank-and file, White veterans were easy scapegoats in the OGPU's witch hunt for saboteurs who were supposedly undermining the productivity of the collective farms. The thousands of Cossacks who originally went abroad with the White armies only to return sometime during the 1920s were the least likely to escape notice by Soviet security forces. Inevitably, the OGPU's crackdown on White veterans affected Cossacks more than the non–Cossack population since the former had a disproportionately large presence in the White armies, particularly in South Russia. Officially, senior and regional Soviet authorities, including the North Caucasus Territory Committee, condemned reprisals against Cossacks that did not take into account their social background. Yet at the same time, that committee violated its own directives by waging an indiscriminate terror campaign against Cossacks in the Kuban.[78]

Of all the former Cossack communities, none seems to have suffered more during the events of 1929–33 than those of the former Kuban Host. In the years following the civil war, the Kuban replaced the devastated Don as the nucleus of what remained of Cossack culture and heritage.[79] Its fertile lands, and its fortune of having escaped the worst ravages of the civil war, enabled the region to bounce back relatively quickly under the NEP. After traveling through the Kuban in 1924, William Henry Chamberlin, a correspondent for the *Christian Science Monitor*, observed that the proud Kuban Cossacks still maintained "something of the psychology of Southerners in America after 1865."[80] From the communist viewpoint, the Kuban, like nearby Ukraine, was a redoubt of unsophisticated yokels glued to their traditions of petty capitalism and misguided separatism. The relative prosperity and cohesion of the stanitsas made their inhabitants especially reluctant to submit to collectivization and provides an explanation as to why the party singled out the Kuban for a campaign of mass terror that was among the worst anywhere in the Soviet state.[81]

Even before the push towards mass collectivization in 1929, Soviet security forces had begun to clamp down on the Kuban Cossacks with extraordinary savageness. During the previous year, the OGPU dispossessed 35,000 "*kulak*" families—mostly Cossacks—of their Kuban farms. Some 600 unfortunate individuals from that group were hastily executed while the rest were loaded onto railcars that carried them into internal exile. Mass evictions of Cossacks from their homes and stanitsas continued sporadically over the following months until they reached a feverish pitch at the end of 1932.[82] The Soviet press blamed the poor crop yields of that autumn on the independent farmers and *kulak*-sympathizers for ruining the Kuban's harvest.[83] Even local Communists who tried to convince their superiors to reduce the grain levies in light of the poor harvest fell under a cloud of suspicion and were purged.[84] In some instances Soviet security forces resorted to "blockading" entire stanitsas—that is, barring any deliveries of fuel, goods or foodstuffs to them—until their inhabitants surrendered enough grain to fill their quotas.[85] Locales suspected by the party of putting up any form of resistance were treated harshly. In order to make the Cossacks more compliant, the OGPU sometimes decapitated the community by liquidating its traditional leaders. At Tikhoretskaya, for example, OGPU troops reportedly hustled 600 elderly Cossacks into the town square, ordered them to shed their clothes and then mowed them down with machine guns.[86]

As though terrorizing the countryside and subjecting much of its population to inevitable starvation were not enough, the North Caucasus Territory Committee dealt another blow to the Kuban by authorizing mass deportations of entire stanitsas. The number of persons exiled from that region to the Far North in the winter of 1932–33 has been estimated to range from 63,000 up to 200,000.[87] The deportations were often conducted in the most inhumane manner as the victims were evicted from their homes after only a few hours' notice and then left waiting in the cold—sometimes for days—for trains to carry them into exile. Those Kuban stanitsas with a record of defiance and whose residents were predominantly Ukrainophone Cossacks were meted the worst treatment. Such was the case of Poltavskaya, which in the years after 1929 saw hundreds of its members deported as *kulaks* while others were persecuted for alleged involvement in Ukrainian separatist activity. Despite the authorities' tightening grip, the majority of Cossack farmers in the stanitsa remained outside of the collectives into late 1932. Finally, in December of that year, the president of the Executive Committee of the North Caucasus Territory issued orders for all of Poltavskaya's 27,000 inhabitants to be exiled to the frozen north. The bewildered Cossacks responded to this decision by taking up arms, but the OGPU quickly crushed their insurrection with characteristic ferocity. In the aftermath, the majority of the Cossacks were exiled, Russians were settled in their place and the community was renamed Krasnoarmeiskaya.[88] Similar fates befell several other Kuban stanitsas, including one where the OGPU simply deported all Cossacks whose surnames began with letters from the first half of the alphabet.[89]

Those Cossacks who were not packed into northbound freight cars during the winter of 1932–33 were left to wallow in fear and famine. The agonizing effects of the latter were felt all across the North Caucasus Territory, including by non–Cossack populations. For instance, the cities of Stavropol and Krasnodar (formerly Yekaterinodar) reported losing respectively 35 percent and 28 percent of their residents. Communities in remote areas fared better if they could supplement their exhausted supplies with wild sources of food, such as one group of villagers in the eastern Don who subsisted on marmots.[90] Although the Soviet government remained silent about the famine in the North Caucasus and elsewhere, whisperings of the catastrophe nonetheless reached Moscow in spring of 1933. To conceal the crisis from the rest of the world, the regime prohibited foreign journalists and most visitors from traveling to the affected regions until the following September. William Henry Chamberlin was among those journalists who journeyed to the North Caucasus and Ukraine shortly after the travel ban was lifted. Upon arriving in a Kuban Cossack village, he observed: "Enormous weeds, of striking height and toughness, filled up many of the gardens and could be seen waving in the fields of wheat, corn and sunflower seeds. Gone were the wheaten loaves, succulent slices of lamb that had been offered for sale everywhere when I visited the Kuban Valley in 1924. At that time every Cossack settlement had its large number of fierce, snapping dogs trained to guard sheep and cattle; now there was an almost ghostly quiet; the bark of a dog was never heard. 'The dogs all died or were eaten during the famine,' was the general explanation of their disappearance."[91] The number of Soviet citizens who perished in the famine of 1932–33 has been estimated at 7,000,000 persons. Of that figure, 5,000,000 are believed to have died in Ukraine and another 1,000,000 in the North Caucasus Territory. In addition to those numbers, perhaps 6,500,000 individuals across the country died as a result of the dekulakization campaign, deportations and mass resettlements carried out in the years following 1929.[92] This carnage proved to be more or less the final word in the struggle between the party and the peasantry. The former, which had partially buckled under universal peasant resistance in 1921, now had the means and determination to impose its will in the countryside.

By the mid–1930s, the Cossack way of life appeared to be essentially extinct. The strongest, proudest stanitsas had been broken up and their survivors were condemned to long days of back-breaking work in remote camps. The meadows upon which they had hunted and pastured their horses were plowed under by the "work brigades" of collective farms. The horses that were once integral to their culture were becoming less common as those on farms were slowly replaced by tractors while others had been consumed during the famine. In the remaining stanitsas, the folksy wisdom of the elders was replaced by the brash exhortations of a much younger, literate generation who were veterans of the Red Army or other party organizations. Most remaining Cossacks, like their peasant neighbors, found themselves subjugated to the "second serfdom" of the collective farms. There was little left distinguish them from ordinary Russian peasants whose speech, dress and experiences were now identical to theirs. Yet, just when it seemed appropriate to write the final obituary of the Cossack people, they were suddenly revived by the very regime which had done so much to destroy them.

Cossack Renaissance

The push towards mass collectivization was merely one component of the First Five-Year Plan, an ambitious project initiated by Stalin to drastically increase the Soviet Union's agricultural and industrial output. The expansion of the country's industrial base was deemed essential by party leaders to ensure the survival of the proletarian dictatorship. Throughout the 1920s, they were convinced that it was only a matter of time before the capitalist countries, particularly Great Britain and France, renewed hostilities against them. While these threats of foreign aggression were exaggerated, those of the following decade were not. In the distant Far East, the Soviets found themselves confronting a new bogeyman in the form of Japan after the Kwantung Army seized Manchuria in 1932. The next year saw the ascension of Adolf Hitler and his virulently anticommunist Nazi Party in Germany. For the remainder of the decade, as ominous clouds of war gathered over Europe and East Asia, the Soviet regime had even more impetus to continue its frenzied efforts to increase its industrial capacity and, by extension, its military capabilities.[93]

Like other leading powers, the Soviet rearmament program during the 1930s emphasized the production of modern hardware such as artillery, tanks and planes. Still, Soviet military planners were astute enough to recognize the limitations of these weapons in the vast regions of their country which were cursed with primitive roads, extreme weather conditions and difficult terrain. They believed that the answer to the Red Army's operational difficulties in these areas was the same as it had been during the civil war and in tsarist times: the deployment of cavalry. Yet, the condition of the Red Army's cavalry arm was disconcerting for one of its most famous rough-riding commanders, Semyon Budyonny. Two key factors appear to have influenced the civil war hero's pessimistic assessment of Soviet mounted units. One was the quantity of horses in the country: following the mass slaughter of horses in the years of collectivization and famine, the number of equine remaining in Soviet lands fell to unprecedented lows.[94] His second concern was the quality of horses available to the Red Army.[95] In pre-revolutionary times, the Russian Empire had a distinctive edge in cavalry over her opponents since it enjoyed access to a rich selection of bloodlines that were as diverse and unique as the people and regions it ruled. Whereas other European cavalries depended almost exclusively on stately Thoroughbreds, Russian war horses often combined the ruggedness of the steppe ponies with the fiery spirit of Arab steeds. The Don horse, which by the twentieth century ranked among the most popular mounts in the tsarist army, was further refined by the addition of Thoroughbred blood to increase its size. Other Cossack hosts favored breeds adapted to local conditions: the Kuban and Terek Cossacks rode sure-footed mountain horses acquired from Circassian highlanders while the Siberian hosts preferred small, shaggy breeds that were unfazed by frigid temperatures and deep snow pack.[96] As one might expect, the fortunes of these Cossack breeds during and after the revolution corresponded closely with that of their masters. Hundreds of thousands fell on the battlefield, starved during retreats or were slain at seaside during the evacuations from South Russia. In the following years, more were butchered either for food or to prevent them from being turned over to collective farms. Collectivization's emphasis on grain production over pasturing livestock and the subsequent efforts to permanently settle nomadic people further depleted the herds of hardy steppe horses. Therefore, as Budyonny called on the Soviet state to improve its mounted units, he urged a revival of careful horse-breeding. Remarkably, he went as far as to commend Cossacks for their animal husbandry skills and their attention to bloodline development.

Budyonny's praise for "Soviet Cossacks"—meaning those Cossacks who broke with the past and embraced collectivization—was the first sign of a seismic shift in the regime's attitudes towards the Cossack people.[97] Just as the tsars had turned rebellious Cossacks into their loyal servitors, the Communists now sought to transform them from pariahs to model patriots of the proletarian state. On 20 April 1936, the Soviet government issued a decree "to remove from Cossacks all previously existing limitations on military service in the ranks of the Peasants' and Workers' Red Army."[98] On the heels of this proclamation, the Soviet Commissar of Defense, Kliment Voroshilov, announced the establishment of five Cossack cavalry divisions in the Red Army. These were formed by renaming two existing formations as the 4th Don and 6th Kuban—Terek Cossack Cavalry Divisions. Three other Cossack cavalry divisions were created from scratch: the 10th Terek—Stavropol, the 12th Kuban and the 13th Don Cossack Cavalry Divisions.[99] Despite their names, eligibility in these formations was not restricted to genuine Cossacks. Rather, they were open to anyone from the traditional Cossack lands of the North Caucasus—with the notable exception of native highlanders. The designation of these divisions as "Cossack" was mostly honorific; intended to inspire their riders with the legendary courage, skills and tenacity of the horsemen of the steppe. Stalin made no attempt to reintroduce the military obligations which had been a prominent feature of Cossack life in the years prior to 1917. The ranks of these formations were to be filled not only with individuals who had Cossack blood coursing through their veins but also with recruits of non–Cossack origin. The latter probably included quite a few outlanders or their descendants who, like Budyonny himself on occasion, were not averse to falsely portraying their ancestors as Cossacks. Indeed, throughout the former Don, Kuban and Terek lands whole rural communities soon called themselves Cossacks regardless of their actual ancestry.[100]

In the months following Voroshilov's announcement, the new and re-anointed Cossacks of South Russia appeared to go out of their way to express their solidarity with the Soviet people. In the Kremlin, party functionaries busily drafting a new constitution were visited by a Cossack delegation which averred their people's readiness to defend the Soviet motherland. Elsewhere in the capital, foreign diplomats were treated to Cossack performances in the opera house. In the dusty towns of the North Caucasus, mounted companies of Cossacks outfitted in their traditional costumes were featured in parades held ostensibly to celebrate their harmony with neighboring peoples and the Communist Party. In the stanitsas, the *dzhigitovka* and folk songs could again be seen and heard. Meanwhile, party leaders in the North Caucasus Territory lauded the "Soviet Cossacks" in speeches and publications for their devotion to the new order and their severance with the past. Generally, these exhibitions were not spontaneous. Most were carefully choreographed by the party to pave the way for the new constitution that was announced on 5 December 1936. Known as the Stalin Constitution, this document portrayed the peoples of the Soviet Union as a vast single community no longer constrained by national or class divisions. From the party's viewpoint, there was no better symbol of this all-encompassing unity than the apparent reconciliation of the former wardens of the tsar with the communist system.[101]

By the late 1930s, then, there existed two very different narratives expounding the ideals, traits and virtues of Cossackry. On one hand was the collage of émigrés who claimed to represent the traditional Cossack heritage. Although united by their hostility towards communism, they agreed on little else. As we have seen, they were deeply divided by those who envisaged the Cossacks' future within a Russian national state and those who aspired for some form of Cossack independence. Opposing this fractured camp was the Communist Party with its view that the revolution had forged a new Cossack; one which no longer clung to antiquated customs and was eager to join the "work brigades" in order to win "the battle for grain." Despite their differences, the rivals had their similarities. For instance, both claimed the prerogative to decide exactly who was a Cossack. The Don government had done so in 1918–19 when it conferred Cossack status upon officers, peasants and outlanders who fought on its behalf. Now, nearly a generation later, the Soviet government made liberal use of Cossack titles to stir its population and soldiers to master the horsemanship and fighting skills which had made those warriors so famous. Essentially, both groups implicitly acknowledged that Cossackry was by definition more than an estate—as it had been characterized during tsarist times—yet was not quite an unalienable trait—such as an ethnicity. For them, it was a status that could be bequeathed when and where they saw fit.[102]

Another similarity which the Soviet Cossacks shared with Cossacks abroad was a sense of bewilderment and confusion in the years leading up to the Nazi—Soviet conflict in Eastern Europe. Whereas the émigrés struggled to make sense of the Nazis' bipolar foreign policy towards Stalin's regime, Soviet Cossacks endeavored to do the same but from the opposite viewpoint. Their perspective, however, was clouded by a new wave of terror which, like a tsunami arising from a serene sea, suddenly engulfed the Soviet Union in the latter 1930s. Indeed, the restoration of Cossack units in the middle of the decade, accompanied by the reestablishment of personal ranks for Red Army officers, seemed to indicate that the regime had finally shed its irrational paranoia of internal enemies. But even as the party was striving to present a gentler face in the interests of public and foreign consumption, behind the scenes its upper ranks were in turmoil as Stalin began eliminating prominent Communists who posed even the slightest challenge to his authority. The vast majority of Soviet citizens had no inkling of what was taking place among the party elite until August 1936, when the press reported that sixteen Old Bolsheviks appeared in a Moscow courtroom, confessed to charges that they had conspired to kill present Soviet leaders, and were marched before a firing squad shortly thereafter. This ignominious fate for such party luminaries—two of the convicts, Grigory Zinoviev and Lev Kamenev, had been among the founding members of Politburo—was nothing short of shocking for peoples across the breadth of the Soviet Union.[103]

The trial of the sixteen Old Bolsheviks in 1936 was merely the first of three highly-publicized show trials that were to be held over the following two years. But as Stalin's former intra-party rivals and colleagues were compelled to admit their involvement in improbable schemes emanating from the exiled Trotsky, Hitler's Gestapo and Japanese imperialists, a wider, less-publicized purge affecting everyone from obscure party officials to lowly workmen gained momentum. A decade later, a post–World War II émigré who lived through the Great Terror described how fear permeated every aspect of life as a student attending an institute in Kharkov: "During the winter of 1937-1938 many professors and students were arrested and expelled from the institute. Friends stopped recognizing each other. One did not greet his acquaintances. One looked at strangers wondering if they too were not 'enemies of the people.'"[104] The dragnet occasionally captured a personality whose execution warranted mention by the press; such was the case with the civil war hero and Marshal of the Soviet Union, Mikhail Tukhachevsky, who was shot on 11 June 1937 after being convicted of espionage by a secret military tribunal. Tukhachevksy's demise touched off a wave of arrests and executions of Red Army personnel, especially in the upper ranks. By that time the terror was devouring its own technicians. Thousands of NKVD operatives, especially non–Russians who had carried out the organization's dirty work since it had been known as the Cheka, experienced the same cycle of arrests, interrogations, executions and exile to labor camps that was familiar to their countless victims. Indeed, two successive NKVD chiefs, Genrikh Yagoda and Nikola Yezhov, would be counted among the over half-million persons who perished in the Great Terror.[105]

Unlike the de-Cossackization of 1919 or collectivization a decade later, the Great Terror did not specifically single out Cossacks or their livelihoods for elimination. Nonetheless, many Cossacks were executed or sent to the dreaded work camps. Some, such as those who were veterans of the White armies or were returned émigrés from abroad, had been targeted for punishment in past waves of terror.[106] But in the late 1930s, the scope for dangerous internal enemies was widened to include former insurgents who had fought the Whites during the civil war as well as anyone who had seen a glimpse of life abroad, including Great War veterans who been held by the Central Powers in a POW camp. Ultimately, anyone and their families whose name was uttered by a prisoner during the hours of intense interrogation and torture by NKVD agents was liable to be detained. The sheer randomness of the purge, combined with the harsh reality that even at this stage most peasants and Cossacks were preoccupied with the unending struggle to feed their families from the meager rations left to them by the collective farms, prevented the outbreak of any widespread resistance.[107] Nevertheless, local uprisings were not unheard of during this period, including in the former Don territory, where in the spring of 1941 some disgruntled Cossacks attempted to form an independent republic of their own in a stanitsa north of Rostov.[108] Although their adventure got nowhere, it was a sign that even at this late stage the restless spirit of their ancestors still flickered among the subdued horsemen of the steppe.

The fresh nightmare of the Great Terror, particularly the fact that hundreds of thousands of individuals had been carted off to camps for spying on behalf of Hitler's Germany, made the announcement of the Nazi—Soviet nonaggression pact even more incomprehensible for Soviet citizens. Suddenly, the swastika-bedecked fascist bogeyman featured in Soviet propaganda for the last six years was now a partner while the British and French were recast into their former role as the motherland's primary foes.[109] This drastic about-face in policy, combined with the decimation of the Soviet officers' corps during the purges,[110] weakened the Red Army by fostering a certain amount of distrust among troops who found themselves subordinated to unfamiliar and often unqualified commanders.[111]

It was under these auspicious circumstances which Cossacks and other peoples living in the Soviet Union found themselves when the German war machine invaded their country during the summer of 1941. Given the fact that Soviet citizens had lived through multiple rounds of famine and terror during the previous two decades, émigré predictions that their compatriots in the Red Army would not defend the extant regime seemed reasonable. Indeed, some émigrés and Western historians have argued that the Red Army's crushing defeats early in the conflict were the result of its soldiers' unwillingness to risk their lives for a murderous regime.[112] But even if that explanation was true for the initial phase of the war—and it is far from conclusive—the Germans, in order to sustain any indigenous Soviet opposition, needed to offer an attractive alternative to communist rule. This, as we shall see, would be difficult under Hitler's policies for the newly-occupied Eastern territories.

13

Invasion

Ostpolitik

For fervent anticommunist Cossack émigrés in Europe, Manchuria and elsewhere, Germany's invasion of the Soviet Union in the summer of 1941 triggered a new wave of optimism in their twenty-four year struggle against Bolshevism. In the coming days, weeks and months, several prominent figures from their community publicly endorsed Germany's *blitzkrieg* in the East. Among the most prestigious of these well-wishers was Krasnov, the former Don ataman, who greeted the news of the invasion by offering prayers for the Führer's success.[1] Two other exiled Cossack atamans, Generals Naumenko (Kuban) and Vdovenko (Terek), echoed Krasnov's sentiment in a message to Nazi Foreign Minister Joachim von Ribbentrop.[2] Not to be left out, Vasily Glazkov's Cossack National Center, claiming to be the voice of all Cossacks abroad, cabled several top Nazis with promises of Cossackdom's enthusiastic support in the struggle against "Judeo-Bolshevism." Over the following months, Glazkov's group rebranded themselves the Cossack National Liberation Movement (KNOD), called upon their compatriots in exile to actively support the campaign against the Red Army, and made attempts to draw the Führer's attention to their cause through letters addressed to his office.[3]

The initial hopes of these aspiring collaborators and other Cossack émigrés was soon tempered by the reality that the mastermind of the massive campaign in the East had no interest in their movement. Indeed, Hitler had developed an acute prejudice against Slavs since his party had first collaborated with White émigrés in the early 1920s. After the failure of his putsch in Munich, the Nazi leader authored an autobiographical manifesto, *Mien Kampf*, where he openly categorized the Slavs as an inferior race utterly beguiled by the "Jewish wirepullers" of the Bolshevik revolution. War with Russia, he argued, was necessary to foil the Jewish-Marxist plot of world domination and roll back the Slavic ethnic frontier which threatened the racial purity of "the Aryan culture-bearer."[4] Moreover, the projected campaign in the East was to have another benefit by opening new regions to German colonization. The Führer lectured that the Reich, in order to truly become a world power, must "secure for the German people the land and soil to which they are entitled on this earth."[5] Those fields, he wrote, "could be obtained by and large only at the expense of Russia."[6] These aims, largely written off at the time of *Mien Kampf*'s publication in 1925 as the eccentric musings of a fringe politician, had by 1941 become Germany's Ostpolitik (Eastern policy). The Führer, who regarded the peoples of Eastern Europe as *untermensch* ("subhuman"), had no desire to make friends in that region.[7]

For Hitler, the notion that the oppressed Eastern peoples should be recruited in his grandiose campaign against the Soviet Union was self-defeating. At a conference on 16 July

1941 he laid down the "iron principle": "We must never permit anybody but the Germans to carry arms! This is especially important; even when it seems easier at first to enlist the support of foreign subjugated nations, it is wrong to do so. In the end this will prove to be our disadvantage unconditionally and unavoidably. Only the German may carry arms, not the Slav, not the Czech, not the Cossack nor Ukrainian!"[8] Not only was he against using Cossacks and other Soviet peoples militarily but also politically. He thought nothing good could come from offering even false hope to the subject races. "By no means," he declared, "should we render our task more difficult by making superfluous declarations."[9] Unlike in the previous war, Germany would make no attempt to exploit regional separatist movements to guise its territorial acquisitions in Eastern Europe. Instead, under Hitler's plan Berlin would rule that area outright through "reichskommissariats" to ensure the Nazi war economy unhindered access to Ukrainian grain, Caucasian oil and other crucial commodities.[10]

Interestingly, not everyone in the upper tiers of the Nazi hierarchy agreed with the Führer's savage approach to establishing German hegemony in Eastern Europe. A leading dissident to Hitler's Ostpolitik was his longtime disciple Alfred Rosenberg, the Baltic German émigré who fancied himself as the party's foreign policy guru. Rosenberg believed that Germany should pursue a more sophisticated program of *divide et impera* in the East. Like Hitler, Rosenberg detested Jews, communists and Great Russians; but unlike his master, he was eager to utilize émigrés and stoke separatist movements among Soviet minorities. His blueprints for the East were designed "to free the German Reich from Pan-Slavic pressure for centuries to come" by partitioning the Soviet Union into four suzerainties each with local self-government: Ostland, which would encompass the Baltic States and Belorussia; an expanded Ukraine which included the Don territory, the Caucasus and a truncated Russia centered on Moscow.[11] In this way, the Great Russian population was to be permanently isolated from those nationalities along her western and southern borderlands and confined to the periphery of Europe. Meanwhile, the Soviet minorities, particularly those traditionally hostile toward Russian and Soviet rule, were to be granted preferential treatment in order to make them more or less willing minions of Berlin. Although Hitler scoffed at Rosenberg's more tactful proposals, the German dictator still appointed him to lead the Reich Ministry for the Eastern Occupied Territories (Ostministrium). Theoretically, that ministry was to be responsible for the civil administration in areas behind the battle zones of the Eastern Front,[12] but in practice Rosenberg's actual powers in the occupied territories were considerably diminished by the Führer's decision to entrust the region's economic and security matters to Reichsmarshall Hermann Göring and Heinrich Himmler, respectively.[13] None of Hitler's henchmen, then, were to enjoy complete dominance over Eastern European affairs, and as a result much confusion, inconsistency and rivalry arose between the various party functionaries, government bureaucrats and military officers who sometimes found themselves at odds with one another as they worked towards their prescribed goals in that embattled region.

Opposition to Hitler's Ostpolitik also existed in the section of the German Ministry of Foreign Affairs which monitored developments in the Soviet Union. The head of this section was the former German ambassador to Moscow, Count Friedrich Werner von Schulenburg, who believed that the Soviet Union could only be vanquished by turning its peoples against Stalin's regime. He also abhorred Nazi racial propaganda, urged that the population in occupied territories be granted local self-government and advocated for Germany to publicly renounce any territorial claims on Russian lands. "Schulenburg's ideas," his colleague Hans von Herwarth observed, "contradicted Hitler's own colonial plans so completely that no compromise between the two was possible." As a result, neither Schulenburg nor the German foreign ministry in general possessed any influence over affairs in the occupied Eastern territories.[14]

There were brief occasions when the Führer appeared ready to adopt the more enlightened policies towards Eastern peoples urged by the likes of Rosenberg or even Schulenburg. In a radio broadcast on the morning of 22 June 1941, as his panzer divisions rolled eastward across the Soviet frontier, the Führer attempted to portray the invasion as a military campaign against "Judeo-Bolshevism" and not the peoples of Russia. Wehrmacht propagandists struck a similar note as they printed leaflets urging Red Army men not to resist "their German liberators."[15] But aside from these shallow appeals, German political warfare in the first critical months of the offensive left much to be desired. This clumsy approach disappointed not only knowledgeable Russophiles like Schulenburg, but also the officers and soldiers of the Wehrmacht who were welcomed at the gates of many villages that summer and autumn by jubilant inhabitants attired in their holiday clothes.[16] "Everywhere we went we were greeted with bread and salt, the traditional Slav symbols of hospitality," recalled Herwarth, then serving as a second lieutenant with the First Cavalry Division. "Even in the poor villages where provisions were in short supply, the peasants generously offered to share their cucumbers, yogurt and bread with individual soldiers as a sign of friendship."[17] Similar observations were made by a corporal with the Waffen-SS Division *Leibstandarte Adolf Hitler* who wrote, "All along the road armfuls of autumn flowers were showered in on us, asters of all colors: red, white, yellow, [and] blue."[18] After such expressions of anticommunist sentiment firsthand, it is no wonder that numerous personnel in the German army became convinced that a cleverer propaganda campaign and more humane policy towards the populace could trigger a revolution that would work in their side's favor.[19]

The reports of German troops being accorded a friendly reception by the civilian population in the Soviet territory made no impression on top Nazi leaders. Therefore, as the frontline troops continued their march east, those villagers and townsfolk who hoped that the new regime would dissolve the collective farms, restore private property and end rule by terror were quickly disillusioned. It soon became apparent to them that the German administrators were in no hurry to break-up the collective farms since the centralization imposed by them made the countryside easier to control. Even more troubling was the special detachments of SS, *Einsatzgruppen*, Security Services and police battalions that descended on the rear areas and began staging mass executions of Jews, suspected communists and others who were singled out for extermination in Hitler's new order. From the perspective of the inhabitants, they had simply exchanged one tyranny for another.[20]

The unwillingness of the German leaders to make any effort to accommodate the aspirations of the Eastern peoples was at least partly attributable to their misplaced confidence that their army would score a quick, decisive victory over the Slavic *untermenschen*. Indeed, in an evaluation of the Red Army at the end of 1939, Germany's top generals gave very low marks to its hardware, commanders and troops. In summary, they concluded, "the Russian 'mass' is no match for an army with modern equipment and superior leadership."[21] These views persisted into the summer of 1941. Hitler, for example, assured one general that the war against the Soviet Union would be won within six weeks.[22] The Wehrmacht's successes in the early months of the campaign merely reinforced these optimistic forecasts. Within a matter of days, the Luftwaffe had decimated the Soviet air force, previously the largest in the world, and assured their side control of the skies for the remainder of year.[23] On the ground, the panzer spearheads sliced through the defenders' lines and advanced with lightning speed, allowing the invaders to take possession of Minsk and Riga before the end of June. Convinced that Soviet forces were irreparably shattered, on 3 July the German army's chief of the general staff, General Franz Halder, wrote in his diary, "It is thus probably no overstatement to say that the Russian campaign has been won in the space of two weeks."[24] The capture of hundreds of thousands of Soviet troops in vast encirclements near Minsk, Smolensk, Kiev and Vyazma seemed to confirm Halder's assessment that the Red Army was as good as destroyed. By the end of September 1941 the German High Command of the Armed Forces (Oberkommando der Wehrmacht, OKW) pegged Soviet losses to be upwards of 2,500,000 men, 22,000 guns, 18,000 tanks and 14,000 aircraft since the start of the campaign.[25] The weeks ahead did not look any brighter for the Red Army. Leningrad, the sacred cradle of the revolution, was virtually cut-off from the rest of Russia. On the other end of the front, the Crimea was isolated from the mainland after the German vanguard reached the Azov coast. By October, Army Group Center was preparing to resume its advance toward Moscow. With victory seemingly assured, Nazi leaders felt no need to mount a serious propaganda campaign among, much less seek assistance from, the *untermenschen*.[26]

Yet, in between the German communiqués announcing the fall of another Soviet city or massive encirclement of enemy troops, there were signs that not everything was going according to their plan. German troops quickly learned that their Red Army opponents were no pushovers. Their panzers were completely outmatched by the larger caliber and wider tread of the Soviet T-34 tank. That tank's thick, sloping armor also rendered it nearly impervious to the rounds fired from the 37 mm high-velocity guns fielded by most of the Wehrmacht's anti-tank companies.[27] No less frustrating for German infantrymen was the dogged resilience of Red Army soldiers who frequently fought to the last man rather than give themselves up.[28] Moreover, by autumn the invaders were coming to appreciate the challenges of operating in a vast country with an unforgiving climate and poor roads. The offensive against Moscow, which was initiated in early October 1941, quickly bogged down as the halcyon autumn weather gave way to driving rains and wet snow which turned the unpaved roads into sticky quagmires.[29] Writing of the challenges his men faced in those weeks, the commander of the Second Panzer Army, General Heinz Guderian, recalled, "The roads rapidly became nothing but canals of bottomless mud, along which our vehicles could only advance at a snail's pace and with great wear to the engines."[30]

One of the most serious challenges faced by the Germans from the early stages of their campaign were shortages of manpower. More and more soldiers were needed not only to replace the unexpectedly high casualties at the front, but also to protect the invaders' communication and supply arteries that stretched across the occupied territories. The Red Army, in contrast, seemed to have near limitless human resources. "At the outset of the war, we reckoned with 200 Russian divisions," Halder confided to his diary on 11 August 1941, "Now we have already counted 360."[31] The commander of Army Group South, General Gerd von Rundstedt, expressed similar amazement at the Soviets' inexhaustible reserves. "It seemed to us that as soon as one force was wiped out," Rundstedt later recalled, "the path was blocked by the arrival of a fresh force."[32]

In order to compensate for their limited manpower, Nazi leaders sought to terrorize the populations in occupied territories into complete submission. From the start, German soldiers were under strict orders to take "ruthless action" and employ "the most extreme methods" against any form of resistance they may encounter in the conquered lands.[33] Supplementary directives merely reiterated this savagery. In September 1941, OKW instructed its soldiers to regard all uprisings as communist insurrections. "As atonement for the life of one German soldier," the directive stated, "a death penalty for 50–100 Communists must generally be considered as proper."[34] Thus, as in the Russian Civil War, horrendous atrocities against the civilian population where justified on the grounds that the victims were "communists" or "Bolsheviks." This system of reprisals proved no more successful at establishing order in the rear of the German forces than it had been a generation earlier. Just as the naked repression of the Cossack atamans and other warlords had compelled many peasants to join anti–White partisans, the violent and exploitative behavior of the Germans ignited a ferocious insurgency that exacted revenge upon the occupiers by ambushing their personnel, supply convoys and trains. The Red Army Stavka began to aid the guerrillas by parachuting experts and infiltrating weapons behind the German front. For its part, Soviet propaganda appealed to the population to defend the motherland; placing greater emphasis on nationalist fervor rather than revolutionary duty.[35] But even as the partisan movement gathered momentum in the latter months of 1941, the Germans by and large remained committed to terror as the best means for safeguarding their rear on the grounds that the population must fear the invaders' counter-measures above all else.[36]

Despite these mounting problems, the German army continued its advance into late autumn. On 23 November, the First Panzer Army entered Rostov, a feat trumpeted by Nazi propaganda as having "opened the gateway to the Caucasus." Just five days later, however, that gate was slammed shut by a Soviet counterattack that forced the Germans to retire thirty miles to the west.[37] Even greater disappointment awaited the Wehrmacht to the north, where Army Group Center was battering its way through snow-draped forests towards the Soviet capital. Like Denikin twenty-two years earlier, Hitler was belatedly resolved on seizing Moscow in the belief that its capture would herald the demise of the Bolshevik regime.[38] Army Group Center came much closer to the Kremlin than the Volunteer Army; having passed beyond the latter's high-water mark, Oryol, in early October. Their lead units even approached within twenty miles of the city, but by that point they lacked the strength to press any further.

On 5 December, just as the German offensive had ground to a halt outside the Soviet capital, the Red Army launched a counterattack against the exhausted invaders with fresh reinforcements recently transferred from the Far East. The Soviet infantrymen, some attired in white camouflage and outfitted in skis, were better prepared for the wintry weather than their German adversaries, many of whom still donned their summer uniforms. "This lack of warm clothes," complained Guderian, "was, in the difficult months ahead, to provide the greatest problem and cause the greatest suffering to our troops."[39] Not only did the German soldiers have to stave off attacking infantry and frostbite as the mercury plunged to thirty degrees below zero (Fahrenheit), but they also had to contend with cold-hardy Red cavalry divisions from the Far East. Consisting of Buryats and former Cossacks from the Transbaikal and Ussuri regions,[40] these horsemen made their presence felt on the battlefield as they helped encircle stranded German formations. By mid–December, the intensity of the unexpected Soviet counteroffensive precipitated a crisis in the German command, which had been convinced only days earlier that its opponent was on the brink of collapse. The commanders-in-chief of both the German Army Supreme Command (Oberkommando des Heeres, OKH) and Army Group Center were sent into early retirement while their colleagues argued for a withdrawal.[41] But Hitler, who personally took charge at OKH, would not hear of it. "The army is not to retire a single step," the Führer ordered, "Every man must fight where he stands."[42] His intervention was decisive. After the war, a senior German officer speculated that any retreat at that point may have degenerated into a panicked rout—*à la* Napoleon[43] or, to use a more recent example, Denikin. But the beleaguered formations of Army Group Center, steeled by the iron will of their Führer, did not fall back and instead hastily improvised hedgehog defensive positions in the frozen countryside.

Even though Hitler's obstinate refusal to authorize a general withdrawal may have warded off a German military collapse during that first winter in Russia, his reflexive tendency to order his armies to hold ground would have grave consequences later in the war. Likewise, he adopted a similar unyielding attitude towards political questions in the East. Although it was obvious that he greatly underestimated the resilience of the Stalinist regime, the Führer was determined to stay the course as far as his Ostpolitik was concerned. Months after that winter's catastrophe, he made it clear that he still had no interest in seeking assistance from the Eastern peoples. "The most foolish mistake we could possibly make would be to allow the subject races to possess arms," he explained to his dinner guests the following April. "History shows that all conquerors who have allowed their subject races to carry arms have prepared their own downfall by so doing."[44]

A growing number of German officers, unlike the Führer, took a more sober and pragmatic view of their military predicament. The unprecedented resurgence of the Red Army, the challenges imposed by the climate, the primitive road network and the persistent guerrilla threat in the occupied territories shook their confidence that the armed might of Nazi Germany was by itself enough to defeat the Soviet colossus. Some generals even dismissed the possibility of resuming the offensive during 1942.[45] By then Captain Wilfried Strik-Strikfeldt, a staff officer with Army Group Center, was already advocating a new approach that would end the self-defeating practices of Ostpolitik and instead stoke a new revolution in Russia. "At that time," Strik-Strikfeldt later wrote, "I, like the other officers, believed that Hitler must ultimately see reason, alternatively that the generals would enforce a sensible solution."[46] It was these hopes which, in late spring 1942, brought together a group of like-minded army officers who were determined to find ways they could improve the treatment of Eastern peoples, utilize them militarily and, ultimately, enforce changes in Germany's Ostpolitik. While some officers appreciated the benefits of these proposals from a utilitarian viewpoint, others, like Strik-Strikfeldt, believed that the war could only "be brought to an end through sincere collaboration with the liberated population."[47] This latter set of officers, though they lacked any formal organization, has been referred to by historians as the "Other Germany" group. They drew encouragement from the practice within the army of recruiting volunteers from among Cossacks and other Eastern peoples. The development of these volunteer formations occurred spontaneously and almost from the outset of the Nazi—Soviet conflict. In it, the Other Germany group saw proof of what a more sensible policy in the East might accomplish.[48]

Cossacks in *Feldgrau*

Although few of the Wehrmacht's senior generals showed much interest in revising the official Ostpolitik prior to the setback in the winter of 1941–42, the exigencies of holding a vast front line while maintaining order in the extensive rear areas compelled a number of local German commanders to deviate from that policy much earlier. With their available personnel overstretched since the early weeks of the campaign, these officers began recruiting much-needed militiamen and support crews from among the Eastern peoples. As a German intelligence officer noted, this method of acquiring additional manpower arose "more from a healthy instinct of self-preservation than for any political motives."[49] However, the overall success of this practice opened the eyes of the German commanders to the potential advantages their side might attain if their policies intelligibly exploited the anti–Soviet mood among the Eastern peoples. In particular, they looked upon the multitudes of war prisoners entering captivity as a potential wellspring of manpower.

By the end of 1941, the Wehrmacht had captured an estimated 3,350,000 soldiers from the Red Army.[50] Although it would be wrong to assume that many gave themselves up out of a sense of disloyalty,[51] the average Soviet POW did have plenty of reasons to at least consider throwing his lot with the Germans. Many had been drafted from villages that had experienced the horrors of collectivization, dekulakization and famines during the previous decade. The harsh reality of Soviet rule was now familiar to them, unlike in the civil war period, and some wistfully hoped that the invaders might offer them a better alternative.[52] The Soviet regime, for its part, did nothing to retain the loyalties of its soldiers once they entered POW camps. It exhibited no concern for their well-being, did not send them parcels through the Red Cross and had abstained from international agreements concerning the humane treatment of war prisoners. It was no secret that Stalin regarded any Red Army personnel who was taken alive to be a traitor. This situation was demoralizing for Soviet POWs, causing one war prisoner-turned-collaborator to reason that "if Stalin refused to have anything to do with us, we didn't want to have anything to do with Stalin."[53]

Aside from political considerations, collaboration could offer Soviet war prisoners more tangible rewards such as their release from the appalling conditions of the POW camps. The Germans were unprepared, and in some cases unwilling, to accommodate the millions of enemy soldiers they took captive. Consequently, many camps, especially early in the war, were nothing more than improvised enclosures without adequate shelter, food or sanitation. Their inmates' situation turned catastrophic during the winter of 1941–42, when upwards of two million Soviet POWs perished from starvation, exposure and epidemics.[54] Through their own gross negligence, the Germans were forced to rule out the possibility that the bulk of their Soviet POWs might serve a useful military, economic or propagandistic purpose.[55]

The volunteers who managed to avoid or escape the hellish POW camps by entering Wehrmacht service were dubbed *Hilfswilligers*, or "Hiwis," by the Germans. At first, Hiwis were assigned to non-combat duties such as batmen, cooks, lorry drivers and stable-hands. Many continued to wear Red Army uniforms devoid of communist insignia, but eventually they were outfitted in *feldgrau* (field gray) uniforms and issued captured rifles. Since this was in direct contravention with the Führer's "iron principle" that no one but Germans should carry arms, the recruitment of Eastern volunteers into the Wehrmacht was carried out clandestinely. For that reason, it is unknown exactly how many Hiwis entered German service. According to one account, by spring of 1942 their numbers may have reached 200,000 and continued to climb.[56]

In the course of the war, nearly all of the major demographic groups in the Soviet Union would be represented among the collaborators, including the Cossacks. Incidentally, the earliest recorded mass defection of a Red Army unit to the Wehrmacht occurred under the auspices of a Cossack, Ivan Nikitich Kononov, a forty-one-year-old major who had spent half of his life in the Red Army. In 1920, Kononov served under Budyonny in the First Cavalry Army and continued his military service and education during the interwar period, culminating with his admission into the Frunze Military Academy in 1935. His advancement in the Red Army was likely aided by his membership to the Communist Party, to which he had belonged since 1927. When the Soviet Union went to war against Finland in 1939, he was given command of the 436th Infantry Regiment and, following that campaign, was awarded the Order of the Red Star. Nearly two years later, when the Germans launched their invasion of the Soviet Union, Kononov again led the 436th Regiment to the front. By all accounts, he appeared to be a loyal, experienced and competent officer—attributes urgently needed by the Red Army following the recent purge of its officer corps.

In August 1941, while overseeing the operations of the 436th Regiment near Mogilev, Kononov, with the connivance of just a few subordinate officers, dispatched an emissary to the opposing Germans with an offer for his unit to change sides. The emissary soon returned a message that the enemy commander, Lieutenant-General Count Max von Schenkendorff, accepted his proposal and personally guaranteed the safety of the major and his men. After receiving this assurance, Kononov proceeded to assemble his regiment, informed his men of his intention to defect and invited them to join him. None, it seems, raised any objection and on 22 August the entire 436th Regiment followed their leader across the front.

The specific motives behind Kononov's defection are unclear. His polished record of service to the revolution did conceal one tragic experience: both his father, a Cossack captain in the tsarist army, and his mother had been shot after Red Guards occupied their Don stanitsa in 1918. Still, this episode was either sufficiently obscure or insignificant to the NKVD as Kononov's career and person, unlike tens of thousands of other Red Army officers, survived the purges of the late 1930s. Did the memory of his murdered parents compel Kononov to abandon the Soviet cause or, like so many others, did he simply become disillusioned with communism's failure to deliver on its utopian promises? While the factors behind his transformation into an active opponent of the communist regime can only be guessed, one aspect is certain: Kononov had set his sights on the ambitious goal of organizing, with German assistance, an anticommunist army to free Russia from Stalin's yoke. With Schenkendorff's permission, he hoped he could begin organizing that army around his men from the 436th Regiment. Although Schenkendorff was not averse to Kononov's proposal, he knew that Germany's political and military leaders were in no mood to set up a "Russian liberation army." To remain in active service, Kononov had to settle for the command of a much smaller unit, dubbed the 102nd Cossack Regiment. The nucleus of this formation was composed of soldiers and officers from the 436th Regiment. In addition, its ranks were augmented by 542 POWs, mostly Cossacks, enlisted from a nearby camp. By the middle of September the strength of 102nd Cossack Regiment stood at nearly 1,800 men and officers.[57]

That autumn, as Kononov led his men in their first operations as auxiliaries with Army Group Center, another force of anti–Soviet Cossacks appeared on the southern end of the Eastern Front. Like Kononov, the leader of this band of rebellious Cossacks, Nikolay Nazarenko, was a Don Cossack. Beyond that similarity, however, the two men had little else in common. As a child, Nazarenko had fled Russia during the civil war and settled as an émigré in Romania. When he came of age, he enlisted in that country's army and slipped back into the Soviet Union as an undercover agent. His intelligence mission, however, came to naught when he was arrested and sentenced to a forced labor camp. After several years in the camp, Nazarenko escaped and made his way to the Caucasus, where he joined an underground anticommunist cell. In the summer of 1941, he and his accomplices, with the aid of forged identity papers, relocated to Taganrog, were mobilized with local factory militias and then hastily sent into battle to assist the hard-pressed Ninth Red Army. Upon reaching the front, Nazarenko's company turned their rifles on neighboring Soviet troops and defected to the XIV Panzer Corps.

After crossing to German lines, Nazarenko was taken to the headquarters of XIV Panzer Corps' commander, General Gustav von Wietersheim. There he asked for he and his men to be allowed to serve alongside the Germans; a modest request in comparison to Kononov's stated desire to organize an anticommunist Russian army. The cautious Wietersheim, however, was reluctant to violate official policy by allowing Slavs to serve openly with the German army. Instead, he urged the Cossacks to pass themselves off as ethnic Germans. Nazarenko refused this suggestion and, after further discussion, convinced Wietersheim to allow his men to fight alongside the Germans as the Cossack Reconnaissance Battalion. Before long the detachment, discernable in *feldgrau* uniforms only by white armbands displaying the letter "K" for *Kosak*, was marching with its patrons towards Rostov.[58]

The defections of Kononov and Nazarenko are but two examples of how Cossacks and other Eastern peoples began serving the German army even before the enlistment of Osttruppen ("Eastern troops") was officially sanctioned by either OKH or OKW. While some of these units were deployed as scouts or raiders against the Red Army, most had to settle for less dashing missions such as escorting Soviet POWs to the rear or protecting railways and roads from guerrillas. By the end of 1941, the invaders were experimenting with numerous militias recruited from deserters or the local civilian population. Indeed, one of their most unusual projects in this field began late that year when the Second Panzer Army, with the approval of its army group headquarters and Ostministerium, established the Autonomous Administrative District of Lokot. With minimal interference from the Germans, the leading collaborators of this self-governing region, located on the edge of the guerrilla-friendly terrain of Bryansk Forest, guarded their villages as well as the Germans' rear with a militia that, by September 1943, approached 10,000 troops supported by 36 field guns and 24 captured T-34 tanks.[59] Overall, the use of indigenous units proved successful by keeping the partisans in check while freeing up German manpower so it could be used elsewhere. It is no wonder then that by the beginning of 1942 the German army, with the approval of Ostministerium and OKW, was openly recruiting POWs of Georgian, Armenian, Turkic and Caucasian extract into four ethnic legions. During the ensuing months, more such formations were planned for the Crimean Tatars, Volga Tatars, Azeris and Kalmyks.[60]

Despite the successful deployments of the 102nd Cossack Regiment and the Cossack Reconnaissance Battalion, the Germans were slow to establish more Cossack formations. While this may be partly attributable to the fact that their forces, except for a brief incursion into the western Don during the previous autumn, had not yet occupied the main Cossack lands, the same could be said for the Caucasian Muslims who were being organized into legions. A more likely reason for the absence of additional Cossack auxiliary formations during this period was the prejudice of the Ostministrium, which at the time was attempting to consolidate the organization of Osttruppen under its aegis. Whereas Rosenberg's ministry was eager to exploit the perceived anti–Soviet tendencies of Ukrainians and various Caucasian peoples, it was reluctant to apply a similar policy towards Cossacks since it refused to accept their claims as a distinct nationality. Germanophile Cossack emigres challenged that position by denying the Slavic origins of Cossacks,[61] and their argument was corroborated by a 1942 study by the SS-operated Wannsee Institute.[62] In addition to removal of that racial stigma, the Cossacks would also benefit from the growing interest among senior army commanders for a more enlightened Ostpolitik, which was being advocated by the likes of Lieutenant-General Schenkendorff and Captain Strik-Strikfeldt.[63] On 15 April even Hitler, who the previous summer had specifically excluded Cossacks as unfit to carry arms on behalf of Germany, assented to the formation of armed Cossack auxiliaries.[64] Despite his about-face, the Führer did impose the condition that they and other Osttruppen must not serve in cohesive units larger than a battalion (750 men).[65] This stipulation, which was obviously designed to prevent any legion from becoming too strong, created a dilemma for Schenkendorff since the 102nd Cossack Regiment under his command was over twice that strength. Rather than risk damaging the morale of the Cossacks by dismantling their unit, Schenkendorff opted instead to skirt the rule by simply renaming the detachment the 600th Don Cossack Battalion. His decision appears to have been successful in avoiding any unpleasantness with its members. Indeed, the unit continued to serve so effectively that in the autumn of 1942 its commander, Kononov, was promoted to the rank of lieutenant-colonel.[66]

At around the same time Hitler approved the recruitment of Cossacks, the German army was attempting to introduce regulations for Osttruppen units. This work was carried out under the direction of Major Count Claus von Stauffenberg of Section II, Organizational Division of OKH. Stauffenberg, who would later acquire fame for his leading role in the July 1944 attempt to assassinate Hitler, subscribed to the Other Germany thesis that the war against the Soviet Union could only be won with the assistance of its peoples. Through the Organizational Division, he hoped to demonstrate that the Eastern peoples, when treated properly, could be valuable allies. His first step towards this goal was to improve the conditions under which the Osttruppen served by issuing them standardized uniforms, insignia, decorations for bravery and better provisions. He then sought to enlarge the number of volunteers in the German army. Since the Ostministrium continued oppose the arming of ethnic Russians, Stauffenberg's section focused on the recruitment of non-Russian peoples. Cossacks were included in the latter category after the SS declared them no longer Slavs. According to Hans von Herwarth, who was assigned to Section II of the Organizational Division earlier that year, the fact that Cossacks were allowed to enroll in the "Eastern battalions" was widely publicized by recruiters and in the camps. "As a result," wrote Herwarth, "thousands of POWs—many of them Russians—took the hint, identified themselves as Cossacks and left the camps."[67]

When Stauffenberg and his associates embarked in their work on behalf of the Osttruppen, they were optimistic that their example, once it showed good progress, would be followed by Ostministrium, the SS and other agencies in charge of the greater part of the occupied Eastern territories. However, they had hardly begun their work when the populations of those lands were confronted with new tribulations in the form of compulsory labor and mass deportations. By early 1942, the Third Reich was in desperate need of workers to replace those men who had been drafted from the factories and fields into the armed forces. To meet these demands, the occupation authorities in the East began recruiting volunteers from the civilian population for work in Germany. When these drives fell short of their quotas, the Germans resorted to forced deportations—frequently in inhumane conditions—of able-bodied men and women to the Reich.[68] Looking back on these methods, Strik-Strikfeldt wrote, "It was all too reminiscent of the way that Stalin's gangs had behaved at the time of forced collectivization."[69]

Therefore, despite the push by Stauffenberg and the Other Germany group for a "saner" Eastern policy in 1942, the brutal, unpopular practices from the previous year only worsened. By then much of the civilian population in the occupied Eastern territories were thoroughly disillusioned with German rule. Even though the invaders did make concessions such as the belated promise of agrarian reform, these were received with considerable skepticism.[70] The drafting of civilians for labor in the Reich's industrial enterprises was especially unpopular, and it was not unheard of for persons to flee into the forests and take their chances with the partisans rather than risk deportation to a factory in Germany.

Just when it seemed that the army's efforts to enlist more Osttruppen would be crippled by the dwindling numbers of willing and enthusiastic volunteers among Eastern peoples, the Wehrmacht launched a new offensive during the summer of 1942. This campaign, which was directed against the lower Volga and North Caucasus, provided fresh opportunities for officers like Stauffenberg to test their ideas since it brought the Germans into new areas that had not yet experienced Nazi misrule. Moreover, the setting of these new battles handed them one other advantage since it enabled them to make direct contact with peoples who possessed a strong tradition of resistance to communism. Foremost among these groups were the Cossacks.

The Stanitsas Under the Swastika

Even before he launched his war with Russia, Hitler made it clear that his only interest in the Caucasus was control of its abundant oil resources.[71] This was a stark contrast to most of the conquered Eastern territories, where he harbored outlandish plans to reduce the native population to ignorant helots, crisscross the land with autobahns and transform the Crimea into a German Riviera.[72] Subsequently, as Army Group A, an offshoot of Army Group South, began overrunning the North Caucasus during the Germans' 1942 summer offensive, Stauffenberg and his associates exploited Hitler's disinterest in that region to obtain for themselves extensive powers concerning its occupation and administration. Their efforts led to a Führer directive issued on 8 September authorizing the establishment of puppet regimes for Caucasian ethnicities while entrusting control of the region to the commander of Army Group A, General Wilhelm List. By then Stauffenberg had recruited the former German military attaché to Moscow, General Ernst Köstring, as the "General in Charge of Caucasian Affairs." From that post, Köstring was able to prohibit deportations for compulsory labor, assure the humane treatment of POWs and introduce self-government in certain locales. Stauffenberg's group was also fortunate that the two plenipotentiaries from Ostministrium assigned to its staff, Otto Bräutigam and Gerhard von Mende, were knowledgeable and sympathetic to the region's peoples.[73] Together, these men trumpeted the promise to restore private property and abolish collective farms in leaflets dropped over enemy territory and in posters plastered in public squares throughout the occupied settlements.[74]

Militarily, the Germans made stunning progress after they recaptured Rostov on 23 July 1942. Within a fortnight, their vanguard covered over two-hundred miles to take Stavropol and encroach upon the oilfields around Maykop. The former capital of the Kuban Host, Krasnodar, fell to them on 12 August. Their momentum, however, ebbed when they reached the Caucasian foothills. Not only did they find themselves operating in mountainous, woody terrain that was more favorable to the defenders than the flat steppe, but they also had to contend with serious supply issues. Petrol became so scarce at times that camels were used in place of lorries to distribute fuel to the thirsty panzers at the front. After the Battle of Stalingrad got underway in late summer, List's replacement as commander of Army Group A, General Paul Ludwig Ewald von Kleist, saw his front weakened by the diversion of motorized troops, anti-aircraft corps and most of his air squadrons northward to the quagmire along the Volga.[75] As a result of these complications, the German advance

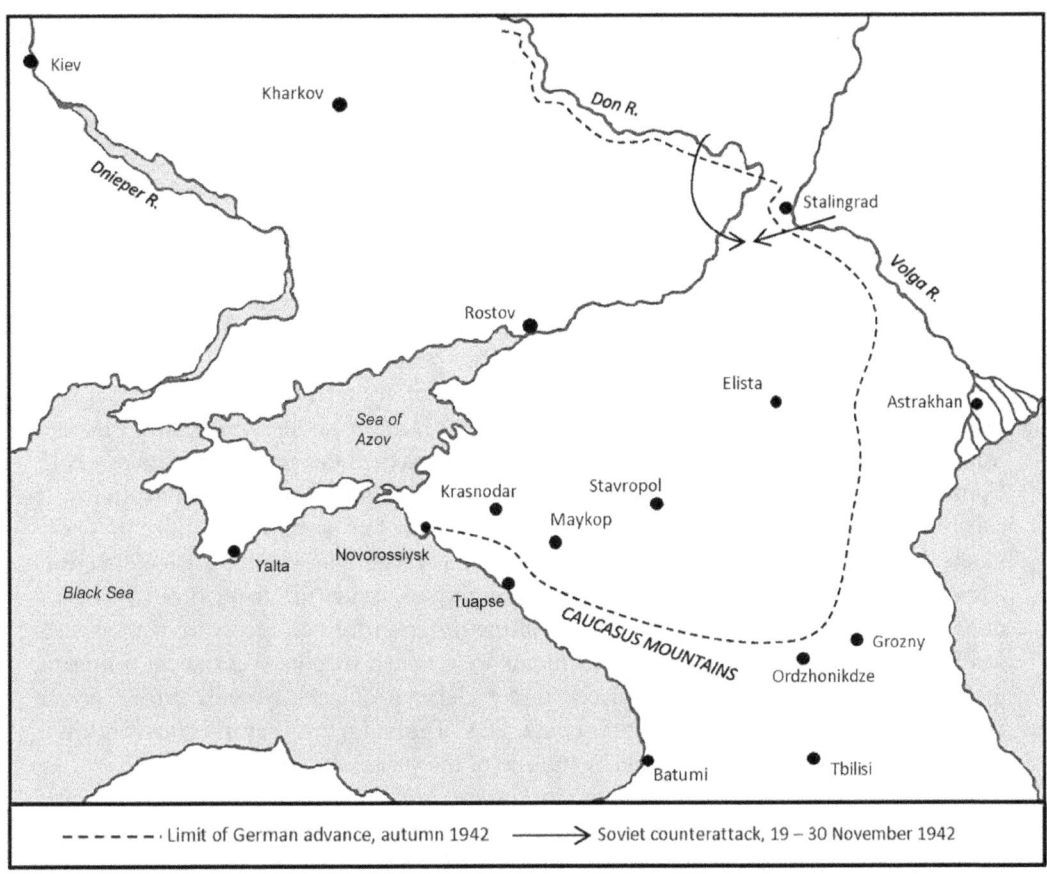

The War in South Russia and the North Caucasus, 1942.

in the North Caucasus bogged down in the autumn of 1942, and their progress arrived to a complete halt in November.

Nonetheless, the invading forces, before they were brought to a standstill, succeeded in occupying most of the Don and Kuban Cossack homelands as well as a fragment of the former Terek Cossack Host. Historians have long disagreed over how the Germans were received by Cossacks and other peoples of the North Caucasus. During the Cold War, Western historians, relying primarily on German and postwar émigré sources, tended to equate the Cossacks' and natives' long record of grievances against the communist regime with pro–German sentiment.[76] Yet, while Wehrmacht propaganda promising the dissolution of collective farms, reopening of religious shrines and offers of self-determination certainly appealed to some Cossacks, highlanders and nomads; it is doubtful whether a majority of the population from any group actively collaborated with enemy.[77] At the other extreme of this controversy are the writings of Soviet historians which essentially parrot the claims of the state-controlled press that all Caucasian peoples were invariably united with the rest of the country in its opposition to the "Hitlerite robbers."[78] Stalin, however, clearly did not buy into his own propaganda since later in the war he had entire Caucasian ethnic groups deported on charges that they collaborated with the enemy. Besides this extreme example, further evidence of the populations' flagging devotion to the Soviet regime can be seen in the impotence of the partisan movement in the North Caucasus. Although party officials had months to anticipate the occupation and prepare underground organizations in the region,[79] these efforts came to naught as the projected partisan movements there mostly withered away without active support from the civilian population. Lacking recruits and basic supplies, guerrilla activity in the North Caucasus was largely restricted to the marshy Kuban River delta and the rugged countryside around Krasnodar even though plenty of other areas were conducive for partisan warfare.[80] In light of these observations, it is reasonable to surmise that the North Caucasians peoples were generally wary of fully committing to either side. Their overall stance may described as one of passive neutrality at least until events allowed them to predict with certainty the outcome of the present struggle.

Despite the prevalence of caution among the peoples of the North Caucasus, there were individuals and factions who threw away all discretion in the presence of the German "liberators." Underground anticommunist organizations in the stanitsas were aroused from their long hibernations as the invaders approached the Don and Kuban lands in 1942. Upon the Wehrmacht's arrival, their members quickly made the leap from conspirators to collaborators. The Germans, for their part, were much better prepared to utilize these elements than they had been during the previous year. For example, a lieutenant-colonel from Army Group A's staff, Wesel von Freytag-Loringhoven, made the formation of Cossack units more systematic by organizing a recruiting program for volunteers from the stanitsas. In most instances, these new detachments were issued surplus Wehrmacht uniforms, took an oath to Hitler, and were placed under German officers. At least three German lieutenant-colonels, Joachim von Jungschutz, D. R. Lehmann and Baron Hans von Wolff, presided over regimental-sized units by the end of the year.

While the Germans, with few exceptions, were careful to appoint their own personnel to lead these military detachments, they did allow Cossacks to organize and command local militias. Shortly after capturing Novocherkassk on 22 June, self-appointed representatives of the Don Cossacks were granted permission to form a field staff to oversee the formation of armed self-defense units in the former Don Host.[81] This group soon elected a forty-six-year-old engineer, Sergey V. Pavlov, as their field ataman. Pavlov possessed an impressive record of service in the White armies during the civil war and, remarkably, managed to evade the prying eyes of Soviet security organs in the twenty years since that upheaval. As field ataman of the Don Cossacks, he helped organize a security force composed of ten regiments and numerous squadrons armed mostly with weapons captured from the Red Army. This achievement was even more impressive when one considers that the Soviets, whenever they retreated from an area, usually forced any able-bodied males among the civilian population to evacuate with them. This practice was calculated to leave few recruits available to either the enemy or any collaborators. Nonetheless, Pavlov succeeded to scratch his units together from men who hid themselves during the Soviet withdrawal and war prisoners taken by the Germans. The latter endeavor presented its own challenges as a number of POWs were eager to falsely claim a Cossack background in order to escape the awful camps. While the Germans, as we have seen, were not averse to disguising ethnic Russian volunteers as Cossacks, Cossack patriots were too proud to allow this indiscretion to continue. Thus, to weed out pretenders, Pavlov appointed a commission to certify the true origin of each applicant by having them answer questions specific to Cossack history and traditions.[82] Such was the latest attempt by anticommunist Cossacks to determine who was fit to bear the Cossack designation.

Although the Don Cossacks were allowed to establish their own militia, the goal of

These young Osttruppen, possibly Kuban Cossacks, appear to be in good spirits as they listen to an interpreter (right, back to camera) in the German-held Kuban bridgehead during 1943. Several of the men are wearing *kubanka* caps embossed with the Nazi eagle (akg-images / Sammlung Berliner Verlag / Archiv).

achieving some level of independence remained elusive. On 15 November, Cossack leaders in Novocherkassk formally asked Berlin to recognize the sovereignty of the Don.[83] To their disappointment, this request was denied since neither the German government nor Ostministrium was prepared to grant Cossacks self-rule. On the other hand the army, having fewer scruples, did just that in a small district in the neighboring Kuban. There the military administrators attached to Army Group A, with the approval of the quartermaster general in Berlin, established a self-governing district on 1 October. This so-called "Cossack Republic," with a population of 160,000, was organized along the stanitsa model on an experimental basis. Since it proved successful at maintaining law and order, its advocates in the army intended to expand its borders during the following year. However, those plans were never put into practice since by then the tide of the battle had turned decisively against Germany. Throughout its brief duration, the existence of the self-governing Cossack district was not widely advertised, most likely to conceal it from Rosenberg and his hirelings who had not been consulted on the project. As a result, most Cossack émigrés probably did not learn about it until after it was terminated.[84]

As in the Don, collaborationist Cossacks in the former Kuban and Terek lands used the opportunity afforded by the German occupation to elect field atamans of their own. The man chosen by the Terek Cossacks for that post was, like Pavlov, a veteran of the White army by the name Nikolay L. Kulakov. He was a double amputee, having lost both of his legs in the civil war, and was among those left behind during Denikin's chaotic evacuation of Novorossiysk in early 1920. During the following two decades he concealed himself in a hidden cellar below his house with the help of his wife, who threw Soviet investigators off his trail by claiming that her husband had died of his wounds. He remained in hiding until the rearguard of Red Army pulled out of his stanitsa late in the summer of 1942. At that opportune moment, Kulakov emerged from his hideout, summoned his fellow Terek Cossacks to make war upon the communists and befriended the Germans.[85]

Not long after his "resurrection," Kulakov met with a German lieutenant-colonel by the name of Helmuth von Pannwitz. The forty-four-year-old Pannwitz had been dispatched to the North Caucasus by OKH in the last week of September to investigate the practicality of creating a large Cossack cavalry formation. Having conferred with Kleist and Köstring, he found both generals receptive to his project. He also reviewed various German-sponsored ethnic battalions and was most impressed by the bearing of Lieutenant-Colonel Jungshutz's Cossack regiment.[86] That experience seems to have convinced Pannwitz that his idea of creating an effective Cossack cavalry formation to fight on the side of Germany was a realistic goal. Upon reporting his findings to Field Ataman Kulakov, the Terek leader urged Pannwitz to proceed with his project immediately.

As it turned out, that first meeting between the German lieutenant colonel and the Terek field ataman marked the beginning of a lasting friendship. Indeed, Pannwitz possessed many qualities which enabled him to win the confidence and admiration of Kulakov and other like-minded Cossacks. His childhood home, in Upper Silesia, was located on the Liswarta River which had marked the frontier with Russian Poland. As a youth, he was fascinated by the sight of the Cossack border guards patrolling the opposite bank. By the time the First World War broke out in August 1914, Pannwitz was enrolled at cadet school. The following October, when he turned sixteen, he graduated from the Prussian Royal Cadet Corps and enlisted in the Emperor Alexander II Uhlan Regiment. Just a few months later he was promoted to second lieutenant and in 1917 he was awarded the Iron Cross, First Class after being wounded amid fighting in the Carpathian Mountains. Between the wars, he resided in Poland for several years until rejoining the German army as captain of a cavalry squadron in 1935. By the start of Second World War, then, his background had already imbued him with all the prerequisites to become a successful commander of Cossacks: seasoning as a cavalry officer, recognition for valor in battle, fluency in the Russian language and, last but not least, an acute sense of appreciation for Slavic peoples.

Pannwitz's military career continued its interminable progress during the Second World War. In the campaigns in Poland and France, he commanded a partly motorized reconnaissance detachment. He remained in that role into the summer of 1941, when his unit at times scouted as far as 90 miles ahead of its division. By the end of that summer, he had been promoted to lieutenant-colonel and awarded the Knight's Cross to the Iron Cross. A few weeks later he was recommended for the Oak Leaves clasp to the Knight's Cross but this decoration was withheld after refusing to embark on a mission he considered suicidal for him and his men. In November, he was waylaid by an illness that forced him to give up his field command. When he returned to active duty the following month, he was attached to OKH as an advisor on mobile troops, where he remained into the summer of 1942. During that time, he became convinced that the Hiwis serving as noncombatants or in small counter-insurgency detachments were being underutilized by Germany. Subsequently, he independently developed a plan to form large frontline units from the Eastern volunteers, particularly Cossacks, to serve alongside Wehrmacht troops and help rally the Soviet peoples to the German cause. Although it conflicted with Hitler's earlier order restricting Osttruppen formations to battalion strength, the proposal caught the eye of General Kurt Zeitzler, the new chief of staff at OKH, who sent Pannwitz to the North Caucasus in September to broach his idea to the staff of Army Group A.

After "selling" his project to Zeitzler, Kleist and Cossacks like Kulakov, Pannwitz's next step was to head to Berlin to begin laying the groundwork for a Cossack cavalry division. He arrived there in early October but his work was soon cut short when he was summoned back to the Eastern Front after Germany's military fortunes suddenly took a drastic turn for the worst.[87]

The crisis which warranted Pannwitz's return to Russia began on 19 November, when the Red Army launched a massive, double-pronged counteroffensive on the flanks of Army Group B, whose strength was concentrated on capturing the industrial center of Stalingrad. By then the struggle for the city, which for the second time in twenty-five years earned it comparisons with the First World War siege of Verdun,[88] had been raging for three months. During that time, the seesaw street fighting in Stalingrad assumed a symbolic importance to both sides completely out of proportion to its strategic value. The operations there easily overshadowed the fighting in the Caucasus, even though the latter contained abundant grain, oil and mineral resources coveted by both sides.[89] Just when the battle in the ruined city appeared to be settling into a stalemate, the successful Soviet counterstrokes on its outskirts swung the contest in the defenders' favor. Four days after launching their attack, the jaws of the Red Army closed at Kalach, 50 miles west of Stalingrad, completing the encirclement of the German Sixth Army and neighboring formations—almost 300,000 men in all. In the following weeks, the Red Army invested considerable energies into widening its ring around the trapped Axis troops by pushing further westward, thereby threatening the main supply line of Army Group A, which ran through Rostov, in the process.[90] Pannwitz's assignment was to avert further disaster in this crucial sector of the front.

Pannwitz arrived in the Don territory just as Field Marshal Erich von Manstein, as commander of the newly-formed Army of the Don, was orchestrating Operation Winter Tempest in a vain bid to rescue the imperiled Sixth Army. Pannwitz immediately set about cobbling together a task force from an armored brigade, Romanian cavalry brigade, Romanian artillery battery and, last but not least, about 1,000 Cossacks from Ataman Pavlov's self-defense units. With this ad hoc formation, he sought to block the First Red Army's push towards Novocherkassk, where Manstein's headquarters was located, and secure the extended right flank of the Fourth Panzer Army, which on 12 December had launched its drive to break through to the Stalingrad pocket. In the ensuing days, Pannwitz's force succeeded in checking the Red advance and ending the threat to the southern flank of the Fourth Panzer Army. It also bagged 3,000 enemy prisoners. Although this achievement did not save Manstein's relief effort, which was repulsed before reaching the Stalingrad pocket, his handling of the task force earned Pannwitz a Romanian decoration, Order of Michael the Brave, Third Class, as well as his long overdue Oak Leaves for his Iron Cross.[91] The operation also brought recognition to the Cossacks' valor and was another demonstration of what they might accomplish if they were capably led, treated with dignity and, most importantly, given a chance.

Soviet Cossacks in the Great Patriotic War

Despite the noted successes of German policies in attracting recruits from the stanitsas and permitting a degree of self-rule in at least one Cossack district, depictions that the Cossack population was thoroughly anticommunist in the Second World War were no more accurate than similar claims made of them in the Russian Civil War. Indeed, the majority of Cossacks fought with, and not against, the Red Army during Russia's "Great Patriotic War." As mentioned earlier, in 1936 the Soviet government lifted its restrictions against Cossacks and established five Cossack cavalry divisions in the Red Army. Although these formations held a substantial number of individuals who were of non–Cossack ancestry, an undetermined number of *bona fide* Cossacks were serving in these divisions upon the outbreak of the war; and many more were to be conscripted in the following years.[92]

While the popular image of the Second World War is one of tanks charging across battlefields, cavalry did find a niche on the Eastern Front. The Red Army, in particular, made extensive use of horsemen; fielding at least 200,000 towards the beginning of the conflict and five times that many by its end.[93] They were, admittedly, vulnerable in the open country against a well-armed and prepared enemy. For example, on 16 November 1941 the Soviet 44th Cavalry Division was slaughtered by machine guns and artillery fire when it attempted to charge the positions of the German 106th Infantry Division near Klin. In that action, the defenders did not even suffer any casualties.[94] But, as the deployment of horsemen in the Soviet counteroffensive around Moscow proved just a few weeks later, cavalry could still be effective in terrain or weather unfavorable to the operation of vehicles. While German tank crews had to light fires beneath their vehicles' engine hulls just to get them started in the bitter cold,[95] Soviet cavalrymen, mounted on horses bred from hardy steppe ponies, were still able to maneuver and help drive the enemy back from the capital.[96]

Soviet successes with cavalry continued as the conflict entered its second year. In early 1942, the 1st Guards Cavalry Corps, commanded by Major-General Pavel A. Belov, terrorized the rear of Army Group Center for several months and even evaded a pursuing force of seven divisions.[97] That summer, as the armored spearheads of Army Group A fanned out across the North Caucasus, the 17th Kuban Cossack Cavalry Corps, under the command of Lieutenant General Nikolay Y. Kirichenko, repeatedly distinguished itself in defensive operations and local counterattacks against the invaders.[98] Later in the war, during an interview with an American correspondent, Kirichenko attributed the success of his Cossacks to the "dependable mobility" provided by their horses. As he explained it, "Where the tank cannot pass, where the human foot cannot tread, the horse can make its way."[99]

Still, the Soviet Cossack divisions, despite their skilled riders and clever use of difficult terrain, were not enough to prevent the enemy from overrunning most of the North Caucasus region during the summer of 1942. During those critical months, when the Germans once again seemed unstoppable, Stalin sought to improve the Red Army's performance through measures ranging from the abolishment of political commissars to the introduction of epaulets and gold braid to officer uniforms.[100] In another throwback to tsarist days, elite formations in the Red Army were designated as "guard" units. This distinction was soon bestowed upon Kirichenko's men, who were renamed the 4th Guards Kuban Cossack Corps, for their role in repulsing the German Seventeenth Army's attacks along the highway leading to Tuapse.[101] Finally, in case offers of decorations and honorific titles were not enough incentives, a decree was read to all Red Army troops on 30 July in which the phrase "Not a step backward" became the order of the day. On the Soviet homefront, communist propagandists employed the slogan "Everything for the front, everything for victory" to remind the civilian population of what was expected of them in the war economy.[102]

Despite Stalin's blanket rejection of further retreats, Soviet forces in the North Caucasus, rather than make a suicidal stand against a much better-equipped enemy, continued to give ground into that autumn. To deprive the enemy of as much resources as possible, party territorial committees shipped industrial equipment, grain and hundreds of thousands heads of livestock outside the threatened districts. What could not be removed from the enemy's path was destroyed. Under this policy, the oil derricks near Maykop were wrecked and nearby oil stockpiles were set ablaze.[103] These scorched-earth tactics, however, were frequently hampered by the rapidity of the German advance, confusion among local officials and, at least in some instances, the reluctance of the population to evacuate or destroy their livestock and crops.[104]

While German accounts sometimes claim that the troops from Army Group A were given a rapturous welcome by residents in villages and even in towns like Krasnodar, Soviet sources allege that such spectacles were deliberately staged by the Nazi invader for propaganda purposes.[105] Whatever the truth, any genuine enthusiasm the Cossacks and other North Caucasians peoples might have held towards the Germans largely dissipated in the following weeks and months of the occupation. Disillusionment quickly set in as the invaders suppressed local newspapers and failed to deliver manufactured goods from Central Europe. In districts where the retreating Soviets had stripped the countryside of foodstuffs, shortages and hunger arose which the Wehrmacht, with its overburdened supply lines, could not alleviate. Most distressing of all was the occupiers' slow progress in breaking up the collective farms. In many areas, the promised land reforms were begun only in December, weeks after Army Group A had been halted and the Sixth Army had been encircled at Stalingrad.[106] Those developments, which cast serious doubt on the Soviets' ultimate defeat, gave Cossacks and other peoples a powerful incentive to remain aloof from the Germans even as their most earnest desire, the liquidation of the collective farms, was on the verge of being realized.

As a result of its economic and, most of all, military shortcomings in the North Caucasus, the German army fell short of its goal of transforming that region's peoples, including its Cossacks, into dependable allies. Russian historians from the Stalin to Putin eras regard the Cossacks as overwhelmingly loyal to the motherland. Indeed, a German officer taken prisoner by the Red Army was said to express disappointment in the failure of anticommunist propaganda to generate widespread enthusiasm among the Cossack population.[107]

As in the civil war, anticommunist propaganda in the stanitsas was countered by fanatics who remained faithful to the Soviet cause. These were mainly represented by partisans who took to the mountains or marshes, emerging ever so often to raid an enemy patrol or supply dump. Since the steppe regions were ill-suited for guerrilla warfare, partisan activity during most of the occupation was confined mostly to a few select areas of the North Caucasus. One partisan hotbed was in the mountains just outside of Krasnodar, where Cossacks were counted among the guerrillas.[108] They faced immense challenges in the summer and early fall of 1942 when the local population by and large preferred not to take sides in the struggle. The partisans' operations became easier later in the year after the German offensive lost momentum and disillusionment with occupation set in among civilians. As the return of Soviet power appeared more likely, many North Caucasians clearly distanced themselves from the occupiers and, in an effort to prove their loyalty, began lending support to partisan or underground groups. Subsequently, as the civilians grew less cooperative, German policy in the region hardened until it was little different from the rapacious Ostpolitik practiced in other occupied Eastern territories.[109]

One final explanation behind the Germans' tepid reception in the Cossack homeland was that their restoration of atamans and promises of autonomy appealed only to a shrinking demographic. The policies and practices of de-Cossackization, collectivization and deportations which occurred under communist rule had permanently transformed the stanitsas. One historian has even argued that Cossackdom had ceased to exist by the latter 1930s.[110] While that view may be extreme, it can be said with certainty that the Cossack people were barely recognizable after these calamities. The Soviet government's 1936 "rehabilitation" of Cossacks was not a boost but rather another blow to the famed horsemen of the steppe. After that announcement, the Cossack identity became more ambiguous than ever as nearly anyone residing in the North Caucasus—as long as they were not a highlander—could refer to themselves as "Cossacks." Descendants of non–Cossacks felt no nostalgia for the military traditions and stanitsa politics which had once featured so prominently in the Cossack way of life. There was not even the certainty that these new "Soviet Cossacks" possessed basic horse-riding skills.[111] If the bulk of these newly-minted Cossacks harbored anti–Soviet sympathies, it was because they desired control of the land and not a return to old Cossack customs. Such a sentiment was not exclusive to Cossacks and was probably widespread throughout much of the rural population in the Soviet Union.

Outnumbered by pretenders and tied to collective farms, true Cossacks had almost no influence in the homelands. Their regional administration and military apparatus, which had enabled them to rapidly field armies during civil war, had been extinguished for over two decades and could not be rebuilt during the brief six-month German occupation of the North Caucasus. Gradually, the Germans, defectors and émigrés were forced to accept the reality that their incipient anticommunist movement among Cossacks faced even greater hurdles than that from a generation earlier. There was no way around the fact that the Pavlovs and Kulakovs of the Second World War wielded considerably less power than the Krasnovs and Dutovs of the civil war.

14

Regroup

Flight from the Caucasus

By the end of 1942, the German disaster at Stalingrad placed the over 400,000 Axis troops in the North Caucasus in a precarious position. Their advance in that theater had already stalled in mid–November amid increasing logistical difficulties, mounting enemy resistance and the depletion of manpower as supporting units were transferred northward to the Stalingrad inferno. Nonetheless, even after it was clear that the invaders could push no further, General von Kleist was ordered by Hitler to hold his army group's positions. It was not until the final days of year when the Führer relented by allowing Kleist to withdraw. This permission came not a moment too soon as Soviet forces in the region kicked off 1943 with an offensive along the Terek River. Over the course of the following month, Army Group A continued to pull out of the North Caucasus.[1]

For the population in the armies' paths, the shifting fortunes of war brought immense hardship. Determined to leave nothing of use to the enemy, the evacuating Germans abandoned their earlier policy of restraint and respect towards people and property in the North Caucasus. Suddenly, stores of grain were set alight, livestock was requisitioned, public buildings were mined, orchards were leveled and valuable implements were smashed to pieces at machine-tractor stations.[2] The local population's agony did not end with the arrival of the Red Army. Whenever a slice of Soviet territory was liberated from the invaders, denunciations and interrogations ensued as the NKVD began its frenzied effort to round up suspected traitors.[3]

The honeymoon between the Germans and the majority of the North Caucasian population—in so far there ever was one—was long over by the time the evacuation began in early 1943. Still, thousands of Cossacks and Caucasian natives chose to uproot their families and take flight along the slushy roads as the Wehrmacht pulled out of their districts. The reasons why they chose to do so are varied. Some may have been unwilling to give up the religious freedoms and economic opportunities they had acquired during the brief German occupation. Most of these refugees, however, were probably motivated to flee out of fear of Soviet reprisals. Kleist, at the behest of Ostministrium representative Otto Bräutigam, aided the civilians' flight by establishing an agency to direct and provide relief to the Caucasian refugees.[4] Estimates for the total number of Cossacks who fled alongside the Wehrmacht that winter on foot, horseback or in rickety wagons pulled by oxen or camels vary, but it seems probable that that figure was in the tens of thousands.[5] Other than the fact that they were falling back from a victorious Red Army, their plight bore little similarity to the White retreat through the North Caucasus in 1920. The German troops, unlike those of Denikin, did not panic and continued to put up resistance as they withdrew. The weather was also milder for the Germans and the wayward refugees than it had been for the Whites. Some were able to escape from the North Caucasus through Rostov, which Manstein's Army Group Don kept open by stubbornly resisting the Red Army's efforts to reach the Azov coast.[6] After the Soviets finally captured Rostov on 14 February, the remaining Germans and evacuees were able to escape from the Kuban by crossing over into the Crimea via the narrow Kerch Strait—a route which Denikin's shattered forces had failed to utilize. Indeed, the disparity between the two withdrawals could not be more evident than in how the two commanders fared after their operations were complete. Denikin's military career, as we have seen, ended following the White debacle in the North Caucasus, but Kleist, in recognition for having successfully extracted his armies from that region, was promoted to the rank of field marshal.[7]

Not all Cossack collaborators opted to leave their homeland that winter. A few brave warriors, convinced that the German withdrawal was only a temporary setback, tried to vanish into the countryside in order to carry out guerrilla attacks until the invaders returned.[8] Although the Germans retained a bridgehead in the Kuban from which Hitler intended to launch a renewed offensive in the North Caucasus, that plan came to naught. By late summer of 1943, the Red Army had unquestionably gained the initiative on the Eastern Front and, during the following September, the Germans withdrew from their remaining positions in the Kuban region.[9]

For the time being, the majority of Cossack refugees from the North Caucasus were directed by the Germans to set up camp at Kamenets-Podolsk in southwestern Ukraine.[10] There they bided their time hoping, like the White émigrés a generation before them, that their present situation was temporary. They believed that sooner, rather than later, they would return triumphantly to their homeland.

The Genesis of the Cossack Cavalry Division

The grave reverses experienced by the Wehrmacht in the winter of 1942–43, like those suffered a year earlier, provided another impetus to those officers and officials who sought to modify Germany's Ostpolitik. Even before the debacle at Stalingrad, Otto Bräutigam composed a top-secret memorandum which sharply criticized the failure of his countrymen to capitalize on the evident unpopularity of communism among Eastern peoples. "Were the war being conducted only for the smashing of Bolshevism," the Ostministrium official declared, "then it would have been decided long ago in our favor." The predicament in which Germany now found herself, he reasoned, had materialized because "our political policy has forced both Bolshevists and Russian nationals into a common front against us."

In order to assuage the discontent among the masses in the occupied territories, Bräutigam outlined several possible actions which he felt should be undertaken by Germany. Among these measures was a plan conceived by Wehrmacht propagandists to mimic Charles de Gaulle's Free French movement by setting up a "Free Russia" equivalent under a captured Red Army lieutenant general, Andrey Vlasov.[11] Several weeks earlier, the towering and bespectacled Vlasov had launched his controversial career as a collaborator by publicly declaring his opposition to Stalin. In subsequent months, Vlasov and his organization passed further milestones that once seemed unthinkable: he was portrayed as the commander of a "Russian Liberation Army," became chairman of a Russian National Committee and one of his most ardent German backers, Captain Wilfried Strik-Strikfeldt, was appointed to lead a training school for Russian officers and propagandists at Dabendorf, twenty miles outside of Berlin. By the beginning of 1943, Vlasov's anticommunist appeals were being disseminated in leaflets sown over the Eastern Front as well as in Russian-language newspapers distributed to Russian workers and soldiers already serving the German war machine.[12] In February, he made a tour of the occupied regions behind Army Group Center. While passing through Mogilev, he visited the 600th Don Cossack Battalion and made a favorable impression on its troops and their commander, Lieutenant-Colonel Kononov. Frustrated by the size restrictions imposed on Eastern formations since the previous year, Kononov and his men optimistically interpreted Vlasov's appearance as a sign that the Germans had at last recognized error of their ways.[13] For them, other collaborators and the German officers who despaired over their side's utter failure to nurture the anti–Stalin opposition among Eastern peoples, the emergence of Vlasov seemed too good to be true. And it was.

At this stage, much of the Vlasov movement was a hoax. The former Soviet general himself lived under a perpetual cloud of suspicion; at times both the OKW and Gestapo were itching to arrest him. He was only spared this humiliation thanks to his influential friends in the army and later in the SS.[14] In reality, his much-hyped Russian Liberation Army consisted of nothing more than the battalions of Osttruppen scattered across the expanse of the Eastern Front. Neither Vlasov nor his closest associates had any control over their deployment. This arrangement was perfectly fine with Hitler. As late as June 1943, the Führer declared, "We will never build up a Russian army, that is a phantom of the first order."[15] The Vlasovites also lacked any real freedom in their political activity. In their hearts, Vlasov and most of his inner circle sympathized with the program of the National Labor Alliance (NTS), with whom they established a working relationship. But ultimately, it was the Germans who had the final say in the content of the manifestos and appeals published by the Russian National Committee.[16]

Still, the fact that the so-called *untermenschen* were finally permitted to establish a visible anticommunist movement of their own, even an impotent one, was quite a deviation from the Führer's earlier refusal to even pay lip-service to such aspirations.[17] For Cossacks, Berlin's more acquiescent attitude towards Slavs and other Eastern peoples promised them new opportunities for expanding their military and political activities; especially since the Nazis regarded them as more racially-desirable than Great Russians. Earlier, when Pannwitz had originally begun his planning for a Cossack cavalry division in the autumn of 1942, he had only the backing of the German army chief of staff. But when he returned to that task in January 1943, he did so with the knowledge and approval of the Führer. His recent decoration with Oak Leaves for his Iron Cross, it seems, had aroused Hitler's curiosity in the potentialities of fielding a large Cossack formation under such a proven, competent officer.[18] Still, his work in the next few months would not be without some imposing hurdles. Erich Koch, the ruthless Reichskommissar for Ukraine, vehemently opposed the plan for a Cossack division and tried to obstruct its formation on his territory. Fortunately for Pannwitz, the army's need for troops enabled him to override Koch's objections and begin gathering his Cossack volunteers at the town of Kherson, on the lower Dnieper. To deflect the suspicions of other anti–Slav Nazis, Pannwitz's nascent formation was named Cavalry Task Force Pannwitz (Reiterverband Pannwitz) in order to conceal the nationality of its recruits. Hardly had he overcome that challenge before he was pulled away again, this time to the Crimea to defend Feodosia from the threat of an amphibious landing by Soviet forces. There, with the help of Kuban, Don and Terek Cossacks under Field Ataman Kulakov, he succeeded in securing the vicinity of the Black Sea port. In the meantime, the task of laying the groundwork of the Cossack division was left to his subordinates. A difficulty which they and Pannwitz encountered was locating German officers whose attitudes towards Eastern peoples were not warped by racist propaganda. With one exception, all Cossack regiments were to be commanded by Germans. The problem of finding suitable officers was partially resolved by incorporating existent Cossack detachments, including their German officers, into the division. Other positions were filled with German cavalry officers, especially those from Austrian backgrounds. Still, the task of acquiring enough qualified German officers who did not regard the Cossacks as racially inferior took many months to overcome.[19]

Shortly after Pannwitz was able to take leave of the Crimea, on 23 April, OKW officially recognized the Cossack division and ordered it to begin training at Mława, about 80 miles north of Warsaw. Thereafter, Cossack detachments began converging on that town from all over the Eastern Front. Thousands of Cossacks, including the 760 who had formed the original contingent of Cavalry Task Force Pannwitz, arrived there from Kherson. From Army Group South came the regiments commanded by Jungschutz, Lehmann and Wolff. Kononov's 600th Cossack Battalion, which continued to hold the distinction of being the only sizable unit in the Wehrmacht officered entirely by Cossacks, was dispatched to there from Mogilev. Nazarenko's battalion and the Terek Cossacks under Kulakov also joined the mix. Others were volunteers recruited from POW camps or the refugees who had been screened by a commission to verify each man's Cossack background and political reliability. In all, approximately 10,000–15,000 Cossack troops collected at Mława. It was an impressive feat, and one that was made possible only by the intervention of the Führer's headquarters since many German formations were reluctant to let go of their Cossack auxiliaries.[20]

The task of molding this collection of Cossack refugees, war prisoners and irregulars into a cohesive division would not be easy. These men hailed from any one of several hosts and varied considerably in age; photographs of the recruits show gray-bearded Cossacks mingling among boyish-faced youths. Some arrived at the camp donning Wehrmacht uniforms and helmets while others were dressed in rags. Those who had previously fought with the Germans often carried an assortment of firearms ranging from Mausers to rifles captured from the Red Army or partisans.[21] Among this gaggle were egotistical pretenders claiming that either the Germans or a certain group of Cossacks had recognized them as field ataman.[22] Adding to the general confusion and distrust among these groups were the subversive activities of Soviet operatives who succeeded in infiltrating the division's ranks.[23]

Under another commander, the Cossack division might never have come together, but Pannwitz was no ordinary officer. From his earlier observations in the North Caucasus, he knew that the Cossacks would follow and obey officers who earned their trust and respect.[24] To that end, he showed considerable sensitivity toward their customs and Orthodox faith. As one of his colleagues put it, Pannwitz "associated himself heart and soul with Cossack traditions."[25] Prior to the war, he had displayed a penchant for collecting uniforms from historic Prussian regiments.[26] As a Cossack commander, he put that indulgence for costumes to good use by wearing *cherkesskas*, *papakhas* and other traditional Cossack garments for ceremonial occasions. Indeed, he marked his promotion to major-general, announced on 1 June, in Cossack attire. He also sought to purge the division of its most problematic elements. German officers and non-commissioned officers who displayed prejudice or arrogance towards the Cossacks were replaced. According to Lieutenant Nazarenko, he encouraged interactions between Germans and Cossacks since he considered such exchanges "absolutely essential for the creation of a unified spirit."[27] As for the pro-Soviet elements which infiltrated the division, a counterintelligence unit was formed to comb them out and curb their activities. In his limited spare time, he took excursions to Mochówo, about 50 miles southwest of Mława, where he visited with the families of some enlisted Cossacks who settled there to be closer to their sons, husbands and brothers. A training regiment, initially under the command of Colonel Alexander von Bosse, was established at that camp as well as an informal "cadet corps" that was set up to groom underage Cossacks for eventual admission into the ranks of the Cossack division.[28]

Still, Pannwitz's energetic and enlightened style of leadership alone was not enough to boost the morale of the Cossacks during their roughly three-and-a-half-month training at Mława. In particular, the high-handed treatment accorded to them by local German authorities outside the division was a sharp reminder to Cossack recruits that many Germans regarded them, at best, as second-class citizens.[29] At one point, Pannwitz grumbled to his friend, General Baron Horst von Buttlar-Brandenfels, then chief of the Operations Department at OKW, about the unending challenges his men faced as long as the insolent practices of Ostpolitik were allowed to continue. "At the time he complained particularly about the fact that the [German] Government's policy held up no national aim for his division," Buttlar-Brandenfels testified after the war, "and he made other complaints about the difficulties incurred by the members of his division at that time who were partly on the road and had to be settled."[30] Such concerns were indicative of the deep obligations which Pannwitz and other like-minded German officers felt towards the Cossack and Caucasian warriors who chose to retreat with the Wehrmacht earlier that year. "Having cut themselves off from their homelands, these loyal soldiers became entirely our responsibility," wrote Lieutenant von Herwarth.[31]

Although Pannwitz was unable to overrule Hitler's orders, he did seek other ways to lift the spirits of his division. In particular, he turned to émigré Cossacks for advice and assistance. This decision had some clear benefits; the old émigrés could, after all, easily relate to those homesick Cossacks who wondered whether they would ever see their homeland again. A possibly even greater advantage was the prestige which some old émigrés, even after a generation abroad, still held among Cossacks from the Soviet Union. Nonetheless, this strategy did carry the risk of further disrupting the division's delicate cohesion by injecting yet another distinct group into its already diverse mix since, as we shall see, many émigrés had their own ideas about how to construct a Cossack liberation movement.

Worlds Collide: Émigrés and Defectors

Since Hitler had no desire to entertain the aspirations of the Russian Diaspora, Cossack émigrés were initially excluded from any role in the war effort against the Soviet Union. Just days before the invasion began, German police placed travel restrictions on all émigrés, including Cossacks, to bar them from entering the soon-to-be-occupied Eastern territories.[32] Few measures could have injured the morale of the émigrés more than placing their "liberated" homeland off-limits to them. As a result, most Cossack émigrés were sidelined. One exception was Poltavets-Ostranitsa, the chief of the National Ukrainian Cossack Organization, who remained a confidant of Alfred Rosenberg. Still, neither Poltavets-Ostranitsa nor the Ostminister possessed the leverage they needed to temper the brutal German occupation of Ukraine.[33] Cossack émigrés claiming to represent their compatriots in the North Caucasus and further east were in an even more unfavorable position since they could not even count on the sympathy of Rosenberg. As we have seen, the Ostminister initially dismissed their ethnic assertions and instead regarded them as simply another breed of contemptible Russians.

The fortunes of Cossack émigrés began to brighten with the onset of 1942. The proven dependability of Cossack defectors, such as Kononov's detachment, and the grievous setbacks experienced by the Wehrmacht during the previous winter, made German commanders amenable to increasing the number of Cossack auxiliaries. Unable to resist this trend and concerned that his agency might be left out, the Ostminister decided to jump on the Cossack bandwagon. First, he elevated the Cossacks' status in his projected new order by reversing his earlier judgment that Cossacks and Russians were one and the same. Next, he established the Cossack Central Office, headquartered in Berlin, in a bid to consolidate all Cossack political and military activity in the Reich and its occupied territories. If his project succeeded, it would have extended the Ostministrium's influence into émigré communities, occupied stanitsas and among Cossack volunteers at the front. This objective, however, was hindered by Rosenberg's decision to collaborate with émigrés whose politics were more palatable to his personal tastes rather than that of Cossacks in general. Since he remained an advocate of dismantling the Russian colossus, he initially aligned the Cossack Central Office with the separatist politics of Vasily Glazkov's Cossack National Liberation Movement (KNOD). Before long, KNOD propaganda detailing its ideas of a German-sponsored "Cossackia" was disseminated via the Cossack Central Office to POW camps, Osttruppen and stanitsas throughout the occupied Eastern territories.

Besides its propaganda duties, the Cossack Central Office was also responsible for enlisting Cossack volunteers in Hitler's anticommunist crusade. Except during the brief occupation of the North Caucasus in 1942, the only available pools of potential Cossack recruits for most of the war were émigrés, refugees and war prisoners. Even so, the results of the Cossack Central Office's recruiting drives were worse than expected, and this engendered considerable disappointment in Nikolaus Himpel, the man appointed by Rosenberg to supervise the organization. Himpel realized that for the Cossack Central Office to acquire influence among Cossack émigrés and defectors it needed a much wider appeal than that offered by the controversial Glazkov. Gradually, he set his sights on General Pyotr Krasnov, the former Don ataman and one of the most prestigious Cossack émigrés, as the best candidate to inspire Cossacks to take up arms on behalf of Germany.[34]

Krasnov, now in his early seventies, had visibly aged since having risen to prominence during the civil war. He no longer sported a well-trimmed mustache or short-cropped hair, his eyesight was failing and he walked laboriously with a cane.[35] Yet, despite his physical deterioration, his desire to destroy Bolshevism remained as fervent as it had been when he led the All-Great Don Host against its Red opponents in 1918. That legacy, combined with the additional acclaim he acquired in exile as a novelist, were key factors behind Himpel's interest in him. Yet, it was one of Krasnov's lesser appreciated traits—namely, his political dexterity—which made him the perfect fit to lead the Cossack Central Office. During his tenure as Don ataman, he walked a political tightrope between the Germans and the pro–Allied Volunteer Army. As an émigré, he did the same with the Francophile Supreme Monarchist Council and the German-oriented Aufbau. Although it would be a stretch to claim that he was universally popular, he made few bitter enemies and was generally respected among Cossacks.[36]

In 1937, Krasnov left France, where in previous years NKVD operatives had regularly targeted prominent White émigrés, to reside in more secure living quarters outside of Berlin.[37] From there, he followed Nazi Germany's campaign against the Soviet Union, and particularly any flickers of rebellion among Stalin's subjects, with keen interest. In December 1941, he sent a letter to Kononov praising his decision defect and serve the anticommunist cause.[38] During the following year, it was the turn of the defectors to fawn over the civil war hero when Krasnov welcomed a Don Cossack delegation dispatched to the German capital by Field Ataman S. V. Pavlov. Their meeting apparently went well until the delegation invited their host to lead their effort to raise new Cossack forces. At that point, the former ataman quickly turned down their offer on the excuse of his poor health.[39] Other considerations may have also factored into Krasnov's decision. One was that he may have been mindful of the restrictions which made it difficult for old émigrés to enter the occupied Eastern territories. Another possibility was his inherent distrust of Soviet defectors; a sentiment that was prevalent among old émigrés.[40]

The old émigrés quite frankly held a number of reservations about the anticommunist movements that were taking shape in the occupied Eastern territories. Since the Germans did not officially permit the émigrés to visit those lands until the summer of 1942,[41] these organizations originated among Soviet defectors without much participation from the exiles. Most émigrés doubted that their compatriots, after decades of living under a regime which ruthlessly suppressed private initiative and independent thought, were capable of organizing a viable resistance movement. Others, leery of Soviet provocations, distrusted the defectors as undercover communist agents. Another complication was that émigrés and defectors, after having been estranged from one another for more than a generation, had significant cultural, social and above all political differences that were difficult to bridge. Ever since they abandoned their homelands, émigré leaders had thought of themselves as curators of their people's heritage. They were convinced that only they could restore their people's culture and institutions in a pure, unadulterated form. In their opinion the defectors, though they might have good intentions, were irretrievably corrupted by Marxist influences. On the other hand, some defectors felt that only *they* could offer a practical program to rally their kinfolk to the anticommunist cause. In their eyes the émigrés, at best, were simply too long removed from their homeland to understand its current character and needs. At worst, the émigrés might want to restore the pre-revolutionary order or were completely beholden to the Germans.[42]

As events played out, Cossack leaders did not get a very large window of opportunity to see which group, the émigrés or defectors, possessed greater appeal to the masses in the North Caucasus. It was not until the German evacuation of that region was already underway in January 1943 when Krasnov was approached by Himpel with an offer to lead the underperforming Cossack Central Office. At first the former Don ataman, wanting nothing to do with the brand of radical separatism promulgated by Glazkov and Ostministrium, turned down the proposal. As in the civil war, Krasnov, though eager to extol the unique heritage of the Cossacks, never denied their close kinship with the Russian people.[43] His acquaintances, likewise, detested Glazkov's movement but urged him to reconsider his decision so that he might use the position to curtail separatist propaganda. Krasnov yielded to their argument and, on 25 January, he was inducted as chief of the Cossack Central Office. His appointment immediately caught the attention of OKH. At the latter's behest, he authored an appeal two days later calling upon Cossacks to fight alongside Germany. To appease his bosses at Ostministrium, his statement was carefully worded to avoid any suggestion that the Cossacks were bound to take up arms on behalf of the Russian national cause.[44]

Initially, Krasnov remained in the background when Pannwitz began inviting old émigrés to Mława during the summer of 1943. Even so, less-prominent Cossack exiles from all over German-occupied Europe answered the call. Those who had spent the interwar period in Yugoslavia were especially valuable as officer material since many had been educated at one of the three cadet schools established in that country by the exiled White army. Cossack emigrés who were veterans of the tsarist army were recruited to serve in Pannwitz's personal bodyguard.[45] The émigrés, then, quickly acquired key positions of influence in the division even though luminaries like Krasnov abstained from an active role in the division. That, however, would change as the formation prepared to embark for the front.

By September 1943, Pannwitz's First Cossack Cavalry Division was approaching the end of its training. It was organized into two cavalry brigades, each with three cavalry regiments. Of the six regiments, two consisted of Don Cossacks, two of Kuban Cossacks, one of Terek Cossacks and one, the 2nd Siberian Regiment, was a catch-all unit of Cossacks originating from hosts east of the Volga River.[46] Each brigade possessed a battalion of horse-drawn artillery while the entire formation was supported by reconnaissance, engineer, signal, medical and replacement training battalions along with a veterinarian company. For lighter moments, the division also included a mounted band to accompany it in parades and ceremonies.[47]

Like other Osttruppen, the Cossacks' main desire was to serve on the Eastern Front, where the future of their homeland was being decided. Instead, the division received orders to prepare for battle not against communists in Russia but rather against communists in Croatia. The factors behind the decision to send the Cossacks to the Balkans are unclear though one historian, Peter Huxley-Blythe, has asserted that it was made at the behest of their commander, Pannwitz. According to him, Pannwitz latched onto the idea of leading his division into Croatia after he realized that it would not be permitted to serve in a *bona fide* Russian liberation army on the Eastern Front.[48] In any case, Pannwitz was concerned how the marching orders for Croatia would be received by his division. In order to make this news more palatable to them, he decided it would be best if it was delivered to them by someone who enjoyed their full confidence and admiration. He knew that the man best qualified for the task was Krasnov, who accepted the general's invitation to visit the training grounds at Mława in early September.

The arrival of Krasnov, which shortly preceded that of the Kuban ataman, General Vyacheslav G. Naumenko, to the Cossack division was an occasion for parades, songs and stirring speeches. These émigré leaders, who for more than twenty years had yearned to see a Cossack army again take the field against the Bolsheviks, were naturally thrilled by the spectacle of well-drilled Cossack soldiers riding past them. Krasnov, appreciative of Pannwitz's efforts in building the Cossack division, readily complied with the latter's request to break the news to the soldiers that they were headed for Croatia and not the Eastern Front.[49] In his speech, he expertly spun this news by portraying the Red partisans in the Balkans as an extension of the international Bolshevik conspiracy which enslaved their homeland. Indeed, a Cossack soldier later admitted that these links between the communists in Russia with those in Croatia "to some extent smoothed over Cossack unhappiness with being sent there."[50]

Krasnov also depicted the deployment to the Balkans as a temporary assignment; implying that the Cossacks would eventually be sent to the Russian front.[51] Although this was not to be, he should not be faulted for misleading the men since he probably truly believed that the division would someday see action in Russia. He had no way of knowing that just a few days later, after the division had boarded trains for southeastern Europe, an intense controversy erupted among top German military circles concerning the use of Osttruppen.

This imbroglio began at a conference on 14 September when Himmler attributed recent Soviet gains to desertion among the Osttruppen. This allegation provoked an enraged Hitler to demand that the Osttruppen—which by then numbered approximately 800,000 men—be immediately disarmed and employed only as laborers. OKH, at the behest of the General der Osttruppen, General Heinz Hellmich, resisted the order on the grounds that the Eastern volunteers were, on the whole, reliable and that their demobilization would place the Wehrmacht at an even greater manpower disadvantage. Eventually, the two sides reached a compromise where the Osttruppen could continue to serve in combat roles in theaters other than the East so that they would not be tempted to desert to their compatriots in the Red Army.[52] For the First Cossack Cavalry Division, this decision mitigated the chances that it would ever see action in Russia.

As a result of this controversy, most Osttruppen—including those Cossack battalions not incorporated into Pannwitz's division—were redeployed to France in late 1943 and early 1944 to guard against the threat of an amphibious landing by the Western Allies. After being sent to a strange, faraway land to fight for a cause which they felt was not their own, the morale among these volunteers plummeted. To boost their spirits, Vlasov, as commander of the mythical Russian Liberation Army, published an open letter indicating that the decision behind their redeployment to the West was not final.[53] Still, the transfer of the Osttruppen from the Eastern Front to Western Europe made it difficult to hide that fact that Nazi leaders had deep reservations about them and were quite insensitive towards their aspirations. "Had they been mere mercenaries, their disillusionment would have been less," wrote Herwarth of the Osttruppen. "They were idealists, however, and hence their disenchantment was the more profound."[54] While his observation may over-romanticize the motivations of the Eastern volunteers, there can be little doubt he was correct in his assessment that the unending series of real or perceived slights weighed heavily upon their minds and their fighting abilities.

15

Catastrophe

Refugees in Retreat

While Pannwitz was busy consolidating various Cossack formations and recruits into a battle-ready division, the Cossack refugees who left their homeland with the retreating Germans during the winter of 1942–43 faced the excruciating task of putting their lives back together as best as they could. Like all émigrés, they hoped that events would transpire in a manner that would allow them to return to their stanitsas sooner rather than later and, for that reason, they were unwilling to fully unpack into their new surroundings. Indeed, the news from the front was not all bad when they concentrated in the vicinity of Kamenets-Podolsk in late winter and early spring of 1943. In mid–March, a counterattack by Army Group South retook the industrial city of Kharkov.[1] This victory, along with warmer weather and the deployment of a new generation of armored vehicles, such as the Panzer V Panther and Panzer VI Tiger tanks, seemed to presage further successes for the Wehrmacht in the upcoming months. But Germany's main effort that summer, the offensive against the Kursk salient, sputtered out in only a matter of days and was answered by a powerful Soviet counterthrust that pushed most of Army Group South across the Dnieper River by mid-autumn.[2] Those events made it clear to all that the Wehrmacht no longer held the initiative on the Eastern Front. For the Cossack refugees at Kamenets-Podolsk, the German failure at Kursk and the ensuing drive of Soviet forces deep into Ukraine compelled them to resettle behind a quieter sector of the front.

The Cossack refugees were directed northward to Novogrodek (Navahrudak), 90 miles east of Minsk.[3] By spring of 1944, an estimated 25,000 Cossack refugees had collected in the vicinity of that Belorussian town.[4] Naturally, their morale was low; it was after all the second time within a year that they were forced to relocate to a new region. Two factors, however, improved their outlook. The first was their sense of security at Novogrodek. When they arrived, the local partisan movement was insignificant; a stark contrast to more wooded parts of Belorussia. To their east, the frontlines of Army Group Center deflected one Red Army assault after another during the winter of 1943–44.[5] For those first months, the troubles of the war seemed far away. The second factor which lifted their spirits was the charismatic leadership of S. V. Pavlov, who was elected field ataman that winter by this throng of wandering Cossacks. Under his direction, the German occupation authorities again allowed the Cossacks to form new settlements, which they called "Cossachi Stan," on the stanitsa model and provided them arms to organize their own self-defense militias.[6] Although Pavlov assured his followers that one day they would be able to return to their liberated homeland, he was not content to simply wait for a brighter future. To improve the refugees' present lot, he encouraged the construction of a school, hospital and church. The clergy among them organized the settlements into a Cossack diocese. In the surrounding countryside, the Cossacks planted fields and grazed cattle just as they would have done if they were back in the steppe. The entire experience awakened in them a sense of defiance and pride; emotions which their ancestors surely felt when they fled from Muscovy into the wilderness centuries ago. Hence, after local guerrillas began to step up their activity in late spring of 1944, the Cossacks responded energetically to this threat by organizing four infantry regiments.

Unfortunately for the refugees, their pleasant existence at Novogrodek ended abruptly that summer. The first reminder of the violent realities of the nearby Eastern Front came on 17 June when Field Ataman Pavlov was killed while riding to a nearby village. According to Kuban Ataman V. G. Naumenko, who was present in Cossachi Stan during the tragedy and its subsequent investigation, Pavlov had been shot off his horse by Belorussian policemen who mistook the field ataman and his escort for Soviet partisans.[7] Despite that official conclusion, alternate tales attributing Pavlov's untimely demise to partisans or even an agent-provocateur among his own men persisted long after the incident. Whatever the cause, a leader of his caliber proved irreplaceable. The void left by him was filled by his chief-of-staff, Timofey I. Domanov, a forty-six-year-old Don Cossack colonel with an uncertain background. Some sources allege that he was a teacher and former Red Army major prior to his collaboration with the Germans; others claim that he was a veteran of the Don Army who was employed in various managerial roles in the Caucasus between the wars.[8] According to another account, postwar interrogations by the Soviet military counterintelligence agency known as SMERSH established that Domanov was a NKVD operative charged with organizing resistance behind German lines. If indeed he made such a confession, it should not be accepted at face-value. There is no evidence that Domanov attempted to undermine the invaders; instead he helped them by recruiting Cossack auxiliary units after the Wehrmacht reached Pyatigorsk in 1942.[9] Regardless of his checkered past, he was apparently genuinely committed to the anticommunist cause. As a leader, his primary flaw was that he lacked his predecessor's magnetism. Indeed, he was not elected but rather was appointed field ataman by Naumenko and Major Müller, the German liaison officer to Cossachi Stan.[10] But even if Domanov had been more charismatic, he could not escape the fact that Pavlov had left him enormous shoes to fill. Moreover, his inauguration as field ataman coincided with the start of a massive Soviet offensive in eastern Belorussia that led to hardships which would have been trying for any leader in his position.

The Red Army attack, codenamed Operation Bagration, opened on 22 June, just five days after Pavlov's death. The Soviet forces, enjoying a huge superiority in troops, artillery, armor and warplanes, quickly smashed through the front of Army Group Center. The defenders' losses were staggering; in just the first twelve days of the offensive German casualties soared to over 300,000. Most of the German Fourth Army was encircled east of Minsk, which fell to the Red Army on 3 July. Five days later the Soviets seized Baranovichi, just 40 miles south of Novogrodek.[11] By then the Cossacks at Novogrodek had loaded their families onto horse-drawn carts and, driving their herds alongside them, were in a frenzied flight from the onrushing enemy. "We left Novogrodek hurriedly, pressed on all sides by Bolsheviks and partisans," recalled a female Cossack refugee. "We often went along mined roads, captured partisans being led at the front of the column. This was a frightful trip with masses of blown-apart people and horses."[12] Eventually, the Cossack caravan reached the town of Zduńska Wola in western Poland. From there, most boarded trains to northern Italy, where they were directed by the Germans to Tolmezzo, a town nestled in the Alps. The selection of Tolmezzo, nearly 1,000 miles from Novogrodek, as the Cossacks' destination was apparently the work of Himmler's SS, which by that time was taking a curious interest in all Cossacks residing in German-controlled territory. The area was chosen for Cossachi Stan since it was outside the borders of Hitler's Greater Germany yet far enough away from any front to put them beyond any immediate danger. The SS intended to use the Cossacks to police the surrounding mountainous countryside and help suppress local anti-fascist partisans who were becoming increasingly bold as Allied forces in Italy inched northward.

To prepare Tolmezzo and neighboring villages for the arrival of the Cossack refugees, SS troops descended on these communities and evicted their unlucky Italian residents from their homes. This operation unintentionally aided the recruiting effort of local guerrillas since some the dispossessed Italians, having nowhere else to go, joined the insurgency. What remained of the local population, then, was anything but welcoming when the column of exhausted Cossack refugees dragged themselves into Tolmezzo during September 1944. In addition to vengeful guerrillas, the members of Cossachi Stan also faced the immediate problem of locating enough forage in the area's sparse pastures for the more than 3,000 head of livestock they brought with them. Ten miles to the north, at Paluzza, a similar scenario unfolded as the Germans settled about 4,000 Caucasians in that municipality and then left them to organize their own administration and defense. Comprised mostly of survivors of shattered Ostlegions, this group was a heterogeneous mix of Georgians, Armenians, Azeris, Ossetians and a sprinkling of Circassians. Not surprisingly, their ethnic, linguistic and religious dissimilarities fostered plenty of internal discord among them. By comparison, Domanov's Cossacks, though ragged, desperate and amalgamated from several hosts, seemed disciplined and orderly. None of this mattered, however, to the local Italian population. They despised all of the refugees as menacing heathens; a view that was reinforced by the sight of exotic costumes, sheathed sabers and the occasional camel in the herds of both groups.[13]

Politics in *Götterdämmerung*

The Wehrmacht's difficulties in containing the Red Army from mid–1943 onward had a significant impact on official German attitudes and policies towards Eastern peoples. For the Cossacks, these events mirrored the actions of Denikin, who made extensive concessions to them when his armies were confronted with total defeat.[14] On 10 November 1943, just four days after the Germans lost Kiev and along with it any hope of holding the enemy at the Dnieper, the chief of OKW, Field Marshal Wilhelm Keitel, and Ostminister Alfred Rosenberg issued a joint proclamation to the Don, Kuban, Terek and Zaporozhian Cossacks promising them the right to observe their customs, settle their homelands and lead an "independent life." In exchange, they called upon "all Cossacks to work together as comrades with Germany … to organize a Europe of freedom and order."[15] The pledges made by the document, which echoed the guarantees made to Cossacks in the charters issued by the tsars, were of little practical significance. By then German Army Group South had evacuated all Cossack regions and was continuing to reel before Soviet forces. There was no indication that Berlin would be in a position to make good on its assurances to the Cossacks any time soon.

Like the Vlasov movement, the November 1943 proclamation was another example of how military expediency was slowly taking precedent over Hitler's Ostpolitik. Pragmatism alone, however, cannot entirely explain as to why such sweeping promises were made to the Cossacks. Interestingly, the proclamation came only days after Keitel's chief of staff at OKW, General Alfred Jodl, gave a speech in which he urged that the recruitment of alien peoples "be examined with the greatest caution and skepticism." While assessing the performance of the Osttruppen, he stated, "Our experiences were good while we were ourselves attacking successfully." But he went on to add, "They became bad when the position changed for the worse and we were compelled to retreat."[16] Jodl's comments, then, suggest that his boss's decision to sign the declaration on behalf of OKW was motivated by increasingly favorable attitudes specific to the Cossacks and not towards Osttruppen in general. In a sense, the Cossacks, through a combination of their fabled warrior past and contemporary reports exalting their performance as auxiliaries, had acquired the status of pets in the eyes of their doting German masters.

Even though Cossack collaborators could not fully cash in on the key promises of the November 1943 proclamation as long as German forces remained outside of the North Caucasus, they still managed to acquire some benefits from it. Most importantly, the cooperation which it had fostered between OKW and Ostministrium enabled a union of Cossack military and political organizations which, up to that point, had functioned mostly in completely separate spheres. It was in this spirit that, on 31 March 1944, the new General der Osttruppen, General Ernst Köstring,[17] summoned the formation of a Cossack Central Administration; a body that was intended to give the appearance of a Cossack government-in-exile. Though it replaced Ostministrium's Cossack Central Office, it retained that organization's eminent head, Krasnov, as its chief. Its "ministries" were filled with other atamans who had risen to prominence amid the Nazi—Soviet conflict: V. G. Naumenko, N. L. Kulakov and S. V. Pavlov (until his death later that year). Krasnov was even allowed to appoint a military staff; though it lacked any control over the deployment of Pannwitz's division or any of the other Cossack battalions scattered across occupied Europe. The Cossacks may have been the Germans' preferred pets, but even pets have leashes.[18]

Although Krasnov was the natural choice to oversee the newly-minted Cossack Central Administration, his leadership was not without controversy. In what was now a familiar dilemma, the Cossacks were broadly divided between those who desired autonomy within a Russian state and others, mostly followers of the Cossack National Liberation Movement (KNOD), who wanted nothing less than complete independence for the Cossack territories. True to his character, Krasnov was skittish on this topic. He almost certainly desired some form of close ties to Russia, but he was careful not to alienate the separatists. He knew that the latter still had powerful patrons in Ostministrium. For that reason, he met with KNOD's mastermind, Vasily Glazkov, in Berlin during July 1944. Although Krasnov refused Glazkov's demand to implement a separatist ideology for the Cossack Central Administration, he did agree to appoint three KNOD members to the organization's "ministries" of foreign affairs, internal affairs and propaganda. In exchange, Krasnov was to be recognized as "Supreme Ataman."

When the compromise between Krasnov and Glazkov was announced in an order dated 2 August 1944, it immediately triggered a backlash of protests among Cossack troops and refugees. Most commanders of Cossack formations, including Pannwitz, were Slavophiles and advocates of reconstructing a Russian national state. They opposed Ostministrium's goal of permanently breaking-up the Eastern territories. Pannwitz, for his part, refused to distribute KNOD propaganda to his troops and had threatened to arrest the fiery Ukrainian nationalist, Stepan Bandera, when he tried to stir up anti–Russian feelings among the Cossacks during a speaking tour in Croatia.[19] Subsequently, the separatist program acquired little traction among Cossack soldiers, and many expressed their displeasure with Krasnov's arrangement in petitions to his office. Key personnel, including Naumenko and General Semyon N. Krasnov, a nephew to the Supreme Ataman and the chief of staff of his shadow military headquarters, also objected to the concessions accorded to the separatists. Even Himpel, the German go-between for the Cossacks and Ostministrium, voiced his dismay with the order; a surprising development in light of his employer's long-standing preference for Glazkov. But by this stage Himpel understood that the Cossacks were useful to Germany only if they fought her enemies and not among themselves. From his earlier experience with the Cossack émigrés, he apparently felt that working with the separatists was not conducive towards that goal. Another consideration for Himpel, as well as Krasnov, was Ostministrium's waning authority by the end of that summer. The Red Army offensive which devastated Army Group Center had chased most German forces beyond the Soviet Union's former frontier, leaving hardly any Eastern occupied territories under Rosenberg's jurisdiction. With Ostministrium fading into irrelevance, retaining the support of KNOD was no longer imperative. The Supreme Ataman wisely decided it was much more critical to placate the Cossack fighting men and their commanders. Subsequently, on 29 August, he rescinded his previous order by denying the KNOD members any influential role in the Cossack Central Administration.[20]

Even after the Cossack Central Administration adopted a policy decisively in favor of retaining the Cossacks' close ties with Russia, its relations with the Vlasov movement remained uneasy. Although the former Red Army general and his supporters could not boast of any proclamations or military formations comparable to those of the Cossacks, their movement nonetheless gained momentum as the Allied armies closed in on Central Europe. Even Himmler, a longtime champion of the *untermensch* racial theory, was intrigued by the idea of employing Vlasov as a "wonder weapon" against the Soviet onslaught. On 16 September 1944 the two men held a meeting during which Himmler—according to Vlasov's version of the talks—stated his readiness to make the Russian Liberation Army a *bona fide* formation of ten divisions. Moreover, Vlasov believed the SS leader authorized him to unite all collaborationist organizations among Eastern peoples into a single movement. Subsequently, he upgraded his impotent Russian National Committee into a more inclusive Committee for the Liberation of the Peoples of Russia (KONR). It was his hope that all Eastern peoples with anticommunist sympathies would submit to his new organization. This included the Cossacks, for whom Vlasov and his associates set up a central headquarters in the anticipation that their formations would be transferred to the auspices of KONR.[21]

Disappointment soon set in for Vlasov and his disciples. Instead of the ten divisions promised in their meeting, Himmler quickly whittled that number down to three and then later two. No less distressing was the refusal of the German Ministry of Foreign Affairs, Ostministrium, OKW and Osttruppen headquarters to accept Vlasov as the legitimate spokesman for the various Eastern peoples.[22] Despite these frustrations, the Russian general plodded on with his immediate goal of forging a political program for the new KONR. With Himmler's blessing, the committee convened its inaugural meeting in the Bohemian capital of Prague on the afternoon of 14 November 1944.[23] This gathering produced the Prague Manifesto which outlined KONR's aims as "the overthrow of Stalin's tyranny," followed by the "discontinuation of the war and an honorable peace with Germany," and finally the "creation of a new free People's political system without Bolsheviks and exploiters." Many of its goals, such as "the establishment of a national-labor system," were borrowed from earlier NTS programs. On the all-important national question, the document was contradictory. While it included the promise of self-determination to the nationalities, it also emphatically stated, "The Committee for the Liberation of the Peoples of Russia regards the *unification of all national forces and their subordination to the common cause of destroying Bolshevism as the prerequisite for victory.*"[24] The KONR leaders calculated that a unified front of the anticommunist peoples of the East would be in a stronger position to press their case regardless of the outcome of the war—even in the likelihood of an Allied victory. To some non–Russian peoples, however, this call for unity smacked of Great Russian chauvinism. Nonetheless, over a dozen individuals of non–Russian ethnicity were among the thirty-seven signatories to the manifesto, though most of these persons were relatively obscure. For example, at least two Cossacks, Lieutenant General E. M. Balabin and the former commander of the Don Corps, Lieutenant General F. F. Abramov, were among the signatories of the document even though neither had a substantial role in any of the main Cossack political and military organizations then in existence.[25]

Vlasov, for his part, was eager to enlist recognized Cossack leaders in his committee. Earlier that year, he had met with General Andrey Shkuro and was pleased to find the civil war hero amenable towards the goals of his liberation movement. Krasnov, however, was a different story. He had first conferred with Krasnov, then leader of the Cossack Central Office, in September 1943. Back then the Cossack leader, ever mindful of his masters in Ostministrium, refused to submit to Vlasov's command.[26] Their second round of meetings, held over a year later on 7 and 9 December 1944, did not proceed any more smoothly. Krasnov, as was his habit on hot-button political issues, was evasive towards Vlasov's call for unity.

Why was the Supreme Ataman, who only a few months earlier had severed his ties with the separatists and oriented the Cossack Central Administration towards a pro–Russian program, still unwilling to fully cooperate with the increasingly dynamic Vlasov movement? One possibility is that he chose to remain outside of KONR in order to appease his German backers who, for one reason or another, looked unfavorably on the project. Indeed, Köstring, who was instrumental in founding the Cossack Central Administration, never really embraced the Vlasov movement. According to his aide-de-camp, Lieutenant von Herwarth, his aloofness towards the ex–Soviet general resulted from his doubts over whether Hitler would ever allow ethnic Great Russians form their own army. Subsequently, Köstring thought it was wiser invest his limited resources in the Cossack, Caucasian and other ethnic battalions sanctioned by the Führer.[27] Another consideration was Krasnov's negative attitude towards Vlasov. According to one account, the Supreme Ataman loathed Vlasov and accused him of being "a Bolshevik at heart."[28] His lingering distrust of the Soviet defectors who populated the upper tiers of KONR is understandable; during the interwar period he and many other émigrés had their hopes repeatedly dashed by anticommunist conspiracies that were later exposed as elaborate frauds orchestrated by Soviet agents. Whatever the actual reason, Krasnov's refusal to support KONR made him appear out of touch in the eyes of Vlasov's backers. In summarizing the disagreements between the two men, Strik-Strikfeldt wrote, "There was a vast gulf between Vlasov's approach and the wild fantasies of the aging Cossack general."[29]

It was not only the Vlasovites who were disappointed by Krasnov's refusal to join KONR. The majority of Cossack troops and refugees, many of whom had clamored against the inclusion of the separatists in the Cossack Central Administration, now demanded to know why their leader had decided to keep Vlasov at an arm's length.[30] Over the following months this issue, more than any other, was to hound Krasnov. Undoubtedly, the controversy was fueled in part by Vlasov's rising fortunes in the final months of the war. On 28 January 1945, Vlasov was able to formally take command of the Armed Forces of KONR, which at the time consisted of the fully-equipped First KONR Division and a nascent Second KONR Division. During the following month, a small armored detachment from the First KONR Division began skirmishing against the Red Army on the Eastern Front.[31] These developments enhanced Vlasov's prestige among those Eastern peoples, including the Cossacks, who found themselves within the shrinking boundaries of Hitler's empire. By this late stage, few could have believed that a German military victory in the war was a realistic possibility, yet Krasnov's goal of resurrecting the lost Cossack way of life in the North Caucasus was dependent on such an outcome. On the other hand, the Vlasov movement sought to foment a revolt within the Red Army that would spread throughout the Soviet Union and force a regime change in Moscow. Although the chances for this scenario were remote, it was for the Cossack refugees and millions of other displaced Eastern peoples the only plausible, desirable path left open to them.

Overall, the politics of the anti–Soviet Cossacks in World War II were hardly less tumultuous than they had been during the Russian Civil War; a circumstance that was made all the more peculiar by the fact that Cossack leaders in 1944 held substantially less authority than their predecessors twenty-five years earlier. The most contentious issue, the question of whether Cossacks should seek a completely independent state or an autonomous status within a federated, non-communist Russia, was a riddle unresolved from the civil war. Even though neither solution appeared likely, it still had real-world implications in defining the Cossacks' relations with the forces of the Russian liberation movement that came into existence during the war's final months. In contrast, other hot-button topics from the revolution were barely touched by anticommunist Cossacks in the Second World War. If, for example, the Cossack collaborators did succeed in imposing their rule on the North Caucasus, how would this affect the large outlander populations in those territories? Were they to be deported, assimilated or tolerated? Moreover, what was to become of the native highlanders, particularly in the eastern districts of the former Terek Host, who had settled Cossack lands after 1920? Finally, precisely who would be considered a Cossack in the post–Soviet order? In other words, were Cossacks to be defined according to their pre–1917 legal status as an estate, the Don government's 1918 declaration that the classification belonged only to those who fought against Bolshevism or by the Soviet government's 1936 proclamation which applied the label to nearly every resident in the North Caucasus? These questions were left unanswered by the anticommunist Cossack leaders since they were of minor significance while they and their German patrons remained far beyond the borders of their homeland. They do, however, offer a glimpse into the daunting political challenges which the Cossack collaborators faced if their movement had somehow managed to shed its surreal existence.

The Croatian Cauldron

While Cossack politicians busied themselves with formulating a program for their people once their homeland was liberated from communism, Cossack soldiers continued to put their lives on the line for that cherished goal. This was especially true for the men of the First Cossack Cavalry Division after they were transferred from the Mława camp to the western Balkans in September 1943. Their assignment to that corner of Europe was among the least desirable for soldiers in the Wehrmacht.[32] This was because the territory that had comprised the state of Yugoslavia had, since the summer of 1941, become the theater of a multisided, take-no-prisoners style civil war embedded within the wider world war.

The Cossacks were deployed to Croatia, which had proclaimed its independence on 10 April 1941, just four days after the Wehrmacht began its invasion of Yugoslavia. Throughout its existence, it was a creature of Berlin: German agents had encouraged the Croatian declaration of independence to undermine Yugoslav resistance, much of the country was occupied by either the Italians or Germans and, after November 1942, its armed forces were under German operational control.[33] The presence of outside Axis forces was required since the ruling party, the ultranationalist Ustaša, lacked popular support among Croats[34] and was detested by the Serbian minority in its realm.[35] Immediately after assuming power, the Ustaše embarked on an ethnic-cleansing program intended to eradicate the Orthodox Serbs from "Greater Croatia," which included the ethnically-heterogeneous regions of Bosnia and Herzegovina. Within months, their militias and supporters deported over 100,000 Serbs to occupied Serbia, confined thousands of others to inhumane concentration camps or simply massacred the inhabitants of Serbian villages. In order to survive the Ustaša terror, the persecuted population could either convert to Roman Catholicism or take up arms with the guerrilla bands taking shape in nearby woods and mountains. With a tradition of armed resistance dating back to the Turkish occupation of their homeland, it should not be surprising that many Serbs chose the latter option.[36]

Croatia and Neighboring Lands, 1943 - 1945

The resistance groups in former Yugoslavia, like those which developed in the occupied Eastern territories, got their start from army units and personnel bypassed during the Germans' swift military campaign. After the Yugoslav army surrendered to the invaders on 17 April 1941, the German frontline divisions were speedily withdrawn to prepare for the invasion of the Soviet Union. The troops which were brought in to occupy the subdued country consisted of older men with poor training and low-grade equipment. With these formations ill-prepared to combat the incipient resistance movement, the guerrillas gained a crucial respite that they used to build their networks and plan their forthcoming operations.[37] Another factor which worked in the insurgents' favor was the deportations and atrocities carried out against Serbs and other groups, all of which compelled the persecuted peoples to join or at least sympathize with the resistance. From the outset, however, the guerrillas themselves were broadly split into two unfriendly camps: the Četniks, whose followers tended to be royalists or Serb nationalists loosely controlled by Colonel Draža Mihailović, and the pro-communist Yugoslav Partisans under Josip Broz, better known by the nickname of Tito. After Germany attacked the Soviet Union, both insurgent groups swung into action to demonstrate their solidarity with the Allied cause. A German officer, writing of the situation in occupied Serbia that summer, observed that "placards and leaflets summoned people all over the country to plunder, sabotage and riot."[38] Railways were mined, telephone communications were cut and other infrastructure used by the Axis was demolished. The situation was no better in neighboring Croatia, which was ostensibly under the control of the pro–German Ustaša regime. In late October the German plenipotentiary general in Zagreb, Edmund Glaise von Horstenau, glumly reported, "The fighting capacity of the Croatian troops is diminishing so much that they can no longer hold their own against the insurgents."[39]

To combat the resistance in the lands of former Yugoslavia, the OKW applied the same counter-insurgency policies used in the occupied Eastern territories; meaning that all resistance was to be considered communist in origin and mercilessly suppressed.[40] Local German and Italian commanders, however, saw advantages to differentiating between the Partisans and Četniks; particularly after the latter concluded that their most dangerous enemy might be the communist Partisans and not the Axis occupation forces. The Italians were the first to accept the Četniks as an ally against Yugoslav Partisans; even going as far as providing them arms, ammunition and funds to organize additional units.[41]

By the time Pannwitz's Cossacks arrived in Croatia, Italy was no longer a factor in the Balkans since that country had surrendered just a few weeks earlier on 8 September 1943. The void left by the Italians in Slovene and Croatian territories was a further drain on German manpower as the Wehrmacht had to dispatch more troops to these lands in order to protect the river and railway routes which connected the Reich with valuable bauxite, copper and lead mines in Serbia as well as its sizable garrison in Greece. The Germans also sought to strengthen their presence along the Adriatic coast to thwart any Allied landings which might take place there.[42] The crisis compelled them to finally enter into uneasy alliances with local Četnik groups against Tito's Partisans. This policy revision was abhorred by the Croats, not least because Četnik detachments were accused of carrying out brutal reprisals against Croat villagers. The Cossack newcomers, with their fearsome reputation, were hardly more popular with either the Croatian civilians or the Ustaša regime.[43]

Once in Croatia, the First Cossack Cavalry Division, numbering about 13,000 Cossacks and 4,500 Germans,[44] was subordinated to the German Commander-in-Chief of Southeast Europe, Field Marshal Baron Maximillan von Weichs. They were immediately incorporated into Weichs' counter-insurgency campaign against Tito's Partisan army, which was believed to be 100,000–180,000 strong.[45] With the 1st Cossack Cavalry Brigade deployed in the vicinity of the Croatian capital of Zagreb and the 2nd Cossack Brigade stationed further east in Bosnia, the division's primary objective was to minimize partisan disruption of traffic along the roads and especially the railway linking Zagreb and Belgrade. Various regiments were also assigned to supporting roles in a series of offensives intended to clear various districts of guerrilla activity. The first of these, Operation Fruska-Gora, was launched in October 1943 against an insurgent stronghold northwest of Belgrade. Although that action succeeded in sweeping the insurgents from that locale, its success was indecisive. The Partisans, rather than give battle, simply slunk away and survived to fight another day. This strategy of denying their enemies a hard target was one they would use repeatedly. For the Cossacks and others involved in the counter-insurgency operations, it was nothing short of frustrating.

Pannwitz's Cossacks participated in several more anti-partisan sweeps during the remainder of 1943 and into early 1944. Occasionally, their quarry fought back. For example, the 2nd Siberian Cossack Cavalry Regiment, a portion of which was mounted on bicycles due to a lack of horses, was battered after an engagement that winter against Titoists near the town of Petrinja. That regiment acquired its revenge of sorts on 29 March 1944 when in another battle it destroyed a Partisan battalion north of Sisak. Although that triumph came at the steep cost of 21 Cossacks and 10 Germans killed, it earned the division recognition in a Wehrmacht communiqué. A few weeks later, in May 1944, the 1st Cossack Cavalry Brigade, which included the 1st Don, 2nd Siberian and 4th Kuban Cossack Cavalry Regiments, marched alongside units of the German Second Panzer Army in an operation, codenamed "Schach," to eliminate guerrilla strongholds in the mountains of central Croatia. Once again, the Titoists evaded the bulk of the attacking forces though they did manage to encircle the 2nd Siberian Cossack Cavalry Regiment. The latter, however, was able to battle its way out of the predicament with help from the 369th Infantry Division, a composite formation of Germans and Croats. Such narrow escapes, combined with the enemy's ability to seem everywhere and nowhere, added to the distress experienced by the Cossack troops.[46]

From the German perspective, the Cossacks acquitted themselves well in battle; earning themselves the nickname of "the North Caucasian Fire Brigade."[47] Nonetheless, their overall record in Croatia was marred by atrocities; especially against villages suspected of supporting the Partisans. Like their forbearers, the men of the First Cossack Cavalry Division seemed unable to resist the temptation to plunder whenever the opportunity presented itself. These incidents were made worse by the psychological strain of the guerrilla war and the prevalence of wine cellars or distilleries in the countryside. Amid some alcohol-fueled rampages, the Cossacks committed widespread rape and slaughter without regard as to whether their victims were in anyway associated with the guerrillas. Cottages and barns were also put to the torch. News of these awful deeds stoked considerable outrage among the Croatian population and compelled Glaise von Horstenau to lobby Hitler—unsuccessfully—for the Cossack division's recall from the country.[48] But such conduct was hardly unique to the Cossack division. For example, in nearby Serbia and Bosnia-Herzegovina, Waffen-SS formations comprised of ethnic Germans and Muslims indigenous to those lands committed similar atrocities in the name of anti-guerrilla warfare.[49] Nonetheless, Pannwitz tried to enforce stricter discipline by establishing a special divisional court-martial to investigate alleged criminals within the ranks. This tribunal was kept quite busy amid the divisions' first two months in Croatia, during which time it handed down no less than twenty death sentences in each of the six regiments. Those convicted of milder offensives were punished by solitary confinement or flogging. Despite these measures, Cossack troops continued to be implicated in heinous acts as late as December 1944, when a spate of rapes and looting in the northern Croatian town of Đurđevac left 26 residents dead.[50] It is no wonder then that Lieutenant von Herwarth, whose memoir tends to portray Osttruppen in the most favorable light, succinctly described Pannwitz's Cossacks as a "rough lot."[51]

The Cossacks' record of maltreatment of civilians provided plenty of fodder for Partisan propagandists. The latter's newsheets relished in gory details and exaggerations of such incidents in order to incite the population against the Cossacks and, by extension, their German and Ustaše allies. Even so, the Partisans' readiness to portray the Cossacks as bloodthirsty horsemen did not stop them from appealing to the steppe warriors to defect to their side. Indeed, the Yugoslav Partisan movement, almost from its inception, combined a watered-down version of communism with revived ideals of Pan-Slavism. Fitzroy Maclean, who slipped into occupied Yugoslavia as the head of a British Military Mission around the same time as the Cossack Division, believed that this political formula was a crucial factor behind their movement's success. "They succeeded in inducing their followers to forget the old internecine feuds and hatreds," Maclean observed, "and, by throwing together Serbs, Croats, Slovenes, Montenegrins and the rest in the fight against the common enemy, produced within their own ranks a new sense of national unity."[52] The Partisans' Slavophilism was also projected onto any and all things Russian. As a result the Cossacks, long regarded by foreigners as quintessential Russians, were an object of intense fascination for the guerrillas, who called upon their Cossack brothers to join them in the struggle against the German "oppressors of Slavs."[53]

During their operations in Bosnia, the Cossacks too acquired an affinity for their Serbian co-religionists. Aside from their common faith, many Cossacks remembered that Serbia had historically been one of Russia's dearest allies, and the old émigrés among them certainly could not forget that Serb-dominated Yugoslavia had generously welcomed thousands of White refugees at a time when few other countries were willing to accept them. These feelings made it difficult for them to stomach the Ustaša militias' indiscriminate violence against Serbian civilians or their destruction of Orthodox churches. Still, most could not reconcile their hatred of communism in order to desert to the Partisans; only about 250 are believed to have done so during their stay in Croatia. They were able to find more common ground with the pro–Serb Četniks but, as already mentioned, the latter and German occupation forces were practically fighting on the same side by the time the Cossack division was tossed into the Yugoslav maelstrom.

During the opening months of 1944, the spirits of the Cossack troops were raised by visits from their civil war heroes and prominent German officers. Representing the former were Ataman Naumenko and General Shkuro, who arrived in Croatia to review the Cossack regiments during January. In the next two months German Generals Glaise von Horstenau, who had earlier complained to the Führer about the Cossacks' misbehavior, and Köstring stopped by to observe the division as well. Herwarth, who accompanied Köstring in a car ride to review a Cossack regiment just outside Zagreb, was impressed by the mounted horsemen which escorted them along the route. "Every five hundred yards or so," Herwarth wrote, "two fresh Cossacks would appear and gallop wildly along with us until they were replaced by the next pair."[54] The visiting dignitaries were also treated to elaborate ceremonies and parades in which the Cossacks could showcase their military prowess. Cossack culture was also on full display as various regiments, including their German officers, donned tra-

Gen. Andrey Shkuro (left, in black uniform) watches two soldiers from the First Cossack Cavalry Division perform a traditional folk dance amid their tour in Croatia, 1944. Standing to the right of Shkuro is the division's commander, Gen. Helmuth von Pannwitz, and the commander of the 5th Don Regiment, Lt. Col. Ivan Kononov (in black cap) (akg-images).

ditional Caucasian costumes. The men also dazzled their guests by performing the *dzhigitovka* and serenading them with choirs.[55] These colorful spectacles overawed at least one visitor. After observing the 5th Don Cossack Cavalry Regiment on parade, the chief of staff of the Second Panzer Army, Major-General Helmuth von Grölmann, reportedly remarked, "I thought I had been transported to another world."[56]

The general improvement of the First Cossack Cavalry Division's morale in early 1944 would be dearly needed to hold it together during the tumultuous months ahead. In late May the division played a supporting role in Operation Rösselsprung, a surprise assault on Marshal Tito's headquarters at Drvar in western Bosnia. The raid, which had opened with 500 SS paratroopers descending on the village and its environs, came within a hairsbreadth of capturing the Partisan leader in his cave hideout. As a consolation, the Germans did capture important documents and disrupt the marshal's contact with the scattered Partisan formations. Still, this modest success was unable to stem the movement's momentum in the coming months. Each of the Big Three Allies—Great Britain, the United States and the Soviet Union—had attached a military mission to Tito's headquarters. British and American airplanes flying from Italy were regularly dropping advisors, arms, munitions, boots, food and medical supplies to the Partisans.[57] As a result, on 10 July the 1st Cossack Cavalry Brigade, in an anti-guerrilla sweep towards Metlika, in present-day southeast Slovenia, encountered Partisan detachments that were far better equipped and led than those they had fought in previous engagements. Nonetheless, the brigade's three regiments executed a carefully-planned attack that enabled them to take Metlika six days later. At the same time, the 2nd Cossack Cavalry Brigade, comprised of the 3rd Kuban, 5th Don and 6th Terek Cossack Cavalry Regiments, was tied down in a series of merciless—and ultimately futile—counterinsurgency raids in Bosnia.[58]

Beside the aid the Partisans were receiving from the Western Allies, another factor working in their favor was the brightening prospect of an Allied, and especially Soviet, victory in the wider war. Since mid-1943, the unrelenting advance of the Red Army on the Eastern Front boosted the Titoists' morale and made recruiting easier. By April 1944, Soviet troops of the 2nd and 3rd Ukrainian Fronts were at Romania's eastern frontier, and after they renewed their attacks in August they compelled two of Germany's partners, Romania and Bulgaria, to seek terms with Moscow and switch their allegiance to the Allies. The defection of these countries essentially opened up most of south-central Europe to the Red Army, enabling it advance to the Danube River in the western Balkans. Along the way, the Soviet troops linked up with Partisan groups in Serbia and together they captured Belgrade on 20 October.[59] "It was now plain to Hitler that the Balkans could no longer be defended," wrote General Guderian, then OKH Chief of Staff, of these disasters.[60] At that point the Führer finally ordered the beleaguered Wehrmacht divisions in the Balkans to begin withdrawing to northward, where Guderian hoped they might be available for the defense of Germany. He was to be sorely disappointed. The Partisans, along with British and American airmen operating from bases in Italy, had no intention of allowing the Germans to evacuate their sizable forces from Greece and other areas unscathed.[61] Meanwhile, other Wehrmacht units stationed in the western Balkans, including Pannwitz's Cossacks, had to remain there to keep an escape route open for the Germans retreating from the south.

Generally, the performance of the Cossack division in Croatia met the expectations of its German commanders and backers. As a result of its solid martial reputation, by mid-1944 it had captivated the second-most powerful man in the Third Reich, Heinrich Himmler. As the head of the German police, Security Service and Schutzstaffel (SS), Himmler oversaw activities ranging from intelligence and surveillance to enforcement of the regime's racial policy and administration of the concentration camps. His SS organization, in particular, was an omnipotent one that included an armed component, the Waffen-SS, which functioned as the private militia of the Nazi Party.[62] The presence of the Waffen-SS on the frontlines, fighting shoulder to shoulder with the army, was intended, among other things, to enhance Himmler's prestige and earn his place among the warrior-heroes in the Nazi Valhalla.[63] After July 1944, when he added Commander of the Reserve Army and Chief of Army Ordnance to his titles, the Reichsführer-SS was in an ideal position to play out his eccentric fantasies.[64] By then, he had become fixated on the battle-tested Cossack division and was determined to incorporate it into his Waffen-SS.

Sponsorship by the SS

As a loyal disciple of Hitler, Himmler was obsessed with National Socialist racial theories. Originally, his SS was supposed to embody a racial elite, and until the outbreak of the war, its membership was restricted to those who were deemed "Germanic" and could meet a high physical standard. The organization's ideology also preached intolerance against supposedly primitive or parasitic races, such as Slavs and Jews.[65] A glimpse of Himmler's utter disregard for Slavic *untermenschen* can be found in an October 1943 address to high-ranking SS officers at Posen (Poznań, Poland) where he declared: "What happens to a

Russian, to a Czech does not interest me in the slightest. What the nations can offer in the way of good blood of our type, we will take, if necessary by kidnapping their children and raising them here with us. Whether nations live in prosperity or starve to death interests me only in so far as we need them as slaves for our Kultur; otherwise, it is of no interest to me. Whether 10,000 Russian females fall down from exhaustion while digging an anti-tank ditch interests me only in so far as the anti-tank ditch for Germany is finished."[66] Such bombast was disconcerting for German commanders of Osttruppen units, including Pannwitz. For him, the acceptance of Nazi racial theories by German officers and soldiers were a source of dysfunction in the early existence of the Cossack division. Indeed, a late 1943 investigation into the low morale among some Cossacks attributed that problem to the prejudices they endured from German soldiers in the division's support units. Subsequently, Pannwitz and his officers implemented strict penalties for any German who denigrated Cossacks or Slavs—at a time when Himmler was still publicly spewing such demagogic remarks.[67]

Nonetheless, Germany's deteriorating military situation eventually compelled even an outspoken race-baiter like Himmler to revise his attitude towards Eastern peoples. By the time of his Posen address, the Waffen-SS was no longer able to obtain sufficient recruits from Nordic volunteers and had turned to conscripts and peoples once considered racially unsuitable, including Slavs.[68] Earlier that year, a Waffen-SS division had been formed of Ukrainian volunteers from Galicia.[69] Later, the remnant of the Russian Liberation People's Army, a conglomeration of Russians, Ukrainians, Belarusians and Poles who had served as a counter-insurgency militia in the Autonomous District of Lokot, was granted entry into the ranks of the Waffen-SS.[70] With the addition of so many Soviet peoples into the organization, the SS headquarters in Berlin set up an "Eastern Volunteers Desk," headed by Waffen-SS Major Fritz Rudolf Arlt. Arlt's efforts to guide the SS into adopting a more sophisticated approach towards Eastern peoples quickly won the support of Köstring. Around the same time, a SS propagandist, Günther d'Alquen, was allowed to proceed with a scheme designed to encourage desertion from the 2nd and 3rd Ukrainian Fronts as they were preparing their plunge into the Balkans. His operation, codenamed "Skorpion," centered on the distribution of leaflets advertising the existence of the Russian Liberation Army and signed by a Vlasovite general, Georgey N. Zhilenkov. Although this psychological warfare produced only a modest bump in the Red Army deserters, it convinced the likes of Arlt and d'Alquen that the SS must be more accommodating towards collaborators. Indeed, d'Alquen is credited with persuading Himmler to meet with Vlasov in September which, as we have seen, led to the establishment of KONR and its armed formations in the following months.[71]

The anti–Slav demagoguery of Himmler and his SS were well-known to collaborators like Vlasov, making them wary of the Reichsführer's approaches. But after they overcame their initial hesitation, they readily accepted his assistance in building their political and military organizations; if for no reason other than a lack of better options. Few, however, deceived themselves into believing that the recent change of heart experienced by the SS was due to anything but "purely practical considerations."[72]

Pannwitz too was initially suspicious when the Reichsführer expressed an uncanny interest in his Cossack division. After all, even though the SS had not classified Cossacks as Slavs since 1942,[73] the fact was that these horsemen, who blended ethnic and cultural elements of Slavic, Turkic and Circassian peoples, were the antithesis of the racial purity ideal preached by Führer.[74] Still, Himmler had long shown a fascination towards Cossacks. In early 1943 he, alongside Hitler, had supported Pannwitz's efforts to organize a Cossack division.[75] Moreover, the SS, as previously mentioned, looked after the welfare of the Cossack refugees who fled from Novogrodek to Tolmezzo after the collapse of Army Group Center during the summer of 1944. It was amid that disaster, in July, when Pannwitz was unexpectedly approached by Arlt with a proposal to transfer the First Cossack Cavalry Division from the Wehrmacht to the Waffen-SS. Pannwitz, it seems, was not eager to tie his men to the fortunes of the SS but at the same time he recognized that Himmler could provide valuable assistance in solving the division's chronic supply shortages.[76] Indeed, in recent months his Cossacks were required by necessity to ration their ammunition.[77] Pannwitz then, regardless of his personal attitude towards the SS, had a powerful incentive to explore to Arlt's offer.

Late the following month, the topic of transferring the Cossack division to the Waffen-SS was again discussed; this time in a meeting between Himmler, Pannwitz, and the latter's chief of staff, Schultz. Even in these talks Pannwitz was hesitant to accept Himmler's invitation to place the division under the Waffen-SS. "I have been in the army since I was fifteen," he explained to the Reichsführer-SS, "To leave it now would seem to me like desertion."[78] Unwilling to give up easily, Himmler sweetened his offer by unveiling a plan to augment the division into a corps by consolidating all Cossacks in the German army under Pannwitz's command. The latter finally agreed to the Cossack division's incorporation into the Waffen-SS, though on the stipulation that its leaders and officers would not be replaced with SS personnel.[79] This condition was perfectly acceptable to Himmler since the Waffen-SS, which was then growing by leaps and bounds, lacked enough trained officers of its own to lead its new formations. In fact, the conversion of the Cossack division into a SS unit brought fewer changes than might have been expected. For example, unlike earlier Waffen-SS recruits, the Cossacks did not receive any formal ideological indoctrination nor were SS runes sewn onto their uniforms. From the perspective of one historian of the Waffen-SS, the future Cossack corps and other formations cobbled together by Himmler at this stage of the war "were SS corps in name only."[80]

As a result of the deal between Himmler and Pannwitz, the division began to receive additional manpower during the autumn of 1944. A handful of recruits were released war prisoners or forced laborers but most came from existing Cossack battalions within the Wehrmacht. Some were transferred from the Eastern Front, where a few had been retained by local German commanders despite Hitler's earlier order that all Osttruppen were to be withdrawn from that theater. Many arrived from France, where they had been employed in building and manning the defenses intended to repel the anticipated Anglo-American invasion. Prior to the Normandy landings in June 1944, the Western Allies received intelligence indicating the presence of "a large Russian element that has been forced to serve with the German armies in the West."[81] To induce these troops to desert, the Allied propagandists printed leaflets promising their speedy repatriation to the Soviet Union. This appeal was counterproductive since many Osttruppen, regardless of whether they entered German service voluntarily or under duress, knew that a sentence of hard labor or death likely awaited them if they were handed over to Soviet authorities. Later that summer, after the British and American armies had landed and began hacking their way through the hedgerows of northern France, they captured thousands of Soviet peoples, including Cossacks, in German uniform. Interrogations of these prisoners revealed that they had little enthusiasm for fighting against the Western Allies.[82] For instance, the Wehrmacht's 570th Cossack Battalion, which actually contained only a minority of *bona fide* Cossacks, surrendered to the advancing Allies at the first opportunity.[83] Essentially, the Cossack battalions in the West were being thrown away and, from the German perspective, could be put to better use elsewhere. With

Himmler's help, some of these battalions, along with those in other theaters of the war, were salvaged through their transfer to Croatia to form the ranks in Pannwitz's new corps.

In late September 1944, the Cossack division was officially upgraded to the XIV SS Cossack Cavalry Corps. Rather than form new units from scratch, the two existing brigades were simply enlarged into divisions. Thus the 1st Cossack Cavalry Brigade was expanded into the First Cossack Cavalry Division with Colonel Konstantin Wagner, a career German officer who had led the 1st Don Regiment, as commander. Likewise, the 2nd Cossack Cavalry Brigade became the Second Cossack Cavalry Division with Pannwitz's former chief-of-staff, Major Hans Joachim von Schultz, at the helm. Ultimately, Himmler, to his credit, delivered on his promise to augment and reequip Pannwitz's formation that autumn, but unfortunately for the Cossacks, this did not improve their outlook since their enemies were able to augment their strength many times more.

In the coming months, as the Soviets and their allies pressed against Croatia's eastern frontiers, the focus of the Cossack corps shifted from tracking down Partisans in the country's interior to holding the Yugoslav, Bulgarian and Red Army divisions at the line formed by the Drava River. Had the Soviet 3rd Ukrainian Front made a concerted effort to reach the Adriatic, the Cossacks, German occupation forces and Ustaša militias might have been forced to withdraw from Croatia altogether. Instead, after sweeping through Romania, Bulgaria and the eastern fringe of Yugoslavia, most of that front's armor swung northward to support the Red Army's operations against more strategically-valuable targets in Hungary. The rugged terrain of the Dinarian Alps, which favored defensive warfare and restricted the mobility of tanks, probably factored into the Soviet decision to bypass that region. However, the Soviet 3rd Ukrainian Front did assign a number of rifle divisions as well as those of their Yugoslav and Bulgarian allies to secure its left flank by maintaining pressure on the remaining Axis forces along the Adriatic littoral. Such was the situation on 25 December 1944, when the Cossack corps exchanged fire with the Red Army in what one writer has called "the last engagement of the Russian Civil War."[84] In that action, the Second Cossack Cavalry Division battled the 133rd Soviet Infantry Division to prevent it from securing a bridgehead on the east bank of the Drava River near Pitomača. In fighting that at times devolved into hand-to-hand melees with bayonets and sabers, the Cossacks fought with the desperate determination of a cornered beast. Despite heavy losses, the Cossacks succeeded in denying the Soviets a bridgehead. For their valor, Colonel Kononev, whose 5th Don Cossack Cavalry Regiment endured the brunt of the engagement, and other officers were awarded the Iron Cross, First Class. Although the Cossacks could claim victory in this battle against the Red Army, which was destined to be the only significant clash between them during the war, it would have no bearing on the outcome of the conflict.[85]

Two months after the battle of Pitomača, on 25 February 1945, Pannwitz's formation was re-designated as the XV SS Cossack Cavalry Corps. By then a third division was being organized that included a shock brigade, formed around veterans of the 5th Don Cossack Regiment as well as two regiments of *plastun*. The commander of this new division was a Baltic German colonel, Alexander von Renteln. As a former tsarist cavalry officer who had seen action against the Bolsheviks in Estonia during the civil war, he was a natural fit to lead anticommunist Cossacks. Since 1942, Renteln commanded a regiment of Cossack infantry that for most of the war was known as the 360th Grenadier Regiment. In 1943, instead of being incorporated into Pannwitz's division, Renteln's Cossacks were sent to France where they were deployed along a quiet sector of coastline in the Bay of Biscay. They remained there into the following year and, subsequently, avoided the brunt of the Normandy invasion and ensuing Allied advance. Throughout much of their time in the Wehrmacht, the uniforms of the 360th Grenadier Regiment identified them as members of the Vlasov's Russian Liberation Army. Since by the time Renteln and his Cossacks were joined to the XV SS Cossack Cavalry Corps the war was entering its final months, the third division that was to be built around them never became fully operational.

As winter transitioned into spring that year, the XV SS Cossack Corps continued to skirmish with the Red Army and its allies situated on the east bank of the Drava River. Simultaneously, they had to deal with emboldened guerrillas operating in their rear. In early March 1945 the 4th Kuban Cossack Cavalry Regiment, fighting alongside the Eleventh Luftwaffe Field Division, launched an attack over the Drava as a diversion to the main German offensive further north in Hungary. Later that month, a Cossack charge against a Bulgarian artillery battery destroyed numerous guns and took 450 prisoners but thereafter they found themselves increasingly hard-pressed as Germany's collapse was imminent and her enemies closed in from all directions.[86]

Outwardly, the Cossack troops and their German officers exuded confidence in their side's ultimate victory. Their performance on the battlefield showed no indication that the men felt they were risking their lives for a lost cause.[87] It helped that their overall stellar service was recognized by the German Commander-in-Chief of Southeast Europe, Field Marshal Baron von Weichs, as well as his successor, Colonel-General Alexander von Löhr, both of whom paid their respects to the Cossack corps amid visits during those tumultuous months.[88] Yet, Pannwitz knew by then that his country's defeat was only a matter of time. A Cossack corps, even one equipped by the all-powerful SS, could not single-handedly reverse the tide of the war. It is likely that Pannwitz—and Cossack collaborators who saw the writing on the wall—began looking for options that might save the members of the corps from the clutches of the vindictive Red Army. Unable to challenge Allied military supremacy, they began to place their hopes in a number of political outcomes; many of them unrealistic. These schemes, as we shall see, were born out of desperation, but the position of the Third Reich and those who had staked their future on it was, in the spring of 1945, nothing if not desperate.

16

Repatriation

The Last Ataman

Even in the bleakest moments of their campaign, the men of the XV SS Cossack Cavalry Corps could take solace in knowing that their commander was always looking out for them. Pannwitz's attentiveness to their welfare was conveyed through his actions, such as in the early days of the division's training, when he stipulated that orders within the regiments were to be given in Russian and not German.[1] From the summer of 1943 onwards, he dignified Cossack customs and imagery by adopting their native costume for ceremonial occasions. To ensure that the sacrifices of his men were given fair recognition, he lobbied General Köstring for them to be eligible for the same medals and decorations that were awarded to German soldiers.[2] He took immense pride in his Cossacks' accomplishments and was convinced that their success demonstrated the grave errors of Germany's inhumane Ostpolitik. "With my division I have shown how we should have acted everywhere on the grand scale," he wrote in a January 1945 letter to his wife. "My Cossacks are as faithful and brave as ever, which is almost beyond understanding in the present situation."[3]

His assertion of his Cossacks' devotion to him was no exaggeration. During the previous year Field Ataman Kulakov had inducted Pannwitz into the Terek Cossack Host as a gesture of gratitude for his "wise leadership and fatherly care for cementing of the Cossack family."[4] Later, on 5 April 1945, Pannwitz received an even greater honor when an all-Cossack krug was convened in the corps' operational base at the northern Croatian town of Virovitica. There, delegates from each regiment within the XV SS Cossack Cavalry Corps elected their commander as their overall field ataman in a ceremony that seemed as anachronistic as the medieval surroundings of the chateau where this event was held.[5] Few could help overlook the significance of the spectacle. "The election of a foreigner, a German, was unprecedented," observed historian Samuel Newland. "Thus they passed over the heroes of another age, such as Kulakov, Shkuro and Krasnov, and chose instead a German general."[6]

Despite the festive atmosphere of the celebration at Virovitica, events in the coming days would have a sobering effect on the men of the Cossack corps and especially their commander. The Red Army was by then at the Oder River and well within striking distance of Hitler's capital. Looking ahead to what may follow in the wake of Germany's looming defeat, various Cossack leaders and German officers in the corps staked their hopes on a last-minute falling-out between the capitalist powers of the West and the Soviet Union. Optimistic Nazis, Ustaše, Vlasovites and Četniks were making a similar bet; their expectations were buoyed by memories of the undeclared war between the Allies and the Bolsheviks in the wake of the previous world war.[7] To improve the chances that his Cossacks might be integrated into any postwar anticommunist crusade, in late March Pannwitz had sent a delegation led by Kononov and Kulakov to confer with General Vlasov, whose leadership was soon recognized by the Virovitica krug. At the very least, Pannwitz hoped that the corps' inclusion into Vlasov's KONR would help deflect some of the stigma the corps might receive due to its association with the vanquished Germans and, in particular, the Waffen-SS.[8]

When the delegation from the Cossack corps arrived in Vlasov's headquarters on 31 March, they found the KONR leader, like Pannwitz, simply trying to hold his organization together amid Germany's imminent collapse. By then Allied bombings had forced the Russian general to transfer the seat of KONR from Dabendorf to the Bohemian spa resort of Karlovy Vary. It would not be the last time he would be compelled to relocate his headquarters before the end of the war.[9] Just three days earlier KONR, at what would be its final meeting, had resolved to concentrate is armed divisions in Innsbruck, Austria. From there, its leaders intended to decide whether they should turn west and surrender to the Western Allies or head southeast in order to continue the struggle against Tito's Partisans in Yugoslavia.[10] Despite these plans, Vlasov was depressed by his prospects and was in the habit of drowning his sorrows with liquor. "Inwardly he was a broken man," Captain Strik-Strikfeldt wrote of one of his last meetings with the Russian general, "He pulled himself together when he had to exercise authority, but he knew that this was the end."[11] In these macabre surroundings, Kononov convinced the ex-Soviet general that they must distance themselves from the Germans as much as possible to have any chance of garnering sympathy from the Western Allies. As a first step, they agreed that they would need to replace all German officers in the Cossack corps with Cossack or Russian officers. Eventually, the Cossack corps was officially accepted into KONR on 28 April and a week later Vlasov designated Kononov as its new commander. None of these arrangements, however, had any real impact on the corps since the war ended just days later. Moreover, there is reason to doubt whether the Cossack soldiers would have willingly accepted the replacement of the genuinely-popular Pannwitz with Kononov, who was regarded as self-serving in some circles.[12]

After being promoted to the rank of major general by Vlasov, Kononov continued to float around the KONR leader's entourage into the final days of the war.[13] During his absence from the Cossack corps, the unit began its withdrawal from Croatia. Earlier, in late March, Pannwitz and his divisional commanders had agreed among themselves that the Cossacks must at all costs avoid surrendering to the Soviets or the Yugoslav People's Army. Instead, they decided that the corps, in accordance with KONR's vague plans, should retreat through Slovenia and into Austria.[14] There it might be to able link up with Vlasovites, Četniks and nationalist Czechs and form a multinational redoubt against further communist encroachment into Europe.[15] Even if the redoubt failed to materialize, Pannwitz knew that by heading northwest the corps would at least be within reach of the Western Allies; from whom he felt he could obtain acceptable terms for surrender.

The exodus of the various Cossack, Wehrmacht, Ustaše and even some Četnik detachments was set into to motion on 13 April after enemy forces ruptured the front in far southeastern Croatia. That development, combined with the fall of Vienna to the Red Army on that same day, rendered the position of the remaining German and collaborationist forces in the Balkans untenable.[16] By the end of the month, these elements were pushing northwestward, frequently harassed by insurgents along the way. "Often when our men were badly wounded in these clashes," a veteran of the Russian Protective Corps recalled of the retreat, "they would beg to be finished off with a *coup de grâce* from a pistol rather than fall into the hands of Soviet troops."[17] The Cossack corps did not begin its withdrawal until 3–4

May when the First Cossack Division pulled out of its positions and rode along the Drava valley towards Austria. It experienced relatively little trouble during its journey; only at the Slovenian town of Celje did it have to battle its way through communist guerrillas attempting to block its route. On the other hand, the Second Cossack Division had held back for two days to cover the withdrawal of the First Cossack Division. When it did finally begin its retreat, the division not only had to fight a rearguard action against the Bulgarian and Yugoslav army detachments nipping at its heels but it also had to contend with the Partisans ahead of them seeking to cut off their escape. Despite being surrounded at times, the Cossacks from the Second Division turned down all enemy appeals for them to surrender.[18]

Most of the corps had not yet reached Austria when Germany's unconditional surrender went into effect on 8 May 1945. Although all German forces were instructed to cease active operations and remain in their present positions, Pannwitz refused to abide by these terms since he knew his Cossacks could expect no mercy if they surrendered to Tito's troops. They, along with their Wehrmacht and Ustaše allies, continued their fighting retreat until they crossed the Austrian frontier. For a full week after the war's end, until May 15, bedraggled columns of Cossacks, Germans and Croats flowed into Austria in a desperate effort to place themselves out of reach of both Tito and Stalin.[19]

When Pannwitz received confirmation of Germany's capitulation on 8 May, he immediately sought to arrange the Cossacks' surrender with the British, whose divisions were racing northward into Austria from Italy in order to prevent the Red Army and Yugoslavs from occupying additional lands. To initiate contact, he sent Lieutenant-Colonel von Renteln and a small retinue ahead of the corps to negotiate directly with the Supreme Allied Commander of the Mediterranean, Field Marshal Harold Alexander. The selection of Renteln for this task was not accidental; he had known Alexander since 1919 when they had campaigned against the Red Army in the Baltic region. It was Pannwitz's earnest hope that Renteln's past camaraderie with Alexander would improve the corps' chances of being granted favorable terms of surrender. This scheme, however, got nowhere. When Renteln and his escort reached British lines, their pleas to be taken to the field marshal's headquarters were ignored and the group was taken into captivity.[20]

When, by 10 May, Pannwitz had still not heard back from Renteln, he realized he could not wait any longer. That morning he and his adjutant attached a white sheet to his staff car and motored ahead of the First Division to make contact with the British and arrange for the corps' surrender. After encountering a reconnaissance unit from the Eleventh British Armored Division, the general was escorted to the headquarters of the First King's Royal Rifle Corps in Völkermarkt. Pannwitz had hoped the British would accept the Cossacks' surrender on the condition that they would not be turned over to the Red Army, but the major in command of the rifle corps, Major Henry Howard, would have none of it. The British officer demanded nothing less than the Cossack corps' unconditional surrender; a stipulation that was being required of all German military formations. After this curt exchange, Pannwitz was invited to return to his corps and lead them into captivity on the following day. The German general, while certainly uneasy about placing his men in British custody without a guarantee that they would not be repatriated to the Soviet Union, had no other option. With the Yugoslavs in pursuit and the Red Army only about hundred miles to the north, he knew that the British represented the corps' only chance for survival.

The next day, 11 May, Pannwitz led the First Cossack Cavalry Division towards Völkermarkt in accordance with Howard's instructions. Once they were safely inside British lines, but before reaching the town, Pannwitz suddenly ordered his regiments into parade formation. Within minutes, the division's band retrieved its instruments and the Cossacks, arranged four abreast, began riding past their commander and the British officers standing at his side. This spectacle, Pannwitz hoped, would impress the Cossacks' soon-to-be captors by showcasing their pageantry and discipline. Maybe—just maybe—it would convince them of the corps' value and of the need to preserve it. After the parade, the Cossacks handed over their arms at a collection point on the edge of Völkermarkt. Their column then proceeded through the town and continued westbound along the Drau (Drava) valley for sixteen miles until St. Veit an der Glan. From there, most of them were directed to ride another sixteen miles west to Feldkirchen. However, Pannwitz and his staff, along with the 4th Kuban Cossack Regiment, were sent ten miles north to Althofen. Both areas were under the supervision of the British Sixth Armored Division.

The procession of Cossacks tossing their weapons into piles of discarded arms outside of Völkermarkt and then riding forward to either Feldkirchen or Althofen continued in spurts over the next several days. Indeed, the Second Division did not reach British lines in Austria until 12 May. In the preceding days, it had been badly mauled amid fighting with the Partisans during which several squadrons had lost contact with the main body. Ultimately, the remnants of the division joined Pannwitz and the 4th Kuban Cossack Regiment at Althofen.[21]

Though interned by the British, the Cossacks certainly did not feel as though they were prisoners. They were not closely guarded nor were they corralled in enclosures at either Feldkirchen or Althofen. They were simply instructed to limit their movement within defined boundaries. Surrounded by mountain valleys in full bloom and abundant sunshine, they leisurely bivouacked in fields and attended to their mounts. Some among them, however, did begin to fret over their future. Foremost among those was Pannwitz. Even as he maintained a calm composure when in sight of his men and officers, behind the scenes he desperately tried to extract some assurance from senior British officers that the corps would not be turned over to the Soviets. He tried to explain the Cossacks' plight in a letter he dispatched with Renteln's group and in later meetings with their captors. As he pleaded with the British, there was no shortage of omens pointing at the corps' likely fate. Several days after the Cossacks' surrender, Lieutenant-Colonel von Renteln rejoined the corps at Althofen without ever making contact with Field Marshal Alexander. This and the general disinterest shown by senior British officers towards the Cossacks' dilemma aroused a sense of dread within him. British personnel who befriended the corps' German officers also began to drop hints that the latter might want to get away while it was still possible. The most candid warning came on 15 May when the corps' senior officers were summoned to the headquarters of the British Sixth Armored Division in Klagenfurt. There the division's commander, Major-General Horatius Murray, informed them of the probability that the Cossacks would be handed over to the Soviets. He advised the German officers to walk away if they wanted to avoid their men's impending fate.[22]

The German officers of the Cossack corps had several justifications, if they so chose, for abandoning the corps at that point. By then, all signs indicated that the Cossacks would be repatriated to the Soviet Union. In that case the corps would be destroyed with or without them. Since the German personnel were not and never had been citizens of the Soviet Union, the Western Allies were under no obligation to turn these men over to Stalin. If they did enter the custody of the Red Army or NKVD, they likely faced execution or years of hard labor. Moreover, by this time some among the Cossack rank-and-file *wanted* the German personnel removed from their posts. Agitators from the 5th Don Cossack Regiment, which had been officered solely by Cossacks throughout the war, had begun demanding that the entire corps should be led by Cossacks. They were apparently convinced by the argument put forth by their former commander, Kononov, and Vlasov that the formation would be preserved by the Western Allies if the Cossacks disassociated themselves from the Germans. Pannwitz did not attempt to suppress these dissidents. On the contrary, he gave them and the rest of the corps a chance to make their voices heard by inviting delegates from each regiment to Althofen to elect a new field ataman. Despite the 5th Don Cossack Regiment's campaign against the corps commander, Pannwitz retained enough support among the other regiments to win reelection. Still, tensions between the Cossacks and other German officers continued to simmer. As a result, many officers resigned their posts and then slipped away. According to one source, nearly 500 Germans would leave the corps in the coming days.[23]

Even if the Cossack agitators had succeeded in their bid to dismiss Pannwitz and rest of the German officers, that action would not have impacted their ultimate fate. On the same day that Pannwitz was reelected field ataman, Soviet and British officers met at Wolfsberg to arrange the handover of the Cossacks and other Soviet nationals in Austria to the Red Army. The two parties agreed that the Cossacks should be delivered to the Austrian town of Judenburg on the Mur River, which marked the demarcation line between the British and Red Armies.[24] This arrangement was made in the spirit of the Yalta Agreement, signed on 11 February 1945, which had effectively decided the Cossacks' future. Under its terms, the Soviet Union and Great Britain were obligated to inform the other whenever they found their citizens, maintain these persons in camps or concentration points separate from enemy war prisoners and allow the other's repatriation representatives access to these camps or points of concentration. Ultimately, it was intended to return the citizens to their homeland as speedily as possible.[25] Neither Britain nor the United States appear to have foreseen the possibility that many of Stalin's former subjects might not want to return to the Soviet Union as they made no provisions for those who preferred to remain abroad. When confronted with this dilemma among anticommunist Cossacks in the immediate aftermath of the war, the British high command decided in favor of compulsory mass-repatriations to avoid the tedious alternative of examining cases individually. Their decision was at least partly motivated by an eagerness to appease their Soviet allies, which is apparent from an order of the day issued by the commander of the Fifth Corps, Lieutenant-General Charles Keightly. "It is of the utmost importance that all the officers and particularly senior commanders are rounded up and that none are allowed to escape," announced Keightly. "The Soviet forces consider this as being of the highest importance and will probably regard the safe delivery of the officers as a test of British good faith."[26]

Not everyone in the British army was comfortable with the forthcoming operation. Some guards who had developed a liking for their former enemies in the days since the end of the war again alerted certain officers that the bulk of the corps was due to be transferred to an enclosed camp at Weitensfeld, about seventeen miles west of Althofen. Their message was clear: time was running out for them to make their getaway. Among the recipients of that warning was Colonel Wagner, the commander of the First Division, who immediately relayed the message to Pannwitz and urged him to flee. But for Pannwitz there could be no question of deserting the Cossacks just days after they reelected him field ataman. The Cossacks had stood by him when all seemed lost and he was determined to repay that loyalty. He did, however, grant the other officers the freedom to decide for themselves whether they should remain with their men or desert.

As a result of these exchanges, Pannwitz was probably not surprised when on the morning of 26 May a pair of British staff cars and two lorries rolled into the village of Mühlen, where he had recently set up his headquarters. After exiting their staff cars, the British officers informed the German general that he was no longer in command of the corps and placed him under arrest. He and his remaining staff were then led to the vehicles and whisked away.[27]

Wagner, along with a number of other German and Cossack officers with the First Division, had finally heeded the many warnings and deserted the previous evening. They had little trouble in escaping as most British personnel at this stage turned a blind eye towards such attempts. The Cossack troops, however, seemed to have little inkling of what was in store for them even as the first batches of them boarded three-ton trucks which hauled them to Weitensfeld on the morning of 27 May. It was only after they reached that camp when their captors informed them that they would be turned over the Soviets the next day. As this news spread through the ranks, the mood within the camp immediately grew somber. Cossacks who had been carefree up to that point became despondent. The Welsh Guardsmen at Weitensfeld, unlike the soldiers at either Althofen or Feldkirchen, kept their distance and made no effort to befriend the inmates. Throughout the following night, searchlights scanned the camp's perimeter; the guards no longer took a lackadaisical approach toward escape attempts.

When the trucks returned the following morning, the Cossacks in the camp made one last attempt to plead their case to the senior British officer, Colonel Rose Price. They strenuously objected to their repatriation, emphasizing that only death and suffering awaited them in the Soviet Union. Some bared their chests and asked the British kill them right there instead of turning them over to the Red Army. These arguments got nowhere. Price had his orders and he was determined to follow through with them. Eventually, the divisional priests climbed into the trucks and most of the Cossack soldiers followed. However, a few dozen Cossacks, led by Major Vladimir Ostrovsky, refused to cooperate by sitting on the ground. They remained in their spots even when Welsh Guardsmen were called in and raised their rifles in front of them. When this intimidation tactic failed, Price gave orders to have the resisters bound and forcibly hauled onto the trucks. At that point, Ostrovsky and his followers, seeing that further resistance was useless, stood up and boarded the remaining trucks.[28]

Once the vehicles were en route to Judenburg, the Cossacks had few opportunities to make a last-minute escape. The trucks they were transported in carried a pair of armed guards in addition to a driver and co-driver. Along the winding fifty-mile route from Weitensfeld and other locations, British guards manned intersections and other stretches of road where the trucks might be expected to slow down. The convoys were also escorted by motorcyclists armed with sub-machine guns and light armored vehicles. Along the way, some Cossacks tossed their watches, rings and other valuables on the roadside to avoid having to turn these over to the NKVD. A couple Cossacks did leap out of the speeding trucks in a desperate escape attempt, and although there is no account of the British guards firing on them, these would-be fugitives often sustained a crippling injury during their landing which prevented them from completing their getaway.[29]

Among the first prisoners from the XV SS Cossack Cavalry Corps turned over by the British were Pannwitz and his remaining staff.[30] In the last days of May and first days of June 1945, 17,702 persons affiliated with the corps, including 47 women, 5 children and 7 priests, went into Soviet captivity at Judenburg.[31] One by one, the British trucks carried them across the town's stone bridge spanning the Mur River and into the Soviet zone, where they disembarked from the vehicles under heavy guard. Among those delivered to the Soviets were old émigrés who had fled revolutionary Russia, lived in Yugoslavia or Western Europe between the wars and joined the division as officers. Only belatedly did the British give second thought to handing over émigrés who were in no way due to be repatriated according to the terms of the Yalta Agreement. When this point was made known to the British Sixth Armored Division, its personnel stopped several of its trucks before they reached Judenburg and let go any Cossack who claimed to be a prewar émigré regardless of whether or not the individual could offer any evidence. Among those fortunate enough to be spared in this manner was Major Ostrovsky, who led the resistance to loading at Weitensfeld.[32] But nothing could be done for multitudes of émigrés who had already crossed the bridge over the Mur.

While the decision of the British and Americans to forcibly repatriate Cossacks and other Soviet nationals after the war has been condemned by many historians,[33] no aspect of these operations is more deserving of criticism than the delivery of prewar émigrés to the Red Army. One is inclined to ask then why the British handed over old émigrés to the Soviets even when this action was not required by the Yalta Agreement? While no one can be absolutely certain, one theory is that the émigrés were deliberately turned over to Soviets out of a desire to appease Stalin. It must be remembered that in May and June of 1945 the Western Allies were still eager to cultivate good relations with the Soviet dictator in the hope that he might yet permit self-determination and free elections in Central and Eastern European territories occupied by the Red Army. Most of all, they were eager to acquire Soviet assistance into the ongoing war against Japan. According to this line of thought, then, the old émigrés were handed over as a gesture of goodwill by the Western Allies; possibly as a means of convincing their paranoid ally once and for all that they had no desire to embark on any anticommunist adventures.

A second theory attributes the handover of the old émigrés to an error made by the British amid their haste to observe the terms of the Yalta Agreement. Considering that post-war repatriation operations between the Allies involved millions of displaced peoples, it is understandable to see why an option to review cases individually was regarded as impractical. Given the sheer numbers involved, the chaos of war-ravaged Europe and the likelihood that many Nansen passports or other identification papers were lost in the migrations or conflagration of war, it was perhaps inevitable that mistakes would be made. Yet, it is unlikely that the repatriation of old émigrés can be entirely written off as a simple, albeit tragic, blunder. When the Cossack soldiers were informed by the British of the decision to send them back to their homeland, many émigrés among them angrily waved Nansen passports and French or Yugoslav citizenship papers before their British captors. Similar scenes took place when the Cossacks under Field Ataman Domanov, who had also retreated into an area of the Drau valley about seventy miles west of Pannwitz's corps, were subjected to forced repatriation. Notably, whereas the bulk of old émigrés serving under Pannwitz were rather undistinguished and could be overlooked, several who had joined Domanov's group were men who had won fame in the civil war and whose names were recognizable to senior British officers and leaders. As we shall see, these celebrities, with few exceptions, were handed over to the Soviets as nonchalantly as the obscure émigrés who officered Pannwitz's corps.[34] Those old émigrés who were spared mostly owed their salvation to decisions made by local commanders and belated timing; only after the bulk of the Cossacks had been repatriated did the British pause and reconsider their decision to handover old émigrés.

The Valley of Death

While Pannwitz preserved his command over the Cossack corps until that unit effectively ceased to exist, the same could not be said for Krasnov in his role as Supreme Ataman of the Cossack Central Administration. Since the final months of 1944, he had been facing increasing pressure from his fellow Cossacks to merge their liberation movement with Vlasov's Committee for the Liberation of the Peoples of Russia. Despite Vlasov's growing appeal to a wide swath of anticommunist Cossacks, Krasnov remained fixated on the better rewards that had been promised by the Germans exclusively to Cossacks. He continued to face a torrent of sharp criticism for his policy even after he and his entourage evacuated Berlin in February 1945 and joined Cossachi Stan in Tolmezzo. Although Krasnov nominally subordinated himself to Field Ataman T. I. Domanov upon his arrival in the settlement, he did not cease his attempts to steer the policies of the Cossack liberation movement towards his own pseudo-separatist views. For example, he and his aides organized an anti-Vlasov propaganda campaign and tried to intercept any KONR media destined for Cossachi Stan.[35] He capped off these efforts on 15 March with an open letter to Vlasov where he challenged the KONR leader to clarify his position towards the promises made to the Cossacks by the Germans in their 10 November 1943 proclamation.[36] His reluctance to place Cossack interests under the umbrella of KONR even at this stage is indicative of his deep-seated reservations towards the former Red Army general.

Although there is no account of the Vlasov camp penning a reply to Krasnov's letter, the controversy within Cossachi Stan refused to fade away. Kuban Ataman Naumenko made his disagreement with Krasnov public by announcing that the Kuban Cossacks would recognize Vlasov's leadership. Krasnov retaliated by ordering the Kuban Cossacks to ignore their ataman's decree.[37] Domanov also favored a union with KONR. Like Major-General Kononov, the field ataman and his supporters believed that the Cossacks had to accept the inevitability of Third Reich's defeat and disassociate themselves from their soon-to-be vanquished sponsors. They felt that by joining KONR the Cossacks, Russians and other Eastern peoples could present a strong, united front that would at least earn the respect of the Western Allies. This argument, it seems, won over the majority of ordinary Cossacks. As this became apparent to Krasnov, he acknowledged that he no longer represented the will of most Cossacks and stated his intention to withdraw from public service. Not long afterwards, in the 26 April edition of Cossachi Stan's newspaper, Domanov announced that the "free Cossacks" would recognize the political leadership of KONR.[38]

The last-minute entry of the Cossack irregulars and refugees into KONR's fold was of no more benefit to them than it had been for the men of the Cossack corps. Throughout the month of April, signs of Germany's imminent collapse could be seen all around them: to their north the Red Army was sweeping into Austria while to their south British and American forces in Italy were thrusting northward. Closer to their settlement, anti-fascist partisans lurking in the mountains above Tolmezzo and nearby villages redoubled their attacks against the unwelcome Cossacks. In one raid, they set fire to a military hospital with many wounded Cossacks trapped inside.[39] The day after Domanov proclaimed his people's affiliation with KONR, three emissaries from the partisans visited his headquarters with demands for the Cossacks to lay down their weapons and evacuate the area. The field ataman, not wanting to fight the approaching British army, agreed to a compromise where the Cossacks would leave Tolmezzo but retain their weapons.[40] That night, in the dark, early morning hours of 28 April, the men and women of Cossachi Stan set off on yet another mass retreat that by now seemed all too frequent in the history of anticommunist Cossacks. Although this trek, which took them through the Alpine wilderness of northern Italy into southern Austria, was not as epic as their journey from Novogrudek or those taken by their elders across the Northern Caucasus or Siberia a generation earlier, it was hardly less tragic. Italian guerrillas, ignoring the armistice arranged by their emissaries, harassed the column from the outset; thereby forcing Domanov's regiments to guard the front and rear of the caravan. As the Cossacks ascended along the winding mountain roads, a cold rain fell and then turned to a wet snow at the higher elevations; soaking and chilling the unfortunate refugees. The wintry precipitation added to their woes by making the narrow paths perilously slick for the horses and carts.

On 3 May the front of the caravan descended from the Plöcken Pass onto the Austrian village of Mauthen. Since the village and its surroundings lacked enough green pasture land for the Cossacks' herds, the refugees continued to plod northward into the Drau (Drava) valley. In the meantime, Krasnov and Domanov met at a hotel in Mauthen-Kötschach to debate their next move. From the window of the hotel, Krasnov watched the procession of Cossacks stream through the village. "Only now did he see that these regiments did not have the appearance of troops by any concept of our time," wrote one of his aides. "This was a rag-tag group dressed in various uniforms, many in civilian clothes, with household junk on their carts and pigs and sheep along with them."[41] Equally disheartening for him was the sight of retreating German units in the same pitiful condition. At that moment, it was apparent even to Krasnov that any further resistance was useless. The war was over. In his discussions with Domanov, he conceded that the Cossacks' only remaining option was to negotiate their surrender with the British and American forces pushing northward from Italy. The two men agreed that the British, due to the past anti–Bolshevik activities of Churchill and Field Marshall Alexander, were more likely than the Americans to show sympathy towards the anti–Soviet Cossacks.[42] Subsequently, they dispatched a woman interpreter, Olga Rotova, to accompany General Leonide V. Vasiliev and his aide-de-camp, Lieutenant Nikolay N. Krasnov, a grandson of the former Supreme Ataman, to make contact with the British in northern Italy. With a white sheet flapping from their car, the delegation retraced their journey through the mountain passes littered with horse carcasses and broken wagons left behind by their peoples' flight. After encountering the British vanguard, they were forwarded to the commander of the 78th Infantry Division, General Robert Arbuthnott, who had recently set up his headquarters in Tolmezzo, the same town that the Cossacks had evacuated only a week earlier.

The Cossack delegation met with Arbuthnott as well as Brigadier Geoffrey Musson of the 36th Infantry Brigade. Both British officers listened to Vasiliev's assurances that the Cossacks had nothing but peaceful intentions towards the Western Allies. He went on to explain that they sought only to continue the struggle against communism by joining Vlasov's Armed Forces of KONR. Unmoved by Vasiliev's speech, both British generals demanded the Cossacks to surrender their arms immediately. When Vasiliev replied that this decision could only be made by Field Ataman Domanov, Musson stated his willingness to personally clear up the matter with the Cossack leader the next morning. In the meantime, the British generals and the Cossack guests continued their discussions over tea. After being accorded such friendly treatment, the three Cossacks were upbeat over their prospects under the British and were eager to pass this news on to rest of the refugees.[43]

That evening, the delegation headed by Vasiliev, escorted by British vehicles, returned to Domanov's headquarters in Mauthen-Kötschach. The three delegates immediately related their pleasant experience with the British generals to Domanov and Krasnov. According to one of Krasnov's aides, the delegation reported that they had received a promise from the British that under no circumstances would the Cossacks be handed over to the Soviets.[44] Based on this and other accounts, Cossack historians and memoirists have ever since condemned the subsequent actions of the British in the Drau Valley as treacherous.[45] In retrospect, it is improbable that any senior British officers gave the Cossacks such a direct guarantee, although it is possible that the delegates read too much into their hosts' hospitality. At the very least, they probably felt that the upstanding British would spare the Cossacks from compulsory repatriation on moral grounds. Such impressions were reinforced the next morning when Brigadier Musson arrived at Domanov's headquarters and made an allowance for the retreating Cossacks to retain their arms for self-protection against fanatical SS guerrillas that might be at large. That evening, units from Musson's 36th Infantry Brigade began arriving in the area to assume control of the Cossack refugees.[46]

While the Cossack leaders were busy arranging their surrender to the British, the soldiers and refugees under them made their camps in the Drau valley along a fifteen-mile stretch of highway from Oberdrauburg to Lienz. As elsewhere, local townsfolk and farmers were uneasy about a mass of 22,000 hungry foreigners settling in their midst.[47] Indeed, when the Cossacks first moved into Austria, they encountered token resistance from some local authorities who sought to keep them from entering their districts.[48] Matters were not helped by the breakdown of discipline among the retreating column. Amidst the general confusion, some Cossacks took it upon themselves to plunder local farms or hold-up homebound German soldiers. According to Lieutenant Krasnov, the worst offenders were the 4,800 Caucasians who joined the Cossacks amid their retreat from northern Italy. Before the evacuation got underway, German officers had deserted the mutinous Caucasians, leaving an old émigré, Sultan Kelech Ghirey, to exercise command over this unruly group. A veteran of the tsarist army's famous Caucasian Cavalry Division and hero of the Russian Civil War, Ghirey was well-qualified for the post but even he had trouble imposing control over the disjointed Caucasians. Since most Austrians viewed Cossacks and Caucasians as one and the same, the latter's poor behavior seemed to confirm rumors among locals that the Cossacks on the whole were nothing more than a horde of ruffians.[49]

Beginning in the second week of May Domanov's Cossacks settled into an uncertain limbo. They were haunted by fears of repatriation while remaining hopeful that they would be granted asylum. With each passing day in the valley, however, their minds were put at ease. The camps they inhabited, like those of the Cossack corps further to the east, were not enclosed. Moreover, they were only loosely-guarded by only two British battalions. A few Cossacks distrusted British intentions enough to walk away from the camps, but those with families mostly stayed put and tried to make the best of a difficult situation. "They laid out little vegetable gardens and settled down to keep house," observed Lieutenant Krasnov.[50] Born in 1918 and taken out of revolutionary Russia as an infant, Krasnov had grown up in Yugoslavia where he attended cadet school, served in the Yugoslav Army and was taken prisoner by the Germans in April 1941. Upon his release from captivity, he joined collaborationist units to fight against communism.[51] Émigrés such as himself who lived abroad most of their lives took comfort in the speculation that they were sure to be spared even if the British turned over former Soviet citizens.[52]

His grandfather, the former Supreme Ataman, was also optimistic about their future. Even if the British had no use for a formation of anticommunist Cossacks, the elder Kransov was certain that they would, at the very least, permit the Cossacks to settle somewhere outside the Soviet Union. But as a precaution, he took to his pen to plead the Cossacks' case to Field Marshal Alexander. In his trademark sensational prose, Krasnov tried to arouse understanding for the Cossacks' plight by reminding Alexander how he had once fought on their side in the struggle against Bolshevism. After its completion, Krasnov entrusted the letter with a British officer for delivery to the field marshal's headquarters.[53]

In mid–May another prestigious émigré joined Domanov's Cossacks when General Andrey Shkuro and 1,400 of his men were brought to Lienz. Several days earlier, on 10 May, Shkuro and the Cossack reserve regiment he had commanded since the previous autumn had surrendered to the British north of the town of Spittal. The arrival in Lienz of this famous war hero, who held the British Order of the Bath for his exploits during the Russian Civil War, reinforced the notion among Cossacks that the British had no intention of handing them over to the Soviets.[54]

This sense of security appears to have been encouraged by the British themselves. Officers from the 8th Battalion, Argyll and Sutherland Highlander Regiment, which was tasked with supervising the camps in the area from Oberdrauburg to Lienz, encouraged the Cossacks to restart their newspaper, set up schools and handed out candy to the children when they made their daily inspections of the camps. On 15 May the Cossacks' rations improved with the arrival of Red Cross personnel bearing food and other basic necessities. On Sundays they held Orthodox masses outdoors in the spring sunshine while British soldiers looked on approvingly. In moments of leisure, the Cossacks impressed their captors by performing *dzhigitovka* acrobatics, dancing and singing in choirs.[55] Not since their stay at Novogrudek had the Cossacks been in such high spirits.

While many Cossacks took comfort in the kind treatment they received from the British, their leaders remained uneasy. Days turned into weeks following the dispatch of Krasnov's letter to Field Marshal Alexander and still the Cossack leaders heard nothing back from the Supreme Allied Commander of the Mediterranean. On 24 May the British seized some of the camps' horses on the grounds that the Cossacks, as prisoners of war, were no longer the animals' rightful owners. Upon hearing of this incident, Krasnov again petitioned in writing to Alexander for his personal intervention. On the following day, a British detachment confiscated the assets of the Cossacks' field bank located in Lienz.[56] Word also reached them that Vlasov and his First KONR Division, after surrendering to the U.S. Army in Bohemia, had been turned over to the Soviets. In the meantime, Lieutenant Krasnov became convinced that Domanov had some premonition of what was about to happen to them. The field ataman visited the highlanders' headquarters in Lienz often, noted Krasnov, and "each time he came out his face was gloomier and his step heavier. He seemed to shrink into himself, but he did not share his thoughts with anyone."[57]

Their pessimism increased on 27 May when the British ordered the Cossack leaders and officers to handover their sidearms. Since Domanov's Cossacks had been a unit of irregulars, the British had been rather generous towards them with respect to their weapons. The rank-and-file was not asked to turn in their arms until a week after their formal surrender.[58] That evening, more troubling news came in the form of a notice that all Cossack leaders and officers were to be transported to Oberdrauburg where Field Marshal Alexander would address them at a conference. This suspicious order alarmed many, including the wife of the ex-Supreme Ataman, Lydia Krasnova. "I felt that something big and terrible was coming," she later wrote, "Such a tortured, unfathomable despair lay on my heart."[59] However, her husband, along with Domanov, did their utmost to put these anxieties at ease. They instructed the officers to obey the order and assured their families that they would return the following evening. It is possible that they believed the conference was being organized in response to their recent letter to the British field marshal.

On 28 May, 1,475 officers from the camps converged, as instructed, in Lienz where they boarded sixty British lorries which they expected to take them to the conference. They began to have doubts about their real destination after armed jeeps and motorcycles joined the procession of eastbound trucks. When some Cossacks raised questions about the escort, the accompanying guards told them that this extra security was necessary to protect them from SS guerrillas. But their apprehensions proved justified when the trucks arrived to a stop at Spittal, where they were unloaded and confined to a POW camp previously used by the Germans. There they learned that the British intended to deliver them to the Soviets in Judenburg on the following day.[60]

Unrest broke out among the Cossack officers after they found themselves behind barbed wire waiting to be handed over to their sworn enemies. Some began hurling allegations which persisted long after the incident that Domanov had been aware of British intentions and had an active role in the entire deception. According to his accusers, he hoped to obtain a reprieve from either the British or the Soviets as a reward for delivering the anticommunist Cossacks to the NKVD.[61] Although there is no evidence to substantiate this claim, Domanov's reputation among Cossacks never recovered. "He either gave up the Cossacks carelessly or on purpose—God only knows," alleged the daughter of Kuban Cossack colonel.[62] In the meantime, other officers tore off all insignia from their uniforms in order to conceal their ranks from the NKVD. Eventually, some calm was restored by General Krasnov who pleaded with the men to preserve their dignity as officers. According to some accounts,[63] he penned one last appeal to Field Marshal Alexander though it is doubtful whether this letter, if written, was even forwarded by the British officers in charge of the Spittal camp.[64]

When the British trucks arrived on the morning of 29 May to haul the prisoners to Judenburg, they found that several Cossacks had committed suicide during the night by hanging or lacerating their wrists.[65] The rest were uncooperative. After the British were unable to persuade Domanov to order his officers to board the trucks, a platoon of soldiers approached the Cossacks to begin dragging them onto the trucks. The prisoners, however, made this exceptionally difficult by sitting on the ground with their arms linked together. When one soldier was bitten in the hand after pulling a Cossack away from his comrades, the British lost their patience and began bludgeoning the prisoners with rifle butts or poking them with fixed bayonets. After this brief, one-sided melee, the Cossack officers reluctantly began climbing into the trucks.

At Judenburg, the British delivered Domanov's officers in the same manner they had used with the men from the XV SS Cossack Cavalry Corps a day earlier. Each truck drove across the bridge over the Mur and dumped its human cargo in the Soviet zone. The empty trucks then trundled back across the river into the British zone. A couple of Cossacks made last minute attempts to end their lives within full view of the Red Army and NKVD officers waiting to receive them. One did so by making a dash for the side of bridge which stood nearly 100 feet over the Mur, where he jumped and landed with a thud on the rocky bank below. He was retrieved and thus entered Soviet custody not-quite-dead. Another Cossack, after stepping off a truck amid a chorus of revolutionary anthems blaring from nearby loudspeakers, immediately pulled out a razor and sliced open his throat.[66]

For the NKVD, the greatest prizes to fall in their hands were not defectors like Domanov but rather the old émigrés; the "White Guardists" who had once been blamed for so many of their country's woes. Indeed, one Red Army general at Judenburg reportedly expressed astonishment that the British turned over the old émigrés when they were not bound to do so under the terms of the Yalta Agreement.[67] According to Cossack sources, nearly seven out of every ten officers briefly held in the camp at Spittal were old émigrés.[68] Moreover, among these men were some of the most recognizable names from the White movement: four members of the Krasnov family, including the former Don ataman, his son, nephew and grandson; Shkuro and Sultan Ghirey.[69]

Once in Soviet custody, these men, along with Domanov, were separated from the others and confined to a steel mill alongside other high-profile prisoners, including Pannwitz and his senior officers who had been turned over on the previous day. Because P. N. Krasnov and Shkuro aroused considerable fascination among Red Army personnel, particularly those who had fought against them in the civil war, that evening the two men were brought to a house in which several Soviet officers were billeted. For the next several hours, the Red Army officers traded stories and informally interviewed the two Cossack generals. For most of the time, though, the high-profile prisoners remained in the steel mill where, according to Lieutenant Krasnov, they were treated with "exaggerated politeness" by the NKVD and SMERSH personnel looking after them. Shkuro, with his bawdy sense of humor, became popular with both the prisoners and their Soviet captors. "I think of Andrey Shkuro with gratitude," recalled Lieutenant Krasnov, "his jokes and his cheerfulness kept all our spirits up. There were moments when we quite forgot the tragedy of our situation." On the other hand, the NKVD officers showed nothing but contempt for Domanov and other former Soviet citizens who collaborated with the enemy. "Domanov ... was a nonentity here," wrote Lieutenant Krasnov. "No one was in the least interested in him. It almost seemed as though no one even noticed him."[70]

After being held in the steel mill for two days, the high-profile prisoners were taken out of Judenburg and eventually brought to Moscow. Many other officers, however, never made it alive out of Judenburg. According to the younger Krasnov, prior to being transferred to the Soviet capital, his group was forced to watch the execution by firing squad of a German officer from Pannwitz's corps.[71] Others were dispatched by the same method in the steel mill where the senior officers had been held. To drown out the volleys of gunfire, the NKVD revved the engines in a nearby fleet of vehicles. This effort to conceal the prisoners' fate from the outer world was not very successful. "Day and night, executions were carried out beneath the sounds of running engines," recalled one Austrian resident.[72] Just across the Mur River, the ears of British sentries also picked up barks of gunfire originating from some unseen location in the Soviet sector of the town.[73]

In the meantime, it became clear to the officers' families and other Cossack refugees still camped in the Drau valley that something sinister had happened to their men. The morning after the officers' departure, their anxieties were confirmed when British officers in Camp Peggetz had translator Olga Rotova announce to the worried families that their men would not be returning and that they would be repatriated to their homeland beginning the next day.[74] Unsure of their next move, the bewildered Cossacks elected a temporary ataman, hung black flags in their encampments, began a hunger strike and drafted petitions addressed to Britain's King George VI, King Peter of Yugoslavia, the Vatican and the headquarters of the International Red Cross. Some constructed large placards bearing English inscriptions proclaiming "We prefer hunger and death here than return to the Soviet Union!"[75] The émigrés among them confronted British officers with their Nansen passports or certificates of Yugoslav citizenship. Some may have believed that their prayers and demonstrations were having an effect when, on the following day, the British postponed their delivery to Judenburg. In fact, this delay did not come about by divine intervention or by their captors having second thoughts; rather, it was made at the Soviets' request as their facilities and rolling stock at Judenburg was overwhelmed by the thousands of prisoners they received there in previous days.[76]

The repatriation operations resumed on 31 May, when the British began rounding up 3,000 Caucasians at Dellach and sent them to Judenburg. On the following day it was the Cossacks' turn. The members of Cossachi Stan were jittery since having learned of their impending fate three days earlier. "Many wanted to run away," recalled a young Cossack mother, "but most stayed in the camp in the conviction that there could be neither a massacre nor forced removal of defenseless people."[77] Hundreds of them, moving individually or in small groups, did flee from the open camps into the nearby wooded slopes. Those Cossacks that remained behind at Camp Peggetz decided to hold an Orthodox mass on the day scheduled for loading. Some joined this throng of worshippers out of the belief that the British soldiers would not disrupt religious services.[78] Therefore, when soldiers from the Argyll and Sutherland Highlander Regiment descended on that camp at daybreak on 1 June, they found about 4,000 Cossacks worshipping in its square. After it became clear that the Cossack priests had no intention of ending the service in a timely manner, platoons of highlanders moved in. To the soldiers' dismay, they encountered well-organized passive resistance as the crowd huddled together with its strongest members, including cadets from Cossachi Stan's military school, arranged on the outside. Once again, the soldiers had to resort to swinging their rifles and prodding with bayonets to isolate persons or small groups from the mass of people. These unfortunates were then dragged to the tarpaulin-covered trucks which hauled the prisoners a short distance to a waiting train in Lienz. There the Cossacks were unloaded from the vehicles and locked in cattle wagons that would take them rest of the journey to Judenburg. In the meantime, the trucks returned to Camp Peggetz to pick up the next batch of unfortunate prisoners.

As the operation progressed, the increasingly frustrated British soldiers hit the uncooperative Cossacks ever harder, leading to panic which spread throughout the camp. Field altars were toppled and holy icons fell in the dirt. At one point, as the frightened crowd pressed against a fence, the barrier broke and opened a momentarily unguarded escape route for those clamoring to getaway. "Horror took hold of everyone," recalled Rotova, "like rabbits being chased, they ran here and there."[79] Some headed for the woods while others ran across a nearby bridge spanning the Drau River. Various accounts claim that at least one desperate Cossack mother tossed her children into the roiling waters of the Drau and then jumped in after them.[80] The number of Cossacks who perished that day as a result of such suicidal actions or from the brutal treatment accorded by their captors is unknown. The estimated figure ranges from a few dozen reported by the British to the improbable figure of 700 claimed by Cossack survivors. Regardless of the actual number, many Cossack deaths went unreported as some simply withdrew into the nearby forests, pulled out revolvers they had stashed away and shot their horses or families before turning the weapons on themselves.[81] Those whose remains were found in and near the camps were interred in a cemetery at Lienz which remains in place to this day. Nearly any visitor will note that this small graveyard, readily distinguishable by the Orthodox crosses standing over its gates, seems out of place in this corner of predominantly Catholic Austria.[82]

Scenes similar to those in Peggetz also occurred in other camps in the Drau valley on 1 June. However, the operations proceeded much more smoothly in the following days as the remaining Cossacks, apparently resigned to their fate, were more cooperative in boarding the trucks. The entire ordeal was a source of mental anguish for many British troops who could not readily forget the shrieking women, crying children and old men collapsing to the ground under their blows. Having been fed a diet of wartime propaganda that trumpeted the feats of their Soviet ally while downplaying the tyranny of "Uncle Joe," they could not comprehend why the Cossacks so stubbornly resisted being sent back to their homeland. Camp interpreter Rotova, recalling her earlier exchanges with the highlanders, wrote, "All were surprised that we hated Stalin and argued with me, trying to convince me that he was a remarkable man and that it was only thanks to him that they defeated the Nazis."[83] The less sympathetic among the British, in an effort to justify the operation, concluded that the only explanation for the Cossacks' reluctance to return to the Soviet Union was that they wanted to avoid punishment for their treasonous activities and war crimes.

By 7 June, approximately 35,000 Cossacks from Pannwitz's cavalry corps and Domanov's group had been turned over to the Soviets in Judenburg. The majority of Domanov's followers were hauled to Judenburg by train where they were unloaded in the British zone and then herded over the bridge at the Mur River into the custody of the waiting NKVD. Every now and then a Cossack prisoner, unable to continue walking towards the red flags and blaring loudspeakers, chose instead to hurl himself off the side of the bridge. The vast majority, however, completed the crossing, where they were relieved of any luggage and valuables after their first few steps in the Soviet zone.

At times, Soviet authorities were convinced that the British were only half-heartedly holding up their end of the Yalta Agreement by more or less allowing significant numbers of Cossacks to escape. In order to placate their ally, throughout the remainder of June 1945 detachments of British soldiers went into the forests and mountains surrounding the Drau valley to track down Cossack fugitives. Their pursuits were occasionally aided by local Austrians who offered tips on the whereabouts of the runaways. According to British sources, by the end of the month 1,356 Cossack fugitives had been captured and taken to Judenburg. Shortly after one large batch of these prisoners was delivered to the Soviets on 16 June, the British soldiers were startled by the chatter of machine gun fire from an unseen location in the Soviet zone. They could only surmise what became of the unfortunate prisoners.

Despite British efforts to accommodate Soviet demands that they hunt down and turn over Cossack fugitives at large in Austria, a considerable number of escapees—possibly as many as 2,000—managed to evade their pursuers and avoid repatriation. Some slipped away with assistance from British officers or soldiers who provided them with false documents identifying them as old émigrés or gave them directions to avoid the posts guarding the passes leading out of the valley. Others received valuable help from sympathetic Austrians who gave them food and a hideout. To lessen the likelihood of encountering British soldiers, they traveled along the snowline in the mountains and avoided footpaths.[84] Aside from these scattered, relatively sparse survivors, little else remained of the anticommunist Cossack resistance that had existed in some form on the European stage since 1917. It would, however, linger for just a bit longer on the other end of the Eurasian landmass.

Lightning War in the East

The Soviet—Manchurian frontier that had been a hot-zone for border conflicts during the 1930s was, paradoxically, quiet throughout much of Second World War. The Red Army, preoccupied with repelling the German invasion from the west, had no desire to become engaged in that distant theater. On the other hand, many Japanese officers in the Kwantung Army were still eager to avenge their humiliation at Khalkhin Gol by launching an offensive against the Soviet Far East. For a brief few months, it looked as though they might get their chance. In August 1941, well before Hitler's invasion lost its momentum, the Kwantung Army flexed its muscles by staging military maneuvers near Manchukuo's northwest frontier. Unlike the Germans, the Japanese were prepared from the start to make extensive use of the Russian émigrés if they found themselves at war against the Soviet Union. With help from Ataman Semyonov and the leader of the Russian Fascist Union, Konstantin Rodzaevsky, they recruited about 2,000 émigrés to carry out dangerous operations behind Soviet lines. They also provided Rodzaevsky with a small staff and funds to generate propaganda aimed at undermining Soviet morale.[85] These preparations, however, arrived to nothing since the military leaders in Tokyo had different ideas. Not wanting to risk another showdown with the Red Army so recently after the latter had demonstrated its superiority in land warfare at Khalkhin Gol, they instead directed their ambitions to the south and east. After the Japanese fleet's surprise attack on Pearl Harbor brought the United States in to the war in December 1941, Tokyo also had an interest in preserving peace in Northeast Asia.

For the Cossack communities in Manchuria, particularly those in the Trekrechye, the dwindling likelihood of war with the Soviet Union in the early 1940s brought a sense of relief. They had not forgotten how, just over a decade earlier, an ill-conceived adventure by the Manchurian warlord Zhang Xueliang led to a brief but devastating Soviet occupation of Trekrechye. From time to time, Semyonov's recruiters still visited their stanitsas in order to enroll idealistic young Cossacks for future operations against the Soviet Union, but such activity was soon curtailed by the Japanese as the military situation of the Axis powers became direr. Indeed, by 1943, the hard-pressed Japanese had become less tolerant of anticommunist ventures among the White Russians out of fear that such endeavors might be regarded as hostile provocations by the Soviets. Nonetheless, when General Vlasov's announcement of his Russian liberation movement reached the émigré press in Manchuria that spring, Semyonov could not resist coming out publicly in support of the rogue general. When his endorsement of Vlasov appeared in a May edition of a Harbin émigré newspaper, his Japanese sponsors were flabbergasted. They promptly clamped down on anticommunist political activity among the émigrés by making an example not of Semyonov but of his rival, Rodzaevsky. Subsequently, the *vozhd* was briefly detained and his party, the Russian Fascist Union, was disbanded.[86]

The disappearance of the Russian Fascist Union in summer of 1943 was mourned by few in the émigré community; least of all the Cossacks.[87] Non-Cossack émigrés in Manchuria who had once flocked to Rodzaevsky were not disturbed by the demise of his political party since by then they faced more pressing matters as the Manchurian countryside was stripped of grain, coal and other resources in order to meet the needs of Japan's industry and armed forces. For the large émigré community in Harbin, finding adequate food and heating fuel during the long winters became a daily challenge. As a result of these privations, Japan's ongoing campaigns in the Pacific and China became evermore unpopular with the émigrés. Meanwhile, reports of the Red Army's feats against the Nazi war machine began to arouse a keen sense of pride for their homeland. Indeed, wartime changes within the Soviet Union itself made them question whether they had been wrong all along about Stalin's regime. In particular, Moscow's patriotic appeals to Russian nationalism, the relaxed persecution of the Orthodox Church, the restoration of officer ranks in the Red Army and the termination of the Comintern convinced many émigrés that the Bolshevik government was evolving into a Russian one. So smitten had they become of their homeland that a significant number of them went as far as to take the once-unthinkable step of applying for Soviet citizenship through consulates in Harbin and elsewhere.[88]

For their part, the Soviets did not exploit this outpouring of patriotism among the Far Eastern émigrés until early 1945. In February, a Soviet radio station began broadcasting to White Russians in Manchuria. Its programming promised amnesty to the émigrés while spreading xenophobic messages about the Japanese. Just a few weeks later, copies of a pro–Soviet newspaper began appearing in Harbin. For the émigrés and Japanese alike, these were the first omens that the Red Army was shifting its attention to the Far East. More were to follow. The Japanese soon learned that at Yalta Stalin had committed his country to entering the war against them after Germany's defeat. Later, they received reports that their neutrality pact with Moscow had been publicly derided by the Soviet Foreign Minister, Vyacheslav Molotov, on 5 April. During the following month, Japanese intelligence was able to confirm that the Red Army's build-up of men and materiel along the Soviet—Manchurian border was well underway.[89]

By August 1945, the Kwantung Army still possessed a respectable strength on paper of 787,600 troops, 1,215 tanks, 1,800 aircraft and 6,700 heavy guns. But what these numbers did not reveal was that its best divisions had long ago been transferred to island outposts to stem the American advance in the Pacific. Perhaps as much as half of Kwantung Army's remaining manpower consisted of unreliable Chinese conscripts or raw recruits unfit for frontline duty. Its tanks and aircraft were outdated, especially compared to the latest Soviet models, and short on fuel. Meanwhile, the Red Army had amassed an impressive force of over 1,500,000 men, 5,500 tanks, 3,800 aircraft and 26,000 guns arrayed on three sides of Manchuria.[90]

White Russians in Manchuria who remained hostile to communism and sensed the coming catastrophe had few good options available to them. Those who sought to leave Manchukuo were prevented from doing so by the Japanese, who denied them the necessary passports. Some continued to place their faith in Japanese military might. For example, nearly 4,000 Russian and Cossack émigrés remained in the ranks of the Japanese-sponsored Asano Brigade, but its numbers and élan were hardly enough to make up for the Kwantung Army's deficiencies.[91]

On the night of 8–9 August, less than three days after the Japanese city of Hiroshima was destroyed by an atomic bomb, the Red Army launched its invasion of Manchuria. After Soviet armor broke through the frontiers, its progress was more likely to be hindered by logistical difficulties than enemy resistance. Those points where the Japanese did put up a determined defense, such as at Hailar, were simply bypassed by the onrushing tanks.[92] Since the Soviet attack began with no advance warning and unfolded so rapidly, the Cossacks at Trekrechye had almost no chance to flee their settlements. But many showed no inclination to get away and instead welcomed the Red Army as liberators to their stanitsas. Similar events occurred at Harbin on 18 August as émigrés waving red flags took to the streets to greet Soviet troops when they entered the city. Evidently, many White Russians in Manchuria, whether because of their rough treatment by the Japanese, overtures made to them by Soviet propagandists or a combination thereof, were ready to embrace Stalin's regime.[93]

Instinctively, prominent White Russians knew better than to trust the promises of amnesty made by Soviet propaganda. On 13 August a number of them, including Rodzaevksy, evacuated Harbin on a special train furnished by the Japanese. That train just barely managed to stay ahead of the Soviet forward detachments sweeping southward. Its passengers were able to heave a sigh of relief only after they arrived safely in Tianjin at the end of the month.[94] Semyonov, who remained in Darien during the invasion, was not so fortunate. On 24 August Soviet naval units and paratroopers landed in the Japanese-controlled port. There are three versions of how the ataman was captured. According to one account, Semyonov flew out of Darien in the same manner he escaped from Chita when that town fell to the Reds in 1922. Only this time his plane landed at an airfield in Changchun without realizing that the Red Army was already there. A second version claims he made no attempt to escape and instead welcomed his Soviet captors to his Darien villa, where he dined with them and made some light-hearted table-talk before being hauled away. A final version claims he attired himself in his full uniform before turning himself into Soviet troops at a local railroad station. Regardless of how his arrest unfolded, after his capture he was stuffed into a plane and flown to Moscow.[95]

Besides Semyonov, thousands of other White Russians marked for capture or liquidation by the NKVD and SMERSH were trapped by the speed of the Soviet conquest of Manchuria. Their hit lists included members of Russian Fascist Union, ROVS, the Union of the Cossacks in the Far East, the Asano Brigade and other anticommunist or collaborationist organizations. In these efforts, the NKVD received valuable assistance from operatives within these organizations. For example, the commander of the Asano Brigade, an Armenian colonel by the name of Gurgen Nagolen, was actually on the Soviets' payroll. While more prominent prisoners were transported to Moscow, Chita or Khabarovsk for show trials, thousands of ordinary émigrés who had once been a member of these organizations or served in a White army were carted off to Gulag camps.[96] Those not arrested outright were exhorted by Soviet repatriation commissions to return to the motherland. Many families eventually gave into these appeals only to be arrested as they crossed the Soviet frontier.[97] These ex-Semyonovites and other émigrés from the Far East presented a pathetic sight to Lieutenant Krasnov, who encountered them during his years as a prisoner in the labor camps. "They had long since abandoned all illusions of anything better," wrote Krasnov, "all they strove for now was to be assimilated by and disappear into the main body of the Soviet Union."[98]

Interestingly, the Soviet repatriation campaign in the Far East was so effective that even high-profile émigrés who escaped the Red Army onslaught were lured back into Soviet-occupied territory. Among these was Rodzaevsky, who was convinced to go back on the assurances he received from a Soviet agent that his past transgressions would be forgiven. After writing a letter to Stalin in which he depicted himself as a born-again communist, the former fascist leader crossed into the Soviet Union from China on October 1945. He was immediately arrested and hauled to Moscow.[99]

Ultimately, the fate of the Cossack and Russian emigres in Manchuria, despite their outpouring of pro–Soviet sentiment in the summer of 1945, proved hardly less different than the devoutly anticommunist Cossacks of Domanov or Pannwitz. Regardless of whether they returned to their homeland forcibly or voluntarily, thousands of Cossacks living in the Trekrechye area and other rural communities along the Chinese Eastern Railway were conveyed to the labor camps. Much of the émigré community in Harbin also disappeared into the Gulag. The few thousand émigrés in China who resisted repatriation or were passed over by the NKVD did not remain in that country for long. As Mao Zedong's Communists gained the upper hand in that country's civil war, the White Russians emigrated a second time, often to more distant havens such as Australia or the United States.[100] By 1950, the once-thriving Cossack community in Manchuria, like those in Yugoslavia and Bulgaria, had faded into history.

Epilogue

Retribution

Near the conclusion of Pyotr Krasnov's epic novel, *From Double Eagle to Red Flag*, the protagonist, General Aleksandr N. Sablin, is intercepted by the Cheka while en route to enlist with the Volunteer Army in South Russia. After being hauled to Petrograd, Sablin's captors try to pressure him to serve in the Red Army as a "military specialist," but nothing—not threats of torture, death or reprisals against his kin—succeed in breaking his resistance to their demands. When the Chekists realize the futility of their intimidation efforts, they resort to torturing their uncooperative prisoner using the "glove trick"; a method where the victim's hands are blanched in a vat of boiling water until the skin can be peeled off. After inflicting this agony upon the general, his tormentors finally end his painful misery by having him shot.[1] Sablin's grisly demise reflects the popular perception of "revolutionary justice" in the imaginations of the old émigrés: unspeakable cruelties that, in contrast, made death appear to be the more attractive option. At the time of the novel's publication in 1921, neither Krasnov nor his fellow émigrés could have foreseen that one day many of them would be delivered into the bowels of the Soviet penal system which they so dreaded; least of all with the connivance of the Western Allies.

Generally, most Cossacks repatriated in May and June 1945 were accused of similar crimes: rendering aid to enemies of the Soviet Union and plotting to overthrow the Soviet government; yet, the treatment and punishments meted out to them by their captors varied considerably. Indeed, the factors which appear to have had the greatest influence over their fates were not the precise nature of their alleged misdeeds but rather their military ranks and notoriety. Trophy prisoners like the Krasnovs, Shkuro and Semyonov, as have seen, were flown to Moscow and locked up in the Lubyanka or other high-security prisons. Over the following months, they endured a series of sporadic interrogations by the NKVD or its successor, the MVD, aimed at extracting a confession or other information that would tie their crimes to an elaborate, vast conspiracy against the Soviet state. While the NKVD was officially barred from resorting to the physical tortures which its Chekist predecessors had inflicted on the fictional Sablin, it employed more artful tactics, such as sleep deprivation, intimidation and isolation to breakdown the prisoners.[2] Lieutenant Nikolay Krasnov, who was briefly imprisoned in the Lubyanka along with his famous grandfather, wrote that such "methods of indirect pressure have an oppressive, disintegrating effect and prepare the ground splendidly for despair, panic and cowardice."[3] His recollection provides some insight as to why a number of high-profile political prisoners signed confessions or provided incriminating though dubious information once in Soviet custody.

Once the interrogators were finished with the prisoners, the latter were sent before the Military Collegium of the Supreme Court of the Soviet Union. This court was presided over by Colonel General Vasily V. Ulrikh, the same man who had directed the show trials of the Old Bolsheviks and Marshal Tukhachevsky during the previous decade. Ironically, after having condemned the men who helped establish the Bolshevik regime, Ulrikh would pass similar judgment onto its oldest adversaries. But unlike the show trials staged during the Great Terror, which were covered by the Soviet press and observed by foreign diplomats, the proceedings against the Cossack leaders and top Vlasovites were mostly hidden from public view. In fact, the trials, which spanned a few days at most, were usually not reported in the press until after their sentences had been carried out; and even then the news was relegated to a brief announcement. This was how readers of the 2 August 1946 edition of *Izvestiya*, the government's official newspaper, learned that General Vlasov and his closest deputies had been hanged after making their appearance before the special court.[4]

At the end of that month it was Ataman Semyonov's turn. The trial of the Cossack warlord began on 26 August and was lumped together with that of seven other defendants nabbed by the Soviets in the Far East at the end of the war, including the fascist leader Rodzaevsky. Although five of the defendants were either fascists or figures from the long-extinct Kolchak government, they were collectively labeled as "Semyonovites" by the state prosecutor—no doubt a bitter final humiliation for those among them who despised the ataman. The NKVD interrogators had apparently done their work well as the accused men all pled guilty to plotting an armed struggle against the Soviet Union and other crimes. One day after the verdict was read, on 30 August, Semyonov went to the gallows while five others, including Rodzaevsky, were given a more honorable form of capital punishment via firing squad. Several of the ataman's adult children were also unlucky enough to be captured by the Soviets. Three of his daughters were sentenced to years of hard labor while his son Mikhail, who had been born abroad and never set foot in the Soviet Union prior to his arrest, was charged with treason and shot.[5]

Four and a half months later, on 17 January 1947, the Communist Party's newspaper, *Pravda*, announced that Generals Pyotr N. Krasnov, Andrey G. Shkuro, Semyon N. Krasnov, Helmuth von Pannwitz, Sultan Kelech Ghirey and Timofey I. Domanov had been hanged after having admitted to providing aid to the Germans and "White Guardist units" during the Great Patriotic War. Unfortunately, it is impossible to verify *Pravda*'s claim that the defendants confessed or acknowledged their actions as crimes. However, writers sympathetic to the Cossack cause have cast doubt on that report by noting that trial of the Cossack leaders, which began and ended on 15 January, was exceptionally brief.[6] In contrast, the trial of the "Semyonovites," most of whom were prisoners of much lesser prestige but were apparently more cooperative in the witness stand, lasted for three days.

Domanov, Semyonov and P. N. Krasnov were not the only Cossack leaders who fared badly at the end of the Second World War. N. L. Kulakov, Pannwitz's trusted friend and Field Ataman of the Terek Cossacks, was reportedly killed in a shoot-out with guerrillas near the Austrian frontier in May 1945.[7] The longtime Terek ataman, General Vdovenko, though senile and in failing health, was no luckier. He had been captured by the Soviets shortly after the fall of Belgrade in 1944 and presumably died in captivity.[8] Another casualty worthy of note was Skoropadsky, the all-but-forgotten hetman who nominally ruled Ukraine for seven and a half months in 1918. In the final weeks of the war, he was among the passengers killed while exiting Berlin aboard a train that was struck by a bomb from an Allied warplane.[9]

While the most distinguished prisoners who entered Soviet captivity were often held for a year or more before being sentenced, relatively unknown Cossack senior officers were punished swiftly. Because of their obscurity, the NKVD felt no need to stage a show trial on their behalf—the world would not miss these nameless men. At the same time, because of their high military rank, the NKVD regarded them as incorrigible "enemies of the people" who could not be reformed through corrective labor. As a result, many were killed shortly after their repatriation—even before they were brought back across the Soviet frontier. The preferred method of their execution was, as seen in the previous chapter, by firing squad.[10]

The fate of the tens of thousands of Cossack junior officers, soldiers and refugees who entered Soviet custody but were not marked for outright execution was no less tragic. At Judenburg and other collection points in Central Europe, Soviet repatriation commissions strung out welcoming banners and blared patriotic music from loudspeakers to reassure the returnees that their homecoming would be a joyous occasion. Any illusions the repatriates formed from these displays, however, quickly evaporated once they proceeded beyond the reception areas. Most were crammed into eastbound trains, where they were confined for weeks or months in unsanitary conditions with minimal food or water. In the summer, the wagons were stuffy and felt like the inside of an oven, but for those who traveled in them during the winter each was essentially "an icebox on wheels."[11] This spate of horrors usually came to an end only in the depths of Siberia or Central Asia, when the prisoners emerged from one nightmare and into another: the Gulag.

Upon reaching the correctional labor camps, the Cossack prisoners entered a labyrinth that was completely alien to them. The camp system possessed its own jargon, lore and pecking order. For instance, they quickly learned that they and other political prisoners were dubbed "*kontriks*"—a play on the word "counter-revolutionaries"—and condemned to the lowest category in the prisons' hierarchy. The guards frequently denigrated them as "fascists" and "Hitlerites," and these taunts were sometimes parroted by rival prisoner gangs. Still, other inmates often could not help but be fascinated by the Cossacks and other repatriates who flooded their remote camps in 1945 and the following years. Aleksandr Solzhenitsyn, himself a prisoner at the time, wrote in his monumental work *The Gulag Archipelago* that the appearance of old émigrés among the repatriates "was very like a dream: the resurrection of buried history."[12]

The actual work the Cossack prisoners were sentenced to perform depended on the region and camp to which they were sent. Lieutenant Nikolay Krasnov, who was shipped off to the Gulag in December 1945 after spending the preceding months in various Moscow prisons, toiled on a collective dairy farm, graded a railway bed, harvested timber, constructed an oil distillery and mined coal during his ten years in various Siberian and Central Asian work camps. Despite the exhaustive hours, gnawing hunger, back-breaking work and harsh climate typical of most camps, Krasnov survived his experience thanks to a combination of his youth—he was only twenty-seven years of age when he was turned over to the NKVD at Judenburg—and fitness. However, thousands of other repatriated Cossacks, including his father, expired long before their sentence was up.[13]

The sentence of hard labor was a punishment which the repatriated Cossacks shared with millions of other Soviet citizens returned willingly or forcibly to their homeland. Altogether, at least 5,000,000 Soviet nationals were stranded in foreign lands at the close of the Second World War. Collaborators such as the Vlasovites and Cossacks who fought in German-sponsored military formations represented only a minority of that figure. Most were simply persons who had been deported to Central Europe as forced laborers, former Red Army soldiers captured by the Germans or refugees simply trying to escape the onslaught; in other words, individuals who were swept up in the maelstrom of the war through no fault of their own. Nonetheless, even if they had not voluntarily rendered aid to the enemy, many had some inkling of the severe penalties awaiting them if they fell into Soviet hands. For that reason, anywhere from 1,000,000 to 2,000,000 displaced Soviet citizens may have desired to remain abroad after May 1945.[14] Stalin and his cronies, however, were determined to prevent them from doing so. There were several possible reasons as to why the Soviet leadership wanted to these persons returned. One consideration was that such a massive defection of ordinary citizens might have formed an émigré community that was even larger than the one which existed abroad after the revolution. Such an outcome would have been a major humiliation for a regime which styled itself as a champion for the exploited masses. Another factor was the concern that the non-returners would be recruited by a foreign power, such as the United States, into an anticommunist military role—something that was certainly an aspiration among Pannwitz's Cossacks, the Vlasovites and some old émigrés.[15] A final consideration for the return of Soviet nationals was the state's need for slave laborers to replace those prisoner-workers in the Gulag who died, became infirm or were amnestied. Essentially, the repatriates, as far as Soviet authorities were concerned, were useful as "units of labor" that could be ruthlessly exploited for the state's benefit.[16]

For many *kontriks*, regardless of whether they were Cossacks or other repatriates, the nadir of their experiences in the Gulag began at the close of the 1940s, when political prisoners regarded as exceptionally dangerous by the MVD were isolated from rest of the Gulag population and confined into "special camps." These institutions differed from ordinary camps in that they were surrounded by taller barbed-wire enclosures, employed stricter guards, possessed longer work days and drastically limited correspondence with family and friends outside the camps.[17] Among those transferred to a special camp in the remote Siberian taiga was Nikolay Krasnov. For him, the special camps' most dehumanizing aspect was the numeric system used to identify each prisoner. "Pieces of cloth, with the prisoner's personal number in large letters on it, were sewn on the front and back of his upper garment, also above the right knee on his trousers, and on the front of his cap," wrote Krasnov. "We looked like envelopes plastered with stamps."[18]

It was under these dreadful conditions that Krasnov and his fellow *kontriks* toiled, day in and day out, until 5 March 1953. On that date the guards abruptly forced the prisoners to leave their worksites and return to the camp early. There the inmates noticed that the red flag waving above the administration building was lowered to half-mast. It was not long before they learned why: Stalin had died. Nearly all Gulag memoirs are in agreement that from that moment onward the camps were never the same.[19] Krasnov, writing of that day, recalled:

> In the evening we were allowed to go out and get our food from the kitchens. On the faces of the heads of the camp, military and civilian, there were expressions of complete bewilderment. Their eyes wandered, they were pale. They clutched their guns.
> The night passed quietly, but the next day, less than twenty-four hours after Stalin's death, everything was radically changed.
> During the entire day there was not a yell. Gone was all trace of: "Get going! No talking! Lie down! Put your hands in back of you!"[20]

Despite the guards' jitters, Stalin's passing did not portend a radical new order; the slaves were not transformed into masters. But his successors did begin the process of scaling down the cumbersome camp system. Within weeks they amnestied nearly a million Gulag prisoners; a year later they abolished the special camps and foreign prisoners were allowed to receive parcels from abroad.[21]

On 17 September 1955, Nikita Khrushchev's government issued an amnesty towards repatriates in the camps that, over the next several months, led to their release or being given lighter sentences. For many Cossack prisoners, it was a bittersweet milestone. Most had seen family members or friends waste away in the Gulag. Although they had survived, their bodies and health were frequently ravished by years of overexertion, malnourishment and abuse, leaving some practically disabled. Those that tried to return to their families or former stanitsas in the Soviet Union became a burden on their relatives and communities. They were shunned by old friends and potential employers who feared that any association with these former "enemies of the people" would put themselves in the crosshairs of the local authorities and secret police. Overall, the released Cossacks found it difficult to integrate into society and were doomed to the status of pariahs.[22]

Among the Cossacks released by the Khrushchev government's amnesty were old émigrés who had held foreign citizenship. Initially, to actually leave the Soviet Union and gain entry into a foreign land, they needed to make contact with relatives living abroad or "their governments." These requirements were imposing hurdles since many prisoners had lost track of their acquaintances amid the confusion of the world war and the isolation forced upon them by camp regimens. Moreover, the governments which they had served or been citizens of were frequently no longer extant. Such was the predicament faced by Nikolay Krasnov and other Cossacks who had been Yugoslav citizens prior to the war. The royal government there had been supplanted by Tito's Communists. As relations between Tito and Stalin deteriorated in the postwar years, Cossacks and other Russian citizens remaining in the country were subjected to increased persecution and expulsion. Subsequently, the remnants of the Cossack communities in Yugoslavia melted away as their members dispersed to neighboring countries or to the West.[23] This meant that the postcards which Krasnov and other desperate Cossack prisoners sent through the Red Cross to friends and families whom they believed to be in Yugoslavia never reached their addressees.[24] Krasnov was fortunate that a few of his postcards did reach his cousin in Stockholm who, with assistance from the Swedish Red Cross, managed to secure his freedom at the end of 1955.

It was only after he had gone abroad when Krasnov was fully able to see the changes and population shifts that had affected the Russian Diaspora during the decade he spent trapped behind the Iron Curtain. His wife was living in Argentina, his mother in the United States and the country where he had grown up, Yugoslavia, was virtually off-limits. Subsequently, he remained in Stockholm, where he wrote *The Hidden Russia*, a memoir of his experiences in the Gulag. After saving enough money for a trans-Atlantic voyage, he finally reached Argentina in September 1956. There he was able to reunite with his wife, Lili Krasnova, who had successfully evaded repatriation. He took up work as a draftsman and was active in the small Cossack émigré community in Buenos Aires. But like so many survivors of the camps, he was plagued by physical ailments throughout the remainder of his life. These were likely a contributing factor to his death in 1959 at the age of only forty-one.[25]

Other old Cossack émigrés who were unjustly repatriated to the Soviet Union, survived the labor camps and then returned to the West in the mid–1950s made an effort to obtain some compensation for their harrowing ordeal. In December 1957, a group in Vienna calling itself "the Union of Cossack Officers emigrated in 1920 who returned from the Soviet concentration camps in 1956–57" sent a petition to Britain's Queen Elizabeth II pleading for assistance for having been "quite undeservedly delivered into the hands of the Red Army in the town of Judenburg by your Majesty's Armed Forces." Such assistance was badly needed after their spell in the Siberian labor camps since, in their words, "We have grown old and contracted sicknesses there and now are unable to work." The petition closed with the names of fourteen survivors from the camps along with that of the president of the union.[26] Several months later, their request was politely rejected in a short letter transmitted through the British Embassy in Vienna. The following year, the Union of Cossack Officers prevailed upon British author Peter Huxley-Blythe to submit another petition to the Queen explaining in greater detail their forced repatriation and plight. When he sent this letter and other documents to the British Prime Minister on 4 September 1958, Huxley-Blythe pointed out that the compensation for the handful of officers might be obtained from the money that had been seized by British troops from the Cossacks' field bank in Lienz during May 1945. This solution, he hoped, would be palatable to the government since it would spare British taxpayers from having to support the men. British officials, however, refused to be swayed by this or any argument.[27] Their government, along with that of the United States,[28] was unwilling to concede that it had committed any wrongdoing by forcibly repatriating émigrés, war prisoners and other displaced persons at the end of the war.

Although officials in London and Washington showed no remorse for their governments' conduct towards Soviet nationals in the postwar period, that was not necessarily the case for their soldiers and officers who had carried out those policies. Almost fifteen years after the Allied victory in Europe, a witness to a few compulsory repatriation operations, U.S. General Frank Howley, wrote, "The cries of these men, their attempts to escape, even to kill themselves rather than to be returned to the Soviet Union against which they had fought still plague my memory."[29] On the other hand, a British battalion commander, Colonel A. D. Malcolm, whose unit directly participated in the repatriation of Domanov's Cossacks, was less sympathetic towards the repatriated peoples. Defending his unit's actions in a letter to Huxley-Blythe, Malcolm condemned the entire population of Cossachi Stan—including its sizable civilian contingent of women, children and the elderly—as "traitors to their country." Yet, regardless of how deserving he felt the Cossacks were of their fate, he was still careful to deflect any personal responsibility for the operation. "I was only a battalion commander and only had to carry out orders to administer some of the Russians and put them in lorries and trains," Malcolm explained, "I took no political or policy decisions which were the responsibility of the Army or Corps Commander."[30] According to Huxley-Blythe, the failure of men like Malcolm and their governments to reassess their attitude towards members of the Russian liberation movement during and after the Second World War led the remaining émigrés to become completely disillusioned with the West. Writing in the 1950s, he asserted that Russian émigrés "are equally anti–West as they are anticommunist."[31]

Interestingly, the plight of the Cossack people was not completely shunned by the U.S. government during the height of the Cold War. On 17 July 1959, President Dwight Eisenhower approved the observance of Captive Nations Week. Among those nations that resolution specifically cited as enslaved by "Communist imperialism" was "Cossackia," which stood out as a curious anomaly among the names of Poland, Czechoslovakia, Latvia and other states with a more solid claim to past sovereignty.[32] While it may seem that the inclusion of their homeland into this resolution might have been celebrated by most Cossacks abroad, according the Huxley-Blythe the mention of Cossackia along with Ukraine, Georgia and other lands was more likely to offend their patriotic sensibilities. One group of anticommunist émigrés went as far as to claim that the resolution showed that the United States, like Hitler, aimed to dismember Russia.[33]

Even if many Cossack and Russian émigrés were thoroughly disenchanted with the West after the Second World War, those feelings did not stop scores of them from settling there. Despite the Western Allies' commitment to deporting Soviet nationals, thousands of them did manage to avoid being sent back to their homeland with the help of sympathetic Allied soldiers or by posing as Ukrainians, Poles, old émigrés or other groups who were sometimes exempted from compulsory repatriation.[34] Among the old émigrés who managed to avoid repatriation was Kuban Ataman V. G. Naumenko, who was in Munich when the fighting ended in Europe. He eventually emigrated to the United States, remained Kuban ataman until 1958 and died in 1980 at the age of 97.[35] Another prominent Cossack leader who escaped Stalin's wrath was the Red Army defector Major-General Ivan Kononov. After undertaking his mission to Vlasov's headquarters in April 1945, Kononov never rejoined the XV SS Cossack Cavalry Corps in Croatia and thus avoided sharing its fate. In the war's aftermath, he took advantage of the prevailing disorder and confusion to acquire several false aliases and leave Europe. He eventually settled in Australia.[36]

Regardless of how they avoided repatriation, most émigrés—whether they belonged to the first wave (1920) or the second wave (1945)—let go of their dream of overthrowing Stalin's dictatorship. The Soviet Union's ascendancy to superpower status, combined with the forcible repatriation carried out by the Western Allies, made the émigrés painfully aware of their inconsequential role in international diplomacy. In some instances, old émigrés even jumped on the pro–Soviet bandwagon to applaud the feats of the regime they once detested. Their enthusiasm, one non-returner noted, was "all based on ignorance about life in the Soviet Union."[37] But this lack of real information did not stop many émigrés from projecting their own hopes onto the intentions of the ruling party. Some convinced themselves that Stalin had effectively abandoned Marxism, internationalism and atheism in favor of Russian national ideals. Others were certain that the government was on the verge of offering amnesty to the émigrés, which would enable them to return home as free men. This upsurge of Soviet patriotism among the old émigrés was evident not only in the destitute Far Eastern communities but also among the comparatively well-off émigrés in France. In the White Russian enclaves in Paris and other cities, an increasing number of old émigrés penned pro–Soviet editorials in their postwar press or readily hired themselves as informants to undercover NKVD operatives.[38]

This outpouring of pro–Soviet sentiment made life in postwar France increasingly intolerable for those émigrés who remained unwavering in their opposition to the communist regime. Another factor weighing heavily on their minds was the looming fear that the Western Powers might yet force them to return to their homeland. Subsequently, many non-returners did not settle in Western Europe but instead migrated onto the United States, Canada and even more distant locations such as Australia or Argentina. Some old émigrés followed them, including General Denikin. After having kept a low-profile while living in southeastern France during World War II, the former AFSR commander and his wife decided to take leave of the tumultuous émigré community in that country and head for the United States. Not long after his arrival in New York in December 1945, Denikin sent a letter to the then U.S. Army Chief of Staff, General Eisenhower, pleading in vain for the Western powers to cease compulsory repatriations of non-returners. Eventually, he settled in Ann Arbor, Michigan, where he died in 1947.[39]

After the war, a few dedicated anticommunists persisted in their decades-long struggle against the Soviet Union by remaining active in the NTS, which continued to advertise its program of national-labor solidarity to peoples trapped behind the Iron Curtain through smuggled newspapers and radio broadcasts.[40] But these individuals were the exception, not the norm. By and large, most Russian and Cossack émigrés abandoned their hope of one day returning to their liberated homeland. Subsequently, they placed much less emphasis on preserving their language and culture than the Diaspora of the interwar period, leading them and their offspring to assimilate more readily into their host countries.[41] Most of their associations that remained active after 1945 frequently de-emphasized politics and instead focused their resources on socio-cultural endeavors.[42] Yet, despite their disengagement from the anticommunist struggle or migration to distant corners of the globe, the émigrés still received occasional reminders that the Soviet motherland had not forgotten about them. For example, after Moscow declared amnesty toward the non-returners in 1952, Soviet diplomats in Australia, in a renewed drive to lure former citizens back home, had nostalgic pamphlets and other forms of propaganda distributed throughout that country's émigré community.[43]

The Soviet victory in the war which effectively shattered the Cossack community abroad was also bittersweet for their compatriots who remained in the Soviet Union and had faithfully served their communist masters during the conflict. In early 1945, anticipation for a new, brighter future was widespread among Soviet citizens as fascism was on the verge of being crushed while the leading capitalist states, Britain and the Unites States, were their country's allies. At last, they felt, their country was on the path to achieving national security and a peaceful coexistence within the wider global community. The *raison d'être* for the regime's policies of reckless collectivization, breakneck industrialization and stifling repression appeared to have disintegrated. The Soviet economy could finally concentrate on improving the lives of its citizens by producing consumer goods instead of churning out armaments. The most optimistic even expected that their victory would win them greater personal and political freedoms. But all of those hopes were soon dashed. A new arms race—the nuclear arms race—was initiated by the atomic bombings of Hiroshima and Nagasaki in August 1945, and the Soviets were once again relegated to the role of playing catch-up. Relations between Stalin and his erstwhile allies rapidly cooled; in 1948 the two camps had their first major standoff in the Berlin crisis. By then the Cold War was well underway. For the average Soviet citizen, it meant that old threats were replaced by new ones which the regime used to justify further deprivations, sacrifices and tyranny.

The Cossacks in the Soviet Union were not only disillusioned by the same unrealized hopes as other Soviet citizens, but also by their slide into obscurity. In the months following the surprise German attack, Soviet propagandists had seized upon the dashing performance of the Cossacks and other Red Army horsemen as a bright spot amid a seemingly endless spate bad news from the front.[44] But by the end of the conflict, it became clear that the laurels of victory, at least as far as the regime was concerned, belonged to only one hero: Generalissimo Stalin. No division, group or commander could dare to outshine him. Moreover, steady advances in technology and tactics during the war's latter operations indicated that the future of mobile warfare unquestionably belonged to mechanized vehicles, not horses. With the country no longer in need of heroes or horsemen, the Cossacks had outlived their usefulness. Quietly, the Soviet government undid its 1936 decree and nullified the Cossack identity a second time.[45] Suddenly, the non-native populations of the North Caucasus region which had previously reveled in their association with the famed steppe warriors, even if only in name, found themselves "demoted" to the status of ordinary citizens.

Despite this and other letdowns, the Cossacks in the Soviet Union fared well in comparison to many of their neighbors. Several months after the Red Army drove the Wehrmacht out of the North Caucasus region in 1943, Stalin singled out certain ethnic groups for wholesale deportation on the grounds that they had collaborated *en masse* with the invader.

The first to be meted out this punishment were the Karachays in November, and they were followed by the Kalmyks later that winter. In February 1944 it was the turn of the Chechens and Ingush even though most of their autonomous republic had been spared from German occupation. During the next month the Balkars were rounded up and finally, in May, the Crimean Tatars were shipped into internal exile. Altogether, these operations represented a massive undertaking that carried off approximately 1,000,000 persons from their home districts to remote "special settlements" in Central Asia or Siberia. The autonomous republics and provinces of the deported ethnicities were abolished while their towns and villages were renamed. Russians, Ukrainians and other nationalities regarded as "reliable" were moved in their place. Most of the exiled peoples were not permitted to return to their native districts until the mid-1950s, but the Crimean Tatars and the Volga Germans, who were deported in 1941, were not granted that freedom until the 1980s.[46]

Given the preponderance of ostensibly Cossack formations in the German army,[47] Stalin's decision to exile entire ethnicities on charges of collaboration but not Cossacks appears irrational. In fact, the allegation that these groups were guilty of betraying the motherland to the enemy was likely nothing more than a convenient excuse to settle scores with various minorities which appeared too restive. Their cultures, from the perspective of the Kremlin, were regarded as incompatible with the concept of the new Soviet man, *Homo sovieticus*. To make them conform to the new order, the targeted North Caucasian peoples were deprived of their autonomy and livelihoods that were inextricably bound with their homelands by resettling them in remote, unfamiliar and often barren surroundings. The high death rates experienced by exiled groups during that process was regarded as an undesirable yet tolerable outcome.[48]

Stalin and his inner circle felt no need to enact similar reprisals against Cossacks. That is not to say that individual Cossacks suspected of having been too friendly with the invaders went unpunished; but the Cossack people as a whole were spared condemnation as traitors. Soviet authorities recognized that de-Cossackization policies, whether carried out officially or surreptitiously in the 1920s, had succeeded. By the eve of the Great Patriotic War, the Cossack identity had been harnessed purely for the interests of the state. Those qualities that had once partially defined Cossacks, such as limited self-rule, military service and tax-exempt privileges, had not been revived. True, a flicker of the old ethos did emerge in form of the anticommunist Cossack movements led by S. V. Pavlov, T. I. Domanov and a handful of others, but their venture was little more than a nuisance. It certainly lacked the vigor of the "Cossack counterrevolution" launched by Kaledin, Kornilov and Dutov a generation earlier. In any case, with the Cossacks unceremoniously written into extinction soon after the war, it seemed doubtful whether the old Cossack spirit would make an appearance ever again.

Resurrection

For more than four decades following the Soviet victory in the Second World War, virtually nothing was heard from Cossacks—or groups claiming Cossack ancestry—in the Soviet Union. Throughout that period their homelands, by all appearances, remained tranquil with one significant exception: the unrest which rocked Novocherkassk for two days in the summer of 1962. That incident was sparked by a government announcement on 1 June that meat and dairy products would undergo a considerable price hike. This news, which came on the heels of recent wage cuts, prompted about 200 workers at the Budyonny Novocherkassk Electric Locomotive Plant to walk off the job that morning. By noon, the number of protesting workers had swelled to 1,000, and on the following morning a crowd of nearly 7,000 demonstrators gathered at the factory. By then troops from the North Caucasian Military District had occupied the locomotive works and nearby roads, but their presence was not enough to deter the crowd from marching from the factory to the center of Novocherkassk. Indeed, they continued to push forward even after encountering Soviet tanks parked in their path. A bloodbath was avoided there only because the commander of the tank crews refused an order to fire on the unarmed crowd. Most of the demonstrators converged on the city square in front of the palace that had once served as the headquarters of the Don Host and now was home to the offices of local party leaders. When the chairman of the city executive committee refused to negotiate with the demonstrators, the crowd broke into the building and, according to Soviet authorities, ransacked its interior. The municipal police headquarters and a branch of the State Bank were also attacked around the same time. Eventually, reliable security forces arrived in Novocherkassk, cleared the square with machine guns, instituted a curfew and continued to patrol the city days afterward. The KGB reported that about two dozen persons were killed in this crackdown, although participants have claimed that the actual figure was much higher.[49]

While chroniclers are occasionally unable to resist the temptation to link this brief disturbance in the former Don Cossack capital as a final spasm of the long Cossack struggle against Soviet tyranny,[50] a closer examination of the available evidence suggests that its origins lay squarely with the working-class. Its instigators were workers who rallied to slogans that were variations of "Meat, butter, higher wages." According to eyewitnesses, the procession of demonstrators waved red flags, carried portraits of Lenin and sang revolutionary hymns as they marched into the heart of Novocherkassk. Neither they nor Soviet investigators attributed the unrest to some nefarious Cossack conspiracy. The alleged "banditry" which the demonstrators engaged in was confined to the city and industrial district of Novocherkassk. It had no echoes in the nearby countryside. The Cossacks remained quiet; not even an insurrection in their own backyard could arouse them from their dormancy.[51]

The victims of the Novocherkassk massacre did have one thing in common with the countless Cossacks who had fallen in their struggle against the Soviet regime: regardless of how much their story was suppressed or how deep their remains were buried, they were never quite forgotten. Indeed, this aspect was shared by all victims of the violent appropriation, terror, famine, genocide, collectivization, slavery, exile, purges and paranoia sponsored by Lenin and his successors. When, in 1987, Communist Party General Secretary Mikhail Gorbachev included the country's history in the realm of *glasnost* (openness), he hoped to restore the people's faith in the Leninist-Marxist system by rejecting the stifling repression of Stalinism. But as historians, journalists and the intelligentsia embarked on thorough investigations of Soviet history, they were unable to overlook the evidence that bloody repressions were not confined to Stalin's reign. Indeed, the concentration camp system, Red Terror and de-Cossackization all developed under Lenin's watch. The Novocherkassk massacre occurred under Khrushchev while the last camp for political prisoners closed down only in 1992. Through *glasnost*, Gorbachev had unwittingly poked holes in a dam which undermined the integrity of the entire structure, eventually causing it to burst.[52]

For Gorbachev and other "Soviet patriots," one of the most troubling forces uncorked by the liberal-democratic reforms was that of nationalism. The cabal in the Kremlin had not imagined that the new freedoms would threaten the unity of the Soviet state since they firmly believed the official line that the party had long ago created a "Soviet people" who enjoyed a familial bond untroubled by ethnic animosities.[53] But this expectation soon dissipated as national ferment in the Baltic, Caucasus and other borderlands began tugging at the country's national seams. For the center, perhaps the most unexpected development was the emergence of Cossack spokesmen who joined the chorus of ethnicities demanding greater self-determination and even rehabilitation.

The evolution of Cossack organizations during *glasnost* began innocently enough. Their origins can be traced to informal gatherings among the intelligentsia and enthusiasts who wanted to rediscover the history and culture of Cossacks. As local clubs established links with each other, their organizations grew larger and more sophisticated. In 1989, a group dedicated to the Don Cossacks was formed; this was shortly followed by a similar organization on behalf of the Kuban Cossacks. Gradually, their activities evolved from preserving the Cossacks' past to restoring it. At first they revived old folk songs and horse-riding skills, but soon these "neo-Cossacks" began embarking on activities with a more political and even military bent. In the spring and summer of 1990, putative Cossack representatives from the Don, Terek, Kuban, Urals and Siberian hosts conferred to develop a general Cossack political program. Their efforts bore fruit in June of that year with the establishment of the Union of Cossacks in Russia, an umbrella association claiming to represent all Cossack interests. Under its guidance, Cossack activists in the borderlands began summoning their traditional assemblies. In October, the Kuban Cossacks convened a rada, and the Cossacks from the Don and other extinct hosts followed suit by organizing krugs at regional and local levels in the coming months.[54]

The Union of Cossacks in Russia identified its interests with the Communist Party and ultimately the Soviet Union. Subsequently, statists—meaning those who, like the White generals, desired to hold the state together at all costs—lent the Cossack movement their support as a useful counterweight to the separatist aspirations of the minorities in the North Caucasus and other contested borderlands. Regional Soviet authorities gratefully accepted assistance from Cossack militiamen in their efforts to contain demonstrations, strikes and other forms of unrest which rocked their districts. At the statewide level, the Ministry of Defense reintroduced Cossack formations to the Soviet army. To the casual observer, it may have appeared as though that the Cossacks, in a repeat of 1905, were by and large lining up on the side of reaction through their defense of a faltering regime.[55]

In reality, Cossack political activity was no more monolithic in 1990 than it had been at the beginning of that century. This became evident in late November of that year, when a council of Cossacks convened in Krasnodar and refused to view their peoples' past relations with the Communist Party through rose-colored lenses. The conference brazenly called upon the Soviet government to abandon its past stereotypes of Cossacks as "a reactionary force," officially recognize the earlier atrocities against Cossacks as genocide and acknowledge the Cossacks' right to the same forms of "national self-expression" that was granted to other ethnic groups. Their demands were realized the following April, when the Supreme Soviet's decree "On the Rehabilitation of Repressed Peoples" specifically mentioned Cossacks among those peoples subjected to "unlawful and criminal acts of repression" against them. This was followed by another decree a few months later which granted Cossacks the right to reestablish their traditional forms of government, make claims on their former lands and, among other things, establish university chairs in Cossack history. These conditions, particularly those promising the return of Cossack lands, were a source of grave concern for the non-Cossack population living in the areas affected by the decree. Indeed, in the

Terek region and southern Kuban, local disputes erupted as Cossacks tried to regain ownership of lands which they claimed had been expropriated from them almost seventy years earlier.[56] These tussles became even bitterer when they involved natives, such as Chechens, Ingush or Circassians, who argued that the contested lands had originally been stolen from their ancestors by Cossack colonists. Understandably, they regarded themselves, and not the Cossacks, as the victims most deserving of compensation.

Following their success in their campaign for rehabilitation, the anticommunist Cossacks founded the Union of Cossack Hosts in Russia and Abroad in July 1991. Its ostensible purpose was to represent all Cossacks who were persecuted or went into exile during the communist period. However, like their forerunners in the civil war period, the anticommunist Cossacks in the early 1990s were able to agree on little besides their hostility to Marxism. Some, like the Kuban politicians in 1919, sought to secure additional rights by arguing that their people were a distinct ethnicity. The radicals among them even aspired to the worn dream of creating an independent "Cossackia." Others preferred to style themselves as selfless patriots upholding Russian interests, Orthodoxy and "order" in the restive borderlands.

After the collapse of the Soviet Union at the end of 1991, anticommunism became the dominant ideological strain among modern Cossacks. But for the time being it remained an open question as to whether most Cossacks would veer towards the separatists or the Russian nationalists. Gradually, proponents of the latter cause won out. At the end of 1992, a meeting of Cossack representatives from the eleven hosts declared their readiness to defend the integrity of the Russian Federation, which at the time was threatened by separatist movements among Chechens, Tatars and even Siberians. Furthermore, they sweetened their offer by expressing their desire to be directly subordinate to the head of state—an arrangement reminiscent to the Cossacks' mythical bond with the tsars. Although Russian President Boris Yeltsin was hardly a chauvinist, there was no shortage of reasons for him to look favorably upon their proposal, including the possibilities of wooing problematic conservatives his side, co-opting the Cossacks as a positive force for the country's fledging democracy and, if nothing else, upholding the boundaries of the Russian Federation. Ultimately, Yeltsin accepted their offer by granting the Cossacks official security duties, thus putting them on path towards the privileged status which they enjoy today.[57]

The efforts of post–Soviet Russia to transition into a stable, Western-style democracy eventually foundered amid political bedlam, economic turmoil and ultimately disillusionment. In addition to these challenges were the clashes which occasionally flared up in Russia's borderlands: the Abkhazian-Georgian conflict (1992–1993), the wars in Chechnya (1994–1996, 1999–2009), the South Ossetian conflict (2008) and the war in eastern Ukraine (2014–present). Cossack paramilitary detachments of the official and unofficial variety have made appearances in each of these struggles as well as others that were fought well beyond the frontiers of the Russian Federation: the Transnistria War (1992), Bosnian War (1992–1995) and Syrian civil war (2011–present).[58]

For a significant segment of Russia's population, the humiliating loss of the Soviet empire and its superpower status, combined with the adversities and disorders that seemingly stemmed from efforts to model their governing system after the democratic West, spawned an acute identity crisis in the post–Soviet era. Indeed, just as the "Eurasianist" émigrés of the 1920s blamed the calamity of the Russian Revolution on the importation and mutation of foreign ideas such as Marxism, Russian conservatives tend to regard the attempt to transplant liberal democracy in the country as no less delusional and the source of its post-Soviet troubles.⁵⁹ These "patriotic forces," as they view themselves, fear not only the imposition of a Western-style government but also the infiltration of pop culture, tolerance for homosexuals and demographic trends which threaten to usurp the preponderance of ethnic Russians in some districts of the country. Against this current of change and modernity, they have found an ally in the Cossack movement. For them, the Cossacks are not simply national mascots but also defenders of tradition, decency and order. In the Russian Far East, conservatives looked at the formation of Amur and Ussuri Cossack detachments as a possible solution against Chinese, Japanese and South Korean commercial penetration of their region.⁶⁰ Campaigns to implement Cossack patrols have been even more vigorous in the North Caucasus, where relations between Russians and other ethnic groups have always been fraught. There Cossacks routinely patrol districts for illegal Muslim migrants even though they are officially barred from carrying weapons or even asking for identity papers.⁶¹ These restrictions, however, do not unduly concern Cossacks or their supporters. For example, in 2012, the governor of Krasnodar territory, Aleksandr N. Tkachev, explained the inherent value of Cossack patrols to skeptical law enforcement officers by declaring, "What you cannot do, a Cossack can."⁶² It is little wonder then that opponents of the Kremlin and human-rights observers have frowned upon the neo-Cossack movement in recent years as its members intimidate Muslim workers, brawl with protesters, crackdown on LGBTQ rallies and raid art exhibits which they deem inappropriate. On the other hand, these same activities have won the Cossacks accolades from their supporters who view them as defenders of Russian society against Western decadence and unsavory immigrants.⁶³

In addition to serving as the conservative vanguard in Russia's "culture wars," Cossack groups have also championed the cult of personality which has arisen around the country's current president, Vladimir Putin. For the Russian strongman, the Cossacks are the perfect standard-bearers for his propaganda machine which seeks to restore the country's imperial splendor by idolizing the past and ignoring the dismal realities of the present. No better examples of this aim exist than the grandiose parades held in Red Square each year on 9 May to commemorate the Soviet victory in the Second World War. These spectacles are engineered to be intoxicating for those Russians who mourn their loss of empire, diminished geopolitical influence and continuing economic woes.⁶⁴ This ruse appears to have had its intended effect on ultra-nationalist Cossacks. One such group, the Irbis Cossacks, has honored Putin by immortalizing his likeness in a Caesar-esque bust. The Irbis Cossacks have also made headlines by conferring honorary Cossack status on Donald Trump following his victory in the 2016 U.S. presidential election. According to the group's ataman, the latter action was taken out of consideration for Trump's record of favorable—one might even say flattering—comments towards Putin throughout his campaign. Their offer, however, was withdrawn in early 2018 after the Trump presidency failed to meet the Cossacks' expectations of ushering in a new era of harmonious Russian—U.S. relations.⁶⁵ For the Irbis Cossacks, at least, the Cossack identity remains as intricately tied to politics as it had been in Krasnov's All-Great Don Host a century earlier.

While the Kremlin spares no expense to remind its citizens of their grandparents' triumph in the Great Patriotic War, other events of the past that were no less significant for the country and its people are hardly given any attention at all. This became apparent in early 2017, when the centennial of the February Revolution that toppled the ancient Romanov dynasty passed by seemingly unnoticed by the country's state-controlled media.⁶⁶ The modern Cossack movement, it seems, is also afflicted with similar bouts of selective amnesia. One does not need to delve very far into Cossack history to see that the xenophobic and authoritarian outlook of neo-Cossacks is at odds with the multicultural and egalitarian ethos of their early founders and most famous rebel leaders. Even relatively recent history is accorded inconsistent treatment: modern Cossacks take immense pride in their country's feats in World War II even as Cossack paramilitaries idolize figures such as General Shkuro, a German collaborator who is still officially regarded as a war criminal by the Russian government.[67]

In Western media, most coverage of the neo-Cossacks evokes flashbacks of their early twentieth-century stereotype by depicting them as loyal janissaries of a new Russian tsar—the enigmatic Putin. Subsequently, it is easy to overlook the fact that the Cossack ethos is not and never was exclusively bound to one nation, party or individual. Reminders of this fact appeared during the 2014 EuroMaidan protests in the Ukrainian capital of Kiev, where demonstrators donned Zaporozhian costumes, styled their hair in a forelock, carried portraits of Hetman Khmelnytsky and even declared themselves Cossacks.[68] Arguably, the anti–Moscow, democratic and independent spirit of the Euromaidan protesters was perhaps more faithful to early Cossack traditions than the blind obedience to authority preached by their Russian counterparts. But in recent years there were occasions which revealed that even Russian elements are not always comfortable with their Cossack allies. In 2013, Russia's Federal Security Service (FSB) suppressed a group of Cossack mercenaries that was participating in Syria's civil war. Two years later, the proclamation of a Cossack republic in eastern Ukraine's embattled Luhansk district triggered a brief internecine struggle between Cossack detachments and pro–Russian separatists fighting the Ukrainian army. The skirmishing between the erstwhile allies ended only after the Cossacks were driven from the disputed area.[69] Thus it would be wrong to assume that the aims of neo-Cossacks always mirror those of the Russian government and Russian nationalists. Indeed, among the conclusions that can be drawn from the Cossacks' past struggle against communism is that their temperament, as the tsarist officers and even their atamans learned, can be quite unpredictable. That lesson is one that their current patrons, particularly those in the Kremlin, should not forget.

Glossary of Terms, Acronyms and Abbreviations

AFSR (Armed Forces of South Russia): official name of the White armies of South Russia from January 1919 to March 1920.

aoul: Caucasian native village.

ARA (American Relief Association): charitable organization which carried out famine relief in Soviet Russia from 1921 to 1923.

ataman: Cossack chieftain.

atamanschina: Cossack warlordism.

Aufbau (Aufbau: Wirtschafts—politische Vereinigung für den Osten): Reconstruction: Economic—Political Organization of the East; a conspiratorial organization of anticommunist émigrés which collaborated closely with the German National Socialist (Nazi) Party from 1920 to 1923.

Bolshevik Party: radical faction of the Russian Social Democratic Labor Party. The party formally changed its name to the Russian Communist Party (Bolshevik) in early 1918.

Četniks: Yugoslav royalist and Serb nationalist insurgents in occupied Yugoslavia during World War II. Though pro–Allied in ideology, various Četnik detachments frequently collaborated with Italian and German occupation forces against the Yugoslav Partisans.

Cheka: Soviet secret police from 1917 to 1922.

cherkesska: cloak with decorative cartridge holders traditionally worn by various Caucasian peoples and adopted by Kuban and Terek Cossacks.

Cossachi Stan: "Cossack land"; name given to the community of anticommunist Cossack refugees and irregulars who migrated between Novogrodek (Belarus), Tolmezzo (Italy) and Lienz (Austria) in 1944–45.

Dalburo: Far Eastern Bureau of the Russian Communist Party.

Donburo: Don Bureau of the Russian Communist Party.

dzhigitovka: a form of trick riding popular among Cossacks and other Caucasian peoples to exhibit their equestrian skills.

FER: Far Eastern Republic; a Soviet-dominated buffer state in Eastern Siberia and the Russian Far East from 1920 to 1922.

Gulag: Russian acronym for the "Main Administration of Corrective Labor Camps and Labor Settlements."

hetman: title for supreme leader; used by Zaporozhian and Ukrainian Cossacks.

Hiwi: German acronym for *Hilfswilligers*, meaning "willing to help." The term Hiwi was applied to Soviet peoples who voluntarily (and in some instances reluctantly) collaborated with the Wehrmacht.

host (*voisko*): the highest Cossack administrative unit; each possessed its own armed force.

Kadet (Constitutional Democrat) Party: liberal-center Russian political party in the early twentieth century.

Kappelite (kappelovtsy): soldiers and officers who had fought under General V. O. Kappel. Many Kappelites were anti–Bolshevik workers from the Volga and Ural regions.

KNOD: Cossack National Liberation Movement; a separatist-oriented Cossack émigré group during World War II.

Komuch: Russian acronym for the Committee of Members of the Constituent Assembly, an anti–Bolshevik government formed in Samara during 1918.

KONR: Committee for the Liberation of the Peoples of Russia; an anticommunist organization for Russians and other Soviet peoples active from 1944 to 1945.

kontrik: Gulag slang for "counterrevolutionary" that was applied to some groups of political prisoners.

krug: a Cossack assembly founded on nominally democratic principles.

kubanka: a shorter version of the *papakha* wool cap traditionally worn by Kuban Cossacks.

kulak: well-to-do peasant.

***lineitsy* Cossacks**: Cossacks of the line. In the northwest Caucasus, the *lineitsy* Cossacks inhabiting the fortified settlements inland were fused together with the more numerous Black Sea (Ukrainian) Cossacks along the coast to create the Kuban Cossack Host.

Menshevik Party: moderate faction of the Russian Social Democratic Labor Party.

military revolutionary committee (MRC): Revolutionary military organs responsible for organizing and defending rebellions in a city or region. MRCs were often created on behalf of soviets and dominated by members of the Bolshevik Party although there were instances of Cossack rebels and other socialists creating their own MRCs.

MVD: Ministry of Internal Affairs of the Soviet Union after 1946. One of its primary functions was the administration of the Gulag system.

nagaika: short whip employed by Cossacks as a non-lethal form of crowd control in pre-revolutionary Russia

National Ukrainian Cossack Organization (NUCO): organization of Ukrainian nationalists and émigrés, many of whom claimed Cossack ancestry. The NUCO was active from 1917 into World War II and maintained a general anticommunist, anti–Polish and pro–German outlook throughout its existence.

Natsionalnoe Trudovoy Soyuz (NTS): National Labor Alliance. Originally, this anticommunist émigré organization was named Natsionalnoe-trudovoi soyuz novogo pokolenya (NTSNP, i.e., National Labor Alliance of the New Generation) and its followers were referred to as "Solidarists."

NKVD: People's Commissariat for Internal Affairs; its functions included operation of the Soviet secret police and Gulag from 1934 to 1946.

non-returner: Label applied to those Soviet citizens (often former POWs, collaborators, forced laborers and refugees) who remained abroad after World War II.

Ober Ost: Supreme Command of German Forces in the East (World War I).

OGPU: Soviet secret police from 1923 to 1934.

OHL (Oberste Heeresleitung): German Supreme Army Command (World War I).

OKH (Oberkommando des Heeres): Supreme command of the German army (World War II); formally subordinate to Oberkommando der Wehrmacht.

OKW (Oberkommando der Wehrmacht): Supreme command of the armed forces of Germany in World War II.

old émigrés: Émigrés who fled from areas of the former Russian empire prior to World War II (mainly during the years 1917–22).

Orgburo: Organization Bureau of the Bolshevik Party Central Committee.

Ostministrium: Reich Ministry of the Occupied Territories in the East (World War II).

Ostpolitik: German policy toward the Soviet Union in World War II.

Osttruppen: "Eastern troops"; general term applied to Soviet peoples who fought for Germany in World War II.

outlander (*inogorodnye*): term for the non–Cossack, non-native population of a host. Outlanders included everyone from recently-arrived settlers to the descendants of Russian peasants whose families had resided in the host for several generations.

papakha: shaggy wool hat traditionally worn by some Cossack and Caucasian groups.

plastun: Cossack infantry.

POW: prisoner of war.

rada: term for a legislative assembly in Ukraine or in the Kuban Cossack Host.

revkom: revolutionary committee.

ROND (Russkoe Osvoboditelnoe Natsionalnoe Dvizhenie): Russian National Liberation Movement; a fascist-oriented Russian émigré organization active in Germany during the 1930s.

ROVS (Russky Obshche-Voynsky Soyuz): Russian General Military Union; an émigré organization of White army veterans established in 1924.

Semyonovite (*Semyonovtsy*): soldiers and officers who fought under Ataman Grigory Semyonov.

Sibobduma: Siberian Regional Assembly, 1917–18.

SMERSH: Soviet counterintelligence agency from 1943 to 1946.

Socialist Revolutionary (SR) Party: loosely-organized Russian political party in the early twentieth century favored by the peasantry.

Sovnarod: Union for the Return to the Motherland; an organization founded by Russian émigrés to facilitate their repatriation to Soviet Russia in the 1920s.

stanitsa: a Cossack settlement ranging in size from few hundred up to tens of thousands of individuals. As an administrative unit, stanitsas sometimes encompassed several smaller nearby settlements.

Stavka: Supreme headquarters of the Imperial Russian Army (World War I) and later the Red Army (World War II)

untermenschen: "subhumans"; a term applied to most Slavs and other groups viewed as undesirable in Nazi racist ideology.

Ustaša: Croat ultranationalist party which, with Axis backing, ruled the Independent State of Croatia from 1941 to 1945.

vozhd: "leader"; title used by some Russian fascist leaders.

Wehrmacht: Armed forces of Nazi Germany.

zemstvo: autonomous local and regional assembly in Russia from 1864 to 1917. During the Russian Civil War, some anti–Bolshevik governments attempted to reestablish zemstvos.

Chapter Notes

Preface

1. The association of the Cossacks and the White armies can be found in almost any general history of the Russian civil war, including such classics as William Henry Chamberlin's *The Russian Revolution*, Vol. 2 (New York: Grosset & Dunlap, 1965), Evan Mawdsley's *The Russian Civil War* (New York: Pegasus, 2007) and George Stewart's *The White Armies of Russia* (New York: Russell & Russell, 1970). For more in-depth analyses of the Cossacks' turbulent relations with the White movement, see Peter Kenez's two volumes *The Civil War in South Russia: The First Year of the Volunteer Army* (Berkeley: University of California Press, 1971) and *The Defeat of the Whites* (Berkeley: University of California Press, 1977).

2. Literature on anti-Soviet Cossacks in the Second World War is less thorough than that for the Russian civil war. The subject is briefly addressed by two works which cover Nazi collaborators of all nationalities: David Littlejohn's *Foreign Legions of the Third Reich*, Volume 4 (San Jose, CA: R. James Bender Publishing, 1987) and Christopher Ailsby's *Htiler's Renegades: Foreign Nationals in the Service of the Third Reich* (Duiles, VA: Brassey's Inc., 2004). These, along with François de Lsannoy's *Les Cosaques de Pannwitz* (Château de Damigry: Heimdal, 2000) offer great photo essays of Cossacks in the Wehrmacht. Peter Huxley-Blythe's *The East Came West* (Caldwell, ID: The Caxton Printers, 1964) is a subjective retelling of the Cossacks' anti-Soviet campaign in World War II. For a scholarly account on the subject, however, one would need to turn to Samuel Newland's, *Cossacks in the German Army 1941–1945* (Portland, OR: Frank Cass, 1991).

Introduction

1. Tharoor, Ishaan, "Sochi Olympics Stirs Nationalism of an Exiled People," *Time*, 6 February 2014, http://time.com/4864/sochi-olympics-russia-circassians/, Retrieved 9 March 2015.

2. Forsyth, James, *The Caucasus* (New York: Cambridge University Press, 2013) 284–294; Bullough, Oliver, "Sochi 2014Winter Olympics: The Circassians Cry Genocide," *Newsweek*, 21 May 2012, http://www.newsweek.com/sochi-2014-winter-olympics-circassians-cry-genocide-64893, Retrieved 16 March 2015.

3. Quoted in Tharoor, Ishaan, "Sochi Olympics Stirs Nationalism of an Exiled People," *Time*, 6 February 2014.

4. Quoted in Tharoor, Ishaan, "Sochi Olympics Stirs Nationalism of an Exiled People," *Time*, 6 February 2014.

5. Steven Lee Myers, *The New Tsar* (New York: Alfred A. Knopf, 2015) 323–324.

6. Myers, *The New Tsar*, 434–437. One of Putin's critics, Boris Nemtsov, labeled the Games as a "festival of corruption" after his investigation estimated that half of the $51 billion spent on the preparing Sochi for the Olympics was stolen or squandered. Despite the massive budget overruns, not all of the construction was completed in time for the games.

7. Smith-Spark, Laura and Nick Paton Walsh, "United States reveals 'specific' threats to Olympic Games," *CNN*, 4 February 2014, http://www.cnn.com/2014/02/04/world/europe/russia-sochi-winter-olympics/, Retrieved 9 March 2015.

8. Luhn, Alec, "The Cossacks Ride Again," *Slate*, 31 January 2014.

9. Lee, Jolie, "Who are Russia's Cossack Militiamen in Pussy Riot Beating?," *USA Today*, 20 February 2014.; Flintoff, Corey, "Russia's Cossacks Ride Back From History as 'Patriots,'" *National Public Radio*, 22 February 2014, http://www.npr.org/2014/02/22/280964932/back-from-history-russias-cossacks-rise-as-patriots, Retrieved 3 February 2015.

10. Myers, *The New Tsar*, 455.

11. Luhn, Alec, "The Cossacks Ride Again," *Slate*, 31 January 2014.

12. Lee, Jolie, "Who are Russia's Cossack Militiamen in Pussy Riot Beating?," *USA Today*, 20 February 2014, https://www.usatoday.com/story/news/nation-now/2014/02/20/cossack-militiamen-pussy-riot-sochi/5636603/.

13. Keating, Joshua, "Cossacks Return to the World Stage," *Slate*, 15 April 2014, www.slate.com/blogs/the_world_/2014/04/15in_sochi_and_ukraine_cossacks_return_to_the_world_stage.html, Retrieved 15 April 2015.

14. Lee, Jolie, "Who are Russia's Cossack Militiamen in Pussy Riot Beating?," *USA Today*, 20 February 2014; Keating, Joshua, "Cossacks Return to the World Stage," *Slate*, 15 April 2014; Flintoff, Corey, "Russia's Cossacks Ride Back From History as 'Patriots,'" *National Public Radio*, 22 February 2014.

15. Myers, *The New Tsar*, 457–481.
16. Shuster, Simon, "Meet the Cossack 'Wolves' Doing Russia's Dirty Work in Ukraine," *Time*, 12 May 2014, http://time.com/95898/wolves-hundred-ukraine-russia-cossack/.
17. Myers, *The New Tsar*, 472.
18. Tharoor, Ishaan, "The Evidence that may Prove Pro-Russian Separatists Shot Down MH17," *Time*, 20 July 2014; Windrem, Robert and Mike Brunker, "MH17 Shootdown: Russian Cossack Leader Made 'Spies' Phone Call," *NBC News*, 24 July 2014, http://www.nbcnews.com/storyline/ukraine-plane-crash/mh17-shootdown-russian-cossack-leader-made-spies-phone-call-n163311. An investigation by the Dutch Safety Board later confirmed the allegation that MH17 was felled by a Buk surface to air missile fired from rebel-held territory. See MH17 (brochure), Dutch Safety Board, October 2015.
19. Windrem, Robert and Mike Brunker, "MH17 Shootdown: Russian Cossack Leader Made 'Spies' Phone Call," *NBC News*, 24 July 2014.
20. Hanson, Victor Davis, "What Makes Vladimir Run?," *Strategika*, Issue 21, Hoover Institution, 18 February 2015, http://www.hoover.org/research/what-makes-vladimir-run, Retrieved 4 March 2015.
21. Gregory, Paul R., "We Can End Russia's War Against Ukraine," *Strategika*, Issue 21, Hoover Institution, 18 February 2015, http://www.hoover.org/research/we-can-end-russias-war-against-ukraine, Retrieved 5 March 2015.
22. William Penn Cresson, *The Cossacks: Their History and Country* (New York: Brentano's, 1919) 5.
23. For example, see Vasily Glazkov's *History of the Cossacks* (New York: Robert Speller & Sons, 1972) or Nicholas Feodoroff, *History of the Cossacks* (Commack: Nova Science Publishers, 1999).
24. For example, see British Brigadier Huddleston Noel Hedsworth Williamson's observations in *Farewell to the Don*, edited by John Harris (New York: The John Day Company, 1971) 46–47; Shane O'Rourke, *Warriors and Peasants* (New York: St Martin's Press, 2000) 136.
25. Longworth, *Cossacks*, 36–40; O'Rourke, *Cossacks*, 40–41; 50–52.
26. W. P. Cresson, *The Cossacks: Their History and Country* (New York: Brentano's, 1919) 95.
27. Longworth, *Cossacks*, 24; O'Rourke, *Cossacks*, 40.
28. *Ibid.* 29; Albert Seaton, *The Horsemen of the Steppes* (London: The Bodley Head, 1985) 46–49; Phillip Longworth, *The Cossacks* (New York: Holt, Rinehart and Winston, 1969) 13–14.
29. Seaton, *Horsemen*, 50–51.
30. Seaton, *Horsemen*, 68–71, 127. The Terek Cossacks, especially in their early history, were sometimes referred to as Grebensk Cossacks after the ridge (*greben'*) on which they built their settlements.
31. Seaton, *Horsemen*, 62, 67–68.
32. Robert H. McNeal, *Tsar and Cossack* (London: Macmillan Press, 1987) 16–17.
33. O'Rourke, *Cossacks*, 63–65.
34. Longworth, *Cossacks*, 82–87; Seaton, *Horsemen*, 98–104.
35. Longworth, *Cossacks*, 88–89; Willard Sunderland, *Taming the Wild Field* (Ithaca: Cornell University Press, 2004) 26.
36. Seaton, *Horsemen*, 56–57, 104–106, 109–110; O'Rourke, *Warriors and Peasants* (New York: St. Martin's Press, 2000) 32–37; Longworth, *Cossacks*, 39–42, 154.
37. Nicholas Feodoroff, *History of the Cossacks* (Commack: Nova Science Publishers, 1999) 79.
38. Longworth, *Cossacks*, 25–26; W. G. Glaskow, *History of the Cossacks* (New York: Robert Speller & Sons, 1972) 89.
39. Longworth, *Cossacks*, 159; Seaton, *Horsemen*, 110.
40. Seaton, *Horsemen*, 110.
41. Longworth, *Cossacks*, 159–170; Seaton, *Horsemen*, 111–112.
42. Longworth, *Cossacks*, 97–123; O'Rourke, *Cossacks*, 67–87.
43. O'Rourke, *Cossacks*, 99–109; Longworth, *Cossacks*, 130–149.
44. O'Rourke, *Cossacks*, 112–132; Longworth, *Cossacks*, 187–223.
45. O'Rourke, *Cossacks*, 64, 102–103; Longworth, *Cossacks*, 215.
46. Seaton, *Horsemen*, 114.
47. James Forsyth, *The Caucasus* (New York: Cambridge University Press, 2013) 237–249; Robert McNeal, *Tsar and Cossack* (London: Macmillan Press, 1987) 18–19.
48. Seaton, *Horsemen*, 136–137; 173–175; James Forsyth, *The Caucasus* (New York: Cambridge University Press, 2013) 246–248.
49. O'Rourke, *Cossacks*, 136–137; Seaton, *Horsemen*, 141.
50. Longworth, *Cossacks*, 235–240.
51. Longworth, *Cossacks*, 249.
52. McNeal, *Tsar and Cossack*, 6–7.
53. O'Rourke, *Cossacks*, 140–142; Seaton, *Horsemen*, 182–183.
54. McNeal, *Tsar and Cossack*, 3, 13.
55. Cresson, *The Cossacks*, 228.
56. Seaton, *Horsemen*, 185.
57. Glaskow, *Cossacks*, 33–35.
58. Evan Mawdsley, *The Russian Civil War* (New York: Pegasus Books, 2007) 19; Peter Holquist, *Making War, Forging Revolution* (Cambridge: Harvard University Press, 2002) 8; Peter Kenez, *Civil War in South Russia, 1918* (Berkeley, University of California Press, 1971) 38–39. Accounts differ on the exact proportion of Cossacks to outlanders in the Don Territory in 1914–1917. The figures given by Mawdsley and Holquist place the Don Cossacks at about 36–39 percent of the host's population. Kenez gives a slightly more optimistic figure—from the Cossack viewpoint—of 49 percent. All agree, however, that the Cossacks of the Don represented a minority of the populations of their homelands.
59. McNeal, *Tsar and Cossack*, 12–21.
60. McNeal, *Tsar and Cossack*, 103–110; O'Rourke, *Warriors and Peasants*, 43. The Cossacks also opposed the zemstvo proposals on the account that it would abrogate their tax-exempt status, one of their most endeared privileges under the tsarist regime.

61. McNeal, *Tsar and Cossack*, 109–110. The restoration of a host krug appeared among the demands of some Don Cossacks as early as 1881.

Chapter 1

1. O'Rourke, *Cossacks*, 209.
2. McNeal, *Tsar and Cossack*, 113–114, 193–194.
3. McNeal, *Tsar and Cossack*, 40; O'Rourke, *Cossacks*, 185; Seaton, *Horsemen* 199.
4. Ward Rutherford, *The Russian Army in World War I* (London: Gordon Cremonesi, 1975) 20.
5. McNeal, *Tsar and Cossack*, 72–73.
6. McNeal, *Tsar and Cossack*, 181–188; O'Rourke, *Warriors and Peasants*, 82–87.
7. McNeal, *Tsar and Cossack*, 181–188; O'Rourke, *Warriors and Peasants*, 87–90.
8. McNeal, *Tsar and Cossack*, 103–110; Cresson, *The Cossacks*, vii–viii.
9. O'Rourke, *Cossacks*, 185–188.
10. Quoted in Edward Sokol, *The Revolt of 1916 in Russian Central Asia* (Baltimore: The John Hopkins Press, 1954) 62–63.
11. O'Rourke, *Cossacks*,190–193.
12. McNeal, *Tsar and Cossack*, 74–75.
13. Sergey Starikov and Roy Medvedev, *Philip Mironov and the Russian Civil War*, trans. Guy Daniels (New York: Alfred A. Knopf, 1978) 14–15.
14. O'Rourke, *Cossacks*, 198–199.
15. McNeal, *Tsar and Cossack*, 77–84.
16. McNeal, *Tsar and Cossack*, 127–153.
17. For example, after the civil war, Sergey Syrtsov, a Bolshevik activist from Rostov, continued to label the Cossacks as "the janissaries of the imperial family." Quoted in Starikov and Medvedev, trans. Daniels, *Philip Mironov*, 8.
18. Marina Yurlova, *Cossack Girl* (New York: The Macaulay Company, 1934) 19.
19. Sergei Kournakoff, *Savage Squadrons* (Boston: Hale, Cushman & Flint, 1935) 34–35.
20. Starikov and Medvedev, trans. Daniels, *Philip Mironov*, 16.
21. Rutherford, *Russian Army*, 35. Red placards had to be used to announce the outbreak of war since the majority of the conscripts were illiterate. See W. Bruce Lincoln, *Passage Through Armageddon* (New York: Simon and Schuster, 1986) 25. On peasant attitudes towards the war, see Lincoln, 45–46, and Major-General Alfred Knox, *With the Russian Army*, 1914–1917 (New York: Arno Press, 1971) 50.
22. Seaton, *Horsemen*, 205–209; O'Rourke, *Cossacks*, 209.
23. Louis DiMarco, *War Horse* (Yardley: Westholme Publishing, 2008), 310. Quoted in Knox, *Russian Army*, 496.
24. Rutherford, *Russian Army*, 20, 45–46, 57, 261.
25. DiMarco, *War Horse*, 314.
26. Roman Jarymowycz, *Cavalry from Hoof to Track* (Westport: Praeger Security International, 2008) 124, 131.
27. Vladimir Littauer, *Russian Hussar* (Shippensburg: White Mane Publishing, 1993) 105.
28. M. Phillips Price, *War & Revolution in Asiatic Russia* (New York: The Macmillan Company, 1918) 157.
29. The Russian problem with having too many mounted units at the front is discussed in Norman Stone's *The Eastern Front 1914-1917* (New York: Charles Scribner's Sons, 1975) 34–36 and Knox, *Russian Army*, 506. According to one source, by 1917 the Russian army's required over 4,000 railcars per day to haul forage for its cavalry, artillery and draft horses at the fronts. See Littauer, *Russian Hussar*, vi–vii.
30. O'Rourke, *Cossacks*, 209; Rutherford, *Russian Army*, 187. According to Littauer, other Russian cavalry formations (hussars, dragoons and lancers) were dismounted more readily than the Cossacks. Just before the revolution, two squadrons from each Russian cavalry regiment were converted into the nuclei of new infantry regiments. Although Cossack regiments were spared this reorganization, they and the remaining Russian cavalry units were still ordered out of their saddles and into the trenches when needed. Littauer, *Russian Hussar*, 220.
31. Knox, *Russian Army*, 99. On another occasion, Knox witnessed a Cossack flogging a Russian soldier for pillaging a house in East Prussia. See Knox, *Russian Army*, 75.
32. Rutherford, *Russian Army*,151, 196, 261. At that time, anti-Semitism was prevalent throughout Russia. The diaries of Major-General Alfred Knox, a British liaison officer on the Eastern Front, contain many references of violence against Jews and Russian suspicions of Jewish treachery. See Knox, *Russian Army*, 73, 120, 171.
33. Florence Farmborough's *Nurse at the Russian Front* (London: Constable, 1970) 72, 83, 103–105, based off the author's diaries, offers an eye-witness account of the 1915 retreat and the Cossacks' behavior. At the outbreak of the war, the Russian Stavka issued several proclamations vaguely promising increased freedoms to various peoples in East Central Europe, including the Poles and Ukrainians. See C. Jay Smith, Jr., *The Russian Struggle for Power, 1914-1917* (New York: Greenwood, 1956) 8–20.
34. Glaskow, *Cossacks*, 110–111; Trut, Vladimir, "Some Aspects of the Russian Cossacks' Participation in the First World War," *Bylye Gody*, 2014, No 33 (3), https://doaj.org/article/bee3ba98cbba4017a9b55b9f21a69adb, accessed 7 October 2015.
35. Knox, *Russian Army*, 343. On page 338 of the same account, Knox noted that Kuban Cossack cavalry failed to prevent another German cavalry raid from seizing 3,000 head of cattle along with the divisional transports of two Russian corps.
36. Yurlova, *Cossack Girl*, 184–185.
37. For a study on the proliferation of rumors in Russia during the First World War, see "The Desacralization of the Monarchy: Rumors and 'Political Pornagraphy' during World War I," by Boris Kolonitsky, translated by Nathaniel Knight in Igal Halfin (ed.), *Language and Revolution* (London: Frank Cass Publishers, 2002).
38. Knox, *Russian Army*, 216–222, 270.
39. Lincoln, *Passage Through Armageddon*, 249–259.

40. Writing after the war, one tsarist general wrote that during the blockade Russia "became a sort of barred house, which could be entered only through the chimney." See Nicholas Golovine, *The Russian Army in the World War* (New Haven: Yale University Press, 1931) 37.
41. Knox, *Russian Army*, 426.
42. Rutherford, *Russian Army*, 223–224.
43. Quoted in Knox, *Russian Army*, 334.
44. Lincoln, *Passage Through Armageddon*, 22,
45. Sokol, *Revolt of 1916*, 77–78, 84, 111.
46. Sokol, *Revolt of 1916*, 33–44.
47. Sokol, *Revolt of 1916*, 114–120.
48. Sokol, *Revolt of 1916*, 94, 121–129.
49. The figure of 300,000 Kazakhs and Kyrgyz who left for China is given by Richard Pipes, *The Formation of the Soviet Union* (Cambridge: Harvard University Press, 1964) 83–84. In *The "Russian" Civil Wars*, Jonathon Smele, citing Soviet figures, put the number of natives who fled to Xinjiang at 250,000. See Smele, *"Russian" Civil Wars*, 20. Edward Sokol's history of the rebellion, *The Revolt of 1916 in Russian Central Asia*, does not attempt to estimate the total number of native refugees who fled into Xinjiang.
50. Sokol, *Revolt of 1916*, 129–137.
51. Pipes, *Formation of the Soviet Union*, 84; Sokol *Revolt of 1916*, 154–155.
52. Quoted in Sokol, *Revolt of 1916*, 94.
53. Sokol, *Revolt of 1916*, 115–117.
54. Sokol, *Revolt of 1916*, 154. The formation of the new Cossack settlements, as well as the all-Russian district in Semirechye, was disrupted by the outbreak of the revolution in February 1917.
55. Jonathon Smele, *The "Russian" Civil Wars* (New York: Oxford University Press, 2015) 17–21.
56. Rutherford, *Russian Army*, 223–224.
57. Allan Wildman, *The Old Army and the Soldiers' Revolt* (Princeton: Princeton University Press, 1980) 126.

Chapter 2

1. Shane O'Rourke, *The Cossacks* (Manchester: Manchester University Press, 2007) 212–215; Allan Wildman, *The Old Army and the Soldiers' Revolt* (Princeton: Princeton University Press, 1980) 121–126. In addition to the immediate Petrograd garrison was a further 152,000 troops in the vicinity of the capital for a total force of 332,000 troops. Since the Cossacks comprised less than one percent of that figure, the attention accorded to their defection was drastically disproportionate to their actual numbers.
2. Frank Golder, *War, Revolution and Peace in Russia* (Stanford: Hoover Institution Press, 1992) 34–35; 41–42.
3. Wladimir S. Woytinsky, *Stormy Passage* (New York: Vanguard Press, 1961) 248.
4. W. Bruce Lincoln, *Passage Through Armageddon* (New York: Simon and Schuster, 1986) 317–343; Allan Wildman, *The Old Army and the Soldiers' Revolt* (Princeton: Princeton University Press, 1980) 121–158.
5. The memoirs of White generals claim that the men at the front were "dumbfounded" and "thunderstruck" by the news of the Tsar's abdication, and while that may be true, the soldiers appear to have quickly recovered from their initial shock and embraced the revolution. See General Anton Denikin, *The Russian Turmoil* (Westport: Hyperion Press, 1973) 57; General Peter Wrangel, *Always with Honour* (New York: Robert Speller & Sons, 1957) 14.
6. Marina Yurlova, *Cossack Girl* (New York: The Macaulay Company, 1934) 195.
7. Trut, Vladimir, "Russian Cossacks' Participation in the First World War," *Bylye Gody*.
8. O'Rourke, *Cossacks*, 165–166.
9. Richard Pipes, *The Formation of the Soviet Union* (Cambridge: Harvard University Press, 1964) 50–51.
10. Peter Holquist, *Making War, Forging Revolution* (Cambridge: Harvard University Press, 2002) 55–56; 66–75.
11. Phillip Longworth, *The Cossacks* (New York: Holt, Rinehart and Winston, 1969) 286; Peter Kenez, *Civil War in South Russia: The First Year of the Volunteer Army* (Berkeley: University of California Press, 1971) 43–44.
12. Cresson, *The Cossacks*, 150–151, 232. According to Cresson, the proposal to return to the original name of "Cossacks of the Yaik" was approved, but it seems to have made no difference as nearly all histories of the period refer to the community as the Ural Cossack Host.
13. Longworth, *Cossacks*, 288; Holquist, *Making War*, 68.
14. Holquist, *Making War*, 51–61.
15. Kenez, *Volunteer Army*, 40.
16. Holquist, *Making War*, 84–85.
17. Wildman, *Soldiers' Revolt*, 265–266; Denikin, *Russian Turmoil*, 149–150; Holquist, *Making War*, 73.
18. Peter Holquist, "From Estate to Ethnos: The Changing Nature of Cossack Identity in the Twentieth Century," Nurit Schleifman (editor) *Russia at a Crossroads* (London: Frank Cass Publishers, 1998) 92–96; Holquist, *Making War*. 85. For more on the development and content of Order Number One, see Wildman, *Soldier's Revolt*, 182–198.
19. Peter Kenez, *Civil War in South Russia: The Defeat of the Whites* (Berkeley: University of California Press, 1977) 113–115; Kenez, *Volunteer Army*, 43; O'Rourke, *Cossacks*, 152–153.
20. Quoted in Lincoln, *Passage*, 357–358.
21. Orlando Figes, *A People's Tragedy* (New York, Viking, 1997) 378–384; Lincoln, *Passage Through Armageddon*, 354–369.
22. Holquist, *Making War*, 65–66, 73; Kenez, *Volunteer Army*, 41. The Don Krug initially agreed with Kaledin's view by declaring the Don Host "an indivisible part of the great Russian people's republic" that should be granted "wide local autonomy." See O'Rourke, *Cossacks*, 219.
23. Holquist, *Making War*, 83.
24. Wildman, *Soldier's Revolt*, 332–372.
25. A firsthand account of one of Kerensky's theatrical speeches to mutinous soldiers can be found in Kournakoff, *Savage Squadrons*, 327–333.

26. *Paper Relating to the Foreign Relations of the United States: 1918: Russia*, Volume I (Washington: U.S. Government Printing Office, 1931) 99–104.
27. O'Rourke, *Cossacks*, 221.
28. Kournakoff, *Savage Squadrons*, 315–316.
29. Figes, *People's Tragedy*, 413. The Women's Battalion of Death was a shock battalion consisting entirely of women volunteers. It was formed after the February Revolution in the hope that it would shame male soldiers into remaining at the front. Although it rarely achieved that intended effect, the Women's Battalion continued to serve the Provisional Government and was among its defenders in the Winter Palace during the Bolshevik coup in November 1917.
30. Louise Erwin Heenan, *Russian Democracy's Fatal Blunder* (New York: Praeger, 1987) 109–124.
31. Kournakoff, *Savage Squadrons*, 333.
32. Terence Emmons and Bertrand Patenaude (editors), *War, Revolution and Peace in Russia: The Passages of Frank Golder, 1914–1927* (Stanford: Hoover Institution Press, 1992) 82.
33. Figes, *People's Tragedy*, 423–438.
34. Heenan, *Fatal Blunder*, 120–124.
35. Richard Luckett, *The White Generals* (London: Routledge & Kegan Paul, 1987) 61–64; Figes, *People's Tragedy*, 442–443; Allan Wildman, *The Road to Soviet Power and Peace* (Princeton: Princeton University Press, 1987) 98. An account of Kornilov's escape, as told by the general himself, can be found in the diaries of Major-General Alfred Knox. See *With the Russian Army 1914–1917* (New York: Arno Press, 1971) 488–490.
36. Wildman, *Soviet Power*, 123–143, 153–156.
37. William Henry Chamberlin, *The Russian Revolution*, Volume I (New York: Grosset & Dunlap, 1965) 200–205.
38. Luckett, *White Generals*, 66–67, 72–73.
39. Figes, *Peoples' Tragedy*, 449–452.
40. Chamberlin, *Russian Revolution*, Volume I, 215.
41. Holquist, *Making War*, 91–92.
42. Chamberlin, *Russian Revolution*, Vol. I, 213–214.
43. Chamberlin, *Russian Revolution*, Vol. I, 216–217; Luckett, *White General*, 79–81; Wildman, *Soviet Power*, 195–196.
44. Woytinsky, *Stormy Passage*, 355.
45. Figes, *People's Tragedy*, 453–459; Lincoln, *Passage Through Armageddon*, 419–425.
46. James Bunyan and H. H. Fisher, *The Bolshevik Revolution 1917–1918* (Stanford: Stanford University Press, 1965) 24.
47. Wildman, *Soviet Power*, 213–215, 225.
48. Sergey Starikov and Roy Medvedev, *Philip Mironov and the Russian Civil War*, translated by Guy Daniels (New York: Alfred A. Knopf, 1978) 33.
49. Holquist, *Making War*, 92.
50. Bunyan and Fisher, *Bolshevik Revolution*, 76–77. In the days prior to the coup, the question of whether the moment was ripe for an uprising was openly debated in the revolutionary press. Meanwhile, everyone from the assistant commander of the Petrograd military district to U.S. Ambassador David Francis speculated that any Bolshevik move would likely fail.
51. Bunyan and Fisher, *Bolshevik Revolution*, 79.
52. Alexander Kerensky, *The Catastrophe* (New York: D. Appleton and Company, 1927) 328–339; Bunyan and Fisher, *Bolshevik Revolution*, 116–118.
53. Figes, *People's Tragedy*, 481–289; Luckett, *White Generals*, 92.
54. Alexander Kerensky, *The Catastrophe* (New York: D. Appleton and Company, 1927) 337–340.
55. Allan Wildman, *The Road to Soviet Power and Peace* (Princeton: Princeton University Press, 1987) 193–196, 217–218, 264, 294–296.
56. Woytinky, *Stormy Passage*, 356.
57. Wildman, *Soviet Power*, 295–298; James Bunyan and H. H. Fisher, *The Bolshevik Revolution 1917–1918* (Stanford: Stanford University Press, 1965) 141–142.
58. Kerensky, *Catastrophe*, 344.
59. Kerensky, *Catastrophe*, 346; Wildman, *Soviet Power*, 298; Bunyan and Fisher, *Bolshevik Revolution*, 144.
60. Quoted in Woytinsky, *Stormy Passage*, 381–382.
61. Kerensky, *Catastrophe*, 348–352; Woytinsky, *Stormy Passage*, 382–383.
62. Wildman, *Soviet Power*, 298–300; Bunyan and Fisher, *Bolshevik Revolution*, 162.
63. Wildman, *Soviet Power*, 302–304; Kerensky, *Catastrophe*, 355.
64. Quoted in Bunyan and Fisher, *Bolshevik Power*, 161–162.
65. Bunyan and Fisher, *Bolshevik Power*, 150–165, 198–210; Wildman, *Soviet Power*, 305–306.
66. Kerensky, *Catastrophe*, 360–366. He soon slipped out of Russia disguised as a seaman.
67. Farmborough, *Nurse at the Russian Front*, 343.
68. Quoted in Cresson, *The Cossacks*, 207.
69. Peter Kenez, *Civil War in South Russia, 1918* (Berkeley: University of California Press, 1971) 46, 140; Richard Luckett, *The White Generals* (London: Routledge & Kegan Paul Ltd., 1987) 93. Various sources place the length of Krasnov's incarceration at this time between 5 days and one month.
70. Quoted in Bunyan and Fisher, *Bolshevik Revolution*, 407.
71. O'Rourke, *Cossacks*, 229.
72. Bunyan and Fisher, *Bolshevik Revolution*, 407; Evan Mawdsley, *The Russian Civil War* (New York: Pegasus, 2007) 17–18.
73. Bunyan and Fisher, *Bolshevik Revolution*, 404. When news of the Bolshevik uprising in the capital reached Novocherkassk on 7 November 1917, Kaledin declared that his government would assume "full executive power in the region of the Don."
74. Kenez, *Volunteer Army*, 59.
75. General Anton Denikin, *The White Army*, trans. Catherine Zvegintzov (Gulf Breeze: Academic International Press, 1973) 26.
76. Chamberlin, *Russian Revolution*, Vol. I, 342–346; Wildman, *Soviet Power*, 379–405.
77. Denikin, *White Army*, 22–25; Luckett, *White Generals*, 95.

78. Kenez, *Volunteer Army*, 68.
79. Denikin, *Russian Turmoil*, 246.

Chapter 3

1. James Bunyan and H. H. Fisher, *The Bolshevik Revolution 1917–1918* (Stanford: Stanford University Press, 1965) 118–119.
2. Bunyan and Fisher, *Bolshevik Revolution*, 147–148.
3. Bunyan and Fisher, *Bolshevik Revolution*, 80–81, 407–408; Phillip Longworth, *The Cossacks* (New York: Holt, Rinehart and Winston, 1969) 291.
4. O'Rourke, *Cossacks*, 230.
5. Paul Robinson, *The White Russian Army in Exile* (Oxford: Clarendon Press, 2002) 4.
6. Peter Kenez, *Civil War in South Russia, 1918: The First Year of the Volunteer Army* (Berkeley, University of California, 1971) 62–64.
7. Quoted in Kenez, *Volunteer Army*, 65–66.
8. Quoted in Bunyan and Fisher, *Bolshevik Revolution*, 407.
9. Quoted in Bunyan and Fisher, *Bolshevik Revolution*, 407–409.
10. Cresson, *The Cossacks*, 217.
11. Bunyan and Fisher, *Bolshevik Revolution*, 416–417; Peter Holquist, *Making War, Forging Revolution* (Cambridge: Harvard University Press, 2002) 120–123.
12. General Anton Denikin, trans. Catherine Zvegintzov, *The White Army* (Gulf Breeze: Academic International Press, 1973) 30.
13. Kenez, *Volunteer Army*, 76–84.
14. Quoted in Eduard Dune, *Notes of a Red Guard*, trans. Diane Koenker and S. A. Smith (Chicago: University of Illinois Press, 1993) 98–99.
15. Bunyan and Fisher, *Bolshevik Revolution*, 417–418. According to Peter Kenez, Chernetsov probably did not consult Kaledin before attacking Kamenskaya. See *Volunteer Army*, 89–91. However, Peter Holquist believes that Kaledin authorized the operation to gain the upper hand in the negotiations. See *Making War*, 124–127.
16. Dune, *Red Guard*, trans. Koenker and Smith, 60–61, 96–97.
17. Bunyan and Fisher, *Bolshevik Revolution*, 419–420; Kenez, *Volunteer Army*, 91–94; Holquist, *Making War*, 127–128; General Aleksandr Lukomsky, *Memoirs of the Russian Revolution*, trans. Mrs. Vitali (Westport: Hyperion Press, 1975) 144.
18. Quoted in Bunyan and Fisher, *Bolshevik Revolution*, 420.
19. Lukomsky, *Memoir*, 148.
20. Kenez, *Volunteer Army*, 94–95; Holquist, *Making War*, 127–130; Lukomsky, *Memoir*, 148–149.
21. Bunyan and Fisher, *Bolshevik Revolution*, 450. On 1 March 1918 the U.S. Consul in Kiev reported than an estimated 300–400 officers were executed by the Bolsheviks just a few days after they took the Ukrainian capital.
22. Evan Mawdsley, *The Russian Civil War* (New York: Pegasus, 2007) 17–18.
23. Bunyan and Fisher, *Bolshevik Revolution*, 423.
24. Bunyan and Fisher, *Bolshevik Revolution*, 407.
25. Kenez, *Volunteer Army*, 104–108.
26. Quoted in Denikin, *White Army*, 45.
27. Denikin, *White Army*, 54–56.
28. Quoted in Denikin, *White Army*, 80.
29. Denikin, *White Army*, 49, 56–59.
30. Kenez, *Volunteer Army*, 108–111; Denikin, *White Army*, 78, 82–83.
31. Denikin, *White Army*, 86–101.
32. Denikin, *White Army*, 105–110.
33. Dimitry Lehovich, *White Against Red* (New York: W. W. Norton & Company, 1974) 47, 83–84.
34. Mawdsley, *Russian Civil War*, 20.
35. Kenez, *Volunteer Army*, 153.
36. Holquist, *Making War*, 129–130; Kenez, *Volunteer Army*, 118–119.
37. Bunyan and Fisher, *Bolshevik Revolution*, 251, 258–259, 264, 510.
38. Max Hoffman, *War Diaries and Other Papers*, Volume I (London: Martin Secker, 1929) 207.
39. Bunyan and Fisher, *Bolshevik Revolution*, 510, 513, 517–520.
40. Brent Mueggenberg, *The Czecho-Slovak Struggle for Independence 1914–1918* (Jefferson: McFarland, 2014) 146–147.
41. Holquist, *Making War*, 131.
42. Kenez, *Volunteer Army*, 119–120.
43. Bunyan and Fisher, *Bolshevik Revolution*, 664–665.
44. Holquist, *Making War*, 132.
45. Kenez, *Volunteer Army*, 120.
46. The Red Cossack leader, Lieutenant-Colonel Filip Mironov, explained the anti-Bolshevik rebellion's origins in spring 1918 by writing: "Front line Cossack came back to their homes, and there, being out of reach of the political centers, with no education in politics, their primitive level of understanding let them succumb in the end to the influence of their fathers and grandfathers, coupled also with the counterrevolutionary priesthood and officers—and went over, without realizing it themselves, to side with the enemies of the people." Quoted in A. B. Murphy, *The Russian Civil War* (New York: St. Martin's Press, 2000) 146. For more on the role of elders in Cossack society, see Maurice Hindus, *The Cossacks* (New York: Doubleday, Doran & Company, 1945) 231–232.
47. Kenez, *Volunteer Army*, 119–122; Holquist, *Making War*, 135–140, 146.
48. Kenez, *Volunteer Army*, 122–123.
49. For a glimpse of how the military preparedness permeated Cossack livelihood, see Marina Yurlova, *Cossack Girl* (New York: The Macaulay Company, 1934) 19–20.
50. Mawdsley, *Russian Civil War*, 87.
51. Peter Holquist, "Making Cossacks Counter-Revolutionary: The Don Host and the 1918 Anti-Soviet Insurgency," Igal Halfin (editor), *Language and Revolution* (London: Frank Cass Publishers, 2002) 87–90.
52. Bunyan and Fisher, *Bolshevik Revolution*, 423.
53. Bunyan, *Intervention, Civil War and Communism in Russia* (New York: Octagon Books, 1976) 293–294.

54. Bunyan and Fisher, *Bolshevik Revolution*, 394-397. At the Third Congress of the Soviets (23-31 January 1918), Stalin, as Commissar of the Nationalities, summed up the Bolsheviks' attitudes toward self-determination: "The principle of self-determination should be limited in such a way as to make it applicable to only the toilers and not to the bourgeoisie. Self-determination must be a means of attaining socialism..."

55. Bunyan, *Intervention*, 123-125.
56. Bunyan, *Intervention*, 157-171.
57. Bunyan and Fisher, *Bolshevik Revolution*, 666. Shortly after the Don Cossack uprising put that region's grain out of Bolshevik reach, the revolt of the Czecho-Slovak Legion occurred and quickly severed another important grain-producing region, Western Siberia, from the Soviet Republic.

Chapter 4

1. General Baron P. N. Wrangel, *Always With Honour* (New York: Robert Speller & Sons, 1957) 45.
2. General Aleksandr Lukomsky, *Memoirs of the Russian Revolution*, trans. Mrs. Vitali (Westport: Hyperion Press, 1975) 187.
3. James Bunyan, *Intervention, Civil War and Communism in Russia* (New York: Octagon Books, 1976) 177-179.
4. Reshetar, John, *The Ukrainian Revolution 1917-1920* (Princeton: Princeton University Press, 1952) 115.
5. Michael Kellogg, *The Russian Roots of Nazism* (Cambridge: Cambridge University Press, 2005) 52-53; Reshetar, *Ukrainian Revolution*, 122-130.
6. Reshetar, *Ukrainian Revolution*, 143-207.
7. A. B. Murphy, *The Russian Civil War* (New York: St. Martin's Press, 2000) 18. In a telegram dated 13 April 1918, Antonov-Ovseyenko accused soviets in the Donets Basin of prematurely abandoning their districts and proposed "energetic measures" to stop such flights.
8. Major-General Max Hoffmann, *War Diaries and Other Papers*, Volume I, trans. Eric Sutton (London: Martin Secker, 1929) 216.
9. Peter Holquist, *Making War, Forging Revolution* (Cambridge: Harvard University Press, 2002) 146-147.
10. Paul Robinson, *The White Russian Army in Exile* (Oxford: Clarendon Press, 2002) 8. On 5 September 1914 the tsarist government had signed a treaty with Britain and France which prohibited any of them from seeking a separate peace with any enemy. On 23 November 1917, shortly after the Soviet government made clear its intentions to open formal negotiations with the Central Powers, the Allied missions at Stavka reminded the Russian Army's Commander-in-Chief, General Dukhonin, of this treaty in a futile protest. See James Bunyan and H. H. Fisher, *The Bolshevik Revolution* (Stanford: Stanford University Press, 1965) 245.
11. General Anton Denikin, *The White Army*, trans. Catherine Zvegintzov (Gulf Breeze: Academic International Press, 1973) 123.

12. Peter Kenez, *The First Year of the Volunteer Army* (Berkeley: University of California Press, 1971) 123-132.
13. Bunyan, *Intervention*, 33-34.
14. Holquist, "Making Cossacks Counter-Revolutionary," Halfin, ed., *Language and Revolution*, 93.
15. The Gregorian calendar, long in use in Western countries, was introduced to Russia by the Bolsheviks on 13 February 1918. It replaced the Julian calendar which was 13 days behind the Gregorian calendar.
16. Kenez, *Volunteer Army*, 138-140.
17. Bunyan, *Intervention*, 35-36.
18. George Brinkley, *The Volunteer Army and Allied Intervention in South Russia* (Notre Dame: University of Notre Dame Press, 1966) 46.
19. Denikin, *White Army*, 152.
20. Bunyan, *Intervention*, 35-36.
21. Quoted in Bunyan, *Intervention*, 42-44. For more on Krasnov's letters to Kaiser Wilhelm II, see Kenez, *Volunteer Army*, 142-143.
22. Richard Luckett, *The White Generals* (London: Routledge, 1987) 159-160.
23. Kenez, *Volunteer Army*, 142, 169; Denikin, *White Army*, 152.
24. Quoted in Bunyan, *Intervention*, 36-37.
25. Bunyan, *Intervention*, 37-38.
26. Reshetar, *Ukrainian Revolution*, 185-187; Kenez, *Volunteer Army*, 146-148. A translation of Krasnov's appeal to the Kaiser can be found in Bunyan, *Intervention*, 42-44.
27. James Bunyan and H. H. Fisher, *The Bolshevik Revolution* (Stanford: Stanford University Press, 1965) 403.
28. Bunyan, *Intervention*, 44-46.
29. Kenez, *Volunteer Army*, 154; Reshetar, *Ukrainian Revolution*, 187.
30. Bunyan, *Intervention*, 46; Murphy, *Civil War*, 27.
31. Kenez, *Volunteer Army*, 154-156.
32. Denkin alludes to the uneasy relationship with Krasnov by writing "Continual friction with the Don Ataman, due to his political orientation, the divergence of our strategic views and his personal qualities, further complicated our temporary sojourn in the Don territory." Denikin, *White Army*, 156.
33. Luckett, *White Generals*, 160; Kenez, *Volunteer Army*, 176; Kellogg, *Russian Roots*, 56-57.
34. Quoted in Kenez, *Volunteer Army*, 156-157.
35. Lukomsky, *Memoir*, 200.
36. Lukomsky, *Memoir*, 203-204.
37. Bunyan, *Intervention*, 47-50.
38. Kenez, *Volunteer Army*, 149-150, 157.
39. Kenez, *Volunteer Army*, 153, 167-169.
40. Bunyan, *Intervention*, 43.
41. Holquist, "Making Cossacks Counter-Revolutionary," Halfin (ed.) *Language and Revolution*, 89-97.
42. Bunyan, *Intervention*, 43.
43. Bunyan, *Intervention*, 34.
44. Kenez, *Volunteer Army*, 174-175.

45. Sergey Starikov and Roy Medvedev, *Phillip Mironov and the Russian Civil War*, trans. Guy Daniels (New York: Alfred A. Knopf, 1978) 68–76. Due to their continued service in the Red Army, Mironov and his followers were among those purged from the Cossack estate by the All-Great Don Host.
46. Bunyan and Fisher, *Bolshevik Revolution*, 568–569; Martin McCauley, *The Russian Revolution and the Soviet State 1917-1921* (London: The Macmillan Press, 1975) 140–146.
47. Bunyan and Fisher, *Bolshevik Revolution*, 569–570; McCauley, *Russian Revolution*, 150.
48. Kenez, *Volunteer Army*, 174.
49. Luckett, *White Generals*, 183.
50. Mawdsley, *Russian Civil War*, 88.
51. Kenez, *Volunteer Army*, 173–174.
52. Mawdsley, *Russian Civil War*, 92.
53. Brovkin, *Bolsheviks in Russian Society*, 226–227.
54. Mawdsley, *Russian Civil War*, 89–90.
55. Quoted in McCauley, *Russian Revolution*, 149.
56. Kenez, *Volunteer Army*, 174.
57. Denikin, *White Army*, 164.
58. Denikin, *White Army*, 158, 162–163. Denikin estimated the number of Red troops to his south to be as high as 80,000–100,000 men.
59. Kenez, *Volunteer Army*, 169–170; Denikin, *White Army*, 162–163.
60. Denikin, *White Army*, 165–175.
61. Denikin, *White Army*, 176–177; Luckett, *White Generals*, 185–186; Mawdsley, 94.
62. Denikin, *White Army*, 185.
63. Denikin, *White Army*, 185–187; William Henry Chamberlin, *The Russian Revolution*, Volume 2 (New York: The Macmillan Company, 1965) 139–140.
64. Denikin, *White Army*, 185–187.
65. Luckett, White Generals, 186–189; Mawdsley, *Russian Civil War*, 94.
66. Denikin, *White Army*, 176–180.
67. Murphy, *Russian Civil War*, 253.
68. Kenez, *Volunteer Army*, 181–182.
69. Denikin, *White Army*, 179–180. In his memoirs, Denikin refers to Shkuro as "a brave, rollicking, scatter-brained man of somewhat loose morals."
70. Kenez, *Volunteer Army*, 182.
71. Denikin, *White Army*, 195–200; Luckett, *White Generals*, 191–192; Kenez, *Volunteer Army*, 185; Chamberlin, *Russian Revolution*, Vol. 2,141, 144–146.
72. Maurice Hindus, *The Cossacks* (New York: Doubleday, Doran & Company, 1945) 93–101.
73. Quoted in Dune, *Red Guard*, trans. Koenker and Smith, 222.
74. James Forsyth, *The Caucasus* (New York: Cambridge University Press, 2013) 281. Russia's war to complete the conquest of Dagestan and Chechnya is dated 1818–71.
75. Richard Pipes, *The Formation of the Soviet Union* (Cambridge: Harvard University Press, 1964) 93–95; James Forsyth, *The Caucasus* (New York: Cambridge University Press) 275–281.
76. M. Phillips Price, *War & Revolution in Asiatic Russia* (New York: The Macmillan Company, 1918) 295.
77. Pipes, *Formation of the Soviet Union*, 95–98; Lukomsky, *Memoir*, 138.
78. Pipes, *Formation of the Soviet Union*, 195–198; Peter Kenez, *The Defeat of the Whites* (Berkeley, University of California Press, 1977) 124–126; Forsyth, *Caucasus*, 361–365.
79. Denikin, *White Army*, 205.
80. Kenez, *Defeat of the Whites*, 126–127.
81. Pipes, *Formation of the Soviet Union*, 214.
82. Denikin, *White Army*, 210.
83. Kenez, *Defeat of the Whites*, 127–128.
84. Denikin, *White Army*, 202–203.
85. Bunyan, *Intervention*, 47–48.
86. Dimitry Lehovich, *White Against Red* (New York: W. W. Norton & Company, 1974) 330–331.
87. Bunyan, *Intervention*, 48–50.
88. Kenez, *Volunteer Army*, 177; Denikin, *White Army*, 190. The Whites' favorable policies towards the Cossacks did not come without a cost for the latter. From the start, Denikin's draft was designed to net far more Cossacks than outlanders. In his first call-up from Yekaterinodar, for example, Denikin ordered conscription for ten classes of Kuban Cossacks compared to only two classes for the outlanders.
89. Chamberlin, *Russian Revolution*, Vol. 2, 141.
90. Under the new election law, only Cossacks, members of mountain tribes and "original inhabitants," meaning well-established and wealthier non-Cossacks, were allowed to vote. Kenez, *Volunteer Army*, 220–221.
91. Chamberlin, *Russian Revolution*, Vol. 2, 141; Kenez, *Volunteer Army*, 221–222.
92. Lukomsky, *Memoir*, 205–207.
93. Kenez, *Volunteer Army*, 223–230.
94. Lehovich, *White Against Red*, 246-2 47.
95. Denikin, *White Army*, 206.
96. Reshetar, *Ukrainian Revolution*, 174–176; Bunyan, *Intervention*, 22–26.
97. Chamberlin, *Russian Revolution*, Vol. 2, 126.
98. Mark Cornwall, editor, *The Last Years of Austria-Hungary* (Exeter: University of Exeter Press, 2002) 161. The share of Ukrainian grain which Austria-Hungary actually received was only 46,225 tons.
99. Specifically, Article XII of the Armistice called for the German troops in Russia to return to Germany "as soon as the Allies shall think the moment suitable, having regard to the internal situation of these territories." Quoted in John M. Thompson, *Russia, Bolshevism and the Versailles Peace* (Princeton: Princeton University Press, 1966) 23–32.
100. Hoffmann, *War Diaries*, 246.
101. Bunyan, *Intervention*, 29–32; Reshetar, *Ukrainian Revolution*, 192–207; Kellogg, *Russian Roots*, 60–63. For a memorable though fictionalized account of Skoropadsky's flight from Kiev, see Mikhail Bulgakov's classic novel, *White Guard*, trans. Marian Schwartz (New Haven: Yale University Press, 2008) 113–115.

102. Mawdsley, *Russian Civil War*, 120.
103. Denikin, *White Army*, 239.
104. Mawdsley, *Russian Civil War*, 164; Schleifman, *Russia at a Crossroads*, 97.
105. Chamberlin, *Russuan Revolution*, Vol. 2, 132.
106. H. N. H. Williamson, *Farewell to the Don* (New York: The John Day Company, 1971) 89-92.
107. Kenez, *Volunteer Army*, 263-264; Lehovich, *White Against Red*, 272.
108. Denikin, *White Army*, 215; Miliukov, *Russia Today and Tomorrow*, 123. Miliukov cited the Treaty of London, signed by Great Britain, France and Russia on 4 October 1914, as the basis for the Allies' legal obligation to assist the anti-Bolshevik Russians.
109. Brinkley, *Allied Intervention in South Russia*, 79.
110. Denikin, *White Army*, 227-228.
111. Lehovich, *White Against Red*, 215.
112. Kenez, *Volunteer Army*, 265-267.
113. Sergey Starikov and Roy Medvedev, *Philip Mironov and the Russian Civil* War (New York: Alfred A. Knopf, 1978) 89.
114. Kenez, *Volunteer Army*, 267-270; Lehovich, *White Against Red*, 273-274.

Chapter 5

1. Shane O'Rourke, *The Cossacks* (Manchester: Manchester University Press, 2007) 42-45.
2. Alan Wood, ed., *The History of Siberia* (Routledge: London, 1991) 17-27.
3. Albert Seaton, *The Horsemen of the Steppes* (London: The Bodley Head, 1985) 175-176.
4. Seaton, *Horsemen*, 177-179; O'Rourke, *Cossacks*, 150-151. The four decades from 1850 to 1890 not only saw the establishment of the Transbaikal, Amur, Semirechye and Ussuri Hosts in Asiatic Russia, but also the reorganization of existing Cossack settlements in the North Caucasus region into the Kuban and Terek Hosts.
5. O'Rourke, *Cossacks*, 151-152.
6. O'Rourke, *Cossacks*, 188-189; John Stephan, *The Russian Far East* (Stanford: Stanford University Press, 1994) 62-63.
7. Evan Mawdsley, *The Russian Civil War* (New York: Pegasus, 2007) 145.
8. Seaton, *Horsemen*, 209, 248.
9. John Albert White, *The Siberian Intervention* (Princeton: Princeton University Press, 1950) 46. Male peasant immigrants to Siberia typically received between 20 and 40 acres of land. By comparison, Cossacks in the Far East received 100 acres of land per man. See also: O'Rourke, *Cossacks*, 188.
10. Bobrick, *East of the Sun* (New York: Poseidon Press, 1992) 378-381.
11. Wood, ed., *Siberia*, 140-153.
12. For example, the percentage of Cossacks in the Amur district fell from 85 percent in 1859 to just 18 percent by 1897. See Stephan, John, *The Russian Far East*, 62-63.
13. O'Rourke, *Cossacks*, 217.
14. Richard Pipes *The Formation of the Soviet Union* (Cambridge: Harvard University Press, 1964) 86.
15. M. P. Price, *War & Revolution in Asiatic Russia* (New York: The Macmillan Company, 1918) 272; Pipes *Formation of the Soviet Union*, 82-85.
16. Paul Dotsenko, *The Struggle for a Democracy in Siberia* (Stanford, Hoover Institution Press, 1983) 3-4.
17. Jonathon Smele, *Civil War in Siberia* (New York: Cambridge University Press, 1996) 15-19.
18. Wood, ed., *Siberia*, 144-153, 159-160.
19. Vladimir Brovkin, ed., *The Bolsheviks in Russian Society* (New Haven: Yale University Press, 1997) 123.
20. Wood, ed., *Siberia*, 163-164.
21. Dotsenko, *Struggle for a Democracy*, 14-15.
22. Smele, *Civil War*, 18-20, 25.
23. Jamie Bisher, *White Terror* (New York: Routledge, 2005) 33.
24. O'Rourke, *Cossacks*, 241.
25. Bisher, *White Terror*, 96.
26. Mawdsley, *Russian Civil War*, 236.
27. Bisher, *White Terror*, 23-32.
28. John Ward, *With the "Die-Hards" in Siberia* (London: Cassell, 1920) 238.
29. General Baron Pytor Wrangel, *Always With Honour* (New York: Robert Speller & Sons, 1957) 6.
30. Bisher, *White Terror*, 35-42.
31. James Palmer, *The Bloody White Baron* (New York: Basic Books, 2009) 74-80; Bisher, *White Terror*, 42-44.
32. George Kennan, *Russia Leaves the War* (Princeton: Princeton University Press, 1956) 303-305; James Morley, *The Japanese Thrust into Siberia* (New York: Columbia University Press, 1957) 14.
33. Bisher, *White Terror*, 46-48.
34. Bisher, *White Terror*, 60-79; Morley, *Japanese Thrust*, 193-197.
35. Morley, *Japanese Thrust*, 110-121, 188, 208-210; White, *Siberian Intervention*, 193.
36. Bisher, *White Terror*, 96; Stephan, *The Russian Far East*, 120-121.
37. Stephan, *The Russian Far East*, 119-120.
38. Nik Cornish, *The Russian Army and the First World War* (Gloucestershire: Spellmount, 2006) 194; Peter Pastor and Samuel Williamson, Jr., ed., Ivo Banac, "South Slav Prisoners of War in Revolutionary Russia," *Essays on World War I* (New York: Brooklyn College Press, 1983) 132.
39. Pastor, Peter, ed., Josef Kalvoda, "Czech and Slovak Prisoners of War in Russia during the War and Revolution," *Essays on World War I*, 215-229.
40. Victor Fic, *The Bolsheviks and the Czechoslovak Legion* (New Dehli: Abhinov Publications, 1978) 5-23.
41. Fic, *Bolsheviks and the Czechoslovak Legion*, 220-231, 249-261.
42. Bunyan, *Intervention*, 91.
43. Fic, *Bolsheviks and the Czechoslovak Legion*, 277-282, 314-322.
44. Francis McCullagh, *A Prisoner of the Reds* (New York: E. P. Dutton, 1922) xi.

45. Fic, *Bolsheviks and the Czechoslovak Legion*, 320–324.
46. Henry Baerlein, *The March of the Seventy Thousand* (London: Leonard Parsons, 1926) 135.
47. Gustav Bečvar, *The Lost Legion* (London: Stanley Paul, 1939) 129–131.
48. Morley, *Japanese Thrust*, 255. By the end of the summer Kalmykov was reported to have only 400 men under his command. See John Ward, *With the "Die-Hards" in Siberia* (London: Cassell, 1920) 10–12.
49. Bisher, *White Terror*, 78–88.
50. Bunyan, *Intervention*, 283–290.
51. Bunyan, *Intervention*, 293–295.
52. Kennan, *Russia Leaves the War*, 478–481.
53. George Kennan, *The Decision to Intervene* (Princeton: Princeton University Press, 1958) 358.
54. Kennan, *Decision to Intervene*, 312–317, 408–413. To be fair, it must be noted that the French were not the only ones who ordered the Czecho-Slovaks to support the anti-Bolshevik Russians. American officials in Russia, including Ambassador David Francis, also encouraged the legionaries operating in the Volga and Ural regions to suspend their withdrawal to the east.
55. Ward, *With the "Die-Hards,"* 1–3.
56. Bunyan, *Intervention*, 283, 329–334; Dotsenko, *Struggle for a Democracy*, 37–38.
57. Dotsenko, *Struggle for a Democracy*, 41–44.
58. Bunyan, *Intervention*, 333–334.
59. Bunyan, *Intervention*, 336–337.
60. Bunyan, *Intervention*, 342–343.
61. Quoted in John Silverlight, *The Victor's Dilemma* (New York: Weybright and Talley, 1970) 80.
62. Bunyan, *Intervention*, 348–349.
63. Bunyan, *Intervention*, 352–356.
64. Bunyan, *Intervention*, 362–365.
65. Paul Dotsenko, *The Struggle for Democracy in Siberia* (Stanford: Stanford University, 1983) 52.
66. Bunyan, *Intervention*, 360.
67. Ward, *With the "Die-Hards,"* 104–105, Dotsenko, *Struggle for a Democracy*, 53–54.
68. Dotsenko, *Struggle for a Democracy*, 46–47, 54.
69. Ward, *With the "Die-Hards,"* 108.
70. Dotsenko, *Struggle for Democracy*, 61.
71. Smele, *Civil War*, 102–107.
72. Ward, *With the "Die-Hards,"* 129–130.
73. V. P. Butt, A. B. Murphy, N. A. Myshov and G. R. Swain, *The Russian Civil War* (New York: St. Martin's Press, 1996) 17–20; Ward, *With the "Die-Hards,"* 143.
74. Pipes, *Formation of the Soviet Union*, 161–162.
75. Bunyan, *Intervention*, 371–373.
76. Bunyan, *Intervention*, 373; Smele, *Civil War*, 111–113. Colonel John Ward, the commanding officer of the British battalion then in Omsk, went out of his way to ensure the safety of the two SR directors. See Ward, *With the "Die-Hards,"* 135–136.
77. Morley, *Japanese Thrust*, 77–82.
78. White, *Siberian Intervention*, 195.
79. Quoted in Bunyan, *Intervention*, 315.
80. Bisher, *White Terror*, 114–115, 139, 158–160, 163–166; Ward, *With the "Die-Hards,"* 79–83.
81. Dmitri Alioshin, *Asian Odyssey* (New York: Henry Holt and Co., 1940) 48.
82. Bisher, *White Terror*, 100–101.
83. General William Graves, *America's Siberian Adventure* (New York: Peter Smith, 1941) 90.
84. Palmer, *Bloody White Baron*, 92–93.
85. Bisher, *White Terror*, 139, 145.
86. Bunyan, *Intervention*, 358.
87. Smele, *Civil War*, 189–190; Ward, *With the "Die-Hards,"* 144–145; Bisher, *White Terror*, 127–131, 174–177.
88. Bisher, *White Terror*, 116, 123.
89. *Papers Relating to the Foreign Relations of the United States: 1919: Russia* (Washington, U.S. Government Printing Office, 1937) 485–488.
90. Bisher, *White Terror*, 114, 136–137.
91. Graves, *America's Siberian Adventure*, 86. Semyonov was eventually elected *pokhodny ataman* of the three Far Eastern Cossack hosts and given the honorary title of ataman by the Ural and Siberian Cossacks. See Bisher, *White Terror*, 105–106.
92. For examples of Japanese brutality towards ordinary Russians, see Ward, *With the "Die-Hards,"* 54 and *Papers Relating to the Foreign Relations of the United States: 1919: Russia* (Washington, U.S. Government Printing Office, 1937) 468–472.
93. George Stewart, *The White Armies of Russia* (New York: Russell & Russell, 1970) 258–261; Graves, *America's Siberian Adventure*, 128–137.
94. Palmer, *Bloody White Baron*, 87.
95. Alioshin, *Asian Odyssey*, 10.
96. Bisher, *White Terror*, 188–191, Palmer, *Bloody White Baron*, 107–109.
97. *Papers Relating to the Foreign Relations of the United States: 1919: Russia* (Washington, U.S. Government Printing Office, 1937) 474–475.
98. Bisher, *White Terror*, 194–196. British Colonel John Ward, despite providing an unfavorable description of the ataman, nonetheless commented that he "is one of the most striking personalities I have met in Russia." See Ward, *With the "Die-Hards,"* 238.
99. Ward, *With the "Die-Hards,"* 148.
100. Smele, *Civil War*, 181–182, 187. The Whites' victory at Perm was less impressive than it appeared to be. For example, according to Smele, many of the prisoners claimed by the Whites were actually Russian POWs repatriated from Germany attempting to return their homes in Siberia.
101. Smele, *Civil War*, 168–171; Ward, *With the "Die-Hards,"* 150–155.
102. Bečvar, *Lost Legion*, 199.
103. *Papers Relating to the Foreign Relations of the United States: 1919: Russia* (Washington, U.S. Government Printing Office, 1937) 196, 199.
104. Mawdsley, *Russian Civil War*, 132.
105. Smele, *Civil War*, 300–301; Pipes, *Formation of the Soviet Union*, 162–164.
106. Smele, *Civil War*, 229–240, 307–314.
107. Mawdsley, *Russian Civil War*, 142.
108. Smele, *Civil War*, 318, 480–484.
109. *Papers Relating to the Foreign Relations of the United States: 1919: Russia* (Washington, U.S. Government Printing Office, 1937) 206–207.
110. Mawdsley, 149.
111. *Papers Relating to the Foreign Relations of the*

United States: 1919: Russia (Washington, U.S. Government Printing Office, 1937) 464–465.

112. According to Peter Kenez, Cossacks still made up 50–60 percent of the units when the Armed Forces of South Russia reached the peak of its strength in autumn of 1919. See Kenez, *The Defeat of the Whites* (Berkeley: University of California Press, 1977) 110. Not all historians agree with that assessment, however. Jonathon Smele estimated the percentage of Cossacks in the AFSR much lower at only 32 percent. See Smele, *Civil War*, 530. Whatever the true figure, it can be stated with certainty that the ratio of Cossacks in Kolchak's armies were much lower than in Denikin's.

113. Luckett, *White Generals*, 265.

114. Stewart, *White Armies*, 258.

Chapter 6

1. Peter Kenez, *The Defeat of the Whites* (Berkeley: University of California Press, 1977) 30.

2. Sergey Starikov and Roy Medvedev, *Philip Mironov and the Russian Civil War*, trans. Guy Daniels (New York: Alfred A. Knopf, 1978) 81–91.

3. Dune, *Red Guard*, trans. Koenker and Smith, 140–141.

4. Starikov and Medvedev, *Philip Mironov*, trans. Daniels, 81–91.

5. Peter Kenez, *The First Year of the Volunteer Army* (Berkeley: University of California Press, 1971) 270–271.

6. Richard Luckett, *The White Generals* (London: Routledge & Kegan Paul Ltd., 1987) 254–255; William Henry Chamberlin, *The Russian Revolution*, Vol. 2 (New York: Grosset & Dunlap, 1965) 209–211.

7. General Baron Peter Wrangel, *Always With Honour* (New York: Robert Speller & Sons, 1957) 69–70.

8. General Anton Denikin, *The White Army*, trans. Catherine Zvegintzov (Gulf Breeze: Academic International Press, 1973) 255–256.

9. Quoted in W. P. Coates and Zelda Coates, *Allied Intervention in Russia 1918–1922* (London: Victor Gollanz Ltd., 1935) 255.

10. Luckett, *White Generals*, 258; Kenez, *Defeat of the Whites*, 36.

11. George Brinkley, *The Volunteer Army and Allied Intervention in South Russia* (Notre Dame: University of Notre Dame Press, 1966) 113–145; Chamberlin, *Russian Revolution*, 213–214.

12. A. B. Murphy, *The Russian Civil War* (New York: St. Martin's Press, 2000) 107.

13. V. P. Butt, A. B. Murphy, N. A. Myshov and G. R. Swain, *The Russian Civil War* (New York: St. Martin's Press, 1996) 47.

14. James Bunyan, *Intervention, Civil War and Communism in Russia* (New York: Octagon, 1976) 37–38.

15. Peter Holquist, *Making War, Forging Revolution* (Cambridge: Harvard University Press, 2002) 177–181; Starikov and Medvedev, trans. Daniels, *Philip Mironov*, 54, 102.

16. Starikov and Medvedev, trans. Daniels, *Philip Mironov*, 115–118. In *Making War, Forging Revolution*, Peter Holquist has estimated that 10,000 to 12,000 Don inhabitants were executed by the Bolsheviks in early 1919.

17. Murphy, *Russian Civil War*, 107.

18. Quoted in Starikov and Medvedev, trans. Daniels, *Philip Mironov*, 150.

19. Starikov and Medvedev, trans. Daniels, *Philip Mironov*, 118–120.

20. V. P. Butt et al, *The Russian Civil War*, 62–63; A. B. Murphy, *Russian Civil War*, 109.

21. Starikov and Medvedev, trans. Daniels, *Philip Mironov*, 122–124.

22. Brovkin, ed., *Bolsheviks in Russian Society*, 165.

23. Denikin, trans. Zvegintzov, *White Army*, 254.

24. Quoted in V. P. Butt et al, *The Russian Civil War*, 58–68.

25. V. P. Butt et al, *The Russian Civil War*, 50–55.

26. Starikov and Medvedev, trans. Daniels, *Philip Mironov*, 126–127; Murphy, *Russian Civil War*, 112.

27. Quoted in Starikov and Medvedev, trans. Daniels, *Philip Mironov*, 149. This source quotes Mironov's entire 31 July 1919 letter to Lenin on pages 147–153.

28. Murphy, *Russian Civil War*, 116–117.

29. Starikov and Medvedev, trans. Daniels, *Philip Mironov*, 186–187.

30. Chamberlin, *Russian Revolution*, Vol. 2, 217, 242–244.

31. Starikov and Medvedev, trans. Daniels, *Philip Mironov*, 130–131.

32. Denikin, trans. Zvegintzov, *White Army*, 274.

33. Wrangel, *Always With Honour*, 6.

34. Marion Aten and Arthur Orrmont, *Last Train over Rostov Bridge* (New York: Julian Messner Inc., 1961) 67–84.

35. George Stewart, *The White Armies of Russia* (New York: Russell & Russell, 1970) 175–176; Evan Mawdsley, *The Russian Civil War* (New York: Pegasus, 2007) 171–172.

36. Mawdsley, *Russian Civil War*, 172.

37. Wrangel, *Always With Honour*, 89.

38. George Brinkley, *The Volunteer Army and Allied Intervention in South Russia* (Notre Dame, University of Notre Dame Press, 1966) 107–112; Denikin, trans. Zvegintzov, *White Army*, 279.

39. Mawdsley, *Russian Civil War*, 173–175.

40. Chamberlin, *Russian Revolution*, Vol. 2, 247–248; Brovkin, ed., *Bolsheviks in Russian Society*, 181–182.

41. Denikin, trans. Zvegintzov, *White Army*, 283.

42. Luckett, *White Generals*, 292. The original objective of Mamontov's raid had been to attack the Eighth and Ninth Red Armies in their rear.

43. Brigadier H. N. H. Williamson, John Harris, ed., *Farewell to the Don* (New York: The John Day Company, 1971) 158.

44. Kenez, *Defeat of the Whites*, 44.

45. Chamberlin, *Russian Revolution*, Vol. 2, 249.

46. Mawdsley, *Russian Civil War*, 214. W. H. Chamberlin provides somewhat higher figures for the two sides: 112,600 for the AFSR and 186,000 Red Army men. See Chamberlin, *Russian Revolution*, Vol. 2, 275–276.

47. Mawdsley, *Russian Civil War*, 208; Lehovich, *White Against Red*, 295–297; C. E. Bechhofer, *In Denikin's Russia* (London: W. Collins & Sons, 1921) 105.
48. Forsyth, *Caucasus*, 413–417; Brinkley, *Volunteer Army*, 174, 194–210; Denikin, trans. Zvegintzov, *White Army*, 330.
49. Williamson, *Farewell to the Don*, 51–52.
50. Denikin, trans. Zvegintzov, *White Army*, 330.
51. Lehovich, *White Against Red*, 264–265, 347.
52. Kenez, *Defeat of the Whites*, 118–119.
53. Kenez, *Defeat of the Whites*, 119–120. A brief sketch of Ryabovol's murder from the Cossack viewpoint can be found in W. G. Glaskow, *History of the Cossacks*, 120.
54. Kenez, *Defeat of the Whites*, 55–65, 129–131.
55. Wrangel, *Always With Honour*, 90–92.
56. Kenez, *Defeat of the Whites*, 135.
57. Denikin, trans. Zvegintzov, *White Army*, 298.
58. Wrangel, *Always With Honour*, 103.
59. Wrangel, *Always With Honour*, 104–106; Chamberlin, *Russian Revolution*, Vol. 2, 260–261; Kenez, *Defeat of the Whites*, 136–137; Bechhofer, *In Denikin's Russia*, 146.
60. Chamberlin, *Russian Revolution*, Vol. 2, 285–286.
61. Wrangel, *Always With Honour*, 106; Kenez, *Defeat of the Whites*, 137–138.
62. Denikin, trans. Zvegintzov, *White Army*, 298.
63. Chamberlin, *Russian Revolution*, Vol. 2, 261.
64. Pipes, *Russia Under the Bolsehvik Regime*, 110.
65. Pipes Richard, *Russia Under the Bolsehvik Regime* (New York: Alfred A. Knopf, 1993) 100–108; Chamberlin, *Russian Revolution*, Vol. 2, 228–231. Prominent Bolsheviks of Jewish origin included Trotsky, Zinoviev, Kamenev, Sverdlov and Sokolnikov. In the following year, 1920, the Jews in western Ukraine would again endure another series of bloody pogroms. Some of these were committed by the invading Poles while Cossacks, now serving in the First Cavalry Army under Budyonny, were responsible for plenty of others. For an eyewitness account of this violence, see Isaac Babel, *1920 Diary*, translated by H. T. Willetts (New Haven: Yale University Press, 1995).
66. Lehovich, *White Against Red*, 327–330.
67. "The Fastov Pogrom," *The Nation*, Vol. 111, No 2892, 646–647.
68. Pipes, *Russia Under the Bolsehvik Regime*, 108–109.

Chapter 7

1. Quoted in McCauley, *Russian Revolution and the Soviet State*, 244–247.
2. Mawdsley, *Russian Civil War*, 220.
3. Quoted in Butt et al, *Russian Civil War*, 62–63.
4. Quoted in Murphy, *Russian Civil War*, 90–91.
5. Quoted in Mawdsley, *Russian Civil War*, 220.
6. Starikov and Medvedev, trans. Daniels, *Philip Mironov*, 140–145, 159. The difficulties encountered by famed Red Cossack commander Filip Mironov in outfitting a planned Don Cossack cavalry corps during the summer of 1919 stand as the best example of Bolshevik reluctance to permit anti-White Cossacks to fight in large, powerful units.
7. Williamson, *Farewell to the Don*, 202.
8. Mawdsley, *Russian Civil War*, 220.
9. Murphy, *Russian Civil War*, 174–175.
10. Kenez, *End of the Whites*, 218.
11. Kenez, *End of the Whites*, 165–166; Lehovich, *White Against Red*, 334–335, Prince A. Lobanov-Rostovsky, *The Grinding Mill* (New York: The Macmillan Company, 1935) 358–359.
12. Luckett, *White Generals*, 332–337.
13. Mawdsley, *Russian Civil War*, 221.
14. Wrangel, *Always With Honour*, 111–115.
15. Denikin, trans. Zvegintzov, *White Army*, 330–331, Kenez, *Defeat of the Whites*, 220; Aten and Orrmont, *Last Train*, 194–208.
16. Quoted in Wrangel, *Always With Honour*, 115. Denikin's account also mentions the disagreement between the two commanders. See Denikin, trans. Zvegintzov, *White Army*, 332.
17. Kenez, *End of the Whites*, 223.
18. Williamson, *Farewell to the Don*, 214.
19. Luckett, *White Generals*, 287, 352.
20. Williamson, *Farewell to the Don*, 214.
21. Kenez, *End of the Whites*, 222.
22. Williamson, *Farewell to the Don*, 211.
23. Williamson, *Farewell to the Don*, 211–225, 232, 255.
24. Murphy, *Russian Civil War*, 192.
25. Luckett, *White Generals*, 348. Many sources disagree on the exact dates when these cities were occupied by the Reds in 1920. The dates of 5–6 January 1920 have been provided for the fall of Taganrog and 7–9 January for Rostov and Novocherkassk.
26. Williamson, *Farewell to the Don*, 247; Mawdsley, *Russian Civil War*, 221.
27. Quoted in Murphy, *Russian Civil War*, 188.
28. Kenez, *End of the Whites*, 225–228; Chamberlin, *Russian Revolution*, Vol. 2, 284–285.
29. Denikin, trans. Zvegintzov, *White Army*, 337.
30. Chamberlin, *Russian Revolution*, Vol. 2, 282.
31. Kenez, *End of the Whites*, 229–230; Chamberlin, *Russian Revolution*, Vol. 2, 285.
32. Quoted in Lehovich, *White Against Red*, 376.
33. Chamberlin, *Russian Revolution*, Vol. 2, 285–286; Kenez, *End of the Whites*, 232–235; Lehovich, *White Against Red*, 376.
34. Brinkley, *Allied Intervention in South Russia*, 225–233.
35. Kenez, *End of the Whites*, 237.
36. Bechhofer, *In Denikin's Russia*, 122.
37. Thompson, *Russia, Bolshevism and the Versailles Peace*, 359–360.
38. Chamberlin, *Russian Revolution*, Vol. 2, 286–287; Kenez, *End of the Whites*, 238–239; Mawdsley, *Russian Civil War*, 223.
39. Denikin, trans. Zvegintzov, *White Army*, 344–345.
40. Lukomsky, trans. Vitali, *Memoirs*, 246.
41. Williamson, *Farewell to the Don*, 246. In Williamson's own words, "The posters showing Red atrocities which were supposed to encourage

recruiting had only increased terror and made matters worse."
42. Denikin, trans. Zvegintzov, *White Army*, 346–347; Chamberlin, *Russian Revolution*, Vol. 2, 287; Mawdsley, *Russian Civil War*, 223.
43. Williamson, *Farewell to the Don*, 262. C. E. Bechhofer wrote of similar observations in his account. See *In Denikin's Russia*, 196, 217.
44. Bechhofer, *In Denikin's Russia*, 174; Williamson, *Farewell to the Don*, 274.
45. Brinkley, *Allied Intervention in South Russia*, 225–227; Kenez, *End of the Whites*, 239–245.
46. Denikin, trans. Zvegintzov, *White Army*, 347.
47. Kenez, *White Army*, 251.
48. Lehovich, *White Against Red*, 385–386.
49. Aten & Orrmont, *Last Train*, 320.
50. Williamson, *Farewell to the Don*, 279–280.
51. Chamberlin, *Russian Revolution*, Vol. 2, 287–288.
52. Williamson, *Farewell to the Don*, 282.
53. Denikin, trans. Zvegintzov, *White Army*, 353; Kenez, *End of the Whites*, 252; Chamberlin, *Russian Revolution*, Vol. 2, 287–288.
54. Luckett, *White Generals*, 252–253; Kenez, *End of the Whites*, 252; Chamberlin, *Russian Revolution*, Vol. 2, 287–288.
55. According to Evan Mawdsley, 19,300 Volunteers and 11,850 Cossacks were evacuated from Novorossiysk. See Mawdsley, *Russian Civil War*, 224. General Wrangel uses slightly different figures: 25,000 Volunteers and 10,000 Cossacks. See Wrangel, *Always With Honour*, 138. Denikin's figures for the total number of men evacuated from the North Caucasus are 35,000–40,000 along with 100 field guns and 500 machine guns. See Denikin, trans. Zvegintzov, *White Army*, 357.
56. Wrangel, *Always With Honour*, 137–138.
57. Brinkley, *Allied Intervention in South Russia*, 231–233.
58. Denikin later wrote that the Supreme Krug, which had collaborated with him in forming the South Russian Government, "knew how to demoralize the Cossacks but was powerless to make them fight." See Denikin, trans. Zvegintzov, *White Army*, 339. In general, the Volunteer Corps held similar negative attitudes towards the South Russian Government. See Lehovich, *White Against Red*, 390.
59. Lehovich, *White Against Red*, 379–384, 391–394.
60. Wrangel, *Always With Honour*, 137–138, 169–171, 182–183; Brinkley, *Allied Intervention in South Russia*, 234.

Chapter 8

1. Smele, *"Russian" Civil Wars*, 139.
2. Mawdsley, *Russian Civil War*, 236–237; Chamberlin, *Russian Revolution*, Vol. 2, 203–204, 419–423; Peter Hopkirk, *Setting the East Ablaze* (London: John Murray, 1984) 99–100. Figures for the number of refugees who crossed in Xingjian with Annenkov and Dutov vary from 30,000–50,000.
3. Unless noted otherwise, information in this section is from Smele, *Civil War in Siberia*, 521–541.
4. Mawdsley, *Russian Civil War*, 145.
5. *Papers Relating to the Foreign Relations of the United States: 1919: Russia* (Washington, U.S. Government Printing Office, 1937) 514.
6. *Papers Relating to the Foreign Relations of the United States: 1919: Russia* (Washington, U.S. Government Printing Office, 1937) 514.
7. Bobrick, *East of the Sun*, 328–329.
8. Yurlova, *Cossack Girl*, 256.
9. Quoted in Baerlein, *Seventy Thousand*, 235.
10. Bečvar, *Lost Legion*. 214–215.
11. Yurlova, *Cossack Girl*, 257.
12. Smele, *Civil War in Siberia*, 450–470.
13. Smele, *Civil War in Siberia*, 533–544.
14. Coates and Coates, *Allied Intervention in Russia*, 228; McCullagh, *Prisoner of the Reds*, 24.
15. Petroff, *Forgotten War*, 227–231; Smele, *Civil War in Siberia*, 544–550; Mawdsley, *Russian Civil War*, 154–155.
16. Mawdsley, *Russian Civil War*, 230; Butt, *Russian Civil War*, 150–152.
17. McCullagh, *Prisoner of the Reds*, 3–5, 15, 18.
18. *Papers Relating to the Foreign Relations of the United States: 1919: Russia* (Washington, U.S. Government Printing Office, 1937) 274–277.
19. Smele, *Civil War in SIberia*, 572.
20. *Papers Relating to the Foreign Relations of the United States: 1919: Russia* (Washington, U.S. Government Printing Office, 1937) 231–232.
21. Pipes, *Russia Under the Bolshevik Regime*, 45.
22. Dotsenko, *Struggle for a Democracy*, 84–86.
23. Bečvar, *Lost Legion*, 225–231.
24. Smele, *Civil War in Siberia*, 590–592.
25. Dotsenko, *Struggle for a Democracy*, 108.
26. Smele, *Civil War in Siberia*, 591–592, 596–598.
27. McCullagh, *Prisoner of the Reds*, 22.
28. McCullagh, *Prisoner of the Reds*, 65–66.
29. Petroff, *Forgotten War*, 239.
30. Smele, *Civil War in Siberia*, 602–605.
31. *Papers Relating to the Foreign Relations of the United States: 1919: Russia* (Washington, U.S. Government Printing Office, 1937) 235.
32. Bisher, *White Terror*, 208–212; Smele, *Civil War in Siberia*, 605–625.
33. *Papers Relating to the Foreign Relations of the United States: 1919: Russia* (Washington, U.S. Government Printing Office, 1937) 232.
34. Smele, *Civil War in Siberia*, 655–666.
35. Bisher, *White Terror*, 194–196; Littauer, *Russian Hussar*, 278.
36. Dotsenko, *Struggle for a Democracy*, 84–85.
37. *Papers Relating to the Foreign Relations of the United States: 1919: Russia* (Washington, U.S. Government Printing Office, 1937) 514–522.
38. *Papers Relating to the Foreign Relations of the United States: 1919: Russia* (Washington, U.S. Government Printing Office, 1937) 546–547; Smele, *Civil War in Siberia*, 567–570.
39. Bisher, *White Terror*, 207–215.
40. Ernest Dupuy, *Perish by the Sword* (Harris-

burg: The Military Service Publishing Company, 1939) 260-267.

41. Baerlein, *Seventy Thousand*, 261-262.

42. Bisher, *White Terror*, 216-218. Other sources are even more pessimistic about Semyonov's strength. N. G. O. Pereira wrote that Semyonov probably had only 4,000 men under him that winter and that the number Semyonovites never exceeded 10,000. See Vladimir Brovkin (editor), *The Bolsheviks in Russian Society* (New Haven: Yale University Press, 1997) 132.

43. Canfield F. Smith, *Vladivostok Under Red and White Rule* (Seattle: University of Washington Press, 1975) 15-18; Bisher, *White Terror*, 223.

44. Bisher, *White Terror*, 120, 230-231, 263; Stephan, *The Russian Far East*, 139.

45. Smele, *Civil War in Siberia*, 667.

46. Smith, *Vladivostok*, 19-20, 24-26.

47. Smith, *Vladivostok*, 33-34.

48. Bisher, *White Terror*, 232-240; Smith, *Vladivostok*, 18-19, 29-30.

49. Quoted in Coates and Coates, *Allied Intervention in Russia*, 243.

50. Smith, *Vladivostok*, 35-43; Bisher, *White Terror*, 245-248, 259. According to John Stephan, *The Russian Far East*, 145-146, Bochkarev was a Don Cossack. Most of the men he commanded, however, were probably Ussuri Cossacks.

51. Bisher, *White Terror*, 249-251.

52. Bisher, *White Terror*, 260.

53. Smith, *Vladivostok*, 56-57.

54. Palmer, *Bloody White Baron*, 112-116.

55. Quoted in Alioshin, *Asian Odyssey*, 18.

56. Ferdinand Ossendowski, *Beasts, Men and Gods* (New York: E. P. Dutton, 1923) 239-247.

57. Ossendowski, *Beast, Men and Gods*, 104; Bisher, *White Terror*, 266-271.

58. Quoted in Wrangel, *Always With Honour*, 297.

59. Bisher, *White Terror*, 263-264.

60. Smith, *Vladivostok*, 67-75.

Chapter 9

1. Wrangel, *Always With Honour*, 151.

2. Kenez, *Defeat of the Whites*, 253, 260; Wrangel, *Always With Honour*, 139. According to Wrangel, Slashchev's 3,000 infantry and 2,000 cavalry faced 9,000 troops of the Thirteenth Red Army.

3. Wrangel, *Always With Honour*, 95.

4. Wrangel, *Always With Honour*, 219.

5. Kenez, *Defeat of the Whites*, 293-295.

6. Wrangel, *Always With Honour*, 162-163.

7. Wrangel, *Always With Honour*, 236-244; Kenez, *Defeat of the Whites*, 296-297.

8. Kenez, *Defeat of the Whites*, 295-296.

9. Wrangel, *Always With Honour*, 214; Chamberlin, *Russian Revolution*, Vol. 2, 315.

10. Wrangel, *Always With Honour*, 173-175.

11. Chamberlin, *Russian Revolution*, Vol. 2, 323; Wrangel, *Always With Honour*, 189-201.

12. Mawdsley, *Russian Civil War*, 263.

13. Chamberlin, *Russian Revolution*, Vol. 2, 323.

14. Wrangel, *Always With Honour*, 151, 204, 214, 228-233.

15. Wrangel, *Always With Honour*, 115, 231, 235; Denikin, *White Army*, 255-256.

16. Kenez, *Defeat of the Whites*, 297-299.

17. Brinkley, *Allied Intervention in South Russia*, 261; Wrangel, *Always With Honour*, 241-243, 254; Pipes, *Russia Under the Bolshevik Regime*, 177-183.

18. Chamberlin, *Russian Revolution*, Vol. 2, 325-327; Kenez, *Defeat of the Whites*, 299-302; Wrangel, *Always With Honour*, 249-273, 287-288.

19. Mawdsley, *Russian Civil War*, 269.

20. Wrangel, *Always With Honour*, 305-306.

21. Wrangel, *Always With Honour*, 300.

22. Wrangel, *Always With Honour*, 300, 309; Starikov and Medvedev, trans. Daniels, *Philip Mironov and the Russian Civil War*, 197-209; Mawdsley, *Russian Civil War*, 270.

23. Wrangel, *Always With Honour*, 307-312, Chamberlin, *Russian Revolution*, Vol. 2, 330-332.

24. Wrangel, *Always With Honour*, 324-327. According to Wrangel's figures, 145,693 persons fled the Crimea with him. However, a historian of the White Russian army in the interwar period puts that figure slightly higher at 149,000. Paul Robinson, *The White Russian Army in Exile 1920-1941* (Oxford: Clarendon Press, 2002) 31.

25. Smele, "Russian" Civil Wars, 171.

26. Smith, *Vladivostok*, 68-95.

27. Smith, *Vladivostok*, 109-110, Bisher, *White Terror*, 283.

28. Alioshin, *Asian Odyssey*, 183.

29. Peter Hopkirk, *Setting the East Ablaze*, 127-129.

30. Alioshin, *Asian Odyssey*, 237-238.

31. Bisher, *White Terror*, 274-281.

32. Alioshin, *Asian Odyssey*, 260-261.

33. Alioshin, *Asian Odyssey*, 267.

34. Alioshin, *Asian Odyssey*, 267-269; Bisher, *White Terror*, 274-281.

35. Smith, *Vladivostok*, 111-112.

36. This version of Bochkarev's Kamchatka adventure is from John Stephan's *The Russian Far East*, 160. In *Vladivostok Under Red and White Rule*, 124-125, Canfield Smith offers slightly different account of the Whites' Kamchatka expedition. According to Smith, Bochkarev arrived in Petropavlovsk in September (instead October) 1921 and was killed by local villagers (instead the GPU) in the summer of 1922 (instead of spring 1923).

37. Smith, *Vladivostok*, 121-164. The estimated number of Russian evacuees from Vladivostok is given in Bisher, *White Terror*, 285.

38. Butt, *Russian Civil War*, 185. According to Canfield Smith's account, *Vladivostok Under Red and White Rule*, Glebov's looting spree occurred in Vladivostok. See Smith, *Vladivostok*, 164.

39. Smith, *Vladivostok*, 164-165.

40. Butt, *Russian Civil War*, 186. The number of soldiers and refugees given here is according to Diterikhs own estimates. Jamie Bisher (*White Terror*, 286) has placed the number of White Russians to cross into Manchuria at Hunchun as high as 16,000.

41. Butt, *Russian Civil War*, 177-185.

42. Butt, *Russian Civil War*, 190–192. In autumn of 1921, approximately 900 persons who had fled Russia with Wrangel's army were delivered to Vladivostok by British shipping. Most of these individuals had lived or been stationed in Asiatic Russia prior to the civil war. See Smith, *Vladivostok*, 121–122.
43. Butt, *Russian Civil War*, 202–206.
44. Mawdsley, *Russian Civil War*, 285–287.
45. O'Rourke, *Cossacks*, 253.

Chapter 10

1. Lukomsky, *Memoirs of the Russian Revolution*, 253. "Tsargrad" was the old Russian name for Constantinople.
2. For figures on the Russian Diaspora (1917–22), see Paul Robinson, *The White Russian Army in Exile 1920-1941* (Oxford: Clarendon Press, 2002) 16, Catherine Andreyev and Ivan Savický, *Russia Abroad: Prague and the Russian Diaspora, 1918-1938* (New Haven: Yale University Press, 2004) xi.
3. G. O. Matsievsky, "Political Life of the Cossacks in Emigration: Tendencies and Features," *Modern Studies of Social Problems*, 2013, No 3 (23), www.sisp.nkras.ru, 3; O. V. Ratushnyak, "Adaption of the Cossack Emigrants to the Style of Living Abroad," *Historical and Social-educational Ideas*, 2014, 6 (6_2): 156, DOI:10.17748/2075-9908-2014-6-6_2-156-158.
4. Wrangel. *Always With Honour*, 326.
5. Norman Stone and Michael Glenny, *The Other Russia* (London: Faber and Faber Limited, 1990) 173–175, 200–205.
6. Wrangel, *Always With Honour*, 269.
7. Robinson, *White Russian Army*, 33.
8. Lobanov-Rostovksy, *The Grinding Mill*, 374.
9. Wrangel, *Always With Honour*, 316–317, 321.
10. Robinson, *White Russian Army*, 34–35; Wrangel, *Always With Honour*, 338; Matsievsky, "Cossacks in Emigration," 3; W. C. Huntington, *The Homesick Million: Russia-out-of-Russia* (Boston: The Stratford Company, 1933) 13.
11. Robinson, *White Russian Army*, 35–42.
12. Wrangel, *Always With Honour*, 319.
13. Wrangel, *Always With Honour*, 338–341; Robinson, *White Russian Army*, 39–43.
14. Robinson, *White Russian Army*, 40–42.
15. Matsievsky, "Cossacks in Emigration," 6; Ratushnyak, "Cossack Emigrants," 156.
16. Coates and Coates, *Armed Intervention in Russia*, 356.
17. Matsievsky, "Cossacks in Emigration," 6.
18. Matsievsky, "Cossacks in Emigration," 7.
19. Robert Johnston, *New Mecca, New Babylon* (Montreal: McGill-Queen's University Press, 1988) 149.
20. Robinson, *White Russian Army*, 42. In *The Gulag Archipelago*, Aleksandr Solzhenitsyn writes that all of the Cossack émigrés were arrested upon their return to Soviet Russia. See Solzhenitsyn, *The Gulag Archipelago*, trans. Thomas P. Whitney (New York: Harper & Row, 1974) 39. Many, if not most, would in fact be detained during the periods of forced collectivization and purges which followed in the late 1920s and 1930s.
21. Wrangel, *Always With Honour*, 341–342.
22. Robinson, *White Russian Army*, 65–66.
23. Robinson, *White Russian Army*, 45–46; Wrangel, *Always With Honour*, 343.
24. Catherine Andreyev and Ivan Savický, *Russia Abroad: Prague and the Russian Diaspora, 1918-1938* (New Haven: Yale University Press, 2004) 45–47.
25. Quoted in Wrangel, *Always With Honour*, 342.
26. Robinson, *White Russian Army*, 46.
27. Robinson, *White Russian Army*, 86–94; Wrangel, *Always With Honour*, 344.
28. Kellogg, *Russian Roots of Nazism*, 123–126; 145–150, 160; Robinson, *White Russian Army*, 113–115.
29. Miliukov, *Russia Today and Tomorrow*, 126.
30. Johnston, *New Mecca, New Babylon*, 37; Huntington, *Homesick Million*, 176–180.
31. Robinson, *White Russian Army*, 58–62.
32. Quoted in Huntington, *Homesick Million*, 182.
33. Robert Johnston, *New Mecca, New Babylon*, 91–92; Robinson, *White Russian Army*, 24–26.
34. Robert C. Williams, *Culture in Exile: Russian Émigrés in Germany, 1881-1941* (Ithaca: Cornell University Press, 1972) 147–148, 289; Reshetar, *Ukrainian Revolution*, 206. According to Williams (350–352), after 1927 Skoropadsky did eventually secure an annual subsidy of 12,000 reichmarks from the German government.
35. Glazkov, *History of the Cossacks*, 102.
36. Glazkov, *History of the Cossacks*, 3–4.
37. Glazkov, *History of the Cossacks*, 18.
38. Schleifman, *Russia at a Crossroads*, 99–101.
39. Matsievsky, "Cossacks in Emigration," 4; Robinson, *White Russian Army*, 51–54.
40. Andreyev and Savický, *Russia Abroad*, 47.
41. Robinson, *White Russian Army*, 54.
42. Robinson, *White Russian Army*, 61–62.
43. Huntington, *Homesick Million*, 259–260; Matsievsky, "Cossacks in Emigration," 8.
44. Wrangel, *Always With Honour*, 346–347; Huntington, *Homesick Million*, 239–243.
45. Robinson, *White Russian Army*, 62, 99.
46. Robinson, *White Russian Army*, 129–130. Some Russian émigrés have speculated that Wrangel, who was only age 49 when he died, was poisoned by Soviet agents. However, evidence for this hypothesis is lacking.
47. Matsievsky, "Cossacks in Emigration," 4–5.
48. Robinson, *White Russian Army*, 83.
49. Quoted in Stone and Glenny, *The Other Russia*, 282–285.
50. Wrangel, *Always With Honour*, 348.
51. Lobanov-Rostovsky, *The Grinding Mill*, 381.
52. Williams, *Culture in Exile*, 252–281.
53. Williams, *Culture in Exile*, 145.
54. Marc Raeff, *Russia Abroad: A Cultural History of the Russian Emigration 1919-1939* (New York: Oxford University Press, 1990) 29–32.
55. Raeff, *Russia Abroad*, 4–6, 37–38.
56. Woytinsky, *Stormy Passage*, 403.
57. Matsievsky, "Cossacks in Emigration," 10–11.
58. Stone and Glenny, *The Other Russia*, 327–333; Anne Applebaum, *Gulag: A History* (New York: Doubleday, 2003) 124.

59. Raeff, *Russia Abroad*, 24–25; Johnston, *New Mecca, New Babylon*, 85–88; Huntington, *Homesick Million*, 108.
60. Matsievsky, "Cossacks in Emigration," 9; Raeff, *Russia Abroad*, 9.
61. Huntington, *Homesick Million*, 58.
62. Seaton, *Horsemen of the Steppe*, 204.
63. Nikolay Tolstoy, *Victims of Yalta* (London, Hodder and Stoughton, 1977) 164–165.
64. General Pyotr Krasnov, *From Double Eagle to Red Flag*, trans. Erik Law-Gisiko (New York: Duffield and Company, 1926) xii; Williams, *Culture in Exile*, 291–293.
65. Huntington, *Homesick Million*, 260–261.
66. Huntington, *Homesick Million*, 30–32, 66–69.
67. Matsievsky, "Cossacks in Emigration," 5; Huntington, *Homesick Million*, 58, 66–69.
68. Raeff, *Russia Abroad*, 122–123; Matsievsky, "Cossacks in Emigration," 3; Robinson, *White Russian Army*, 81–82. Included among the officer schools in Yugoslavia was the Don Cossack Alexander III Cadet Corps.
69. Andreyev and Savický, *Russia Abroad*, 178–179; Tomasevich, Jozo, *War and Revolution in Yugoslavia, 1941–1945: Occupation and Collaboration* (Stanford: Stanford University Press, 2001) 16.
70. Andreyev and Savický, *Russia Abroad*, 45–51.
71. Boris Raymond and David Jones, *The Russian Diaspora 1917-1941* (Lanham: The Scarecrow Press, 2000) 24; Huntington, *Homesick Millions*, 72–73; Stone and Glenny, *The Other Russia*, 269–271.
72. Johnston, *New Mecca, New Babylon*, 81–82; Huntington, *Homesick Million*, 72.
73. Alioshin, *Asian Odyssey*, 20.
74. Leonid Petrov, "Out of the Frying Pan, Into the Fire: Russian Immigrants in China," Asian Studies Association of Australia, 2002, Accessed 11 June 2015, http://community.fortunecity.ws/meltingpot/champion/65/immigrants/htm; Chamberlin, *Russian Revolution*, Vol. 2, 203; Hopkirk, *Setting the East Ablaze*, 100.
75. For estimates on the number of Russian émigrés living in Manchuria during the 1920s, see Petrov, "Out of the Frying Pan, Into the Fire" and John Stephan, *The Russian Fascists* (New York: Harper & Row, 1978) 37.
76. Raymond and Jones, *Russian Diaspora*, 48–50; Petrov, "Out of the Frying Pan, Into the Fire," Stone and Glenny, *The Other Russia*, 208.
77. Quoted in Stone and Glenny, *The Other Russia*, 204.
78. Stephan, *Russian Fascists*, 38–39, 188–191; Stone and Glenny, *The Other Russia*, 218–219, Patrikeeff,—*Russian Politics in Exile*, 31, 173; Owen Lattimore, *Manchuria: Cradle of Conflict* (New York: Macmillan, 1935) 248–249.
79. Lattimore, *Manchuria: Cradle of Conflict*, 247.
80. Stone and Glenny, *The Other Russia*, 217; John Stephan, *The Russian Fascists* (New York: Harper & Row, 1978) 45.
81. Stephan, *Russian Fascists*, 44; 188–191.
82. Bisher, *White Terror*, 297.
83. Hopkirk, *Setting the East Ablaze*, 215–233; Vladimir and Evdokia Petrov, *Empire of Fear* (New York: Frederick A. Praeger, 1956) 59–66; Petrov, "Out of the Frying Pan, Into the Fire."
84. Matsievsky, "Cossacks in Emigration," 7–8.
85. Robinson, *White Russian Army*, 99–100.
86. Raeff, *Russia Abroad*, 9.
87. Robinson, *White Russian Army*, 131, 141.
88. Robinson, *White Russian Army*, 64–74.
89. Robinson, *White Russian Army*, 75; Matsievsky, "Cossacks in Emigration," 6–7.
90. Andreyev and Savický, *Russia Abroad*, 48.
91. Petrov, "Out of the Frying Pan, Into the Fire."
92. Matsievsky, "Cossacks in Emigration."
93. Smele, *"Russian" Civil Wars*, 226, 350–351.
94. Smele, *"Russian" Civil Wars*, 228.
95. Bisher, *White Terror*, 287.
96. Robinson, *White Russian Army*, 141–147, 190–213.
97. Stephan, *Russian Fascists*, 117–118.

Chapter 11

1. Huntington, *Homesick Million*, 175–180.
2. Kellogg, *Russian Roots of Nazism*, 153, 167. According to Kellogg, Horthy's government maintained close ties to Aufbau during the early 1920s.
3. Kellogg, *Russian Roots of Nazism*, 160–163.
4. Williams, *Culture in Exile*, 178.
5. Kellogg, *Russian Roots of Nazism*, 41, 55, 124, 127–131; Williams, *Culture in Exile*, 160–181; Stephan, *Russian Fascists*, 12–14.
6. Kellogg, *Russian Roots of Nazism*, 185–190.
7. Stephan, *Russian Fascists*, 117–118.
8. Raymond and Jones, *The Russian Diaspora*, 135; Kellogg, *Russian Roots of Nazism*, 187.
9. Kellogg, *Russian Roots of Nazism*, 187–188.
10. Williams, *Culture in Exile*, 218–220; Kellogg, *Russian Roots of Nazism*, 209–212.
11. Wrangel, *Always With Honour*, 13.
12. Robinson, *White Russian Army*, 115–126.
13. Robinson, *White Russian Army*, 167–175.
14. Quoted in Huntington, *Homesick Millions*, 191.
15. Boris Dvinov, *Politics of the Russian Emigration* (Santa Monica: Rand, 1955).
16. Robinson, *White Russian Army*, 175–182; Stephan, *Russian Fascists*, 28–30.
17. Johnston, *New Mecca, New Babylon*, 93–94, 119–120; Catherine Andreyev, *Vlasov and the Russian Liberation Movement* (Cambridge: Cambridge University Press, 1987) 181–182.
18. Stephan, *Russian Fascists*, 91–136.
19. Kellogg, *Russian Roots of Nazism*, 250.
20. Kellogg, *Russian Roots of Nazism*, 250–251.
21. Unfortunately, there is no complete history of the NTS since many of its records were lost during the Second World War as the result of arrests, conspiratorial activities and Allied bombings. In the English language, the most objective study of the NTS and its activities from its formation to 1945 is found in Catherine Andreyev's *Vlasov and the Russian Liberation Movement*, 183–193. *Politics of the Russian Emigration*, by the Menshevik and émigré author Boris

Dvinov, also contains a detailed though more critical review of the organization on pages 111-193.

22. Quoted in Dvinov, *Politics of the Russian Emigration*, 118-119.

23. Dvinov, *Politics of the Russian Emigration*, 130-145.

24. Johnston, *New Mecca, New Babylon*, 151-152.

25. Williams, *Culture in Exile*, 331-363; Dvinov, *Politics of the Russian Emigration*, 127, 141-151; Kellogg, *Russian Roots of Nazism*, 251-256; Andreyev, *Vlasov and the Russian Liberation Movement*, 187-189.

26. See "The Struggle of Ideas" in Chapter 11.

27. Biographical information on Vasily Glazkov is from Samuel Newland, *Cossacks in the German Army 1941-1945* (Portland, OR: Frank Cass, 1991) 96-97.

28. Glazkov, *History of the Cossacks*, 64.

29. Glazkov, *History of the Cossacks*, 26.

30. Glazkov, *History of the Cossacks*, 72-107.

31. Newland, *Cossacks in the German Army*, 96-97.

32. Degtyarev, Sergey I. and Vadim A. Nesterenko. "The Cossack Issue in the Plans of the German Command during the Second World War," *Propaganda in the World and Local Conflicts*, 2015; 4(2) 82-94 (In Russ.) DOI: 10.13187/pwlc.2015.4.82.

33. Stephan, *Russian Fascists*, 49-58.

34. Stephan, *Russian Fascists*, 35-39; Stone and Glenny, *The Other Russia*, 222-229.

35. Bisher, *White Terror*, 297-298.

36. Patrikeeff, *Russian Politics in Exile*, 80-84.

37. Patrikeeff, *Russian Politics in Exile*, 85-89.

38. Patrikeeff, *Russian Politics on Exile*, 99-101.

39. Patrikeeff, *Russian Politics on Exile*, 92-99, 107.

40. Lattimore, *Manchuria: Cradle of Conflict*, 249-250.

41. Stephan, *Russian Fascists*, 60-62.

42. Stephan, *Russian Fascists*, 68-70, 139-153, 174-176.

43. Stephan, *Russian Fascists*, 178-179, 195-197.

44. Bisher, *White Terror*, 286-292.

45. Bisher, *White Terror*, 300.

46. Stephan, *Russian Fascists*, 43-44, 67-68, 164-167; Bisher, *White Terror*, 298.

47. Stephan, *Russian Fascists*, 160, 178-180.

48. Stephan, *Russian Fascists*, 195-199.

49. Bisher, *White Terror*, 300; Stephan, *Russian Fascists*, 195-199; Stephan, *Russian Far East*, 234.

50. Petrov, "Out of the Frying Pan, Into the Fire."

51. Cordier, Sherwood, "Red Star vs. the Rising Sun," *World War II*, July 2003, 30-36; Stephan, *Russian Fascists*, 198-199.

52. Stephan, *Russian Fascists*, 203-204.

53. Johnston, *New Mecca, New Babylon*, 130-131.

54. Stephan, *Russian Fascists*, 206-207.

55. Johnston, *New Mecca, New Babylon*, 121-123.

56. Quoted in Lehovich, *White Against Red*, 450-452.

57. Johnston, *New Mecca, New Babylon*, 114-120. As Johnston points out, many right-wing Russian émigrés also sympathized with the anti-Semitism of the Nazis. According to Andreyev, *Vlasov and the Russian Liberation Movement*, 187-189, the NTS did not officially subscribe to anti-Semitism.

58. Quoted in Dvinov, *Politics of the Russian Emigration*, 121-122.

59. Johnston, *New Mecca, New Babylon*, 157-162.

60. Among them was Second Lieutenant Nikolay N. Krasnov, a grandson of the former Don ataman, who went on to collaborate with the Germans by serving in the Russian Protective Corps and later joined Domanov's Cossacks at Tolmezzo, Italy. See Lannoy, *Les Cosaques de Pannwitz*, 197.

61. The figures used here for the invasion force are from David Glantz and Jonathon House, *When Titans Clashed* (Lawrence, KS: University Press of Kansas, 2015) 34.

62. Sven Steenberg, *Vlasov* (New York: Alfred A. Knopf, 1970) 43-44.

63. Dvinov, *Politics of the Russian Emigration*, 127.

64. Matsievsky, "Cossacks in Emigration, 12.

65. Fitzroy Maclean, *Eastern Approaches* (London: Jonathon Cape, 1949) 330-331.

66. Andreyev and Savický, *Russia Abroad*, 179.

67. Jozo Tomasevich, *War and Revolution in Yugoslavia 1941-1945: Occupation and Collaboration* (Stanford: Stanford University Press, 2001) 191-193.

68. See Chapter 15.

69. Dvinov, *Politics of the Russian Emigration*, 26, 122.

70. Erich Kern, *Dance of Death*, translated by Paul Findlay (London: Collins, 1951) 106-107.

Chapter 12

1. Ossendowski, *Beast, Men and Gods*, 28; Alioshin, *Asian Odyssey*, 83.

2. Murphy, *Russian Civil War*, 187, 213-216.

3. Dune, trans. Koenker and Smith, *Notes of a Red Guard*, 209.

4. Babel, *1920 Diary*, 63-65.

5. Holquist, *Making War, Forging Revolution*, 200-201, 282.

6. Quoted in O'Rourke, *The Cossacks*, 261-262.

7. O'Rourke, *The Cossacks*, 260-262.

8. Pipes, *Formation of the Soviet Union*, 223-225, 242-247; O'Rourke, *The Cossacks*, 263; Forsyth, *The Caucasus*, 462.

9. Aleksandr Skoryk, "Repressive Policies of the Bolsheviks in the Cossack Regions of Southern Russia in the Conditions Collectivization: Principles, Methods, Results," *Bylye Gody*, Vol. 26, 2012, 1.

10. Skoryk, "Repressive Policies of the Bolsheviks," 1-2.

11. Vladimir Brovkin, "Mobilization, Utilization and the Rhetoric of Liberation: Bolshevik Policy Toward Women," Vladimir Brovkin, ed., *Bolsheviks in Russian Society*, 222-225.

12. Forsyth, *The Caucasus*, 461.

13. Holquist, "From Estate to Ethnos," Schliefman, ed., *Russia at a Crossroads*, 101; O'Rourke, *The Cossacks*, 263-264.

14. Holquist, "From Estate to Ethnos," Schliefman, ed., *Russia at a Crossroads*, 98-99.

15. Forsyth, *The Caucasus*, 461.

16. Holquist, *Making War, Forging Revolution*, 255-263; Starikov and Medvedev, *Philip Mironov*, 214.

17. Pipes, *Russia under the Bolshevik Regime*, 370–372.
18. H. H. Fisher, *The Famine in Soviet Russia* (New York, The Macmillan Company, 1927) 486–489.
19. Forsyth, *The Caucasus*, 436–438.
20. O'Rourke, *The Cossacks*, 264–266.
21. "Peasant Rebellions: Origin, Scope, Dynamics and Consequences," Vladimir Brovkin, ed., *The Bolsheviks in Russian Society*, 169.
22. Delano Dugarm, "Peasant War in Tambov Province," Vladimir Brovkin, ed., *The Bolsehviks in Russian Society*, 177.
23. O'Rourke, *The Cossacks*, 266.
24. See Chapter 10.
25. Holquist, *Making War, Forging Revolution*, 269–270.
26. Starikov and Medvedev, *Philip Mironov*, 215–233.
27. Brovkin, ed., "Peasant Rebellions," *Bolsheviks in Russian Society*, 172; Robert Conquest, *The Harvest of Sorrow* (New York: Oxford University Press, 1986) 51.
28. Brovkin, ed., "Peasant Rebellions," *Bolsheviks in Russian Society*, 172; Robert Conquest, *The Harvest of Sorrow* (New York: Oxford University Press, 1986) 177–198; Pipes, *Russia under the Bolshevik Regime*, 388–389. While all sources agree that the anticommunist rebellion in Western Siberia involved tens of thousands of insurgents, they differ considerably on the exact number involved. Accounts also disagree on whether the uprising began in January or February of 1921.
29. Pipes, *Russia under the Bolshevik Regime*, 379–386.
30. Pipes, *Russia under the Bolshevik Regime*, 391–398, 403–409.
31. Longworth, *The Cossacks*, 319.
32. Strong, Anna Louise, "Modern Farming—Soviet Style" Labor Research Association (New York, International Pamphlet, 1930) 5.
33. Holquist, *Making War, Forging Revolution*, 260–266.
34. Fisher, *Famine in Soviet Russia*, 497, 504.
35. See Table 28 in Danilov, trans. Figes, *Rural Russia under the New Regime* (London: Hutchinson, 1988) 276.
36. Fisher, *Famine in Soviet Russia*, 475–479. Since 1900, the Russian Empire had experienced two regional crop failures: along the Volga in 1906 and in the vicinity of the Urals in 1911. Each disaster threatened the food security of roughly twenty million people living in those areas, but the tsarist government was able to alleviate the crises by dipping into grain reserves or transferring food surpluses from other regions into the affected zone.
37. Fisher, *Famine in Soviet Russia*, 51, 86–95.
38. Quoted in Miliukov, *Russia Today and Tomorrow*, 238–241.
39. Fisher, *Famine in Soviet Russia*, 97–98, 106–109, 229; Miliukov, *Russia Today and Tomorrow*, 242–258.
40. Conquest, *Harvest of Sorrow*, 53–54.
41. Fisher, *Famine in Soviet Russia*, 51–61, 226–227, 292, 326–327; Conquest, *Harvest of Sorrow*, 55–56. Moscow's decision to export grain out of the country was undertaken against of the pleas of ARA officials.
42. Fisher, *Famine in Soviet Russia*, 374–377.
43. Danilov, trans. Figes, *Rural Russia under the New Regime*, 276.
44. Conquest, *Harvest of Sorrow*, 70.
45. Lynne Viola, *Peasant Resistance under Stalin* (New York: Oxford University Press, 1965) 48–49.
46. Despite claims that Cossack costume and songs were outlawed by the Communists during the 1920s, most historians have stated otherwise. For example, see Holquist, "From Estate to Ethnos," Schleifman, ed., *Russia at a Crossroads*, 101 and Longworth, *The Cossacks*, 322. Remarkably, Maurice Hindus, whose works have been criticized for pro-Soviet bias, was among those who charged that Cossack dress and music were illegal during the 1920s. See Hindus, *The Cossacks*, 105–106.
47. Hindus, *The Cossacks*, 102.
48. Danilov, trans. Figes, *Rural Russia under the New Regime*, 111–115.
49. Forsyth, *The Caucasus*, 461.
50. Danilov, trans. Figes, *Rural Russia under the New Regime*, 142–153.
51. Danilov, trans. Figes, *Rural Russia under the New Regime*, 163.
52. See Table 16 in Danilov, trans. Figes, *Rural Russia under the New Regime*, 174.
53. Strong, "Modern Farming—Soviet Style," 3–6; Chamberlin, *Russia's Iron Age*, 68–69.
54. Danilov, trans. Figes, *Rural Russia under the New Regime*, 161–163.
55. Conquest, *Harvest of Sorrow*, 107–108.
56. Danilov, trans. Figes, *Rural Russia under the New Regime*, 157.
57. See Table 28 of grain harvests and yields in Danilov, trans. Figes, *Rural Russia under the New Regime*, 276.
58. Viola, *Peasant Rebels under Stalin*, 21, 74.
59. Conquest, *Harvest of Sorrow*, 87–93; Chamberlin, *Russia's Iron Age*, 356–357.
60. Danilov, trans. Figes, *Rural Russia under the New Regime*, 175–176.
61. Conquest, *Harvest of Sorrow*, 87–95.
62. Conquest, *Harvest of Sorrow*, 109–112.
63. Viola, *Peasant Rebels under Stalin*, 25–28.
64. Viola, *Peasant Rebels under Stalin*, 28–29.
65. Viola, *Peasant Rebels under Stalin*, 67–99.
66. Chamberlin, *Russia's Iron Age*, 73–74. The percentages are calculated from figures reported in *Pravda* on 28 January 1934. Similar figures may also be found in Viola, *Peasant Rebels under Stalin*, 70.
67. Danilov, trans. Figes, *Rural Russia under the New Regime*, 268–269.
68. Chamberlin, *Russia's Iron Age*, 77.
69. Viola, *Peasant Rebels under Stalin*, 100–131.
70. Conquest, *Harvest of Sorrow*, 153.
71. Viola, *Peasant Rebels under Stalin*, 132–204.
72. Anne Applebaum, *Gulag: A History* (New York: Doubleday, 2003) 47–91; Chamberlin, *Russia's Iron Age*, 51–53; Conquest, *Harvest of Sorrow*, 138–142.
73. Conquest, *Harvest of Sorrow*, 276.

74. Petrov and Petrov, *Empire of Fear*, 227.
75. Fischer, *Thirteen Who Fled*, 42.
76. Chamberlin, *Russia's Iron Age*, 82.
77. Conquest, *Harvest of Sorrow*, 188–198; Stephan, *Russian Far East*, 191.
78. Skoryk, "Repressive Policies of the Bolsheviks," 2–4.
79. O'Rourke, *Cossacks*, 253.
80. Chamberlin, *Russia's Iron Age*, 347.
81. Conquest, *Harvest of Sorrow*, 219–220.
82. Forsyth, *The Caucasus*, 445–446.
83. Forsyth, *The Caucasus*, 445–446.
84. Conquest, *Harvest of Sorrow*, 276; Viola, *Peasant Rebels under Stalin*, 225.
85. Chamberlin, *Russia's Iron Age*, 86.
86. Forsyth, *The Caucasus*, 446.
87. Forsyth, *The Caucasus*, 446; Conquest, *Harvest of Sorrow*, 277.
88. Conquest, *Harvest of Sorrow*, 276–278.
89. Forsyth, *The Caucasus*, 446–447.
90. Conquest, *Harvest of Sorrow*, 280.
91. Chamberlin, *Russia's Iron Age*, 82–84.
92. Conquest, *Harvest of Sorrow*, 306.
93. Chamberlin, *Russia's Iron Age*, 41–48, 194–195.
94. Viola, *Peasant Rebels under Stalin*, 70.
95. Olga Rvacheva, "Formation of the Soviet Cossacks Community in the South of Russia in the mid-1930s—early 1940s," Vestnik Volgogradskogo Gosudarstvennogo Universiteta. Seria 4. Istoria, Regionovedenie, Mezdunarodnye Otnosenia (2014; (3)81–92 DOI 10.15688/jvosu4.2014.3.9).
96. Seaton, *Horsemen of the Steppe*, 202–203; DiMarco, *War Horse*, 319–320.
97. Rvacheva, "Formation of the Soviet Cossacks."
98. Hindus, *Cossacks*, 111.
99. Holquist, "From Estate to Ethnos," Schliefman, ed., *Russia at a Crossroads*, 104.
100. Seaton, *Horsemen of the Steppe*, 233–234.
101. Hindus, *Cossacks*, 111–112; Holquist, "From Estate to Ethnos," Schliefman, ed., *Russia at a Crossroads*, 103–104; Rvacheva, "Formation of the Soviet Cossacks."
102. Holquist, "From Estate to Ethnos," Schliefman, ed., *Russia at a Crossroads*, 99–105.
103. Joel Carmichael, *Stalin's Masterpiece* (London: Weidenfeld and Nicolson, 1976) 28–38.
104. Louis Fischer and Boris Yakovlev, ed., *Thirteen Who Fled*, trans. Gloria and Victor Fischer (New York: Harper & Brothers, 1949) 146.
105. Joel Carmichael, *Stalin's Masterpiece*, 130–189.
106. O'Rourke, *Cossacks*, 276.
107. Carmichael, *Stalin's Masterpiece*, 176–179, 157; Viola, *Peasant Rebels under Stalin*, 207.
108. Antony Beevor, *Stalingrad* (New York: Penguin, 1999) 88.
109. Hagen, Mark von, "Soviet Soldiers and Officers on the Eve of the German Invasion: Toward a Description of Social Psychology and Political Attitudes," Robert Thurston and Bernd Bonwetsch (ed.) *The Peoples War* (Chicago: University of Illinois Press, 2000) 199.
110. Carmichael, *Stalin's Masterpiece*, 183–184.

According to Carmichael, a third of the officer corps was arrested and many of those were executed. The senior ranks of the Red Army officer corps were eliminated at a higher proportional rate than the lower ones.

111. Hagen, Mark von, "Soviet Soldiers and Officers on the Eve of the German Invasion: Toward a Description of Social Psychology and Political Attitudes," Robert Thurston and Bernd Bonwetsch (ed.) *The Peoples War* (Chicago: University of Illinois Press, 2000) 195–200.
112. George Fischer, *Soviet Opposition to Stalin* (Cambridge: Havard University Press, 1952) 3–6. For examples of émigrés claims that early defeats were the result of widespread disloyalty, see Fischer, ed., *Thirteen Who Fled*, 38–39, 72.

Chapter 13

1. Matsievsky, "Cossacks in Emigration," 13–14.
2. Degtyarev, Sergey I. and Vadim A. Nesterenko. "The Cossack Issue in the Plans of the German Command during the Second World War," *Propaganda in the World and Local Conflicts*, 2015; 4(2) 82–94 (In Russ.) DOI: 10.13187/pwlc.2015.4.82.
3. Degtyarev, Sergey I. and Vadim A. Nesterenko. "The Cossack Issue in the Plans of the German Command during the Second World War," *Propaganda in the World and Local Conflicts*, 2015; 4(2) 82–94 (In Russ.) DOI: 10.13187/pwlc.2015.4.82; Matsievsky, "Cossacks in Emigration," 13–15.
4. Hitler, trans. Manheim, *Mien Kampf*, 655–659.
5. Hitler, trans. Manheim, *Mien Kampf*, 652.
6. Hitler, trans. Manheim, *Mien Kampf*, 139–140.
7. Dallin, Alexander, *German Rule in Russia* (London: The Macmillan Press, 1981) 68–70.
8. *Nazi Conspiracy and Aggression*, Vol. VII, 1086–1093.
9. *Nazi Conspiracy and Aggression*, Vol. VII, 1086–1093.
10. Jürgen Thorwald, *The Illusion: Soviet Soldiers in Hitler's Army*, trans. Richard and Clara Winston (New York: Harcourt Brace Jovanovich, 1975) 3–13. For Hitler's determination to extract as much foodstuffs and oil as possible from the occupied East, see "Guiding Principles for the Economic Operations in the newly occupied Eastern territories" in *Nazi Conspiracy and Aggression*, Vol. IV (Washington: United States Government Printing Office, 1948) 263–271.
11. *Nazi Conspiracy and Aggression*, Vol. III, 692–693. According to one source, Rosenberg proposed a fifth partition, Turkistan, to be based in Central Asia. See Jürgen Thorwald, *The Illusion: Soviet Soldiers in Hitler's Army*, 9–13.
12. Jürgen Thorwald, *The Illusion: Soviet Soldiers in Hitler's Army*, trans. Richard and Clara Winston (New York: Harcourt Brace Jovanovich, 1975) 3–13; Dallin, *German Rule in Russia*, 46–49; *Nazi Conspiracy and Aggression*, Vol. IV, 634–636.
13. Jürgen Thorwald, *The Illusion: Soviet Soldiers in Hitler's Army*, trans. Richard and Clara Winston (New York: Harcourt Brace Jovanovich, 1975) 3–13;

Dallin, *German Rule in Russia*, 46–49; *Nazi Conspiracy and Aggression*, 634–636.

14. Hans von Herwarth with S. Frederick Starr, *Against Two Evils* (New York: Rawson, Wade Publishers, Inc., 1981) 211–214.

15. Dallin, *German Rule in Russia*, 64–67. Recent events, and not propaganda, appear to have been far more important in shaping the peoples' attitudes towards the arrival of German forces. For example, most sources agree that the German invaders were frequently welcomed by local inhabitants of towns and villages in the former Baltic States and eastern Poland, all which had fallen under Soviet occupation only in 1939. Populations further east, which had endured Bolshevik tyranny since the conclusion of the Russian Civil War, showed markedly less enthusiasm for invaders.

16. Dallin, *German Rule in Russia*, 64. The extent to which various Soviet peoples greeted the oncoming Germans is controversial. According to Dallin, the invaders received their warmest welcome in the areas only recently occupied by the Red Army in 1939. Still, accounts written by German soldiers (see below) and Soviet "nonreturners" after the war claim that such favorable demonstrations towards the invader were frequent even to the east of the Soviet Union's pre-1939 frontier. See Louis Fischer, ed., *Thirteen Who Fled*, 97.

17. Herwarth, *Against Two Evils*, 201.

18. Erich Kern, *Dance of Death*, translated by Paul Findlay (London: Collins, 1951) 76–77.

19. Wilfried Strik-Strikfeldt, *Against Stalin and Hitler*, trans. David Footman (London: Macmillan, 1970) 24–26.

20. Strik-Strikfeldt, trans. Footman, *Against Stalin and Hitler*, 63–64.

21. *Nazi Conspiracy and Aggression*, Vol. VI, 977–1002.

22. Hans von Herwarth with S. Frederick Starr, *Against Two Evils* (New York: Rawson, Wade Publishers Inc., 1981) 222. Another example of the supposed six-week schedule for Operation Barbarossa can be found in Strik-Strikfeldt's memoir, *Against Stalin and Hitler*, 23.

23. Alan Clark, *Barbarossa* (New York: William Morrow and Company, 1965) 50.

24. Halder, *War Diary*, 444–448.

25. Clark, *Barbarossa*, 142–145; Liddell Hart, *The Other Side of the Hill* (London: Cassell & Company, 1973) 269, 277, 283. As Alan Clark points out, Soviet historians have disputed some of these figures as much too high.

26. Halder, *War Diary*, 554, 557–559.

27. Clark, *Barbarossa*, 54.

28. Halder, *War Dairy*, 418, 431–436.

29. Halder, *War Diary*, 543–545, 551–553; Liddell Hart, *Other Side of the Hill*, 248–249.

30. General Hienz Guderian, *Panzer Leader*, trans. Constantine Fitzgibbon (London: Michael Joseph, 1952) 233.

31. Halder, *War Diary*, 506.

32. Liddell Hart, *Other Side of the Hill*, 265.

33. *Nazi Conspiracy and Aggression*, Vol. V, 871–875.

34. *Nazi Conspiracy and Aggression*, Vol. I, 339–341.

35. Clark, *Barbarossa*, 151–155; Glantz and House, *When Titans Clashed*, 84–85.

36. *Nazi Conspiracy and Aggression*, Vol. VII, 49–53.

37. Quoted in Liddell Hart, *Other Side of the Hill*, 281–282.

38. Liddell Hart, *Other Side of the Hill*, 284–285. Unlike his generals, Hitler attached no great importance to Moscow as an objective for most of 1941. See Halder, *War Diary*, 293–294, 484–488.

39. Guderian, *Panzer Leader*, trans. Fitzgibbon, 237.

40. Clark, *Barbarossa*, 170.

41. Halder, *War Diary*, 594–598.

42. Liddell Hart, *Other Side of the Hill*, 288–289.

43. Liddell Hart, *Other Side of the Hill*, 289.

44. Gerhard Weinberg and H. R. Trevor-Roper, ed., trans. Norman Cameron and R. H. Stevens, *Hitler's Table Talk*, 318–321.

45. Liddell Hart, *Other Side of the Hill*, 294–295.

46. Strik-Strikfeldt, trans. Footman, *Against Stalin and Hitler*, 80. According to Strik-Strikfeldt's memoir (*Against Stalin and Hitler*, 52, 56), the initial commander of Army Group Center, Field Marshal von Bock, and his successor, Field Marshal von Kluge, both appreciated the advantages of a more practical Ostpolitik by late 1941 and early 1942. Nazi Propaganda Minister Josef Goebbels also subscribed to the utilitarian viewpoint from 1942 onward. See Fischer, *Soviet Opposition to Stalin*, 11–15. The head of the OKH intelligence branch known as Foreign Armies East, General Reinhard Gehlen, also describes in his memoirs how numerous officers of the German General Staff and field commanders all desired a radical change in Ostpolitik during the winter of 1941–1942. See Reinhard Gehlen, *The Service*, trans. David Irving (New York: World Publishing Company, 1972) 81–82.

47. Strik-Strikfeldt, trans. Footman, *Against Stalin and Hitler*, 57–58.

48. Fischer, *Soviet Opposition to Stalin*, 16–17.

49. Gehlen, *The Service*, trans. Irving, 81.

50. Robert Thurston, "Cauldrons of Loyalty and Betrayal: Soviet Soldiers' Behavior, 1941 and 1945," Thurston and Bonwetsch, ed., *The People's War* (Chicago: University of Illinois Press, 2000) 239–245.

51. The fealty of the average Red Army soldier at the outset of the Soviet—Nazi war is a controversial subject among historians. During the early Cold War, American historians reasoned that the Red Army men were by and large unmotivated to risk their lives for the Stalin's oppressive regime. As a result, the Soviet troops were eager to desert or surrender at the first opportunity which, according to this theory, contributed substantially to the droves of Red Army soldiers who entered German captivity in 1941. This assessment was corroborated by the accounts of "new" émigrés—Soviet citizens who remained abroad after the war—which alleged that the Red Army was riddled with low morale and disloyalty at outset of the conflict. See George Fischer, *Soviet Opposition to Stalin* (Cambridge: Harvard University Press, 1952) 4–6. German accounts, however, are filled with exam-

ples and reports of staunch resistance from encircled Soviet soldiers long after the latter had been cut off their rear. See Halder, *War Diary*, XX. A German infantryman, later promoted to a lieutenant, may have put it best when he stated that the Red Army men were unpredictable: at times they fought with suicidal determination while on other occasions they gave themselves up after offering only token resistance. See Gottlob Bidermann, *In Deadly Combat* (Lawrence: University Press of Kansas, 2000) 115. According to an in-depth study on the loyalty of Soviet soldiers in the first months of the war, an estimated 3 out 4 Red Army men who entered captivity in 1941 did so as a result of being trapped in a major encirclement by enemy forces. In other words, the bulk of these soldiers were taken prisoner only when further resistance would prove futile. See Robert Thurston, "Cauldrons of Loyalty and Betrayal: Soviet Soldiers' Behavior, 1941 and 1945," Robert Thurston and Bernd Bonwetsch, ed., *The Peoples War* (Chicago: University of Illinois Press, 2000) 238–239. Regardless of the prevailing mood among Red Army troops in 1941, it is incontestable that at least tens of thousands (out of millions) eventually entered into German service.

52. Louis Fischer, ed., *Thirteen Who Fled*, trans. Gloria and Victor Fischer (New York: Harper & Brothers Publishers, 1949) 11, 238. One Russian prisoner who remained abroad after the war asserted that, "I am sure that not only I but 70 to 80 per cent of the Soviet population hoped for the defeat of their regime and awaited the Germans, their enemies, as liberators from the Communist 'paradise.'"

53. Quoted in Mikhail Koriakov, *I'll Never Go Back*, trans. Nicholas Wreden (New York: E.P. Dutton, 1948) 128.

54. Robert Thurston, "Cauldrons of Loyalty and Betrayal: Soviet Soldiers' Behavior, 1941 and 1945," Thurston and Bonwetsch, ed., *The People's War* (Chicago: University of Illinois Press, 2000) 239–245.

55. *Nazi Conspiracy and Aggression*, Vol. II, 126–130.

56. The estimates of Hiwi strength during 1942 can be found in Christopher Ailsby's *Hilter's Renegades: Foreign Nationals in the Service of the Third Reich* (Dulles: Brasseys, 2004) 119–120. Hitler addressed the subject of arming Eastern peoples at a *führer* conference on 26 July 1941, where he stated his "iron principle" that "We must never permit anybody but the Germans to carry arms! This is especially important; even when it seems easier at first to enlist the support of foreign subjugated nations, it is wrong to do so. In the end this will prove to be our disadvantage unconditionally and unavoidably. Only the Germans may carry arms, not the Slav, not the Czech, not the Cossack nor the Ukrainian!" See *Nazi Conspiracy and Aggression*, Vol. VII.

57. Peter Huxley-Blythe, *The East Came West* (Caldwell: The Caxton Printers, 1964) 15–19; Samuel Newland, *Cossacks in the German Army* (Portland: Frank Cass, 1991) 94.

58. Newland, *Cossacks in the German Army*, 90–92.

59. David Littlejohn, *Foreign Legions of the Third Reich*, Vol. IV (San Jose: R. James Binder Pubishing, 1987) 309–312; Cooper, *Nazi War Against Soviet Partisans*, 112–113.

60. Littlejohn, *Foreign Legions*, Vol. IV, 250; *Nazi Conspiracy and Aggression*, Vol. IV, 55–58, 65–75.

61. For example, see Glazkov, *History of the Cossacks*, 3–15.

62. Dallin, *German Rule in Russia*, 298–302; Newland, *Cossacks in the German Army*, 104. The initial reluctance of various German agencies to recognize Cossacks as a distinct group can be seen by their absence in a September 1941 OKW directive regarding the categorization of Soviet POWs. See *Nazi Conspiracy and Aggression*, Vol. IV, 65–75.

63. Cooper, *Nazi War Against Soviet Partisans*, 109–110; Strik-Strikfeldt, *Against Stalin and Hitler*, 52.

64. Dallin, *German Rule in Russia*, 299. Interestingly, Hitler's approval of the Cossacks auxiliaries occurred just four days after he informed dinner guests that only the Germans, not the subject races, should be permitted to carry arms. Such contradictions between the Führer's words and actions were not unusual.

65. Ailsby, *Hitler's Renegades*, 123.

66. Huxley-Blythe, *East Came West*, 20.

67. Herwarth, *Against Two Evils*, 215–221.

68. The decrees on compulsory labor in the occupied territories can be found in *Nazi Conspiracy and Aggression*, Vol. 1, 347–350, 361–362, 408–412.

69. Strik-Strikfeldt, *Against Stalin and Hitler*, 64.

70. Dallin, *German Rule in Russia*, 60. Nazi propaganda belatedly promised agrarian reform in the occupied territories during February 1942; albeit with significant caveats. See Tatarov, Azamat, "Restoration Attempt of Private Landed Property in the North Caucasus in the Conditions of the Nazi Occupation (August 1942-1943)," *Historical and Social-Educational Ideas*, 2015, 7 (8): 76.

71. Thorwald, *The Illusion*, 13.

72. Weinberg, ed., *Hitler's Table Talk*, 6–7, 20–24, 98–99, 318–321.

73. Herwarth, *Against Two Evils*, 223–231.

74. Tatarov, Azamat, "Restoration Attempt of Private Landed Property in the North Caucasus in the Conditions of the Nazi Occupation (August 1942–1943)," *Historical and Social-Educational Ideas*, 2015, 7 (8) : 76. In another example of the slightly moderating trend in Ostpolitik in early 1942, the German announced the abolition of collective farms in occupied Eastern territories on 26 February. See Dallin, *German Rule in Russia*, 334–335.

75. Liddell Hart, *Other Side of the Hill*, 303–305.

76. For example, see the postwar survey conducted by German researchers of anti-German and anti-Soviet attitudes among Cossacks reproduced in Huxley-Blythe, *East Came West*, 21.

77. See Aleksandr Nekrich, *The Punished Peoples*, trans. George Saunders (New York: W. W. Norton & Company, 1978). On the subject of collaboration among the Kalmyks, Nekrich points out that even West German historians, who had a tendency to inflate and romanticize the number of Kalmyks who

entered German service, estimated that no more than half of the Kalmyk population became collaborators. Other sources put that figure drastically smaller. See Nekrich, *Punished Peoples*, 74–75.

78. For example Major-General (later promoted to a Marshal of the Soviet Union) A. A. Grechko, who presided over various commands amid the defense of the Caucasus, later wrote in his history of the battle that, "The friendship of the peoples of the Caucasian republics with all the peoples of the USSR withstood the severe tests imposed on it by this gigantic struggle." His account makes no mention of widespread disloyalty among any Caucasian peoples even though the NKVD, following the German occupation, deported whole communities on the basis of their alleged collaboration with the enemy. See Grechko, *Battle for the Caucasus*, 9. Alexander Werth, a British correspondent in the USSR during most of the war, recorded how the press gave much publicity to the supposedly enthusiastic turnout of Caucasian peoples at "anti–Fascist meetings" held throughout the region in 1942. See Werth, *Russia at War*, 531–532.

79. Andrey Grechko, *Battle for the Caucasus* (Moscow: Progress Publishers, 1971) 57.

80. Cooper, *Nazi War Against Soviet Partisans*, 61, 100. Hans von Herwarth attributed the near-absence of partisans in the North Caucasus as a successful outcome of Stauffenberg's enlightened policy. See Herwarth, *Against Two Evils*, 231.

81. Newland, *Cossacks in the German Army*, 98–99; Lannoy, *Les Cosaques de Pannwitz*, 21–23.

82. Huxley-Blythe, *East Came West*, 26–30.

83. Degtyarev, Sergey I. and Vadim A. Nesterenko. "The Cossack Issue in the Plans of the German Command during the Second World War," *Propaganda in the World and Local Conflicts*, 2015; 4(2) 82–94 (In Russ.) DOI: 10.13187/pwlc.2015.4.82.

84. Dallin, *German Rule in Russia*, 298–302; Newland, *Cossacks in the German Army*, 138–139.

85. Huxley-Blythe, *East Came West*, 23–26.

86. François de Lannoy, *Les Cosaques de Pannwitz* (Château de Damigry: Heimdal, 2000) 21–25.

87. Biographical details on Helmuth von Pannwitz can be found in *The German Generals of World War II*, Friedrich Wilhelm von Mellenthin (Norman, OK: University of Oklahoma Press, 1977) 40–52.

88. Werth, *Russia at War*, 451. As mentioned earlier, the city, then known as Tsaritsyn, was nicknamed "the Red Verdun" for repulsing Krasnov's Don Army in 1918.

89. Werth, *Russia at War*, 522.

90. Clark, *Barbarossa*, 241–247; Werth, *Russia at War*, 411–439.

91. Mellenthin, *German Generals*, 45–46; Huxley-Blythe, *East Came West*, 32–33; Lannoy, *Les Cosaques de Pannwitz*, 27.

92. O'Rourke, *Cossacks*, 277.

93. DiMarco, *War Horse*, 338.

94. Glantz and House, *When Titans Clashed*, 105.

95. Guderian, *Panzer Leader*, 248.

96. Clark, *Barbarossa*, 41, 138–139; Werth, *Russia at War*, 535.

97. Halder, *War Diary*, 621–624.

98. Grechko, *Battle for the Caucasus*, 68–71.

99. Hindus, *Cossacks*, 16.

100. Werth, *Russia at War*, 389, 399–401. This was the second time that Red Army did away with its political commissars. The first time was in 1940, although the institution was reinstated the following year.

101. Grechko, *Battle for the Caucasus*, 79.

102. Grechko, *Battle for the Caucasus*, 52–54.

103. Grechko, *Battle for the Caucasus*, 55–56.

104. For example of an evacuation gone awry in the Kalmyk Autonomous Soviet Socialist Republic, see Nekrich, *The Punished Peoples*, 69–71.

105. Hindus, *Cossacks*, 137–139.

106. Tatarov, Azamat, "Restoration Attempt of Private Landed Property in the North Caucasus in the Conditions of the Nazi Occupation (August 1942–1943)," *Historical and Social-Educational Ideas*, 2015, 7 (8): 77; Naumenko, *Great Betrayal*, 54–55.

107. Olga Rvacheva, "Formation of the Soviet Cossacks Community in the South of Russia in the mid-1930s—early 1940s," Vestnik Volgogradskogo Gosudarstvennogo Universiteta. Seria 4. Istoria, Regionovedenie, Mezdunarodnye Otnosenia (2014; (3)81–92 DOI 10.15688/jvosu4.2014.3.9).

108. Hindus, *Cossacks*, 153.

109. Cooper, *Nazi War Against Soviet Partisans*, 104–105.

110. Albert Seaton, in *The Horsemen of the Steppes*, 237, wrote that true Cossackdom died in 1920.

111. Seaton, *Horseman of the Steppes*, 327.

Chapter 14

1. Liddell Hart, *Other Side of the Hill*, 316–317; Grechko, *Battle for the Caucasus*, 185–205; Beevor, *Stalingrad*, 274; Werth, *Russia at War*, 529.

2. Hindus, *Cossacks*, 139–140, 167–168; Cooper, *Nazi War Against Soviet Partisans*, 105; Clark, *Barbarossa*, 303. Accounts emanating directly from or sympathetic to anti-Soviet Cossacks often downplay German atrocities in the North Caucasus. Therefore, the testimony of an Kuban Cossack in Naumenko's compilation *Great Betrayal* (51–59) is all more interesting since it casts light on German misdeeds during their later occupation of the North Caucasus.

3. Koriakov, *I'll Never Go Back*, 140; Fischer, ed., *Thirteen Who Fled*, 151; Werth, *Russia at War*, 567.

4. Thorwald, *The Illusion*, trans. Richard and Clara Winston, 76–77.

5. According to Samuel Newland (Newland, *Cossacks in the German Army*, 131), 14,000 Cossacks fled from the region that winter, a figure which seems too low when one considers that migrations of Cossack refugees later in the war involved 20,000–30,000 individuals. On the other hand, Peter Huxley-Blythe (Huxley-Blythe, *East Came West*, 36) put the total number of refugees from the North Caucasus, including Cossacks, Circassians and Kalmyks, at the excessive figure of over one million.

6. Clark, *Barbarossa*, 279–282.

7. Liddell Hart, *Other Side of the Hill*, 316.

8. Huxley-Blythe, *East Came West*, 36.

9. Grechko, *Battle for the Caucasus*, 312–352.
10. Huxley-Blythe, *East Came West*, 54–55.
11. *Nazi Conspiracy and Aggression*, Vol. III, 242–251.
12. Strik-Strikfeldt, *Against Stalin and Hitler*, 95–100; Fischer, *Soviet Opposition to Stalin*, 32–38.
13. Sven Steenberg, *Vlasov*, 69–76.
14. Steenberg, *Vlasov*, 91–92, 130; Gehlen, *The Service*, trans. Irving, 89.
15. *Nazi Conspiracy and Aggression*, Vol. III, 959–960.
16. On the cooperation between the Vlasovites and the NTS, see Steenberg, trans. Farbstein, *Vlasov*, 29–67, 110–111, 126–127, 163–164, 185.
17. See Chapter 13.
18. Mellenthin, *German Generals*, 46. Pannwitz's Oak Leaves were awarded to him by the Führer in person on 15 January 1943. During the occasion, Hitler had asked the lieutenant-colonel about his Cossacks, indicating some knowledge of Pannwitz's project.
19. Newland, *Cossacks in the German Army*, 110–114; Huxley-Blythe, *The East Came West*, 57–59; Lannoy, *Les Cosaques de Pannwitz*, 27.
20. Newland, *Cossacks in the German Army*, 112–121.
21. Huxley-Blythe, *The East Came West*, 57–58. Photos of the Cossack division can be found in Lannoy, *Les Cosaques de Pannwitz*.
22. Naumenko, Vyacheslav G., *Great Betrayal*, trans. William Dritschilo (CreateSpace Independent Publisher, 2015 edition; first published in New York by Slavic Publishing House, 1962) 42–43.
23. Newland, *Cossacks in the German Army*, 124.
24. See Chapter 14.
25. Mellenthin, *German Generals*, 47.
26. Mellenthin, *German Generals*, 42.
27. Naumenko, *Great Betrayal*, 38.
28. Huxley-Blythe, *The East Came West*, 53–68.
29. Herwarth, *Against Two Evils*, 266. Officially, Cossacks and Caucasians were to be spared the worst treatment but it its likely that few local authorities bothered to distinguish these groups from Slavic "*untermenschen*."
30. *Trial of the Major War Criminals before the International Military Tribunal*, 14 November 1945–1 October 1946, Volume XV (Nuremberg: International Military Tribunal, 1947), 567–568.
31. Herwarth, *Against Two Evils*, 236.
32. *Nazi Conspiracy and Aggression*, Vol. IV, 112–114.
33. Kellogg, *Russian Roots of Nazism*, 263–265.
34. Huxley-Blythe, *East Came West*, 43–45; Newland, *Cossacks in the German Army*,138–139.
35. Nikolay N. Krasnov, *The Hidden Russia* (New York: Henry Holt and Company, 1960) 19.
36. See Chapter 12.
37. Newland, *Cossacks in the German Army*, 95.
38. Huxley-Blythe, *East Came West*, 19.
39. Naumenko, *Great Betrayal*, 77.
40. Strik-Strikfeldt, *Against Stalin and Hitler*, 157.
41. Dallin, *German Rule in Russia*, 113–114.
42. Two men affiliated with the Vlasov movement, M. A. Zykov and G. N. Zhilenkov, showed considerable distrust towards the old émigrés. See Steenberg, *Vlasov*, 44–46, 55–62.
43. Huxley-Blythe, in *The East Came West*, 43–44, attributes the following quote to Krasnov: "The Cossacks! Are they an exclusive nationality? Perhaps a distinct tribe? No, they are Russians who possess their own traditions." Even in 1944, when Krasnov was catering to Cossack separatists, he wrote, "Among the peoples of Russia there are branches: Great Russians, Ukrainians, Belorussians and there are also Cossacks…," seemingly implying that "Russia" and the "Cossacks" were inseparable. See Glazkov, *History of the Cossacks*, 13.
44. Huxley-Blythe, *East Came West*, 43–44, 47–48.
45. Newland, *Cossacks in the German Army*, 115–116; Robinson, *White Russian Army in Exile*, 81–83. For photos of Pannwitz's bodyguard, see Lannoy, *Les Cosaques de Pannwitz*, 100–103.
46. Lannoy, *Les Cosaques de Pannwitz*, 35.
47. Newland, *Cossacks in the German Army*, 121–123; Lannoy, *Les Cosaques de Pannwitz*, 34–35.
48. Huxley-Blythe, *East Came West*, 61–62.
49. Huxley-Blythe, *East Came West*, 63–64.
50. Naumenko, *Great Betrayal*, 57.
51. Littlejohn, *Foreign Legions of the Third Reich*, 277.
52. Newland, *Cossacks in the German Army*, 60–61. The estimated number of Osttruppen serving with the Germans by the latter part of 1943 ranges from 500,000 to 1,000,000. See Littlejohn, *Foreign Legions of the Third Reich*, 330; Ailsby, *Hitler's Renegades*, 172.
53. Littlejohn, *Foreign Legions of the Third Reich*, 330–331.
54. Herwarth, *Against Two Evils*, 264.

Chapter 15

1. Clark, *Barbarossa*, 304–306.
2. Werth, *Russia at War*, 703; Glantz and House, *When Titans Clashed*, 217–229.
3. Navahrudak (Nowogródek) was controlled by Poland until the Soviet invasion of that country in September 1939, after which it was incorporated into the Belarusian SSR.
4. The figure of 25,000 Cossacks at Novogrodek is from Newland, *Cossacks in the German Army*, 133. Huxley-Blythe, in *The East Came West*, 54–55, gives a much higher total of 100,000 refugees at Novogrodek.
5. Glantz and House, *When Titans Clashed*, 255.
6. Newland, *Cossacks in the German Army*, 131–133, Huxley-Blythe, *East Came West*, 67.
7. Naumenko, *Great Betrayal*, 98–103, 259–267.
8. Tolstoy, *Victims of Yalta*, 151–152; Huxley-Blythe, *East Came West*, 54–55, 67–69.
9. Lannoy, *Les Cosaques de Pannwitz*, 173.
10. On the appointment of Domanov, see Naumenko, *Great Betrayal*, 103–104.
11. Glantz and House, *When Titans Clashed*, 256–278; Werth, *Russia at War*, 778–786.
12. Naumenko, trans. Dritschilo, *Great Betrayal*, 63.
13. Newland, *Cossacks in the German Army*, 135–

136; Tolstoy, *Victims of Yalta*, 152–153; Naumenko, *Great Betrayal*, 89.

14. See Chapter 8.

15. The 10 November 1943 proclamation is reproduced in Newland, *Cossacks in the German Army*, 140.

16. *Nazi Conspiracy and Aggression*, Vol. VII, 920–976.

17. Köstring was appointed General der Osttruppen on 1 January 1944 after his predecessor, General Hellmich, requested another assignment. See Thorwald, *The Illusion*, trans. Richard and Clara Winston, 181 and Herwarth, *Against Two Evils*, 262. According to Herwarth, who served as Köstring's aide-de-camp until the end of the war, the official title of the post was changed to General der Freiwilligenverbände (Volunteer units).

18. Newland, *Cossacks in the German Army*, 141.

19. Newland, *Cossacks in the German Army*, 96–98; Steenberg, trans. Farbstein, *Vlasov*, 155–156.

20. Huxley-Blythe, *East Came West*, 50–51; Newland, *Cossacks in the German Army*, 96–98. On the NTS employment of Ostministrium's propaganda center (Wustrau) and the Wehrmacht's propaganda center (Dabendorf), see Fischer, *Soviet Opposition to Hitler*, 20, 69. There is no better evidence of Ostministrium's decline than the resignation which Rosenberg tendered to Hitler on 12 October 1944. The Nazi dictator, who was increasingly estranged from his ministers in the aftermath of the failed 20 July 1944 plot to assassinate him, did not reply to the offer. The Ostminister and his office were shunted aside, but not dissolved, for the remainder of the war. Dallin, *German Rule In Russia*, 626–630.

21. Catherine Andreyev, *Vlasov and the Russian Liberation Movement* (Cambridge: Cambridge University Press, 1987) 62–63.

22. Steenberg, *Vlasov*, 143–148; Strik-Strikfeldt, *Against Stalin and Hitler*, 207–209.

23. Fischer, *Soviet Opposition to Stalin*, 85–90.

24. Fischer, *Soviet Opposition to Stalin*, 194–200. Emphasis in original. Despite the manifesto's demand for the "subordination" of the nationalities to KONR, historian Catherine Andreyev believed that Vlasov and his circle were genuinely committed to granting considerable self-determination to the nationalities. See *Vlasov and the Russian Liberation Movement*, 127.

25. Fischer, *Soviet Opposition to Stalin*, 90.

26. Steenberg, *Vlasov*, 117–118, 124.

27. Herwarth, *Against Two Evils*, 289–290.

28. Dallin, *German Rule in Russia*, 656.

29. Strik-Strikfeldt, *Against Stalin and Hitler*, 210.

30. Huxley-Blythe, *East Came West*, 51–53.

31. Littlejohn, *Foreign Legions of the Third Reich*, 334–335; Fischer, *Soviet Opposition to Stalin*, 95–97.

32. Paul Hehn, *The German Struggle Against Yugoslav Guerillas in World War II* (New York: East European Quarterly, 1979) 3.

33. Tomasevich, *War and Revolution in Yugoslavia*, 52, 242–247, 278.

34. In exchange for power and Axis sponsorship, the Ustaše regime handed over large tracts of Croatian territory to Italy, agreed to place an Italian royal on the Croatian throne and was forced to accept Italian military occupation in nearly half of its territory. For the majority of Croats, these concessions to their traditional enemy were too much to bear. See Tomasevich, *War and Revolution in Yugoslavia*, 239.

35. According to Tomasevich, Serbs comprised about 30 percent of the population of the Croatian state. Other ethnic groups, including Moslems (about 15 percent), Germans (2.5 percent), Jews and Gypsies (less than 1 percent for both) were also represented. *War and Revolution in Yugoslavia*, 335.

36. Tomasevich, *War and Revolution in Yugoslavia*, 380–415.

37. Hehn, *German Struggle Against Yugoslav Guerrillas*, 18–28.

38. Hehn, *German Struggle Against Yugoslav Guerrillas*, 21.

39. Quoted in Hehn, *German Struggle Against Yugoslav Guerrillas*, 73.

40. *Nazi Conspiracy and Aggression*, Vol. I, 339–341.

41. Tomasevich, *War and Revolution in Yugoslavia*, 142–144, 254–256; Hehn, *German Struggle Against Yugoslav Guerrillas*, 1.

42. Tomasevich, *War and Revolution in Yugoslavia*, 221; Hehn, *German Struggle Against Yugoslav Guerillas*, 3.

43. Tomasevich, *War and Revolution in Yugoslavia*, 254, 308–310.

44. Newland, *Cossacks in the German Army*, 143.

45. Stevan K. Pavlowitch, *Hitler's New Disorder* (New York: Columbia University Press, 2008) 191, 215. Partisan sources frequently claimed to have much higher numbers of fighters under the command; sometimes as many as 200,000–300,000.

46. Newland, *Cossacks in the German Army*, 150–153; Lannoy, *Les Cosaques de Pannwitz*, 61–67.

47. Mellenthin, *German Generals*, 48.

48. Newland, *Cossacks in the German Army*, 150–153; Tomasevich, *War and Revolution in Yugoslavia*, 303–306; Lannoy, *Les Cosaques de Pannwitz*, 61–67.

49. George Stein, *The Waffen SS* (Ithaca, NY: Cornell University Press, 1966) 179-184, 273–274.

50. Newland, *Cossacks in the German Army*, 150–153; Tomasevich, *War and Revolution in Yugoslavia*, 303–306.

51. Herwarth, *Against Two Evils*, 293.

52. Maclean, *Eastern Approaches*, 330–331.

53. Hehn, *German Struggle Against Yugoslav Guerillas*, 77; Tomasevich, *War and Revolution in Yugoslavia*, 230–231, 314.

54. Herwarth, *Against Two Evils*, 293.

55. Newland, *Cossacks in the German Army*, 155.

56. Quoted in Lannoy, *Les Cosaques de Pannwitz*, 69. Lannoy's book contains several photographs taken during visits by Naumenko, Shkuro and Glaise von Horstenau.

57. Newland, *Cossacks in the German Army*, 158–160; Tomasevich, *War and Revolution in Yugoslavia*, 314. After the attack at Dvar, the British airlifted Tito to the Allied-held Dalmatian island of Vis, where he was able to set up a more secure headquarters for the next several months. See Maclean, *Eastern Approaches*, 449–454.

58. Lannoy, *Les Cosaques de Pannwitz*, 67.

59. Werth, *Russia at War*, 816–824; Glantz and House, *When Titans Clashed*, 248–252.
60. Guderian, *Panzer Leader*, trans. Fitzgibbon, 368.
61. Tomasevich, *War and Revolution in Yugoslavia*, 752; Guderian, *Panzer Leader*, 368, 374; Maclean, *Eastern Approaches*, 470–497.
62. Stein, *Waffen SS*, xxvi–xxxii.
63. Stein, *Waffen SS*, 102. According to General Guderian (*Panzer Leader*, trans. Fitzgibbon, 422), Himmler also aspired to win Germany's highest military honor, the Knight's Cross.
64. Stein, *Waffen SS*, 227.
65. Stein, *Waffen SS*, 121–130.
66. *Nazi Conspiracy and Aggression*, Vol. IV, 558–572.
67. Newland, *Cossacks in the German Army*, 150–153; Tomasevich, *War and Revolution in Yugoslavia*, 303–306.
68. Stein, *Waffen SS*, 179.
69. Littlejohn, *Foreign Legions of the Third Reich*, 29–30; Stein, *Waffen SS*, 185–187. For a while, Himmler pretended that these men were neither Ukrainians nor Slavs and instead referred to them as "Galicians." Only in early 1945 was this division re-designated as "Ukrainian."
70. Littlejohn, *Foreign Legions of the Third Reich*, 309–312.
71. Thorwald, *The Illusion*, trans. Richard and Clara Winston, 187–204.
72. Strik-Strikfeldt, *Against Stalin and Hitler*, 161.
73. See Chapter 14.
74. Hitler, *Mien Kampf*, 285–329.
75. Newland, *Cossacks in the German Army*, 110.
76. Thorwald, *The Illusion*, trans. Richard and Clara Winston, 193.
77. Huxley-Blythe, *East Came West*, 82–84.
78. Quoted in Mellenthin, *German Generals*, 48–49.
79. Newland, *Cossacks in the German Army*, 141–145; Lannoy, *Les Cosaques de Pannwitz*, 69–73. The Waffen-SS had its own ranks and insignia independent of the Wehrmacht, but these were never used in the Cossack corps. For example, Pannwitz was given the rank of SS Grüppenführer though he never wore the uniform of that rank.
80. Stein, *Waffen SS*, 210–211.
81. Quoted in Nicholas Bethell, *The Last Secret* (New York: Basic Books, 1974) 2.
82. Tolstoy, *Victims of Yalta*, 45–47. According General F. W. von Mellenthin (*German Generals*, 38), by the end of October 1944 the Western Allies had captured approximately 28,000 Eastern peoples serving with the Wehrmacht.
83. Newland, *Cossacks in the German Army*, 156–158.
84. Tolstoy, *Victims of Yalta*, 227.
85. Newland, *Cossacks in the German Army*, 161–162; Huxley-Blythe, *The East Came West*, 84–87. Sources differ on whether the Cossacks were the defenders or attackers in this battle.
86. Lannoy, *Les Cosaques de Pannwitz*, 46–55, 77–78.
87. Newland, *Cossacks in the German Army*, 164.
88. Lannoy, *Les Cosaques de Pannwitz*, 78.

Chapter 16

1. For a perspective of Pannwitz from a veteran of the corps, see Lieutenant Nazarenko's testimonial in Naumenko's *Great Betrayal*, 37–38. Pannwitz's decision to use the Russian language was not without complications since not all of the division's German officers spoke Russian. As a result, interpreters had to be used as intermediaries between these officers and their men. See Lannoy, *Les Cosaques de Pannwitz*, 34.
2. Lannoy, *Les Cosaques de Pannwitz*, 67. At Hitler's behest, Cossacks and other Eastern peoples serving in the Wehrmacht were initially barred from receiving or wearing German medals and war badges, including the Iron Cross. From 1942–44, soldiers in Eastern battalions could only be awarded the "Decoration for Bravery and Merit for the Eastern Peoples." It was not until 1944 when Cossacks and other Eastern peoples finally became eligible to receive the Iron Cross. See Littlejohn, *Foreign Legions of the Third Reich*, 347–351 and Herwarth, *Against Two Evils*, 264.
3. An excerpt from this letter is reproduced in Mellenthin, *German Generals*, 49.
4. Lannoy, *Les Cosaques de Pannwitz*, 164–165.
5. Lannoy, *Les Cosaques de Pannwitz*, 78.
6. Newland, *Cossacks in the German Army*, 164–165.
7. Newland, *Cossacks in the German Army*, 166; Tomasevich, *War and Revolution in Yugoslavia*, 762.
8. Steenberg, trans. Farbstein, *Vlasov*, 182. Lannoy, *Les Cosaques de Pannwitz*, 79. Kononov's visit to Vlasov, which ultimately enabled him to escape the fate of the XV SS Cossack Cavalry Corps, is not without controversy. Some writers and historians have speculated that Pannwitz sent Kononov on a mission to Vlasov in order to relieve himself of a troublesome and ambitious subordinate. Others have claimed that Kononov sought to meet Vlasov on his own terms in the hope that the KONR leader would place him in command of the Cossack corps.
9. Fischer, *Soviet Opposition to Stalin*, 92; Steenberg, trans. Farbstein, *Vlasov*, 190. On 20 April 1945 Vlasov transferred his headquarter to the Bavarian town of Füssen.
10. Steenberg, trans. Farbstein, *Vlasov*, 182.
11. Strik-Strikfeldt, *Against Stalin and Hitler*, 227–229.
12. Huxley-Blythe, *East Came West*, 91–92. Colonel N. Nazarenko, an early Cossack collaborator and head of the Cossack War Veteran Association, expressed considerable distrust in Kononov during an interview conducted by Samuel Newland. Nazarenko believed Kononov was overly ambitious and even cast doubt on his credentials as a Don Cossack. See endnote in Newland, *Cossacks in the German Army*, 188.
13. Steenberg, trans. Farbstein, *Vlasov*, 183–184, 202–203.
14. Mellenthin *German Generals*, 50.
15. Strik-Strikfeldt, *Against Stalin and Hitler*, 227–228; Steenberg, trans. Farbstein, *Vlasov*, 190.

16. Tomasevich, *War and Revolution in Yugoslavia*, 752.
17. Grigoriev, Vladimir A., "With the Russian Corps," Stone and Glenny, *The Other Russia*, 243.
18. Huxley-Blythe, *East Came West*, 93–94.
19. Tomasevich, *War and Revolution in Yugoslavia*, 754–756; Newland, *Cossacks in the German Army*, 167–168.
20. Newland, *Cossacks in the German Army*, 167. In the closing days of the war, the Vlasovites also sent emissaries to Field Marshal Alexander without any success. See Steenberg, trans. Farbstein, *Vlasov*, 190–191.
21. Huxley-Blythe, *East Came West*, 95–97; Tolstoy, *Victims of Yalta*, 227–230. Unfortunately, these accounts do not agree on exact dates or details concerning the surrender of the XV SS Cossack Cavalry Corps.
22. Tolstoy, *Victims of Yalta*, 230–231; Lannoy, *Les Cosaques de Pannwitz*, 187–188.
23. Huxley-Blythe, *East Came West*, 99–100; Lannoy, *Les Cosaques de Pannwitz*, 188–189.
24. Tolstoy, *Victims of Yalta*, 233; Huxley-Blythe, *East Came West*, 99–100; Lannoy, *Les Cosaques de Pannwitz*, 188–189.
25. *Foreign Relations of the United States: Diplomatic Papers: The Conferences at Malta and Yalta, 1945* (Washington: United States Government Printing Office, 1955) 416–418.
26. Quoted in Bethell, *The Last Secret*, 91.
27. Tolstoy, *Victims of Yalta*, 233; Huxley-Blythe, *East Came West*, 101–102.
29. Tolstoy, *Victims of Yalta*, 238–243.
30. Tolstoy, *Victims of Yalta*, 234–236.
31. Tolstoy, *Victims of Yalta*, 234. Once again, the accounts differ on the date when Pannwitz taken into Soviet captivity. Tolstoy put that date at 28 May 1945, when the rest of the corps began to be turned over. But according to Huxley-Blythe, in *The East Came West*, 101–102, the commander of the Cossack corps was turned over on the same day of his arrest, 26 May.
31. Tolstoy, *Victims of Yalta*, 236.
32. Tolstoy, *Victims of Yalta*, 245–247.
33. For example, see Nikolay Tolstoy's *Victims of Yalta*, Julius Epstein's *Operation Keelhaul*, Nicholas Bethell's *The Last Secret* and Peter Huxley-Blythe's *The East Came West*. The Americans, however, do seem to have been more cautious about handing over old émigrés than their British counterparts.
34. On controversy surrounding the repatriation of old émigrés, see Tolstoy, *Victims of Yalta*, 249–253 and Lannoy, *Cosaques de Pannwitz*, 190.
35. Naumenko, *Great Betrayal*, 104–107.
36. Huxley-Blythe, *East Came West*, 51–53.
37. Naumenko, *Great Betrayal*, 107.
38. Huxley-Blythe, *East Came West*, 52–53.
39. Naumenko, *Great Betrayal*, 261.
40. Naumenko, *Great Betrayal*, 126–129, 132–136.
41. Naumenko, *Great Betrayal*, 113.
42. Tolstoy, *Victims of Yalta*, 154–158.
43. Nikolay N. Krasnov, Jr, *The Hidden Russia* (New York: Henry Holt, 1960) 11; Tolstoy, *Victims of Yalta*, 158–159.
44. Naumenko, *Great Betrayal*, 113.
45. For example, the Ataman Naumenko published his compilation of survivor and witness testimony of the repatriation of the anti-Soviet Cossacks under the title of *Great Betrayal*. Lieutenant N. N. Krasnov, in his memoir *The Hidden Russia*, entitled a chapter *Betrayal at Lienz* (9–31).
46. Tolstoy, *Victims of Yalta*, 159–160.
47. The figure of 22,000 for Domanov's Cossacks is from British figures used by Nicholas Bethell in *The Last Secret*, 82. Tolstoy (*Victims of Yalta*, 161) has given a slightly higher number of 23,000 while the Cossacks estimated their numbers much larger at 30,000–35,000. Efforts to count the Cossacks in the Drau valley were made difficult by the loose organization of their camps and the relative freedom of movement they enjoyed just prior to repatriation.
48. Tolstoy, *Victims of Yalta*, 156–157.
49. Krasnov, *Hidden Russia*, 10. An incident of Cossacks robbing retreating German soldiers is described in Naumenko, *Great Betrayal*, 113.
50. Krasnov, *Hidden Russia*, 12–13.
51. Lannoy, *Les Cosaques de Pannwitz*, 197.
52. Krasnov, *Hidden Russia*, 12.
53. Tolstoy, *Victims of Yalta*, 163.
54. Tolstoy, *Victims of Yalta*, 164–165.
55. Tolstoy, *Victims of Yalta*, 166–168.
56. Epstein, *Keelhaul*, 76–77; Tolstoy, *Victims of Yalta*, 169.
57. Krasnov, *Hidden Russia*, 14.
58. Huxley-Blythe, *East Came West*, 122, 127. According to Tolstoy (*Victims of Yalta*, 169–170) the majority of Cossacks were not disarmed until 27 May, but this seems unlikely since by then plans were moving forward to round-up the Cossack officers on the following day.
59. Naumenko, *Great Betrayal*, 156–157.
60. Huxley-Blythe, *East Came West*, 131–132; Krasnov, *Hidden Russia*, 21.
61. For more on this controversy, see Bethell, *Last Secret*, 103–104.
62. Naumenko, *Great Betrayal*, 129–131.
63. Naumenko, *Great Betrayal*, 270–275.
64. Tolstoy, *Victims of Yalta*, 180–182; Huxley-Blythe, *East Came West*, 139. Domanov, according to Soviet interrogators, was a former NKVD operative who was supposed to organize resistance against the Germans during their occupation of the Caucasus. All evidence, however, indicates that Domanov worked against the Soviet regime from 1942 onward.
65. Bethell, *Last Secret*, 114.
66. Tolstoy, *Victims of Yalta*, 184.
67. Tolstoy, *Victims of Yalta*, 250.
68. Naumenko, *Great Betrayal*, 144.
69. Tolstoy, *Victims of Yalta*, 250–251. According to a pair of Caucasian witnesses, the British offered to spare Ghirey as an old émigré when they began detaining officers from the Caucasian camp. Ghirey declined to abandon his men but another prominent veteran of Wrangel's army, General Kuchuk Ulagay, accepted the offer and survived the ordeal. See Naumenko, *Great Betrayal*, 170–172.

70. Krasnov, *Hidden Russia*, 40.
71. Krasnov, *Hidden Russia*, 42.
72. Naumenko, *Great Betrayal*, 172–174.
73. Tolstoy, *Victims of Yalta*, 186.
74. Tolstoy, *Victims of Yalta*, 199.
75. Naumenko, *Great Betrayal*, 183–184. The hunger strike, placards, black flags and other demonstrations against forced repatriation are corroborated by numerous other accounts from survivors of Cossachi Stan.
76. Tolstoy, *Victims of Yalta*, 201–202.
77. Naumenko, *Great Betrayal*, 199.
78. Naumenko, *Great Betrayal*, 198; Bethell, *Last Secret*, 128.
79. Naumenko, *Great Betrayal*, 206.
80. Naumenko, *Great Betrayal*, 206; 234. Similar murder-suicides were reportedly carried out in the forests as a parent (usually the father) dispatched the entire family before turning their sidearm on themselves.
81. Tolstoy, *Victims of Yalta*, 203–213; Bethell, *Last Secret*, 142–144. Olga Rotova's account, which for the most part is consistent with that of other witnesses to the events at Camp Peggetz, claims 700 Cossacks fell victim to beating, trampling, drowning or other forms of suicide on 1 June 1945. See Naumenko, *Great Betrayal*, 210.
82. Bethell, *Last Secret*, 158; Lannoy, *Cosaques de Pannwitz*, 184.
83. Naumenko, *Great Betrayal*, 192.
84. Tolstoy, *Victims of Yalta*, 213–222; Bethell, *Last Secret*, 148–157; Naumenko, *Great Betrayal*, 132–136, 170–172, 198–203.
85. Stephan, *Russian Fascists*, 314–316.
86. Stephan, *Russian Fascists*, 317–320.
87. See Chapter 12.
88. Stephan, *Russian Fascists*, 320–321.
89. Stephan, *Russian Fascists*, 320–324; Werth, *Russia at War*, 926–927.
90. Glantz and House, *When Titans Clashed*, 349, Stephan, *Russian Fascists*, 321–324, 349.
91. Stephan, *Russian Fascists*, 322–323.
92. Glantz and House, *When Titans Clashed*, 352.
93. Stephan, *Russian Fascists*, 334–335.
94. Stephan, *Russian Fascists*, 329–332.
95. The versions of Semyonov's capture can be found in Stephan, *Russian Fascists*, 333–334 and Bisher, *White Terror*, 310. These two works, however, disagree on whether Semyonov and his associates were brought to Moscow or to Khabarovsk to stand trial.
96. Stephan, *Russian Fascists*, 342–343; Bisher, *White Terror*, 310.
97. Solzhenitsyn, *Gulag Archipelago*, 85.
98. Krasnov, *Hidden Russia*, 288.
99. Stephan, *Russian Fascists*, 332–351.
100. Stone and Glenny, *The Other Russia*, 220–221.

Epilogue

1. Krasnov, *From Double Eagle to Red Flag*, 753–810.
2. Applebaum, *Gulag*, 134–145.
3. Krasnov, *Hidden Russia*, 58.
4. Steenberg, trans. Farbstein, *Vlasov*, 225–226.
5. Stephan, *Russian Fascists*, 351–354; Stephan, *Russian Far East*, 245; Bisher, *White Terror*, 311. The two lesser defendants tried with Semyonov's group were handed fifteen- and twenty-year terms in the Gulag camps.
6. Huxley-Blythe, *East Came West*, 140–142, Lannoy, *Cosaques de Pannwitz*, 195–197.
7. Steenberg, trans. Farbstein, *Vlasov*, 217.
8. Krasnov, *Hidden Russia*, 127.
9. Reshetar, *Ukranian Revolution*, 206.
10. Bethell, *Last Secret*, 160–163; Tolstoy, *Victims of Yalta*, 402–403.
11. Krasnov, *Hidden Russia*, 148.
12. Solzhenitsyn, *Gulag Archipelago*, 262.
13. Krasnov, *Hidden Russia*. For another account of the Cossacks' experience inside the Gulag, see Bethell, *Last Secret*, 160–163. For general description of conditions in the labor camps, see Anne Applebaum's *Gulag*.
14. Estimates for the number of Soviet nationals among displaced citizens and the figures of those who had to be forcibly repatriated are variable. Julius Epstein (*Keelhaul*, 71) estimated that 6,000,000–7,000,000 Soviet nationals were repatriated in the aftermath of the Second World War. Of those, he believed that 1,500,000–2,000,000 were returned against their will. Robert Thurston, in his essay "Cauldrons of Loyalty and Betrayal: Soviet Soldiers' Behavior, 1941 and 1945" (Thurston and Bonwetsch, *The People's War*, 235–257) has written that the number of Soviet nationals in German-controlled areas near the end of war was closer to 5,000,000 and that their resistance to repatriation has been inflated by Western authors.
15. Epstein, *Keelhaul*, 20–21.
16. Applebaum, *Gulag*, 30–31, 54–56, 73–75.
17. Applebaum, *Gulag*, 466.
18. Krasnov, *Hidden Russia*, 189.
19. Applebaum, *Gulag*, 476–483.
20. Krasnov, *Hidden Russia*, 213.
21. Applebaum, *Gulag*, 476–483, 506–507; Krasnov, *Hidden Russia*, 272.
22. Tolstoy, *Victims of Yalta*, 409; Lannoy, *Cosaques de Pannwitz*, 197.
23. Ratushnyak, O. V., "The Cossack Émigré in 1945–1960," Krasnodar, *Historical and Social Educational Ideas*, 2016, Vol. 8, No. 3, Part 2, 59–68, DOI: 10:17748/2075-9908-2016-8-3/2-59-68. (In Russian).
24. Krasnov, *Hidden Russia*, 271–272.
25. Krasnov, *Hidden Russia*, 297–334; Lannoy, *Cosaques de Pannwitz*, 197.
26. For full text of the petition, see Huxley-Blythe, *East Came West*, 203–204.
27. For full text of these documents, see Huxley-Blythe, *East Came West*, 205–210.
28. A 8 February 1955 resolution introduced by Congressman Albert Bosch (R-NY) to form an committee to investigate the postwar compulsory repatriation of Soviet nationals went nowhere. Huxley-Blythe, *East Came West*, 171.

29. See foreword by Brigadier General (ret.) Frank Howley in Krasnov, *Hidden Russia*, ix–x.

30. Huxley-Blythe, *East Came West*, 210–213. Malcolm's letter also vehemently disputes the accounts of Cossack survivors that excessive force was used to compel members of Cossachi Stan to board trucks and trains.

31. Huxley-Blythe, *East Came West*, 219.

32. Public Law 86-90, Joint Resolution 111: Providing for the designation of the third week of July as "Captive Nations Week," Government Publishing Office, 17 July 1959, www.gpo.gov/fdsys/pkg/STATUTE-73/pdf/STATUTE-73-pg212.pdf.

33. Huxley-Blythe, *East Came West*, 219. It should be pointed out that here that Huxley-Blythe was well-connected with Cossack and Russian émigré groups that held right-wing political views.

34. Ratushnyak, O. V., "The Cossack Émigré in 1945–1960," Krasnodar, *Historical and Social Educational Ideas*, 2016, Vol. 8, No. 3, Part 2, 59–68, DOI: 10:17748/2075-9908-2016-8-3/2-59-68. (In Russian).

35. de Lannoy, *Cosaques de Pannwitz*, 227–228.

36. Huxley-Blythe, *East Came West*, 92.

37. Koriakov, trans. Wreden, 214.

38. Koriakov, trans. Wreden, *I'll Never Go Back*, 194–217. Most old émigrés gradually lost their pro-Soviet enthusiasm during 1945–1947 as the Communist regime reverted to its prewar levels of repression. See Andreyev, *Vlasov and the Russian Liberation Movement*, 171–172.

39. Ratushnyak, O. V., "Adaption of the Cossack Emigrants to the Style of Living Abroad," *Historical and Social-educational Ideas*, 2014, 6 (6_2): 156, DOI:10.17748/2075-9908-2014-6-6_2-156-158. On Denikin's final years, see Lehovich, *White Against Red*, 450–494. The full text of his letter to Eisenhower can be found in Epstein, *Operation Keelhaul*, 213–215.

40. For a survey of the postwar activities of the NTS, see Gordon Young's *The House of Secrets* (New York: Duell, Sloan and Pearce, 1959).

41. Ratushnyak, O. V., "Adaption of the Cossack Emigrants to the Style of Living Abroad," *Historical and Social-educational Ideas*, 2014, 6 (6_2): 156, DOI:10.17748/2075-9908-2014-6-6_2-156-158.

42. Ratushnyak, O. V., "The Cossack Émigré in 1945–1960," Krasnodar, *Historical and Social Educational Ideas*, 2016, Vol. 8, No. 3, Part 2, 59–68, DOI: 10:17748/2075-9908-2016-8-3/2-59-68. (In Russian).

43. Petrov and Petrov, *Empire of Fear*, 261–263.

44. Werth, *Russia at War*, 711.

45. Forsyth, *The Caucasus*, 718.

46. For a study of these operations, see *The Punished Peoples* (New York: W. W. Norton, 1978) by Soviet dissident author Aleksandr Nekrich.

47. For example, in early 1943 the Cossacks held second-place among Osttruppen battalions formed along broad ethnic lines. Their 24 battalions was surpassed by the Turkic peoples with 33 battalions but was still well ahead that of other favored peoples, including the North Caucasians who ranked third with 13 battalions. See chart in Gehlen, *The Service*, 86.

48. Applebaum, *Gulag*, 426–427.

49. On the 1–2 June 1962 incident in Novocherkassk, see the online archive "Seventeen Moments in Soviet History" at http://soviethistory.msu.edu/novocherkassk-massacre-texts and David Remnick, *Lenin's Tomb* (New York: Random House, 1993) 414–419.

50. Stratfor Global Intelligence, "Russia Again Cautiously Embraces the Cossacks," 20 September 2015, www.stratfor.com/analysis/russia-again-cautiously-embraces-cossacks. Accessed on 23 October 2015.

51. "Seventeen Moments in Soviet History," http://soviethistory.msu.edu/novocherkassk-massacre-texts; David Remnick, *Lenin's Tomb* (New York: Random House, 1993) 414–419.

52. See Remnick, *Lenin's Tomb*, 47–50, 399–400; Applebaum, *Gulag*, 556–563.

53. Remnick, *Lenin's Tomb*, 60.

54. O'Rourke, *Cossacks*, 282, Forsyth, *Caucasus*, 718–719; Olga V. Rvacheva, "The Cossack Restoration Movement in the South of Russia in the Early 1990s: Organization, Ideas and Participants," 2016 (In Russ.) DOI:10.15688/jvolsu4.2016.4.13.

55. Ure, *Cossacks*, 231; Forsyth, *Caucasus*, 719–720.

56. O'Rourke, *Cossacks*, 283–284; Forsyth, *Caucasus*, 720.

57. Kislitsyn, S. A., "Phenomenon of Cossack Estate Quasi-Statehood and its Significance," *Historical and Social Educational Ideas*, 2016; Vol. 8, no. 4, Part 1, 78–86 (In Russ.) DOI: 10.17748/2075-9908-2016-8-4/1-1-78-86; Forsyth, *Caucasus*, 720.

58. Forsyth, *Caucasus*, 720, 734.

59. Interestingly, Eurasianism experienced a revival during the 1990s among Russians seeking to justify the preservation or restoration of the Soviet empire. See Dunlop, *The Rise of Russia and the Fall of the Soviet Empire*, 290–293.

60. Stephan, *Russian Far East*, 300.

61. Ellen Barry, "The Cossacks Are Back. May the Hills Tremble." *The New York Times*, 16 March 2013, www.nytimes.com/2013/03/17/worl/europe/cossacks-are-back-in-russia-may-the-hills-tremble.html. Accessed on 24 February 2014; Luhn, Alec, "The Cossacks Ride Again," *Slate*, 31 January 2014, http://www.slate.com/articles/news_and_politics/roads/2014/01/cossacks_will_patrol_the_sochi_olympics_vladimir_putin_is_drafting_these.html, Retrieved 3 February 2015; Dan Peleschuk, "Russia's Cossacks Return," *Public Radio International/GlobalPost*, 5 May 2013, www.pri.org/stories/2013-05-05/russia-s-cossacks-return. Accessed 24 May 2017.

62. Tkachev's quote appears in two sources: Luhn, Alec, "The Cossacks Ride Again," *Slate*, 31 January 2014, http://www.slate.com/articles/news_and_politics/roads/2014/01/cossacks_will_patrol_the_sochi_olympics_vladimir_putin_is_drafting_these.html, Retrieved 3 February 2015 and Barry, Ellen, "The Cossacks are Back. May the Hills Tremble.," *The New York Times*, 16 March 2013, http://www.nytimes.com/2013/03/17/world/europe/cossacks-are-back-in-russia-may-the-hills-tremble.html. Retrieved 24 February 2014.

63. Luhn, Alec, "The Cossacks Ride Again," *Slate*, 31 January 2014, http://www.slate.com/articles/news_and_politics/roads/2014/01/cossacks_will_patrol_the_sochi_olympics_vladimir_putin_is_drafting_these.html, Retrieved 3 February 2015; Peleschuk, Dan, "Russia's Cossacks Return," *Public Radio International/GlobalPost*, 5 May 2013, www.pri.org/stories/2013-05-05/russia-s-cossacks-return. Accessed 24 May 2017.

64. Bershidsky, Leonid, "Russia is Losing World War II," *Bloomberg View*, 8 May 2015, http://www.bloombergview.com/articles/2015-05-08/russia-is-losing-world-war-ii?cmpid=yhoo, Retrieved 8 May 2015.

65. See BBC News, "Donald Trump: Why the next U.S. President in popular with Cossacks," 19 November 2016, www.bbc.com/new/world-europe-38029642. Accessed on 26 April 2017. Matt Payton, "Donald Trump has been made an honorary Russian Cossack," *The Independent*, 12 November 2016, www.independent.co.uk/news/world/americas/donald-trump-russian-cossack-vladimir-putin-us-president-elect-election-victory-a7413601.html. Accessed 26 April 2017. This group is the Irbis Cossacks based in a village north of St. Petersburg. A few months later, in April 2017, the Irbis Cossacks considered withdrawing the honor after then President Trump commenced a round of missile strikes against airbases controlled by Russia's Syrian ally. Continued fallout over Syria eventually led them to strip President Trump of Cossack status in April 2018. See David R. Sands, "Russian warrior clan strips Trump of 'honorary Cossack' status," *The Washington Times*, 11 April 2018, https://www.washingtontimes.com/news/2018/apr/11/trump-no-longer-honorary-cossack/. Accessed 6 February 2019.

66. Mikhail Zygar, "Putin Likes to Pretend 1917 Never Happened," trans. Julia Ioffe, *The Atlantic*, 1 April 2017, https://www.theatlantic.com/international/archive/2017/russia-putin-revolution-lenin-nicholas-1917/521571. Accessed 3 April 2017.

67. Simon Shuster, "Meet the Cossack 'Wolves' Doing Russia's Dirty Work in Ukraine," *Time*, 12 May 2014, http://time.com/95898/wolves-hundred-ukraine-russia-cossack/. Accessed on 22 October 2014. Interestingly, the German commander of the XV SS Cossack Cavalry Corps, General Helmuth von Pannwitz, was rehabilitated on 17 July 1996. A similar request to rehabilitate Shkuro, Pytor Krasnov and the Cossack generals executed with them, however, was rejected during the following year. Lannoy, *Les Cosaques de Pannwitz*, 253–255.

68. Hanna Kozlowska, "'Cossack' at the Heart of Kiev Protests Refuses to Give In," *Foreign Policy*, 27 January 2014, www.foreignpolicy.com/2014/01/27/cossack-at-the-heart-of-kiev-protests-refuses-to-give-in. Accessed 4 February 2015.

69. Stratfor Global Intelligence, "Russia Again Cautiously Embraces the Cossacks," 20 September 2015, http://www.stratfor.com/analysis/russia-again-cautiously-embraces-cossacks. Accessed on 23 October 2015.

Bibliography

Original Documents and References

Bunyan, James, ed., *Intervention, Civil War and Communism in Russia* (New York: Octagon, 1976).

Bunyan, James, and H. H. Fisher, *The Bolshevik Revolution* (Stanford: Stanford University Press, 1965).

Butt, V. P., A. B. Murphy, N. A. Myshov and G. R. Swain, *The Russian Civil War* (New York: St. Martin's Press, 1996).

Chief of Counsel for Prosecution of Axis Criminality, *Nazi Conspiracy and Aggression*, Vol. I—XIII (Washington: United States Government Printing Office, 1947-1948).

McCauley, Martin, *The Russian Revolution and the Soviet State 1917-1921* (London: The Macmillan Press, 1975).

Murphy, A. B., *The Russian Civil War* (New York: St. Martin's Press, 2000).

Publications of the Department of State, *Papers Relating to the Foreign Relations of the United States: 1918: Russia* (Washington: U.S. Government Printing Office, 1931).

Publications of the Department of State, *Papers Relating to the Foreign Relations of the United States: 1919: Russia* (Washington: U.S. Government Printing Office, 1937).

Trial of the Major War Criminals before the International Military Tribunal, 14 November 1945-1 October 1946, Volume XV (Nuremberg: International Military Tribunal, 1947).

Memoirs and First-Person Accounts

Alioshin, Dmitri, *Asian Odyssey* (New York: Henry Holt and Co., 1940)

Aten, Marion, and Arthur Orrmont, *Last Train over Rostov Bridge* (New York: Julian Messner Inc., 1961)

Babel, Isaak, *1920 Diary*, trans. H. T. Willetts (New Haven: Yale University Press, 1995).

Bechhofer, C. E., *In Denikin's Russia* (London: W. Collins & Sons, 1921).

Bečvar, Gustav, *The Lost Legion* (London: Stanley Paul, 1939).

Denikin, General Anton, *The Russian Turmoil* (Westport: Hyperion Press, 1973).

Denikin, General Anton, *The White Army*, trans. Catherine Zvegintzov (Gulf Breeze: Academic International Press, 1973).

Dotsenko, Paul, *The Struggle for a Democracy in Siberia* (Stanford, Hoover Institution Press, 1983).

Dune, Eduard, *Notes of a Red Guard*, trans. Diane Koenker and S. A. Smith (Chicago: University of Illinois Press, 1993).

Farmborough, Florence, *Nurse at the Russian Front* (London: Constable, 1970).

Fischer, Louis, editor, and Boris A. Yakovlev, subeditor, *Thirteen Who Fled*, trans. Gloria and Victor Fischer (New York: Harper & Brothers Publishers, 1949).

Gehlen, General Reinhard, *The Service*, trans. David Irving (New York: World Publishing Company, 1972).

Golder, Frank, *War, Revolution and Peace in Russia* (Stanford: Hoover Institution Press, 1992).

Graves, General William, *America's Siberian Adventure* (New York: Peter Smith, 1941).

Guderian, General Heinz, *Panzer Leader*, trans. Constantine Fitzgibbon (London: Michael Joseph Ltd., 1952).

Halder, Franz, Charles Burdick and Hans-Adolf Jacobsen, ed., *The Halder War Diary 1939-1942* (Novato, CA: Presido Press, 1988).

Herwarth, Hans von, with S. Frederick Starr, *Against Two Evils* (New York: Rawson, Wade Publishers, Inc, 1981).

Hoffmann, Major-General Max, *War Diaries and Other Papers*, trans. Eric Sutton (London: Martin Secker, 1929).

Kerensky, Alexander, *The Catastrophe* (New York: D. Appleton and Company, 1927)

Kern, Erich, *Dance of Death* (London: Collins, 1951).

Knox, Major-General Alfred, *With the Russian Army 1914-1917* (New York: Arno Press, 1971).

Koriakov, Mikhail, *I'll Never Go Back*, trans. Nicholas Wreden (New York: E. P. Dutton & Company, 1948).

Kournakoff, Sergei, *Savage Squadrons* (Boston: Hale, Cushman & Flint, 1935).

Littauer, Vladimir, *Russian Hussar* (Shippensburg: White Mane Publishing, 1993).

Lobanov-Rostovsky, Prince A., *The Grinding Mill* (New York: The Macmillan Company, 1935).

Lukomsky, General Aleksandr, *Memoirs of the Russian Revolution*, trans. Mrs. Vitali (Westport: Hyperion Press, 1975).

Maclean, Fitzroy, *Eastern Approaches* (London: Jonathan Cape, 1949).

McCullagh, Francis, *A Prisoner of the Reds* (New York: E. P. Dutton, 1922).

Naumenko, Vyacheslav G., *Great Betrayal*, trans. Wil-

liam Dritschilo (CreateSpace Independent Publisher, 2015 edition; first published in New York by Slavic Publishing House, 1962.)
Ossendowski, Ferdinand, *Beasts, Men and Gods* (New York: E. P. Dutton, 1923).
Strik-Strikfeldt, Wilfried, *Against Stalin and Hitler*, trans. David Footman (London: Macmillan, 1970)
Ward, John, *With the "Die-Hards" in Siberia* (London: Cassell, 1920).
Williamson, Brigadier H. N. H., John Harris, ed., *Farewell to the Don* (New York: The John Day Company, 1971).
Woytinsky, Wladimir S., *Stormy Passage* (New York, Vanguard Press, 1961).
Wrangel, General Baron Peter, *Always With Honour* (New York: Robert Speller & Sons, 1957).
Yurlova, Marina, *Cossack Girl* (New York: The Macaulay Company, 1934).

Secondary Sources

Ailsby, Christopher, *Htiler's Renegades: Foreign Nationals in the Service of the Third Reich* (Duiles, VA: Brassey's Inc., 2004).
Andreyev, Catherine, *Vlasov and the Russian Liberation Movement* (Cambridge: Cambridge University Press, 1987).
Andreyev, Catherine, and Ivan Savický, *Russia Abroad: Prague and the Russian Diaspora, 1918-1938* (New Haven: Yale University Press, 2004).
Applebaum, Anne, *Gulag: A History* (New York: Doubleday, 2003).
Baerlein, Henry, *The March of the Seventy Thousand* (London: Leonard Parsons, 1926)
Beevor, Antony, *Stalingrad* (New York: Penguin, 1999).
Bethell, Nicholas, *The Last Secret* (New York: Basic Books, 1974).
Bisher, Jamie, *White Terror* (New York: Routledge, 2005).
Bobrick, Benson, *East of the Sun* (New York: Poseidon Press, 1992).
Brinkley, George, *The Volunteer Army and Allied Intervention in South Russia* (Notre Dame: University of Notre Dame Press, 1966)
Brovkin, Vladimir (editor), *The Bolsheviks in Russian Society* (New Haven: Yale University Press, 1997).
Carmichael, Joel, *Stalin's Masterpiece: The Show Trials and Purges of the Thirties—the Consolidation of the Bolshevik Dictatorship* (London: Weidenfeld and Nicolson, 1976).
Chamberlin, William Henry, *The Russian Revolution*, Vol. 2 (New York: Grosset & Dunlap, 1965).
Chamberlin, William Henry, *Russia's Iron Age* (Boston: Little, Brown and Company, 1934).
Clark, Alan, *Barbarossa: The Russian—German Conflict 1941-1945* (New York: William Morrow and Company, 1965).
Coates, W. P., and Zelda Coates, *Armed Intervention in Russia 1918-1922* (London: Victor Gollanz Ltd., 1935).
Conquest, Robert, *The Harvest of Sorrow* (New York: Oxford University Press, 1986).
Cooper, Matthew, *The Nazi War Against Soviet Partisans 1941-1944* (New York: Stein and Day, 1979).

Cornish, Nik, *The Russian Army and the First World War* (Gloucestershire: Spellmount, 2006).
Cornwall, Mark, editor, *The Last Years of Austria-Hungary* (Exeter: University of Exeter Press, 2002).
Cresson, William Penn, *The Cossacks: Their History and Country* (New York: Brentano's, 1919).
Danilov, Viktor, *Rural Russia under the New Regime*, trans. Orlando Figes (London: Hutchinson, 1988).
DiMarco, Louis, *War Horse* (Yardley: Westholme Publishing, 2008).
Dunlop, John B., *The Rise of Russia and the Fall of the Soviet Empire* (Princeton: Princeton University Press, 1993).
Dupuy, Ernest, *Perish by the Sword* (Harrisburg, PA: The Military Service Publishing Company, 1939).
Dvinov, Boris, *Politics of the Russian Emigration* (Santa Monica: Rand, 1955).
Emmons, Terrence, and Bertrand Patenaude (editors), *War, Revolution and Peace in Russia: The Passages of Frank Golder, 1914-1927* (Stanford: Hoover Institution Press, 1992).
Epstein, Julius, *Operation Keelhaul* (Old Greenwich, CT: The Devin-Adair Company, 1973).
Feodoroff, Nicholas, *History of the Cossacks* (Commack: Nova Science Publishers, 1999).
Figes, Orlando, *A People's Tragedy* (New York, Viking, 1997).
Fischer, George, *Soviet Opposition to Stalin* (Cambridge: Harvard University Press, 1952).
Fisher, H. H., *The Famine in Soviet Russia 1919-1923* (New York: The Macmillan Company, 1927).
Forsyth, James, *The Caucasus* (New York: Cambridge University Press, 2013).
Glantz, David and Jonathon M. House, *When Titans Clashed* (Lawrence, KS: University Press of Kansas, 2015).
Glaskow, W. G., *History of the Cossacks* (New York: Robert Speller & Sons, 1972).
Golovine, Nicholas, *The Russian Army in the World War* (New Haven: Yale University Press, 1931).
Grechko, Andrey A., *Battle for the Caucasus*, trans. David Fidlon (Moscow: Progress Publishers, 1971).
Heenan, Louise Erwin, *Russian Democracy's Fatal Blunder* (New York: Praeger, 1987).
Hehn, Paul, *The German Struggle Against Yugoslav Guerillas in World War II* (New York: East European Quarterly, Boulder, 1979).
Hindus, Maurice, *The Cossacks* (New York: Doubleday, Doran & Company, 1945).
Hitler, Adolf, *Mien Kampf*, trans. Ralph Manheim (New York: Houghton Mifflin, 1971).
Holquist, Peter, *Making War, Forging Revolution* (Cambridge: Harvard University Press, 2002).
Hopkirk, Peter, *Setting the East Ablaze* (London: John Murray, 1984)
Huntington, W. C., *The Homesick Million: Russia-out-of-Russia* (Boston: The Stratford Company, 1933).
Huxley-Blythe, Peter, *The East Came West* (Caldwell, ID: The Caxton Printers, 1964).
Jarymowycz, Roman, *Cavalry from Hoof to Track* (Westport: Praeger Security International, 2008).
Kellogg, Michael, *The Russian Roots of Nazism* (Cambridge: Cambridge University Press, 2005).

Kenez, Peter, *The Defeat of the Whites* (Berkeley: University of California Press, 1977).

Kenez, Peter, *The First Year of the Volunteer Army* (Berkeley: University of California Press, 1971).

Kennan, George, *The Decision to Intervene* (Princeton: Princeton University Press, 1958).

Kennan, George, *Russia Leaves the War* (Princeton: Princeton University Press, 1956).

Lannoy, François de, *Les Cosaques de Pannwitz* (Château de Damigry: Heimdal, 2000).

Lattimore, Owen, *Manchuria: Cradle of Conflict* (New York: The Macmillan Company, 1935).

Lehovich, Dimitry, *White Against Red* (New York: W. W. Norton & Company, 1974).

Liddell Hart, B. H., *The Other Side of the Hill* (London: Cassell & Company, 1973).

Lincoln, W. Bruce, *Passage Through Armageddon* (New York: Simon & Schuster, 1986).

Littlejohn, David, *Foreign Legions of the Third Reich*, Volume 4 (San Jose, CA: R. James Bender Publishing, 1987).

Longworth, Phillip, *The Cossacks* (New York: Holt, Rinehart and Winston, 1969).

Luckett, Richard, *The White Generals* (London: Routledge & Kegan Paul Ltd., 1987).

Mawdsley, Evan, *The Russian Civil War* (New York: Pegasus, 2007).

McNeal, Robert, *Tsar and Cossack* (London: Macmillan Press, 1987).

Mellenthin, General Friedrich Wilhelm von, *German Generals of World War II* (Norman, OK: University of Oklahoma Press, 1977).

Milyukov, Pavel, *Russia To-day and To-morrow* (New York: The Macmillan Company, 1922).

Morley, James, *The Japanese Thrust into Siberia* (New York: Columbia University Press, 1957).

Mueggenberg, Brent, *The Czecho-Slovak Struggle for Independence 1914-1918* (Jefferson, NC: McFarland, 2014).

Myers, Steven Lee, *The New Tsar* (New York: Alfred A. Knopf, 2015).

Newland, Samuel, *Cossacks in the German Army 1941-1945* (Portland, OR: Frank Cass, 1991).

O'Rourke, Shane, *The Cossacks* (Manchester: Manchester University Press, 2007).

O'Rourke, Shane, *Warriors and Peasants* (New York: St. Martin's Press, 2000).

Palmer, James, *The Bloody White Baron* (New York: Basic Books, 2009).

Pastor, Peter, and Samuel Williamson, Jr., ed., *Essays on World War I* (New York: Brooklyn College Press, 1983).

Patrikeeff, Felix, *Russian Politics in Exile* (New York: Palgrave Macmillan, 2002)

Pavlowitch, Stevan K., *Hitler's New Disorder* (New York: Columbia University Press, 2008).

Petroff, Serge, *Remembering a Forgotten War* (Boulder: East European Monographs, 2000).

Pipes, Richard, *The Formation of the Soviet Union* (Cambridge: Harvard University Press, 1964).

Pipes, Richard, *Russia Under the Bolshevik Regime* (New York: Alfred A. Knopf, 1993).

Price, M. Phillips, *War & Revolution in Asiatic Russia* (New York: The Macmillan Company, 1918).

Remnick, David, *Lenin's Tomb: The Last Days of the Soviet Empire* (New York: Random House, 1993).

Reshetar, John S., Jr., *The Ukrainian Revolution 1917-1920* (Princeton: Princeton University Press, 1952).

Robinson, Paul, *The White Russian Army in Exile 1920-1941* (Oxford: Clarendon Press, 2002).

Rutherford, Ward, *The Russian Army in World War I* (London: Gordon Cremonesi, 1975).

Schleifman, Nurit, ed., *Russia at a Crossroads* (London: Frank Cass, 1998).

Seaton, Albert, *The Horsemen of the Steppes* (London: The Bodley Head, 1985).

Smele, Jonathon, *Civil War in Siberia* (New York: Cambridge University Press, 1996).

Smele, Jonathon, *The "Russian" Civil War* (New York: Oxford University Press, 2015).

Smith, C. Jay, Jr., *The Russian Struggle for Power, 1914-1917* (New York: Greenwood, 1956).

Smith, Canfield F., *Vladivostok Under Red and White Rule* (Seattle: University of Washington Press, 1975).

Smith, Graham and Vivien Law, Andrew Wilson, Annette Bohr and Edward Allworth, *Nation-building in the Post-Soviet Borderlands* (Cambridge: Cambridge University Press, 1998).

Sokol, Edward, *The Revolt of 1916 in Russian Central Asia* (Baltimore: The John Hopkins Press, 1954)

Solzhenitsyn, Aleksandr I., *The Gulag Archipelago*, Volumes I-II, trans. Thomas P. Whitney (New York: Harper & Row, 1974).

Starikov, Sergey, and Roy Medvedev, *Philip Mironov and the Russian Civil War*, trans. Guy Daniels (New York: Alfred A. Knopf, 1978).

Steenberg, Sven, *Vlasov*, trans. Abe Farbestein (New York: Alfred A. Knopf, 1970).

Stein, George, *The Waffen SS* (Ithaca, NY: Cornell University Press, 1966).

Stephan, John, *The Russian Far East* (Stanford: Stanford University Press, 1994).

Stephan, John, *The Russian Fascists* (New York: Harper & Row, 1978).

Stewart, George, *The White Armies of Russia* (New York: Russell & Russell, 1970).

Stone, Norman, *The Eastern Front 1914-1917* (New York: Charles Scribner's Sons, 1975).

Stone, Norman, and Michael Glenny, *The Other Russia* (London: Faber & Faber Limited, 1990).

Thompson, John M., *Russia, Bolshevism and the Versailles Peace* (Princeton: Princeton University Press, 1966).

Thorwald, Jürgen, *The Illusion: Soviet Soldiers in Hitler's Army,* trans. Richard and Clara Winston (New York: Harcourt Brace Jovanovich, 1975).

Thurston, Robert W. and Bernd Bonwetsch, ed., *The People's War* (Chicago: University of Illinois Press, 2000).

Tolstoy, Nikolay, *Victims of Yalta* (London: Hodder and Stoughton, 1977).

Tomasevich, Jozo, *War and Revolution in Yugoslavia, 1941-1945: Occupation and Collaboration* (Stanford: Stanford University Press, 2001).

Viola, Lynne, *Peasant Rebels under Stalin* (New York: Oxford University Press, 1996).

Weinberg, Gerhard and H. R. Trevor-Roper, ed., *Norman Cameron and R. H. Stevens, trans., *Hitler's Table Talk* (New York: Enigma, 2008).

Werth, Alexander, *Russian at War* (New York: Avon, 1965).

White, John Albert, *The Siberian Intervention* (Princeton: Princeton University Press, 1950).

Wildman, Allan, *The Old Army and the Soldiers' Revolt* (Princeton: Princeton University Press, 1980).

Wildman, Allan, *The Road to Soviet Power and Peace* (Princeton: Princeton University Press, 1987).

Williams, Robert C., *Culture in Exile: Russian Émigrés in Germany, 1881–1941* (Ithaca: Cornell University Press, 1972).

Wood, Alan, ed., *The History of Siberia* (Routledge: London, 1991).

Young, Gordon, *The House of Secrets* (New York: Duell, Sloan and Pearce, 1959).

Journals

Degtyarev, Sergey I. and Vadim A. Nesterenko. "The Cossack Issue in the Plans of the German Command during the Second World War," *Propaganda in the World and Local Conflicts*, 2015; 4(2) 82–94 (In Russ.) DOI: 10.13187/pwlc.2015.4.82

Kislitsyn, S. A., "Phenomenon of Cossack Estate Quasi-Statehood and its Significance," *Historical and Social Educational Ideas*, 2016; Vol. 8, no. 4, Part 1, 78–86 (In Russ.) DOI: 10.17748/2075-9908-2016-8-4/1-1-78-86.

Matsievsky, G. O., "Political Life of the Cossacks in Emigration: Tendencies and Features," *Modern Studies of Social Problems*, 2013; 3 (In Russ.) DOI: 10.12731/2218-7405-2013-3-7

Ratushnyak, O. V., "Adaption of the Cossack Emigrants to the Style of Living Abroad (1920s to the 1960s)"; *Historical and Social-educational Ideas*, 2014; 6 (6_2):156–158 (In Russ.) DOI:10.17748/2075-9908-2014-6-6_2-156-158.

Ratushnyak, O. V., "The Cossack Émigré in 1945–1960"; *Historical and Social Educational Ideas*, Krasnodar, 2016, Vol. 8, No. 3, Part 2, 59–68 (In Russ.) DOI: 10:17748/2075-9908-2016-8-3/2-59-68.

Rvacheva, Olga V., "The Cossack Restoration Movement in the South of Russia in the Early 1990s: Organization, Ideas and Participants," 2016 (In Russ.) DOI:10.15688/jvolsu4.2016.4.13.

Rvacheva, Olga V., "Formation of the Soviet Cossacks Community in the South of Russia in the mid–1930s—early 1940s," Volgograd State University, 2014. Vestnik Volgogradskogo Gosudarstvennogo Universiteta. Seriâ 4. Isotriâ, Regionovedenia, Meždunarodnye Otnoešeniâ, 2014; (3) 81–92 (In Russ.) DOI: 10.15688/jvolsu4.2014.3.9.

Skoryk, Aleksandr, "Repressive Policies of the Bolsheviks in the Cossack Regions of Southern Russia in the Conditions Collectivization: Principles, Methods, Results," *Bylye Gody* (In Russ.) 2012; 26(4): 42–47.

Tatarov, Azamat, "Restoration Attempt of Private Landed Property in the North Caucasus in the Conditions of Nazi Occupation (August 1942—January 1943)," *Historical and Social-educational Ideas*, 2015; 7(8): 75–79. (In Russ.) DOI: 10.17748/2075-9908-2015-7-8-75-79.

Trut, Vladimir, "On the Participation of Don Cossacks in World War II in 1941," *Bylye Gody*. (In Russ.) 2015; 36(2): 428–433.

Trut, Vladimir, "Some Aspects of the Russian Cossacks' Participation in the First World War" *Bylye Gody* (In Russ.) 2014; 33(3): 335–340.

Newspaper, Magazine, Pamphlet and Website Articles

Barry, Ellen, "The Cossacks are Back. May the Hills Tremble.," *The New York Times*, 16 March 2013, http://www.nytimes.com/2013/03/17/world/europe/cossacks-are-back-in-russia-may-the-hills-tremble.html. Retrieved 24 February 2014.

Barry, Ellen, "Georgia says Russia Committed Genocide in the 19th Century," *The New York Times*, 20 May 2011, http://www.nytimes.com/2011/05/21/world/europe/21georgia.html, Retrieved 16 March 2015.

Bullough, Oliver, "Sochi 2014Winter Olympics: The Circassians Cry Genocide," *Newsweek*, 21 May 2012, http://www.newsweek.com/sochi-2014-winter-olympics-circassians-cry-genocide-64893, Retrieved 16 March 2015.

Cordier, Sherwood, "Red Star vs. the Rising Sun," *World War II*, June 2003, 30–36.

"The Fastov Pogrom," *The Nation* (111): 2892, 646–647.

Flintoff, Corey, "Russia's Cossacks Ride Back From History as 'Patriots,'" *National Public Radio*, 22 February 2014, http://www.npr.org/2014/02/22/280964932/back-from-history-russias-cossacks-rise-as-patriots, Retrieved 3 February 2015.

Gregory, Paul R., "We Can End Russia's War Against Ukraine," *Strategika*, Issue 21, Hoover Institution, 18 February 2015, http://www.hoover.org/research/we-can-end-russias-war-against-ukraine, Retrieved 5 March 2015.

Hanson, Victor Davis, "What Makes Vladimir Run?," *Strategika*, Issue 21, Hoover Institution, 18 February 2015, http://www.hoover.org/research/what-makes-vladimir-run, Retrieved 4 March 2015.

Keating, Joshua, "Cossacks Return to the World Stage," *Slate*, 15 April 2014, www.slate.com/blogs/the_world_/2014/04/15in_sochi_and_ukraine_cossacks_return_to_the_world_stage.html, Retrieved 15 April 2015.

Kozlowska, Hanna, "'Cossack' at the Heart of Kiev Protests Refuses to Give In," *Foreign Policy*, 27 January 2014, http://foreignpolicy.com/2014/01/27/cossack-at-the-heart-of-kiev-protests-refuses-to-give-in, Retrieved 4 February 2015.

Lee, Jolie, "Who are Russia's Cossack Militiamen in Pussy Riot Beating?," *USA Today*, 20 February 2014.

Luhn, Alec, "The Cossacks Ride Again," *Slate*, 31 January 2014, http://www.slate.com/articles/news_and_politics/roads/2014/01/cossacks_will_patrol_the_sochi_olympics_vladimir_putin_is_drafting_these.html, Retrieved 3 February 2015.

Shuster, Simon, "Meet the Cossack 'Wolves' Doing Russia's Dirty Work in Ukraine," *Time*, 12 May 2014, http://time.com/95898/wolves-hundred-ukraine-russia-cossack/.

Smith-Spark, Laura and Nick Paton Walsh, "United States reveals 'specific' threats to Olympic Games," *CNN*, 4 February 2014, http://www.cnn.com/2014/02/04/world/europe/russia-sochi-winter-olympics/, Retrieved 9 March 2015.

Strong, Anna Louise, "Modern Farming—Soviet Style," Labor Research Association (New York: International Pamphlets, 1930).

Syuda, Pytor, "The Novocherkassk Tragedy, June 1–3 1962," "Seventeen Moments in Soviet History" (1988, online archive), http://soviethistory.msu.edu/1961-2/novocherkassk-massacre/novocherkassk-massacre-texts/the-novocherkassk-tragedy, Retrieved 26 April 2017.

Tharoor, Ishaan, "Sochi Olympics Stirs Nationalism of an Exiled People," *Time*, 6 February 2014, http://time.com/4864/sochi-olympics-russia-circassians/, Retrieved 9 March 2015.

Windrem, Robert and Mike Brunker, "MH17 Shootdown: Russian Cossack Leader Made 'Spies' Phone Call," *NBC News*, 24 July 2014, http://www.nbcnews.com/storyline/ukraine-plane-crash/mh17-shootdown-russian-cossack-leader-made-spies-phone-call-n163311.

Zygar, Mikhail, "Putin Likes to Pretend 1917 Never Happened," trans. Julia Ioffe, *The Atlantic*, 1 April 2017, https://www.theatlantic.com/international/archive/2017/russia-putin-revolution-lenin-nicholas-1917/521571. Accessed 3 April 2017.

Index

Numbers in *bold italics* indicate pages with illustrations

Abramov, Fyodor 158, 171, 178, 189, 257
Abramov, Nikolay 189
Alekseyev, Mikhail 42, 48–53, 56, 58, 64, 66, 71, 83, 87, 175
Alexander, Harold 271–272, 278–280
Alexander II, Tsar 18, 23
Alexander III, Tsar 19
All-Cossack Agrarian Union 177, 183
All-Russian Fascist Organization 194
All-Russian Provisional Government (ARPG) 103–105
American Expeditionary Force to Siberia 107–109, 149–153, 200
American Red Cross 171
American Relief Administration (ARA) 211–212, 301
Amur Cossacks 21, 23, 25, 34, 90–91, 94, 97–98, 108, 186, 299
Andijan uprising (1898) 23
Annenkov, Boris 94, 112, 142–143, 184, 188
Anti-Comintern Pact 202
anti-Semitism 26, 154, 190–191, 224–226, 264; *see also* pogroms
Antonov-Ovseyenko, Vladimir 52, 54, 59, 84
Arbuthnott, Robert 277
Arkhangelsky, A.P. 189
Arlt, Fritz Rudolf 265–266
Armed Forces of South Russia (AFSR) 87, 115–141, 156–157, 159, 206, 293, 301
Asano Brigade 201, 285–286
Asano Takashi 201
Astrakhan Cossacks 16, 19, 21, 23, 157–158
Attila the Hun 12
Aufbau 175, 191–192, 248, 301
Avksentev, A.V. 104–105

Babel, Isaak 206
Balabin, E.M. 257
Bandera, Stepan 255
Bashkir National Council 105
Baydalakov, Viktor 194–195, 204
Belov, Pavel A. 240
Berthelot, Henri 85
Biskupsky, Vasily 192

Black Sea Cossacks 36, 82, 91, 127, 135–136
Bochkarev, V.I. 153, 167
Bogaevsky, Afrikan 115–116, 124, 132–136, 177–178
Boldyrev, Vasily 104, 107
Bolshevik, Bolshevism *see* Communist Party of Russia (Bolshevik)
Bosse, Alexander von 247
Bräutigam, Otto 234, 243–244
Bread Peace 60, 83
Brest-Litvosk, Treaty of 59–62, 64, 130
Brinkley, George 68
Brotherhood of Russian Truth 185–186, 189, 192
Broussaud, Gen. 172–173
Brusilov, Aleksey 27
Budyonny, Semyon 130–134, 137, 162, 206, 219–220, 230
Budyonny Novocherkassk Electric Locomotive Plant 296
Bukretov, Gen. 127, 135, 141, 158
Bulavin, Kondrati 15–16
Bureau of Russian Émigré Affairs 199
Buttlar-Brandenfels, Baron Horst von 247

Catherine II, Empress 16, 34
Central Asian revolt of 1916 28–30
Central Rada (Ukraine) 60, 64–65, 83–84
Četniks 260, 262, 269–270, 301
Chamberlin, William Henry 217–218
Changing Landmarks movement 176
Charles XII, King 15
Charpy, Gen. 172
Cheka 119, 149, 208–210, 222, 287, 301
Cheremisov, Gen. 43–45
Chernetsov, Vasily 53–54
Christian Science Monitor 217
Circassians, genocide against 5–6
collectivization 1, 212–222, 230, 233, 242, 294, 296
Comintern *see* Communist International
Committee for the Liberation of the

Peoples of Russia (KONR) 256–258, 265, 270, 276–277, 279, 302
Committee of Members of the Constituent Assembly (Komuch) 100–105, 110, 147, 302
Communist International 190, 198, 285
Communist Party (Bulgaria) 187–188
Communist Party of Russia (Bolshevik) 1–3, 8, 24, 32, 38–41, 48, 49, 52–59, 64–68, 71–74, 80, 85, 87, 107–109, 115, 121–123, 126, 129–141, 156–157, 159, 169, 171–172, 176, 190, 198, 205–224, 228, 230, 240, 250, 253, 256–257, 267, 269, 288, 301; activities among émigrés 173, 178, 182, 187–189, 285; activities among ethnic minorities 62, 80, 207; 111, 124; administration of Don region 59–61, 117–120; decline 296–298; propaganda among Cossacks 50–51, 69, 113–*114*, 117, 206; seizes power 42–47; in Siberia 88, 92–95, 99–103, 110, 143, 145, 147–148, 151–154, 163–168, 184; in Ukraine 55–56, 64–65, 83–84
Communist Party (Yugoslavia) 182, 204–205, 260, 271
Congress of the United Stanitsas 62, 100
Constituent Assembly 42, 49, 71, 100, 102–103, 110, 175, 177, 190
Cossachi Stan 252–254; 276–283, 292, 301
Cossack Central Administration 255–257, 276
Cossack Central Office 248–249, 255, 257
Cossack National Center 195–196, 203, 224
Cossack National Liberation Movement (KNOD) 224, 248, 255–256, 302
Cossack Union *see* Union of Cossacks
Cresson, William Penn 10, 12, 18, 52
Czecho-Slovak Legion 98–106, 110, 146–153, 183

Dalburo 152–153, 301
d'Alquen, Günther 265

341

de-Cossackization 8, 118–120, 143, 207, 222, 242, 295–296
de Martel, Count 162
Denikin, Anton 40, 49, 57, 112, 148, 157–159, 163, 174, 190, 204, 228–229, 238, 243–244, 254; Allied backing 85–86, 143; as commander of AFSR 87, 113–141; as commander of Volunteer Army 58–59, 66, 70–71, 74–83; in exile 203, 293
Denisov, S.V. 66–67
Directory (Ukraine) 84
Diterikhs, Mikhail 143–146, 167–168, 184, 187, 190
Domanov, Timofey I. 253–254, 275–283, 286, 288, 292, 295
Don Army, Don Cossack Army *see* Don Cossacks
Don-Caucasian Federation 70
Don Cossacks 9, 21, 24, 30, 75, 91, 122, 141, 158–159, 162, 178, 189, 195, 232–233, 245, 253, 296; anticommunist uprising (1918) 61–63, 65–69; anticommunist uprising (1919) 117–120; early history 10–19; in exile 171–172, 181, 188; after February Revolution 33–42; in German army 250, 263, 272–273; in German occupation 236, 249; liberation from Soviets 72–74, 120–121, 124–125; military collapses 84–86, 113–117, 131–135, 137–140; after October Revolution 42–60; in post-Soviet era 297; relations with White generals 70–71, 86–87, 135–136, 157; in Soviet Union 210, 220
Don Executive Committee 33–35, 37
Don Expeditionary Corps 119
Don MRC 59–60
Don Soviet Republic 60, 67, 118
Donburo 118, 301
Drozdovsky, M.G. 67, 71
Duan Qirui 96–97
Dukhonin, Nikolay 48–49
Dune, Eduard 54, 206
Dutov, Aleksandr 48, 52, 56, 95, 101, 105, 110–111, 142–143, 184, 188, 242, 295
dzhigitovka 181, 212, 221, 263, 279, 301

Eichhorn, Gen. von 64, 83
Eisenhower, Dwight 292–293
Elizabeth II, Queen 291–292
Eurasianist movement 176, 298
EuroMaidan protests 8, 300

famine of 1921–22 (RSFSR) 211–212
famine of 1932–33 (USSR) 216–218
Far Eastern Republic (FER) 153–155, 163–168, 301
February Revolution 31–34, 39, 93, 299
Federal Security Service (FSB) 300
Filimonov, A.P. 56, 58, 76, 82–83, 126–127

First All-Russian Conference of Toiling Cossacks 207
First Cossack Cavalry Division 249–251, 271; deployment in Balkans 258–264; development 244–247; transfer into Waffen-SS 266–267; *see also* XIV SS Cossack Cavalry Corps; XV SS Cossack Cavalry Corps
First Five-Year Plan 219
First Kuban Campaign (Icy March) 55–59, 71, 75–76, 115
Flight MH17, Malaysia Airlines 9
Fostikov, Gen. 160–161, 164, 171
Free Cossack movement (1917–18) 55–56, 64
Freytag-Loringhoven, Wesel von 236

Gajda, Radola 99–100, 104, 110, 150
Gamov, Vasily 97–98
George VI, King 281
Gestapo 222, 245
Ghirey, Sultan Kelech 278, 281, 288
Glaise von Horstenau, Edmund 260–262
glasnost 296–297
Glazkov, Vasily G. 195–196, 224, 248–249, 255–256
Glebov, Gen. 267–268
Golubov, V.S. 55, 59, 61
Gorbachev, Mikhail 296
Göring, Hermann 225
GPU 167; *see also* OGPU
Graves, William 107–108
Great Terror 221, 228
Green movement 138, 140, 161
Grölmann, Helmuth von 263
Guchkov, Aleksandr 33–34, 37
Guderian, Heinz 227–228, 264
Gudonov, Tsar Boris 13
Gulag (Main Administration of Corrective Labor Camps and Labor Settlements) 215–216, 286, 289–291, 301

Halder, Franz 227
Harris, Ernst 112
Hellmich, Heinz 251
Herwarth, Hans von 225–226, 233, 247, 251, 257, 262
Hilfswilligers, Hiwis 230, 238, 302
Himmler, Heinrich 225, 251, 254, 256, 264–267
Himpel, Nikolaus 248–249, 256
Hitler, Adolf 194, 203–204, 219, 222–223, 236, 238, 243–244, 247–248, 251, 254, 257–258, 261, 264, 266, 269, 284, 292; early political career 191–192; Ostpolitik 195–196, 224–229, 234; support for Cossack division 232–233, 245, 265
Hoffmann, Max 59, 65
Hoover, Herbert 211
Horthy, Miklós 174, 191
Horvath, Dmitry 96–97, 107
Howard, Henry 271

Howley, Frank 292
hunghutze 185, 196, 200
Huxley-Blythe, Peter 250, 292

Icy March *see* First Kuban Campaign
Imarat Kavkaz 5–6
International Olympic Committee (IOC) 5–6
Irbis Cossacks 299
Ivan the Terrible, Tsar 11, 13
Ivanov (-Rinov), P.P. 29, 102–103, 144, 189
Izvestiya 288

Janin, Maurice 146
Jin Shuren 186
Jodl, Alfred 255
July Days 38
Jungschutz, Joachim von 236, 238, 246

Kadet (Constitutional Democrat) Party 37, 39, 103–105, 203, 302
Kalabukhov, A.I. 127
Kaledin, Aleksey M. 1, 34–35, 56, 60–61, 66, 68, 70, 73, 88, 92, 95, 112, 295; anticommunist activities 48–53; as conservative icon 36–40; death 53–55; in Kornilov affair 40–42
Kalinin, Mikhail 207
Kalmykov, Ivan P. 112, 149–150, 153, 167, 190; atrocities 106–109; death 151–152; early career 97–98, 100
Kamenev, Lev 221
Kamenskaya MRC 54, 59
Kappel, Vladimir 147, 152
Kappelites 152–155, 164–165, 167, 302
Karaulov, M.A. 80
Katanaev, Maj. 105
Kazem-Bek, Aleksandr 194
Keightly, Charles 273
Keitel, Wilhelm 254–255
Kerensky, Aleksandr 37–48, 175
Khalkhin Gol, battle of 202, 284
Khmelnytsky, Bohdan 15–16, 300
Khrushchev, Nikita 291, 296
Kirichenko, Nikolay Y. 240
Kleist, Paul Ludwig Ewald von 234, 239, 243–244
Knox, Alfred 26, 28, 104
Koch, Erich 245
Kochubey, Ivan 77
Kolchak, Aleksandr 96, 111–113, 116, 119, 126, 150, 152–153, 158–159, 163, 166, 174, 184–185, 190, 201, 209, 288; downfall 145–149; relations with Cossacks 107–110, 142–144; seizes power 104–105;
Komuch *see* Committee of Members of the Constituent Assembly
Kononov, Ivan N. 233, 245–246, 248–249, **263**, 293; defection 230–232; efforts to disassociate with Germans 270, 273, 276
KONR *see* Committee for the Liberation of the Peoples of Russia

Index

Kornilov, Lavr G. 1, 43–45, 49, 52, 87, 95, 112, 295; as conservative icon 36–40; revolt 40–42; as Volunteer Army commander 53–58
Köstring, Ernst 234, 238, 255, 257, 262, 265, 269
Kozitsyn, Nikolay 9
Krasilnikov, I.N. 104–105, 147
Krasnov, Nikolay N. 277–279, 281, 286–287, 289–291
Krasnov, Pyotr N. 1, 92, 118, 122, 165, 224, 242, 250, 269, 299; as commander of Third Cavalry Corps **44**–47, 50; death 288; as Don ataman 67–74, 84–87, 113–115; during interwar period 181–182, 190, 192; as head of Cossack Central Office 248–249; repatriation 276–281; as Supreme Ataman 255–258, 276; writings 181–182, 287
Krasnov, Semyon N. 256, 288
Krasnova, Lili 291
Krasnova, Lydia 279
Krylenko, Nikolay 49, 52
Krymov, Gen. 40–41
Kuban Cossacks 1, 3, 19, 21, 24–25, 31, 63, 79, 81, 87–88, 91, 102, 112, 117, 120–124, 131–133, 140–141, 143, 181, 220, 245, 250, 254, 276, 280; in exile 171–172, 174, 179; after February Revolution 34–36; in German army 261, 264, 268, 272; origins 36; participation in pogroms 127–128; in post-Soviet era 297–299; relations with White movement 55–59, 69–71, 74–77, 82–83, 125–127, 134–138, 156–163, 177; in Soviet Union 209, 212–218, 240; under German occupation 234–237
Kulakov, Nikolay L. 237–239, 242, 245–246, 255, 269–270, 288
Kun, Béla 163
Kuropatkin, Aleksey N. 29
Kutepov, Aleksandr 133, 158, 171–172, 188–189
Kwantung Army 199, 219, 284–285

Lazo, Sergey 96, 153
Lehmann, D.R. 236, 246
Lenin, Vladimir I. 1, 32, 38, 47–50, 60, 87, 94, 120, 130, 146, 175, 207, 209–210, 296
lineitsy Cossacks 36, 82, 91, 126, 136, 302
List, Wilhelm 234
Litvinov, Maksim 211
Lloyd George, David 137
Lobanov-Rostovsky, Prince 179
Löhr, Alexander von 268
Ludendorff, Erich 191
Lukomsky, Aleksandr 54–55, 64, 71, 170

Maclean, Fitzroy 262
Makhno, Nestor 83, 120, 131–132, 158–159
Malcolm, A.D. 292
Mamontov, Konstantin 122–123, 127, 131–132
Mamontov Raid 122–123, 127, 130
Manstein, Erich von 239, 244
Mao Zedong 286
Mark V (tank) 121, 139
Masaryk, Tomáš 98
May-Maevsky, V.Z. 115, 120, 132
Mazepa, Ivan 15–16
Melnikov, N.M. 136
Mende, Gerhard von 234
Menshevik Party 35, 50, 60, 175, 302
Merkulov, Nikolay 164–167
Merkulov, Spiridon 165–167
Mihailović, Draža 260
Miller, E.K. 189
Milyukov, Pavel 36–38, 64, 175, 203
Mironov, Filip 42, 73, 113–114, 120, 162, 206, 209
Molotov, Vyacheslav 285
Moscow State Conference 39–40
Murray, Horatius 272
Mussolini, Benito 191, 193–194
Musson, Geoffrey 277–278
Myers, Steven Lee 7

Nagolen, Gurgen 286
Nansen, Fridtjof 179, 188
Napoleon I, Emperor 17, 182
National Labor Alliance (NTS) 194–195, 200, 203–204, 245, 256–257, 293
National Ukrainian Cossack Organization (NUCO) 64–65, 176, 302
Naumenko, Vyacheslav G. 126, 177, 224, 250, 253, 255–256, 262, 276, 293
Nazarenko, Nikolay 231–232, 246
Nazarov, A.M. 55
Nazi Party (German National Socialist Workers' Party) 194–196, 203–204, 219–221, 251, 264, 265, 269, 283–284; collaboration with White émigrés 191–193, 204–205; Eastern policy 224–229; views on Cossacks 245
Nazi-Soviet nonaggression pact 202–204, 222
New Economic Policy (NEP) 210, 212–214, 217
Newland, Samuel 269
Nicholas I, Tsar 18
Nicholas II, Tsar **17**, 24, 28, 65, 175
NKVD 186, 202, 222, 231, 243, 248, 253, 272, 274, 280–283, 286–289, 293, 302
North Caucasus Defense Council 124
Novo-Dmitrovskaya agreement 57–58, 70, 76
Novocherkassk massacre 295–296
Novoselov, Aleksandr 104

Ober Ost 59–60, 65–66, 303
October Revolution 2–3, 42–48, 51, 52, 56, 67, 88, 94, 173
OGPU 173, 180, 185, 188–189, 215, 217–218, 303
OKH (German Army Supreme Command) 228, 232–233, 238–239, 249, 251, 264, 303
OKW (German High Command of the Armed Forces) 227, 232, 245–247, 254–256, 260, 303
Order Number One 35
Ordzhonikidze, Grigory 80
Orenburg Cossacks 18, 23, 34, 91, 168, 188; anticommunist uprisings (1917–18) 48, 56, 62, 93, 95, 100–101; in Kolchak's army 105, 110–111, 113, 142–143; origins 16, 21, 88
Organization for Security and Cooperation in Europe 9
Ostministrium (Reich Ministry for the Eastern Occupied Territories) 225, 232–234, 237, 243–244, 248–249, 255–257, 303
Ostpolitik 224–229, 232, 241, 244, 247, 254, 269, 303
Ostrovsky, Vladimir 274–275
Osttruppen 232–234, **237**–238, 245, 248, 250–251, 255–256, 262, 265–266, 303
Otani, Gen. 106
Other Germany group 229, 233
outlanders 21, 33, 37, 54–57, 59, 61–62, 68, 72, 80–82, 84, 87, 92, 102, 113, 125, 130, 177, 220–221, 258, 303; conflicts with Cossacks 22, 34–35, 48, 52–53, 76–77, 79; origins 18–19; Soviet policy towards 118, 160, 209–210

Pannwitz, Helmuth von 252, 255, **263**, 276, 283, 286, 290; biographical sketch 238–239; as commander of XV SS Cossack Cavalry Corps 267–273; as commander of First Cossack Cavalry Division 245–247, 249–251, 258–267; in Soviet captivity 274–275, 281, 288
Panzer V Panther (tank) 252
Panzer VI Tiger (tank) 252
partisan movements 77, 94, 185, 196, 208–210, 222, 250; on Eastern Front (1941–45) 228, 232, 234–236, 241, 246, 252–253; in Italy (1944–45) 254, 276; in North Caucasus (1918–21) 80, 135, 138, 140, 161, 209; in Russian Far East (1919–22) 149–154, 163, 167; in Siberia (1918–21) 103, 107, 109, 146–148, 209; in Tambov Province (1920–21) 209; in Ukraine (1918–20) 83–84, 120, 123, 131–132; *see also* Green movement; Partisans, Yugoslav People's Army
Partisans, Yugoslav People's Army 258–264, 267, 270–272
Pavlov, Gen. 137
Pavlov, Sergey V. 236–239, 242, 249, 252–253, 255, 295

Pellé, Gen. 173
Penza Agreement 99
People's Revolutionary Army (PRA) 153–155, 166–168
Peter I, Tsar 15, 67–68, 176
Peter II, King 281
Petliura, Symon 84, 117, 124
Philips Price, Morgan 79
Podtelkov, Fyodor 54, 59, 67
pogroms 83, 112, 127–128
Pokrovsky, Viktor 56–57, 82–83, 126–127
Politburo 214, 221
Political Center 147–148
Polkovo Heights, battle of 45–47
Poltavets-Ostranitsa, Ivan 65, 176, 192, 247
Poole, F.C. 86
Popov, P.K. 55, 66
Prague Manifesto 256–257
Pravda 211, 288
Price, Rose 274
Provisional Government (Russia, 1917) 32–48, 50, 64, 67, 93, 95, 98, 128
Provisional Zemstvo Government 151–154, 164
Pugachev, Emelian 15–16, 18
Pussy Riot 6–*7*
Putin, Vladimir V. 6–10, 241, 299–300

Rasputin, Grigory 27
Razin, Stenka 15–16, 18
Red Army 2, 62, 72, 74, 100, 103–106, 110–112, 117–126, 130, 134–142, 147–152, 156–166, 172, 176, 184–187, 198–210, 215, 219–224, 227–232, 236–246, 251–258, 264, 267–276, 280–293; Cossacks serving with 72–73, 86, 114–115, 220, 130, 206, 294; foreigners serving with 96; in North Caucasus (1918–21) 71, 75–83; partisans serving with 84, 109, 120, 153, 228; propaganda directed at 226, 265; purge 222; reforms 73
Red Cross 107, 171, 230, 279, 281, 291
Red Guards 41–48, 50, 53–56, 60–62, 67, 95–99, 146, 231
Renault factory strike (1916) 29
Renteln, Alexander von 267–268, 271–272
Revolution of 1905 23–24, 129, 181, 297
Ribbentrop, Joachim von 224
Riga Agreement 211
Rodzaevsky, Konstantin V. 196, 199–201, 284–286, 288
Romanov, Grand Duke Kirill V. 191–192
Romanov, Tsar Mikhail 13
Romanov, Grand Duke Nikolay N. 175, 191, 193
Romanova, Viktoria 191
Romanovsky, I.P. 126
Rosenberg, Alfred 192, 225–226, 232, 237, 247–248, 254, 256

Rotova, Olga 277–278, 281–283
Rozanov, Sergey 149–151
Rundstedt, Gerd von 227
Russian Diaspora 2, 62, 68, 186–189, 221–223, 232, 235, 237, 242, 244, 298–299; Cossacks in 170–174, 176–185; collaboration with Germany 190–193, 224–225, 247–254, 262; collaboration with Japan 196–203, 284–286; fascism among 193–196; political outlook 174–176, 254–258, 203–205; pro-Soviet tendencies 176, 293, 285–286; repatriation efforts 172–173, 187–189, 275–283, 287, 289–294
Russian Fascist Party 196, 199
Russian Fascist Union 201
Russian General Military Union (ROVS) 187, 193, 195, 286, 303; attitudes towards Nazis 204; origins 178–179; Soviet penetration 187, 189
Russian Liberation Army 244–245, 251, 256, 265, 268
Russian National Committee 244–245, 256
Russian National Council 175
Russian National Liberation Movement (ROND) 194, 203, 303
Russo-Japanese War 23
Ryabovol, N.S. 125

SA-11 Buk (surface-to-air missile) 9
Sakharov, Konstantin 145
Schenkendorff, Count Max von 231–233
Scheubner-Richter, Max von 192
Schickedanz, Arno 192
Schulenburg, Count Friedrich Werner von 225–226
Schultz, Hans Joachim von 266–267
Second Kuban Campaign 74–77
Semirechye Cossacks 19, 21–22, 25, 28–29, 33, 88–89, 91, 93, 142, 186, 207
Semyonov, Grigory M. 1, 100, 112, 148–149, 164–168, 189–190, 198, 200, 284; atrocities 106–107; capture and death 286–288; conflicts with Allied forces 150–151; conflicts with other anticommunists 107–109, 164–166, 200–201; driven from Chita 152–155; early career 95–98
Semyonov, Mikhail 288
separatist movements 69–70, 76, 218, 225, 297; among Cossacks 37, 81–83, 124–127, 135–136, 158, 177, 195, 217, 248–249, 255–257, 276, 298; Bolshevik attitudes toward 207; in Russo-Ukrainian border conflict 8–10, 300
Sheng Shicai 186
Shkuro, Andrey G. 122, 269; capture and death 281, 287–288;

collaboration with Germans 257, 262–**263**, 279, 300; in exile 181; in Russian Civil War 76–77, 82, 120, 123, 131, 138
Siberian Cossacks 21, 39, 91, 110–111, 188; early history 88; in the First Cossack Cavalry Division 261; in Kolchak coup 102–105; in Russian Civil War 94, 143–147
Siberian Provisional Government 102–104
Siberian Regional Conference 93
Sibobduma 93, 100, 104, 303
Sidorin, Vladimir 115, 119, 124–125, 132–133, 137, 139, 157, 175
Sino-Soviet conflict (1929) 197–199
Skoblin, Nikolay 189
Skoropadsky, Pavel 65, 69–70, 83–85, 176, 190, 192, 288
Slashchev, Y.A. 156, 158
Slate 7
Sochi Games *see* Winter Olympic Games
Social Revolutionary (SR) Party 35, 50, 54, 93, 100, 103–105, 146–150, 153, 175, 209–210, 303
Solzhenitsyn, Aleksandr 289
Sopwith Camel (plane) 121
Sorokin, Ivan 75
South Russian Government 136, 140
Soviet of People's Commissars (Sovnarkom) 48, 50, 52, 69 117
Sovnarkom *see* Soviet of People's Commissars
Sovnarod *see* Union for the Return to the Motherland
Special Council 126, 134–136
Stalin, Josef 74, 204–205, 231, 233, 241, 244–245, 249, 256, 271, 275, 283, 296; attitudes toward POWs 230, 272–273; as Commissar of Nationalities 208; death 290; as General Secretary 219–221, 225, 229, 235, 240, 284–286, 291–295; in Great Terror 222
Stalin Constitution 220–221
Stalingrad, Battle of 234, 239, 241, 243–244
Stauffenberg, Count Claus von 233–234
Strik-Strikfeldt, Wilfried 229, 232–233, 244–245, 257, 270
Supreme Krug 135–137
Supreme Monarchist Council 175, 191–193, 248
Syrový, Jan 146
Syrtsov, Sergey 118–120

Tchaikovsky, Nikolay 136
Terek Cossacks 21–24, 31, 33, 69, 117, 181, 220, 254, 269, 288; anticommunist uprisings among 75, 79–81; demographics of homeland 19, 79, 124; early history 13–15; in exile 177, 182; in German army 245–246, 250, 264; participation in pogroms 127–128;

in post-Soviet era 297–298; in Soviet Union 207–208, 213, 220; under German occupation 235, 237–238; in White movement 121, 125–126, 131, 135–136, 141, 157–158, 163
Terek-Mountain government 79–80
Terek People's Soviet Socialist Republic 80
Time of Troubles 10, 13
Timofeyevich, Yermak 88, 182
Timoshenko, I.P. 135
Tito, Josip Broz 260–264, 270–271, 291
Tkachev, Aleksandr N. 299
Transbaikal Cossacks 21, 23, 121, 201, 216, 228; after February Revolution 34, 94; early history 89–91; in exile 185–186; in White movement 95–98, 106–110, 143, 151–155, 164–168
Trekrechye Cossacks 184–185, 198, 201, 216, 284–286
Trifonov, Valentin 120
Trotsky, Leon 46, 59, 67, 222; as Commissar of War 73–75, 99, 113, 130
Trump, Donald J. 299
Tukhachevsky, Mikhail 222, 288
Tundutov, Prince Danzan 70
Turkestan Soviet Republic 111, 142

Ukrainian National Union 84
Ulagay, Sergey 77, 133, 141, 161
Ulrikh, Vasily V. 288
Umarov, Doku 5–6
Ungern-Sternberg, Baron Nikolay Roman von 95, 106–107, 154, 165–166, 200
Union for the Resurrection of Cossackdom 177, 179, 195
Union for the Return to the Motherland (Sovnarod) 188, 303
Union of Cossack Hosts 34, 38, 43, 47, 92
Union of Cossack Hosts in Russia and Abroad 298
Union of Cossacks 177–178, 187
Union of Cossacks in Russia (1990–92) 297

Union of Cossacks in the Far East 186–187, 201
Union of Mountain Peoples 79
Union of the Southeast 69
Union of Young Russia (Young Russians) 194–195, 203
United Council of the Don, Terek and Kuban 177
Ural Cossacks 16, 21, 23, 34, 47–48, 56, 101, 105, 111, 122, 142
USA Today 7
Ussuri Cossacks 21, 23, 25, 40, 91, 228, 299; in exile 186; origins 90; in White movement 95–98, 100, 105, 107–108, 143, 149–152, 164
Ustaša 259–262, 267, 270–271, 304

Validov, Zek 105
Vasiliev, Leonide V. 277–278
Vdovenko, Gen. 177, 225, 288
Verzhbitsky, Gen. 165
Vikzhel (All-Russian Union of Railwaymen) 46–47
Vladimir the Great 170
Vlasov, Andrey 254, 265, 268–269, 273, 277, 284, 289–290, 293; capture and death 279, 288; early anticommunist activity 244–245, 251; relations with Cossacks 256–258, 270, 276
Voitsekhovsky, Sergey 147, 149, 152–153
Volunteer Army 63, 68, 74, 78, 80, 86, 113, 158, 201, 228, 287; in AFSR 116, 121, 122–123, 131–133; beginnings 49–55; in Icy March 55–59; relations with Allies 66; relations with Cossacks 70–71, 81–83, 85, 115, 126; in Second Kuban Campaign 74–77
Vonsiatsky, Anastase 194, 200–201
Voroshilov, Kliment 74, 220

Waffen-SS 205, 226, 261, 264–266, 270
Wagner, Konstantin 267, 273–274
Wehrmacht 2, 204, 244, 246–248, 251–253, 266, 268, 304; invasion of Soviet Union 204–205, 224–230; in North Caucasus region 234–243, 294; in occupied Yugoslavia 259–264, 270–271; propaganda campaigns 226, 254, 265
Weichs, Baron Maximillan von 260–261, 268
Wietersheim, Gustav von 232
Wilhelm II, Kaiser 27, 68–69, 72, 85
Williamson, H.N.H. 124, 138
Wilson, Woodrow 101, 106
Winter Olympic Games (2010) 6
Winter Olympic Games (2014) 5–7
Wolff, Baron Hans von 236, 246
Woytinsky, Wladimir S. 44–45
Wrangel, Baron Pyotr 64, 77, 95, 135, 183, 187, 190, 193; as Caucasian Army commander 116–117, 121–123; confrontation with Kuban Rada 126–127; in the Crimea 140–141, 154, 156–163; disputes with Denikin 132–133; in exile 170–175, 177–179, 182; relations with Cossacks 121, 157–158, 175, 177, 183

XIV SS Cossack Cavalry Corps 267
XV SS Cossack Cavalry Corps 267–275, 280, 293

Yagoda, Genrikh 222
Yalta Agreement 273, 275, 281, 283
Yang Zengxin 142–143
Yanukovych, Viktor 8
Yeltsin, Boris 298
Yezhov, Nikola 222
Young Russians *see* Union of Young Russia
Yugoslav People's Army *see* Partisans
Yurlova, Marina 24, 27

Zaporozhian Cossacks 10, 15–16, 36, 65, 254
Zeitzler, Kurt 238–239
Zhang Xueliang 197–199, 284
Zhang Zuolin 166, 168, 185–186, 197
Zhilenkov, Georgey N. 265
Zhukov, Grigory 202
Zinoviev, Grigory 221
Zinoviev, V.M. 104–105